# The Archaeology of Britain

*The Archaeology of Britain* is a comprehensive and up-to-date introduction to all the archaeological periods covering Britain from early prehistory to the Industrial Revolution. It provides a one-stop textbook for the entire archaeology of Britain and reflects the most recent developments in archaeology both as a field subject and as an academic discipline.

Chapters are:

- accessibly written by experts in the relevant field;
- organised in chronological order;
- followed by two-level bibliographies, the first providing core reading material and the second a more detailed guide to the subject area;
- highly illustrated with photographs, maps, graphs and tables.

This collection is essential reading for undergraduates in archaeology, and all those interested in British archaeology, history and geography.

**John Hunter** is Professor of Ancient History and Archaeology at the University of Birmingham. He has wide research interests covering heritage management, forensic archaeology and late Iron Age and Viking settlement. His most recent book is *Fair Isle: the Archaeology of an Island Community* (1996). **Ian Ralston** is Professor of Archaeology at the University of Edinburgh. His principal archaeological interests lie in the later prehistory of Scotland and in the Iron Age of Western Europe. His most recent publication is, with K. J. Edwards, *Scotland: Environment and Archaeology* (1997).

# The Archaeology of Britain

## An introduction from the Upper Palaeolithic to the Industrial Revolution

Edited by
John Hunter and Ian Ralston

First published 1999
by Routledge
11 New Fetter Lane, London EC4P 4EE

Simultaneously published in the USA and Canada
by Routledge
29 West 35th Street, New York, NY 10001

Reprinted 1999, 2000, 2001, 2002, 2003

*Routledge is an imprint of the Taylor & Francis Group*

Typeset in Garamond by Keystroke, Jacaranda Lodge, Wolverhampton
Printed and bound in Great Britain by
Bell & Bain Ltd, Glasgow

*British Library Cataloguing in Publication Data*
A catalogue record for this book is available from the British Library

*Library of Congress Cataloging in Publication Data*
The archaeology of Britain : an introduction from the Upper
    Palaeolithic to the Industrial Revolution / edited by John Hunter
    and Ian Ralston.
        p.    cm.
    Includes bibliographical references and index.
    1. Great Britain—Antiquities.  2. Excavations (Archaeology)—
    Great Britain.  I. Hunter, John, 1949–  .  II. Ralston, Ian.
    DA90.A715   1999
    936.1—dc21                                      98–24844
                                                       CIP

ISBN 0–415–13587–7 (hbk)
ISBN 0–415–13588–5 (pbk)

# Contents

*List of figures* vii

*List of contributors* xi

*Preface* xiv

*Chapter One*

BRITISH ARCHAEOLOGY SINCE THE END
OF THE SECOND WORLD WAR 1
Ian Ralston and John Hunter

*Chapter Two*
THE LATEGLACIAL OR LATE AND FINAL UPPER PALAEOLITHIC
COLONIZATION OF BRITAIN 13
Nicholas Barton

*Chapter Three*
HUNTER-GATHERERS OF THE MESOLITHIC 35
Steven Mithen

*Chapter Four*
THE NEOLITHIC PERIOD, *c.* 4000–2500/2200 BC:
CHANGING THE WORLD 58
Alasdair Whittle

*Chapter Five*
THE EARLIER BRONZE AGE 77
Mike Parker Pearson

*Chapter Six*
THE LATER BRONZE AGE 95
Timothy Champion

*Chapter Seven*
THE IRON AGE 113
Colin Haselgrove

*Chapter Eight*
ROMAN BRITAIN: THE MILITARY DIMENSION  135
W. S. Hanson

*Chapter Nine*
ROMAN BRITAIN: CIVIL AND RURAL SOCIETY  157
Simon Esmonde Cleary

*Chapter Ten*
EARLY HISTORIC BRITAIN  176
Catherine Hills

*Chapter Eleven*
THE SCANDINAVIAN PRESENCE  194
Julian D. Richards

*Chapter Twelve*
LANDSCAPES OF THE MIDDLE AGES:
TOWNS 1050–1500  210
John Schofield

*Chapter Thirteen*
LANDSCAPES OF THE MIDDLE AGES: CHURCHES,
CASTLES AND MONASTERIES  228
Roberta Gilchrist

*Chapter Fourteen*
LANDSCAPES OF THE MIDDLE AGES:
RURAL SETTLEMENT AND MANORS  247
Paul Stamper

*Chapter Fifteen*
THE HISTORICAL GEOGRAPHY OF BRITAIN FROM AD 1500:
LANDSCAPE AND TOWNSCAPE  264
Ian Whyte

*Chapter Sixteen*
THE WORKSHOP OF THE WORLD: THE INDUSTRIAL
REVOLUTION  280
Kate Clark

*Chapter Seventeen*
REELING IN THE YEARS: THE PAST IN THE PRESENT  297
Timothy Darvill

*Index* 316

# Figures

| | | |
|---|---|---:|
| 1.1 | The recording of military monuments | 2 |
| 1.2 | Aerial photography as a major factor in increasing the number of known sites | 4 |
| 1.3 | The development of urban archaeology | 7 |
| 2.1 | Comparison of ice accumulation rates and palaeotemperature | 15 |
| 2.2 | Creswellian artefacts from Three Holes Cave, Devon | 16 |
| 2.3 | Distribution of Creswellian findspots | 17 |
| 2.4 | Reindeer baton from Gough's Cave | 20 |
| 2.5 | Cut-marks on a human lower jaw bone from Gough's Cave | 22 |
| 2.6 | A horse's head engraved on a rib fragment from Robin Hood Cave | 23 |
| 2.7 | Final Upper Palaeolithic artefacts | 25 |
| 2.8 | Distribution of Final Upper Palaeolithic penknife point findspots | 27 |
| 2.9 | Final Upper Palaeolithic 'long blade' artefacts from Scatter 'A', Three Ways Wharf | 30 |
| 2.10 | Distribution of Final Upper Palaeolithic 'long blade' findspots with bruised blades | 31 |
| 2.11 | Engraved horse mandible from Kendrick's Cave | 32 |
| 3.1 | Location of Mesolithic sites mentioned in text | 35 |
| 3.2 | Pollen diagram from Star Carr illustrating changing vegetation | 36 |
| 3.3 | Changes in sea-level of the North Sea in the Early Holocene | 37 |
| 3.4 | Chipped stone artefacts from Star Carr and Kinloch, Rum | 39–40 |
| 3.5 | Organic and coarse stone artefacts from Mesolithic sites | 41 |
| 3.6 | Non-utilitarian artefacts from Mesolithic sites | 42 |
| 3.7 | Excavations at Farm Fields, Rum | 47 |
| 3.8 | Excavations at Gleann Mor, Islay | 48 |
| 3.9 | Excavations of the hut at Mount Sandel | 49 |
| 4.1 | Reconstruction of one of the phases of occupation at Loch Olabhat, North Uist | 64 |
| 4.2 | The primary burials in the Radley oval barrow, Oxfordshire | 66 |
| 4.3 | The chambers of the West Kennet long barrow, Wiltshire | 68 |
| 4.4 | Reconstructions of two phases of the Street House long barrow, Cleveland | 69 |
| 4.5 | Excavation of bone deposits at Windmill Hill | 70 |
| 4.6 | The Dorset Cursus on Bottlebush Down, seen from the air | 71 |
| 4.7 | Excavations on Site IV within the henge at Mount Pleasant, Dorset | 73 |
| 5.1 | Metalwork chronologies for the Earlier Bronze Age | 79 |
| 5.2 | An unprovenanced bronze flat axe with geometric incised decoration | 80 |

5.3 Ceramic chronologies for the Late Neolithic, Early and Middle Bronze Ages 81
5.4 A beaker and associated non-perishable grave goods from the Green Low round barrow in Derbyshire 82
5.5 Styles of Early Bronze Age storage pots used as cremation containers 83
5.6 Assemblage variation within the Trevisker series 84
5.7 Early Bronze Age house plans from the Western Isles 85
5.8 Different types of round barrows on Normanton Down, Wiltshire 86
5.9 The sequence of funerary events at Hemp Knoll barrow, Wiltshire 87
5.10 The triple-ditched barrow at Irthlingborough, Raunds 88
6.1 Examples of bronzes of the Wilburton assemblage 97
6.2 Examples of bronzes of the Ewart Park assemblage 98
6.3 Deverel-Rimbury pottery 99
6.4 Pottery of the Post-Deverel-Rimbury undecorated phase 100
6.5 Simplified plans of Mucking North Ring and Lofts Farm 100
6.6 Plan of Black Patch Bronze Age settlement 101
6.7 Simplified plan of Bronze Age land divisions on Dartmoor 102
6.8 The Dover Bronze Age boat during excavation 104
7.1 Selected Iron Age brooch types 114
7.2 Different types of circular structures 116
7.3 Rectilinear and curvilinear settlement enclosures 118
7.4 Open and aggregated settlement plans 119
7.5 Danebury in its early and developed stages 121
7.6 Plans of territorial oppida 122
7.7 Plans of Iron Age shrines and sacred enclosures 123
7.8 Grave plans from Wetwang Slack and Westhampnett 124
7.9 Selected iron tools 126
7.10 Selected Iron Age pottery 127
7.11 Inscribed Iron Age coins 129
8.1 Tombstone of Tadius Exuperatus 138
8.2 Aerial photograph of the fort, annexe and temporary camps at Malling 139
8.3 Distribution of first-century AD Roman forts in Britain 140
8.4 Site plans: fortresses 142
8.5 Site plans: forts 144
8.6 Site plans: fortlet and towers 145
8.7 Ardoch fort, Perthshire 146
8.8 Aerial photograph of the fort and *vicus* at Old Carlisle, Cumbria 148
8.9 Plan of the Gask frontier 150
8.10 Frontiers across the Tyne–Solway and Forth–Clyde 151
8.11 Distribution of Saxon Shore forts and late Roman forts and coastal watchtowers 154
9.1 Comparative distribution of civilian towns and long-term military sites in Roman Britain 158
9.2 Plan of the *civitas*-capital at Silchester, Hampshire 161
9.3 Public buildings at Silchester 162
9.4 Plan of a 'small' town, Water Newton, Cambridgeshire 163
9.5 Plans showing the development of the Gorhambury villa 165
9.6 Settlement and landscape of the Roman period around Chalton, Hampshire 166
9.7 Plan of temple and associated buildings at Uley, Gloucestershire 167

| | | |
|---|---|---|
| 9.8 | Drawing of the Hinton St Mary mosaic | 169 |
| 9.9 | Plan of Walesland Rath, Pembrokeshire | 170 |
| 9.10 | Late Roman timber churches at Lincoln | 174 |
| 10.1 | Map of kingdoms and tribal areas mentioned in text | 177 |
| 10.2 | Perception of King Alfred | 180 |
| 10.3 | Cremation burials at Spong Hill | 183 |
| 10.4 | Anglo-Saxon grave from Kent | 185 |
| 10.5 | Sutton Hoo from the air | 185 |
| 10.6 | Aerial view of fort at Dundurn, Perthshire | 186 |
| 10.7 | Model of Anglo-Saxon monastery of St Paul, Jarrow | 190 |
| 10.8 | A Middle Saxon road with timber buildings, London | 192 |
| 11.1 | Cuerdale, Lancashire: part of the early tenth-century silver hoard | 196 |
| 11.2 | The burial at Balladoole in the Isle of Man | 199 |
| 11.3 | The Middleton Cross, St Andrew's Church, Middleton | 200 |
| 11.4 | Ribblehead, N. Yorks: an artist's reconstruction of the Viking Age farmstead | 201 |
| 11.5 | Norse buildings at Jarlshof, Shetland | 202 |
| 11.6 | Excavated buildings at Coppergate, York | 204 |
| 12.1 | The undercroft beneath the chapel on medieval London Bridge | 212 |
| 12.2 | An oak board from a twelfth-century waterfront, Seal House, Thames Street, London | 217 |
| 12.3 | A revetment of 1270–90 excavated at Trig Lane, London | 218 |
| 12.4 | Three medieval buildings at the Cornmarket, Oxford | 219 |
| 12.5 | Three houses and a latrine in thirteenth-century Kirk Close, Perth | 220 |
| 12.6 | An engraved piece of animal bone from Milk Street, London | 221 |
| 12.7 | Late thirteenth-century tokens found near Billingsgate, London | 223 |
| 12.8 | Torksey, Lincolnshire: an aerial view of the shrunken medieval river port | 224 |
| 13.1 | Sequence of church constructions at Raunds, Northamptonshire | 232 |
| 13.2 | Composite ground-plan of St Peter's church, Barton-upon-Humber | 233 |
| 13.3 | Reconstruction of defences and timber buildings at Hen Domen, Montgomeryshire | 236 |
| 13.4 | Castle Acre, Norfolk | 236 |
| 13.5 | Bodiam Castle, Sussex | 237 |
| 13.6 | Norton Priory, Cheshire | 239 |
| 13.7 | Fountains Abbey, North Yorkshire, from the north-east | 240 |
| 13.8 | Fountains Abbey, North Yorkshire: the wool-house | 241 |
| 13.9 | Little Maplestead, Essex: church | 242 |
| 14.1 | Pillar-and-stall coal mining exposed at Coleorton, Leicestershire | 248 |
| 14.2 | A late medieval cruck-built longhouse | 252 |
| 14.3 | Home Farm, Wardhouse, Aberdeenshire | 253 |
| 14.4 | The village of West Whelpington in the early fifteenth century | 254 |
| 14.5 | Thirteenth-century terraced longhouses at Springwood Park | 255 |
| 14.6 | Open fields of Doddington, Northamptonshire | 259 |
| 14.7 | Medieval industrial activity at Stanion, Northamptonshire | 261 |
| 14.8 | The timber piers of the great bridge at Hemington, Leicestershire | 262 |
| 15.1 | Shieling huts, Lewis, Scotland | 267 |
| 15.2 | Montacute House, Somerset | 268 |
| 15.3 | A deserted bastle house and *fermtoun* site, Glenochar, upper Clydesdale | 268 |
| 15.4 | Crathes Castle, Aberdeenshire | 269 |

| | | |
|---|---|---:|
| 15.5 | Garden and landscaped park, Mellerstain, Scottish Borders | 272 |
| 15.6 | Engine house of tin mine, Helston, Cornwall | 273 |
| 15.7 | Mullion Cove, Cornwall | 275 |
| 15.8 | Royal Crescent, Bath | 278 |
| 16.1 | The entrance to Beamish Museum | 283 |
| 16.2 | The Iron Bridge, Shropshire | 284 |
| 16.3 | Ironworks at Bonawe, Argyll | 286 |
| 16.4 | Copper-working landscape at Parys Mountain, Anglesey | 287 |
| 16.5 | Engine house, Cornwall | 289 |
| 16.6 | Anderton boat lift, Cheshire | 291 |
| 16.7 | Reconstruction of a coal waggon on a wooden waggon way, Causey, Durham | 292 |
| 16.8 | The great barn at Leighton, Wales | 293 |
| 16.9 | Kilns at Gladstone Pottery Museum, Stoke-on-Trent | 294 |
| 16.10 | Slip-glazed chamber pot | 295 |
| 17.1 | Bronze Age round barrow cemetery on King Barrow Ridge, Amesbury | 298 |
| 17.2 | Main components of the archaeological resource | 301 |
| 17.3 | Visitors at Stonehenge, Wiltshire | 302 |
| 17.4 | Relationship of controls over developments impacting on archaeological deposits | 305 |
| 17.5 | The management cycle applied to archaeological situations | 307 |
| 17.6 | Protecting a section of Iron Age rampart, Badbury Rings, Dorset | 310 |
| 17.7 | Restoration and consolidation at Lulworth Castle, Dorset | 311 |
| 17.8 | The Morwellham Quay Heritage centre, Devon | 311 |
| 17.9 | Roman gatehouse at South Shields, Tyne and Wear | 312 |
| 17.10 | Excavations at Silchester, Hampshire | 313 |

# Contributors

**John Hunter**, formerly Reader in Archaeology at Bradford, took up the Chair in Ancient History and Archaeology at the University of Birmingham in 1996. He specialises in Viking studies and has carried out multi-period fieldwork in Scotland, particularly in Orkney and Fair Isle, on which he has published *Fair Isle, the archaeology of an island community*. He also has interests in cultural resource management and in forensic archaeology which he has helped to develop as a recognised sub-discipline. *Studies in crime: an introduction to forensic archaeology* appeared in 1994.

**Ian Ralston** taught at the University of Aberdeen before moving to Edinburgh, where he is now a Professor of Archaeology. A former Chairman of the Institute of Field Archaeologists, his research interests include Scottish archaeology (notably its later prehistory), the Iron Age of France and applied archaeology. He recently co-edited *Scotland: environment and archaeology 8000 BC–AD 1000* and has previously edited *Archaeological resource management in the UK: an introduction* with John Hunter.

**Nicholas Barton** is a Senior Lecturer in the Department of Anthropology at Oxford Brookes University. His main areas of research are in Palaeolithic and Mesolithic archaeology. He is currently writing up research on the human uses of caves in the Wye Valley, Herefordshire, and is co-director with Professor Christopher Stringer of the Gibraltar Caves Project. He sits on the UISPP Commission for the European Upper Palaeolithic and has recently published *Stone Age Britain*.

**Timothy Champion** is a Professor of Archaeology at the University of Southampton, and a former President of the Prehistoric Society. His research interests include the later Bronze Age and Iron Age of western Europe, the evolution of complex societies, and the contemporary understanding of the past. Recent publications (as co-editor) include *Nationalism and archaeology in Europe* and *England's coastal heritage*.

**Kate Clark** lectured in industrial archaeology at the Ironbridge Institute, was Monuments Manager for the Ironbridge Gorge museum and whilst there, collaborated with Judith Alfrey on a major research project, published as *Landscape of industry* (Routledge: 1994). Since then she has been Conservation Officer for the Council for British Archaeology and is now Head of the Historical Analysis and Research Team at English Heritage. Her research interests lie in industrial archaeology, and the integration of buildings and landscapes as a basis for conservation.

**Timothy Darvill** is Professor of Archaeology in the School of Conservation Sciences, Bournemouth University. His research interests focus on archaeological resource management and the Neolithic period in northern Europe. He is currently Director of the Billown Neolithic Landscape Project on the Isle of Man and Chairman of the Directors of the Cotswold Archaeological Trust. His publications include *Ancient monuments in the countryside* and *Prehistoric Britain from the air*.

**Simon Esmonde Cleary** teaches archaeology at the University of Birmingham, principally on the Roman period in Europe. His research interests centre on the transition from the 'high' Roman Empire to Late Antiquity and the early mediaeval period; including the ways in which these are reflected in the archaeological record and how this affects our perceptions. His publications include *The ending of Roman Britain*. He is currently undertaking fieldwork on the Roman and mediaeval town of St-Bertrand-de-Comminges in south-western France.

**Roberta Gilchrist** is a Professor of Archaeology at the University of Reading, and archaeological consultant to Norwich Cathedral. Her research focuses on the archaeology of medieval England (particularly buildings and church archaeology), and on the study of gender in the past. Her publications include *Gender and material culture: the archaeology of religious women* (Routledge: 1994) and *Contemplation and action: the other monasticism*.

**Bill Hanson** is a Senior Lecturer in Archaeology at the University of Glasgow and is a former President of the Council for Scottish Archaeology. His research interests include Roman Britain, particularly the impact of the conquest on the indigenous population and on the landscape, Roman frontiers in the western empire and aerial reconnaissance. He is co-author of the standard text on the Antonine Wall – *Rome's north-west frontier: the Antonine Wall*.

**Colin Haselgrove** is now a Professor of Archaeology at Durham University, where he has taught since 1977. His research interests include the Iron Age of Britain and France, particularly coinage; the Roman impact on indigenous societies; and field survey techniques. He recently co-edited *Reconstructing Iron Age societies*.

**Catherine Hills** has been a Lecturer in the Department of Archaeology at Cambridge University for many years, where she is currently Head of Department. Her main interests are Anglo-Saxon archaeology, Europe and Scandinavia in the first millennium AD and the relationship between history and archaeology. She has excavated the Anglo-Saxon cemetery of Spong Hill in Norfolk, the reports on which are published in the series *East Anglian archaeology*.

**Steven Mithen** is Reader in Early Prehistory at the University of Reading. Between 1988 and 1998 he directed the Southern Hebrides Mesolithic Project and is currently a co-director of an Early Prehistory project in south Jordan. He has particular research interests in the use of computer simulation in archaeology, and cognitive archaeology. His books include *Thoughtful foragers: a study of prehistoric decision making* and *The prehistory of the mind*. He is editor of *Creativity in human evolution and prehistory* (Routledge: 1998).

**Mike Parker Pearson** lectures in archaeology at the University of Sheffield. He was previously an Inspector of Ancient Monuments for English Heritage. His current fieldwork projects include the excavation and survey of Early Bronze Age to nineteenth-century settlements on South Uist in the Western Isles, the study of funerary monumentality in southern Madagascar, and the excavation of a Neolithic rock shelter burial site near Sheffield. He is author of *Bronze Age Britain*.

**Julian Richards** completed his doctorate on Anglo-Saxon funerary practices at Staffordshire University Computing Department. After a spell at the University of Leeds he moved to York where he teaches and researches Viking archaeology and computer applications and is Director of the Archaeology Data Service. He has excavated Anglo-Scandinavian settlements in the Yorkshire Wolds and is now working on a Viking barrow cemetery in Derbyshire. He is the author of *Viking age England*.

**John Schofield** is Curator of Architecture at the Museum of London. He has been digging in and writing about the City of London since 1974. His main interests are in urban archaeology of all periods and in the relationships between archaeology and documentary history. He has written *The building of London from the Conquest to the Great Fire*, *Medieval London houses* and, with Alan Vince, *Medieval towns*.

**Paul Stamper** works as an Inspector of historic parks and gardens for English Heritage. In the 1980s he was Assistant Director of excavations at Wharram Percy (Yorkshire), and his research interests have always focussed on the rural landscapes of the Middle Ages. He is the author of *Historic parks and gardens of Shropshire*, a county on which he worked for many years on the staff of the *Victoria County History*. He has recently co-edited *The age of transition: the archaeology of English culture 1400–1600*.

**Alasdair Whittle** is a Professor of Archaeology in the School of History and Archaeology at Cardiff University. He has researched widely on the Neolithic period in Britain, directing field-work projects from Shetland to Wessex, and Europe. His recent publications include *Europe in the Neolithic: the creation of new worlds* and *Sacred mound, holy rings*.

**Ian Whyte** taught at University College Swansea and the University of Glasgow before moving to Lancaster where he is now Professor of Historical Geography. His research interests include landscape change in Britain during the post-medieval period, and the economic and social development of early modern Scotland. His recent books include *Scotland before the Industrial Revolution: an economic and social history c1050–c1750* and *Climatic change and human society*.

# Preface

The idea for the approach taken in this book emerged in late 1994 as the editors compared wounds that were the outcome of their previous collaborative editorial effort. Discussion, typical of many of the time, included comparing statistics on rising student numbers, and noting the very different archaeological world – both academic and practical – that faced the new intakes of students, compared to that which had been encountered some twenty years previously. Talk then turned to the concomitant need to make readily accessible suitable literature for students at the outset of their undergraduate careers, in access classes preparing for university entrance, and for those taking A-level and similar courses and their teachers. The format and contents of this book, an attempt to encapsulate the British archaeological record and its present-day interpretation in an introductory and accessible way, represent the outcome of subsequent thoughts, but honed and improved by anonymous referees, by the various contributors and by the staff at Routledge, initially Diana Grivas, and subsequently Vicky Peters and Nadia Jacobson.

No work of this kind could be put together without a team effort, and the contributions of our colleagues, who have authored the substance of what follows, were obviously essential for the completion of the project. Their telephone calls, e-mails and other communications were also of great help in the shaping of its contents. To those who contributed swiftly and to specification, to those who were not so swift off the mark and required cajoling, as well as to the few who felt the need to draw attention to editorial delays as we sometimes struggled to find time to fit the compilation of this work into other responsibilities, we offer our grateful thanks. We trust they find the final product to their liking, but any deficiencies still present are our responsibility.

Thanks are also due to our partners, Margaret and Sandra, for once more tolerating the trauma of editing during the evenings and weekends and to Ellie, Natalie, both Toms, Ben and (intermittently) Edward for putting up with fathers once again preoccupied with other matters.

We hope that the following pages encourage new students and interested amateurs in their interest and involvement in British archaeology, and that colleagues across the widening spectrum of archaeological endeavour and beyond find value in the contents.

John Hunter and Ian Ralston
Warwickshire – Kinross-shire
August 1997

*Chapter One*

# British archaeology since the end of the Second World War

## Ian Ralston and John Hunter

### INTRODUCTION

As with so many subjects, archaeology, and in particular British archaeology, has been the subject of greater involvement and awareness than was the case in the years around 1950. University departments teaching archaeology have grown from a mere handful to nearly thirty today, the subject itself has developed from a traditionally historical or Classical base to include natural, physical and computing sciences, and its scope has expanded to embrace, for example, standing buildings, underwater remains and whole landscapes. By way of a measure, *British Archaeological Abstracts*, first published in 1968, noted fewer than 300 articles that year, while its successor, *British Archaeological Bibliography*, abstracted nearly five times as many in 1996. Furthermore, long-established, county-based archaeological societies – the mainstay of the amateur involvement in which British archaeology has its roots – have been joined by an increasing range of special-interest groups; these are recorded in the annual reviews published by *Current Archaeology*. This amateur involvement became radically 'professionalized' with the appearance of whole new sectors of archaeological endeavour both in local authorities and, most notably, in archaeological units. The latter bodies first conducted 'rescue' fieldwork on behalf of state agencies, but now, together with archaeological companies and consultants, fulfil the needs of a wide range of developers. This is a product of legislative and planning changes by which developers have been required by government to conduct archaeological investigations within the framework of the 'polluter pays' principle.

The same awareness of 'heritage' has also seen archaeology's remit widening in both scope and detail; its chronological interests lap up against the present, with industrial archaeology (its history is sketched in Chapter 16) now including redundant plant of all kinds reflecting the quantum leaps of twentieth-century technology in methods of energy generation, transportation and bulk processing. A new field of enquiry susceptible to archaeological approaches comprises, for instance, the surviving concrete and other military defences of twentieth-century Britain (e.g. Brown *et al.* 1995). Thus the remaining tank-traps and other defensive installations on the beaches around which today's mid-career archaeologists played as children are now a focus of attention (Figure 1.1). Some are Scheduled Ancient Monuments. In sum, archaeology is defined more broadly, and the archaeological community that researches, manages and monitors this resource is substantially larger and more diverse than it was a generation ago. Even though many archaeological jobs remain precarious, far more individuals earn their living from British archaeology in one of its many guises than was the case in 1950.

***Figure 1.1*** The recording of military monuments. Remains from the Second World War now fall within the recognized scope of archaeology. Military remains at Brockhill, Redditch, Worcestershire.
*Source:* Birmingham University Field Archaeology Unit

## DEVELOPING SCIENCES

There have also been radical changes in the development and sophistication of scientific method and in the intellectual climate in which archaeology has been conducted since the end of the 1940s. New techniques and their routine application have made significant contributions, for example to the understanding of previous environments and subsistence regimes, to sourcing the raw materials from which artefacts were made, and to providing absolute dates for archaeological materials. Many techniques are now exercised routinely, and archaeology continues to draw extensively on other areas of expertise, often in the creation of sub-disciplines that have now evolved in their own right, such as palaeobotany and osteoarchaeology. These new approaches and developments are not in themselves a principal concern in this volume and can be well pursued as individual features elsewhere (see, for example, Renfrew and Bahn 1996). They do, however, reflect archaeology's holistic nature and their results are incorporated in many ways in the following chapters.

## Dating

The issue of obtaining dates may stand as particularly symptomatic of the scale of changes since the 1940s. The fixing of chronology has always been an archaeological preoccupation, and many standard archaeological methods – from site stratigraphies to artefact typologies – contain amongst their primary purposes the establishment of relative chronologies, i.e. the demonstration that building A precedes building B, or that grave C is later than grave D. However, the approaches available for providing absolute dates for archaeological materials immediately after the Second World War were little changed since the nineteenth century and involved correlations with documentary sources. These historical connections become possible from Roman Britain with early chronicles, hagiographies and the emerging written record and, more reliably, with the later histories, accounts and documents of the Middle Ages. However, for pre-Roman times, chronology could still be established in only relative terms; it was interpreted on the basis of perceived artefact analogy or founded on the premise of diffusionist theory, often based on the clumsy 'three-age' development of technological progression from stone through bronze to iron. Alternatively, cross-dating was possible, ultimately with literate civilizations, but only intermittently and only as far back as the emergence of Middle Eastern civilizations some five millennia ago.

Major advances followed in biological, physico-chemical and geological sciences, notably with Libby's 1949 discovery of radiocarbon dating which depended on measuring the decay rate of the radioactive isotope of carbon in organic materials. Although the hypotheses on which the technique was developed have required modification, notably in the 'radiocarbon revolution' of the 1970s when the need for major correction factors was recognized, the measurement of thousands of absolute dates has been of primordial importance in securing and modifying the chronology of prehistory. Radiocarbon measurement from archaeological materials requires adjustment or calibration according to the derived dates of sequences of tree-rings (dendro-chronology) which mirror inconsistencies in the amount of radiocarbon in the atmosphere through time.

The effects of these calibrated dates have been both to push back in time the start dates for various innovations, and to lengthen the timespans of various segments into which the archaeological record is traditionally sub-divided. Thus, in the mid-1950s, the Neolithic period was considered on the best evidence then available to have endured for several centuries either side of 2,000 BC; early radiocarbon dates pushed this back to around 3000 BC; while recent calibrated dates place the British Earlier Neolithic even earlier (see Chapter 4). Radiocarbon dates have also been instrumental in demonstrating that the initial interpretations of some elements in the archaeological record were awry (e.g. Fairweather and Ralston 1993). Dendrochronology is also valuable in its own right, although its scope is restricted by the need for suitable preservation of wood in archaeological contexts. Sequences can provide dates correct to the nearest year; they have a particular role to play in post-Roman periods where structural timbers may survive and when radiocarbon dates become of decreasing value.

## Other technical innovations

Other techniques, too, have made important contributions to the refocusing of research agenda. Developments of the aqualung and the drysuit, for example, have physically extended the scope of British archaeology into lakes and coastal waters, as witness work on the *Mary Rose* and on Scottish crannogs, while the widespread application of aerial photography (Wilson 1982) has had a major impact on the quantity of sites now recorded. New categories of site have also been identified from the air, particularly as cropmarks in free-draining soils in the agricultural lowlands (as far north as the Moray Firth) of eastern and southern Britain (Figure 1.2). The technique has become more refined and versatile, and it currently underpins most regional sites and monuments records. Through the identity of former field and land boundaries, aerial imagery has been able to illustrate the vast extent of some systems of earlier settlement and landuse; it has been in part responsible for the shift away from the study of individual monuments and their artefacts to the investigation of whole landscapes and of their infrastructure (Darvill *et al.* 1993). In its turn this has had a direct influence in matters of heritage management.

***Figure 1.2*** Aerial photography has been a major factor in increasing both the number of known sites and in emphasizing the importance of landscape study. Aerial view of the Don Valley, Aberdeenshire, showing pit defined enclosure (foreground) and ring-ditch set amongst geomorphological marks.
*Source:* Aberdeenshire Archaeological Services

In the uplands and other zones where above-ground survival of monuments and landscapes is optimum, the use of electronic distance measuring equipment has simplified the task of mapping multiperiod features (Mercer 1991). The finer detail in such zones has been recognized through the refinement of fieldwork strategies, supported by sophisticated three-dimensional software and, most recently, by the application of geographical information systems (GIS) which allow landscapes and monuments to be investigated in terms of their physical and spatial relationships.

Not least of these relationships is the time/depth dimension which, given the importance attached to non-invasive strategies, is becoming increasingly pursued by geophysical means. Geophysical survey technology in part derives from post-war military developments and quickly became adapted as an archaeological technique in its own right. Its history and applications are well documented (e.g. Clark 1996), with magnetometry and resistivity methods being most commonly used on archaeological sites for both research and commercial evaluation. Some recent advances have centred on the determination of depth (e.g. using pseudosections), but in common with aerial and other remote sensing techniques, the effectiveness of geophysical survey is determined by the specific character and condition of the buried remains. This in turn biases understanding of period culture, in that some periods are likely to be more 'visible' than others.

Similarly, some periods or environmental settings are more favoured by taphonomic process than others, such as wetlands, or those that simply have more to offer through deep stratigraphy. Some of the following chapters are characterized by archaeological remains that are fragile; in others there are solid walls and durable materials. We can study only what survives or what we are able to locate, and our knowledge of the different periods is skewed accordingly.

## The environmental dimension

The degree to which the land and environments of Britain have been shaped and reshaped by previous human communities across millennia is becoming apparent through the investigation of some components of these landscape palimpsests, in concert with parallel, sometimes integrated, studies by palaeoenvironmentalists. Many approaches are now available, and many sub-disciplines – including the study of sub-fossil midges, beetles, pollen and plant macrorests, and aspects of geomorphology – contribute; dendrochronology, as well as furnishing absolute chronology, is important also for studies of climate change. A substantial literature has been generated and is summarized in numerous works (e.g. Evans 1975; Simmons and Tooley 1981; Bell and Walker 1992; for Wales, Taylor 1980; for Scotland, Edwards and Ralston 1997). In general, the integration of environmental and archaeological studies has been taken further for prehistory than for subsequent periods, but exceptions to this rule are becoming ever more frequent, notably in the analysis of urban deposits. Because of the enhanced possibilities of preservation they offer, and the particular scope for the integration of archaeological and environmental studies, threatened examples of Britain's wetlands have been particular targets for archaeological study (Coles 1992). These include more especially lowland peat mosses and estuarine and other inter-tidal zones. Particularly influential work, such as that undertaken in the Somerset levels and at Flag Fen, near Peterborough, is mentioned in the succeeding chapters.

## CHANGING PERSPECTIVES

Equally relevant are the various ways by which archaeologists have believed the past can be studied. These have implications for the way in which archaeology is conducted in the field, and there have been a number of reassessments of what archaeological approaches to the physical record bequeathed by earlier communities may be able to achieve. Intellectual fashions have changed, not only as some archaeologists have absorbed theoretical developments in neighbouring disciplines in the social sciences and elsewhere, but also as they reconsider the nature and potential meanings of the structures and materials contained within the emerging archaeological record. Such 'changing configurations' (Renfrew 1974) have perhaps been most prominent in the study of prehistory, not least because its 'text-free' status – the absence of contemporary historical documents – means that archaeologists do not have a perceived requirement to integrate their studies at a variety of levels with those of historians and others.

In later periods, these changes in theoretical stance met greater resistance, partly in view of traditional approaches based on artefact typology, and partly through the presence of the written record which enabled the material past to be artificially compartmentalized. Also, the more recent the period, the shorter in general has been the tradition of independent archaeological research. An indication of this is offered by the foundation dates for the major period-based societies in Britain, those for medieval, post-medieval and industrial archaeology being amongst the most recent, whereas the prehistoric has (along with the Roman) been one of the periods with the longest traditions of archaeological study and investigation.

## Culture history

In the 1950s, the dominant framework for prehistoric studies was provided by the cultural-historical approach, most usually associated in Britain with Vere Gordon Childe, Professor at Edinburgh from 1927, and subsequently at the Institute of Archaeology in London University. This perspective prevailed until the 1960s; its great achievements included the fuller recognition and ordering of archaeological assemblages, in part through more extensive and systematic excavation.

The latter was a legacy of, amongst others, Mortimer Wheeler, and of Gerhard Bersu. Bersu's excavations, most celebratedly at Little Woodbury, Wiltshire (discussed in Chapter 7), allowed the import of the best of contemporary continental practice, including techniques appropriate to the recovery of the stances of former earthfast timber structures, as well as furnishing new interpretations. Wheeler's campaigns at Maiden Castle, Dorset, published mid-way through the Second World War (1943), were a demonstration of other technical innovations, and provided the archaeological support for Wheeler's vision of British Iron Age developments, as well as showing the potential for public involvement in what was then a distinctly minority interest. In the 1950s, larger-scale open-area excavations, as at Yeavering, Northumberland (Hope-Taylor 1977), became feasible and, particularly in subsequent decades, were much more numerous in the countryside. Some sites were excavated at a scale that made them 'laboratories' for their own period of use, such as West Heslerton or Wharram Percy in North Yorkshire (see Chapters 10 and 14 respectively); others, like Jarlshof in Shetland (Hamilton 1956), became used as a regional control for predicting structural change in multiperiod settlements. Much of the best field archaeology became avowedly multidisciplinary, as the potential contribution of physical and biological scientists was increasingly recognized; Grahame Clark's promptly published project at Star Carr, Yorkshire, considered in Chapter 3, was particularly influential in this regard.

Much of the pattern of cultural developments recognized, described and refined during this period, has survived into later usage. What has since changed, in some instances substantially, are the modes of explanation favoured to account for changes seen in the archaeological record. The use of invasion theory found much favour, particularly in periods involving recorded Germanic or Scandinavian movement. Although still important for some horizons and periods, its use as the primary means to account for change came under sustained, and often successful, attack (Clark 1966).

From the late 1960s, a change in emphasis marked the way in which the archaeological record was interpreted by a number of influential figures in the discipline. Radiocarbon dating had already pointed towards errors in the chronology of British prehistory, and the writing of culture history was no longer the primary focus. Archaeology, in some views at least, 'lost its innocence' (Clarke 1973) during this period, but as with the other realignments noted here, the new agenda and approaches were far from universally accepted. Important manifestos, like David L. Clarke's *Analytical Archaeology* (1968), drew on American practice more closely to link archaeological interpretation to dominant perspectives within cultural anthropology, borrowing its vocabulary in the process. Primary aims now included the study of archaeologically recognizable changes in cultural systems, often interpreted from changing spatial patterns in the data, and attention was paid to those sub-systems considered most detectable from archaeological evidence. Particular targets were subsistence economics and the recognition of social change; as a result, the recovery and analyses of appropriate datasets immediately became of high priority. A distinctly positivist attitude to reading the archaeological record is characteristic of some writing, often called the 'New Archaeology', during this period.

The period since 1980 has seen major developments in the consideration of fresh ways of approaching the archaeological record, and of conveying its meanings. In contradistinction to the New Archaeology of the 1960s and 1970s, frequently termed 'processual', subsequent archaeological theorizing can be labelled 'post-processual' – a term that obscures a burgeoning range of post-modern theoretical stances and agendas. Included amongst external strands that have contributed are social theory, ethnoarchaeological studies, certain kinds of historical practice (particularly that concerned with long-term evolutionary rhythms and often associated with the *Annales* school in France), feminism and gender studies, and attempts to analyse material culture recovered archaeologically as encoded messages, akin to literary texts (e.g. Hodder 1986; Shanks and Tilley 1987, 1992; Barrett 1995). These approaches have undoubtedly influenced the writing of some of the contributors here; this gives some indication of the competing theoretical approaches to the subject matter and the degree to which these vary according to the data and traditions of the periods under study.

## Archaeology in the field

In terms of fieldwork, the period dominated in interpretive terms by these 'processual' approaches was broadly coeval with the upsurge in 'rescue archaeology' (Rahtz 1974), a development spurred by the recognition by some archaeologists of the impact of government and private sector attempts to renew Britain's infrastructure. Although individual government projects – such as the wartime building of Heathrow airport and the creation of a rocket range on the Outer Hebrides in the 1950s – had been preceded by systematic salvage excavation, this was the exception rather than the rule. Urban renewal projects, especially in the cores of London and some historic cities in England, and the building of the motorway network, were major spurs to the case being accepted for increased state support for preliminary archaeological work, and many large-scale field projects were undertaken because of such perceived threats. It is arguable that the scale of change in the urban cores of many British towns and cites is unlikely to be repeated for many years into the future, with concomitant effects on the range of opportunities for urban archaeology (Figure 1.3). Much of what we know of medieval towns stems from the opportunity presented by this urban regeneration (see Chapter 12). Much new information was generated, but its assimilation into wider syntheses was not, in many instances, accorded high priority.

*Figure 1.3* Urban archaeology developed rapidly under the 'rescue' banner of the 1970s and early 1980s and provided the basis for much of our knowledge of medieval towns. Excavation at Long Causeway, Peterborough.
*Source*: Birmingham University Field Archaeology Unit

The restructuring of field archaeology to counter the increasing erosion of the archaeological record occurred differently in the constituent parts of the country; its development was *ad hoc* and inconsistent, and archaeologists today are still burdened by its legacy. Some parts of Britain received greater archaeological attention and resources than others, based on local demands at the time, not on a rational analysis of longer term need. Only Wales developed a coherent, fully-nationwide system, whilst funding (tied to present day population sizes rather than to archaeological resources or the scale of the threats to them) was most generous in England (see Chapter 17). This biasing is inevitably reflected in the work carried out and in the distribution of data recovered. The unevenness of the record emerges too in the chapters that follow; but it afflicts some periods more than others and is also a measure of the frameworks within which research has taken place as much as regional disparity of resources. For example, at chronological extremes, studies of Mesolithic hunter-gatherers have for long drawn on evidence from across Britain, whereas innovation and change in the Industrial Revolution is characterized as much in south Wales and west-central Scotland as in some parts of England. Contrastingly, the existence of a first-millennium AD Anglo-Saxon zone of Germanic influence in central and eastern England, and broadly Celtic influences in contemporary northern and western zones of Britain, have contributed to traditions of relatively independent archaeological study. In some areas, too, the study of some periods is only now generating overviews: the first-ever synthesis of medieval Scotland from an archaeological perspective (Yeoman 1995) appeared only while the present work was in preparation.

The period since 1980 has also seen substantial alterations in the way in which the practice of field archaeology is structured; and many current archaeologists face new kinds of problems, not always of an 'academic' kind, in examining the record (Hunter and Ralston 1993; Chapter 17 here). Some have railed against these changes, seeing the outcome as one in which British archaeology 'finds itself in a curious position of self-doubt and indecision' (Biddle 1994, 16). Changes have included a significant trend away from large-scale excavation in favour of small field evaluation exercises, designed in part to test for archaeological remains with a view to protecting them *in situ* rather than excavating them. The driving force has been the enactment of European Union directives in British regulations, and the publication of new advice on archaeology in relation to planning matters by central government. Archaeological remains in Britain are now considered as a finite, non-renewable resource for protection for future elucidation by active management rather than benign neglect, and for use for public enjoyment and education. In many ways they have become less of an exploitable raw material for the nourishment of archaeological research.

## DISSEMINATING THE RECORD

The diverse development of British archaeology has undoubtedly benefited from the publication of overviews, and several of the following chapters make reference to key texts that have served as markers of particular approaches or as 'snapshots in time'. Several of these are either major period-based syntheses, or studies of longer timespans (e.g. Renfrew 1974; Megaw and Simpson 1979; Bradley 1984; Longworth and Cherry 1986; Darvill 1987). These, and others written for more specialist readerships (e.g. Vyner 1994), have enabled archaeologists both to take stock and to formulate new hypotheses, and allow students to assimilate information and perspectives that are normally diffused through a wide range of publication outlets. This is a continuing process, and recent years have seen in particular important series of introductory accounts, either period-based or framed round major sites, emerging from English Heritage and Historic Scotland (e.g. Bewley 1994; Ashmore 1996), some of which are noted in the following chapters.

The gap in the currently available overviews that this book was designed to address was for a single volume that provided a panorama of the archaeology of Britain from the Stone Age through to the nineteenth century. This was devised as a team effort to reflect the number of fields of expertise now essential to the study of British archaeology. No single archaeologist could realistically hope to master the entirety of the record to be considered, and the volume additionally demonstrates the range of sub-disciplines involved, the approaches taken, and the results obtained, both regionally and by period, by environmentalists, documentary historians and other specialists in their areas of major interest. The book also provides the opportunity for archaeologists to achieve the necessary awareness of data types, problems and approaches taken in periods and geographical areas other than those in which their own interests are focused.

Any overview also requires some definition of the word 'British' in its title, particularly given recent concerns on the impacts of nationalism and imperialism, as experienced in Britain during the time of archaeology's evolution, on the discipline's form and the way in which its discourses are framed (Champion 1996; Atkinson *et al.* 1996). This volume is intended to address the record for Britain as a geographical region, rather than as the 'archaeology of a nation'. In some respects this also runs counter to differences in the practices and approaches of the various state agencies concerned with archaeological matters, despite the fact that the primary archaeological legislation, the *Ancient Monuments and Archaeological Areas Act 1979*, applies universally.

The emphasis of this book is on Britain (rather than on England, but excluding Ireland) and on a definition of archaeology that spans the full range of contemporary studies. It includes those more modern periods for which a substantial historical record is also available, excepting those military remains (above) now being collated in the *Defence of Britain* project and which will undoubtedly appear in any future edition. Pressure of space means that there has been one conspicuous casualty: the Lower and Middle Palaeolithic periods are omitted, in part because the remains from these periods were not produced by *Homo sapiens sapiens*, and in part because of the hugely long timescales of their records. Their absence also allows adequate space for medieval and more recent times. Consideration of the record in this account thus begins with the Upper Palaeolithic evidence from the terminal stages of the last glaciation.

Ireland, too, has its own traditions of archaeological research, often and logically embracing both Eire and the counties of Ulster. For some periods, Irish comparanda demonstrate that links across the Irish Sea, or along the western seaways to both Britain and Ireland, were important; and selective instances of such features are mentioned here. A multiperiod archaeological account of the British Isles in their north-west European setting remains a task for the future; perhaps the current work, and recent syntheses of Irish material, will encourage such a development, which will be made easier by the inclusion from 1997 of Irish literature in what is now *British and Irish Archaeological Bibliography*.

This volume is intended as a readable introduction to British archaeology written by contributors who not only have a formidable grasp of their own subject areas, but who also have first-hand experience of teaching students and developing teaching from their personal research and that of their colleagues. Their brief was to provide an attractive, readable volume rather than a clinical textbook, one that would reflect their own enthusiasms and not be overburdened with methodological debates and considerations of techniques. They are also all familiar with the changes that have occurred in, and continue to impact on, teaching practices and learning strategies in higher education, and with pressure on library resources, the need for suitable basic texts, and the declining purchasing power of current students, particularly those entering the tertiary system later in life.

The substantial rise in student numbers in university departments over recent years has increased the demand for books but has also caused a shift in the types of book required. Student-centred learning, and competing demands on academic staff time, have brought about the need for students to acquire a basis of knowledge on which academic staff can confidently build, and on which perceptions and hypotheses can be set. In some senses, this volume is a practical reaction to the requirements of late twentieth-century higher education – the need to draw together and make accessible basic themes and to provide opportunities for students to obtain and begin to question current views.

The text is divided into chronologically linked chapters, each of which is designed to stand in its own right, but with overall chronology running in a single calendrical sequence, thus avoiding the admixture of uncalibrated radiocarbon dates and calendrical dates obtained from historical sources that students, plunged into the discipline for the first time, tend to find confusing. Throughout, these chapters are framed in terms of chronologies in calendrical years, from whatever source (including radiocarbon) the dates were originally obtained. The sole exceptions are the remoter periods of prehistory, where dating depends substantially on radiocarbon determinations, for which calibration procedures are as yet relatively untried.

This is a wide-ranging volume, which breaks new ground in the chronological span of its coverage for the geographical area under consideration. Fifty years ago, its scope, dependent on the breadth and depth of archaeological research that underpin its contributions, would not have seemed either appropriate or achievable to many of the archaeologists of the time. Ten years ago, the chapters might have read very differently and the available range of the archaeological data for some chapters would have been distinctly less. The central difficulty faced by all the contributors has lain in determining how to wrestle with the expansion of knowledge, the changing interpretations and the wealth of data, to bring it into a condensed form. As a result, the chapter structures were specifically engineered to make this possible. Individual contributors were asked to address specific elements within their own specialisms, namely principal chronological sub-divisions; major and typical data types; changing perceptions since the Second World War; relevant advances in archaeological science; key sites and assemblages; current perceptions and the British evidence in a wider geographical framework. The aim was to encourage a degree of consistency throughout the volume in regard to the subject matter, but not in the least to force authors to approach this from any particular theoretical perspective. This standardization of content but not of approach, discussed briefly above in relation to recent developments in archaeological theory, has been allowed neither to smooth out the characteristics of individual periods, nor seriously to impinge on individuals' perceptions of what they considered important to lay before the reader.

There are inevitably some differences in the way in which contributions to this book sit within a much wider geographical framework. In those dealing with early prehistory, southern connections are uppermost, not least because Britain was for long a north-western peninsula of the continental landmass, whereas later periods have European links of different strengths, and from different directions, from western continental coastlands in the Later Bronze Age to Norse Scandinavia. In the Roman period, contrastingly, Britain was an outlying province of a continental-scale Empire. During the periods considered in the final chapters, the influences are even wider and the context, latterly that of British imperial expansion, almost global.

There is no common database that can supply a consistent set of material for all periods. The archaeological records for most periods exhibit idiosyncratic or high-profile remains that in some instances drew early antiquarians to them – such as stone circles, villas, brochs – and started the process of cultural definition that provides the near-inescapable framework for the chapter sub-divisions employed here. Much of the way in which archaeologists define culture periods still reflects the traditional responses initially attributable to early antiquarians, and to historians' sub-divisions for most recent periods. Whilst the development of a much securer chronological framework through radiocarbon dating, and new perspectives derived from archaeological approaches to, for example, social change might have permitted a radical alternative framework to be devised, this can be left to others, on another occasion. The primary purpose here is to present a guide to current archaeological interpretations of the sites in Britain's landscapes, and the artefacts in its museums.

Despite the breadth of coverage, each chapter has been deliberately restricted in its bibliography. Each has two levels of bibliography: a set of some five key titles that encapsulate the evidence of, and approaches to, the period under consideration; and a further set of about 25 titles that allows for greater detail or specialization. The criteria set were that all citations should be to works likely to be readily accessible in university libraries. This, it is anticipated, should assist students to embark on their own research for essay writing and other practical course requirements. It will also give more highly motivated students opportunities to begin to consider particular approaches or periods that are absent or less stressed in the particular academic environments in which they are studying.

In another context, John Updike wrote that 'the fate of all monuments is to become . . . a riddle'. Whilst their interpretation undoubtedly poses challenges, the following chapters represent something of the range of archaeological approaches to the physical fabric left by earlier societies that is now being attempted. Medieval monasteries, for example, once viewed primarily as building layouts and as repositories for the study of the development of architectural styles, are now frequently approached as constituent parts of economic landscapes and as arenas for evolving ritual practices. Similarly, castles, formerly considered essentially as fortifications and as keys to changing military tactics and equipment, may now be viewed as symbols of elite power and as central elements in organized economic hinterlands from which they drew resources. Comparable changes are evident for artefactual study, where some archaeologists are now much more readily prepared to hypothesize on social and ritual roles than was the case in the years immediately after the Second World War. Medieval artefacts, for example, viewed solely as fodder for art historical studies, have in recent decades been increasingly studied as keys to technology, as products of exchange and trade, and as indicators of social relations and stratification.

As archaeological evidence accumulates, the very diverse characteristics of different places, sites and objects, conventionally described in the same way, are writ large. This is a book that encapsulates archaeological change in many forms – a 'snapshot' of how we have been thinking, excavating and learning in the late 1990s.

## Bibliography

Ashmore, P.J., 1996. *Neolithic and Bronze Age Scotland.* London: Batsford / Historic Scotland.

Atkinson, J.A., Banks, I. and O'Sullivan, J. (eds) 1996. *Nationalism and archaeology.* Glasgow: Cruithne Press.

Barrett, J.C., 1995. *Some challenges in contemporary archaeology.* Oxford: Oxbow = Oxbow Lecture 2.

Bell, M. and Walker, M.J.C., 1992. *Late Quaternary environmental change: human and physical perspectives.* Harlow: Longman Scientific and Technical.

Bewley, R., 1994. *English Heritage Book of prehistoric settlements.* London: Batsford / English Heritage.

Biddle, M., 1994. *What future for British archaeology?* Oxford: Oxbow = Oxbow Lecture 1.

Bradley, R.J., 1984. *The social foundations of prehistoric Britain: themes and variations in the archaeology of power.* London: Longman.

Brown, I., Burridge, D., Clarke, D., Guy, J., Hellis, J., Lowry, B., Ruckley, N. and Thomas, R., 1995. *20th century defences in Britain; an introductory guide.* York: Council for British Archaeology = Practical Handbooks in Archaeology 12.

Champion, T.C., 1996. 'Three nations or one? Britain and the national use of the past', in Díaz-Andreu, M. and Champion, T.C. (eds) *Nationalism and archaeology in Europe.* London: UCL Press, 119–145.

Clark, A., 1996. *Seeing beneath the soil.* London: Routledge.

Clark, J.G.D., 1966. 'The invasion hypothesis in British archaeology', *Antiquity* 40, 172–189.

Clarke, D.L., 1968. *Analytical archaeology*. London: Methuen.

Clarke, D.L., 1973. 'Archaeology: the loss of innocence', *Antiquity* 47, 6–18.

Coles, B. (ed.) 1992. *The wetland revolution in prehistory*. Exeter: University of Exeter for the Prehistoric Society and W.A.R.P. = Wetland Archaeology Research Project Occasional Paper 6.

Darvill, T.C., 1987. *Prehistoric Britain*. London: Batsford.

Darvill, T.C., Gerrard, C. and Startin, B., 1993. 'Identifying and protecting historic landscapes', *Antiquity* 67, 563–574.

Edwards, K.J. and Ralston, I.B.M. (eds) 1997. *Scotland: environment and archaeology 8000 BC–AD 1000*. Chichester: John Wiley.

Evans, J.G., 1975. *The environment of early man in the British Isles*. Berkeley: University of California Press.

Fairweather, A.D. and Ralston, I.B.M., 1993. 'The Neolithic timber hall at Balbridie, Grampian Region, Scotland: the building, the date, the plant macrofossils', *Antiquity*, 67, 313–323.

Hamilton, J.R.C., 1956. *Excavations at Jarlshof, Shetland*. Edinburgh: HMSO.

Hodder, I., 1986. *Reading the past: current approaches to interpretation in archaeology*. Cambridge: Cambridge University Press.

Hope-Taylor, B.K., 1977. *Yeavering; an Anglo-British centre of early Northumbria*. London: HMSO. = Department of the Environment Research Report 7.

Hunter, J.R. and Ralston, I.B.M. (eds) 1993. *Archaeological resource management in the UK: an introduction*. Stroud: Alan Sutton / Institute of Field Archaeologists.

Longworth, I. and Cherry, J. (eds) 1986. *Archaeology in Britain since 1945*. London: British Museum Publications.

Megaw, J.V.S. and Simpson, D.D.A. (eds) 1979. *An introduction to British prehistory from the arrival of Homo sapiens to the Claudian invasion*. Leicester: Leicester University Press.

Mercer, R.J., 1991. 'The highland zone: reaction and reality 500 BC–2000 AD', *Proceedings of the British Academy* 76, 129–150.

Rahtz, P.A. (ed.) 1974. *Rescue archaeology*. Harmondsworth: Allen Lane.

Renfrew, A.C., 1974. 'Changing configurations in British prehistory', in Renfrew, A.C. (ed.) *British prehistory: a new outline*. London: Duckworth, 1–40.

Renfrew, A.C. and Bahn, P., 1996. *Archaeology: theories, methods and practice*. London: Thames and Hudson. 2 edn.

Shanks, M. and Tilley, C., 1987. *Social theory and archaeology*. Cambridge: Polity Press.

Shanks, M. and Tilley, C., 1992. *Re-constructing archaeology: theory and practice*. London: Routledge. 2 edn.

Simmons, I.G. and Tooley, M.J. (eds) 1981. *The environment in British prehistory*. London: Duckworth.

Taylor, J. (ed.) 1980. *Culture and environment in prehistoric Wales*. Oxford: British Archaeological Reports British Series 76.

Vyner, B. (ed.) 1994. *Building on the past*. London: Royal Archaeological Institute.

Wheeler, R.E.M., 1943. *Maiden Castle, Dorset*. London: Reports of the Research Committee of the Society of Antiquaries 12.

Wilson, D.R., 1982. *Air photography interpretation for archaeologists*. London: Batsford.

Yeoman, P.A., 1995. *Medieval Scotland*. London: Batsford/Historic Scotland.

## Chapter Two

# The Lateglacial or Late and Final Upper Palaeolithic colonization of Britain

## Nicholas Barton

### THE FRAMEWORK

The record of human settlement of Britain in the Palaeolithic can be seen as a series of intermittent episodes, comprising periods of occupation punctuated by intervals when the British peninsula became substantially depopulated or was abandoned. One of the most recent cycles of abandonment and colonization occurred towards the end of the last Ice Age, during the Upper Palaeolithic. In this chapter, evidence for the timing of reoccupation of Britain following the last glacial maximum about 18,000 BP (uncalibrated radiocarbon years ago) will be reviewed. The distribution and nature of human settlement patterns in the Lateglacial will also be considered.

The earliest reappearance of hunter-gatherer populations in Britain following the retreat of the ice sheets of the Dimlington stadial (Table 2.1) seems to have taken place sometime after 13,000 BP (Housley *et al.* 1997). Claims for earlier recolonization have been made on the basis of now discredited radiocarbon dates on human remains from Paviland Cave, West Glamorgan (the so-called 'Red Lady'), and animal bone from Kent's Cavern, Devon. In the case of Paviland, redating of the bone has shown that the male individual was buried some 26,350 ± 550 radiocarbon years ago, well before the maximum of the last glaciation. The date on brown bear (*Ursus arctos*) of 14,275 ± 120 BP from Kent's Cavern appears to record a natural occurrence unconnected with human activities (Jacobi 1980). In consequence, there is at present no evidence that Britain was recolonized before the beginning of Lateglacial interstadial climatic amelioration.

The context for studying early human resettlement patterns in the Lateglacial is provided by information on the absolute chronology of this period. Traditionally, the dating sequence for the Lateglacial has been based on pollen chronozones. The interstadial (warm)/stadial (cool) succession of Oldest Dryas/Middle Weichselian (stadial) – Bølling (interstadial) – Older Dryas (stadial) – Allerød (interstadial) – Younger Dryas (stadial) – Postglacial (interglacial) is still the most widely accepted framework used in Europe (Table 2.1). Correlation of these oscillations on a global scale and even across Europe has, however, proved extremely difficult, due to the varying strengths of the climatic signal from region to region. For example, in Britain few pollen diagrams contain evidence for the Older Dryas stadial. This has led to the development of local terms for describing the Lateglacial succession (Table 2.1).

Alternative means of reconstructing Lateglacial palaeotemperatures are provided by the analysis of fossil beetle faunas, and these have been especially important in identifying periods of very rapid climatic change, when the migration of plants was outstripped by insects. More recently, a

*Table 2.1* British and European sub-divisions of the Lateglacial.

| $^{14}C$ years BP | Pollen zones | NW European chronozones | NW European climatostratigraphic units | British biozones |
|---|---|---|---|---|
| | IV | PREBOREAL | FLANDRIAN INTERGLACIAL | FLANDRIAN INTERGLACIAL |
| 10,000 | III | YOUNGER DRYAS | Transition | LOCH LOMOND STADIAL |
| | | | YOUNGER DRYAS STADIAL | |
| 11,000 | II | ALLERØD | Transition | WINDERMERE INTERSTADIAL |
| 11,800 | Ic | OLDER DRYAS | | |
| 12,000 | Ib | BØLLING | LATEGLACIAL INTERSTADIAL | |
| | Ia | | | |
| 13,000 | | MIDDLE WEICHSELIAN | Transition | |
| | | | LATE DEVENSIAN/STADIAL | DIMLINGTON STADIAL |

highly detailed record of climatic change, derived from the Greenland ice sheet, has been obtained from the GISP-2 ice-core. The climatic signal, in the form of a continuous temperature curve, is calculated from the relative percentages of different oxygen isotopes and dust levels present in the core. This is underpinned by a high precision time-scale based on the counting of annually accumulating layers of ice. So far, direct comparisons between the land and ice-core records have been only moderately successful, but the results of work at Gransmoor in eastern Britain suggest that correlations will increasingly prove possible (Lowe *et al.* 1995) (Figure 2.1).

Part of the difficulty in producing a fine-grained chronology for the Lateglacial is due to the current limitations of the radiocarbon method. Nevertheless, recent progress in using independent dating measurements on tree ring data and uranium-thorium results has allowed a recalibration of radiocarbon dates for the Lateglacial period. By combining these results with the information from annually accumulating laminae within the ice-core, it is possible to show that the Dimlington glaciation ended abruptly 14,500 years ago. This same event is recorded by conventional radiocarbon dates at about 13,000 BP.

Despite the fact that calibration of the radiocarbon record over 10,000 years ago is now theoretically possible (though still largely untested), for the sake of comparability, a chronology based on uncalibrated radiocarbon years is employed here. Thus while the beginning of our present interglacial occurred about 11,500 ice-core years ago, the conventional age equivalent of 10,000 BP will be used.

## LATE UPPER PALAEOLITHIC

### Environmental background

The earliest evidence for reoccupation of Britain after the Last Glacial Maximum is currently provided by a modified bone of red deer (*Cervus elaphus*) from Gough's Cave (Somerset), dating

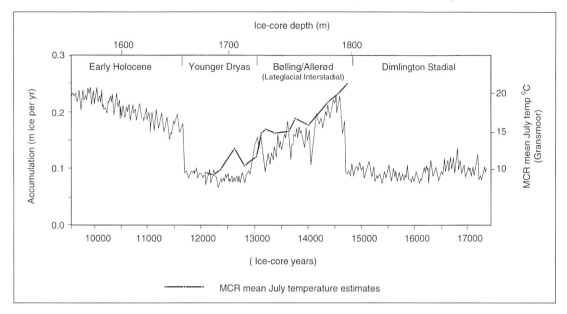

***Figure 2.1*** Comparison of ice accumulation rates from GISP-2, Greenland, and palaeotemperature data from Gransmoor, England.
*Source*: Lowe *et al*. 1995

to 12,800 ± 150 BP. This event can be placed soon after the beginning of the Lateglacial warming at 13,000 BP (Coope and Lemdahl 1995), and it is widely accepted that human populations re-entered the country from the east across the dry land-bridge connecting the British peninsula with the European mainland.

According to annual laminae in the Greenland ice-core and the climatic signal derived from British fossil beetle faunas, the beginning of the Interstadial saw an extremely rapid warming, with mean July temperatures rising by 9–10° C to a maximum of 17° C (Atkinson *et al.* 1987). Although conditions were probably slightly warmer than at present, greater continentality in the climate is implied by lower winter temperatures, which were in the range of 1° C. Evidence from pollen sources shows a considerable time lag in the botanical response to the initial temperature rise. A reflection of the slower vegetational recovery can be found in pollen spectra from the beginning of this period, which show disturbed open-ground species such as *Artemisia* (wormwood/mugwort) only gradually being replaced by low juniper (*Juniperus communis*) scrub. The beginning of the decline in the peak of these open herb-dominated communities is documented at Llanilid, Glamorgan, from around 12,495 ± 70 BP (Walker and Harkness 1990), and was followed by a gradual increase in birch (*Betula*) pollen leading to the main expansion of woodland around 12,000 BP. Thus the warmest part of the Interstadial was associated with an open vegetation dominated by herbs, sedges and grasses and only minimal forest development.

## Material culture and technology

Typological descriptions of artefacts enable comparisons to be made between individual tools or groups of artefacts (assemblages/industries). Many of the terms used today were originally coined by continental prehistorians, and in consequence the following descriptions will include both French or German (in italics) and English forms. Complementing typological studies are those that concern the dynamic processes and states of artefacts at various stages in their 'life-cycle'

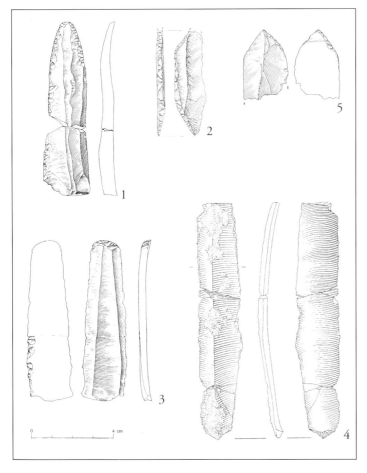

0       4 cm

***Figure 2.2*** Creswellian artefacts from Three Holes Cave, Devon: 1. End-scraper on a blade with scalariform retouch along its lateral margins; 2. Trapezoidal-backed blade (Cheddar point); 3. End-scraper on a blade; 4. Blade with 'spur' (*en éperon*) butt preparation; 5. Truncated blade with heavily worn end (*lame tronquée et usée*).
*Source*: Illustration by Karen Hughes. Courtesy of the British Museum

– from manufacture to discard. This concept is often referred to as the '*chaîne opératoire*', literally the chain of events that links a succession of actions, such as the steps in manufacturing a tool.

The first clearly Late Upper Palaeolithic industry present in Britain appears to have been the *Creswellian*. The term was adopted by Dorothy Garrod in 1926 to distinguish artefacts that were recognizably different in type from those of a contemporary kind in north-west Europe. The description of the Creswellian has recently been revised (Jacobi in Barton *et al.* 1991; Jacobi and Roberts 1992). According to the stricter definition, the Creswellian is characterized by lithic tools known as trapezoidal backed blades (Cheddar points) and variants of this form (Creswell points). Amongst other typical forms are end-scrapers on long, straight blades, which sometimes display additional retouch along their lateral margins. Other tools include piercers, burins, becs (some of them true *Zinken*), *Magdalenian* blades (truncated forms with retouch along their edges), truncated blades with heavily worn ends (*lames tronquées et usées*) and splintered pieces (*pièces esquillées*). A representative selection is shown in Figure 2.2. To date, 28 findspots with characteristic Cheddar points have been identified in England and Wales; none is so far known in Scotland or Ireland (Figure 2.3).

Other features of the Creswellian stone industry are equally distinctive. The debitage (waste) is typified by longer blades that are slightly curved in profile and show that they were detached from cores with a single preferred flaking direction. The butts on the blades are usually faceted, and include evidence of a special preparation technique that leaves a distinct 'spur' on the platforms (Figure 2.2). Flat, diffuse bulbs on the proximal ends of blades indicate a production method using either soft stone or antler hammers.

A fairly wide range of organic artefacts have been recorded in Creswellian contexts. These are made in a variety of materials including deer antler, teeth, bone and mammoth ivory. Rare examples of artefacts made on mammoth products comprise double-bevelled ivory rods (*sagaies*) from Gough's Cave (Somerset) and Kent's Cavern (Devon). Reindeer antler was used to make batons (*batons percés*) at Gough's Cave and scooped-end rods (also *sagaies*) at Fox Hole (Derbyshire) and Church Hole (Creswell Crags, Derbyshire). Products on un-identified antler include parts of three barbed harpoons from Kent's Cavern, while leg bones of arctic hare (*Lepus timidus*) modified for use as pointed awls (*poinçons*) have been recovered at Gough's Cave and Robin Hood Cave (Creswell Crags, Derbyshire). Other organic items include bone needles at Gough's Cave, Church Hole and Kent's Cavern, plus an awl – though not of hare bone – from the latter site. Several fox tooth beads have also been found at Gough's Cave.

Evidence for the method of antler working technology is restricted to a single fragment of antler from Gough's Cave that shows groove and splinter modification. Grooves and cuts on the bones of Whooper swan (*Cygnus cygnus*) from Gough's Cave show how needles were manufactured from bone cores.

## Radiocarbon dating

Until recently, efforts to date the Creswellian have been greatly ham-pered by the limitations of the

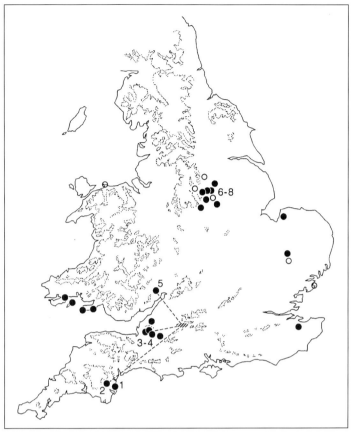

***Figure 2.3*** Distribution of Creswellian findspots: 1. Kent's Cavern; 2. Three Holes Cave; 3. Sun Hole; 4. Gough's Cave; 5. King Arthur's Cave; 6. Robin Hood Cave; 7. Pin Hole; 8. Church Hole. Hachuring indicates potential source of flint raw materials.
*Source*: After Jacobi in Barton *et al.* 1991

conventional methods of determining radiocarbon ages (Campbell 1977). However, since the 1980s, with the advent of AMS (Accelerator Mass Spectrometry) dating which can use extremely small sample sizes, the position has been considerably improved, and it is now possible to outline with greater confidence a basic chronological scheme for the Lateglacial settlement of Britain (Housley *et al.* 1997). The record is based on directly dated human bone, cut-marked bone and teeth, and bone, antler and ivory artefacts.

AMS radiocarbon dates are presented (Table 2.2) for a selection of sites for which reliable associations with Creswellian artefacts exist. Nearly all of them fall between 12,500 and 12,000 BP, and are thus certainly part of the pre-woodland phase of the Interstadial. One of the sites deliberately omitted is Gough's Cave, as this spans a greater number of radiocarbon years and includes artefactual material of clearly later type (see below). Equally problematic, for the moment, is the earliest date on modified bone from Gough's Cave (12,800 ± 150 BP), since it is so far the only date for a Creswellian site that could be significantly older than 12,500 BP. If the date is genuine, it might suggest a potentially earlier phase of occupation in south-west Britain than has hitherto been recognized. Taken as a whole, the AMS dates confirm that human presence

*Table 2.2* Radiocarbon accelerator dates from British Lateglacial findspots.

a) Final Upper Palaeolithic assemblages containing penknife points and related forms

| Age (14C BP) | Age (cal BC) | Lab | Site | Material | Ref |
|---|---|---|---|---|---|
| 11,380 ± 120 | 11,333 ± 125 | OxA-3887 | Broken Cavern | Ulna (*Lepus*) | 22 |
| 11,790 ± 901 | 11,787 ± 104 | OxA-5858 | MG Parlour | Charcoal | B |
| 11,630 ± 120 | 11,603 ± 134 | OxA-5794 | Pixie's Hole | Scapula (*Bos*)* | A |
| 11,910 ± 901 | 11,930 ± 107 | OxA-5795 | Pixie's Hole | Metacarpal (*Bos*) | A |
| 12,070 ± 901 | 12,126 ± 111 | OxA-5796 | Pixie's Hole | Innominate (*Cervus*) | A |

b) selected Creswellian assemblages with trapezoidal/Cheddar points and related forms

| Age (14C BP) | Age (cal BC) | Lab | Site | Material | Ref/AM |
|---|---|---|---|---|---|
| 12,210 ± 160 | 12,296 ± 206 | OxA-535 | Sun Hole | Ulna (*Homo*) | 3 |
| 12,320 ± 130 | 12,440 ± 174 | OxA-1789 | Kent's Cavern | Bone piercer* | 9 |
| 12,250 ± 110 | 12,349 ± 143 | OxA-5692 | Kent's Cavern | Metacarpal* | 22 |
| 12,350 ± 160 | 12,485 ± 217 | OxA-1500 | Three Holes | Bone frag* | 9 |
| 12,260 ± 140 | 12,364 ± 183 | OxA-3208 | Three Holes | Calcaneum (*Lepus*)* | 22 |
| 12,180 ± 130 | 12,262 ± 165 | OxA-3209 | Three Holes | Humerus (*Ursus*)* | 22 |
| 12,150 ± 110 | 12,219 ± 139 | OxA-3890 | Three Holes | Tooth (*Equus*)* | 22 |
| 11,980 ± 100 | 12,012 ± 120 | OxA-3891 | Three Holes | Metatarsal (*Cervus*) | 22 |
| 12,220 ± 110 | 12,311 ± 142 | OxA-4494 | Three Holes | Tooth (*Equus*) | 22 |
| 12,020 ± 100 | 12,065 ± 121 | OxA-3717 | Church Hole | Antler *sagaie** | 18 |
| 12,110 ± 120 | 12,174 ± 149 | OxA-4108 | Church Hole | Femur (*Lepus*)* | 18 |
| 12,250 ± 90 | 12,350 ± 117 | OxA-3718 | Church Hole | Antler *sagaie** | 18 |
| 12,240 ± 150 | 12,335 ± 195 | OxA-735 | Church Hole | Humerus (*Lepus*) | 4 |
| 12,290 ± 120 | 12,403 ± 159 | OxA-1670 | Robin Hood C | Humerus (*Lepus*)* | 9 |
| 12,420 ± 200 | 12,585 ± 280 | OxA-1617 | Robin Hood C | Femur (*Lepus*)* | 9 |
| 12,340 ± 120 | 12,473 ± 162 | OxA-3415 | Robin Hood C | Scapula (*Lepus*)* | 18 |
| 12,450 ± 150 | 12,623 ± 212 | OxA-1619 | Robin Hood C | Humerus (*Lepus*)* | 9 |
| 12,480 ± 170 | 12,669 ± 243 | OxA-1618 | Robin Hood C | Scapula (*Lepus*) * | 9 |
| 12,580 ± 110 | 12,819 ± 164 | OxA-3416 | Robin Hood C | Awl (*Lepus*)* | 18 |
| 12,600 ± 170 | 12,844 ± 254 | OxA-1616 | Robin Hood C | Scapula (*Lepus*)* | 9 |
| 12,350 ± 120 | 12,481 ± 163 | OxA-1467 | Pin Hole | Radius (*Lepus*)* | 9 |
| 12,510 ± 110 | 12,711 ± 160 | OxA-3404 | Pin Hole | Tibia (*Lepus*)* | C |

*Cut-marked or modified bone/antler

*Sources*: References (in): A. Barton and Roberts 1996; B. Jacobi in Fagnart and Thevenin 1997; C. Charles and Jacobi 1994. For reference numbers, see Table 2.3. The calibration method, devised by Weninger, is described in Street *et al.* 1994, 9–13

in Britain probably lagged 500 radiocarbon years or more behind the main phase of Magdalenian settlement of the north-west European mainland.

## Raw material and mobility

The 28 findspots with evidence of Creswellian activity consist mainly of collections from cave sites in the west and mid-central limestone areas of England and Wales, but there is increasing evidence for open-air activity both in these regions and in flatter areas further east (Figure 2.3). In cases where such evidence has been searched for, the preferred raw materials seem to have been good quality flints capable of producing long, straight blades, rather than local rocks of mixed or unpredictable quality.

The use of imported flint is nowhere more apparent than in western Britain, where instances of geologically *in situ* sources of flint are rare. Finds from Kent's Cavern and Three Holes Cave (Devon) include well-made flint blades and tools on long blade blanks. Significantly, although good flint sources are available at Beer (Devon), the only local material employed at Three Holes Cave seems to have been Greensand chert, which occurs at the site almost exclusively in the form of retouched tools (Barton and Roberts 1996). The low quantities of flint debitage with cortication and primary blade waste recorded at both sites further implies that many of the tools and blades were imported as finished items rather than being knapped on the spot. A similar situation has also been described for Gough's Cave (Somerset), where translucent flints appear to have been carried in from sources no nearer than the Vale of Pewsey, on the northern edge of Salisbury Plain (Wiltshire), 60 km to the east (Jacobi in Fagnart and Thevenin 1997). This may also be the source of the flint found in the Devon caves, a minimum distance of 160 km, supporting the contention that Creswellian groups engaged in long-distance movements with correspondingly high residential mobility.

The likelihood that Creswellian groups were not sedentary is strengthened by finds at Gough's Cave of non-local sea shells and pieces of Baltic amber, the nearest known source of which is the North Sea coast. Similarly, comparison of individual artefacts from sites as far apart as Kent's Cavern and Robin Hood Cave (Creswell Crags, Derbyshire) has shown such striking resemblances as to suppose that they were made by a single group (Jacobi in Barton *et al.* 1991). If this is correct, it could give an approximation of the potential size and geography of the annual range exploited by these people.

Interestingly, observations concerning the procurement of non-local rocks for tool making closely match patterns recorded in the continental Late Magdalenian (Arts and Deeben 1987), where long-distance movements of materials have been correlated with greater mobility of hunter-gatherer groups. Amongst various explanations put forward is that raw materials were either exchanged between groups from different territories or that expeditions were deliberately mounted to obtain them. The high quality of much of the raw material at sites in the Central Rhineland suggests the latter as the more likely explanation (Street in Fagnart and Thevenin 1997).

Thus the distribution and use of raw materials in the Creswellian tends to suggest an activity radius of well over 100 km. In such instances, the reduction of nodules into more manageable blade forms would make sense as an economizing measure designed to reduce weight of pieces carried into a more manageable form. The transportability of these toolkits is further emphasized by the fact that the imported implements may show signs of especially heavy use and resharpening.

## Seasonality and subsistence

Evidence linking the exploitation of mammal faunas and human activity is preserved in the form of cut-marks on and other modification to bones, antler and ivory found at Creswellian sites. Species known to have been exploited for meat, raw materials and artefacts included wild horse (*Equus ferus*), red deer (*Cervus elaphus*), arctic hare (*Lepus timidus*), reindeer (*Rangifer tarandus*), mammoth (*Mammuthus primigenius*), Saiga antelope (*Saiga tatarica*), wild cattle (*Bos primigenius*), brown bear (*Ursus arctos*) and lynx (*Lynx lynx*). To this list can probably be added arctic fox (*Alopex lagopus*), red fox (*Vulpes vulpes*) and wolf (*Canis lupus*), although no cut-marks have yet been recorded on Lateglacial bone specimens.

The food species dominantly represented at Creswellian sites is the wild horse. Although wild horses are now extinct, behavioural studies on semi-feral populations in Mongolia reveal that they live in small herds and move constantly between grazing grounds. Today they are adapted to dry, open grassland habitats, but the main restriction on their distribution is the availability of drinking water. The only limitation to their ceaseless mobility is when young foals are present during the spring and early summer. From April to late June, the herds may be highly vulnerable to attack because of frequent resting leaving the tell-tale accumulation of piles of dung in these places. The habits of travelling in single file and of mares deliberately isolating themselves during foaling might have made them equally susceptible to human predation. It is clear that Creswellian groups were highly adept in exploiting wild horses, and evidence of successful hunting in all seasons is indicated by the age profiles of the animals.

Evidence that horse was killed for meat is well documented at Gough's Cave (Parkin *et al.* 1986). Skeletal elements of the head and limb extremities recorded near the entrance of the cave are heavily cut-marked, showing that carcasses were probably dismembered and butchered there with the use of flint knives. Further into the cave, long bone flakes and rib fragments imply different activities, perhaps connected with the smashing and cooking of bone to extract marrow juice and fat. The very thorough method of butchery and filleting suggests that the occupants of the cave were well used to dealing with horse. Once the meat was stripped from the bone, it is apparent that many elements such as the jaws were fractured longitudinally for marrow extraction purposes. Normally meat-poor elements like the head were carefully dissected to remove the brain and the tongue, which may have been considered great delicacies! The stripping-down of the animals also included the removal of the tendons at the back of the legs (for sinew) and of the hooves (possibly for reducing to glue).

The other numerically common species represented in the Gough's Cave fauna are red deer, which seem to have been treated in much the same way as horses, with cut-marks and breakages in identical places on many bones. Opportunities for hunting both these species appear to have been helped by the topography of the gorge, which beyond the cave becomes a narrow winding canyon suitable for driving or corralling animals. Dental evidence provides contradictory indications of the seasonal use of the cave: deer tooth eruption patterns suggest occupation in winter or early spring, whereas incremental banding visible on both deer and wild horse teeth implies that some animals were killed in summer. It thus seems possible that selective hunting took place at various times of year.

Apart from these two large vertebrates, smaller mammals such as the arctic hare were exploited, but probably less for their lean meat than for their pelts and bones as resources for tool making. Bone awls made on hare tibias have been found at a number of Creswellian locations throughout the country (Table 2.2), including Gough's Cave. At Robin Hood Cave, the particularly high numbers of cut-marked hare bones have led to the suggestion that the animals were being processed for their thick winter pelts (Charles and Jacobi 1994).

The use of reindeer bone and mammoth ivory is also attested in the Lateglacial of western and central-midland Britain. It is not known whether either of these animals formed part of the contemporary local fauna. At Gough's Cave, three reindeer antler batons have been recovered (Figure 2.4).

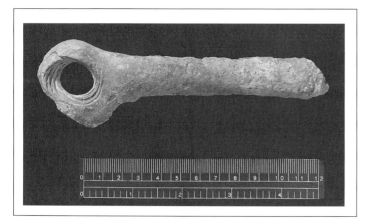

***Figure 2.4*** Reindeer baton from Gough's Cave (Cheddar Gorge, Somerset).
*Source*: Courtesy of the Natural History Museum

Spiral grooving inside the pierced holes may indicate a special function linked with controlling rope movement (e.g. in climbing or for lassooing animals). Such items could have been stored or made on naturally shed antler and need not imply local hunting. Similarly, finds of mammoth ivory *baguettes* at Gough's Cave and Kent's Cavern, and reindeer antler *sagaies* at Church Hole and Fox Hole (Derbyshire), prove only that these materials were brought in by humans and possibly left for some future purpose. Apart from these rare objects, there is in fact very little convincing evidence for caching or storage associated with Creswellian sites. However, if dried meat and fat had been stored, this would doubtless have been in an archaeologically invisible form.

The absence of cut-marked reindeer bone (as opposed to artefacts) from sites dating to the first phase of the Interstadial is an interesting phenomenon. According to Bratlund (in Larsson 1996), contemporary Upper Palaeolithic sites in north-west Europe (*Hamburgian*, Later Magdalenian) invariably contain evidence of either horse or reindeer, but rarely both. When horse dominates the fauna, the seasonal evidence tends to favour summer and winter hunting, whilst reindeer seems to have been trapped predominantly in the autumn and spring. Accordingly, it is theoretically possible that Creswellian sites represent summer and/or winter hunting locations, rather than those used during the intervening seasons. Alternatively, a climatic explanation might be sought for the absence of reindeer in Britain during the warmest part of the Interstadial (Jacobi in Fagnart and Thevenin 1997).

Some additional information on seasonality is forthcoming from Whooper swan (*Cygnus cygnus*) remains recovered at Gough's Cave. One end of a humerus and part of an ulna display grooves and cut-marks connected with the removal of needle blanks. Since this large migratory bird is normally a winter visitor to Britain, its presence at the cave may be taken as plausible evidence for human activity in this season.

Whether the British Creswellian cave sites like Gough's Cave or Kent's Cavern served as 'task locations' or longer term residential sites is difficult to determine on present evidence. Certainly, more than just ephemeral activities seem to be indicated by the range of equipment recorded at both sites. Collectively, they imply sewing and needle making, as well as hide working and the processing of animal carcasses. At the same time, it may be significant that tools like micropiercers (*microperçoirs*), delicate enough for making small incisions in bone and antler, are found at Gough's Cave, one of the few sites where there is direct evidence for engraved items in these materials (see below).

One component, still largely missing from the record, are the Creswellian open-air equivalents of cave sites, which might be predicted to occur in the non-limestone areas in the east of the country. So far, relatively few such findspots are known, but they are likely to include flintwork from Newark (Nottinghamshire), Edlington Wood (Yorkshire), Froggatt (Derbyshire), Lakenheath Warren (Suffolk) and Walton-on-the-Naze (Essex), owing to the presence of blades with typical *en éperon* butts at each of these localities (Jacobi in Fagnart and Thevenin 1997). If these were winter occupation sites, they might be expected to contain evidence of substantial dwelling structures with post-settings, boiling pits and internal fireplaces. Such structures have been found in the German Rhineland at Gönnersdorf, where there is also evidence of winter occupation. On the other hand, if sites were occupied in the autumn and spring, they might be expected to resemble more closely open-air locations in the Paris Basin (e.g. Pincevent; Verberie), where tent-like arrangements have been found alongside outdoor hearths with flat stone cooking slabs.

## Burials

Although human remains have been recorded at a number of Creswellian sites, very few can be proven by AMS dating to be of Lateglacial age. Amongst the examples definitely attributable to this period are an ulna from Sun Hole (Cheddar Gorge, Somerset) dating to 12,210 ± 160 BP (Table 2.2) and human remains from Gough's Cave, which provide three dates on unconserved bones ranging from 11,820 ± 120 BP to 12,380 ± 110 BP. The latter site also has a later inhumation (Chapter 3).

While the few bones and teeth from Sun Hole offer only equivocal evidence of burial, no such doubt exists over the Gough's Cave finds, which represent a remarkable collection of skeletal material intentionally deposited within the cave. The remains comprise at least three adults and two children, aged about 11–13 years and 3–5 years respectively (Currant *et al.* 1989). Although precise details are lacking on some of the original finds, recent work uncovered further human material in a narrow fissure just inside the entrance. Convincing proof that this is probably part of the original burial is provided by a series of refits between bones in the new and old collections. From the associations and fresh condition of the bones, it was also clear that they had not been subject to any major natural disturbance. A new approach to this material concerns the extraction of ancient genetic material from bone collagen and dentine. The underlying hypothesis is that one type of DNA (mtDNA) is inherited exclusively through the maternal line, and that the rate of natural mutation from the parent mtDNA is predictable over time. Using Gough's Cavern teeth, Brian Sykes and colleagues at Oxford University are attempting to build a genetic profile of this Lateglacial population. By estimating the accumulated number of mutations in mtDNA, and comparing individual genetic sequences, they may be able to infer a link between present-day Europeans and these individuals. Results, so far inconclusive, nonetheless produce grounds for optimism.

Even though the bones of the individuals appeared to be closely grouped within the cave, there is no evidence that they represented a single collective inhumation. Rather the remains seem to have been incorporated within a midden deposit consisting of occupation debris of animal bones and flint, bone, antler and ivory artefacts. Further analysis of the human bones revealed that the skeletons had been treated in an extraordinary way prior to deposition (Cook in Barton *et al.* 1991).

From microscopic analysis of cut-marks and scrapes found on the skulls (Figure 2.5), mandibles and some of the post-cranial bones, it could be demonstrated that these had been inflicted after death by the sharp edges of flint knives. The position of the cut-marks shows that the cadavers had been expertly skinned and the joints dismembered soon

**Figure 2.5** Cut-marks on a human lower jaw bone from Gough's Cave (Cheddar Gorge, Somerset).
*Source*: Courtesy of the Natural History Museum

after death. In one case, the incisions made on the inside of the chin leave no doubt that the tongue was removed, before the jaw was detached from the rest of the head.

While today such activities would be considered macabre, none of these practices is necessarily interpretable as proof of cannibalism. Examples of two-stage burial practices and secondary reburial are not uncommon in the prehistoric record. Indeed, the evidence from Gough's Cave merely suggests that the corpses were deliberately skinned and the insides removed, prior to the bodies being dismembered and the remains thereafter perhaps carefully placed in hide sacks around the edges of the cave. Equally valid is the view that since food was plentiful at the time of occupation, there was little need to supplement the diet with human meat. On the other hand, the evidence does not rule out the possibility of ritual consumption of the softer human tissues, as a mark of respect to the dead, a practice known ethnographically amongst tribes in Papua New Guinea. An interesting twist to this interpretation is that some of the post-cranial human remains at Gough's Cave are burnt and are highly fragmented, suggesting further smashing and perhaps cooking. Ultimately, the verdict remains an open one. The only certain means of identifying cannibalism would be a piece of human bone in a human coprolite!

## Art

Despite recurring claims of Palaeolithic cave wall art in Britain, none has so far proved genuine. Nevertheless, the existence of Upper Palaeolithic engravings at the cave of Gouy, near Rouen (Normandy), less than 160 km from the Sussex coast, suggests that Britain was well within range of the cave artists. Gouy Cave is especially interesting because it is in Senonian (Cretaceous) chalk, similar to geological formations found in southern Britain and normally considered unsuitable for the preservation of fragile art. Engravings on the soft chalk walls of horses, bovids, a pig or badger, birds, sexual symbols and stylized figures were made before the natural infilling of the site, which is dated by bone debris to 12,050 ± 130 BP (GifA-92346).

Examples of mobiliary (portable) art objects are known from several Creswellian localities. These include non-figurative abstract engravings on stone, bone and ivory from Gough's Cave, Robin Hood Cave, Pin Hole and, possibly, Mother Grundy's Parlour (Creswell Crags, Derbyshire). Church Hole has a unique example of a notched bone pendant. Regularly spaced groups of delicate incisions on hare tibia awls and on a section of bovid rib from Gough's Cave

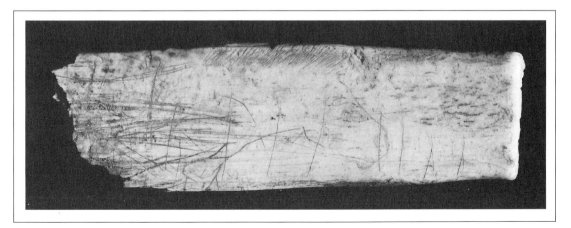

***Figure 2.6*** A horse's head engraved on a rib fragment from Robin Hood Cave (Creswell Crags, Derbyshire).
*Source*: Courtesy of the British Museum

resemble the gradations on a ruler: these items have been variously interpreted as counting tallies, lunar calendars, spacers, message sticks or simply as gaming pieces. Comparable notations have been recorded on pieces of mammoth ivory from the same cave. The only example of figurative art unquestionably connected with the Creswellian is the engraving of a horse on a rib fragment from Robin Hood Cave (Figure 2.6), discovered in 1876. A similar example of an engraved horse from Sherbourne (Dorset) has been discredited as a forgery (Stringer *et al.* 1995).

## FINAL UPPER PALAEOLITHIC

### Environmental background

In the second half of the Interstadial (equivalent to the Allerød, 12–11,000 BP), many British pollen profiles show a marked expansion of birch (*Betula* sp.) (Walker *et al.* 1993). In western Britain, closed birch woodland seems to have developed by about 11,700 BP (Walker and Harkness 1990). This development can be related to the gradual cooling trend detected after 12,500 BP (Atkinson *et al.* 1987).

The evidence for climatic cooling and afforestation are not necessarily in conflict, because the spread of birch may have been favoured by lower summer temperatures combined with moister and less windy weather conditions (Walker *et al.* 1993). According to proxy data from beetle faunas, mean July temperatures fell by up to 2° C (Coope and Lemdahl 1995). Potential evidence for greater climatic instability during this period may be signalled by a clear interruption in the birch curve and a minor increase in juniper between *c.* 11,400–11,300 BP (Walker and Harkness 1990; Walker *et al.* 1993). Significantly, this oscillation seems to be closely matched by an episode of marked cooling in the GISP-2 ice-core (Figure 2.1).

The second phase of the Lateglacial Interstadial thus appears to have been characterized by the development of a woodland (birch and willow) landscape, probably with a mosaic of herbaceous shrub and open grassland species, which seem to have persisted in some upland and northern areas. Despite these vegetational changes, no great turnover of animal species is indicated (see below). This period nevertheless saw the final disappearance of open steppe species such as mammoth (*Mammuthus primigenius*), which may have become extinct in western Europe at about the same time (Street in Fagnart and Thevenin 1997). Amongst the large vertebrates found in Britain dating to this period are red deer (*Cervus elaphus*), elk (*Alces alces*), a large bovid (*Bos* sp.) and possibly roe deer (*Capreolus capreolus*). Wild horse (*Equus ferus*) became less common, while reindeer (*Rangifer tarandus*), if it occurred at all, would have been confined to open tundra in the northern uplands.

### Material culture and technology

Lithic tool assemblages of this period are characterized by curve-backed points (*pointes à dos courbé*) and curve-backed blades (*lames/lamelles à dos courbé, couteaux à dos retouché*). Another important type fossil of the Final Upper Palaeolithic is the penknife point, a curve-backed point variant with additional basal retouch (Figure 2.7). Also suspected of being contemporary are assemblages where one or more of these types are present in combination with thick angle-backed points (*pointes à dos anguleux*) and/or curve-backed bi-points (*pointes aziliennes*). Amongst the other retouched tools present in Final Upper Palaeolithic assemblages are short end-scrapers (*grattoirs courts*), round thumb-nail scrapers (*unguiformes*) and truncation burins. A selection of tool-types is illustrated in Figure 2.7. The appearance of these industries is believed to coincide with the beginning of the forested part of the Lateglacial Interstadial.

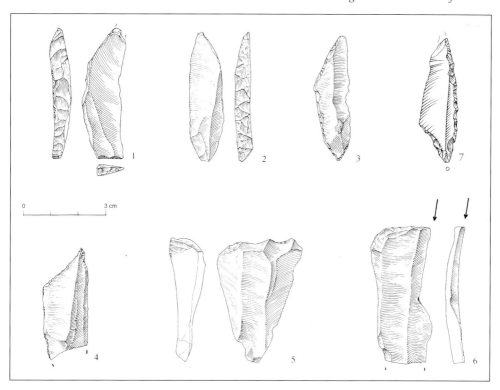

**Figure 2.7** Final Upper Palaeolithic artefacts: 1. curve-backed point with straight proximal truncation; 2. curve-backed point; 3. angle-backed point with oblique basal truncation; 4. piercer; 5. short end-scraper; 6. burin on straight truncation; 7. curve-backed point with additional basal retouch (penknife point). 1–6. Pixie's Hole; 7. Symonds Yat East Rockshelter.
*Source*: Illustrations by Karen Hughes and Hazel Martingell. Courtesy of the British Museum

Analysis of lithic assemblages reveals that they were generally made on smaller raw materials of variable quality. In sites in western Britain, many of the tools are on short blades; the raw material may be of gravel flint and Greensand chert of relatively local origin. The blades tend to display wide, lipped butts; ventral surface features are generally, but not invariably, consistent with a soft stone hammer mode of percussion.

The dating of these assemblages is limited to a handful of sites (Table 2.2). At Broken Cavern (Devon), the retouched tools comprise thick-backed blades, similar to those recorded from the upper hearth at Three Holes Cave nearby. An AMS date on an arctic hare bone from the archaeological layer places the occupation at 11,380 ± 120 years BP. AMS dates have also been obtained on a hearth and adjacent occupation area at Pixie's Hole (Devon), yielding a mean age of *c.* 11,870 years BP (Table 2.2). A broadly similar age may be assigned to the Final Upper Palaeolithic occupation at Mother Grundy's Parlour, where hearth charcoal has been AMS dated to 11,970 ± 90 BP. Although both these sites are earlier than Broken Cavern, the dates would place the human activity in all three within the second phase of the Interstadial. A broadly similar pattern of dates has been recorded for comparable Final Palaeolithic material in northern France and the German Rhineland.

Of less certain identity are assemblages that contain straight-backed blades and bladelets (*lames* and *lamelles à dos*) and shouldered points (*pointes à cran*), such as those from open-air sites at Hengistbury Head (Dorset) and Brockhill (Surrey). The thermoluminescence dating of burnt

*Table 2.3* Selected AMS radiocarbon dates on organic artefacts of the second phase of the Lateglacial Interstadial/early Younger Dryas.

| Age (14C BP) | Age (cal BC) | Lab | Site | Material | Ref/AM |
|---|---|---|---|---|---|
| 11,750 ± 120 | 11,741 ± 137 | OxA-2455 | Victoria Cave | Antler *sagaie* | 14 |
| 11,740 ± 150 | 11,731 ± 171 | OxA-1950 | Leman & Ower | Antler uniserial point | 10 |
| 11,390 ± 120 | 11,351 ± 125 | OxA-1946 | Porth y Waen | Antler uniserial point | 10 |
| 11,270 ± 110 | 11,221 ± 110 | OxA-2456 | Kinsey Cave | Antler artefact | 14 |
| 11,210 ± 90 | 11,169 ± 89 | OxA-2847 | Coniston Dib | Bone point | 14 |
| 11,200 ± 120 | 11,156 ± 118 | OxA-1463 | Dowel Cave | Antler tang | 9 |
| 10,910 ± 150 | 10,871 ± 144 | OxA-517 | Sproughton 1 | Bone uniserial point | 4 |
| 10,810 ± 100 | 10,780 ± 97 | OxA-2607 | Victoria Cave | Antler biserial harpoon | 14 |
| 10,700 ± 160 | 10,664 ± 165 | OxA-518 | Sproughton 2 | Antler uniserial point | 4 |

*Sources*: Apart from references A–C, all the OxA- dates listed here and in Table 2.2 are cited in one of the following datelists published in the journal *Archaeometry*:

AM 3   *Archaeometry* 28, 1 (1986), 116–125
AM 4   *Archaeometry* 28, 2 (1986), 206–221
AM 9   *Archaeometry* 31, 2 (1989), 207–234
AM 10  *Archaeometry* 32, 1 (1990), 101–108
AM 14  *Archaeometry* 34, 1 (1992), 141–159
AM 18  *Archaeometry* 36, 2 (1994), 337–374
AM 22  *Archaeometry* 38, 2 (1996), 391–415
The calibration method, devised by Weninger, is described in Street *et al.* 1994, 9–13

flint artefacts from Hengistbury gave a mean of 12,500 ± 1,150 years ago (Barton 1992), but the wide standard deviation makes the age difficult to interpret. On typological grounds, the assemblages seem to show closest affinity to *Federmesser* industries on the European mainland, especially in northern France and Belgium, where dates suggest attribution to the last few centuries of the twelfth millennium BP. If correct, this implies a much greater diversity in backed tool forms during the Final Upper Palaeolithic than in the Creswellian.

In contrast to the Creswellian, the bone- and antler-work associated with the woodland phase of the Interstadial is more restricted in type. The majority of examples directly dated to this period are uniserial barbed points (Table 2.3).

## Raw materials and mobility

The existence of Final Upper Palaeolithic industries often on short flakes probably reflects different raw material practices from those seen in the Creswellian. In western Britain this is particularly apparent in the assemblages from Three Holes Cave (upper hearth), Broken Cavern and Pixie's Hole, where the small size of artefacts is largely determined by the variable quality of material selected for knapping. Judging from the surface condition and curvature of the cortical flakes, it seems clear that most of the materials were small cobbles derived from local sources. It is also apparent that the rock was transported to the site in the form of whole cobbles, rather than being reduced elsewhere. In the case of Devon, raw materials of this kind can be localized to gravel exposures within 16 km or less of each of the sites.

In other parts of the country, the relationship between size of artefacts and raw material quality may not be so clear-cut. For example, at Symonds Yat East Rockshelter (Gloucestershire), tools made on short flakes and blades were on flint probably imported from up to 80 km away. Even in this case, primary reduction of the small nodules appears to have taken place on site rather than at the point of procurement. Thus, although the potential radius of mobility may sometimes have approached that proposed for the Creswellian, it seems that, in general, Final Upper Palaeolithic groups organized themselves rather differently with regard to lithic raw materials.

That the pattern of raw material use in the Final Upper Palaeolithic may be part of a much wider phenomenon is suggested by observations made in the contemporary continental record. In west-central Germany, for example, the *Federmessergruppen* sites, unlike those of the Magdalenian, are characterized by artefacts made on fist-sized nodules, of variable quality. They contain flints from a mixture of very local Rhine gravels and more distant (>100 km) sources in the Meuse gravels (Street in Fagnart and Thevenin 1997). A similar preference for smaller nodules is evident in contemporary industries in northern France. Although the key to this change in procurement strategy is not fully understood, it is possible that the different approaches to raw material in the Lateglacial should be regarded as complementary solutions to the same problem. That is, the circulation of blanks 'stored' in the form of small, whole nodules (Final Upper Palaeolithic) may have been just as effective, under certain circumstances, as Creswellian transportation of ready-made large blades.

## Geographic distribution and subsistence economy

The majority of the 150 Lateglacial findspots in Britain can be attributed with reasonable certainty to the Final Upper Palaeolithic. Of these, 39 are associated with finds of penknife points (Figure 2.8), while many of the rest are identified by the occurrence of typologically related forms. Apart from being numerically superior to Creswellian examples, they also include a higher percentage of open-air sites and generally have a wider geographical distribution, which extends as far west as islands already isolated by higher sea-level, such as the Scillies. Since the majority of typologically distinctive flint tools such as Cheddar points or penknife points are unlikely to have escaped attention, it seems that this distribution pattern reflects real differences in the territories exploited by both Lateglacial groupings.

The spread of birch woodland and the general shift away from more open environments after about 12,000 BP, must have had an effect on the amount and diversity of available meat sources. Apart from the addition of elk (*Alces alces*), which is known from surprisingly few records, red deer

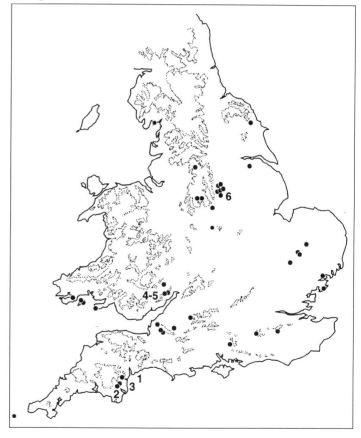

**Figure 2.8** Distribution of Final Upper Palaeolithic penknife point find-spots: 1. Pixie's Hole; 2. Broken Cavern; 3. Three Holes Cave; 4–5. King Arthur's Cave/Symonds Yat East; 6. Mother Grundy's Parlour.
*Source*: After Jacobi in Barton *et al.* 1991

(*Cervus elaphus*), wild aurochs (*Bos primigenius*) and, to a lesser extent, wild horse (*Equus ferus*) continued to be present in the second half of the Interstadial. The rarity of elk may be attributable to its solitary behaviour and the fact that it is a long-distance migrant. The visibility and distribution of these and other animals in the landscape would have been important factors in the type of hunting strategy employed by contemporary human populations. According to some specialists, the introduction of new archery technology may have coincided with the period of woodland development. Certainly, the curve-backed and penknife points would have made highly efficient weapon-heads, and the presence of 'impact fractures' on the tips of some examples lends weight to the idea that these tools were used as projectiles.

Not considered here are edible fruits and plants which must have formed complementary food sources in the human diet, at least on a seasonal basis. Unfortunately, there is no direct evidence for the use of plant foods, due to the extreme fragility of such evidence, but amongst the potentially exploitable resource were wild berries, fruits and a range of edible fungi. It should be noted, however, that Boreal woodland ecosystems are far less productive in terms of plant biomass than open steppe grasslands. They are also characterized by a less stable food chain, with plant (and consequently animal) communities being susceptible to cyclical fluctuations and, sometimes, even catastrophic failures. Thus it is likely that a diversity of plants and animals was exploited, rather than wholesale reliance being placed on a few select species.

Detailed spatial analyses are currently lacking for most Final Upper Palaeolithic sites, but indications from work in progress suggest that bone concentrations at Three Holes Cave and Symonds Yat East Rockshelter coincide closely with those of flint scatters. Much of the bone from these sites is heavily smashed and fragmented, perhaps indicative of systematic crushing of bones and cancellous tissue to extract fat and juice. The presence of a cut-marked bovid scapula at Pixie's Hole certainly confirms that processing of these animals took place at camp-sites.

The only substantial open-air site for which there is evidence of internal spatial organization is at Hengistbury Head, but here interpretation is hampered by lack of any contemporary organic remains. Nevertheless, the distribution of flints revealed discrete areas of activity where blades were first manufactured and then transformed into tools. By refitting core-to-blade sequences, it was also possible to demonstrate a peripheral zone where blanks for tools were prepared and an adjacent zone where tools were used and discarded around a probable hearth (Barton 1992). The circulation of material between outer and inner areas with hearths is a recurrent feature at a number of European sites of this period. Also noticeable at Hengistbury was an overlap in the distributions of end-scrapers and red ochre, including a worked 'crayon'. The possibility that this signified a hide-processing area is supported both by the low edge angles and hooked profiles of the scrapers, typical of a hide-working function, and the well-attested use of red ochre as a colorant of hide and other materials in the ethnohistoric record.

The bone- and antler-work of this period is largely restricted to functional items such as barbed hunting equipment (Table 2.3). The only potential exceptions are four engraved and ochre-stained bone tallies from Kendrick's Cave, Llandudno (Gwynedd). One of these tallies has been directly dated to 11,795 ± 65 BP. The close agreement in age between this and a human bone from the same cave suggests the presence of an inhumation burial. It is noteworthy that the date overlaps at one standard deviation with one of the individuals from Gough's Cave, where similar bone tallies were also recorded. The only other example of non-figurative artwork from this period is an abstract engraving on the cortex of a flint core from Hengistbury (Barton 1992).

## THE END OF THE LAST GLACIATION

### Younger Dryas

A return to much colder conditions in the period 10,800 to 10,000 BP is marked by a dramatic fall of 5–7° C in mean annual sea temperatures in the North Atlantic. Further evidence of climatic deterioration is indicated by the southern limit of winter sea ice which migrated from a position close to Iceland (near where it is today) to a point off the north coast of Iberia. This, coupled with potentially stronger cyclonic activity in the North Atlantic and a northerly wind flow, appears to have provided the right conditions for increased precipitation, much of it probably in the form of snow, feeding local glaciers in the Scottish Highlands and north Wales. According to the GISP-2 ice-core data, the sharp fall in temperatures and the return to a more glacial climate seem to have occurred extremely rapidly, perhaps within as little as a few centuries (Alley *et al.* 1993).

These climatic changes are reflected in the pollen record by evidence for the disruption of birch parkland and increased frequencies of plant communities typical of open tundra. A similar climatic signal is given by the fossil beetle faunas which show that, if anything, temperatures in Britain were slightly cooler than those of western Europe. The latter observation is consistent with the deflection of the warm Gulf Stream currents away from the western European seaboard. The return to more open tundra-like conditions is also indicated by the reappearance of reindeer, as well as several records of steppe pika (*Ochotona pusilla*). The possibility that the climate became progressively more arid in the later part of the Younger Dryas is implied by the occurrence of several different species of *Artemisia*. Such dryness may also have stimulated the growth of wild grasses, creating grazing conditions especially favourable to wild horses and reindeer. Certainly, the few radiocarbon dates on horses of this period all belong to the second half of the stadial.

### Human settlement and the question of continuity of occupation

Recent reviews have drawn attention to the very limited evidence of human activities in the Younger Dryas (Barton in Barton *et al.* 1991; Cook and Jacobi 1994). In fact, there are only three reliable AMS radiocarbon dates that, at two standard deviations, fall wholly within this period. Potentially the most interesting of these comes from a cache of deer bones with cut-marks at Elderbush Cave (Staffordshire) which can be dated to 10,600 ± 110 BP. This date falls close to the thermal minimum of the stadial and, if correctly interpreted, implies that human settlement was not inhibited by even the most extreme cold conditions. Some doubts have been expressed about the Elderbush date, however, because of the uncertain conservation history of the bones used to obtain it.

Much greater confidence can be attributed to two dates from after the period of maximum cold during the stadial (*c.* 10,500 BP). The first comes from a worked reindeer antler object, which has been compared to a 'Lyngby axe', found at Earl's Barton (Northamptonshire). This has been directly dated to 10,320 ± 150 BP. The other is for the older of two dates on wild horse from scatter 'A' at Three Ways Wharf, Uxbridge (Greater London), with an age of 10,270 ± 100 BP. The latter is particularly significant because it is associated with a lithic assemblage.

The lithic artefacts from Three Ways Wharf scatter 'A' (Lewis in Barton *et al.* 1991) include long blades (12 cm or more in maximum length) and a small number of obliquely truncated microliths with basal retouch (Figure 2.9). There can be no doubt about this association, because one of the microliths can be refitted to a long blade core. Amongst the collection, one blade displays heavy battering on its margins. Such edge bruising may have been caused by chopping through antler or by replenishing sandstone hammers, and this artefact is identical to those termed *lâmes machurées* (Barton 1989).

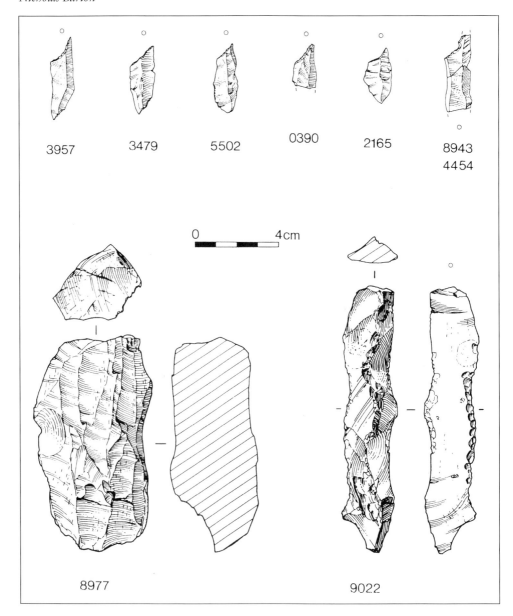

**Figure 2.9** Final Upper Palaeolithic 'long blade' artefacts from Scatter 'A', Three Ways Wharf (Uxbridge, Greater London). Microliths: 3957, 3479, 5502, 0390, 2165, 8943 and 4454; opposed platform blade core: 8977; bruised blade: 9022.
*Source:* Courtesy of CBA/Museum of London

Other assemblages combining long blades and blades with bruised edges are known from 28 findspots in south-eastern Britain and East Anglia (Figure 2.10). Most are located in floodplain or low river valley terrace situations, in places suggesting immediate access to *in situ* sources of flint. Where larger scatters of material have been recorded, as at Sproughton (Suffolk), Riverdale (Kent), Springhead (Kent), Swaffham Prior (Suffolk), Avington VI (Berkshire) and Gatehampton

Farm (Oxfordshire), they usually contain a high proportion of blade waste to retouched tools, the latter making up less than 2 per cent of the assemblage. The absence of hearth structures and burnt flints from all these sites implies that they were occupied for short durations, perhaps mainly relating to knapping and blade manufacture.

Parallels for these British 'long blade' sites can be found in the *Ahrensburgian* of northern Germany, particularly in assemblages of the Eggstedt-Stellmoor group, characterized by 'large' and 'giant' blades (*Gross-* and *Riesenklingen* as defined in Taute 1968). The best known site is Stellmoor, where the ages of nine individually dated reindeer bones and antlers from the Ahrensburgian layer give a pooled age of 9,995 ± 34 BP (Cook and Jacobi 1994). However, Ahrensburgian sites tend to include small tanged points (*Stielspitzen*) and, with the exception of Avington VI, this component is so far missing in British 'long blade' assemblages. In northern France, similar 'long blade' material has been described from the Somme Valley and the Paris Basin, where it

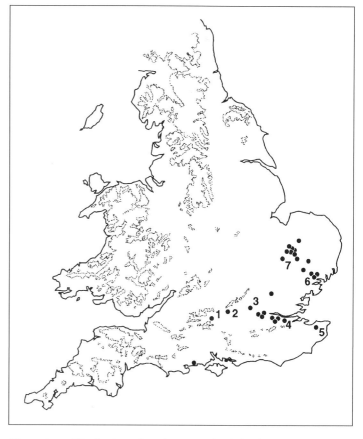

*Figure 2.10* Distribution of Final Upper Palaeolithic 'long blade' findspots with bruised blades (*lames mâchurées*): 1. Avington VI; 2. Gatehampton Farm; 3. Three Ways Wharf; 4. Springhead; 5. Riverdale; 6. Sproughton; 7. Swaffham Prior.

is attributed to the so-called *industries à pièces mâchurées*. These assemblages also display a notable absence of small tanged points. Where bone is preserved in the French sites, it is derived from either wild horse or bovids, rather than reindeer. Four AMS dates on horse teeth from the site at Belloy-sur-Somme in Picardy range from 10,260 ± 160 BP to 9,720 ± 130 BP, and overlap in age with the Three Ways Wharf site.

Other findspots in Britain of potentially comparable age include Risby Warren (Humberside), where small Ahrensburgian points were recorded in an assemblage from above the equivalent of a Younger Dryas Coversand deposit, and Tayfen Road, Bury St Edmunds (Suffolk) and Doniford Cliff (Somerset), where single specimens of Ahrensburgian points are known. At none of these locations, however, were any long blades recovered. Thus it remains to be determined whether the tanged point sites are chronologically equivalent to those of 'long blade' type. The proximity of Risby Warren to the Younger Dryas North Sea shoreline and the similar coastal position of Ahrensburgian sites in southern Scandinavia and northern Germany may point to the seasonal exploitation of various marine food sources in addition to reindeer. Remains of seals, whales and fish have been recorded in some of the Scandinavian sites (Eriksen in Larsson 1996). A date of 9940 ± 100 BP on domesticated dog from Seamer Carr (North Yorkshire), not far from Risby,

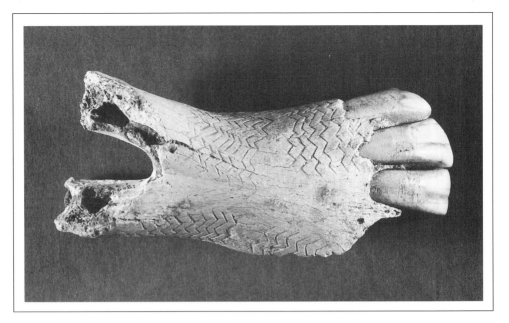

***Figure 2.11*** Engraved horse mandible from Kendrick's Cave (Gwynedd).
*Source*: Courtesy of the British Museum

implies that these animals were employed by humans to assist in hunting or for traction or some other purpose. It seems likely that the assemblages with 'long blades' and those with small tanged points are variants of the same Ahrensburgian technocomplex (Barton 1989).

An interesting group of decorated objects of this period has been recovered from Kendrick's Cave, Llandudno. They comprise a horse jaw incised with a chevron (zig-zag) design (Figure 2.11) and perforated and decorated badger and deer teeth for beads.

In sum, the possibility of a cultural break in human settlement during the Lateglacial in Britain appears to be strongest in the coldest part of the Younger Dryas (*c*. 10,500 BP). However, until this hypothesis can be more fully investigated, it remains possible that occupation continued intermittently throughout this period, perhaps on a scale small enough to be archaeologically invisible.

The end of the Younger Dryas cold stadial is signalled by an episode of intense climatic warming across Britain and western Europe. The rate of most rapid change may have lasted for as little as 50 years (Alley *et al.* 1993). Temperatures at the beginning of the Postglacial (*c*. 10,000 BP) seem to have been as high as or even higher than those of the present day. The appearance of Mesolithic industries containing items of wood-working equipment (axes and adzes) appears to be linked with increased forestation soon after the beginning of this period. It is noteworthy, however, that non-geometric microlith projectiles found in the Early Mesolithic are similar to types found in the Latest Palaeolithic 'long blade' assemblages (Barton in Barton *et al.* 1991), suggesting that division of these groupings may be somewhat arbitrary.

## Acknowledgements
Jill Cook, Andrew Currant and Roger Jacobi are thanked for providing information incorporated in this chapter.

## Key texts

Barton, N., 1997. *Stone Age Britain*. London: Batsford.

Barton, R.N.E. and Roberts, A.J., 1996. 'Reviewing the British Late Upper Palaeolithic: new evidence for chronological patterning in the Lateglacial record', *Oxford Journal of Archaeology* 15, 245–265.

Barton, R.N.E., Roberts, A.J. and Roe, D.A. (eds) 1991. *The Late Glacial in north-west Europe*. London: Council for British Archaeology Research Report 77.

Jacobi, R.M., 1980. 'The Upper Palaeolithic of Britain with special reference to Wales', in Taylor, J.A. (ed.) *Culture and environment in Prehistoric Wales*. Oxford: British Archaeological Reports British Series 76, 15–100.

Lowe, J.J. and Walker, M.J.C., 1997. *Reconstructing Quaternary environments*. London: Longman. 2 edn.

## Bibliography

Alley, R.B., Meese, D.A., Shuman, C.A., Gow, A.J., Taylor, K.C., Grootes, P.M., White, J.W.C., Ram, M., Waddington, E.D., Mayewski, P.A. and Zieginski, G.A., 1993. 'Abrupt increase in Greenland snow accumulation at the end of the Younger Dryas event', *Nature* 362, 527–529.

Arts, N. and Deeben, J., 1987. 'On the northwestern border of the Late Magdalenian territory: ecology and archaeology of early Late Glacial band societies in Northwestern Europe', in Burdukiewicz, J. and Kobusiewicz, M. (eds) *Late Glacial in central Europe. Culture and environment*. Warsaw: Ossolineum, 25–66.

Atkinson, T.C., Briffa, K.R. and Coope, G.R., 1987. 'Seasonal temperatures in Britain during the past 22,000 years, reconstructed using beetle remains', *Nature* 325, 587–592.

Barton, R.N.E., 1989. 'Long blade technology in Southern Britain', in Bonsall, C. (ed.) *The Mesolithic in Europe. Papers presented at the third international symposium, Edinburgh 1985*. Edinburgh: John Donald, 264–271.

Barton, R.N.E., 1992. *Hengistbury Head Dorset. Volume 2: the Late Upper Palaeolithic and Early Mesolithic sites*. Oxford: Oxford University Committee for Archaeology Monograph Series 34.

Campbell, J.C., 1977. *The Upper Palaeolithic of Britain*. Oxford: Clarendon.

Charles, R. and Jacobi, R.M., 1994. 'The lateglacial fauna from the Robin Hood Cave, Creswell Crags: a re-assessment', *Oxford Journal of Archaeology* 13, 1–32.

Cook, J. and Jacobi, R.M., 1994. 'A reindeer antler or "Lyngby" axe from Northamptonshire and its context in the British Late Glacial' *Proceedings of the Prehistoric Society* 60, 75–84.

Coope, G.R. and Lemdahl, G., 1995. 'Regional differences in the Lateglacial climate of northern Europe based on coleopteran analysis', *Journal of Quaternary Science* 10, 391–395.

Currant, A.P., Jacobi, R.M. and Stringer, C.B., 1989. 'Excavations at Gough's Cave, Somerset 1986–7', *Antiquity* 63, 131–136.

Fagnart, J.P. and Thevenin, A. (eds) *Le Tardiglaciaire en Europe du Nord-Ouest*. Actes du 119ième Congrès National des Sociétés Historique et Scientifique. Paris: Editions CTHS.

Garrod, D., 1926. *The Upper Palaeolithic Age in Britain*. Oxford: Clarendon.

Housley, R.A., Gamble, C.S., Street, M.J. and Pettitt, P., 1997. 'Radiocarbon evidence for the Lateglacial human recolonisation of northern Europe', *Proceedings of the Prehistoric Society* 63, 25–54.

Jacobi, R.M. and Roberts, A.J., 1992. 'A new variant on the Creswellian angle-backed blade', *Lithics* 13, 33–39.

Larsson, L. (ed.) 1996. *The earliest settlement of Scandinavia and its relationship with neighbouring areas*. Lund: *Acta Archaeologica Lundensia* Series In 8°, 24.

Lowe, J.J., Coope, G.R., Harkness, D.D., Sheldrick, C. and Walker, M.J.C., 1995. 'Direct comparison of UK temperatures and Greenland snow accumulation rates, 15–12,000 years ago', *Journal of Quaternary Science* 10, 175–180.

Parkin, R.A., Rowley-Conwy, P. and Serjeantson, D., 1986. 'Late Palaeolithic exploitation of horse and red deer at Gough's Cave, Cheddar, Somerset', *Proceedings of the University of Bristol Spelaeological Society* 17, 311–330.

Street, M.J., Baales, M. and Weninger, B., 1994. 'Absolute Chronologie des späten Paläolithikums und des Frühmesolithikums im nördlichen Rheinland', *Archäologisches Korrespondenzblatt* 24, 1–28.

Stringer, C.B., D'Errico, F., Williams, C.T., Housley, R. and Hedges, R., 1995. 'Solution for the Sherbourne problem', *Nature* 378, 452.

Taute, W., 1968. *Die Stielspitzen-Gruppen in nordlichen Mitteleuropa: ein Beitrag zur Kenntnis der späten Altsteinzeit*. Fundamenta Reihe A, 5, Cologne: Böhlau.

Walker, M.J.C., Coope, G.R. and Lowe, J.J., 1993. 'The Devensian (Weichselian) Lateglacial palaeo-environmental record from Gransmoor, East Yorkshire, England', *Quaternary Science Reviews* 12, 659–680.

Walker, M.J.C. and Harkness, D.D., 1990. 'Radiocarbon dating the Devensian Lateglacial in Britain: new evidence from Llanilid, South Wales', *Journal of Quaternary Science* 5, 135–144.

## Chapter Three

# Hunter-gatherers of the Mesolithic

## Steven Mithen

The last Ice Age came to an end 10,000 radiocarbon years ago. Tundra landscapes that supported reindeer herds were colonized by birch and soon became thick deciduous woodland with dispersed fauna including red deer and pine marten. Except in the far north, relative sea-levels rose so that Britain, formerly a peninsula of Europe, had become an island by 8,500 years ago. In this rapidly changing environment, people continued to live by hunting and gathering for several thousand years until agriculture became an established way of life. This period was the Mesolithic (Figure 3.1).

## THE ENVIRONMENTAL CONTEXT FOR MESOLITHIC SETTLEMENT

Eighteen thousand radiocarbon years ago, ice sheets extended southwards to central England, beyond which lay an uninhabited polar desert. As the climate improved, Lateglacial hunters again came northwards (Chapter 2). By 10,000 years ago, the global warming that marks the end of the Pleistocene was established: in a few decades, temperatures rose substantially,

**Figure 3.1** Mesolithic sites referred to in this chapter.

causing more ice to melt and the sea-level to rise. Insects, plants and animals began to colonize, initiating an ecological succession that climaxed with mixed deciduous forest over much of Britain by 8,000 years ago.

Technological changes at the Pleistocene–Holocene (Postglacial) interface are complex and blurred, but by 10,000 years ago people had adopted microliths (discussed below) as a dominant component of their toolkits. The earliest Mesolithic sites, such as Star Carr (Yorkshire) and Thatcham (Berkshire), were created in relatively open landscapes in which birch and pine were the principal trees – probably quite similar to northern Scandinavia today. Palynology demonstrates how the relative amounts of pollen from different trees, herbs and grasses have changed through time (Figure 3.2). Supplementary information can be gained from macro-plant remains, such as seeds and catkin scales, trapped in sediments; in some cases, detailed environmental reconstruction is feasible. At Star Carr, for instance, the Mesolithic hunter-gatherers camped next to reedswamp vegetation fringed by stands of birch. As time passed, the reedswamp was replaced by marsh ferns, and then by sedges and willow. On dry land, ferns were always present amongst birch woodland into which pine infiltrated.

As climate ameliorated further, such woodland was progressively replaced by much denser mixed deciduous woodland, in which hazel, oak, lime and elm were significant. In relatively wet areas, alder and willow flourished. As this vegetation became established, so too did new animal communities in which red deer, roe deer and wild pig were dominant among the larger herbivores.

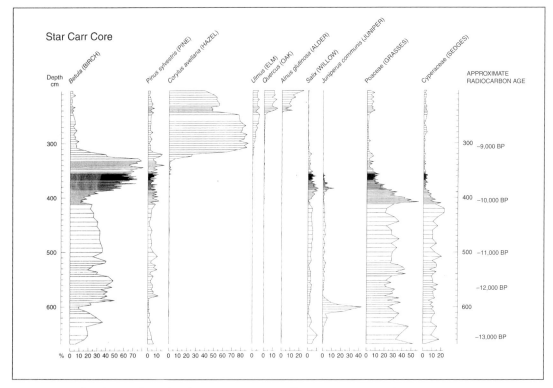

***Figure 3.2*** Pollen diagram from the lake centre at Star Carr, illustrating vegetation change in the Lateglacial and Early to Mid Postglacial.
*Source*: Day, P., 1996. 'Devensian late-glacial and early Flandrian environmental history of the Vale of Pickering, Yorkshire, England', *Journal of Quaternary Science* 11, 9–24

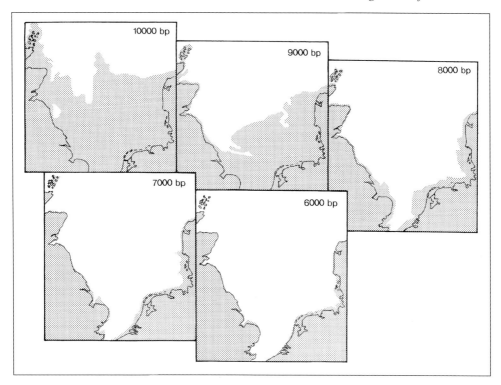

**Figure 3.3** Changes in sea-level of the North Sea in the Early Holocene. These maps show how Britain gradually became detached from the continent, with the flooding of large areas by the encroaching North Sea leading to the loss of substantial hunting territories.
*Source*: Verart, L., 1996. 'Fishing for the Mesolithic. The North Sea: a submerged Mesolithic landscape', in Fischer, A. (ed.) *Man and the Sea in the Mesolithic*. Oxford: Oxford Monograph 53, 291–301

Star Carr's inhabitants could have walked eastwards to what are now the Low Countries and Denmark (Figure 3.3). The rising sea flooded this landscape by 8,500 years ago, separating Britain from the Continent. Rivers that had flowed into the now-submerged land silted up; these drainage changes led to the formation of the East Anglian fens. The rising sea-level established the shorelines of southern England much as they are today, but in the north geographical changes were more complex. There, owing to the removal of the weight of ice, the land was rebounding upwards. By 6,500 years ago, this isostatic rebound began to outpace the rise in sea-level, resulting in a fall in relative sea-level. In many areas of northern Britain, raised beaches, often about 10 m above current sea-level, mark the Late Mesolithic coastline. As with vegetational changes, however, local factors played a role: the former location of glaciers and the local geology influenced local topographic changes.

## THE MESOLITHIC RECORD

Scatters of stone tools and the debris from their manufacture are the most abundant feature of the record. These are found throughout Britain with the exception of the Western and Shetland Isles, although this apparent absence is likely to be due to lack of fieldwork. Additionally, middens – large waste heaps of shells, animal bones and artefacts – are known from coastal locations. These two site types constitute the core of the archaeological record. Both can range from small deposits, suggesting a brief period of activity, to extensive accumulations reflecting either repeated use of a place or long-term activity by a large group of people. Caves and rockshelters were also used.

Stray finds generally indicate little other than that Mesolithic people had been present. In 1931, a barbed bone point was brought up by a trawler some 40 km off the Norfolk coast from a depth of almost 40 m. This findspot on the bed of the North Sea illustrates the major environmental changes that have taken place since the early Postglacial. Trails of Mesolithic footprints found beneath peat on the inter-tidal foreshore of the Severn are an evocative reminder that the ultimate subjects of study of the Mesolithic are not stone tools, animal bones or pollen cores, but people.

## The artefactual record

Chipped stone artefacts dominated in the artefactual record. Figure 3.4 shows typical artefacts from an Early and a Later Mesolithic site. The type artefacts for the period are microliths, small blades, usually of flint, that have been retouched; they occur in a range of shapes and sizes. Microliths are often found in hundreds, and on some sites in thousands. They were probably components of a wide range of tools, including hunting equipment.

Collections including relatively large microliths, either shaped like isosceles triangles or described as 'obliquely blunted points', are referred to as 'broad blade assemblages'. These tend to date to the period before 8,500 years ago, the Early Mesolithic. Notable sites include Star Carr and Thatcham. These microliths are very similar to examples found across northern Europe, referred to as the Maglemosian industry. Mesolithic assemblages later than 8,500 radiocarbon years BP are usually dominated by much smaller microliths. A wider variety of forms, such as scalene triangles and needle points, as at Kinloch (Rum), are recognized. Termed 'narrow blade assemblages', these reflect a cultural development without parallel on the Continent. The period between the appearance of narrow blade assemblages and the Neolithic is referred to as the Late Mesolithic.

This switch in microlith styles remains inadequately explained. It may be the archaeological manifestation of a sequence of changes: the establishment of dense deciduous woodland led to alterations in the behaviour and distribution of game, requiring new hunting strategies that in turn demanded new designs for hunting weapons and consequently new styles of microliths (Myers 1989). Alternatively, the establishment of new cultural traditions of artefact production, which had limited functional significance, may be proposed.

There are regional variations in this basic two-stage Mesolithic sequence. In Scotland, for example, the earliest dated site is attributable to 8,500 radiocarbon years BP. It remains unclear whether there was Early Mesolithic settlement with a Maglemosian technology here, although some broad microliths have been found (Woodman 1989). Maglemosian technology is also absent from Ireland: the Early Irish Mesolithic displays a narrow blade technology. By 7,000 radiocarbon years BP, this had been transformed into an industry dominated by large blades, in which microliths are essentially absent. Within England, there are regional and local variations in microlith forms. For instance, a cluster of Early Mesolithic sites in the Weald produce 'Horsham points', pointed microliths, the base of which have been retouched into a concave form. Elsewhere, certain western sites, such as Cass Ny Hawin (Isle of Man) and Coulererach (Islay) have tanged microliths (Mithen *et al.* in Pollard and Morrison 1996).

While microliths dominate most assemblages, other types of stone tools were important. These include scrapers, burins and awls, known from hunter-gatherer toolkits throughout early prehistory. Flint axes, and their resharpening flakes, are also found, and were no doubt used to acquire wood for bows and huts, and perhaps to make forest clearings. Their absence from Scottish assemblages is probably a reflection of the smallness of available nodules. From coastal

*Figure 3.4*

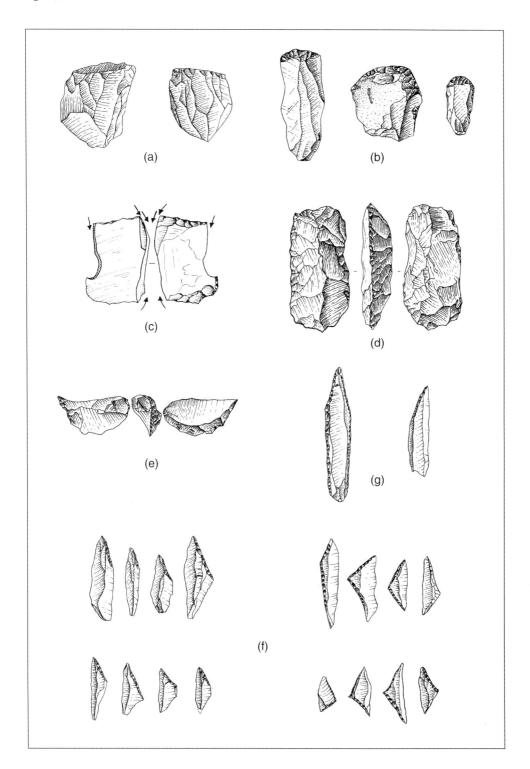

(a)

(b)

(c)

(d)

(e)

(g)

(f)

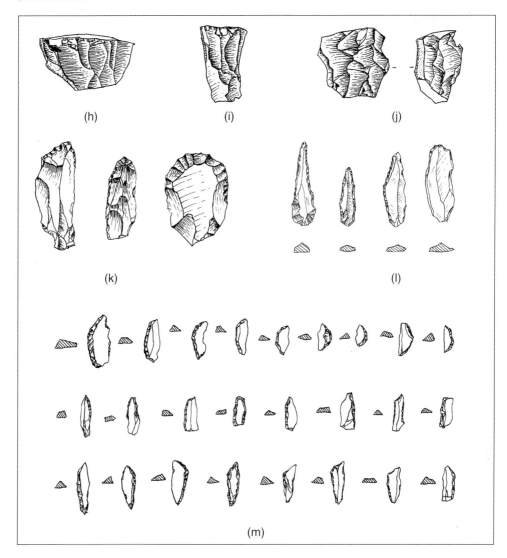

**Figure 3.4 previous page and above** Chipped stone artefacts from Star Carr and Kinloch, Rum: (a)–(g) chipped stone artefacts from Star Carr; (h)–(m) chipped stone artefacts from Farm Fields, Kinloch, Rhum. (a) blade core; (b) scrapers; (c) burin; (d) adze sharpening flake; (f) microliths; (g) borer; (h) conical platform core; (i) blade core; (j) double platform core; (k) scrapers; (l) borers; (m) microliths (top row, crescents; middle row, backed bladelets; bottom row, scalene triangles). Scales: (a)–(g) 1:2, (h)–(l) 2:3, (m) 3:4.
*Sources*: (a)–(g) after Clark 1954; (h)–(m) after Wickham-Jones 1990

---

**Figure 3.5 opposite** Organic and coarse stone artefacts from Mesolithic sites: (a) Barbed antler point from Star Carr (no. 178), c.276mm; (b) Barbed antler point from Star Carr (no. 145), c.180mm; (c) Barbed antler point from Star Carr (no. 150), c.138mm; (d) Bone pin made from the lateral metacarpal bones of elk from Star Carr (no. 160), c.148mm; (e) Mattock head of elk antler from Star Carr (no. 159), c.262mm; (f) Bone/antler harpoons from Oronsay middens, c.124 and 81mm; (g) 'Limpet scoops' made from bone/antler from Caisteal nan Gillean I, Oronsay, c.70mm; (h) Perforated shaped mattock head of red deer antler from Priory Midden, Oronsay, c.150mm.
*Sources*: (a)–(e) after Clark 1954; (f) after Anderson, J., 1895. 'Notice of a cave recently discovered at Oban,

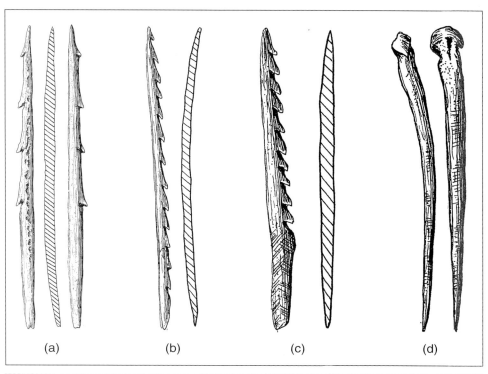

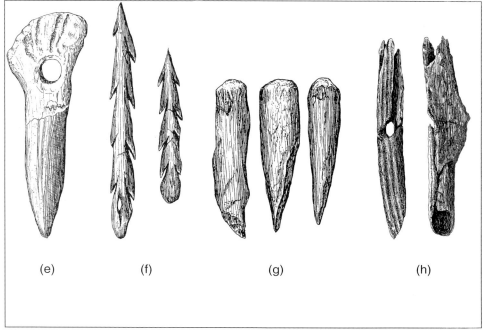

containing human remains, and a refuse-heap of shells and bones of animals, and stone and bone implements',
*Proceedings of the Society of Antiquaries of Scotland* 32, 211–230; (g) after Anderson, J., 1898. 'Notes on the
contents of a small cave or rock shelter at Druimvargie, Oban; and of three shell mounds in Oronsay',
*Proceedings of the Society of Antiquaries of Scotland* 32, 298–311; (h) after Mellars 1987

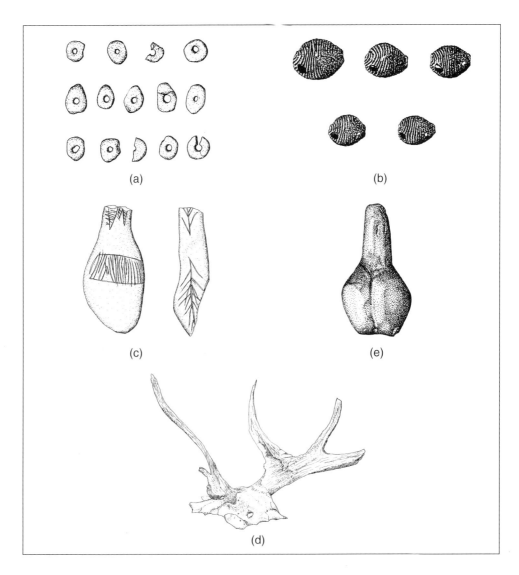

***Figure 3.6*** Non-utilitarian artefacts from Mesolithic sites in Britain: (a) Shale beads from Star Carr; (b) Perforated cowrie shell ornaments from Oronsay; (c) Engraved pebble from Rhuddlan, c.86mm; (d) Red deer antler mask; (e) Shale pebble from Nab Head claimed to represent a phallus, c.104mm.
*Sources*: (a), (d) after Clark 1954; (b) after Mellars 1987; (c) after Berridge, P. and Roberts, A., 1995. 'The Mesolithic decorated and other pebble artefacts: synthesis', in *Excavations at Rhuddlan, Clwyd, 1969–1973, Mesolithic to Medieval*. York: CBA Research Report 95; (e) Jacobi, R., 1980. 'The Early Holocene settlement of Wales', in Taylor, J. A. (ed.) *Culture and Environment in Prehistoric Wales*. Oxford: BAR British Series 76, 131–206

areas in particular, many sites have tools made from coarse types of stone. Often these are minimally altered beach pebbles, and are likely to have been used for detaching or processing shellfish.

Tools made from organic materials are very rare (Figure 3.5). Only Star Carr and a set of middens on the tiny Hebridean island of Oronsay have produced large quantities, although a good sample has recently been acquired from An Corran, a rockshelter on Skye. The most important are barbed points made from red deer antler, and antler mattocks. Barbed points comprise two general types: uniserial points, with one line of barbs, are predominantly found in the Early Mesolithic, while biserial points, often pierced to make harpoon-heads, tend to be shorter and are recovered from Late Mesolithic coastal sites. There is considerable variability within these types: five classes were identified at Star Carr.

Antler mattocks, perforated for hafting, have a working edge made by an oblique transverse truncation of the antler beam (Smith in Bonsall 1989). Those from Star Carr are of elk antler, while other sites produce examples made from red deer. Wear on their working edges includes lustrous polishes, deep and angular striations, and flaking, and is most likely to derive from digging, perhaps to remove roots or raw materials. Three Scottish examples were found associated with whale skeletons, suggesting the removal of blubber.

## Non-utilitarian artefacts

Artefacts of a less utilitarian nature are seldom found (Figure 3.6). A small number of beads include shale examples at Nab Head in Dyfed (David in Bonsall 1989) and pierced cowrie shells from Scottish middens (Simpson in Pollard and Morrison 1996). Red deer antler frontlets, the bone below the antlers pierced so that they could be worn as masks, occur at Star Carr. Such artefacts invite speculation: were they worn by shamans or perhaps as part of hunters' disguise?

Very few decorated objects are known. A shale pebble from Nab Head appears to represent a figurine or a phallus, but this surface find cannot be confidently attributed to the Mesolithic. A piece of red deer antler from Romsey and a *Bos* bone from the Thames are engraved with chevrons – a design frequent on Mesolithic objects from continental Europe; but, again, neither can be definitely attributed to this period. The site of Rhuddlan (Clwyd) produced incised pebbles with geometric designs: one was in a secure Mesolithic context and, in light of their stylistic unity, all are likely to be Mesolithic.

## Site features: pits, postholes and dwellings

While small pits are common on Mesolithic sites, evidence for more substantial structures is rare. The best is from Mount Sandel (Northern Ireland), discussed below. At sites such as Deepcar (Yorkshire) and Morton (Fife: Coles 1971), traces of shelters, perhaps no more than windbreaks, are present. Large depressions on sites including Cass Ny Hawin, Staosnaig (Colonsay: Mithen *et al.* in Pollard and Morrison 1996), and Broom Hill, Hampshire, contain many charred fragments of hazelnut shell, but whether these are the remains of hut floors, or specialized features for the processing of plant foods, is unclear.

## Faunal and floral assemblages

Animal bones are unfortunately infrequent on Mesolithic sites. The only reasonably sized samples come from Star Carr and the Oronsay middens, with smaller but important collections at sites such as Thatcham. Mainland samples are dominated by large herbivore remains – red deer, roe deer, pig, aurochs and elk – species likely to have been regularly hunted.

Human bones are exceedingly rare. One site, Aveline's Hole, a cave in the Mendip Hills, may have been a cemetery, containing over 70 individuals (Smith 1992a). Little, however, survives from work carried out here in the nineteenth and early twentieth centuries. The two best-recorded skeletons were found in a crushed state in 1924, associated with beads made from pig and red deer incisors, and red ochre. Fragments of bone have been dated to 9,000 BP – surprisingly early as continental Postglacial cemeteries generally date after 6,500 BP. The only complete skeleton comes from Gough's Cave, also in the Mendips. These remains, of a young male, are dated to the Early Mesolithic or possibly a little earlier. Bryan Sykes of Oxford University believes that ancient mtDNA (see Chapter 2) from this skeleton shows a remarkable degree of similarity to modern humans, suggesting direct descent.

Elsewhere, human remains are extremely sparse and fragmentary. A small collection of skeletal elements was recovered from the Oronsay middens (Mellars 1987), mostly from Cnoc Coig. These are dominated by head and foot bones which were found dispersed throughout the midden. They seem to indicate mainly adults, with one adolescent and one child represented, and do not appear to derive from intentional burials.

## Environmental evidence

Environmental evidence for Mesolithic activity comes directly from archaeological sites but also from early Postglacial sediments, including those from areas where no Mesolithic sites are currently known (Edwards in Pollard and Morrison 1996). Thus at Loch Lang (South Uist), charcoal, likely to derive from campfires, appears in sediments after 9,000 years ago. Throughout the Western Isles, sediments reveal increased levels of microscopic charcoal after 8,000 BP. This may reflect rising human populations and perhaps deliberate burning of vegetation – although until habitation sites are found, the possibility remains that the fires were natural occurrences during a more arid period (Tipping in Pollard and Morrison 1996). Changes in vegetation visible in the pollen record may also indicate a human presence. At Dallican Water (Shetland), for example, a marked reduction in ferns and tall herbs during the Mesolithic may have resulted from grazing. If so, the likely culprits are red deer: it seems improbable that they could have colonized the Shetland Islands without having been transported in boats.

## Missing evidence

Perhaps the most challenging feature of the record is what is known to be missing. Much of the Early Mesolithic coastline has been inundated by the sea and consequently the role of coastal resources during this period remains unclear. Is the earliest date for the Oronsay middens of *c.* 6,300 years ago simply a reflection of their survival, or is a major economic change indicated at that time? Similarly there are areas where archaeologists can be confident that Mesolithic sites exist, but in highland zones these are deeply buried below peat, or in coastal areas below blown sand.

The rarity of well-preserved sites inhibits the interpretation of surviving artefacts. Microliths must have been fixed in wooden or bone armatures, but only a possible pine arrowshaft from Seamer Carr (North Yorkshire) has survived. Consequently there is limited information on the types of tools they were used for. Offshore islands were reached, although evidence for boats is lacking. A possible paddle was found at Star Carr, but elsewhere in Europe large canoes are known. It must be assumed that similar craft were made here.

Other gaps in the record are more debatable. In the continental Later Mesolithic (Mithen 1994), numerous cemeteries in coastal locations provide evidence for complex burial rituals. Were such cemeteries created in Britain? Aveline's Hole is the only candidate. Similarly, art objects are almost non-existent, yet are plentiful in Europe. It is difficult to believe that Mesolithic societies in Britain did not engrave bone and antler or carve on stone. The extreme rarity of direct evidence frustrates consideration of the non-material aspects of Mesolithic lifestyles.

## INTERPRETATION

Archaeologists face considerable challenges in interpreting the surviving evidence. While all people during the Mesolithic lived by hunting and gathering, that lifestyle is highly variable. Hunter-gatherers can live in small, highly mobile egalitarian groups, or at semi-permanent sites in societies that display significant social differentiation. Archaeological sites can be small, overnight occupations, camps for specialized activites such as hunting, or residential bases; many are likely to be palimpsests from multiple occupations, perhaps each of a different character.

To cope with such complexities in site interpretation, a wide range of methods and techniques is employed. These have changed substantially during the last 50 years, notably with the development of archaeological science.

## DEVELOPMENTS IN MESOLITHIC ARCHAEOLOGY: STAR CARR AS A CASE STUDY

Star Carr is located in the Vale of Pickering, Yorkshire. Its excavation (1949–1951), and publication (Clark 1954) ushered in the modern era of Mesolithic studies. Star Carr has remained at the forefront of Mesolithic studies and is still cited as the 'type site' for the British Mesolithic. In many ways, this status is deserved, for the degree of organic preservation encountered remains unmatched on any other British site. In other ways, however, it is unfortunate. Star Carr does not now appear to have been a major site; it was merely a small hunting camp, occupied on a few occasions, and from which only a limited understanding of the period can be acquired. Ideas about Star Carr have changed since Clark's original publication.

The 1954 volume was of key importance in demonstrating why Mesolithic archaeology has to be a multidisciplinary exercise. It was one of the first publications in which the contribution of zoologists and botanists was seen as critical in understanding archaeological sites. Only later, however, did Clark (1972) offer his interpretation of Star Carr, proposing it as a winter base camp for groups that dispersed into the Pennines or North York Moors during the summer. The season of occupation was determined on the basis of shed antler recovered on site: modern deer shed their antlers between October and March. Clark's interpretation, heavily influenced by the contemporary research environment, drew on the ecology of modern red deer to reconstruct their movements in the Postglacial landscape.

Two radical reinterpretations, both founded on Clark's published data, were proposed within a decade. Far from being a winter base camp, Star Carr was, Pitts (1979) argued, a specialized site for working antler and tanning hides. The high frequencies of end scrapers and awls in the tool assemblage, direct evidence for antler working, and the quantities of birch bark and wood recovered, which he believed were tanning agents, were employed in this hypothesis. As tanning requires warmth, Pitts suggested that this took place in the summer months. The site may thus have been a winter group aggregation site, from which most inhabitants dispersed into the uplands during the summer, although some members continued in occupation to undertake industrial activities.

Shortly thereafter, Andersen and colleagues (1981) proposed that Star Carr had been used for butchery intermittently through the year, with the assemblages of artefacts and bones taking tens or hundreds of years to accumulate. They noted the absence of site maintenance – the clearing away of refuse from the assumed principal occupation area. Had occupation been prolonged, this is likely to have occurred, and consequently they concluded that only short visits were made to the site. They commented on the ephemeral layers within the hearths, again hardly indicative of substantial occupation. The first major concern with site formation processes, and substantial use of observations made on modern hunter-gatherer sites, are apparent. These innovations reflect contemporary thrusts in the subject more generally.

Thereafter, new analyses of the original data were undertaken, mirroring broader developments in Mesolithic archaeology. Dumont (in Bonsall 1989) applied microwear analysis, a method whereby microscopic examination of tool edges may indicate their former use, as different activities such as working wood or hide or cutting meat leave different microscopic traces. This demonstrated that a wide range of tasks had been undertaken, suggesting that arguments for a small set of specialized activities were wrong.

The faunal assemblage (discussed below) was reanalysed by Legge and Rowley-Conwy (1988). Whereas the original report had done little more than identify the species present, sex and age distributions by species, seasonality, body part representation (shown in ethnoarchaeological studies to indicate site function) and cut-marks on the surface of bones were considered. These authors drew heavily on ethnoarchaeology and ecology, demonstrating the remarkable advances in archaeozoology since the 1950s. They concluded that Star Carr had been a spring/summer hunting camp, dismissing the evidence for winter occupation that had once seemed so critical.

High-resolution pollen and sedimentological analyses were undertaken thereafter on a peat monolith from a new trench at Star Carr. Day (1993) examined pollen frequencies, charcoal fragments and mineral content, thus obtaining a more detailed picture of vegetational history and establishing the extent to which this had been influenced by human activity. New radiocarbon dates were acquired by AMS methods and calibrated: an absolute chronology for the occupation was thus secured (Day and Mellars 1994). This research demonstrates that people first occupied the locality *c.* 10, 700 years ago – a thousand years earlier than implied by the uncalibrated dates. During the next 80 years, the lakeside vegetation was burnt, perhaps to encourage new growth and to attract animals. Activity locally then appears to end, to be resumed at 10,550 BP; it then lasted a further 120 years. There thus appear to be two main occupation periods, with Clark's excavation relating to the second.

Day's work confirmed that, while during the Late Mesolithic the immediate vicinity of Star Carr was unoccupied, there was activity elsewhere in the Vale of Pickering; microscopic charcoal particles continued to accumulate in lacustrine sediments. Late Mesolithic occupation of the Vale had already been discovered by Schalda-Hall (1987), who employed extensive test-pitting to show that Clark's site is one of several concentrations of hunter-gatherer activity there.

Star Carr has thus repeatedly provided a test bed for the application of new analytical methods and new theories. New concerns with site formation processes, more sophisticated use of ethnographic analogies, new analytical methods, the calibration of radiocarbon dates, and a recognition of the need to place any site in its regional context are all noteworthy.

## OTHER KEY SITES

### Thatcham, Berkshire

Thatcham is located in the Kennet Valley. Although discovered in 1920, full-scale excavations were not undertaken until 1958–1961. Wymer (1962) identified the assemblage as Maglemosian; radiocarbon dates have since placed this occupation between 10,365 ± 170 and 9480 ± 160 radiocarbon years BP. Located in a topographic situation akin to Star Carr on an ancient lake margin, similar ranges of stone artefacts and fauna were recovered. Red deer, roe deer and wild pig were accompanied by horse and elk, both indicative of cold and relatively open conditions. One major difference from Star Carr is the scarcity of wooden and antler artefacts, especially barbed points.

Further excavations were undertaken in 1989 (Healey *et al.* 1992). These extended the occupation into the Later Mesolithic. Palynological study of nearby sediments indicates small-scale clearings within pine and hazel woodland. Wear traces on newly excavated artefacts suggest that a wide range of activities, using various raw materials, occurred, implying that Thatcham had been a base camp. Its location in a river valley with easy access to varied land and aquatic resources supports this view. Many other Mesolithic sites are now known in the Kennet Valley.

## Oakhanger, Hampshire

Numerous Mesolithic artefact scatters are known at Oakhanger (Jacobi 1981), from sites that span the Early (e.g. Oakhanger II, V, VII, X and XI) and Later (e.g. Oakhanger III, VIII and XX) Mesolithic. Some assemblages are substantial: Oakhanger V provided 85,000 artefacts and site VII 105,678 artefacts; these are in fact parts of a single site now bisected by a road. Most of the material consists of debris from tool making. The tools are dominated by microliths but truncated blades, burins, core adzes and finely serrated blades occur. The quantities of artefacts imply repeated occupations; at site V, six hearths are evident within the artefact distribution. Oakhanger VII, a site for which several radiocarbon dates have a mean of 9045 ± 66 BP, is intriguing: it displays some stratification, with Horsham points appearing in the upper level only. This array of sites indicates that people had repeatedly returned to this part of their landscape, which must have been a favoured location for hunting and gathering.

## Farm Fields, Kinloch, Rum

This, the earliest dated occupation (Wickham-Jones 1990) in Scotland, has uncalibrated dates of 8,500 years BP. Located at the head of a large bay, the site provided a landing place for people crossing, probably in coracles or canoes, to Rum. The island may have been attractive due to the locally available 'bloodstone' – a term used for cryptocrystalline silicas that can be flaked much as flint. Farm Fields (Figure 3.7) is typical of many Mesolithic sites in being a palimpsest of many occupations, incorporating numerous small pits of uncertain function. The artefacts, similar to those from contemporary English sites, are dominated by small geometric microliths, particularly scalene triangles.

It is likely that earlier Mesolithic sites in Scotland await discovery. Glenbatrick on Jura has broad blade microliths that should be contemporary with the Early Mesolithic in England, while a few tanged points may be indicative of Lateglacial occupation, perhaps by far-flung hunting parties.

## The Oronsay middens

Oronsay, a tiny island adjacent to the larger Colonsay, lies in the southern Hebrides. It has six Mesolithic shell middens, a remarkable density that remains unexplained. In recent times, however, the island has been a breeding ground for seals, which

***Figure 3.7*** Excavations at Farm Fields, Rum (Caroline Wickham Jones)

perhaps provided easy killings for Mesolithic coastal foragers. Our principal understanding comes from work during the 1970s, especially at Cnoc Coig midden (Mellars 1987).

Radiocarbon dates show that the middens formed between 6,300 and 4,300 calendar years ago. Aside from mollusc shells, a wide range of remains of marine and terrestrial fauna are attested; the subsistence economy is examined below. A collection of red deer bones is noteworthy, as it is unlikely that deer would ever have lived on Oronsay, or even on Colonsay. It seems that people from Islay and Jura, where occupation was probably based and where deer occur, made intermittent visits to exploit the rich coastal resources.

Artefacts from the middens include those probably used for exploiting coastal resources, such as small antler harpoons, and bevel-ended elongated pebbles ('limpet hammers'), employed, perhaps, for detaching limpets from rocks. The middens lack a microlithic industry, as represented at contemporary sites on nearby islands. This absence probably reflects the specific economic activities undertaken on Oronsay, rather than indicating distinct cultural groups with different tool traditions.

**Figure 3.8** Excavations at Gleann Mor, Islay (Steven Mithen)

## Gleann Mor, Islay

This site (Figure 3.8) provides an important contrast to those already described, which are likely to be palimpsests from multiple occupations. Gleann Mor is a small, discrete scatter consisting solely of stone artefacts and manufacturing waste, that probably represents a single occupation event. Excavated as part of a regional study (Mithen *et al.* in Pollard and Morrison 1996), Gleann Mor is set inland within peat moorland, beneath which the artefacts were sealed. When the site was occupied 6,200 years ago, hazel-dominated woodland would have surrounded the hunter-gatherers. Apart from thousands of waste chippings, the artefacts are again dominated by microliths, which, like the other tools, are preserved in a fresh condition. Microwear study indicates varied uses, outlined below.

Gleann Mor was probably a small hunting camp, occupied for a short period by a group exploiting the Hebridean islands. Other site types in their settlement system are found nearby. Less than 2 km distant, a much larger and probably contemporary site at Bolsay Farm may have been a residential base. The specialized sites of Oronsay, and that at Staosnaig (Colonsay), are located slightly further away; both have dates that overlap those of Gleann Mor. Thus here archaeologists are gaining insights into how Mesolithic people undertook different economic activities at various locations in the landscape.

## Culverwell, Isle of Portland, Dorset

The important site at Culverwell consists of an extensive shell midden, stretching over 300 m² (Palmer in Bonsall 1989), which seems to have formed in a hollow and derives from the exploitation of a wide range of marine molluscs; the absence of fish bones is puzzling. Evidence of dwelling structures is limited to several hearths, what appears to be a substantial cooking pit, and a pavement. The tool assemblage includes an impressive number of picks, made of local Portland chert, perhaps used for removing limpets from rocks, or for extracting chert from outcrops.

Year round occupation may have been possible in light of the likely abundance of coastal resources, and those from nearby woodland environments. Culverwell offers an indication of the substantial nature of some Mesolithic occupation sites in Britain – although quite how much of the site belongs to this period is unclear. The importance of coastal resources is evident at several other south-west English middens, such as Westward Ho! and Blashenwell.

## Mount Sandel, Co Antrim

Dated to *c.* 9,000 radiocarbon years BP, this site is located on a 30 m high bluff overlooking the River Bann (Figure 3.9). Mount Sandel (Woodman 1985) has substantial numbers of microliths dominated by scalene triangles; this is one of the earliest narrow blade assemblages known in the British Isles. Other stone tools include awls, scrapers and axes made on either cores or flakes.

The important evidence for structures consists of a large number of postholes that were dug within an enlarged natural hollow. These postholes evidently relate to numerous structures as some inter-cut, or were cut by other features. They seem to represent substantial circular huts, about 5.5 m in diameter, that contained hearths and pits, perhaps for storage.

### TOOLS, SITE ACTIVITIES, MOBILITY AND SETTLEMENT PATTERNS

Stone tools and manufacturing waste provide the largest body of evidence for the British Mesolithic. The basic types comprise microliths, scrapers, burins, axes and adzes. The simple presence of microliths

*Figure 3.9* Excavations of the hut at Mount Sandel (P. Woodman)

within an assemblage suggests a Mesolithic date – although the possibility that microliths were also made later in prehistory should not be discounted.

## Artefact frequencies, site activities and settlement patterns

The relative frequencies of tool types may indicate the activities that were undertaken at a site. Pitts' use (1979) of the proportions of end-scrapers and burins at Star Carr in arguing for specialized antler working has been noted. In Hampshire, the sites of Iping II and Oakhanger VII have contrasting tool assemblages. Oakhanger VII has more scrapers, serrated blades and truncated pieces than microliths, while microliths far outnumber these types at Iping. Microburins – quite rare at Oakhanger – are more numerous than microliths at Iping, suggesting that (if microliths are indeed for projectiles) hunting weapons were made there, while processing activities, such as cleaning hides, appear dominant at Oakhanger (Jacobi 1981).

Attempts have been made to organize assemblages from throughout Britain into classes relating to past functions. Mellars (1976) published an important interpretation of assemblage variability with regard to settlement patterns. He compiled data on the frequencies of different tool types within assemblages to show that sites fell into three classes: class A sites have assemblages dominated (>80 per cent) by microliths; in class B sites, microliths constitute 30–60 per cent; and class C sites are dominated by scrapers. Class B is by far the most common, being found in upland, lowland and coastal areas; Mellars interpreted these as winter base camps at which several groups of people aggregated. The class A microlith-dominated assemblages, found principally in the uplands of the Pennines and North York Moors, are considered as summer hunting camps. Only three scraper-dominated assemblages were found; the processing of animal hides is assumed to be the major activity indicated.

Barton (1992) recognized a correlation between artefact frequencies, topographic locations and the underlying geology in Early Mesolithic assemblages from central southern England. Sites including Hengistbury and Iping C, which have assemblages that lack tools such as burins, axes and drill bits, are found on high ground and generally occur on sandstone. In contrast, Downton and Thatcham III, on relatively low ground and on silty substrates, have more diverse toolkits. These latter appear to be locations where a wider range of activities was undertaken, compared with the specialized manufacture and use of hunting equipment on the higher sites.

## Microwear analysis and tool function

Microwear analysis, as already described, may give indications of artefact functions. At Gleann Mor, for instance, some microliths were employed as projectile points, identifiable due to tell-tale striations left on their surfaces. Other microliths here had clearly been used in a circular motion, apparently as bits for awls or drills.

While the Star Carr microwear analyses showed that a variety of tasks had been undertaken, few relationships between tool types and specific functions were noted. For instance, 56 scrapers (of 374 from the site) were examined for wear traces: 36 showed signs of use, representing 55 episodes. These were mainly scraping/planing actions, directed principally against hide (40 per cent), bone (22 per cent), antler (22 per cent) and wood (13 per cent). Hints of differences in the morphology of artefacts used on different materials were noted: those used on antler tend to be longer and more curved.

A detailed microwear study was undertaken on artefacts from Thatcham (Healey *et al.* 1992). The results included the identification of a specialist area for bone and antler working. Of six microliths examined, only one appeared to have been a projectile; the remainder had signs of use as borers and piercers.

## Debitage analysis and site function

Tools usually only constitute a small fraction of the artefacts from a site. Much more common is the manufacturing waste, or debitage; indeed retouched tools often form as little as 1 per cent of an assemblage. This division between tools and waste needs careful consideration. At Thatcham, for example, a higher percentage of unretouched artefact edges had been used compared to those that exhibited retouch. 'Debitage' thus includes tools that are not retouched.

Mesolithic sites on Islay illustrate how debitage can be studied. The proportions of tools at Coulererach and Bolsay Farm are very similar. At Coulererach, however, the debitage is dominated by large cores and flakes, often the first detached from the raw material; indeed, several discarded flint beach pebbles had just one or two flakes removed. Nodules were tested for quality and the initial stages of flint knapping took place; there was little concern for efficient use of materials. In contrast, at Bolsay Farm, most cores are small and debitage is dominated by little flakes characteristic of later stages of knapping. It appears that partially worked cores were carried here, to be worked as efficiently as possible before being discarded. Coulererach lay about 100 m from the Mesolithic coastline on which flint pebbles are likely to have been abundant, but Bolsay Farm lies 6 km from this source.

## Debitage analysis and site formation

When debitage can be refitted, more detailed information about knapping methods is obtainable. At Early Mesolithic Hengistbury Head (Barton 1992), for instance, excavations recovered 35,444 pieces of debitage, a considerable number of which have been refitted. Most cores with opposed platforms here displayed uneven use. Refitting also indicates that most, if not all, of the artefacts were contemporary. This is important, as they were found dispersed vertically through wind-blown sand deposits. Examples separated vertically by as much as 0.39 m have been rejoined, demonstrating that their separation is due to post-depositional processes such as trampling and bioturbation. Otherwise, this site might have been interpreted as a series of stratified deposits from successive occupations.

Demonstrating contemporaneity between artefacts and features on a single site can occasion difficulties. The artefacts at Oakhanger III covered more than 100 $m^2$ and surrounded four hearths. Are these hearths and artefacts contemporary and indicative of a relatively large social group, or do they simply reflect repeated visits by a small group? Radiocarbon dating cannot necessarily resolve such problems, as the finest resolution appears to be ± 50 years.

The enormous size of the lithic assemblages at many sites indicates that certain locations were repeatedly visited by Mesolithic foragers. While this may be accounted for purely in functional terms – such as access to materials or good hunting – symbolic relationships with specific places and landscape features linked to the inhabitants' cosmology, about which we know nothing, may be invoked.

## Raw material sources and mobility patterns

Identifying the sources of raw materials found on sites is important in reconstructing past mobility patterns. For instance, Early Mesolithic sites in the Pennines, both in the eastern foothills, such as Deepcar, and on the summits, have artefacts made from a white flint originating in the north Lincolnshire Wolds 80 km away. The frequency (80–99 per cent) of such artefacts matches that found on sites immediately adjacent to the flint sources. Jacobi (1978) suggested that this may reflect direct procurement by groups that exploited the Pennines in summer and the eastern lowlands in winter. Portland chert, contrastingly, is found in only very small frequencies in assemblages even from sites at distances less than 80 km from its source, such as Oakhanger V and VII. Only one blade of Portland chert was identified in the assemblage of 186,000 artefacts there. Jacobi proposed that the distribution mechanism in this case may have been gift exchange.

The distribution of bloodstone, which has its major source on Rum (Wickham-Jones 1990; 1994), is also informative. Assemblages containing bloodstone artefacts come from neighbouring islands, notably Eigg and Skye, and from nearby mainland areas including Ardnamurchan and the shell midden at Risga in Loch Sunart. This pattern may indicate the range over which people from Rum moved during their seasonal cycles. Further away, on Colonsay and Islay for example, bloodstone is absent from Mesolithic assemblages. These islands may, however, have provided sufficient raw materials, so that bloodstone was not required.

Inferences can be drawn from variations in raw material use through time. During the earlier Mesolithic, northern English assemblages are dominated by white flint; subsequently, there was much greater use of poorer quality chert and translucent flint (Pitts and Jacobi 1979). This change may reflect the exhaustion of high-quality sources, perhaps due to increasing population, or their inaccessibility due to rising sea-level or near-impenetrable vegetation. Alternatively, changes in mobility patterns may have been the cause, as later Mesolithic foragers covered smaller distances in the course of their activities and consequently had to rely on local, and poorer quality, raw materials.

## THE MESOLITHIC ECONOMY

The early Postglacial environments of Britain provided a diverse array of foodstuffs. Attempts at gaining a comprehensive understanding of Mesolithic subsistence are fraught by problems of poor preservation and difficulties of interpretation. There are sites that yield a detailed picture of one aspect, such as hunting at Star Carr and coastal exploitation on Oronsay, but a regional series of sites that provides an overall picture of subsistence is lacking.

## Hunting terrestrial game

Star Carr alone has a substantial faunal assemblage and shows that five species were hunted. It is probable that individuals were stalked in thick woodlands, although the possibility that animals were driven into ambushes remains. Legge and Rowley-Conwy (1988) identified 26 red deer, 12 elk, 16 aurochs, 17 roe deer and four pigs in the excavated assemblage. Their relative proportions seemingly reflect the selection of red deer by the hunters. Inferences can be made from bone sizes about the ages of animals that were killed; most red deer were 3- to 4-year-old sub-adults, while roe deer were rather younger when slaughtered. This difference may reflect their social behaviour, particularly the ages at which young deer leave their mothers and consequently become vulnerable to hunting. In the absence of comparable assemblages, it is unclear whether these characteristics are reflections of the local environment or particular function of Star Carr, or general features of the Mesolithic.

Legge and Rowley-Conwy also considered the time of year when Star Carr was occupied by examining seasonal indicators, such as eruption patterns in roe deer mandibles, the crown heights of red deer teeth and the presence of neonatal animals. All such indicators, which assume that growth patterns and reproductive cycles for early Postglacial species and their modern counterparts are comparable, suggest that occupation most probably occurred between May and September. The skeletal parts of red deer represented closely match those of caribou typically found on hunting camps of the Nunamiut in the Canadian Arctic, as opposed to those from their base camps or kill sites. It is therefore proposed that Star Carr played this role in its settlement system, though this conclusion depends, of course, on the relevance of the comparison. Major differences between the Nunamiut and Early Mesolithic environments (tundra versus woodland) and economies (caribou hunting as opposed to that of several species) may invalidate it.

Stalking large game is likely to have been pervasive throughout the British Mesolithic. Expectations as to how this would vary in importance in different environments can be modelled, but as yet cannot be tested with other substantial faunal evidence.

The exploitation of animals may have included something approaching management. Palynological evidence shows that Mesolithic foragers fired vegetation, although whether intentionally or accidentally (from uncontrolled campfires) is unclear. Modern Australian Aborigines employ fire with the express aim of encouraging plant growth and attracting game. Perhaps Mesolithic people acted similarly. At North Gill (North York Moors), a high-resolution pollen sequence demonstrated that during the Late Mesolithic or Early Neolithic, the tree canopy was opened by the removal of oak, willow and alder, allowing shrubs to flower much better. Evidence for the use of fire is absent, and the decline of these species may indicate the acquisition of foliage for wild game (Simmons and Innes 1996). Another form of animal management may have been the transport of some species to offshore islands.

## Shell middens and coastal exploitation

The coastal zone is likely to have been the most productive part of Britain during the Mesolithic. It is not surprising that the largest sites, including Culverwell, are located there. Access to woodland with its large game, as well as marine mammals and fish and the rich resources of the seashore, including crustaceans, seaweeds and shellfish, would have been simple.

The clearest picture of coastal exploitation comes from western Scotland, notably the middens on Oronsay. Others are known from caves and open sites around Oban bay (Argyll), and on other islands (e.g. Ulva Cave off Mull). Such middens typically reveal an immense diversity of species. Red deer and otter, over 30 types of birds, crabs, seals, shellfish and fish are attested on Oronsay. Over 90 per cent of the fish bones come from saithe and testify to marine fishing, although hooks and nets are absent. Limpets dominate the molluscan remains, but periwinkle and dogwhelk are well represented.

Otoliths (ear bones) of fish indicate the season of occupation. As there is a strong correlation between the size of a fish and these bones, and as young saithe grow rapidly, the size distributions of otoliths are indicative of the season(s) of the catches – assuming that spawning occurred at the same time as today. On Oronsay, different middens had distinctive otolith size distributions, implying that they accumulated in different seasons, with summer occupation at Cnoc Sligeach, for instance, while the Priory midden was used from the start of winter until early spring. In fact, all seasons are represented in this set of middens, leading some to suggest that people lived on Oronsay all year round. This seems unlikely in light of its size; a more realistic interpretation is that whenever foragers visited, they chose the optimum site with regard to prevailing winds, tides and the specific resources then available.

Molluscan remains can provide detailed information about foraging patterns. The shape of limpet shells is related to the position on the shore where this mollusc is found: those from its lowest part have relatively flat shells, while those higher up are progressively more conical. Limpets in the Ulva Cave midden are quite flat, indicating that Mesolithic foragers had searched the lowest, and probably most productive, part of the shore (Russell *et al.* in Fischer 1995). Although the shellfish at Ulva were dominated by the three species noted on Oronsay, 19 other species, including tiny ones, were represented. One, the blue-rayed limpet (*Helicon pellucidum*), less than 10 mm in size, is an unlikely foodstuff. This species lives on *Laminaria* spp. (the seaweed kelp, regularly harvested in modern times). It is likely that the Mesolithic foragers were also collecting kelp, perhaps as food.

## The use of plants

A contentious aspect of Mesolithic subsistence concerns the importance of plant foods. Clarke (1976) argued that early Postglacial environments would have been rich in plant foods, which are likely to have made a major contribution to diet. Evidence to support this assertion has slowly been accumulating for the whole of Europe (Zvelebil 1994).

Plant remains survive only if normal processes of decay are halted, which in Britain would mean a totally waterlogged site, the like of which remains absent. Charring also preserves plant foods, although the resulting assemblage is biased: charring depends on the proximity of fire, and many plant foods were probably eaten raw. Even when plant remains are preserved, their recovery from sediments requires sieving through very fine-grained mesh or flotation methods that many early, and some recent, excavations have neglected to employ. In consequence, the limited amounts of plant foods known from Mesolithic sites do not reflect their significance in the diet.

Raspberry seeds from Newferry, wild pear/apple from Mount Sandel and bog bean from Star Carr offer a glimpse of the range regularly exploited.

Only hazelnuts, usually represented by fragments of their charred shells, have been found in large quantities and on many sites. These were probably roasted to improve their flavour and digestibility or to prepare a paste for ease of transport and storage; in this process, some were burnt. The apparent importance of hazelnuts in Mesolithic diets is likely to be more than a factor of preservation and recovery: as a highly nutritious plant food, they were probably intensively exploited and regularly harvested. At sites such as Broom Hill and Staosnaig, hundreds of thousands of charred nuts were deposited in large, circular depressions. As these nuts are presumably only a fraction of those roasted, a very intensive exploitation of hazel trees in the vicinity is implied, especially if, as at Staosnaig, such deposits formed over a number of years rather than centuries.

The importance of plant foods in the diet may be indicated by the evidence for environmental manipulation by igniting vegetation, which increases in frequency during the Later Mesolithic. Firing may have been used to encourage plant growth, and been particularly valuable for hazel. Management of plants may also be indicated by artefacts: amongst other purposes, antler mattocks may have been used to break ground or to weed, so that edible wild plants could flourish.

## The use of cereals?

Numerous pollen cores provide a further contentious aspect of Mesolithic plant use: the exploitation, perhaps cultivation, of cereals. For example, at Cothill Fen, Oxfordshire, a single *Triticum* type (wheat) pollen grain was found at a level dating to *c.* 6,800 radiocarbon years BP (Day 1991), while another cereal type pollen grain was identifed at a level dating to *c.* 5,880 radiocarbon years BP at Machrie Moor, Arran. These may indicate Mesolithic groups experimenting with growing non-indigenous cereals, but some specialists consider that the 'cereal type pollen' was either produced by native wild grasses, or occured in such early contexts due to contamination. Unless cereal grains are found in well-dated, *in situ* Mesolithic contexts, it seems unlikely that this issue will be resolved.

## SOCIAL ORGANIZATION, IDEOLOGY AND THE HUMAN POPULATION

Depressingly little can be stated with confidence about the social organization of Mesolithic hunter-gatherers in Britain, about which archaeologists remain unable to draw inferences from records composed primarily of stone artefacts. Of course, this does not stop speculation, some of which may be correct. For instance, Jacobi (1978) argued that in northern England during the Earlier Mesolithic, two distinct social groups are represented by assemblages with specific frequencies of particular microlith types, and differences in raw material usage. Subtle variations in the retouch of obliquely blunted points, for example, are recognized. Such differences are unlikely to have been functional and, since such equipment is too inconspicuous to have acted as a means of social identification, may reflect largely unconscious social traditions unique to particular human groups. A similar argument may be applicable to other distinctive artefacts, such as Horsham points, found in discrete geographical areas and chronological periods.

Another route into prehistoric social organization is to consider the distribution of prestige goods in order to identify patterns of exchange, but few such items are known. Perhaps the best examples are shale beads, apparently significant artefacts of the Early Mesolithic. At Nab Head I (Dyfed), over 600 have been found (David in Bonsall 1989), made from local material. This seems to have been worked there, given the numbers of perforating tools, unperforated shale discs, and partially-drilled or broken beads recovered. Nab Head may have acted as a production centre for these beads, which were then absorbed into an exchange system, resulting in finds of examples at several inland sites.

Settlement evidence provides few clues as to social organization. The largest sites, such as Culverwell, may represent either a large, semi-sedentary population or many short-term visits, leading to a gradual accumulation of structural features. At present, we do not know which applies, but in future, attempts to look systematically and in detail at the spatial structure of settlements may prove helpful.

Estimating the overall population is also fraught with difficulties. Smith (1992b) has documented the changes in site numbers each millennium during the Lateglacial and early Postglacial, finding that by 7,000 BP, when the available land area was about 270,000 km$^2$, stability had been reached. If the Mesolithic inhabitants lived at population densities (0.01–0.02 persons per km$^2$) similar to ethnographically documented hunter-gatherers in comparable environments, a total population of 2,750–5,500 is implied. Such low figures are a reminder that hunter-gatherers typically have very extensive foraging areas. Indeed, large numbers of sites, such as those from Islay to Rum along Scotland's west coast, may have resulted from a single human group travelling its length. There is an alternative, however: that people were beginning to live a more sedentary lifestyle, especially during the Late Mesolithic. Only future, problem-oriented research will provide an answer.

## OUTSTANDING PROBLEMS

The issue of population size, whether at single settlements or for the country as a whole, encapsulates a set of outstanding problems. Others have been indicated: the role of plant foods in diet; the nature of settlement patterns; and the reasons for variation in microlith form. A considerable amount of innovative research is underway, including experimental knapping to understand the cause of variation in microlith form, and the creation of predictive models for settlement location. The further development of science-based archaeology is likely to have a major impact on our understanding, but new theoretical approaches are also required: few have viewed hunter-gatherer/land relationships other than from functional–ecological perspectives. It is time to consider the symbolic/ideological nature of this relationship – although quite how this can be achieved remains elusive.

It is perhaps only by exploring this issue that an understanding of the transition to the Neolithic will be secured. For 5,000 years, people lived by hunting and gathering with a microlithic technology and without monumental architecture. This hunting and gathering lifestyle probably continued long into the Neolithic (Chapter 4). The loss of microliths from the archaeological record is noteworthy; and the appearance of monuments suggests profound changes in non-subsistence behaviour, perhaps involving entirely new perceptions of the landscape. Of all periods of British prehistory, the Mesolithic has perhaps both the greatest need and potential for innovative research.

## Acknowledgements
Line drawings are by Margaret Matthews and Kirsty Bambridge.

## Key texts
Bonsall, C. (ed.) 1989. *The Mesolithic in Europe*. Edinburgh: John Donald.
Clark, J.G.D., 1954. *Excavations at Star Carr*. Cambridge: Cambridge University Press.
Fischer, A. (ed.) 1995. Proceedings of the *Man, Sea and the Mesolithic conference, Horsholm*. Oxford: Oxbow Monograph 53.

Pollard, T. and Morrison, A. (eds) 1996. *The Early Prehistory of Scotland.* Edinburgh: Edinburgh University Press.

Smith, C., 1992a. *Late Stone Age hunters of the British Isles.* London: Routledge.

Wickham-Jones, C. R., 1994. *Scotland's first settlers.* London: Batsford/Historic Scotland.

## Bibliography

Andersen, J.M., Byrd, B.F., Elson, M.D., McGuire, R.H., Mendoza, R.G., Staski, E. and White, J.P., 1981. 'The deer hunters: Star Carr reconsidered', *World Archaeology* 13, 31–46.

Barton, R.N.E., 1992. *Hengistbury Head Dorset. Volume 2: the Late Upper Palaeolithic and Early Mesolithic sites.* Oxford: Oxford University Committee for Archaeology Monograph Series 34.

Clark, J.G.D., 1972. *Star Carr: a case study in bioarchaeology.* Reading, Mass.: Addison-Wesley Module in Anthropology 10.

Clarke, D.L., 1976. 'Mesolithic Europe: the economic basis', in Sieveking, G. de G., Longworth, I.H. and Wilson, K.E. (eds) *Problems in economic and social archaeology.* London: Duckworth, 449–481.

Coles, J.M., 1971. 'The early settlement of Scotland: excavations at Morton, Fife', *Proceedings of the Prehistoric Society* 37, 284–366.

Day, S.P., 1991. 'Post-glacial vegetational history of the Oxford region', *New Phytologist* 119, 445–470.

Day, S.P., 1993. 'Preliminary results of high resolution palaeoecological analyses at Star Carr, Yorkshire', *Cambridge Archaeological Journal* 3, 129–140.

Day, S.P. and Mellars, P., 1994. '"Absolute" dating of Mesolithic human activities at Star Carr, Yorkshire: new palaeoecological studies and identification of the 9600 BP radiocarbon plateau', *Proceedings of the Prehistoric Society*, 60, 417–422.

Healey, F., Heaton, M. and Lobb, S.J., 1992. 'Excavation of a Mesolithic site at Thatcham, Berkshire', *Proceedings of the Prehistoric Society* 58, 41–76.

Jacobi, R., 1978. 'Northern England in the eighth millennium b.c.: an essay', in Mellars, P.A. (ed.) *The early Postglacial settlement of northern Europe.* London: Duckworth, 295–332.

Jacobi, R., 1981. 'The last hunters in Hampshire', in Shennan, S.J. and Schadla-Hall, R.T. (eds) *The archaeology of Hampshire.* Hampshire: Hampshire Field Club and Archaeology Society Monograph 1, 10–25.

Legge, A.J. and Rowley-Conwy, P.A., 1988. *Star Carr revisited: a reanalysis of the large mammals.* London: Centre for Extra Mural Studies, Birkbeck College.

Mellars, P.A., 1976. 'Settlement patterns and industrial variability in the British Mesolithic', in Sieveking, G. de G., Longworth, I.H. and Wilson, K.E. (eds) *Problems in economic and social archaeology.* London: Duckworth, 375–399.

Mellars, P.A., 1987. *Excavations on Oronsay: prehistoric human ecology on a small island.* Edinburgh: Edinburgh University Press.

Mithen, S., 1994. 'The Mesolithic Age', in Cunliffe, B.W. (ed.) *The Oxford illustrated Prehistory of Europe.* Oxford: Oxford University Press, 79–135.

Myers, A., 1989. 'Reliable and maintainable technological strategies in the Mesolithic of mainland Britain', in Torrence, R. (ed.) *Time, energy and stone tools.* Cambridge: Cambridge University Press, 78–91.

Pitts, M., 1979. 'Hides and antlers: a new look at the gatherer-hunter site of Star Carr, North Yorkshire, England', *World Archaeology* 11, 32–42.

Pitts, M. and Jacobi, R., 1979. 'Some aspects of change in flaked stone industries of the Mesolithic and Neolithic in southern Britain', *Journal of Archaeological Science* 6, 163–177.

Schalda-Hall, R.T., 1987. 'Recent investigations of the early Mesolithic landscape and settlement in the Vale of Pickering, North Yorkshire', in Rowley-Conwy, P., Zvelebil, M. and Blankholm, H.P. (eds) *Mesolithic northwest Europe: recent trends.* Sheffield: Department of Archaeology and Prehistory, Sheffield University, 46–54.

Simmons, I.G. and Innes, J.B., 1996. 'An episode of prehistoric canopy manipulation at North Gill, N. Yorkshire, England', *Journal of Archaeological Science* 23, 337–342.

Smith, C., 1992b. 'The population of Late Upper Palaeolithic and Mesolithic Britain', *Proceedings of the Prehistoric Society* 58, 41–76.

Wickham-Jones, C.R., 1990. *Rhum: Mesolithic and later sites at Kinloch. Excavations 1984–86.* Edinburgh: Society of Antiquaries of Scotland Monograph Series 7.

Woodman, P., 1985. *Excavations at Mount Sandel, 1973–1977.* Belfast: Archaeological Research Monographs 2.

Woodman, P., 1989. 'A review of the Scottish Mesolithic: a plea for normality!', *Proceedings of the Society of Antiquaries of Scotland* 119, 1–32.

Wymer, J.J., 1962. 'Excavations at the Maglemosian sites at Thatcham, Berkshire, England', *Proceedings of the Prehistoric Society* 28, 329–361.

Zvelebil, M., 1994. 'Plant use in the Mesolithic and its role in the transition to farming', *Proceedings of the Prehistoric Society* 60, 35–74.

*Chapter Four*

# The Neolithic period,
# *c.* 4000–2500/2200 BC

## Changing the world

## Alasdair Whittle

### SETTING THE SCENE

In the earlier fourth millennium BC, in woodland near the River Avon, people dug a large pit and deposited in it food remains and artefacts: the bones from several cattle and roe deer, and at least one pig and two red deer; a few beaver and trout bones; some carbonized cereal grains, probably emmer wheat; flint tools and waste; and many broken sherds from about 40 pots (Richards 1990). This pit is at Coneybury, near Stonehenge on Salisbury Plain in Wiltshire. It evokes many recurrent features of the earlier part of the Neolithic period: activity in areas probably not much frequented in the Mesolithic; a woodland setting; absence of residential structures and therefore probably a mobile lifestyle; occasional gatherings of people involving feasting and the use and deposition of novel forms of artefact; and the continuing use of animals and other wild resources alongside domesticated stock and cultivated cereals.

Broadly contemporary with the Coneybury pit, other new features of the earlier Neolithic landscape in this and other regions appeared: shrines or tombs in elongated mounds, echoing the form of the great timber longhouses of the first Neolithic generations on the Continent and containing collections of assorted human bone; and ditched enclosures that defined special places for gathering and ritual, to commemorate the dead, to feast, and to celebrate the domesticity and sociality of the Neolithic world. By about 2500 BC, there were further changes in this area. Several more circular and linear enclosures had been built, the largest, the henge of Durrington Walls (Wiltshire), with a massive circular bank set outside its ditch, containing circular settings of timber uprights around and among which people continued the tradition of depositing food remains and artefacts (Wainwright 1989). By this time, according to radiocarbon determinations, the earthwork enclosure of Stonehenge had also been elaborated with stone settings at its centre in a permanent version of the contemporary timber settings of Durrington Walls and other sites (Cleal *et al.* 1995). This displays many features that recur during the later part of the Neolithic: signs of more people in the landscape, but still the absence of well-defined settlements; a considerable tradition of gatherings and monument building, referring to the past and elaborating the significance of chosen places; and a scale of monument building that raises the question of how such enterprise may have been organized and achieved.

It has become commonplace to entitle chapters on this period 'First farmers' or 'Settling down', as though a new subsistence economy based on domesticated animals and cereals, and a newly sedentary lifestyle based on agriculture, could best define the changes apparent in the Neolithic. This view has been increasingly challenged for some 15 years. Undoubtedly, there were new resources in play, including domesticated cattle, pigs and sheep/goats (the latter not indigenous), and cultivated cereals, principally wheats and barleys (also not indigenous); but their relative importance and impact remain to be established, and substantial rescue and research projects have consistently failed to turn up definitive evidence for permanent or large-scale settlements. The essence of the Neolithic seems to lie elsewhere, in a changing world view involving new notions of time, descent, origins, ancestry, relations with nature, community and shared values and ideals: in changing conceptions of people's place in the scheme of things (Barrett 1994; Bradley 1993; Hodder 1990; Thomas 1991; Tilley 1994; Whittle 1996). These are bound up in part with domestication, but that should not lead us to equate the Neolithic uniquely with mixed farming, nor necessarily with sedentary existence.

The Neolithic period offers both continuities and contrasts with what came before and after it. Mobility and dispersal, a broad-spectrum resource base, and perhaps social ideals such as sharing, can be linked to the Mesolithic lifestyle, while domestication of plants and animals, more frequent woodland clearance, novel artefacts, treatment of the dead and the building of a great variety of monuments, serve to distinguish the Neolithic from the preceding period. The contrasts with what follows, from the Beaker horizon on, may appear superficially extensive: increasing emphasis on individuals in mortuary rites; a greater range of artefacts, some of metal; the demise of major monument building; and a trend in many areas to less wooded landscapes. There are also many continuities, however, and the greatest shift may be sought between the world of the Neolithic and Earlier Bronze Age (considered in Chapter 5) and that of the Later Bronze Age, when the processes of settling down and social differentiation took firmer hold.

In this perspective, traditional terminologies look increasingly unhelpful, but they have their value as labels, and are sanctioned by long use. The simplest division is between an *Earlier Neolithic* and a *Later Neolithic*, separated at *c.* 3000 BC. This accords quite well with major patterns in the development of pottery styles, flint projectile points, and much of the repertoire of southern British monument types. To the *Earlier Neolithic* belong round-based pot styles, some decorated; chipped and polished stone and flint axes; leaf-shaped flint arrowheads; and long barrows, various series of chambered tombs, causewayed enclosures, and cursus monuments. To the *Later Neolithic* belong more profusely decorated round-based pots in the Peterborough tradition and flat-based Grooved Ware pots; waisted, partially polished and other variant stone axes; asymmetrical and transverse flint arrowheads; other portable artefacts including stone and antler maceheads, bone pins, and stone balls; and henges, stone and timber circles, timber palisaded enclosures, early round barrows and ring-ditches, and late cursus monuments.

A next-best approximation is to distinguish *Early Neolithic*, *Middle Neolithic*, and *Late Neolithic*. The Early Neolithic (*c.* 4000–34/3300 BC) displays strong continuity with the Mesolithic in terms of residential mobility and broad-spectrum subsistence, but now involving animal herding and some cereal cultivation with accompanying limited clearance of woodland, broad regional styles of round-based pottery, and axe production but limited circulation (perhaps through gift exchange). The first tombs and shrines, in a variety of regional types of barrow and cairn, with internal structures of wood and stone, were erected; and towards the end of this phase the first causewayed enclosures were built.

The *Middle Neolithic* (perhaps 3400/3300–3000/2900 BC) is marked by both continuing development of these features and the beginnings of replacement and further change. Many of the southern causewayed enclosures (and also modified enclosures as at Flagstones, Dorchester, Dorset, or the first phase of Stonehenge) and most of the largest and most complex chambered tombs, for example of Maes Howe type on the Orkney Islands, were in use, as the largest passage graves in Ireland appear to have been. Regional sequences are not synchronized, however, and construction of chambered tombs may have continued in the north-west after the building of long barrows and chambered tombs in the south had ceased. The strongly linear cursus monuments mostly belong here, representing in some instances elaborations of ideas to do with pre-existing barrows, probably in the realms of the dead and the circulation of spirits (Tilley 1994). The first single or limited-number burials under small barrows or in small ring-ditches date to the end of the Middle Neolithic, while some stone circles could belong this early. Round-based pottery styles include the Ebbsfleet variant of the Peterborough tradition, while in the north, flat-based Grooved Ware may have appeared on Orkney by the end of the Middle Neolithic, perhaps alongside the round-based Unstan Ware.

To the *Late Neolithic* (*c.* 3000/2900–25/2200 BC) belong the end of the Peterborough pottery tradition and the full development of Grooved Ware, now present over the whole country. Late Neolithic monuments include henges and their internal settings, stone and timber circles, and some cursus monuments. Stone rows, some perhaps erected earlier, were incorporated into the layout of ceremonial complexes, such as the West Kennet Avenue attached to Avebury henge in Wiltshire or those at Callanish on Lewis. The monumental mound of Silbury Hill appears to be the north Wiltshire equivalent of the developed phases of Stonehenge. Also pre-Beaker are the palisade enclosures of West Kennet (Whittle 1997), and perhaps too some other examples, though that at Mount Pleasant, Dorchester, Dorset, has later radiocarbon dates but Beaker pottery in deposits contemporary with its decay (Wainwright 1989). A variety of single burials and cremation areas are also known. The date of introduction of Beaker pottery and associated material culture and practices is uncertain; it may well not be as high as 2600 BC (*contra* Chapter 5). If a simple distinction is made between earlier and later Beaker assemblages, only the earlier series can belong with the end of the Late Neolithic. This material is discussed in Chapter 5.

Disappointingly few dendrochronological dates are available for the period, and few radiocarbon dates are of high precision. While the scientific methods await refinement or application, interim goals include monument and artefact sequences (e.g. Kinnes 1979), and studies of regional development.

Both the Earlier–Later and Early–Middle–Late schemes are employed here, although neither does full justice to the regional patterns of landscape and subsistence change across the country, nor to artefact- or site-specific sequences. The general trend seen in pollen and molluscan evidence is one of gradually increasing forest clearance, both in terms of the scale of clearings and their duration, but with considerable local and regional variation. In at least some sequences there are phases of regeneration; the decline of woodland was not relentlessly uninterrupted. In the south, clearance may have been greatest in the vicinity of monument complexes, so that environmental evidence associated with monuments large and small may not be representative of wider landscapes. In some localities, open country may be a by-product of ceremonial activity connected with monument construction, rather than the outcome of an ever-intensifying agricultural economy and a growing population.

Sites with good assemblages of subsistence data are rare from any phase. Causewayed enclosures emphasize domesticated cattle and large southern henges domesticated pigs, but it is not certain that evidence from such special contexts truly reflects contemporary stock keeping. There is little evidence for intensification of cereal cultivation through time. On Orkney, for example, the range of subsistence residues in the distinctive small, nucleated Later Neolithic settlements such as Skara Brae does not seem greatly different to that seen in earlier structures at Knap of Howar, Papa Westray; those apparent may relate in large part to the nature of group composition and to varying tactics for the intake of new land (Sharples in Sharples and Sheridan 1992). Even where stone-built, nucleated houses have been examined, evidence for extensive agriculture is lacking; a broad-based spectrum of cultivation, gathering, herding, hunting and sea fishing is indicated. There is sporadic evidence for scratch ploughs or ards, from the Earlier Neolithic onwards, including the marks preserved under the South Street long barrow, Wiltshire (Ashbee *et al.* 1979). There have been claims for permanent plots or arable fields. The most extensive, the stone-walled systems of western Ireland, appear rather to have contained livestock; and their age remains fully to be established by radiocarbon dating. Irregular stone-walled plots on the Shetland Islands may be Bronze Age or later rather than Neolithic, and the ditched paddocks of Fengate and other sites on the western margin of the East Anglian Fens are now better seen as Later Bronze Age than Late Neolithic.

Regional, topographic and other biases hinder reconstruction. Northern areas have been relatively neglected in terms of major research projects, though that is changing (Barclay 1997; Sharples in Sharples and Sheridan 1992). Much research has concentrated on monuments, both for their interest and importance and because they are generally more easily identifiable than residential occupations. The search for residential sites by means of surface survey, looking principally for lithic scatters, has intensified since the mid-1980s: projects have concentrated on heavily cultivated, thin soils, mainly on the chalk downland of southern England, where monuments also occur. Much less research has been done on coasts, in wetlands and in river valleys. Wetland research, for example in the Somerset Levels (Coles and Coles 1986), has produced spectacular results, not in the identification of domestic sites but in the discovery of successive wooden walkways across fen, fenwood and raised bog, showing organized routes across wet places and wide use of the landscape. Large-scale rescue projects under way in advance of gravel extraction in the Thames and Ouse river valleys promise to reveal much more about valley use.

## CHANGING PERSPECTIVES IN NEOLITHIC STUDIES

Archaeologists have become more reflective of the ways in which assumptions about the Neolithic period are formed. In terms of dominant theory, Neolithic studies reflect post-war trends rather well, and indeed for some 15 years have been in the forefront of theoretical debate.

Initially, the culture-historical model prevailed, best encapsulated by Piggott's classic synthesis *The Neolithic cultures of the British Isles* (1954). The Neolithic was marked by an intrusive agricultural population, arranged in various regional cultural groups, whose artefacts, monuments and development form much of the substance of the book. This was an era of relatively small-scale excavations, for example by Piggott and Atkinson at West Kennet and Wayland's Smithy long barrows and Stonehenge, or by Grahame Clark at the camp at Peacock's Farm, Shippea Hill, on the Cambridgeshire fen-edge. Subsequently, Clark set up larger-scale research excavation at an occupation site at Hurst Fen, Mildenhall, and thereafter large-scale rescue excavations, for example at Durrington Walls henge (Wainwright 1989), were mounted. The application of radiocarbon dating began to lengthen the period, and aerial photography to extend distributions of ploughed-out sites including causewayed enclosures. Fieldwork was concentrated in southern parts of Britain. This bias, created by contemporary perceptions and assumptions as much as by the apparent archaeological richness of the south, persisted for a long time.

In the heyday of processual archaeology, from the late 1960s to the early 1980s, the concern with culture decreased, though research into individual monument and artefact types remained plentiful. A focus on a combination of expansive economy, growing population and changing social structure dominated research. Interpretation of monuments was revived (e.g. Renfrew 1973): these became the territorial markers of sedentary populations concerned with land and resources in competition for space and social position, long barrows and causewayed enclosures for segmentary or tribal society and henges for later chiefdoms. Processual concerns with subsistence ('palaeoeconomy') began to produce better recovery of bone and plant remains, but only on a limited scale. Considerable palynological research was undertaken, in which radiocarbon-dated pollen profiles added much to the understanding of changing landscapes. Palynologists, however, tended to look to the dominant archaeological models in interpreting vegetational changes; earlier ideas of shifting agriculture and shifting settlement were generally disregarded. Large, often prolonged excavations occurred at selected sites, especially southern monuments, such as Hambledon Hill and Crickley Hill causewayed enclosures, Hazleton long barrow and Mount Pleasant henge.

The post-processual theoretical challenge involved Neolithic examples from the outset. Shanks and Tilley (1982) examined the meaning of bone arrangements and sortings in southern long barrows, while Hodder (1982) considered possible conceptual links amongst henges, tombs and houses in the Later Orcadian Neolithic. As in the processual era, it would be misleading to claim theoretical unity. Partly from a theoretical perspective and partly as the results of large-scale survey projects started to become available during the 1980s, the sedentary nature of the Neolithic came increasingly under question, and a dominant role for agriculture was also challenged (Moffett *et al.* 1989; Entwhistle and Grant 1989). The meanings of monuments and their associated practices were emphasized rather than their functions, and material culture was seen as an active agent in promoting individual and sectional interests rather than as a reflector solely of group affiliation. The conceptual and symbolic importance of domestication was emphasized (Hodder 1990; Thomas 1991; 1996). Growing interest in the agency and independence of Neolithic populations viewed as social actors not only encouraged the new consensus of continuity from Mesolithic to Neolithic, replacing the colonization model, but allowed for social changes to have been variable, as opposed to conforming to a universal process, especially in the Later Neolithic (e.g. Barrett 1994). Field research and its publication have remained important (though comparatively little has so far been generated directly by the post-processualist agenda). Recession from the later 1980s reduced the quantity of rescue excavation, but the gravel workings noted above remain important. Since 1980, there has been proportionately more work in the north (Barclay 1997), on monuments and monument complexes in eastern Scotland such as Balfarg, Fife, as well as in Orkney, and on occupation sites there and in the Western Isles.

Some perceptions have not altered much during this phase of research. There is still a strong evolutionary assumption that the pattern of cultural and other changes reflects an underlying process of steady, more-or-less linear progression to greater social complexity and differentiation, as well as to a higher population with a gradually more intensive economy. There is equally a strong belief that the social dynamic driving change was competition for power, or at the very least for social pre-eminence or hegemony. These assumptions have in their turn recently been questioned (e.g. Thomas 1993; Whittle 1996). Further such particularizing investigations, and a more engendered Neolithic archaeology, allied to greater concern for shared values and ideals, may further challenge these assumptions. These new emphases could tie in with the geographically broader range of field research now being undertaken, which may be recognizing a widely spread but highly dispersed population. Future studies may focus on slow change among small-scale, dispersed populations, driven as much by their world view and long ritual cycles as by the demands of growing population or agricultural intensification.

## The Mesolithic–Neolithic transition

Disappointingly, there are so far no sites that give a clear picture of the Mesolithic–Neolithic transition: no stratigraphic sequences that cover the period in question, no reused features. This could change by lucky chance, but meanwhile the evidence available has to be taken at face value. Some population overspill from Neolithic communities in adjacent parts of Europe in the mid or later fifth millennium BC remains envisageable, but the evidence for their source is ambiguous, since Early Neolithic assemblages on this side of the Channel and North Sea bear only general resemblances to their contemporaries on the other. The consensus is now that the indigenous Mesolithic population became Neolithic by adopting new material culture, incorporating new subsistence staples, and developing a new world view. One favoured model proposes that the motivation was economic, demographic or both, leading to a recasting of lifestyle to alleviate pressure on resources. Another model focuses on social competition as the spur to changes in lifestyle.

For this, the Late Mesolithic Ertebølle culture in southern Scandinavia stands as a point of comparison. Unfortunately, relevant data are not plentiful in Britain, to which the loss of some of the contemporary coastline may have contributed (see Chapter 3). The impression is not, however, of packed Late Mesolithic coastal communities, as in parts of the Baltic. Large areas of inland Britain, such as the chalklands, may have been little frequented on a regular basis; demonstrating this by lithics is difficult, and microliths possibly did not continue in use until the end of the Mesolithic sequence. The transition may therefore be from a mobile Mesolithic to a still mobile Neolithic.

Some direct continuities may be suggested. Possible early experimentation with cereal cultivation has been noted (Chapter 3), conceivably as part of a wide spectrum of Mesolithic plant use, including tending and even cultivation (Zvelebil 1994). There is evidence for Mesolithic woodland clearance; some clearings may have persisted until, or been reused in, the Neolithic. A few Neolithic monuments overlie Mesolithic occupation, as at Hazleton on the Cotswolds (Saville 1990), which could imply a closer connection. That may have consisted not of direct residential continuity, but of the maintenance of landscapes with named places, crossed by paths and framed by significant points; in south-west Wales, Neolithic monuments pick out parts of the coastal landscape already containing Mesolithic camps (Tilley 1994).

## Occupations: settlement, residences and structures

Various built structures are known from the Neolithic as a whole, generally consisting of rectangular settings of postholes, rarely longer than 10 m (Darvill and Thomas 1996). In the far north, stone footings, occasionally walling, define a range of structures, from rectangular and squarish to oval and near-circular. It is a curious record. Absent are the great timber longhouses of the first Neolithic of central and western Europe, the *Linearbandkeramik* ('LBK') culture tradition of the mid-sixth millennium BC onward. Such British (and Irish) structures as have been found often occur singly; there is little to indicate that they become more frequent in later phases. They are generally interpreted as houses, and many may indeed have been residences, but they are not normally associated with large accumulations of rubbish or with ancillary structures. At best, these would have been used for short periods of time, or at irregular intervals. Recent evidence from Loch Olabhat, North Uist, illustrates the ambiguities (Armit in Sharples and Sheridan 1992) (Figure 4.1). A succession of rectangular stone footings and middens defines the repeated but probably episodic reuse of a chosen locale. The structures may have been covered by light wooden frames or perhaps only by skin tents. Their use, in a waterside location prone to flooding, may have been seasonal.

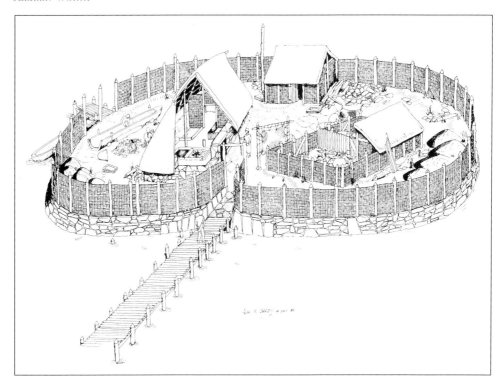

***Figure 4.1*** Reconstruction of one of the phases of occupation at Loch Olabhat, North Uist (Alan Braby).

Some archaeologists consider that more houses will be detected as more fieldwork is undertaken, and that more would have been found were it not for the destructive effects of subsequent land-use. Until now, however, post-built structures have remained rare as research has increased. The staple fare of the settlement record are artefact scatters, often existing only in the top- or plough-soils, and pits, postholes, stakeholes and other features dug into the subsoil. Hurst Fen (Suffolk) is a larger example of a group of pits, while Peacock's Farm, set beside a small river, has lithic scatters on a sand ridge, with small spills of rubbish down its side (Smith *et al.* 1989). These presumably represent camps or bases, of varying duration in any one episode, though in these cases certainly for repeat visits. Shelter is likely to have consisted of skin tents or other light structures that have left little or no subsoil trace.

This is the kind of context to which the Coneybury pit, described above, belongs. The Neolithic inhabitants of Britain moved repeatedly through woodland, making clearings and abandoning them, following cattle herds in particular, and tending – but not always on permanent watch over – stands of cereals. Settlement was based on mobility, or at most on very short-term sedentism. The frame that contained these movements was provided by the created landscape. Monuments were important parts of that frame, and no doubt names of places and paths were others. The wooden trackways of the Somerset Levels indicate how mobility may have been structured. The Sweet Track, for example, was built just before 3800 BC (Coles and Coles 1986). It runs for at least 2 km across wet fen, to take people and perhaps animals out to a small island of dry land. The carefully built single-plank walkway would have needed much timber, but could have been constructed quite quickly by a small group of people. Its significance seems to have been marked, even consecrated, by the deliberate deposition of a rare jadeite axehead beside it. The Sweet Track was preceded by another version, the Post Track, and may have been in use for a relatively short time before being covered by peat growth. It was not directly replaced, though several other hurdle trackways succeed it after a while in the vicinity. This pattern seems to mirror the settlement record as a whole: particular structures and features each of short duration, related to occupation, set within an enduring framework of monuments and other places.

There are interesting changes in the character of lithic scatters during the period. Earlier flint knapping involved careful, planned use of raw material, a trait that later working, when a wider range of materials was employed, generally lacks (Edmonds 1995). In some areas, as around Stonehenge and Avebury (Richards 1990; Thomas 1991), the density and size of Later Neolithic scatters increased compared with earlier examples. This may represent more people staying in these locales for longer periods, but whether as part of a general trend towards increasing sedentism or in connection with the demands of the ritual cycle is hard to say.

Later Neolithic Orkney is the major exception to the general trend. Several sites, including Skara Brae, Rinyo, Links of Noltland and Barnhouse, have stone-walled structures, nucleated to varying degrees, and preserved to impressive height at Skara Brae. The most important recent discovery has been of Barnhouse in the middle of Mainland, not least because it is near the elaborate chambered tomb of Maes Howe and the henges with stone settings at Stenness and Ring of Brogar (Parker Pearson and Richards 1994). Smaller, squarish houses are succeeded by a more varied range, some with carefully arranged doorways, central hearths and wall recesses that echo the layouts of chambered tombs. The Barnhouse houses may have been permanent residences, part of a strategy for taking in the interior of the islands by larger social groups. Their architecture may still reflect structured patterns of movement and behaviour, and also enshrine a cosmology that united people in their daily lives with nature, through a sense of orientation and elements like fire, and with the past, through reference to ancestral tombs and shrines (Parker Pearson and Richards 1994; Richards 1996). The largest structure at Barnhouse, no. 8, was set within an outer wall, and may represent some kind of communal building.

## Axe production sites

Stone and flint axeheads figure prominently in the Neolithic record. Some, perhaps many, were mounted in wooden hafts. The oak planks of the Sweet Track bear their marks. These may have been the all-purpose heavy-duty tool of the Neolithic, but it is clear that the axehead itself carried special significance. One was deposited beside the Sweet Track, and others occur in the ditches of causewayed enclosures, as well as in a range of other contexts (Edmonds 1995). Many axeheads are found far from their place of origin, and must have circulated by various means, including direct acquisition, direct and indirect exchange and perhaps directed trade. Many are isolated discoveries and appear to have been deliberately deposited in the ground. The axe may have stood for several ideas important in the Neolithic world view: independence or prowess in the realm of subsistence; personal (perhaps gender-related) or group identity; the ability to participate in gift exchange and other social interaction; a willingness to give away to other people and to nature rather than to accumulate; and borrowing of the very material of the earth.

Sources of good stone and flint were comparatively limited, with the best stone occurring in the older geologies of the west and north and the best flint from southern English chalk deposits (Edmonds 1995). Numbers of stone and flint sources are known. Some of the former can be traced to actual extraction areas, and in some cases shafts were dug through chalk to exploit good seams of flint. Such 'quarries' and 'mines' were often in places remote from usual settlement zones, even in a mobile system. Group VI axes were made from a volcanic tuff quarried from outcrops high in the Langdale hills of the Cumbrian Lake District. Flint mines in Sussex and in the East Anglian breckland at Grime's Graves may also have been comparatively distant from other settlement. The scale of working seems disproportionate to the needs of everyday existence, though recent excavation at the Group VI workfaces shows that extraction could be small-scale and episodic (Edmonds 1995). This offers a graphic illustration of the non-mundane values that guided many activities.

## Shrines, tombs and graves: monuments to the ancestors and the dead

The past was a vital component of Neolithic world views. Neolithic people may have regarded it in two ways: as evidence, on the one hand, of a timeless natural and social order and, on the other, of the emergence of a new world involving remembered or imagined beginnings, reverence for ancestors, and domestication.

The treatment of the human dead was bound up closely with such views. The record is strewn with occurrences of human remains, often incomplete. These are recovered from occupations as well as in various monument contexts, outlined below. Some formal graves, often for individuals but occasionally for more, are known, as well as the distinctive, regional series of monuments in the form of long or round barrows and cairns, both chambered and unchambered. These constructions often contained the remains of the dead, frequently as collections of incomplete skeletons, variously selected and arranged; but they had other points of reference and therefore other meanings as well.

Formal single burials are relatively rare in the Early Neolithic. Under (and thus predating) the outer bank of the Windmill Hill causewayed enclosure, an adult man was buried in flexed position in an oval pit. He had no grave goods, and the grave pit may have been open for some

***Figure 4.2*** The primary burials in the Radley oval barrow, Oxfordshire (Richard Bradley).

time. From the Middle Neolithic, more frequent single burials, under small mounds or in small enclosures, are encountered in certain regions. At Radley (Oxfordshire), a man and a woman were buried flexed in a pit within a ditched rectangle, which may have bounded a low barrow; they were accompanied by a shale or jet belt-slider and a partially polished flint knife respectively (Bradley 1992) (Figure 4.2). Other pre-Beaker Late Neolithic single burials include the successive inhumations within a deep grave pit, which was capped by a round barrow, at Duggleby Howe, Yorkshire (Kinnes 1979). Beaker funerary rites thus continued existing indigenous practice. Cremations are found throughout the Neolithic, from within the Etton causewayed enclosure to the first phase of Stonehenge.

Human remains occur in other contexts, including the ditches and pits of causewayed enclosures, and later in henges. The excavated 20 per cent of the inner ditch of the Hambledon Hill causewayed enclosure, for example, revealed the remains of some 70 people. These were incomplete, including skulls lacking lower jaws and one truncated torso. The dead may have been exposed, or buried then excarnated, before being redeposited in significant places or circulated among the living, as tokens of indissoluble links with their ancestors.

Something of this kind permeated the use of long barrows and chambered tombs. Rites were very varied, and funerals as such formed only part of them. In some, perhaps many, instances they certainly began with fleshed, recognizable individuals: witness the complete skeleton of an adult man inside the entrance of the north passage of Hazleton (Saville 1990). In others, corpses may, after initial treatments as discussed, only secondarily have been redeposited singly or together within the monuments (Whittle 1991). The end result was collective deposits of varying size, generally comprising the disarticulated and skeletally incomplete remains of a few or tens of people (and exceptionally more, as at Quanterness on Orkney). Monuments may not have been final resting places for all these remains. Some of the incompleteness (for example, too few skulls and longbones) may be accounted for by their successors' circulation through and movements from such monuments (Thomas 1991). In some instances, the emphasis seems to have been on the accumulation, perhaps by successive rites and depositions, of an anonymous mass of intermingled white bone, representing the collectivity of the ancestors. In others, for example in transepted chambered tombs in the Cotswold–Severn area, as at West Kennet long barrow (Figure 4.3), or some of the Orcadian stalled cairns, including Midhowe, attention was certainly given to the placing of individual remains. At West Kennet, the basis of arrangement seems to have been gender and age: males in the end chamber; a predominance of adult males and females in the inner pair of opposed chambers; and principally the old and young in the outer pair (Thomas 1991).

The structures in which these remains were temporarily or permanently stored may have stood for other ideas and associations than with the ancestral dead alone; some had only token human deposits or none at all (Bradley 1993). The terminology that has traditionally labelled them 'tombs' or 'graves' is unhelpful.

All these monuments comprise a mound, cairn or platform, either housing or supporting roofed structures of wood or stone. The actual constructions from region to region and indeed within regions were very varied. Portal dolmens around the Irish Sea had large, stone, box-like chambers, some surrounded by low stone platforms. Court cairns in Ireland, and Clyde cairns in western Scotland, in essence elaborate this form, with larger cairns and divided chambers. Stone chambers set in the ends and sides of long barrows and long cairns occur in many areas, from southern England to the north of Scotland. Round cairns were a mainly northern form, with some in the west and some round barrows in Yorkshire. Many internal chambers or structures were single, and approached directly from outside the monument. In other instances, there was a connecting passage, with the chamber housed well within the mound. Internal spatial complexity

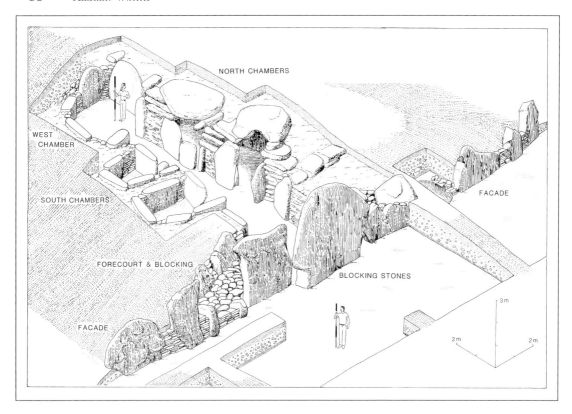

***Figure 4.3*** The chambers of the West Kennet long barrow, Wiltshire.
*Source*: Piggott, S., 1962. *The West Kennet long barrow excavations.* London: HMSO.

characterizes the transepted monuments of the Cotswold–Severn group, some west Scottish monuments, and the developed stalled cairns and Maes Howe round cairns of Orkney (Bradley 1993; Sharples in Sharples and Sheridan 1992; Thomas 1991).

Many individual monuments show a sequence of development, and architectural forms were not static through time. Monuments that ended as long barrows or cairns could begin more simply. At Street House, Cleveland, a high wooden facade concealed two small structures connected with the disposal of human remains; only later, when the facade had been burnt down, was the ensemble covered by a low cairn (Vyner 1984) (Figure 4.4). The first monument at Wayland's Smithy was a short, oval barrow, flanked by ditches. It contained, and may have been preceded by, a banked, probably roofed structure with massive split posts at either end, housing a collective deposit of human remains. Subsequently, this monument was completely incorporated within a larger, trapezoidal mound, with terminal transepted stone chambers and facade (Whittle 1991). The trend through time seems often to have been to greater structural complexity and size. West Kennet long barrow, for example, with its very long mound and transepted chamber space, may post-date less impressive and elaborate constructions in its area. On Orkney, the larger stalled cairns and the Maes Howe cairns, with their passages and central and side chambers, and connections to the largest Irish passage graves, seem to follow short stalled cairns and more simple chambered types.

These architecturally varied monuments stood for ideas, associations and memories. Their forms could encapsulate memories of earlier or contemporary structures: the great timber

***Figure 4.4*** Reconstructions of two phases of the Street House long barrow, Cleveland.
*Source*: Vyner 1984

longhouses of the continental LBK; the huge, elongated shell middens of Late Mesolithic southern Scandinavia and elsewhere, scene of communal gatherings, feastings and burial; and the tents and other dwellings of the insular Late Mesolithic and Early Neolithic. If so, they presented and represented a concept of the past, of an ancestral social order fixed for all time. Their construction brought numbers of people together, and the results were not only highly visible, but enduring. Their locales commemorated and sanctified places perhaps already of long significance, providing conspicuous points of reference in the landscape.

Such powerful symbols were open to contestation. Some dismantlings, burnings and rebuildings could result from hostile activity. Some monuments may have been the focus for inter- or intra-group rivalry. One trend suggested for Orkney is from dispersed small monuments, with modest accumulations of human remains, which served scattered communities, to the grander monuments, more centrally placed, in which the idea of a larger community was expressed by very considerable deposits of bone, some perhaps even robbed from earlier structures (Sharples 1985).

By the Late Neolithic, few if any such constructions were being built, though many were still actively regarded. In terms of mortuary rites, the emphasis began to pass from generalized ancestries to remembered or invented genealogies, intimated by the occurrence of more individual graves with grave goods. How should this be interpreted? It is often seen as witness to greater social differentiation or glossed as 'the rise of the individual', but this should not be seen as a simple process. Individual funerals occurred throughout the Neolithic, and veneration of ancestral pasts continued into the Late Neolithic, in respect for existing monuments and in the enclosure tradition. Genealogical reckoning within the frame of the ancestral order suggests as much a more interdependent, as a more individualized or atomized society.

## Enclosures: bounding the world

When the first enclosures came to be built, their impact, both physical and conceptual, must have been considerable. The outer circuit of the causewayed enclosure on Windmill Hill, for example, had a diameter of some 350 m (Figure 4.5). It belonged to the later Earlier Neolithic or the Middle Neolithic. The evidence indicates that this enclosure was set in open woodland or scrub; it constituted a 'monumental intervention in nature' (Hodder 1990, 260). Moreover, encircling a place with ditches and embankments was a new idea, since earlier monuments here took the form of barrows and related structures. Its source may have lain in earlier ditched enclosures of the continental LBK, and the new practice may have stood for older concepts of community and ancestral order.

As with other monuments, there are variations and unities in the use of causewayed enclosures (Edmonds 1993), which seem to be a mainly southern phenomenon. They consist of circuits of interrupted ditch, with internal banks, generally low and informal; some ditches are backed by palisades, as at Orsett, Essex, or Haddenham, Cambridgeshire. Windmill Hill had three circuits, possibly contemporaneous, possibly successive. Others range from one to four, and there are regional variations in spacing of circuits and enclosed areas. Some sites have seemingly incomplete circuits and others ones that link natural features such as streams and the sides of promontories. On the chalklands, many are set on hilltops or scarps, but there are numerous examples in southern and Midland river valleys, and near the fen-edge of East Anglia. Stone-walled enclosures in the south-west, such as Carn Brea, Cornwall, may be an equivalent form.

***Figure 4.5*** Excavation of bone deposits in the middle ditch of the causewayed enclosure at Windmill Hill (Alasdair Whittle).

These sites do not seem on the whole to have been settlements, though some had restricted occupation within them, perhaps intensifying in later phases of use. They do not generally appear defensive, though the developed circuits of Crickley Hill, on the western Cotswold scarp, and Hambledon Hill (Dorset) may have been so designed. Rather, they too stood for a series of ideas, and were the focus for intense participatory ceremonialism which celebrated key aspects of the earlier Neolithic lifestyle.

Causewayed enclosures too evoked the past, brought people together in their construction and enhanced attachment to place. Their layouts presented a potentially complex and ambiguous symbolism, playing on ideas of inside and outside, access and restriction, belonging and exclusion. There are only limited signs of internal occupation, though artefact scatters and pits do occur, and perhaps even some structures. Within the inner circuit of Hambledon Hill, selected and separate groups of artefacts, including stone axeheads and red deer antler, were deposited in pits. At Etton in Cambridgeshire, deliberately placed deposits including human cremations were found in one internal zone, while occupation traces were recorded in the other; placed deposits in the ditches seem approximately to repeat this zonation.

Such internal deposits were apparently part of a broader use that encompassed the surrounding ditches. In these, there are frequently numerous and varied finds: lithic artefacts and pottery, some human remains, charcoal, some charred plant remains, and, above all, animal bones, especially those of cattle. Few of these categories are regularly represented by whole finds. There are sherds rather than whole pots, and pieces of human skeleton (some complete child burials occur); animal bone deposits often consist of selected parts of more than one animal of more than one species.

Such material may have been middened or stored elsewhere before its deposition. It must come from gatherings, rites and feasting, sometimes involving the large-scale slaughter of animals. Such deposits seem to celebrate various dimensions of the social world: subsistence, eating, sharing, gift giving, relations with neighbours and others, and dealings with ancestors and spirits.

The quantities and character of this material vary from site to site. They can also change from primary to secondary levels within their ditches, as at Maiden Castle (Dorset). They also vary spatially in some enclosures, as already noted at Etton and Hambledon Hill. At Windmill Hill, there is varying emphasis in the three ditch circuits on different deposits and treatment; there are greater quantities of material and more highly processed bone in the innermost circuit, while the outermost has more unusual deposits, including infant burials. The arena of bounded space may have served, either from the outset or as the outcome of repeated deposition, to map major conceptual concerns.

Cursus monuments were another innovation of the Middle Neolithic. Ditched and banked linear enclosures, these often appear to have been constructed in stages, and some at least appear unfinished, with open terminals. They range from

***Figure 4.6*** The Dorset Cursus on Bottlebush Down, seen from the air (Martin Green).

hundreds of metres upwards in length. The longest, the Dorset cursus on Cranborne Chase, runs for almost 10 km (Figure 4.6). Many have been detected on river gravels, and their distribution extends further north than causewayed enclosures (for example, in the complex at Rudston on the Yorkshire Wolds). A related monument in Perthshire, the Cleaven Dyke, which has a central mound or bank as well as flanking ditches, has recently been recognized to be of Neolithic date (Barclay 1997). Some cursus monuments enclose timber and other settings, though these may normally be later additions. The Dorset cursus incorporates pre-existing long barrows in its layout, and that at Dorchester-on-Thames subsumes earlier and smaller ditched features, interpreted as mortuary enclosures. The roles of cursus monuments may have varied. They may have acted as boundary markers, actual or symbolic; they presumably signify woodland clearance. Their form suggests procession, perhaps already a feature of gatherings and rites, now formalized and made permanent. One strong connection appears to have been with the ancestral dead, and there may be some interest in the risings and settings of the sun and moon (Barrett *et al.* 1991). It has been suggested that the Dorset cursus was designed to be experienced from north-east to south-west, towards the great 'death island' formed by the Hambledon Hill causewayed enclosure, a few kilometres away (Tilley 1994).

Whether there was continuity of the enclosure tradition through the Middle into the Late Neolithic is uncertain. Causewayed enclosures were not constructed after *c.* 3000 BC. If there is hiatus, archaeologists might think in terms of the completion of a ritual cycle, with the spirits and ancestors propitiated, and the concept of community well established. If continuity is envisaged, other monument types may be proposed: cursus monuments, stone rows or avenues, early stone circles (such as those encircling Clava cairns of the inner Moray Firth lands) and early henges. Flagstones (Dorset) and the first phase of Stonehenge belong to the early third millennium BC. Both draw on the earlier tradition of interrupted ditches (and Stonehenge has old-style deposits in its primary ditch layers), but have circular or near-circular layouts. This formalization is enhanced in Stonehenge I, the primary monument, by a ring of internal pits, with cremations deposited subsequently, and probably central timber settings.

The enclosure tradition in the Late Neolithic encompasses various elements: henges, with their internal features including stone and timber settings and stone circles; free-standing stone circles and settings; and circular and oval timber palisades. Their distributions are much wider. The Ring of Brogar and Stones of Stenness on Orkney, with ditches, banks and stone circles, mark the northern limit; there are related sites in Ireland. Nearly everywhere formalization is apparent, indicated by concerns for ordering the approach to, entrance into, and movement around these bounded spaces, as well as with their orientations and outward views to horizons and other natural features. Established enclosure traditions were enhanced, both in terms of depositions of food remains and artefacts, and of the increased monumentality of selected sites. The sacred geography, already created, was reinforced. While some henges appear as the first large monuments in their areas, others were added to landscapes long sanctified by older exemplars. Most of the very large henges, such as at Avebury and Mount Pleasant in central-southern England, occur within such established complexes (Figure 4.7). The explanation of this has often been sought purely in terms of political power, but the strength of the sacred traditions of long-lived holy areas should not be underestimated.

Henges generally have ditches inside their earthwork banks. Their sizes vary considerably, attaining considerable diameters (350 m up to nearly 500 m) at Avebury, Mount Pleasant, Durrington Walls and Marden (Wainwright 1989). The smaller henges generally have one entrance, and the larger two, and exceptionally more. These exhibit the general concern for setting, approach and entrance. At Avebury, the approach from the south was by the double stone row of the West Kennet Avenue. A massive stone circle inside the ditch provides the first division

***Figure 4.7*** Excavations on Site IV, a vast post-setting circled by a ditch, within the henge at Mount Pleasant, Dorset (Geoffrey Wainwright).

of internal space, with exceptionally large stones flanking the southern entrance. Two large inner stone circles with central stone settings further sub-divided the enclosed space, and there may also have been timber settings, contemporary or earlier. Within Durrington Walls there were certainly timber settings, the South and North Circles, the former about 40 m in diameter, and consisting of six rings of timbers. Whether these settings were roofed or not is unclear. Deposits of animal bone and artefacts, including sherds of broken Grooved Ware, were made in and adjacent to the South Circle. The general nature of the rites seems to echo much earlier practices, but the setting is more ordered, formalized and restricted.

The following examples come from central-southern England, but it is important to stress that there were also large enclosed monuments, formed by bank and ditch (such as Brogar) or by timber settings (such as Meldon Bridge in the upper Tweed Valley), and significant monument complexes (such as Balfarg, Callanish and Brogar-Stenness-Maes Howe) in other areas. In the south, Durrington Walls was a truly monumental earthwork. It too was added to an area long significant, from the period of long barrows and causewayed enclosures, to the cursus monuments and first phase of Stonehenge; a smaller henge was constructed at Coneybury (Richards 1990). Immediately adjacent lay Woodhenge, a timber setting within a henge-style ditch. During the Late Neolithic, according to radiocarbon dates (Cleal *et al.* 1995), Stonehenge was further monumentalized. Bluestones from south-west Wales and sarsens from north Wiltshire were assembled to create an eternal version in stone of the timber settings seen at Durrington Walls and elsewhere, fixing the ancestral order for all time, making the past timeless, putting the present beyond dispute, and uniting people with nature. In north Wiltshire, the even more monumental construction of Silbury Hill mound was erected, perhaps as a symbol of the earth itself, and as an expression of ideas to do with origins, regeneration and ancestral cycles. Such ideas may have driven this society as much as social or political imperatives, though it may be hard to separate the two dimensions.

Silbury Hill also joined a long-established complex of monuments. There were older barrows and causewayed enclosures in the locality, and simple stone circles and at least one stone row. That row connected Avebury to a smaller setting of timber and stone, the so-called Sanctuary, and between the Sanctuary and Silbury Hill there were two large palisade enclosures, sub-circular and oval. Both stone circles and palisade enclosures belong to the tradition of bounding space, and both seem, like henges, to enhance and formalize that tradition in the Late Neolithic.

## CONTINUITY, CHANGE AND FUTURE RESEARCH

A sense of working with nature and of belonging to a timeless world may have continued from the Mesolithic way of life, as well as traits already mentioned, but there were new ways of doing some things, and not simply tending newly introduced cultivated plants and domesticated animals. Above all, novel ways of thinking about the world, in terms of beginnings, marked time, and the new relations with nature demanded by domestication, mark this period. To what extent were there subsequent changes? The possibility of contesting ritual knowledge and practice has been noted, but on the whole the Earlier Neolithic seems characterized more by various forms of integration and co-operation than by difference or competition. There may have been tensions between social ideals and conceptual schemes: of a timeless past contrasting with marked time, or working with nature clashing with a world in which people had increased control over animals and plants. Some of the practices writ large in the archaeological record may be related to the playing out of such ambiguities. For example, the near-obsession with cattle bone in causewayed enclosure ditches may reflect attempts to come to terms with the changed status of animals. The fact that animal bone was stored, selected, sorted and redeposited – like the human remains in shrines and tombs – could intimate a concern to treat animals and humans similarly.

What further changes occurred? Late Neolithic society has often been proposed as more differentiated than earlier phases; the language has been of chiefdoms, 'ritual authority structures' and the like (e.g. Renfrew 1973; Barrett 1994). The evidence for either economic intensification or major population growth is weak, however, and social reconstruction rests to a large degree on interpretation of monuments and mortuary rites. The beliefs and ideals that created the Neolithic in the first place were probably maintained well into the second millennium BC. Genealogical reckoning was a development of existing ideas about the ancestral past, and its practice may gradually have encouraged an individualism that allowed an ethic of ownership and accumulation. However, landscape changes from the Later Bronze Age onwards have a strongly corporate or communal character, and even then the tradition of shared values must have remained powerful.

## THE EUROPEAN SETTING

Neolithic Britain did not exist in a vacuum. While there was probably direct continuity of population, and the Mesolithic–Neolithic transition in Britain was not quite like that in any continental region, the character of the Earlier Neolithic owed much to continental precedents. The LBK culture brought cereals and domesticated animals to central-west Europe, and, just as importantly, the use of timber longhouses and novel artefacts. The long, slow interaction between the LBK and the south Scandinavian/north European plain Mesolithic led to a convergence of lifestyles. The LBK also impacted on, and was influenced by, indigenous communities in northwest France and elsewhere. From these traditions much was adopted in Britain: ideas, memories, forms of monumental architecture, new styles and kinds of artefact, and new subsistence staples.

The relationship appears not to have involved direct descent from any single area. The general character of Earlier Neolithic Britain has much in common with its contemporaries in western Europe: mobility and dispersal, broad-based subsistence practices, barrows, interrupted ditch enclosures, axes and round-based pottery styles. The repertoires vary from region to region. It seems that there were actively maintained and widely shared value and belief systems that helped to bring the Neolithic into existence and then to consolidate it. Particular horizons of contact, visible for example in the spread of passage grave monuments, may intimate this. In the Late Neolithic, while there was interaction with Ireland, much of the insular record is not matched on the Continent, including henges and Grooved Ware. The trajectories of change there were by now varied and complex (Whittle 1996), but the innovations of the Corded Ware horizon, from *c.* 2800/2700 BC onwards, occurred east of the Rhine, and northern France at least shared with Britain an archaic attachment to older monument forms. When contact with the Continent did come in the Beaker horizon (Chapter 5), this was a renewal rather than a total innovation.

## Key texts
Barrett, J., 1994. *Fragments from antiquity: an archaeology of social life in Britain, 2900–1200 BC*. Oxford: Blackwell.
Bradley, R., 1993. *Altering the earth: the origins of monuments in Britain and continental Europe*. Edinburgh: Society of Antiquaries of Scotland Monograph Series, 8.
Hodder, I., 1990. *The domestication of Europe*. Oxford: Blackwell.
Thomas, J., 1991. *Rethinking the Neolithic*. Cambridge: Cambridge University Press.
Tilley, C., 1994. *A phenomenology of landscape: places, paths and monuments*. Oxford: Berg.
Whittle, A., 1996. *Europe in the Neolithic: the creation of new worlds*. Cambridge: Cambridge University Press.

## Bibliography
Ashbee, P., Smith, I.F. and Evans, J.G., 1979. 'Excavation of three long barrows near Avebury, Wiltshire', *Proceedings of the Prehistoric Society* 45, 207–300.
Barclay, G.J., 1997. 'The Neolithic', in Edwards, K.J. and Ralston, I.B.M. (eds) *Scotland: environment and archaeology, 8000 BC–AD 1000*. Chichester: John Wiley, 127–149.
Barrett, J., Bradley, R. and Green, M., 1991. *Landscape, monuments and society: the prehistory of Cranborne Chase*. Cambridge: Cambridge University Press.
Bradley, R., 1992. 'The excavation of an oval barrow beside the Abingdon causewayed enclosure, Oxfordshire', *Proceedings of the Prehistoric Society* 58, 127–142.
Cleal, R.M.J., Walker, K.E. and Montague, R. 1995. *Stonehenge in its landscape: twentieth-century excavations*. London: English Heritage.
Coles, J. and Coles, B., 1986. *Sweet Track to Glastonbury*. London: Thames and Hudson.
Darvill, T. and Thomas, J. (eds) 1996. *Neolithic houses in northwest Europe and beyond*. Oxford: Oxbow Monograph 57.
Edmonds, M., 1993. 'Interpreting causewayed enclosures in the past and present', in Tilley, C. (ed.) *Interpretative archaeology*. Oxford: Berg, 99–142.
Edmonds, M., 1995. *Stone tools and society*. London: Batsford.
Entwhistle, R. and Grant, A., 1989. 'The evidence for cereal cultivation and animal husbandry in the southern British Neolithic and Early Bronze Age', in Milles, A., Williams, D. and Gardner, N. (eds) *The beginnings of agriculture*. Oxford: British Archaeological Reports S496, 203–215.
Hodder, I., 1982. *Symbols in action*. Cambridge: Cambridge University Press.

Kinnes, I., 1979. *Round barrows and ring ditches in the British Neolithic.* London: British Museum Occasional Paper.

Moffett, L., Robinson, M.A. and Straker, V., 1989. 'Cereals, fruits and nuts: charred plant remains from neolithic sites in England and Wales and the neolithic economy', in Milles, A., Williams, D. and Gardner, N. (eds) *The beginnings of agriculture.* Oxford: British Archaeological Reports S496, 203–215.

Parker Pearson, M., 1993. *Bronze Age Britain.* London: Batsford.

Parker Pearson, M. and Richards, C., 1994. 'Architecture and order: spatial representation and archaeology', in Parker Pearson, M. and Richards, C. (eds) *Architecture and order: approaches to social space.* London: Routledge, 38–72.

Piggott, S., 1954. *The Neolithic cultures of the British Isles.* Cambridge: Cambridge University Press.

Renfrew, C., 1973. 'Monuments, mobilization and social organization in Neolithic Wessex', in Renfrew, C. (ed.) *The explanation of culture change: models in prehistory.* London: Duckworth, 539–558.

Richards, C., 1996. 'Henges and water: towards an elemental understanding of monumentality and landscape in Late Neolithic Britain', *Journal of Material Culture* 1, 313–336.

Richards, J., 1990. *The Stonehenge environs project.* London: English Heritage.

Saville, A. 1990. *Hazleton North: the excavation of a Neolithic long cairn of the Cotswold-Severn group.* London: English Heritage.

Shanks, M. and Tilley, C., 1982. 'Ideology, symbolic power and ritual communication: a reinterpretation of Neolithic mortuary practices', in Hodder, I. (ed.) *Symbolic and structural archaeology.* Cambridge: Cambridge University Press, 129–154.

Sharples, N.M., 1985. 'Individual and community: the changing role of megaliths in the Orcadian Neolithic', *Proceedings of the Prehistoric Society* 51, 59–74.

Sharples, N.M. and Sheridan, A. (eds) 1992. *Vessels for the ancestors.* Edinburgh: Edinburgh University Press.

Smith, A.G., Whittle, A., Cloutman, E.W. and Morgan, L., 1989. 'Mesolithic and Neolithic activity and environmental impact on the south-east fen-edge in Cambridgeshire', *Proceedings of the Prehistoric Society* 55, 207–249.

Thomas, J., 1993. 'Discourse, totalization and "The Neolithic"', in Tilley, C. (ed.) *Interpretative archaeology.* Oxford: Berg, 357–394.

Thomas, J., 1996. 'The cultural context of the first use of domesticates in central and north-west Europe', in Harris, D.H. (ed.) *The origins and spread of agriculture and pastoralism in Eurasia,* London: University of London Press, 310–322.

Vyner, B., 1984. 'The excavation of a Neolithic cairn at Street House, Loftus, Cleveland', *Proceedings of the Prehistoric Society* 50, 151–196.

Wainwright, G.J., 1989. *The henge monuments.* London: Thames and Hudson.

Whittle, A., 1991. 'Wayland's Smithy, Oxfordshire: excavation at the Neolithic tomb in 1962–63 by R.J.C. Atkinson and S. Piggott', *Proceedings of the Prehistoric Society* 57(2), 61–101.

Whittle, A., 1997. *Sacred mound, holy rings. Silbury Hill and the West Kennet palisade enclosures: a Later Neolithic complex in north Wiltshire.* Oxford: Oxbow Monograph 74.

Zvelebil, M., 1994. 'Plant use in the Mesolithic and its role in the transition to farming', *Proceedings of the Prehistoric Society* 60, 35–74.

*Chapter Five*

# The Earlier Bronze Age

## Mike Parker Pearson

### INTRODUCTION

The Earlier Bronze Age is, by and large, a handy shorthand for a specific chronological range
(2600–1400 BC) and for a group of associated artefacts – certain styles of pots, houses, lithic
assemblages, burials, stone monuments and metalwork. Whilst the British Bronze Age can be
divided into a tripartite scheme – Early (2600–1600 BC), Middle (1600–1200 BC) and Late
(1200–700 BC) – it is divided in the present work (see also Chapter 6) into two: the Earlier
(2600–1400 BC) and Later Bronze Age (1400–700 BC). Few archaeologists would still accept the
technological determinism that led Vere Gordon Childe in his 1930 study, *The Bronze Age*, and
others to see technical innovation (in this case the use of bronze) as driving social change, and thus
providing the chronological framework for prehistory. Instead, we recognize that many aspects of
that vanished society, such as monument building and subsistence practices, were similar before
and after the adoption of bronze metallurgy. The British Isles were considerably behind other
parts of Europe in using metals. The smelting of copper had been going on in south-east Europe
for 2,000 years prior to our earliest evidence in Britain. There is no clear indication of a British
Chalcolithic (Copper Age), since both the earliest copper and bronze tools here are dated to the
same broad period of *c.* 2700–2000 BC.

The Earlier Bronze Age has been a crucial period for many of the most important questions and
debates in British and European prehistory. Was the arrival of Beaker pottery due to the
immigration of 'Beaker folk', or was it more the diffusion of an 'ideological package', a group of
new traits associated with new beliefs and practices? Was the great stone monument of
Stonehenge built by Mycenaean architects from the eastern Mediterranean or by indigenous
groups unaware of architectural innovations elsewhere? Was the change from communal to
individual burial indicative of changing notions of individuality? Do the monuments and rich
graves of Wessex indicate the emergence of elites who controlled chiefdoms? Did Bronze Age
metallurgy initiate the freeing of production from political constraint, and thereby instil core
values of freedom and innovation in Western society? In addition, this period has gripped the
imagination of fringe interests in prehistory, such as the 'Earth Mystery' researchers, who consider
that the standing stones and stone circles tap long-forgotten lines of energy unknown to modern
science.

There are many recent books about the British Earlier Bronze Age and its surrounding
centuries (Barrett 1994; Burgess 1980; Burl 1987; Clarke *et al.* 1985; Parker Pearson 1994),

written from different theoretical and empirical perspectives and with different emphases and for various audiences. The following chapter is a brief outline of the various types of evidence and the ways in which archaeologists have used them to understand and write about the lives of these vanished and anonymous people. It adopts the methodology of a contextual analysis, examining the various threads of evidence independently and also weaving them together.

## METALLURGY, METAL AND STONE TOOLS, AND ORNAMENTS

The earliest metal tools in Britain were copper and bronze axes, daggers, awls and halberds (dagger-shaped blades hafted like axes). A bronze axe, associated with a radiocarbon date of *c.* 2300 BC, was found just above the primary silts of the Late Neolithic henge at Mount Pleasant, Dorchester, Dorset (see Chapter 4). However, copper metallurgy in the British Isles seems to have first developed in Ireland.

The earliest true calendar date for metal tools is 2268–2251 BC, established by dendro-chronology on a wooden trackway at Corlea, in Ireland, the timbers of which were felled with a metal axe. The introduction of copper, bronze and gold metallurgy to the British Isles has long been considered to have been associated with people using Beaker pottery. Yet there are signs that metal items may have arrived earlier; in a hoard of copper axes from Castletown Roche in Ireland was a continental import of a form that may pre-date the Beaker horizon.

Various chronological schemes have been proposed for metal and stone artefacts within this period (Burgess 1980; Needham 1988; Roe 1979) (Figure 5.1). There are broad similarities between Burgess's eight industrial stages (1980) and Needham's six metalwork assemblages. Burgess's broad, threefold chronology for the Earlier Bronze Age (1980) defines three periods:

- the *Mount Pleasant phase* (2700–2000 BC) when people used flat axes and Beaker pottery, whilst inhuming rather than cremating their dead. During this period, an arrangement of Welsh blue-stones was erected at Stonehenge (Stonehenge Phase 3i), followed by the sarsens (Phase 3ii).
- the *Overton phase* (2000–1700 BC) when people used flanged axes, flat-tanged daggers, Food Vessels, Collared Urns and Beakers. Some people were buried under mounds with gold and elaborate grave goods (known as the Wessex I phase). There were minor changes at Stonehenge (Phase 3v).
- the *Bedd Branwen phase* (1700–1400 BC) when pottery styles became increasingly regionalized within Britain. Most people were cremated and there were a few with occasional grave goods but not of gold (Wessex II burials).

Though backward in terms of the European adoption of metallurgy, Britain and Ireland were rich in deposits of copper and tin. Early Bronze Age radiocarbon dates for copper extraction have been obtained from charcoal in mining tip deposits at Mount Gabriel in Ireland (*c.* 1800 BC) and at Cwmystwyth in Wales (*c.* 1500 BC) (Blick 1991, 51–59). Mineral exploitation probably began much earlier, but such remains have yet to be found. Similarly, the search is on for Early Bronze Age tin extraction in Cornwall and Devon. The smelting of copper ores can be achieved using bellows in small, charcoal-fired, open-bowl furnaces. The molten metal collects in the bottom in the form of a 'cake'. The earliest flat axes of copper were made by melting this cake and pouring the liquid into a single-piece open mould of stone or fired clay. Bronze was made by adding one part tin to eight parts copper. Two-part moulds enabled the casting of more elaborate axe and dagger forms. Decoration was also employed, notably on axes (Figure 5.2).

There were certain changes in flint knapping from the Late Neolithic. Although Early Bronze Age knapping debris, with its relatively short blades, cannot be easily distinguished from Late Neolithic assemblages, the flintwork includes certain diagnostic items such as thumbnail scrapers,

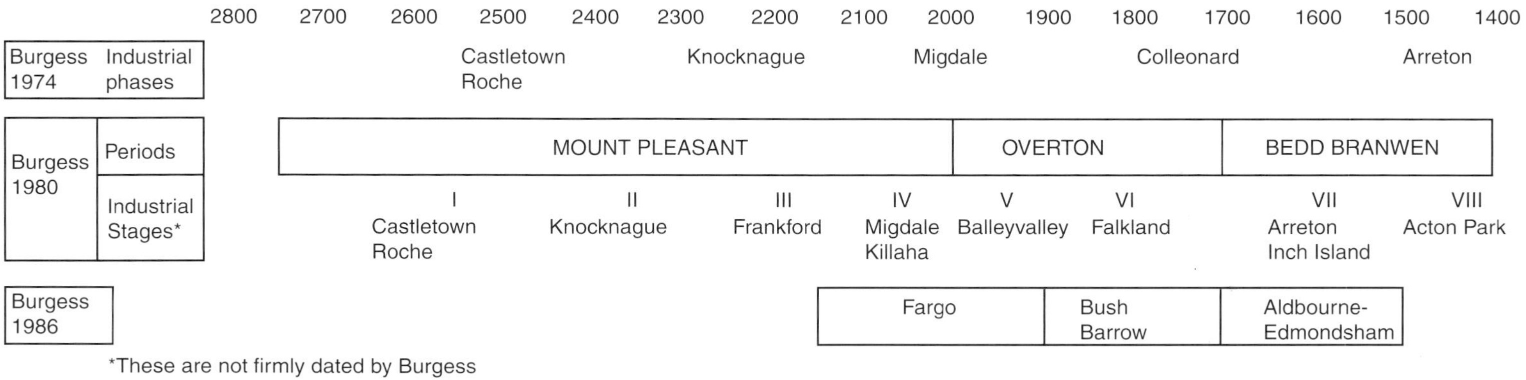

| | 2800 | 2700 | 2600 | 2500 | 2400 | 2300 | 2200 | 2100 | 2000 | 1900 | 1800 | 1700 | 1600 | 1500 | 1400 |
|---|---|---|---|---|---|---|---|---|---|---|---|---|---|---|---|

**Burgess 1974** — Industrial phases:
Castletown Roche | Knocknague | Migdale | Colleonard | Arreton

**Burgess 1980** — Periods / Industrial Stages*:

Periods: MOUNT PLEASANT | OVERTON | BEDD BRANWEN

Industrial Stages*:
I Castletown Roche | II Knocknague | III Frankford | IV Migdale Killaha | V Balleyvalley | VI Falkland | VII Arreton Inch Island | VIII Acton Park

*These are not firmly dated by Burgess

**Burgess 1986**:
Fargo | Bush Barrow | Aldbourne-Edmondsham

**Figure 5.1** Metalwork chronologies for the Earlier Bronze Age.
*Source*: M. Hamilton after Burgess 1980

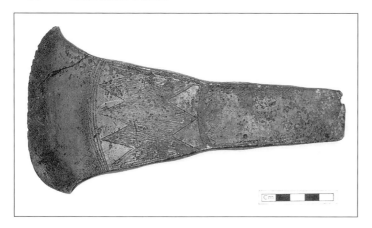

***Figure 5.2*** An unprovenanced bronze flat axe with geometric incised decoration: the narrow butt, slender body and expanded blade are typical features of Burgess's Stage VI (1980), thought to be associated with a new type of axe handle (the knee-shaft handle with forked end).
*Source*: Sheffield City Museum

barbed-and-tanged arrowheads and flaked knives and daggers. These daggers and arrowheads are carefully worked and suggest a division between specialist knapping of prestigious pieces and everyday manufacture of ordinary blades and edges (Edmonds 1995). A similar picture of fine craftsmanship is gained from the ground stone maceheads and battle axes made of flint or igneous rocks. The flaked daggers were copies of copper prototypes, whilst the battle axes were copies not of copper originals but of stone ones from northern and central Europe. Within this tradition of stone working, we should also consider the quarrying and dressing of large stones, such as the use of sarsen mauls to shape the faces of the stones at Stonehenge.

Personal adornment with bead necklaces, boars' tusks, pins, maceheads and polished axes (for these latter items were as much ornaments as practical items) was already commonplace in the Late Neolithic from 3000 BC onwards. It is a major feature of the Earlier Bronze Age, partly because more burial contexts have been investigated and partly because the range of ornamentation increased. Among the most spectacular items are beautiful necklaces of jet or amber beads, especially from Scotland, the 81 gold lunulae (crescent-shaped and decorated sheets probably worn as gorgets) from Ireland, Scotland and south-west England, and the gold cape from a burial mound at Mold in Clwyd. Archaeologists also find dress pins, toggles and buttons which, together with awls and needles, indicate that considerable attention was given to clothing, presumably of leather, wool, cloth and possibly linen. In Ireland, most of the non-perishable dress items are found as hoards or unassociated deposits, whereas in Britain they are more often found as accompaniments to inhumation and cremation burials. This increased concern with personal finery and bodily adornment can be interpreted in many different ways. Some see it as the affirmation of individualism, matching the development of individualized funerary rites (cf. Chapter 4). Others interpret it as the establishment of visible status gradations necessary in chiefdom-style societies. Alternatively, it might represent the challenging and overthrow of traditional authority within communities in which status and power were more fluid and temporary. The 'fancy goods' of Early Bronze Age life form a marked contrast to the pottery and ordinary flintwork that constituted the materials of everyday routines, suggesting that a major distinction was drawn between the public/ceremonial and private/domestic realms of experience.

## POTTERY

Ever since Lord Abercromby's encyclopaedic study of Bronze Age urns early this century, pottery analysis has dominated archaeological research into this period. Subsequent compendia of Beaker pots (Clarke 1970; Gibson 1982), Collared Urns (Longworth 1984), northern Food Vessels and a mass of regional studies have investigated issues of typology, chronology, decorative variation,

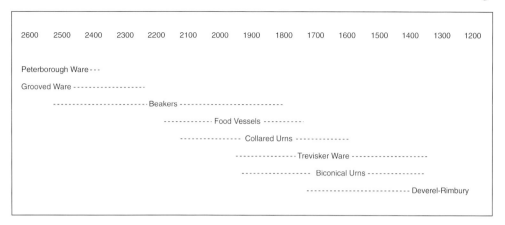

| 2600 | 2500 | 2400 | 2300 | 2200 | 2100 | 2000 | 1900 | 1800 | 1700 | 1600 | 1500 | 1400 | 1300 | 1200 |

Peterborough Ware - - -

Grooved Ware - - - - - - - - - - - - - - - - - -

- - - - - - - - - - - - - - - - - - - - - - -Beakers - - - - - - - - - - - - - - - - - - - - - - - - - -

- - - - - - - - - - - - -Food Vessels - - - - - - - - - - -

- - - - - - - - - - - - - - -Collared Urns - - - - - - - - - - - - -

- - - - - - - - - - - - - - -Trevisker Ware - - - - - - - - - - - - - - - - - - - -

- - - - - - - - - - - - - - - - -Biconical Urns - - - - - - - - - - - - - -

- - - - - - - - - - - - - - - - - - - - - - - - - - - Deverel-Rimbury

**Figure 5.3** Ceramic chronologies for the Late Neolithic, Early Bronze Age and Middle Bronze Age, taking a minimal view of the radiocarbon ranges. Dates are in calibrated years BC.
*Source*: M. Hamilton

regionality, production, distribution, status and deposition. In many respects, the aim of establishing a finely tuned ceramic chronology (Figure 5.3) for the Earlier Bronze Age has not been realized. Even the seven-step sequence proposed in the early 1970s for Beaker decoration, and adopted by some archaeologists, has been undermined by a comprehensive radiocarbon dating programme on Beaker-associated materials (Kinnes *et al.* 1991). The notional sequence of Beaker pottery (2700–1700 BC), Food Vessels (2200–1800 BC), Collared Urns (2000–1700 BC) and Biconical Urns (1800–1400 BC) can be viewed either as a series of chronological overlaps or, less likely, as a chest-of-drawers replacement of one style by another, due to the relative imprecision of the radiocarbon method.

The finely made Beakers stand out from an otherwise crude ceramic tradition, indicating that the coarseness of other Early Bronze Age wares was a matter of cultural preference and not one of prehistoric incompetence. Found throughout Europe, Beakers are identified by their S-shaped profile of an open mouth, narrow neck and bulge in the middle. They are often decorated, mainly in a series of horizontal zones of impressed cord, incised line and impressed comb patterns. Those found in burials (Figure 5.4) may have been made specifically made for the grave. Their poorer fabrics and smooth surfaces indicate that they were to be looked at rather than used (Boast in Kinnes and Varndell 1995). The larger of these funerary vessels often accompany adult male corpses, while small Beakers are often found with the bodies of children (Case in Kinnes and Varndell 1995). Their interpretation as a high-status item has been dismissed; they do not take long to produce and were not sought-after trade items. Even the popular notion that they contained an alcoholic beverage such as mead or an unusual cocktail of alcohol and cannabis may be only a small dimension of their use. Pollen in a grave at Ashgrove (Fife) may derive from mead spilled from a Beaker, but residues from other burials have been interpreted as the remains of floral tributes (Tipping 1994). Elsewhere in northern and eastern Europe, Beaker pots succeed Corded Ware (Chapter 4), and both styles have been interpreted as evidence of invaders or immigrants moving in and replacing indigenous populations. In many parts of Europe, the Beaker forms part of a material culture 'package' (including barbed-and-tanged flint arrowheads, copper or bronze awls, archers' wristguards, and metal or flint daggers) that some archaeologists have interpreted as the material manifestation of a religious cult or ideology rather than a movement of people (Burgess and Shennan in Burgess and Miket 1976). Re-examination of the

***Figure 5.4*** A Beaker and associated non-perishable grave goods from the Green Low round barrow in Derbyshire: (from the left) a bone point; a bone toggle; two bone spatulae; two fragments of bone; a flint scraper; three flint blades; five barbed-and-tanged flint arrowheads; a small flint dagger; a large flint dagger; and two large flint flakes.
*Source*: Sheffield City Museum

invasionist argument that Neolithic people were dolichocephalic (their skulls were longer than they were wide) and Beaker incomers were brachycephalic (short, rounded skulls) has suggested that such changes could result from environmental and genetic changes within an indigenous population (Brodie 1994). Beaker pottery in Britain is not restricted to burials or ceremonial complexes but regularly turns up in settlements from the Hebrides southwards (Gibson 1982). In south-west England, where the geology is suitable for ceramic petrological sourcing, Beakers were made locally and perhaps domestically, and were deposited within no more than a few miles of their likely places of manufacture.

Unlike Beakers, Food Vessels and Collared Urns are not found on the Continent (Figure 5.5). Food Vessels were used throughout much of the British Isles, predominantly with inhumations (in Yorkshire, Scotland and Ireland) and cremation burials (in Wales and north-western England), since settlement sites survive so rarely. They are nearly always found in secondary associations to Beakers, but associated radiocarbon dates indicate a probable chronological overlap of 300–400 years. They are narrow-bottomed pots with straight or bowed sides and an out-turned mouth, and are decorated on their upper parts with twisted cord impressions, incised lines, stabmarks, fingermarks and bone impressions. They divide into three overlapping sizes, the largest perhaps for storage, the middle for cooking and the smaller for eating from.

Collared Urns are similar in shape, decoration and size to Food Vessels, except that the rim is in-turned and slopes down to an external, overhanging collar. Their radiocarbon date range indicates that they appeared some centuries after the first Food Vessels but that use of both forms overlapped in time. When they are found in burial mounds with Food Vessels, they are always in secondary or later deposits within the mound. Such differences may have been social rather than simply chronological. Collared Urns are similarly found throughout Britain.

Cordoned Urns, Encrusted Urns, Biconical Urns and Trevisker pottery are specifically regional styles within the Earlier Bronze Age. Towards the end of this period, a variety of cruder, mainly undecorated bucket-shaped styles appeared, notably Deverel-Rimbury wares in southern England and the Green Knowe style in southern Scotland and northern England. We might also class northern Food Vessel Urns as a regional variant. Cordoned Urns are found in Scotland and Ireland, Encrusted Urns (broadly a style of encrusted decoration used on enlarged Food Vessels) in Scotland, northern England and Ireland, Biconical Urns in lowland England and Trevisker pottery in south-west England. By the end of the Earlier Bronze Age, the repertoire of vessel sizes and forms had increased from twofold or threefold divisions to complex divisions for Deverel-Rimbury and Biconical assemblages of coarse heavy-duty, coarse everyday, cups/bowls and

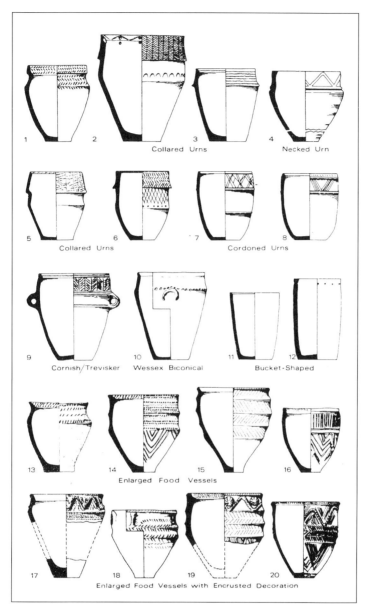

**Figure 5.5** Styles of Early Bronze Age storage pots used as cremation containers.
*Source*: Burgess 1980. Copyright Orion Books

globular fine wares, and for Trevisker wares of large storage, smaller storage, cooking pots and three types of small vessels (Figure 5.6) (Woodward and Parker Pearson in Kinnes and Varndell 1995). The increasing regionality of ceramics can be paralleled by regional styles of Middle Bronze Age palstave axes (Rowlands 1976), and Woodward has shown how Middle Bronze Age defended hilltop settlements such as Ram's Hill (Berkshire) and Norton Fitzwarren (Somerset) in southern Britain lie at the interfaces between these styles, possibly controlling exchange relationships between regions (Ellison 1981). Another interesting interpretation of this growing regionalism

**Figure 5.6** Assemblage variation within the Trevisker series: (from large to small) the large two-handled storage pot (Style 1); the multiple-lugged storage pot (Style 2); the cooking pot (Styles 3 and 4) and the small serving pot (Style 5).
*Source*: Peter Dunn

from the Late Neolithic to the Middle Bronze Age is that the ceramic repertoires might be considered as 'dialects' in material culture, mirroring or playing off linguistic shifts firstly between Britain and the Continent (Food Vessels and Collared Urns) and latterly within the British Isles (Tomalin in Kinnes and Varndell 1995). In other words, they may be the only surviving traces of growing regional differences in local dialects and customs.

It is in south-west and southern Britain that we get the clearest picture of pottery production and distribution. Food Vessels and Collared Urns in Cornwall were predominantly produced from the high-quality and distinctive gabbroic clays of the Lizard peninsula of Cornwall, indicating a centralized production and distribution pattern very different from Beaker wares. Cornish Trevisker Ware was similarly derived from the Lizard gabbro, though Trevisker pottery in Devon probably came largely from two sources of south Devon clay not far from Dartmoor. Trevisker pots made on the Lizard were even moved by sea along the south coast to Wessex (such as the cremation container at Sturminster Marshall, Dorset) and across the Channel to the Pas-de-Calais at Hardelot (Parker Pearson in Kinnes and Varndell 1995). Armorican *vases à anses* came the other way from Brittany to the Isle of Wight and Wessex. Thus the pots support the picture of cross-Channel trade in metalwork (the Salcombe [Devon] and Dover wreck sites) and seafaring as shown by the recent discovery of a Middle Bronze Age sewn plank boat at Dover (see Figure 6.8).

Pots are one of the key artefacts, however lowly, in marking social relationships and rites of passage. They accompanied the corpse (or its burnt remains) to the final resting place; they were involved in the daily rites and routines of food preparation and consumption; and they signalled regional, age, gender and no doubt other social identities. Whilst they were employed in the activities of storage, cooking and serving of food, those essential practices of daily life and relationships, archaeologists can only guess at the complexities of the engendered and status relationships in which they were used. This is partly due to the paucity of excavated settlements and houses.

## HOUSES

There are very few well-preserved Early Bronze Age settlements excavated in Europe, and most of the house remains are found in the western regions of Britain. These are very ephemeral and survive only in exceptional circumstances of preservation or where the scarcity of wood has led to their construction partly in stone. The locality with the greatest potential for preservation is the Western Isles of Scotland, where houses, mostly with stone walls revetted into sand, have been excavated at Northton, Barvas, Dalmore, Alt Chrysal, Cill Donnain and Rosinish (Figure 5.7) (Armit 1996: 88–94; Simpson in Burgess and Miket 1976). Other Earlier Bronze Age stone houses have been excavated in Shetland at Brouster, Ness of Gruting, Yoxie, Stanydale and Benie

Hoose. A burnt down round house (4 m in diameter) and two other probable houses have been excavated at Stackpole Warren in Dyfed. A small, stake-walled house, 5.5 m in diameter, has been found preserved under a Saxon barrow at Sutton Hoo in East Anglia; the supposed houses on the Beaker site at Belle Tout on the chalk downs of Sussex should now be discounted. There are also a few other house remains, claimed from a number of different sites, of variable preservation and likelihood (Gibson 1982).

These houses vary in shape from round to oval to sub-rectangular, with a central hearth but no preferred axial orientation or place for the doorway. The Northton house is 7 m long and 4.5 m wide, whereas one of the Coney Island houses (Co. Armagh, Northern Ireland) is only 2.7 m by 3.3 m. The relatively sunless location and paucity of faunal remains at Dalmore suggests a specialized and perhaps seasonal use. Others may have been occupied all year round, with people living off a mixed economy of wheat and barley along with cattle, sheep and pigs. Houses, however, are more than just shelters and can encode complex cosmologies that may link them to other entities such as the tomb or the human body. The orientation, shape and size of the house can be expected to have had symbolic importance: no society builds houses to random patterns, since there is always an underlying set of rules. Houses are

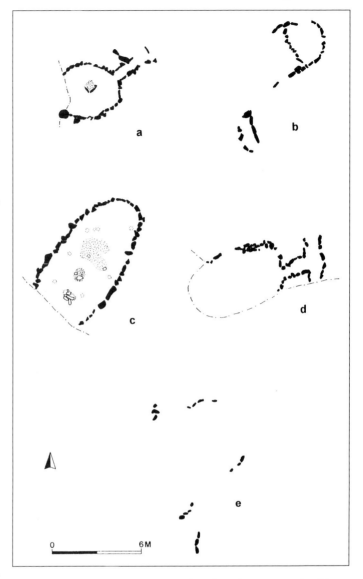

**Figure 5.7** Early Bronze Age house plans from the Western Isles: (a) Dalmore; (b) Northton Structure 1; (c) Northton Structure 2; (d) Barvas; (e) Cill Donnain.
*Sources*: After Armit 1996; Burgess and Miket 1976; and with thanks to M. Hamilton and N. Sharples

different from tombs: they are less symmetrical, smaller and less permanent than the earthen round barrows and cairns in which the dead were placed; perhaps more effort was invested in funerary structures because people would spend eternity in them, in contrast to their short lives in the houses. At the same time, certain aspects of houses may have been similar to tombs: the central burial or cremation in a barrow may have symbolized the role of the hearth within the house. Such similarities and differences may have served to demarcate the realm of the dead from the living and yet present it as a mirror of life. There seems to have been a substantial change in domestic architecture towards the end of the Earlier Bronze Age and in the Middle Bronze Age, when houses were constructed more substantially and in larger sizes. Additionally, settlements were increasingly marked by ditched enclosures and lay within laid-out landscapes of field walls and field banks. The large round houses (up to 7 m in diameter) at Gwithian (Megaw in Burgess and Miket 1976), Trevisker and Trethellan (Nowakowski 1991) in Cornwall, dating from 1800–1200 BC, were solid structures with floor areas in excess of 30 m². Similar changes also appear to have taken place in Ireland, where larger houses are recognized at the end of the Earlier Bronze Age.

In summary, the houses of the British Earlier Bronze Age were not substantial structures, except perhaps in the Western and Northern Isles, nor were they arranged in large settlements but rather formed small, dispersed groups. For much of the Earlier Bronze Age, the permanence and solidity of the tombs, standing stones and stone circles expressed levels of group identity much larger than those at the household level. Early Bronze Age identity was undoubtedly layered and complex, but it was probably most strongly fixed around the larger kin groups and lineages who must have come together to attend funerals and construct monuments. By the Middle Bronze Age, there appeared a number of settlements enclosed by ditches and palisades, such as South Lodge and Down Farm on Cranborne Chase, Dorset (Barrett *et al.* 1991). Not only were houses becoming larger and longer lasting, but the household domain was taking on monumental proportions.

## BURIALS AND FUNERALS

Since the seventeenth century, Early and Middle Bronze Age round burial mounds and cairns have been dug into and excavated by antiquarians and archaeologists. They have a long history of scholarly research and undoubtedly form the most abundant and perhaps significant remains from this period. Their potential for increasing our understanding of social status, sexual and gender differentiation, exchange and power relations has not been ignored (Barrett 1994; Clarke *et al.* 1985; Garwood 1991; Mizoguchi 1992), and recent theoretical studies have benefited from national and local research programmes of round barrow investigations over the last 40 years.

There is an extraordinary diversity of Early Bronze Age funerary practices, though this should not cause surprise given the long time-span, the likely regionalism and the probable complexity of traditions. Bodies might be inhumed or burnt; some inhumations show signs of prior excarnation (the bones partly jumbled from being left to rot before burial); other burials (such as Eynsham and Cassington, both in Oxfordshire) seem not to have been buried under mounds; burial

*Figure 5.8* Different types of round barrows on Normanton Down, Wiltshire: (from the top left) a ditched bowl barrow with an outer bank, a disc barrow, a small barrow (left of the track and partly destroyed by it), a double bell barrow and a bell barrow.
*Source*: Courtesy of the Ashmolean Museum

deposits might be made in small clearance cairns produced by removing stones from fields (at Shaugh Moor, Dartmoor) rather than formal structures; round barrows come in many shapes, such as bowl, bell, disc and pond (Figure 5.8); burials may be multiple within the same grave (Goldington, Bedfordshire); cremations may be placed within pots, by the side of pots or underneath upturned pots; the mounds may have anything between none and three circular ditches cut around them; mounds may be constructed of subsoil or stone or solely of turf (the King Barrows at Stonehenge, Wiltshire); some mounds have stake circles; and the inhumed corpses may be orientated in a number of different directions. Some of these variations are chronological (there was a broad change from inhumation to cremation after 2000 BC), others are procedural (Beaker primary burials often have the head to the north, whereas secondaries may equally be orientated to the south), and others still are regional, such as the wide variety of barrow forms largely confined to the Wessex area. In Scotland, the occurrence of slab-lined graves, termed short cists, beneath mounds or cairns, is common. Whilst barrows normally contain burials, certain mounds (such as the Lockington barrow in Leicestershire) have none at all. Human bones excavated from the Trent at Langford (Nottinghamshire), dated to 2250–2100 BC, and skulls dredged from the Thames suggest that deposition in water was a common rite.

With only the final resting place of the dead available to us, what can be gleaned of the sequence of events that made up the funerary rites of passage is problematic (Figure 5.9). Yet certain fortuitous and extraordinary deposits may have important and interesting implications. Underneath an upturned pot under a barrow at Winterslow G3 in Wiltshire were a bronze razor and a small pile of eyebrow hair

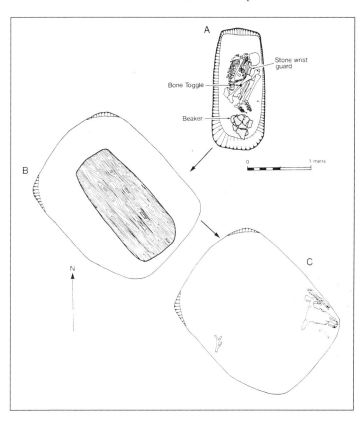

*Figure 5.9* The sequence of funerary events at Hemp Knoll barrow, Wiltshire: the corpse and grave goods are placed in a treetrunk coffin (A) which may have been covered and lowered into the grave (B), which was backfilled to include an ox head and hooves (either an oxhide cloak or a head-and-hooves offering), an antler pick and charcoal.
*Source*: Barrett 1994

(Barrett 1994, 123), suggesting that mourners may have shaved their facial hair as a rite of passage and an act of purification. At Irthlingborough near Raunds in Northamptonshire (Figure 5.10a), buried in alluvial mud, the top of a mound preserved the remains of 184 cattle skulls and smaller numbers of cattle mandibles, shoulder blades and pelves. Most of them were from animals aged around 2 years, probably bullocks. Such numbers can only have derived either from an enormous herd or, more likely, from many different herds, the funerary gifts of many different communities attending the funeral from all over the region (Davis and Payne 1993). The jet

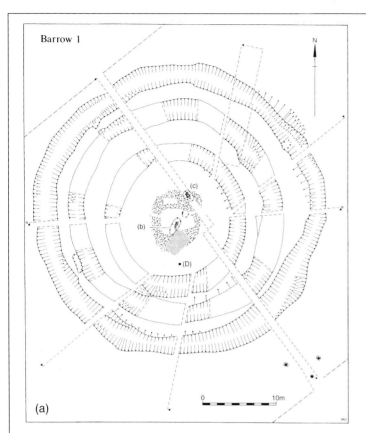

Barrow 1

(a)

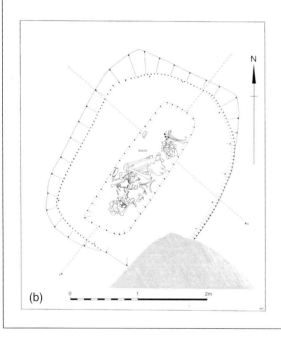

(b)

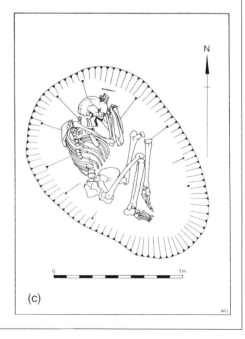

(c)

*Figure 5.10* (a) A plan of the triple-ditched barrow at Irthlingborough, Raunds, Northamptonshire. Under the stone cairn was a central burial and the remains of a wooden structure. There was a second inhumation to the north-east and five cremation pits to the south (D was a Collared Urn containing the ashes of an adult and a teenager along with a horn-hilted bronze dagger). (b) The crouched adult male skeleton in the central burial was accompanied by a group of grave goods below his feet. These comprised a long-necked beaker, three bone spatulae, five conical jet buttons, an unused flint dagger, a flint arrowhead or point, nine unused flint flakes, an amber ring, two 'sponge-finger' stones (one of chalk and one of Langdale rock), a reused stone wristguard and a boar's tusk. (c) The crouched skeleton of an adult, probably male, north-east of the central grave. The only grave good was a bone needle, placed above the head.
*Source*: English Heritage

buttons (of material from Whitby, Yorkshire), the East Anglian flint dagger and the Wessex chalk artefacts found with the body of the adult male in the main burial (Figure 5.10b) indicate the range of these extensive social contacts. Additionally, his bones were disarticulated and his mandible was missing, suggesting that the body had not been buried until long after death. When buried in the mound, his remains were placed in a wooden chamber with evidence of a timber superstructure, possibly a shrine or viewing platform. A second burial of an adult (also probably male), in a separate primary grave, was equipped with only a bone needle (Figure 5.10c).

In the Irthlingborough barrow, the man's Beaker, knife, arrowhead, wristguard, jet buttons, amber ring and assortment of other artefacts support the evidence for a very large funeral that might be accorded to a man of considerable standing and a family or kin group of substantial influence. Yet not all archaeologists would consider this burial to be the most affluent Beaker grave so far discovered. Others, such as the burial at Barnack, Cambridgeshire, or that from Culduthel, Inverness-shire, are associated with small items of goldwork, such as buttons and basket-shaped earrings, stone wristguards with gold studs, daggers with gold pommels, or stone battle axes. How we avoid imposing our own values about precious metals is, of course, problematic. A small amount of goldwork has come from a group of burials from 2200–1900 BC mainly from the Wessex area, known as Wessex I (separate from the later Wessex II group of 1700–1500 BC which is also associated with bronze daggers, stone battle axes and beads of amber and faience but not with gold), and first described as the 'Wessex culture' by Piggott in the 1930s. The most impressive of the Wessex I burials are the Normanton Down group, just south of Stonehenge, especially the Bush Barrow with its gold lozenge, stone mace, three large bronze daggers (one with a pommel inlaid with thousands of tiny gold pins) and a 'baton', all associated with the corpse of an adult man. Other assemblages containing gold artefacts are known from over 25 locations, notably the Clandon barrow in Dorset, and the Lockington barrow in Leicestershire (a large bronze dagger, two gold armrings and two pots found without human remains on the edge of an empty burial mound). There are close similarities with the Kernonen burial and others across the Channel in Brittany (Clarke *et al.* 1985, 129–135). For many archaeologists, these assemblages indicate the existence of chiefs; the Bush Barrow man was even suggested as the architect of Stonehenge until the monument was redated. However, other interpretations are possible. The burying of this personal wealth may actually have prevented the accumulation of hereditary power, and funerals such as Irthlingborough may have acted to disperse and destroy wealth, represented by cattle, in return for personal or family honour and prestige. Perhaps the point was not to keep wealth but to be seen to dispose of it in extravagant gestures at funerals and other ceremonies. Whereas certain archaeologists have considered these burials to have been the products of chiefdom societies in which hereditary elites coerced tribal groups into erecting monuments like Stonehenge (Fleming and Renfrew in Renfrew 1973), there is an equally plausible case for a kin-based, broadly egalitarian yet competitive society, ordered by fine gradations of rank and status and motivated by honour and self-aggrandizement, in which heredity played a less significant role (Parker Pearson and Ramilisonina 1998, 322–3).

Other inferences about social structure from funerary deposits can be made from grave goods and from the relative placing of human remains in burial mounds. Some of the grave goods can be divided on gender lines to suggest that there was a certain division of labour between men and women, symbolized in death. Whilst male graves contain arrowheads, daggers, wristguards, belt rings, amber buttons, flint or stone axes and fire-making tools, female graves are associated with shale and jet beads and the majority of awls and antler picks or hoes; certain items (flint blades, earrings and pebble hammers) are equally shared. Whereas daggers, ornaments and small tools were regularly placed in graves, other items were generally deposited elsewhere. Metal axes, spearheads and halberds are found invariably in boggy contexts as hoards or single finds. These are often in rocky and impressive locations that were evidentially special places. It seems fairly clear that the deposits were votive offerings, occasionally broken and, for certain unknown reasons, inappropriate accompaniments to buried individuals (Needham 1988). Insights into gender and age distinctions can also be gained from the relationship between primary and secondary burials: where adult males are buried first, the later ones may be other adults and children, yet where adult females are buried first, they are rarely followed by adult males (Mizoguchi 1992). The pattern closely matches ethnographic observations of societies with patrilineal systems of descent.

The placing of the dead within the landscape was a complex matter, relating to and even reusing earlier monuments and establishing large areas of sacred space. The large barrow cemeteries in south Dorset, Cranborne Chase, and the Stonehenge area, either side of the River Avon, are far larger than most groups. The western Avon group is built within an area of Neolithic monuments, and most mounds are placed on the edge of an 'envelope of visibility' around Stonehenge. The same referencing of earlier monuments can be found at Avebury (Wiltshire), Irthlingborough and Rudston (Yorkshire). In Ireland, similarly, Earlier Bronze Age barrow cemeteries are placed around the edges of the Neolithic monument complex at the Bend in the Boyne. On the chalklands of Wessex, the predominant locations chosen are downlands often at a distance from the valley-based settlement areas, suggesting that the dead were buried within areas of pasture. Conversely, in the East Midlands, the lighter soils of the river valleys were the principal locations for barrow groups, with each group spaced approximately 10 km along each major river valley. At Irthlingborough, the most intensively investigated of these complexes, the habitation areas (as indicated by flint-knapping debris) were located on the valley sides a short distance away. The carbonized remains of plants from one of these excavated barrows derive from grasses that thrive only when grazing is absent, indicating that animals were kept away from this area.

With the advent of the Middle Bronze Age, cremation was universal and grave goods were largely limited to a single Deverel-Rimbury pot to contain the ashes. The cremated remains were buried in small cemeteries, either of small mounds, or within and around an earlier mound or in unmarked graves, that were located close to settlements. From enclosed settlements like South Lodge and Down Farm on Cranborne Chase (Dorset), it is apparent that the dead were placed in the direction away from the entrances, thereby maintaining a symbolic distinction between the realms of the living and those of the dead (Barrett *et al.* 1991). Their unremarkable remains thus marked the land and fields in which the homestead was situated, rooting people in their land and emphasizing identities at the household level rather than the wider kin groups.

## ENVIRONMENT AND LANDUSE

The landscape of the Early Bronze Age was one that was being continuously reworked and remade. It consisted not only of the forests, wastes, pastures and fields of human occupation but also of the places, monuments and spaces of ancestors and spirits. Neolithic monuments were modified and transformed. For example, in the Western Isles and northern Scotland many Neolithic chambered tombs seem to have been turned into closed monuments by individual Beaker burials (Armit 1996, 94–95). The entrance to the West Kennet chambered tomb in Wiltshire was blocked with huge stones and its chambers filled with chalk rubble and Peterborough and Beaker sherds. Other ancient places were appropriated. In Eastern Scotland, Beaker-accompanied burials were often inserted into, or placed close to, earlier henge monuments, as at Broomend of Crichie, Aberdeenshire. Within the Mount Pleasant henge, a palisaded enclosure of enormous dimensions (800 m long) was constructed, with large tree trunks forming an impenetrable barrier. Another such enclosure was erected with reference to an earlier Late Neolithic monument at Avebury, Wiltshire (see Chapter 4). We might think of them as fortified enclosures, built by Beaker invaders who had taken over existing centres of ritual power, but such enclosures were probably ceremonial spaces for crowds, herds and flocks. The construction of the Stonehenge circles took place within a Late Neolithic circular enclosure and cremation cemetery. Such acts of appropriation, and transformation from wood to stone, may have been designed to incorporate the places of the ancients, rework ancestries and legitimize ancestral power, in much the same way as pagan Saxon cemeteries were often sited on the funerary monuments of the Early Bronze Age.

Another indication of how the natural or given landscape was transformed into a social domain is provided by the rock art of cup-and-ring marks found in northern England and Scotland (Bradley 1993). These curious motifs, pounded onto natural rock faces, are problematic to date and perhaps impossible to decipher, yet there is a patterning in their distribution. In certain areas, the ring motifs are found at higher elevations than the cup marks, which are often found overlooking lowland soils. The larger and more complex designs often overlook the most productive soils in their localities and also are often found in areas with concentrations of henges and ceremonial monuments. In certain stone cist burials within Late Neolithic and Early Bronze Age cairns, some of the stone slabs have been detatched from cup-and-ring mark surfaces and the carvings are generally turned inwards towards the remains of the corpse, perhaps linking the deceased to control of those places.

Barrow groups and cemeteries, as noted, were regularly sited in relation to earlier henges, long barrows, cursuses, stone circles and standing stones. Many of these places of the dead seem to have formed sacred landscapes that were devoid of contemporary settlements, such as the area north-east of Peterborough. Many of these funerary landscapes seem to have been relatively open and suitable for pasture, either on downland or river meadows. The barrow concentrations may well have marked the summer grazing lands for cattle and sheep for different territories, thus embodying the ancestral heartlands of different kin groups. Whilst pastoralism was an important element of Early Bronze Age economy, crops of wheat, barley, pulses, oats and flax were grown. Early Bronze Age cross-ploughing, presumably with a stone-tipped wooden ard, is known from Gwithian in Cornwall (Megaw in Burgess and Miket 1976) and from Rosinish on Benbecula (Shepherd in Burgess and Miket 1976). The lack of houses has led to conjecture that people were semi-sedentary, if not nomadic, and thus largely pastoralists, yet the archaeologist's eye view, somewhere below ground level, probably underestimates the sturdiness and longevity of these small homes.

The Earlier Bronze Age was a time of major expansion and clearance. Whereas evidence from landsnails indicates that substantial portions of the Avebury, Dorchester and Stonehenge areas were already largely cleared of forest, other areas were now being colonized and cleared (Smith 1984). In the Midlands, the Millstone Grit of the Peak District was colonized by users of Food Vessels and Collared Urns. Other uplands, such as Dartmoor and Bodmin moor, were also utilized on a much greater scale than before (Fleming 1988). In these areas, as well as on the chalk downlands and in the river valleys, long, linear boundaries established complex and fixed allotments of land. Extensive and intensive use of the landscape on the Highland edge in eastern Scotland, on a scale not previously apparent, is demonstrable from pollen analysis, anchored by radiocarbon dates, in inland Aberdeenshire.

## STONEHENGE AND OTHER MONUMENTS

The standing stones, stone rows and stone circles of the British Isles have been the subjects of innumerable books, of which a few of the general surveys can be recommended (Burl 1983; 1993; Ruggles and Whittle 1981). Whilst most are thought to date to the Late Neolithic or Early

Bronze Age, very few have been properly investigated and closely dated. Some of those whose construction can be dated with certainty to the Early Bronze Age are two adjacent circles on Machrie Moor, Isle of Arran, which replaced timber circles, the Rollright Stones in Oxfordshire and, of course, Stonehenge (Richards 1991; Cleal *et al.* 1995). These and other monuments have formed the basis for a bewildering range of theories of ley lines, cosmic energy paths, dowsed underwater stream crossings, crop circles, earth mysteries, ancient computers, astronomical markers of star constellations, megalithic units of measurement, and more archaeologically acceptable notions of solar and lunar markers, territorial markers, and legitimation statements. Many archaeologists of the present generation are less virulent in their dismissal of the 'fringe' alternatives than Professors Glyn Daniel and Stuart Piggott were with Alexander Thom's notions of megalithic astronomers (Thom 1971). Nonetheless, a distinction can probably be drawn between the fringe who believe that the ley lines and energy paths actually exist, and the archaeologists who would be prepared to accept that similar beliefs and notions may have been in the heads of prehistoric peoples but that these ideas have no external reality.

Many of these monuments encode solar and lunar observations, indicating not only that the passage of cyclical and presumably linear time (i.e. seasonal time and time counted in years from an origin) was carefully marked but also that these two heavenly bodies were central to a complex cosmology that integrated them with the layout of the land and with the activities of people. This is best illustrated by Stonehenge, which has many sightlines, albeit broadly defined, for movements of the sun and moon (Burl 1983; 1987) besides that of the summer solstice sunrise. Of course, the linking of Druids to Bronze Age Stonehenge is a fallacy. However, there may well have been a group, caste or class of ritual specialists at that time. The question of whether Stonehenge was inspired or engineered by Myceneans can now be rejected; although the evidence currently points in favour of indigenous development, there is the likelihood of indirect links across Europe with the east Mediterranean, so that we cannot view developments in Britain as entirely independent from Europe. In any case, the astronomical sophistication embodied by Stonehenge was not new. Accurate calendrical calculations based on the sun and moon had probably been performed in Britain for over a thousand years prior to the building of Stonehenge. Whilst it seems to have come to embody an *axis mundi*, or centre of the world, Stonehenge may have been not so much an experiment as a memorial, a referential monument to the absolute and unquestionable universality of time and the ancestors in ordering the sacred and mundane routines of people's lives. Whilst its large stones are sarsens, brought probably from the Marlborough Downs of north Wiltshire, the earliest stone circle seems to have been of bluestones from the Prescelly Mountains of Dyfed. There is still a debate amongst geologists as to whether these bluestones were brought to the area by human agency or by earlier glaciers; if the former, and this seems increasingly likely, then the mountains also fit into this elaborate cosmology, perhaps embodying ancestral links with Wales.

## CHANGE

Profound changes can be identified by the end of the Earlier Bronze Age, indicating new conceptions of territory, land, domesticity and identity. The axe, that powerful symbol and tool of Neolithic societies, had been eclipsed by the dagger; by the Middle Bronze Age, this form had become elaborated into long bronze rapiers, which were effective weapons, along with bronze spearheads. As landscapes changed from zones of movement around sacred monuments and burial mounds to fixed places of occupation and unchangeable blocks of agricultural land, so people became rooted at the centres of their increasingly bounded domains (Barrett 1994). Identities also switched in emphasis from individual variations within a geographically uniform material culture to regional expressions of belonging. Changes in metalwork, with regional styles of palstaves, and in pottery, with the introduction of regional urn styles and Deverel-Rimbury styles, heralded a new regionalism. The increase in size and robustness of houses, and the elaboration of food storage, preparation and consumption also point to a new emphasis on the household group and their intimate domestic rituals and routines. Finally, the treatment of the dead was changing from burial or cremation in big groups of large mounds to cremation without grave goods in small cemeteries behind the settlements. The role of the dead had altered from being visibly commemorated ancestral guardians of the wider communities' pastures to local markers of a new sense of place fixed on the homestead. As the transition to the Later Bronze Age approached, people's very nature was changing, as personal identities were defined less by lineage and more by territory. Control over land counted as much as control over people.

## Acknowledgements

I would like to thank the following for permission to use information and illustrations: John Barrett, Colin Burgess, Mike Hamilton, Jon Humble, Niall Sharples, the Ashmolean Museum, Batsford, Blackwell, English Heritage, Orion Press and Sheffield City Museum.

## Key texts

Barrett, J.C., 1994. *Fragments from antiquity: an archaeology of social life in Britain, 2900–1200 BC.* Oxford: Blackwell.
Burgess, C., 1980. *The age of Stonehenge.* London: Dent.
Burgess, C. and Miket, R. (eds) 1976. *Settlement and economy in the third and second millennia BC.* Oxford: British Archaeological Reports 33.
Clarke, D.V., Cowie, T.G. and Foxon, A., 1985. *Symbols of power at the time of Stonehenge.* Edinburgh: HMSO for National Museum of Antiquities of Scotland.
Kinnes, I. and Varndell, G. (eds) 1995. *'Unbaked Urns of Rudely Shape': essays on British and Irish pottery for Ian Longworth.* London: British Museum.
Parker Pearson, M., 1994. *Bronze Age Britain.* London: Batsford/English Heritage.

## Bibliography

Armit, I., 1996. *The Archaeology of Skye and the Western Isles.* Edinburgh: Edinburgh University Press.
Barrett, J.C., Bradley, R. and Green, M., 1991. *Landscape, monuments and society: the prehistory of Cranborne Chase.* Cambridge: Cambridge University Press.
Blick, C.R. (ed.) 1991. *Early metallurgical sites in Great Britain BC 2000 to AD 1500.* London: The Institute of Metals.
Bradley, R., 1993. *Altering the Earth: the origins of monuments in Britain and continental Europe.* Edinburgh: Society of Antiquaries of Scotland Monograph Series 8.
Brodie, N., 1994. *The Neolithic–Bronze Age transition in Britain: a critical review of some archaeological and craniological concepts.* Oxford: British Archaeological Reports British Series 238.
Burl, A., 1983. *Prehistoric astronomy and ritual.* Aylesbury: Shire.
Burl, A., 1987. *The Stonehenge people.* London: Dent.
Burl, A., 1993. *From Carnac to Callanish: the prehistoric stone rows and avenues of Britain, Ireland and Brittany.* New Haven: Yale University Press.
Clarke, D.L., 1970. *Beaker Pottery of Great Britain and Ireland.* Cambridge: Cambridge University Press. 2 vols.
Cleal, R.M.J., Walker, K.E. and Montague, R., 1995. *Stonehenge in its landscape: twentieth century excavations,* London: English Heritage.
Davis, S. and Payne, S., 1993. 'A barrow full of cattle skulls', *Antiquity* 67, 12–22.
Edmonds, M., 1995. *Stone tools and society.* London: Batsford.
Ellison, A., 1981. 'Towards a socio-economic model for the Middle Bronze Age in southern England', in Hammond, N., Hodder, I. and Isaac, G. (eds) *Pattern of the past: studies in honour of David Clarke.* Cambridge: Cambridge University Press, 413–438.
Fleming, A., 1988. *The Dartmoor Reaves: investigating prehistoric land divisions.* London: Batsford.
Garwood, P., 1991. 'Ritual tradition and the reconstitution of society', in Garwood, P., Jennings, D.,

Skeates, R. and Toms, J. (eds) *Sacred and profane: proceedings of a conference on archaeology, ritual and religion, Oxford, 1989.* Oxford: Oxford University Committee for Archaeology Monograph 32, 10–32.

Gibson, A., 1982. *Beaker domestic sites: a study in the domestic pottery of the late third and early second millennia BC in the British Isles.* Oxford: British Archaeological Reports British Series 107.

Kinnes, I., Gibson, A., Ambers, J., Bowman, S., Leese, M. and Boast, R., 1991. 'Radiocarbon dating and British beakers: the British Museum programme', *Scottish Archaeological Review* 8, 35–68.

Longworth, I.H., 1984. *Collared Urns of the Bronze Age in Great Britain and Ireland.* Cambridge: Cambridge University Press.

Mizoguchi, K., 1992. 'A historiography of a linear barrow cemetery: a structurationist's point of view', *Archaeological Reviews from Cambridge* 11(1), 39–49.

Needham, S.P., 1988. 'Selective deposition in the British Early Bronze Age', *World Archaeology* 20, 229–248.

Nowakowski, J., 1991. 'Trethellan Farm, Newquay: the excavation of a lowland Bronze Age settlement and Iron Age cemetery', *Cornish Archaeology* 30, 5–242.

Parker Pearson, M. and Ramilisonina, 1998. 'Stonehenge for the ancestors: the stones pass on the message', *Antiquity* 72, 308–26.

Renfrew, A.C. (ed.) 1973. *The explanation of culture change: models in prehistory.* London: Duckworth.

Richards, J., 1991. *Stonehenge.* London: Batsford/English Heritage.

Roe, F.E.S., 1979. 'Typology of stone implements with shaftholes', in Clough, T.G.M. and Cummins, W.A. (eds) *Stone Axe studies.* London: Council for British Archaeology Research Reports 23, 23–48.

Rowlands, M.J., 1976. *The production and exchange of metalwork in the Middle Bronze Age in southern Britain.* Oxford: British Archaeological Reports 32.

Ruggles, C.L.N. and Whittle, A.W.R. (eds) 1981. *Astronomy and society in Britain during the period 4000–1500 BC.* Oxford: British Archaeological Reports British Series 88.

Smith, R.W., 1984. 'The ecology of Neolithic farming systems as exemplified by the Avebury region of Wiltshire', *Proceedings of the Prehistoric Society* 50, 99–120.

Thom, A., 1971. *Megalithic lunar observatories.* Oxford: Clarendon Press.

Tipping, R., 1994. '"Ritual" floral tributes in the Scottish Early Bronze Age – palynological evidence', *Journal of Archaeological Science* 21, 133–139.

*Chapter Six*

# The Later Bronze Age

## Timothy Champion

### INTRODUCTION

The later part of the second millennium BC was a period of major change in Britain and elsewhere in Europe. The earlier period of the Bronze Age had been characterized by evidence for burials and ritual monuments, but both of these cease at this time. The tradition of individual burial in a barrow died out, and in many parts of Britain there is relatively little evidence for human burial for more than a millennium thereafter. There is also little evidence for any significant activity at the major ceremonial monuments of the Late Neolithic and Earlier Bronze Age after the middle of the second millennium BC.

Instead, the focus of archaeological attention turns to the rapidly increasing evidence for human settlement and for the division and exploitation of the agricultural landscape. There was a significant change in the nature and organization of settlement, resulting in more substantial and more visible sites, and traces of them are now found in much greater numbers in many areas of Britain. Settlements, their structures, and related finds, such as pottery and domestic food waste, now form one of the two main sources of information about Later Bronze Age societies. The other main source is finds of metalwork, especially bronze: these are rare in the settlements, but single finds or collections of items, called hoards, often without any archaeological context, are very numerous.

The Later Bronze Age was a period of radical change in the nature of prehistoric society. It is not necessary to think of a new population arriving from elsewhere with new ideas, but rather to consider a fundamental transformation in the culture of Bronze Age society, with the reorganization of the physical landscape and the introduction of new forms of social interaction.

### CHRONOLOGY

The cessation of the series of burials containing associations of pottery, metalwork and other items, and the fact that much of the metalwork of the Later Bronze Age is found unassociated with other material, mean that chronologies have to be constructed in different ways from previously.

The scheme introduced in the previous chapter can be extended to one final period:

- *the Knighton Heath phase* (1400–1250 BC): end of the burial sequence, predominantly cremations with pottery and few other finds; pottery of the Deverel-Rimbury tradition; metalwork of the Taunton phase.

For the Later Bronze Age, the many finds of bronze metalwork have been used to provide the basis of a chronological scheme, since they can be subjected to careful typological analysis and the hoards offer many examples of associated objects (Burgess 1968; Megaw and Simpson 1979: 242–343; Needham 1996). The characteristic assemblages, named after the findspots of typical hoards, and dated by radiocarbon and by comparison with the sequence worked out in continental Europe, may overlap somewhat and can be arranged chronologically as follows:

- *Taunton* (1400–1250 BC): axes with stop-ridges called palstaves and flanged axes, long rapiers, spearheads; ornaments, including torcs, armlets, bracelets, finger rings and pins; specialist tools for crafts, especially carpentry and metalwork, such as the first socketed axes, socketed hammers, saws, chisels and anvils.
- *Penard* (1300–1100 BC): the first leaf-shaped swords; pegged spearheads.
- *Wilburton* (1150–950 BC): swords, elaborate spearheads, socketed axes, vehicle and horse trappings, and sheet-metal cauldrons (Figure 6.1).
- *Ewart Park* (950–750 BC): swords, regional varieties of spearheads and socketed axes, many types of tools such as knives and gouges, buckets and cauldrons, pins and other ornaments (Figure 6.2).
- *Llyn Fawr* (750–600 BC): the final phase of the Bronze Age industry, overlapping the beginning of the Iron Age: longer swords, heavy socketed axes, and horse trappings.

This well-established scheme (and its equivalents in other regions of Britain) is of restricted use, however, since finds of metalwork on settlement sites or in association with other material such as pottery are comparatively rare. A parallel sequence based on pottery has also been developed for southern Britain, using the evidence of typology, associated finds and radiocarbon to give absolute dates. The phases are:

- Deverel-Rimbury (named after two sites in Dorset: 1500–1000 BC): regional varieties of coarse-ware bucket urns and fine-ware globular urns; Trevisker pottery is a contemporary tradition in south-west England (Figure 6.3).
- Post-Deverel-Rimbury plain ware (1000–800 BC): coarse-ware jars undecorated except for finger-tipping, and finer cups (Figure 6.4).
- Post-Deverel-Rimbury decorated ware (800–600 BC): similar forms with an increased range of incised and inlaid decoration, overlapping the start of the Iron Age.

## CHANGING PERCEPTIONS

The vision of the Later Bronze Age has changed greatly in recent years. New perspectives derive from several different sources: reconsideration of old evidence in the light of developing knowledge, especially for the fixing of a correct chronology for the period; new discoveries in the field; the application of new scientific techniques; and the emergence of new theoretical and interpretative approaches to the prehistoric past.

The first key step was the recognition that the settlement and pottery chronology in favour in the decades immediately after the Second World War was wrong. The relative sequence of metalwork phases has proved to be very robust, but its application to other types of material has been more problematic, because of a lack of good associations. The pottery and settlements of the Deverel-Rimbury phase had been dated to the final period of the Later Bronze Age, but more careful analysis of the evidence eventually demonstrated its true position, confirmed in due course by calibrated radiocarbon dates, before 1000 BC. That left three centuries from 1000 BC to 700 BC in which seemingly the only archaeological material was large quantities of bronze metalwork. This gap was partly filled by reconsideration of material from the beginning of the Iron Age; the pottery tradition previously assigned to the Iron Age in fact begins much earlier, with no significant break in development into the Early Iron Age (see Chapter 7).

Many new Later Bronze Age settlements were discovered from the 1970s onwards. Many sites of this period have left little or no surface evidence, and even their traces in the subsoil are slight; in many cases, it was the development of methods for stripping large areas that allowed such sites to be recognized for the first time. Other important innovations were large-scale surveys that focused on the evolution of Bronze Age landscape organization.

Since metalwork, potentially the most informative evidence for chronology, is seldom found in useful associations, radiocarbon dating has had a very great impact in this period, helped by the absence of the calibration problems that affect its use in the Iron Age. Other scientific methods have also contributed, especially on questions of climate, environment and agricultural economy, but one set of techniques has been of particular significance. Analysis of metalwork, especially bronze, has allowed different sources of metal to be characterized by their trace elements. In this way, the supply and circulation of metal in different regions at different

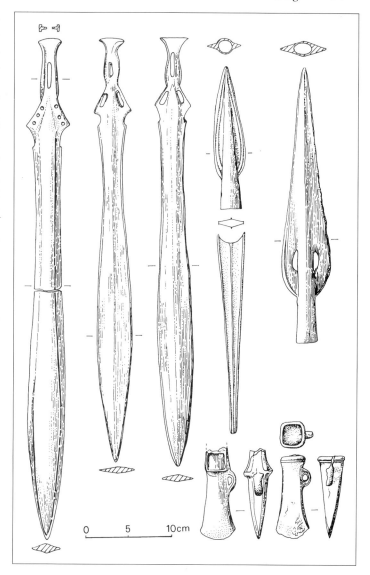

*Figure 6.1* Examples of bronzes of the Wilburton assemblage.
*Source:* Megaw and Simpson 1979, Fig. 6.27

times can be monitored. In some cases, the particular types of metal can be identified with specific geological origins, giving important insights into long-distance exchange in prehistory.

One other scientific development that has had a significant impact is the availability of cheap and effective metal detectors; one of the commonest types of object found with these devices has been Late Bronze Age metalwork. Though many finds have not been reported, and others lack good documentation, in some regions the rate of discoveries has been so fast that it has been almost impossible to keep up with the new information. Though it has not fundamentally changed our knowledge of the types of metalwork and their distribution, it has produced a significant change in our perception of the quantity of metal in circulation in the period.

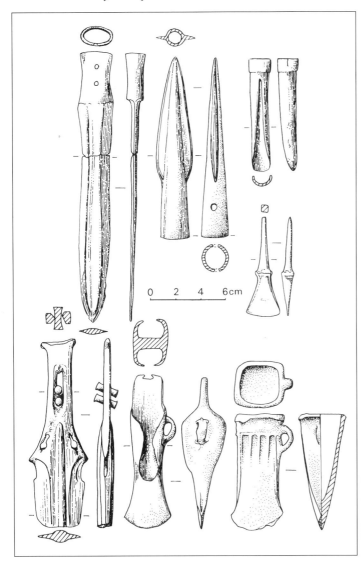

0   2   4   6cm

***Figure 6.2*** Examples of bronzes of the Ewart Park assemblage.
*Source*: Megaw and Simpson 1979, Fig. 6.32

Perhaps the most important changes in perceptions of the Later Bronze Age, however, derive from new theoretical approaches to the understanding of the archaeological record. Greater emphasis has been placed on understanding the patterns in the material record as evidence for the nature of economy and society rather than as an end in itself. Recent studies have focused on questions of economy, ritual and settlement organization. Archaeologists have tended to concentrate on such topics as the changing nature of domestic activities, for example food preparation and consumption, as shown by changes in the styles and shapes of pottery; the development of craft production witnessed by increasing production of specialist tools; or the meaning and value of material culture such as items of bronze and the social contexts in which they were used.

Particular attention has also been paid to the patterns of deposition that have shaped the archaeological record. It is clear that the burials and other deposits of the Late Neolithic and Early Bronze Age were carefully selected and deposited in a highly structured way, and that the meaning of these patterns needs interpretation. It would be easy to think that, with the appearance of settlements as one of the major sources of evidence, much simpler and more obvious processes of loss and waste disposal were involved. It is now clear, however, that some deposits from domestic sites too were carefully structured by their inhabitants. Similarly, recent work on bronze finds has focused on the recognition that these finds are more a product of selective and structured deposition than an indication of production.

## KEY SITES AND ASSEMBLAGES

The archaeological evidence for the Later Bronze Age varies greatly from region to region (Bradley and Bradley 1980). This variation is mostly due to the very uneven coverage of modern archaeological observation. Some regions, such as Wessex and the Thames Valley, have received much attention, but elsewhere, as in Wales, almost nothing is known of contemporary settlement. The key sites are best reviewed on a regional basis.

In eastern England, the earlier part of the period is characterized by small cremation cemeteries with local variants of the Deverel-Rimbury pottery tradition, and some evidence for settlements. At Fengate, Peterborough (Pryor 1991: 52–73), these were associated with extensive field systems laid out around the thirteenth century BC, designed for efficient management of a pastoral cattle economy.

The most striking site of the whole British Later Bronze Age has been excavated at Flag Fen, near Peterborough (Pryor 1991; 1992). As the fens grew wetter and formed a shallow inlet of the sea, a massive timber platform was constructed about 1000 BC in the open water at the mouth of the bay. It was linked to the dry land on either side by an

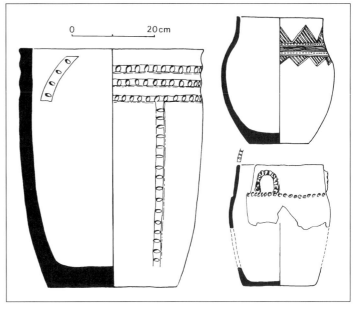

*Figure 6.3*  Deverel-Rimbury pottery.
*Sources: (left and upper right)* Annable, F.K. and Simpson, D.D.A., 1964. *Guide catalogue of the Neolithic and Bronze Age collections in Devizes Museum.* Devizes: Wiltshire Archaeological and Natural History Society, Figs 576 and 566 respectively. (*lower right*) Dacre, M. and Ellison, A., 1981. 'A Bronze Age urn cemetery at Kimpton, Hampshire', *Proceedings of the Prehistoric Society* 47, 147–203, Fig. 19.

alignment of vertical posts more than a kilometre long. In the peat alongside this alignment were found nearly 300 metal items, together with animal bones and pottery, all originally dropped or carefully placed into the water of the bay. The metal items are mainly of bronze, but a few are pure tin; most belong to the Later Bronze Age, but some are of Iron Age date. They include many rings, pins and other small items, as well as swords, spears and daggers, and fragments of bronze helmets. This extraordinary site shows a long-lasting tradition of depositing objects in watery places.

Similar practices are well known from major rivers, especially the Thames, which has a long history of dredging and archaeological observation. The material recovered from the river bed spans a very long period, but there are particular concentrations of Later Bronze Age metalwork in certain stretches. These are not randomly chosen items, but include especially swords and certain types of spearhead. Human skeletal remains have also been found in the river, and again there is a concentration of dated examples in the Later Bronze Age, suggesting a link between the deposition of metalwork in the river and the disposal of at least some of the dead (Bradley and Gordon 1988).

Settlement evidence in the middle and lower Thames Valley suggests a considerable density of population. In the tributary valley of the Kennet, there is a particularly high concentration of sites, such as Aldermaston Wharf, Berkshire (Bradley *et al.* 1980); these are unenclosed clusters of round houses and pits, showing evidence for a mixed agricultural economy and craft activity such as textile production, but little metalwork or other wealth. A very different sort of site also existed in the Thames Valley, as at Runnymede Bridge, Surrey (Needham 1991). Here there was a site with a wooden piled waterfront, producing many bronze objects and other imports such as shale

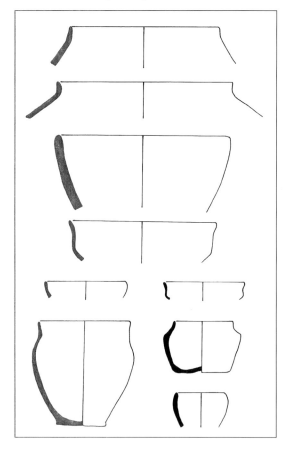

**Figure 6.4** Pottery of the Post-Deverel-Rimbury un-decorated phase.
*Source*: Bradley *et al.* 1980, Fig. 11

and amber, and evidence for metalworking. Sites such as this may have been key links in the exchange system that brought exotic materials into Britain and reworked them and redistributed them into the interior.

In the later period, after 900 BC, a distinctive feature of the settlement evidence of eastern England is a class of defended enclosure, commonest in the region of the lower Thames estuary, but spreading as far north as Thwing, Yorkshire. They were surrounded by impressive defences of timber and earth, with external ditches; some show precisely geometric plans, circular at Mucking North Ring (Bond 1988) and square at Lofts Farm (Brown 1988), both in Essex (Figure 6.5). An excavated example at Springfield Lyons, Essex (Buckley and Hedges 1987), shows a carefully organized interior plan with a large, circular house. There was a large deposit of metalworking debris, including mould fragments for swords, in one of the ditch terminals, but no other evidence for metalworking anywhere on the site.

In southern England, from Sussex to the chalk downlands of Wessex, the evidence is rather more plentiful. Cremation burials with Deverel-Rimbury pottery, either in small barrows or flat cemeteries, continue to the beginning of the first millennium BC, though they are now more common in the river valleys and the coastal lowlands than on the higher chalk downlands where most of the burials of the Earlier Bronze Age had been located. These areas were densely settled, but by the end of the Bronze Age human exploitation had turned areas such as the New Forest (Hampshire) and the Dorset lowlands into acid and unproductive heathlands. Settlement sites have survived better on the chalk, and some can be placed in their context of an evolving agricultural landscape. At South Lodge, in Cranborne Chase, Dorset (Barrett *et al.* 1991), a small settlement developed in a pre-existing field system. One of the most fully excavated sites is at Black Patch, East Sussex (Drewett 1982), where five circular structures were located on one

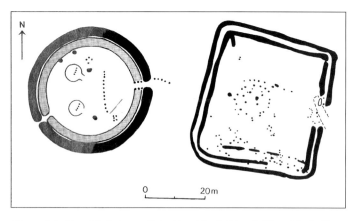

**Figure 6.5** Simplified plans of Mucking North Ring (left) and Lofts Farm (right).
*Source*: (*left*) Bond 1988, Fig. 3 (*right*) Brown 1988, Fig. 4

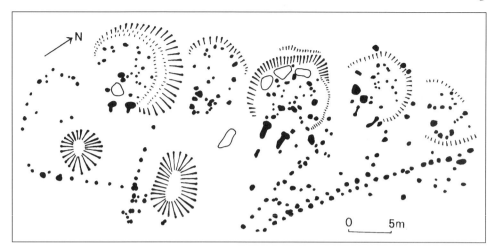

***Figure 6.6*** Plan of Black Patch Bronze Age settlement.
*Source*: Drewett 1982, Fig. 9

settlement platform (Figure 6.6). These have been interpreted as a single household cluster, in which different buildings had different functions, such as sleeping accommodation for various members of the group, as well as being used for eating, food preparation, craft activities and animal shelter. Small settlements made up of such household clusters may have been typical of this region in the late second millennium, while some fortified sites suggest the emergence of new forms of prestige (Ellison 1981).

Settlements of the early first millennium are less well known, but generally comprise unenclosed clusters of round houses with a few small pits for storage and other purposes. A very different type of site has recently been recognized in north Wiltshire, for example at Potterne and East Chisenbury (McOmish 1996); these are very large middens, with high densities of pottery, animal bone and metalwork. They must represent a regional type of high-status site, with an emphasis on the social rituals of feasting. In some areas of the chalk downs, such as Salisbury Plain, long bank and ditch earthworks were constructed, dividing the land into territories each containing settlements, arable and pastoral land (Bradley *et al.* 1994). Towards the end of the Bronze Age, many of these earthworks went out of use, but at some boundary junctions within this system new enclosures were founded, and these played an important role in the emergence of the Iron Age landscape with hillforts.

Further west, one of the most complex examples of Bronze Age land division has been explored on Dartmoor (Fleming 1988). This upland block had been occupied earlier in the Bronze Age, as cairns and stone rows surviving from that period show, but after about 1400 BC the landscape was divided into a pattern of territories that all contained valley land, upland and access to the open moor (Figure 6.7). The unenclosed moorland was separated from the lower land by stone banks, called reaves, and other reaves divided up the territories and defined field systems within them. Settlements were scattered through the territories. By the beginning of the first millennium BC, this upland landscape had been abandoned; climatic deterioration, or human over-exploitation, or a combination of both, had produced an increasingly hostile and peat-covered environment. Settlements and field systems are known elsewhere in the south-west, especially in the upland and marginal areas such as Bodmin Moor and Scilly. In the former, as on Dartmoor, sites were abandoned towards the end of the Bronze Age, and in Scilly much of the occupied area is now under water.

*Figure 6.7* Simplified plan of Bronze Age land divisions on Dartmoor. Land above 500m shaded.
*Source*: Fleming 1988, Fig. 30

Little is yet known about the sites of this period in the Midlands, Wales and the north-west of England. There are a few burials with regional variants of Deverel-Rimbury pottery, but little evidence for settlement sites. By the end of the Bronze Age, hill-top sites were being occupied and defended in the northern Welsh Marches. Sites at Dinorben, Moel-y-Gaer and the Breiddin (Musson 1991) were all occupied by the end of the Bronze Age, but the construction of defences and their development as hillforts may not have occurred until the beginning of the Iron Age.

Settlement evidence is a little better known in the north of England. In north-east Yorkshire, an extensive system of linear earth-works probably dating from around 1000 BC divided the area below the moors into a series of territories or estates with equal access to natural resources (Spratt 1989). A cave at Heathery Burn, Co. Durham, contained a series of ritual deposits of metalwork, including parts of wheeled vehicles (Britton 1971). Sites in the Anglo-Scottish borders, comprising platforms terraced into the hill slope for round houses, belong to the early first millennium BC and earlier; these sites extend well into southern Scotland, where in particular north of the Forth–Clyde isthmus, there are also many hut circles, penannular dry-stone footings for houses, with associated clearances and field walls, some of which certainly belong to this period. At Jarlshof, Shetland, a small, but more nucleated settlement with stone houses has also produced important evidence of metalworking. In parts of Scotland, small kerb cairns covering cremations occur.

One type of site found in many parts of Britain is burnt stone mounds (Buckley 1990). Though best documented in northern and western Scotland and the Isle of Man, they are being found in increasing numbers as far south as the New Forest, and radiocarbon dates place them mainly in the second and early first millennia BC. They comprise mounds or spreads of stone that has been heated; many of them are near a water supply, and in some excavated examples there are water troughs associated with them. Liddle, on South Ronaldsay, Orkney, is a well-excavated example. It is assumed that the stone was heated in a fire and placed in the water to boil it, and several functions have been suggested, such as cooking places or sweat lodges (an analogy with ethnographically recorded practices in North America), though some have a possible link with metalworking. Although they are a very common element of the Bronze Age record, their true function is far from clear, and indeed they may derive from many different operations.

Other key assemblages are not sites but the hoards of bronze. There is great regional and chronological variation in their number and composition, and these topics are discussed below.

## ENVIRONMENT AND AGRICULTURE

The Later Bronze Age was a time of major environmental change. The Late Neolithic and Earlier Bronze Age had been a period of favourable climate, marginally but significantly warmer and drier than today. The prehistoric people of Britain exploited these conditions to extend their farming into new environments, but this expansion was not sustainable, and by the end of the Bronze Age human occupation had contracted drastically. In part this was due to natural causes, in part to previous human activity. Suggestions that the retreat from some northern uplands was sudden, and attributable to dust-clouds from volcanic activity in Iceland, are not widely accepted (Cowie and Shepherd 1997).

Towards 1000 BC, a period of climatic deterioration began. This is seen particularly in the changing rate of growth in peat bogs, and involved a trend to colder and wetter conditions. The growing season for crops was shortened, and existing agricultural practices became increasingly problematic, especially in many upland areas. In some environments, especially those that would become the open upland moors, the increased rainfall, combined with soil changes resulting from human exploitation, produced waterlogging and peat growth. Human over-exploitation also reduced other areas, such as the acid heathlands of the Hampshire–Dorset basin, to their present state. The combination of natural processes and the effects of earlier agriculture resulted in an environment that was increasingly less favourable. All this placed a premium on those soils that were able to withstand more intensive exploitation and sustain their productivity, especially those of the major river valleys and the more fertile lowlands of southern and eastern Britain.

The agricultural economy also shows major changes at this time, though their relationship to climatic, environmental or social pressures is not clear. It was a system of mixed agriculture, exploiting crops and animals in more complex and more intensive ways than before, including new crops, new facilities, and new ways of organizing land use; perhaps most important were new ways of using agriculture for products other than food. Animals were increasingly used for traction, and sheep became for the first time an important source of wool for textiles.

There was a switch in the dominant crop species represented in some regions: emmer wheat gave way to spelt, naked varieties of barley to the hulled varieties, and beans and rye were introduced. The increased emphasis on the division of land into field systems or larger territories may have been due to different causes at different times and places. The erection of boundaries may indicate the growing importance of land as a scarce resource, but it was also a means for its more efficient and intensive exploitation. Agricultural produce was also treated in new ways, with pits and granaries constructed for grain storage; the salt industry allowed the preservation and transport of meat.

Changing attitudes to agriculture and food can also be seen in their increasing involvement in ritual activities. As we will see below, there was a new concern for the preparation and serving of food, much of it concerned with prestige feasting. The growing practice of making special deposits in boundary ditches and storage pits also suggests a focus of ritual very different from that of the Earlier Bronze Age.

## CRAFT, TECHNOLOGY AND TRADE

Much of the output of non-agricultural production in the Bronze Age does not survive, especially items of organic materials, but scattered evidence of raw material extraction, specialist tools and waste products allows a picture of the developing technology and craft skills of the period to be formed.

The flint mines of southern Britain, which had been so important a source of raw material in the Earlier Bronze Age, went out of use. Flint was still used to make tools, but they were simpler and more utilitarian than before; Later Bronze Age flint assemblages often consist of little more than comparatively crude flakes. The explanation of this change is complex: there may have been an alternative and better source, especially metal, for the many different tools needed; alternatively, an elaborate technology was now unnecessary for stone tools as they were no longer used for symbolically important social roles.

Metal ores were exploited at several locations in western Britain. Deep mines for copper are known from Wales, especially at Great Orme, Llandudno, on the north Welsh coast. Analyses of trace elements suggest that a number of western copper sources were used at different times, though copper was also imported from the Continent. Gold, tin and lead were also won, but little is known about their extraction. Other mineral resources exploited include shale from Dorset, used mainly for manufacturing bracelets.

One important new industry was salt boiling. At sites along the east and south coasts from Lincolnshire to Dorset, seawater was heated in fired clay containers to extract the salt, which could then be traded inland. The demand for salt may have arisen from a fashionable taste for salty food, but more probably it was related to a reorganization of food production and a growing need to preserve, store and trade meat.

Organic materials such as cloth and leather are more problematic. Though no actual examples have survived, they certainly provided finished products that played a critical role in domestic and social life. The best evidence for leather working is seen in specialized knives first produced in the Later Bronze Age, suggesting a new level of craft specialism and an increased importance for non-meat products of cattle. Textiles are best demonstrated by spindle-whorls and loom-weights, which become common

*Figure 6.8* The Dover Bronze Age boat during excavation.
*Source*: Courtesy of the Canterbury Archaeological Trust

finds at this point, especially in southern Britain. The main products were presumably clothes. This important new use for sheep as providers of wool would have had a significant effect on their role in the agricultural economy, and textiles would have provided a new medium for decoration and the representation of individual identities.

A little more has survived to demonstrate Bronze Age wood-working skills. A specialized toolkit comprising saws, chisels and gouges made of bronze was produced, as well as the axes which had a variety of functions. The more substantial nature of settlement structures demanded an appropriate level of carpentry, and by the end of the Bronze Age wheeled vehicles were being built. The sewn-plank boats known from Dover (Figure 6.8) and elsewhere show us the achievements of Bronze Age skills, and the mass of material from Flag Fen casts much new light on carpentry techniques.

The industries that have left the most evidence are bronze and pottery making. The range of bronze types produced in the Later Bronze Age, and the developing technologies required to make them, will be discussed in more detail below, but here it can be noted that the bronze industry needed a supply of copper, tin and lead. All these metals were of limited geological distribution and were therefore the focus for long-distance exchange mechanisms. Trace element analysis of copper has revealed the use of sources in western Britain, but much of the bronze metalwork of the Wilburton phase in eastern England was made from a distinctive copper that originated in the Alpine region of continental Europe. This continued to circulate in later periods, increasingly alloyed with metal from other sources as objects were melted down and recycled (Northover 1982). In the later phases of the Bronze Age, large collections of broken bronze items indicate the collection and recycling of scrap metal, in addition to supplies of new metal.

The complexity of the technology, as well as the problems of access to supplies of metal, suggests that bronze working was a specialist skill, and the development of specialized tools such as hammers and anvils supports this. Study of the bronze items themselves indicates that some types, such as tools, ornaments and small spearheads, were made for comparatively local distribution and use, while other larger or more complex types, such as swords, were made by a smaller number of more skilled specialists and distributed more widely.

Pottery production and distribution in southern Britain shows a similar pattern. In the Deverel-Rimbury phase, the coarse-ware jars were made from local materials for local use, while the globular urns and other finer wares were distributed over a wider area. Less is known about the production of vessels in the plain-ware phase, but these again seem mostly to have been of local production. The Deverel-Rimbury and related traditions comprised a very limited range of forms, mainly large jars and some smaller vessels, mostly in finer wares. In the plain-ware phase (Barrett 1980), there is a greatly expanded range of forms, with more jar types, and especially some bowls and cups. These smaller vessels were often made in finer wares with careful surface finishing, and in the final phase these were often decorated. These trends indicate new social uses for pottery, and in particular its role in the serving and consumption of food and drink.

The evidence for some of these crafts, especially textiles and some pottery making, suggests that they were widespread domestic activities. That does not mean that every household practised them, though the majority probably did; it is also likely that such activities were allocated in some way on the basis of age and gender within the household. Other crafts were certainly more specialized; the complexity of the technology, and the skills and practical knowledge needed, the production of specialized tools found in complete toolkits, and the quality of some of the finished products all argue for the existence of specialists. The precise social context in which they worked, and their relationship to other groups in society are unclear. Some may have been full-time specialists, although many were also engaged in agricultural production; some may have worked solely for a particular patron, producing prestige items; while others still were integrated into a more diverse network of social relationships.

The corollary of specialist production and craft industries that use rare raw materials is the need for transport and distribution. Trevisker pottery from Cornwall found in Kent and shale from Dorset at Flag Fen show how such items could travel; and links extended overseas, as Alpine copper, Baltic amber and Irish gold show. As noted above, metal ores from western Britain and the Continent were used to supply other regions, and the extensive imitation of fashions, especially in metalwork, suggests that some items were circulating very widely. Much of this trade is invisible, except through scientific analysis, but occasionally we can catch a glimpse of it. Two collections of metal objects found off the coast of southern England, at Dover, Kent, and Salcombe, Devon, are the result of shipwrecks in the course of such trade. The Dover assemblage consisted mainly of types from France otherwise unknown in Britain, and would have been melted down to cast local forms. Finds of sewn-plank boats, as at Dover or North Ferriby, Yorkshire, are good evidence not only of carpentry and boat-building skills, but also of the importance of sea-borne trade.

## PRODUCTION, USE AND DEPOSITION OF BRONZE

The bronze industry has been intensively studied, not just because bronze objects survive well and are plentiful, but because they contain important evidence for chronology, technology, trade, and many other aspects of Bronze Age society. Interpreting this mass of evidence is not easy, however; there are difficult and interlocking questions relating to supply, production, distribution, use and deposition, many of which are not yet resolved.

Copper and tin sources from the west of Britain were used throughout the Later Bronze Age and there was major importation of Alpine copper from the eleventh century, but the interpretation of this evidence is problematic. Was it a matter of supply and demand, with new sources exploited to meet rising demand for bronze? This is perhaps too modern a view of the prehistoric economy; bronze supply may have been determined by more social or political relationships between south-eastern Britain and the Continent, or there may have been a particular significance attached to imported metal simply because it was from far away. Another problem concerns the abundance or scarcity of supply. The volume of bronze objects found can be read as implying a plentiful supply, but there have been no studies of use wear to test how long objects were in use. The large number of finds from the later phases comprising scrap for recycling may suggest that there were chronic shortages of raw materials. There can be little doubt that control of access to supplies of metal, as well as control of the technical skills to work it, was an important source of power in the Later Bronze Age.

On questions of production, the evidence can be used most clearly for the history of technical progress (Megaw and Simpson 1979: 242–259 and 299–339). The proliferation of socketed spearheads, hammers and axes from the Taunton phase onwards required the use of three-piece moulds to make hollow castings; the replacement of stone and bronze moulds by non-reusable clay ones made larger and more complex castings possible, such as swords. Casting technology was also improved by the addition of a small percentage of lead to the alloy; different alloys were carefully selected for different purposes. The techniques needed to hammer, shape, join, decorate and strengthen large sheet metal objects were also developed, and impressive new items such as cauldrons, shields and helmets were produced.

Questions about the organization of production are more difficult to answer. Finds of bronze objects are determined by patterns of use and loss or deposition, and they are therefore direct evidence for these activities rather than for production. The limited finds of production debris do not tell us much about the social context of manufacture and usage, and even their location does not always coincide with the distribution of finds of similar finished objects.

Two examples can illustrate some further problems in understanding the production and use of bronze. At Flag Fen, many of the items deposited in the water were of poor quality, and unsuitable for functional use; one of the swords was a miniature. Some items were of tin, and there is also nearby evidence for the casting of tin. It is probable that these items were made specially for deposition; their form seems to have been more important than their technical quality, and they had no 'use' except to be deposited. The second example concerns the role of axes in the Later Bronze Age. There are many hoards that contain a large number of axes, many of them broken; at the end of the Bronze Age, there is a particular type of socketed axe found in considerable quantities in Brittany and southern England. These 'Armorican axes' are highly standardized in size and weight, and show little sign of use; some are even made of pure lead. They were produced as standard quantities of metal, for their value as a commodity for exchange rather than as functioning axes, and pose the question whether the large numbers of axes found from earlier phases may have been used in the same way. These examples suggest that caution is required in inferring a utilitarian function from form, or assuming modern concepts of quality, and that archaeologists should in general be careful in trying to apply concepts derived from modern economic systems to the Bronze Age.

The major factors influencing the presence of bronzes in the archaeological record are the patterns of prehistoric deposition and modern recovery. One common method of describing them, using terms such as stray finds, settlement or river finds, or hoards, reveals more about how and where the objects were found than about how or why they were deposited. Many items are found on their own, without further archaeological context; little can be said about such 'stray finds', but this may be due mostly to the circumstances of recovery. Finds from settlement sites are rare, consisting mainly of small or broken items, which might be understood as casual losses, but some such finds suggest more deliberate deposition. The dump of metalworking material in the ditch at Springfield Lyons was a deliberate ritual act, and the finds of metal from a ditch at Petters Sportsfield, Surrey, may have been a similar ritual deposit associated with the abandonment of the site (Needham 1990).

One important locus for deposition was in watery places such as rivers, lakes and bogs (Bradley 1990, 97–154). These may be called hoards if they are found together, for instance in a dried-up fen or a drained lake, but they were assembled as a result of many individual acts of deposition over a long period, made with the intention that the items should not be retrieved. We have already seen the evidence from Flag Fen; there are other concentrations of metalwork elsewhere in the Fens, in the River Thames, in lakes such as Duddingston Loch in Edinburgh, and many other wet places. Previous explanations invoking casual loss in transit or battle must be rejected, and we must recognize a deliberate practice of ritual deposition. Items selected for such deposition were a carefully selected and unrepresentative sample of the available repertoire of bronze, and the meaning associated with individual forms was obviously very significant. The possible implications of such a practice of votive deposits are discussed below.

The final type of bronze find to be considered are the hoards found on dry land. These appear to be deposited in a single act, and therefore raise two separate questions: about the reasons for assembling the collection and the reasons for depositing and not subsequently recovering it. Some of these hoards have been classified on the basis of their contents: 'personal hoards' are the ornaments assumed to have been owned by an individual; 'craftsmen's hoards' contain the tools of a specialist such as a carpenter or metalsmith; and 'merchants' hoards' include newly finished items awaiting distribution. Many hoards, as we have seen, contain scrap or axes representing an exchange commodity, and these were assembled as part of the process of recycling and redistributing bronze metal. Many of these hoards contain items on the periphery of their known distribution, and these hoards are particularly frequent in marginal locations such as the lower Thames Estuary. Like the French objects interrupted in transit by the Dover shipwreck, the items in these hoards may have been assembled for redistribution to another region, their value being more as a commodity for exchange than in their specific form.

This explanation does not fit every such hoard, nor will it account for all the regional and chronological patterns of variation in hoard composition. Above all, it does not address the question of why the hoards were deposited. Some appear to have been deposited within settlements, but many were not. The hiding of hoards for security at times of unrest or danger is a well-known practice, of which a certain proportion were inevitably never found again, and this may account for at least some of the Later Bronze Age finds. Nevertheless, it does conjure up an extraordinary picture of a very disturbed period if so many such concealed hoards were never recovered, and other ideas need to be explored.

Although some items, especially small ones, may have been accidentally lost, and in other cases people may have been prevented from recovering deliberately concealed objects, we should perhaps think of the vast majority of bronze finds as the result of deliberate deposition with no intention of recovery. Whether found singly or in large collections, within settlements or isolated, in wet places or dry, these objects were deposited as part of a widespread and long-lasting practice of ritual deposition. Some evidence for association with the abandonment of sites and the disposal of the dead has been mentioned above, but such acts of deposition may have been part of many different rituals.

These deposits show considerable regional and chronological variation, but some broad patterns emerge, especially in the selection of weaponry. In south-eastern Britain, many hoards include swords with a characteristic long tip (which is responsible for them being named Carp's Tongue swords), spearheads and associated items from belt fittings or even a sort of uniform; this set of equipment is also found in northern and western France. Elsewhere in southern England, spears are the commonest weapons; in much of the midland region there are hoards containing a typical form of barbed spearhead, termed the Broadward type; and in the north, hoards are dominated by swords, particularly of the Ewart Park type.

## LATER BRONZE AGE SOCIETY

The changes in economy, technology, material culture and ritual described above all add up to a major transformation of society in the Later Bronze Age. The ritual monuments and burials that had formed such an important part of the archaeological record of the Earlier Bronze Age, and were the prime focus for the playing out of social relationships and claims to authority at that time, had gone out of use. In their place, new sources of prestige and new social opportunities are apparent.

The general lack of a regularly recoverable burial rite does not mean that human remains were disposed of with any less respect, or that such ceremonies were no longer the occasion of elaborate rituals; it just means that, whatever they did with the dead, we cannot regularly find it (Brück 1995). Deposits in rivers may have been associated with skeletal remains; there is also some evidence for excarnation and continued use of cremation. Whatever methods of disposal were adopted, the ancestors no longer played the same central role as before, and new forms of social activity, with their related material culture, were introduced. Four such themes can be recognized.

The most obvious is the conspicuous consumption of wealth through the ritual deposition of bronze. Such deposits were an indication of an individual's status and, in particular, control over access to rare materials and technologies; whether as part of funeral ceremonies or as gifts to the gods, such deposits could be highly public statements about an individual's identity. To modern eyes, such a practice may seem an inexplicable waste, but the value of bronze may have lain in the status conferred by the ability to acquire it, to possess it and to discard it, and its use in the demonstration of such status, as much as in any functional utility as a tool.

The second theme is warfare. The use of slashing swords and armour suggests a new form of combat, and a new status for the fully armoured warrior. The edges of many swords show signs of use, but the shields and helmets appear too thin to have offered much protection in battle, and may have been more for display, though one shield seems to have been pierced by a spear. The swords and sheet metal armour were certainly some of the most elaborate products of the Bronze Age smiths, requiring many complex skills. Whether such weapons were worn in real battles, or in symbolic rituals of warfare, or simply in showy parade, they were undoubtedly a very obvious symbol of power.

The third theme concerns feasting, the other main function for which sheet bronze was used. Cauldrons and their associated flesh-hooks and buckets represent the material evidence of the ritualized preparation and serving of meat and drink, while finds of pottery and animal bones from some sites have also been interpreted in this way.

Finally, wheeled vehicles represented the most complex technological achievements of the Bronze Age, demanding high levels of skill in carpentry, metalwork, leatherwork and animal management. The uses to which such wagons were put are not clear. There may have been utilitarian versions, but others probably had a significant ritual role; wheeled vehicles have remained a favourite theme for lavish expenditure and symbolic display ever since. The recovery of a hoard of vehicle parts near the summit of Horsehope, Peeblesshire, indicates something of the possibilities.

These new areas of social activity show the relationship between prestige, material culture and technology; the demand for such items was a powerful stimulus to the development of technical skills by innovation and imitation. Control over access to such items and the skill to produce them was an important basis for prestige in Later Bronze Age society and a means of demonstrating it. The importance of feasting links these ideas to the consumption of food, but the full articulation of the system of prestige goods to the agricultural economy is not clear. The intensification of agricultural production, the increasing signs of land division, and the development of the salt industry all suggest that control over the production and distribution of food was also an important feature of Later Bronze Age society.

The material evidence for these prestige activities assumes a high profile in the archaeological record, creating an inevitable emphasis on the hierarchical nature of Later Bronze Age society, but it is not clear how extreme such inequalities were or how they were manifested in daily life. Nor are these relationships the only ones of interest, though they may be the most obvious. The emerging role of specialist craft producers has been discussed above. Relationships of age and gender may also have been changing at this time, and may have been more meaningful for most people's lives, even if it is difficult to detect them archaeologically. The changing nature of pottery produced in the Later Bronze Age, at least in southern Britain, provides one possible insight into such relations, and suggests that the domestic rituals of preparing, serving and consuming food were being ordered in new ways throughout society (Barrett 1989).

## BRITAIN IN WIDER PERSPECTIVE

Britain was not isolated, and we have already seen some of the evidence for contacts in the form of boats and continental imports. The links ran much deeper, however, and can be seen in a wide range of stylistic, technological, economic and ritual developments that affected many areas of temperate Europe at this time (Coles and Harding 1979, 459–532). They are particularly clear in the material culture of the elite, and demonstrate the existence of social relationships through which knowledge of new styles and technologies could be transmitted, and through which the movement of people and objects could be facilitated.

New industries such as salt and textiles were matched by similar developments elsewhere in Europe, as were other changes in the agricultural economy. New crops, more emphasis on storage, increased evidence for territorial division and, ultimately, field systems are all seen throughout Europe, especially in the north and west, though the precise chronology is regionally very variable.

Close contacts with continental Europe can be seen in many features of Bronze Age material culture, most obviously in metalwork, where both style and technology show similar patterns of development (O'Connor 1980). The ornament styles of the Taunton phase link Britain particularly closely to northern Europe, but later connections are to western and central Europe. The bronze industries of southern Britain show especially close links with those of northern France, and the Carp's Tongue sword assemblage is distributed from south-eastern England along the Atlantic coast of Europe. Some new styles are part of even more widespread networks of interaction: complex casting and sheet technologies were developed throughout much of Europe to provide objects for new forms of social prestige, especially vessels, arms and armour. Though the basic themes are standard, there is a high degree of regional variation: cauldrons and flesh-hooks are confined to the west and north-west, while buckets and cups are more common in central Europe; swords and sheet armour are found in most areas, but Britain has only swords, shields and helmets, not the breast-plates and greaves known elsewhere.

Britain can be seen as part of a wider north-west European zone in the later Bronze Age, including parts of northern France and the Low Countries. This zone was united not only by these shared technical and stylistic traditions, but also by common developments in ritual activity. Throughout the region, the long-established Bronze Age burial tradition largely disappeared, and deposition in watery places became common. This north-western zone is sharply differentiated from another cultural province in central Europe, which extended as far west as central and southern France. There the Later Bronze Age, though sharing many of the technical and stylistic innovations, is distinguished by the Urnfield tradition of cremation burials; many of the objects buried with these cremations are precisely the types that turn up in the watery deposits of north-western Europe.

## CURRENT PROBLEMS

One of the main themes of this chapter has been the uncertainty of many current interpretations of the available evidence. The framework for a reliable chronology has been established, and a better understanding is emerging of the nature of some parts of the surviving record. Nevertheless, the picture is very uncertain, and the evidence patchy.

In many areas, little is yet known about the nature of human occupation in the Later Bronze Age. This is particularly true of parts of western and northern Britain. It is precisely these areas that were most affected by the climatic and environmental changes of the late second millennium, and a major problem for the future is to investigate the nature of settlement in these areas, and more fully to assess the extent and speed of changes and the degree to which they may be attributable to external environmental factors rather than internal social forces.

Another problem needing investigation is the regional variability of settlement. Where detailed surveys have been carried out, one regular result has been the very fine-grained variation in the nature of settlement systems and their histories of long-term change. This makes it difficult to extrapolate from one set of evidence to a wider scale, but raises important questions about the social groupings that lie behind such patterns.

Although archaeological understanding of some bronze finds, especially deposits in watery places, has improved enormously in recent years, there are still major problems with other find types, such as dryland hoards, objects from settlements and the many so-called 'stray finds'. These make up a large part of the record, but are still little understood. There are also many questions still to be answered about the organization of bronze production.

Fundamental problems also remain for our understanding of the nature of the changes in Later Bronze Age society. The emergence of new forms of ritual and new sources of prestige and authority, the connections between changes in agriculture and the elite activities of feasting and conspicuous consumption, and the nature of social relationships and differences of age, gender and status are some of the key problems that await more detailed examination.

## Key texts

Barrett, J. and Bradley, R. (eds) 1980. *Settlement and society in the British later Bronze Age*. Oxford: British Archaeological Reports British Series 83.

Bradley, R., 1990. *The passage of arms: an archaeological analysis of prehistoric hoards and votive deposits*. Cambridge: Cambridge University Press, 97–154.

Fleming, A., 1988. *The Dartmoor Reaves: investigating prehistoric land divisions*. London: Batsford.

Megaw, J.V.S. and Simpson, D.D.A. (eds) 1979. *Introduction to British prehistory: from the arrival of Homo sapiens to the Claudian invasion*. Leicester: Leicester University Press, 242–343.

Pryor, F., 1991. *Flag Fen: prehistoric Fenland centre*, London: Batsford and English Heritage.

## Bibliography

Barrett, J., 1980. 'The pottery of the later Bronze age in lowland England', *Proceedings of the Prehistoric Society* 46, 297–319.

Barrett, J., 1989. 'Food, gender and metal: questions of social reproduction', in Sørensen, M.L. and Thomas, R. (eds) *The Bronze Age–Iron Age transition in Europe: aspects of continuity and change in European societies c1200 to 500 B.C.*. Oxford: British Archaeological Reports International Series S483, 304–320. (2 vols).

Barrett, J., Bradley, R. and Green, M., 1991. *Landscape, monuments and society: the archaeology of Cranborne Chase*. Cambridge: Cambridge University Press.

Bond, D., 1988. *Excavation at the North Ring, Mucking, Essex*. Chelmsford: Archaeology Section, Essex County Council.

Bradley, R. and Gordon, K., 1988. 'Human skulls from the River Thames, their dating and significance', *Antiquity* 62, 503–509.

Bradley, R., Lobb, S., Richards, J. and Robinson, M., 1980. 'Two Late Bronze Age settlements on the Kennet gravels: excavations at Aldermaston Wharf and Knight's Farm, Burghfield, Berkshire', *Proceedings of the Prehistoric Society* 46, 217–295.

Bradley, R., Entwistle, R. and Raymond, F., 1994. *Prehistoric land divisions on Salisbury Plain: the work of the Wessex Linear Ditches Project*. London: English Heritage.

Britton, D., 1971. 'The Heathery Burn Cave revisited', in Sieveking, G. de G. (ed.) *Prehistoric and Roman Studies*. London: British Museum Press, 20–38.

Brown, N., 1988. 'A Late Bronze Age enclosure at Lofts Farm, Essex', *Proceedings of the Prehistoric Society*, 54, 249–302.

Brück, J., 1995. 'A place for the dead: the role of human remains in Late Bronze Age Britain', *Proceedings of the Prehistoric Society* 61, 245–277.

Buckley, D.G. and Hedges, J.D., 1987. *The Bronze Age and Saxon settlements at Springfield Lyons, Essex: an interim report*. Chelmsford: Essex County Council.

Buckley, V. (ed.) 1990. *Burnt offerings: international contributions to burnt mound archaeology*. Dublin: Wordwell.

Burgess, C.B., 1968. 'The later Bronze Age in the British Isles and northwestern France', *Archaeological Journal* 125, 1–45.

Coles, J.M. and Harding, A.F., 1979. *The Bronze Age in Europe: an introduction to the prehistory of Europe c.2000–700 B.C.*. London: Methuen.

Cowie, T.G. and Shepherd, I.A.G., 1997. 'The Bronze Age', in Edwards, K.J. and Ralston, I.B.M. (eds) *Scotland: environment and archaeology 8000 BC–AD 1000.* Chichester: John Wiley, 151–168.

Drewett, P., 1982. 'Later Bronze Age downland economy and excavations at Black Patch, East Sussex', *Proceedings of the Prehistoric Society* 48, 321–400.

Ellison, A., 1981. 'Towards a socioeconomic model for the Middle Bronze Age in southern England', in Hodder, I., Isaac, G. and Hammond, N. (eds) *Pattern of the past: studies in honour of David Clarke.* Cambridge: Cambridge University Press, 413–448.

McOmish, D., 1996. 'East Chisenbury: ritual and rubbish in the British Bronze Age–Iron Age transition', *Antiquity* 70, 68–76.

Musson, C.R., 1991. *The Breiddin hillfort: a later prehistoric settlement in the Welsh Marches,* London: Council for British Archaeology Research Report 76.

Needham, S.P., 1990. *The Petters Late Bronze Age metalwork: an analytical study of Thames Valley metal-working in its settlement context.* London: British Museum Press.

Needham, S.P., 1991. *Excavation and salvage at Runnymede Bridge, 1978: the Late Bronze Age waterfront site.* London: British Museum Press.

Needham, S.P., 1996. 'Chronology and periodisation in the British Bronze Age', *Acta Archaeologica* 67, 121–140.

Northover, J.P., 1982. 'The exploration of the long-distance movement of bronze in Bronze and early Iron Age Europe', *Bulletin of the University of London Institute of Archaeology* 19, 45–72.

O'Connor, B., 1980. *Cross-Channel relations in the later Bronze Age.* Oxford: British Archaeological Reports International Series 91.

Pryor, F., 1992. 'Special section: current research at Flag Fen, Peterborough', *Antiquity* 66, 439–531.

Spratt, D.A., 1989. *Linear earthworks of the Tabular Hills, north-east Yorkshire.* Sheffield: J.R. Collis Publications.

*Chapter Seven*

# The Iron Age

## Colin Haselgrove

**INTRODUCTION**

The Iron Age is usually taken as spanning the period from the later eighth century BC until the first century AD. No single archaeological horizon clearly marks the transition from the Late Bronze Age, however, while the Roman conquest took three generations to complete and affected only part of the island. Many attributes once used to define the Iron Age – including the construction of hillforts and the development of a new repertoire of domestic pottery – can now be traced back into the Late Bronze Age. The adoption of iron technology was itself a lengthy process, difficult to follow in its earlier stages due to a lack of relevant evidence. Although the new metal was certainly worked from early in the first millennium BC, it initially seems to have had only limited impact, and it was not until the Later Iron Age that major social and economic changes occurred.

The period is characterized above all by its plentiful and diverse settlement evidence. Over 3,000 dwelling sites survive as upstanding monuments, while almost as many again are recorded as cropmarks. They range from individual farmsteads occupied by a single household to hillforts holding communities of several hundred. The imposing drystone towers (brochs) of Atlantic Scotland are architecturally amongst the most sophisticated structures in Iron Age Europe, while the linear earthwork complexes ('territorial oppida') of south-east England are among the largest. Significant spatial and temporal variations exist: open settlements of village size are characteristic of eastern England, while large hillforts occur primarily in Wessex, the Welsh Marches and eastern Scotland. Many settlement types in western coastal regions are extremely long-lived and so cannot be considered characteristic solely of the Iron Age; these include small defended enclosures called raths and duns and the artificial lake dwellings known as crannogs.

Iron Age landscapes also included field systems, trackways and linear boundaries. Unless directly associated with settlements, these are difficult to distinguish from their Bronze Age and Roman counterparts. An important recent advance has been the recognition in the English–Scottish borders of extensive traces of upland cultivation, termed cord rig. Non-habitation sites are rare, but include Later Iron Age religious sites, as well as production sites for salt, shale and quernstones. Throughout the Iron Age, most of the dead were disposed of in ways that leave no archaeological traces; visible burial rites are restricted to a few regions.

The lack of burials, coupled with the sudden decline in hoarding from the eighth century BC, has significantly affected the nature of surviving Iron Age material culture, most of which comes from settlements, where diagnostic metalwork is relatively rare. Most such objects are isolated

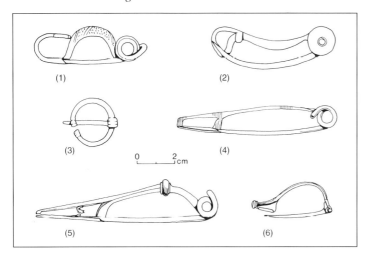

*Figure 7.1* Selected Iron Age brooch types: 1. Early La Tène; 2. Involuted: 3. Penannular; 4. Nauheim; 5. Boss-on-bow; 6. Aucissa.

votive finds from east-flowing rivers like the Thames and Witham, or come from hoards of late date. Even small items like brooches (Figure 7.1) – useful for dating due to their affinities with the continental Hallstatt and La Tène cultures – do not become common until the very end of the period. By default, pottery generally forms the basis of settlement chronology, but outside southern and eastern England and the Scottish islands, it, too, is scarce and shows little typological change over several centuries. Its place was presumably taken by organic containers which survive only in exceptional conditions. Because of soil acidity, sizeable assemblages of animal bone are similarly missing from sites in northern and western Britain. A further contrast with the south and east is the near-total absence of grain storage pits, common in chalk and limestone areas, where they form a major source of artefactual and environmental data.

Based on changes in decorated pottery styles, the Iron Age to the south and east of a line drawn from the Bristol Channel to the Humber is often sub-divided into three phases: Early (*c.* 800/700–300 BC), Middle (*c.* 300–100 BC) and Late (*c.* 100 BC–AD 43/84). To the north and west, the period is difficult to divide into meaningful phases, except at purely local levels. It is sufficient here to distinguish between an Earlier Iron Age, lasting until the fourth century BC, which shares many attributes with the Later Bronze Age, and a Later Iron Age, starting *c.* 300 BC, when insular societies entered a new period of transition. This reached its climax in the first century AD, after Julius Caesar's conquest of northern France and invasions of Britain had brought the south into direct contact with the Roman world.

## THE RECENT DEVELOPMENT OF IRON AGE STUDIES

Until the 1960s, perceptions of the period were shaped by Fox's (1932) classic division of Britain into Highland and Lowland zones. With its poorer soils and climate, the Highland zone was thought to have been sparsely occupied by pastoralists, in contrast to the Lowland zone which was densely populated by mixed farmers. This latter region, nearer the Continent, was also seen as relatively open to externally induced cultural change, unlike the conservative Highland zone where innovations were taken up at best gradually. This emphasis on continental influence accorded with Caesar's mention of Belgic immigrants from northern France, whom archaeologists like Hawkes (1960) saw as responsible for introducing coinage, cremation and wheel-made pottery in the first century BC (during Hawkes' Iron Age C). Earlier invaders were similarly credited with the introduction of iron and of hillforts (Iron Age A), and with the subsequent imposition of continental Early La Tène culture in certain regions (Iron Age B).

In the 1960s, this model was challenged as intellectual fashions changed. In a seminal study, Hodson (1964) argued that few of the supposed invasions were represented by clear-cut archaeological horizons. Instead, he pointed to long-term cultural continuities that distinguished the British Iron Age from that of continental Europe, notably the preference for circular buildings and the lack of burials. With few exceptions, cross-Channel trade provided sufficient explanation for those changes of artefact style that occurred. Support came from radiocarbon dating, which freed northern and western Britain from chronological dependence on sequences developed in areas nearer the Continent. Scottish and Welsh dates showed that Highland zone developments could be as early as in lowland Britain, if not more precocious. These included the occupation of defended hilltop settlements, now shown to have Late Bronze Age origins (Ralston 1979).

Subsequent surveys of the period by Cunliffe (1991; 1995) and others (e.g. Hill 1995a; James and Rigby 1997) have tended to downplay externally induced cultural change, apart from the Late Iron Age, for which intensive contact between south-east England and the Roman world after 50 BC has taken over the role once accorded to Caesar's Belgic settlers. The emphasis has shifted to economic and social questions, prompted in part by Peacock's (1968) use of thin-sectioning to investigate pottery production. This revealed an unexpected degree of centralization in the manufacture of various styles of fine decorated pottery from south-west England, implying that their distributions owed more to regional exchange networks than to cultural factors. Scientific analysis has also provided valuable information on the composition and source of metal artefacts.

As a result of widespread application of flotation techniques, cereal cultivation is now attested widely in the Highland zone, undermining the simple environmental dichotomy advanced by Fox. Mixed agriculture was evidently the preferred subsistence strategy for most communities, but local factors, such as altitude and soil type, were crucial in determining the balance between crops and livestock. Pollen diagrams show significant regional and chronological variations in the nature of the human impact on the landscape during the Iron Age.

Radiocarbon dating was vitally important in liberating Iron Age chronology from its dependence on diffusionist dating principles. Its routine use is gradually providing a satisfactory chronology for different site types, although problems remain. Due to the plateau in the calibration curve *c*. 800–400 cal. BC, dates are very imprecise over the period when iron was coming into wider use. The advent of accelerator dating, however, means that tiny samples of short-lived material like grain – which are more likely to be contemporary with their depositional context than the charcoal needed for conventional determinations – can now be dated. Radiocarbon now underpins the dating of the Wessex ceramic sequence, while archaeomagnetism, dendrochronology and luminescence are also coming into wider use.

## AGRICULTURE AND SETTLEMENT

Systematic investigation of farming settlements began with Bersu's (1940) excavations at Little Woodbury near Salisbury. His report was a model for its time, putting forward a convincing reconstruction of the agricultural role of such sites. As well as showing that the inhabitants lived in large, circular, timber buildings, he identified a range of ancillary structures such as grain storage pits, working hollows, and two- or four-post settings, interpreted as drying racks and raised storage buildings. The sequence of palisaded enclosure later replaced by a banked and ditched compound has turned out to be common, although by no means universal, at Iron Age sites.

Cattle and sheep were the principal livestock, their relative importance varying with the local environment. Pig played a subsidiary role and dog, small horses and domestic fowl were kept. Wild species were of negligible dietary importance, although fish may be under-represented,

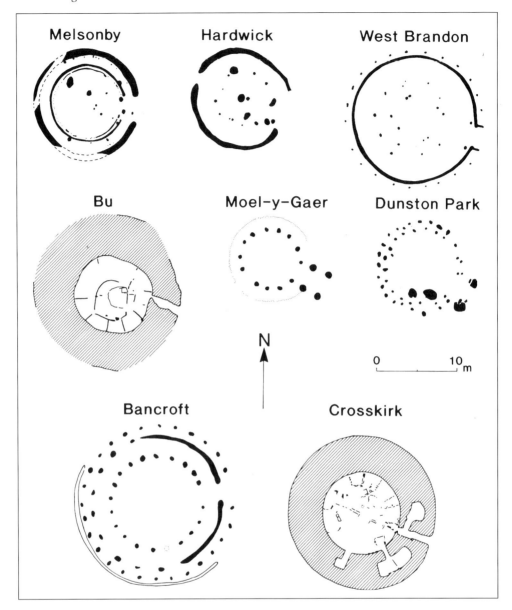

*Figure 7.2* Different types of circular structures.

and many coastal sites depended on shellfish. During the first millennium BC, hulled barley superseded naked barley, and spelt wheat replaced emmer as the main cereal crops, although the timing of these transitions varied considerably. In north-east England, emmer remained the principal wheat on upland sites, long after lower-lying farms had switched to spelt (Van der Veen 1992). In the Late Iron Age, bread wheat began to be grown regularly in regions including the south Midlands, north-east England and south-west Scotland, a development almost certainly linked to the colonization of heavy claylands. Other plant crops included beans, peas, and flax; wild plants such as chess, or rye-brome, were also exploited.

Large-scale settlement excavations are now commonplace; indeed, north-west England is the only sizeable region where such sites remain unknown, while Wessex and the upper Thames Valley are among the most intensively investigated. Most sites reveal evidence of circular domestic buildings, generally between 6 and 15 m in diameter (Figure 7.2). Two main traditions exist: the double-ring and the single-ring forms, in which the main weight of the conical roof was taken respectively on an inner ring of posts and on the wall-head, with or without a central post. Methods of wall construction included stake- and post-rings; ring-grooves to accommodate closely set upright posts or planks; ring-plates; and dry-stone walls. Often only the drainage gullies around such structures remain to mark their positions.

Not all circular buildings were dwellings, some serving other purposes including as shrines. Various regional and temporal trends can be discerned. In southern Britain, very large round-houses are a feature of the earlier first millennium BC, and the average size of buildings diminished markedly thereafter; in the north, substantial dwellings were constructed throughout the period (Hingley 1992). The monumental brochs of Atlantic Scotland and Cornish courtyard houses, both innovations of the Later Iron Age, represent variations on this theme. Rectangular buildings of sill-beam construction are found on many Late Iron Age sites in south-east England, while earlier examples occasionally occur, like the well-preserved wattle and plank-built structures recently excavated at Goldcliff (Gwent). Another structural type found in south-west England and in Scotland is the souterrain: probably primarily for underground storage, these tunnel-like structures may also have had ritual functions.

Enclosed farmsteads occupied by single households were the dominant settlement type in most of Britain. These can be rectilinear, curvilinear or irregular in plan, and enclose between 0.2 ha and more than 1 ha (Figure 7.3). In northern England, small sub-rectangular or D-shaped enclosures like West Brandon (Co. Durham) are characteristic, whereas oval and curvilinear settlements predominate in southern and eastern Scotland. Many settlements in Wales and south-west England have widely spaced multiple embankments – as at Collfryn (Powys) – sometimes accompanied by funnel entrances, a feature shared with the banjo enclosures of Wessex. Such features presumably relate to the needs of animal husbandry, but few such details show clear links to their inhabitants' subsistence base. The small, sub-rectangular enclosure at Fisherwick (Staffordshire), for example, was set in a largely pastoral landscape: identical looking sites elsewhere practised mixed farming.

Many habitation sites passed through both enclosed and open phases, including Bishopstone (Sussex) and Winnall Down (Hampshire), which oscillated between the two. At Dryburn Bridge in East Lothian, a Late Bronze Age palisaded enclosure was succeeded by an unenclosed Iron Age settlement; while at Thorpe Thewles (Cleveland), the enclosed farmstead was superseded by a larger open settlement during the Later Iron Age (Figure 7.4). In some areas, unenclosed settlements were apparently the principal type, as in Scotland north of the Forth, but even in regions where enclosures predominate, open settlements were probably far more common than now appears the case, due to the difficulties of recognizing them as cropmarks. Their size and form varied considerably from individual houses scattered amongst fields, like Kilphedir (Sutherland), or rows of buildings, as at Douglasmuir (Angus) and Roxby (North Yorkshire), to looser aggregations of households each set within their own compound, such as Dalton Parlours (West Yorkshire) or Dragonby (Lincolnshire).

Aggregated settlements were common in eastern England during the Later Iron Age. Such sites pose problems: How many buildings were standing at once? What proportion were residential? What size of household inhabited each dwelling? At some sites like Little Waltham (Essex), frequent rebuilding has created a palimpsest of remains that may exaggerate the actual size of the community at any one time. At Fengate (Cambridgeshire), many buildings were probably

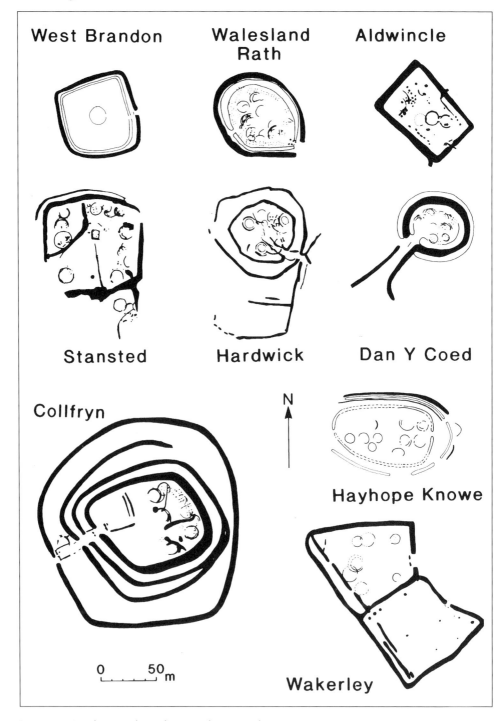

*Figure 7.3* Rectilinear and curvilinear settlement enclosures.

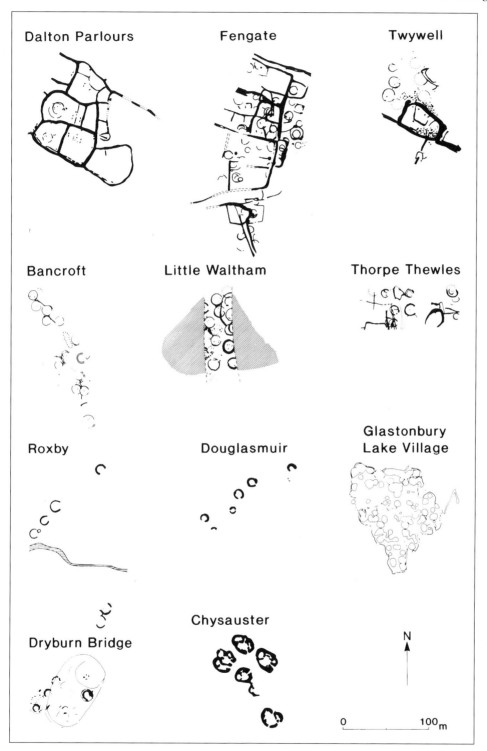

*Figure 7.4* Plans of open and aggregated settlements.

ancillary structures and byres, not houses, and the excavator's estimate of the Later Iron Age population is five households (Pryor 1984). A rather larger population has been suggested for the Glastonbury lake village (Somerset), reaching a maximum of 14 households in the early first century BC, before increasing wet conditions led to contraction and abandonment (Coles and Minnitt 1995). A number of Roman small towns seem to originate in Late Iron Age aggregated settlements, as at Baldock (Hertfordshire).

In the upper Thames Valley of Oxfordshire, different settlement types are seen on the upper and lower gravel terraces (Lambrick 1992). The second terrace is dominated by aggregated settlements like Abingdon Ashville and Gravelly Guy, with separate areas for pit storage and domestic occupation. These sites may have operated communally, each with its strip of arable at the terrace edge, but sharing pasture away from the river. A different settlement type is found on the first terrace, reflecting an expansion of pastoral farming during the Later Iron Age. These are smaller, self-contained ditched or hedged enclosures with funnel entrances, as at Hardwick. Lastly, a scatter of short-lived seasonally occupied sites were established on the floodplain to exploit summer grazing. Seasonal settlements are known elsewhere, some linked to part-time craft specialization, as at Eldon's Seat (Dorset), where Kimmeridge Shale bracelets were manufactured. The wetland settlement at Meare (Somerset) is now interpreted as the site of a seasonal fair.

The main period of hillfort building in southern England occurred during the sixth and fifth centuries BC. However, the defence of hill-tops in Britain has a long and varied history, with construction peaking at different times in different regions. In north and central Wales, for example, the earliest hillforts like the Breiddin (Powys) succeeded Bronze Age enclosures, whereas in East Anglia and the Weald, most hillforts were built in the Later Iron Age. Scottish sites like Eildon Hill North (Roxburghshire) and Traprain Law (East Lothian) were apparently abandoned as centres of habitation before the classic southern British hillforts were even built, although they were reoccupied during the Roman Iron Age and may have retained a ceremonial role during the intervening centuries. In southern England, the earliest hillforts occur from the Cotswolds along the chalk downs of north Wessex as far as the Chiltern scarp.

These early hillforts comprise two main categories: smaller, well-fortified sites with dense internal activity, as at Crickley Hill (Gloucestershire) or Moel-y-Gaer (Powys), and larger hilltop enclosures like Bathampton Down (Avon), with scant evidence of any occupation. At this stage, the defences usually consisted of a single earth or stone rampart, often of box-framed or timber-laced construction, with a relatively simple entrance. After *c.* 350 BC, many early hillforts in Wessex and elsewhere were abandoned, while a smaller number, generally known as developed hillforts, were extended and often massively elaborated. These were usually protected by multiple glacis-style earthworks, constructed so that the external face of each dump rampart formed a continuous profile with a V-shaped ditch, while entrances often consisted of long passages protected by complex outworks. Good examples of developed hillforts include Cadbury Castle (Somerset), Croft Ambrey (Herefordshire), Danebury (Hampshire) and Maiden Castle (Dorset).

Although neither Danebury – where more than half the interior has been excavated – nor Maiden Castle can be considered typical of British sites, between them they exemplify the main features of both early and developed hillforts, as well as illustrating the processes by which certain hillforts rose to dominate their locality between the fourth and second centuries BC. Their earlier occupation phases were characterized by well-ordered layouts, and by possession of substantial food storage capacities. At Danebury (Cunliffe 1993), the northern interior was occupied by rows of four-post storage structures – later replaced by a mass of storage pits – while a limited number of circular buildings were constructed in its southern half and around the circumference (Figure 7.5). At this stage, finds apart from pottery were relatively sparse at either hillfort.

During their developed phases, the defences and entrances of both hillforts were repeatedly maintained and embellished, while the interiors show evidence of intensive occupation of a highly organized character. While the broad outlines of its plan remained unchanged, much of the southern half of Danebury was given over to large four- and six-post structures aligned in rows along internal roads, while circular buildings were now predominantly in the northern part. The centre was cleared and a group of larger rectangular structures, which may have been shrines, was erected. At both sites, the quantity of material deposited increased substantially, attesting a wide range of crafts and extensive external contacts.

The process by which Danebury and Maiden Castle developed into the dominant hillforts in their respective regions is now becoming clearer (Sharples 1991). Initially, this apparently involved the abandonment of weaker hillforts and farmsteads nearby, whose inhabitants moved into the fort. In time, the enlarged communities successfully overcame more distant rivals, whose hillforts were demilitarized and their occupants forced to live in undefended homesteads, leaving a minority of pre-eminent hillforts, each controlling a well-defined territory. Increasingly, the defences came to symbolize the prestige of individual hillfort communities, and defeated neighbours were probably made to labour on the earthworks, thereby reinforcing their dependent status.

By no means all later southern British hillforts conform to this model. In Cambridgeshire, late

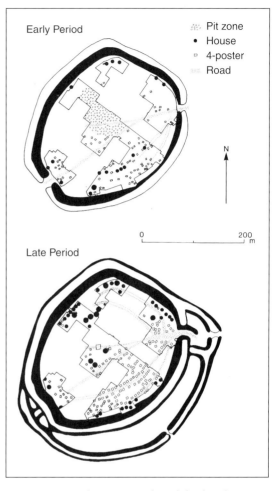

*Figure 7.5*  Danebury in its early and developed stages. *Source*: Cunliffe 1993

ringworks like Arbury and Stonea Camps are almost devoid of occupation, suggesting use for occasional communal gatherings, or in periods of danger. The same is probably true of larger hill-top enclosures dating to the Earlier Iron Age, while – despite the numerous hut circles visible in their interiors – it is difficult to believe that many hillforts at high altitude were ever occupied all year round.

In the second and first centuries BC, a new type of fortified site made its appearance in southern England. Generally known as 'enclosed oppida' (from the term Caesar used to describe fortified sites he encountered in Gaul), they are noticeably larger and more accessible than most hillforts. They range from plateau fortifications such as Bigbury (Kent) and Wheathampstead (Hertfordshire) to slope or valley-bottom enclosures like Oram's Arbour, Winchester, and Salmonsbury (Gloucestershire). Most had been abandoned by the Roman conquest. At some examples, including Braughing-Puckeridge (Hertfordshire) and Canterbury (which appears to succeed Bigbury), fortified enclosures form the nucleus of larger valley-bottom settlements.

In the Later Iron Age, the Bronze Age practice of constructing linear earthworks and landscape boundaries resumed. Examples occur widely in southern Britain, from the Cotswolds to

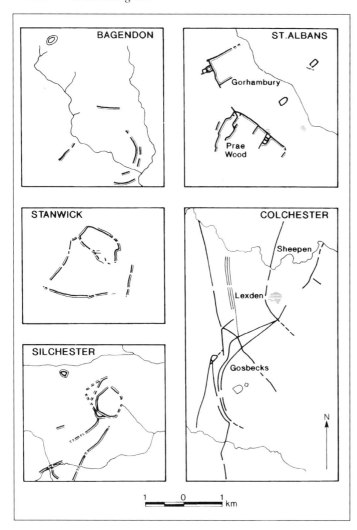

*Figure 7.6* Plans of territorial oppida.

East Anglia and East Yorkshire. The 'territorial oppida' of south-east England – with their imposing but discontinuous earthworks defining large tracts of land around places of social and political importance – must be included in this phenomenon (Figure 7.6). These sites do not represent urban centres in any modern sense. At St Albans (*Verulamium*), much of the delimited area was occupied by individual settlements (both elite dwellings and ordinary farmsteads) and their fields, while other sectors were used for burial, ritual and metalworking. The surrounding earthworks were probably constructed more for symbolic purposes than for defence. Only Silchester (*Calleva*, Hampshire), where a regular street plan was laid out in the late first century BC, has so far yielded evidence for a large nucleated settlement.

Territorial oppida appeared later than the enclosed series and themselves fall into two groups. The first, including Colchester (*Camulodunum*), St Albans and Silchester, were important pre-conquest centres that continued into the Roman period; the second group came to prominence after AD 43 due to their location on the frontiers of the newly established Roman province. Bagendon (Gloucestershire) and Stanwick (North Yorkshire) are examples. Many oppida contained cult centres, while coins bearing their names attest to their political importance. These associations are not surprising, given that the enactment of religious rituals and the reproduction of political power are linked in most traditional societies. Oppida were extensively involved in long-distance trade with the Roman world; in several cases, their rulers had probably entered into formal treaties with the Emperor.

## RELIGION AND BURIAL

Before the first century BC, domestic settlements provided the setting for ritual activity, including feasting and the sacrifice of domestic animals, household objects and sometimes people. Evidence comes in the form of remains periodically deposited in storage pits and at entrances or boundaries (Hill 1995b). On smaller farms, such rituals took place once every few years, but at the hillforts, which represented the main focus of communities, they were noticeably more frequent. These periodic rituals must have played an important social role, reaffirming the obligations between different sectors of the population. Religious beliefs were influential in the laying out of sites: both roundhouse and enclosure entrances are often oriented directly towards either the equinox or the midwinter solstice.

During the Late Iron Age, recognizable shrines and sanctuaries appear in much of southern Britain (Figure 7.7). These range from isolated examples like Harlow (Essex) and Hayling Island (Hampshire) – which with their associated offerings of brooches and coins resemble early Gallo-Roman temples – to rectangular buildings within settlements identified as shrines because they differ from normal domestic structures, as at Danebury, Heathrow (Middlesex) and Stansted Airport (Essex). Many shrines within settlements probably remain un-recognized, because at the time of excavation such structures were not anticipated; examples have been claimed at Baldock and Kelvedon (Essex).

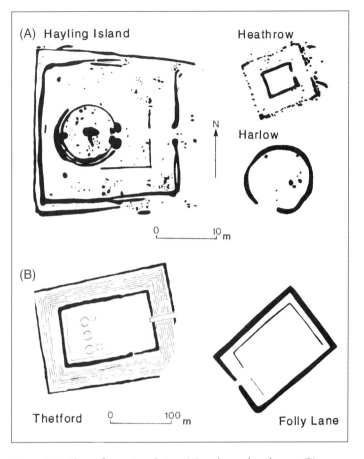

*Figure 7.7* Plans of Iron Age shrines (A) and sacred enclosures (B).

Many archaeologists prefer ritual deposition as the explanation for the spectacular early first-century BC precious metal torc hoards found within a large polygonal enclosure at Snettisham (Norfolk), amounting to over 30 kg of gold (Stead 1991). Other cult enclosures include Fison Way (Norfolk), Gosbeck's, Colchester, and Folly Lane, St Albans. At Folly Lane, a mass of burnt material including chain mail and horse harness was found in a pit beside a shaft at the centre of the enclosure. A cult role must also be inferred for the many water springs that have produced concentrations of Iron Age coins such as Wanborough (Surrey) and Essendon (Hertfordshire), where weapons accompanied the coins. Late Iron Age metalwork finds from lakes and bogs reflect the same general trends, although the objects selected as offerings vary regionally. Amongst the most spectacular votive deposits are the weaponry, horse harness and vehicle fittings from Llyn Cerrig Bach in Anglesey (Fox 1946).

The dead were mainly disposed of by excarnation, or by scattering their cremated remains. The principal exceptions both have strong continental affinities. In the Arras tradition of East Yorkshire, inhumations were placed under small barrows defined by rectangular ditched enclosures, often grouped in large cemeteries like Burton Fleming-Rudston. A few high status graves were accompanied by two-wheeled carts (Figure 7.8), as at Wetwang Slack (Dent 1985). These traits were originally interpreted as evidence of Early La Tène immigrants from northern France, but differences from continental practice are apparent and a plausible alternative is to

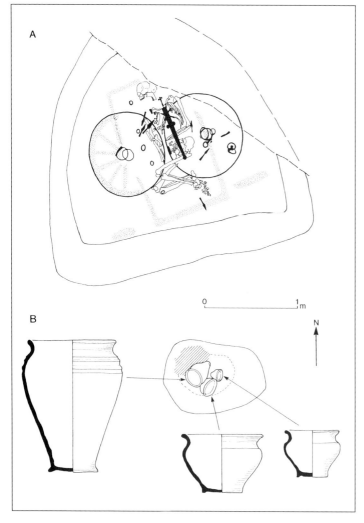

A

B

0    1 m

N

*Figure 7.8* Grave plans: A. cart burial from Wetwang Slack; B. cremation burial from Westhampnett.
*Sources*: A – Dent 1985; B – Fitzpatrick 1997

envisage a ruling group with far-flung contacts adopting exotic burial rites. Although the earliest Arras burials could belong to the late fifth century BC, the tradition peaked in the third and second centuries BC.

The Aylesford cremation rite, introduced into south-east England in the late second century BC, displays close affinities with burial practice in northern France. Burial grounds are typically small, but larger cemeteries are known at King Harry Lane, St Albans, and Westhampnett, near Chichester (Fitzpatrick 1997). Most crema-tions were accompanied by at most two pottery vessels and occasionally items such as brooches or sets of toilet instruments. In some cases, the cremations lay within enclo-sures or clusters that suggest kin-groups. A few richer burials occur, mostly north of the Thames, as at Baldock and Welwyn Garden City (Hertfordshire). Their con-tents emphasize drinking and feasting: Italian wine amphorae and serving vessels are accompanied by indigenous, high status items such as buckets, hearth furniture and gaming sets. Warrior equipment is virtually absent from Aylesford burials, although it does occur in some of the East Yorkshire graves and in a few individual burials else-where. At Mill Hill, Deal (Kent), for example, the grave of a young man dating to the late third century BC contained a sword, shield and bronze head-dress (Parfitt 1995).

Other less prominent Iron Age burial traditions occur in several regions. Cist graves were used in Cornwall between the fifth century BC and the first century AD, while a tradition of crouched inhumation burial developed in Dorset during the first century BC. With the aid of radiocarbon dating, a number of unfurnished inhumation cemeteries are now attributable to the Later Iron Age from places as far apart as Kent and the Lothian plain. Also plausibly of Iron Age date are Lindow Man (Cheshire) and some of the other bog body finds from north-west England, many of whom appear to have been ritually executed (Stead *et al.* 1986).

## PRODUCTION AND EXCHANGE

The manufacture and exchange of finished goods became increasingly complex during the Iron Age (Morris 1994). Three levels of craft activity are identifiable: output to meet individual household or community needs; more specialized products for wider distribution; and luxury goods for the wealthiest sections of society. For most commodities, little or no evidence of production sites has survived, and the finished goods provide our main guide to the organization and scale of activity. Only a minority of craft workers are likely to have been full-time specialists; many activities, such as coastal salt production, metal ore extraction and pottery manufacture, could have been carried out by ordinary agricultural communities at slack times.

Significant technological advances during the Iron Age included the introduction of lathes for turning wooden and shale objects; the potter's wheel; and the ability to make glass beads and bracelets. In bronze-working, the use of lost-wax casting became widespread, and both gilding and tin-plating were introduced late in the period. Other important innovations included the development of the rotary quern for grinding grain and the introduction of iron-tipped plough shares, which greatly facilitated the cultivation of heavier soils.

Successfully forging iron into durable artefacts required new skills and techniques, and was extremely time-consuming, helping to explain why iron objects were relatively scarce until after the mid-first millennium BC. Unlike bronze, iron could not be cast because the available bowl furnaces were unable to achieve sufficiently high temperatures. On smelting, a spongy mass ('bloom') collected in the furnace base, and had to be repeatedly heated and hammered to remove slag and impurities. Since artefacts produced in this way were not inherently superior to bronze, the principal reasons why iron was adopted were presumably that most parts of Britain have access to iron ore and that wrought iron could be forged into shapes that bronze could not. While the earliest iron artefacts – like the sword and sickle from the Llyn Fawr hoard (Glamorgan) – are simply bigger versions of existing bronze types, new tool types, better suited to the tensile properties of wrought iron, were gradually developed, including cutting discs, shaft hole axes, shears, and tongs. Many types of edge tools in use by the Later Iron Age remained essentially unchanged until the Industrial Revolution (Figure 7.9).

Most Iron Age settlements yield evidence of iron smithing, although this may simply indicate that metalworkers visited periodically to make and repair implements. Smelting was generally carried out away from the homestead. Two exceptions are the early Iron Age settlement at Brooklands (Surrey), where areas were set aside for smelting and for forging, and the Later Iron Age defended site at Bryn y Castell (Gwynedd), where furnaces inside the enclosure were used for refining raw blooms; a more extensive iron-working area was located outside. At both sites, the output was probably sufficient only for local needs.

Comparatively few artefacts show evidence for advanced techniques like the deliberate use of steel, or even quenching and tempering, but smiths gradually learned enough about the properties of different ores to choose those best suited for particular tasks; thus implements like adzes and large sickles were generally manufactured from high-phosphorous ores, while high-carbon ores were used for chisels (Ehrenreich 1985). As the period progressed, the best ores – from areas like Northamptonshire and the Forest of Dean – were increasingly exploited. By the third century BC at latest, good quality iron was exchanged over considerable distances as standardized ingots. These were clearly of considerable value, frequently being hoarded or used as offerings. Three main forms are known: sword-shaped bars, spit-shaped bars and ploughshare bars; but detailed examination reveals over 20 types, each potentially indicating a different source. Stone weights found at many Iron Age settlements similarly imply an interest in standardization and equivalence in other spheres of exchange.

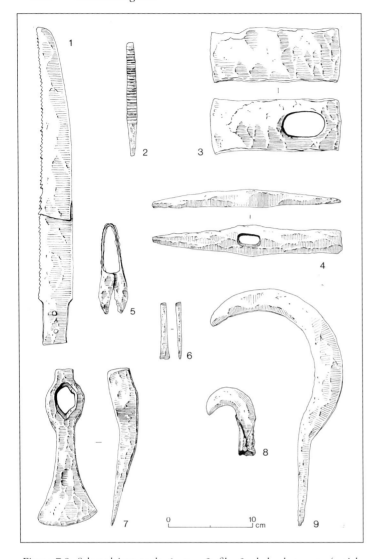

*Figure 7.9* Selected iron tools. 1. saw; 2. file; 3. sledge-hammer; 4. pick; 5. shears; 6. chisel; 7. adze; 8. bill-hook; 9. scythe.
*Sources*: 1, 2, 6–8 – Cunliffe, B.W., 1984. *Danebury: an Iron Age hillfort in Hampshire. The excavations 1969–78.* London: CBA Research Report 52; 3 – Cunliffe, B.W., 1972. 'The late Iron Age metalwork from Bulbury, Dorset', *Antiquaries Journal* 52, 293–308; 4 – author; 5 – Stead, I.M. and Rigby, V., 1989. *Verulamium: the King Harry Lane site.* London: English Heritage Archaeology Report 12; 9 – Fox 1946

As in the Later Bronze Age, many craft activities are represented by only a few specialized tools. Combs, shuttles and needles made of bone and antler, and fired clay spindle-whorls and loom-weights attest to the ubiquity of textile production and leather-working, although the restricted distribution of loom-weights within some aggregated settlements could mean that, here at least, particular households specialized in weaving. With the advent of iron tools, high quality carpentry is evident in house and vehicle construction, while finds from wetland settlements indicate the range of domestic wooden equipment: stave-built, bent-wood, hand-carved and lathe-turned containers are present, as well as ladders, ladles, hurdles and mallets. Meare housed one of the few work-shops for making glass beads known in Iron Age Europe.

The need for timber for construction, fuel and conversion to charcoal implies considerable woodland management. Another commodity in demand, for food storage and perhaps in cooking, was salt. Along the coasts of southern and eastern England, production sites abound. Produced by evaporation from sea water, salt was carried inland in standardized baked-clay ('briquetage') containers. Production and distribution net-works are known as far north as the Tees valley. Inland brine springs were also exploited. As early as the fifth century BC, salt from various West Midlands sources was being distributed up to 50 km away, rising to over 100 km by the Later Iron Age (Morris 1994). At Droitwich (Worcestershire), brine tanks, hearths and vast quantities of briquetage show that by the late first century BC salt production had become a large-scale industry.

Other important crafts included quern and pottery production, and bronze-working. In southern England, the relatively standardized Later Iron Age rotary querns from the Greensand quarry at Lodsworth (West Sussex) were distributed over much greater areas than earlier saddle querns. The latter, variable in shape and size, suggest that an activity once undertaken by individual communities had become more centralized. In northern England, however, the changeover to rotary querns saw greater reliance on local sources, at the expense of high quality products from further afield. Iron Age production thus does not conform to a simple model of increasing centralization through time.

The existing Late Bronze Age fine wares set the tone for Earlier Iron Age ceramic developments in southern Britain (Cunliffe 1991). Alongside coarse wares, most early assemblages contain a significant proportion of decorated forms such as situlate jars with finger-tip impressions, or furrowed bowls, often with a glossy red haematite coating, presumably intended to replicate the metal vessels from which they were copied (Figure 7.10). From the late sixth century BC, partly under continental influence, new forms appeared, including vessels with markedly angular profiles and pedestal bases. The Western Isles too developed distinctive decorated pottery, which was used for most of the later first millennium BC. While most wares were locally produced, a few fine wares, like the distinctive scratch-cordoned bowls of Wessex, were exchanged more widely.

During the Later Iron Age, the

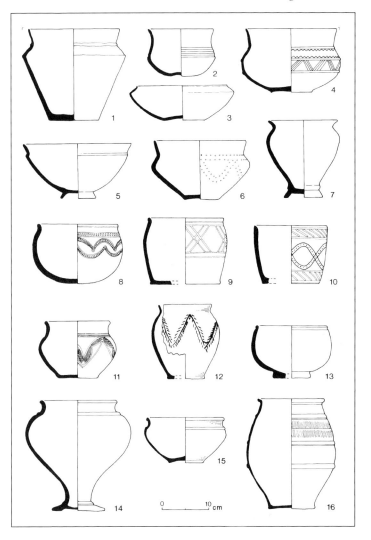

***Figure 7.10*** Selected Iron Age pottery: 1–3. Early Iron Age types; 4. scratch-cordoned bowl; 5–7. angular and pedestal forms; 8. Middle Iron Age decorated bowl; 9–10. saucepan pottery; 11. Glastonbury ware; 12. Western Isles jar; 13. Poole Harbour ware; 14-15. Late Iron Age forms; 16. butt-beaker copy.

*Sources*: 1–10, 12 and 14 – Cunliffe 1991; 11 – Coles, J. M., 1987. *Meare Village East: the excavations of A. Bulleid and H. St George Gray 1932–56*. Exeter: Somerset Levels Papers 13; 13 – Cunliffe, B.W., 1987. *Hengistbury Head, Dorset*, Vol. 1. Oxford: Oxford University Committee for Archaeology Monograph; 15 – Fitzpatrick 1997; 16 – Stead, I.M. and Rigby, V., 1989. *Verulamium: the King Harry Lane site*. London: English Heritage Archaeology Report 12

character of pottery production altered significantly. Over much of southern England, distinctive regional traditions dominated by new forms of decorated jars or bowls emerged, including a distinctive form known as 'saucepan pots'. In some areas, such as the Welsh Marches and south-west England, local workshops all but disappeared in favour of production concentrated at a few locations, wares from which were then exchanged over considerable distances (Morris 1994).

Wessex shows evidence for both local and regional distribution, although by the end of the period potters in the Wareham-Poole Harbour (Dorset) area were supplying highly standardized wares to most of the surrounding region. In much of Britain, however, localized manufacture remained the norm until the Roman conquest.

The introduction of the fast potter's wheel in the late second century BC led to the appearance in eastern and southern England of curvaceous new ceramic forms with horizontal grooves or raised cordons. Not all areas adopted the new technology, and traditional handmade vessels often continued in use alongside finer, wheel-thrown forms. When Roman pottery began to be imported in quantity after *c.* 20 BC, the new shapes – beakers, cups, dishes, flagons, lids and platters – were quickly copied. Although domestic ovens are common on settlements, there is no firm evidence for pre-Roman pottery kilns in Britain, and even wheel-thrown vessels were probably fired in simple bonfire-clamps.

Bronze luxury goods were probably made by a small number of highly skilled and possibly itinerant metalworkers, adept in working both sheet and cast metal, and conversant with continental fashions. At Gussage All Saints (Dorset), a single pit yielded enough casting moulds for 50 sets of horse gear and vehicle fittings, although the context of this operation remains uncertain (Wainwright 1979). Another relatively small settlement, at Weelsby Avenue, Grimsby (Humberside), yielded debris, including failed castings, from the manufacture of horse harness, although here the evidence suggests a longer timespan for production. The main sources of copper, tin and lead seem to have been in the west and south-west, although some metal may have been imported. From the late first century BC onward, imported Roman brass (an alloy of copper and zinc) was often used for decorative metalwork in place of tin bronze.

The categories of decorative metalwork found reflect the same social and ritual preoccupations – feasting, warfare and driving vehicles – as in the Later Bronze Age. Sheet bronze was employed for cauldrons, shields and scabbards, and to clad wooden objects like buckets and tankards, while lost-wax casting was used for chariot fittings and horse harness, and to make components of composite artefacts like mirrors and torcs. A range of decorative techniques such as engraving and repoussé work, adding coloured ornament such as coral and enamel, and plating were all used. Based on the evolving form and decoration of the objects, insular art is divided into five stages (I–V), starting in the fifth century BC and lasting to the early centuries AD (Stead 1996).

Gold and silver objects were rare until the later second century BC, when imported Gallo-Belgic gold coinage began to circulate in south-east England and hoards containing torcs were buried in some numbers. The presence at Snettisham of older torcs indicates that such objects may have been less uncommon in earlier centuries than the archaeological record now suggests. By the later first century BC, most areas of lowland Britain were striking gold and silver coinages (De Jersey 1996). Copper-alloy coinage is, however, confined to south-east England, where struck types replaced cast issues at about this time. Most later coinages bear the name of the issuing ruler in Roman letters (Figure 7.11). No British coin dies have yet been found, but several oppida have yielded baked-clay slab moulds, evidently used for minting or other forms of high status metalworking.

## ECONOMIC AND SOCIAL CHANGES

Climatic and environmental deterioration persisted well into the Iron Age. Continued retreat from upland areas and competition for land in favoured lowlands are likely to have been factors behind the construction of many early hillforts. The prominence of storage facilities confirms the importance of food supplies to such sites, many of which are in areas like southern Scotland

and the Welsh Marches, where resources would have come under pressure sooner than in predominantly lowland regions. The adoption of iron technology may also have been disruptive, undermining the position of the elites who dominated Later Bronze Age society through control of long-distance exchange. In such conditions, larger communities coalesced and competed for the best agricultural land. The territorial control needed to support such communities itself became a significant means of achieving status and power. Given the regional differences in hillfort construction, it is, however, clear that no single explanation suffices and that diverse local factors were important.

*Figure 7.11* Inscribed Iron Age coins: A. gold stater of Tasciovanus. The helmeted horseman on the reverse is brandishing a war trumpet; B. brass coin of Cunobelinus. Beneath the boar on the reverse is the name of his father, Tasciovanus, clearly inscribed; C. bronze coin of Cunobelinus, depicting a boat on the obverse and a winged Victory on the reverse.

From *c.* 400 BC, the climate started to improve, and by the end of the Iron Age was probably similar to today. This must have been significant for the agricultural changes of the Later Iron Age, when many parts of Britain saw widespread expansion of settlement onto heavier, damper soils at the expense of forest and marginal land (Haselgrove 1989). Agricultural intensification is attested by greater use of manuring and crop rotation to maintain soil fertility; ditches for drainage; and by the switch to cereal crops suitable for heavier soils. The dramatic increase in the number of Later Iron Age settlements almost certainly indicates a rising population, although whether as a cause or a consequence of agricultural developments is unclear.

In Wessex, the developed hillforts exerted ever greater dominance over their surrounding territories. Elsewhere, widespread forest clearance and colonization of marginal environments suggest demographic pressure, for which other signs include episodes of hillfort construction in Essex and the Welsh Marches and increased settlement aggregation in eastern England. These pressures were gradually alleviated by rising agricultural production. In many cases, the colonization of new land was accompanied by the laying out of extensive field systems, like the brickwork fields of Nottinghamshire and South Yorkshire (although their dating is contentious) and the co-axial field systems of East Anglia, or by a large-scale landscape reorganization, as in the Trent Valley.

This expansion into thinly settled areas can be linked with increasing specialization of production, seen in the first large-scale exploitation of iron resources in the Weald, the East Midlands and the Vale of York, and in the growth of textile production, glass and shale-working and pottery manufacture in marginal areas like the Somerset Levels and the Isle of Purbeck (Dorset). By the end of the Iron Age, many of these had become full-time specialist enterprises. Settlers in these agriculturally unpromising environments may have developed products for exchange to offset this disadvantage. Another possibility is that such activities were deliberately peripherally located because the external contacts they encouraged were regarded as a threat to the social order (Sharples 1991). Such groups frequently appear more innovative than others, possibly because they lacked the deep-rooted social relationships that characterized already-populous areas.

From 150 BC, southern Britain underwent a series of changes that mark a radical break from the preceding centuries, with Roman power and influence eventually assuming a key role. An early symptom was the circulation of Gallo-Belgic gold, and local cast bronze ('potin'), coinage in south-east England. Around 100 BC, changes intensify significantly: cremation burial and wheel-thrown pottery appear, and widespread imitation of continental coinage and metalwork occurs. Limited immigration from Belgic Gaul may have fostered closer cross-Channel social and political ties. The Late Iron Age also witnessed the restructuring of settlement patterns in Wessex and south-east England. Many new farmsteads in the latter area were associated with agricultural innovations, and noticeably prospered after the Roman conquest compared to many long-established sites.

During the first century BC, a clearer separation between ritual and everyday life is reflected in the appearance of formal shrines and cemeteries (Hill 1995b). A new emphasis on individual status and social ranking is evident in the increasingly differentiated burial rites – in which long-distance ties are often stressed in preference to local ones – and in the greater numbers of personal ornaments found. The conspicuous consumption of wealth through the ritual deposition of valuables in both wet and dry locations rose sharply (Gwilt and Haselgrove 1997). At the same time, coins legends and the emergence of royal sites like Colchester and St Albans suggest greater centralization of political power. Growing Roman involvement in southern Britain – especially after 20 BC – was a major factor in these developments. In return for imported Roman luxuries, the Classical writer Strabo lists corn, cattle, hunting dogs, slaves and metals among exported commodities.

Outside south-east England, the intensity of change during the Later Iron Age varies. In areas such as the Severn Valley and the Vale of York, enclosed settlements were largely replaced by open and aggregated settlements. Elsewhere, however, a tendency towards more massive enclosure is apparent, as in Northumberland and south-east Scotland. Inevitably, the cultural changes in south-east England impinged on neighbouring areas like the Cotswolds, East Anglia and the East Midlands. Romanized material culture appears, for example in occasional rich female burials accompanied by mirrors. These areas probably suffered military and economic predation by their powerful south-eastern neighbours in search of booty and territory. In central-southern England, the organization of the remaining developed hillforts broke down and most of their population dispersed to establish smaller enclosures and field systems, perhaps implying partitioning of land previously communally owned.

In western and northern Britain, the dominant picture is one of stability. Decentralized political conditions appear to have persisted until the Roman advances into Wales, and subsequently northwards. Differences in social and political structures are apparent through the failure of these regions to adopt coinage and in the virtual absence of Roman imports. Some areas such as south Wales, however, exhibit a marked increase in the number of settlements, while elsewhere new settlement types developed, like the courtyard house clusters of Cornwall such as Carn Euny, or Orcadian broch complexes like Gurness and Howe. This implies that some parts of northern and western Britain were experiencing processes of settlement aggregation similar to those that had occurred earlier in many lowland areas. The chronology of the more elaborate brochs remains tentative, not least because of difficulties in relating radiocarbon dates to their construction, but excavations at sites like Crosskirk (Caithness) suggest that their main period of use began around the second century BC.

## Overseas contacts and the wider European context

Despite obvious differences, the rhythm of British Iron Age developments displays significant parallels with the near Continent (Haselgrove 1998). As in the Later Bronze Age, metalwork types indicate close ties between leading elements of society on either side of the Channel, through which technical and stylistic innovations were transmitted. Some supposed differences are more apparent than real: recognizable Iron Age burial rites are absent or discontinuous in many continental areas.

The southern coastline and that of much of East Anglia face the Continent, linking these areas into wider European patterns by relatively short sea crossings. As the Fenland basin presented an obstacle to overland travel, an enduring pattern of maritime contact also developed up the eastern English coastline. The configuration of the western coast makes the Irish Sea one of its principal unifying features and creates a corridor for communication with coastal regions from Brittany to Galicia (Cunliffe 1995).

By the Late Iron Age, sea-going plank boats with sails – known from Caesar's description of Breton vessels and from representations on British coins – were in use around British shores; earlier in the Iron Age, hide craft were probably the dominant form. Substantial logboats like that from Hasholme (East Yorkshire), which could carry over 5 tonnes of cargo, plied inland waterways. Probable Iron Age ports with continental links include Hengistbury Head, Dorset, and Mount Batten on Plymouth Sound.

In temperate Europe, advanced iron technology came into common use during the Hallstatt C period (*c.* 750–625 BC). North-west Europe shares the sudden decline in the hoarding and ritual deposition of metalwork apparent in Britain. Insular Hallstatt C innovations are confined to new sword types (still of copper alloy) and the import of horse gear and objects such as razors. During Hallstatt D (*c.* 625–450 BC), southern British weaponry followed continental fashions, with daggers replacing the sword, while bow brooches began to be used for fastening clothes instead of ring-headed pins. With Belgium and northern France, southern Britain formed a zone that was occasionally penetrated by prestige goods from the Mediterranean, like the Etruscan beaked flagon from near Northampton and the Attic red-figure kylix recovered from the Thames near Reading. These exotica presumably arrived through gift exchange via southern Germany or eastern France.

The Early La Tène period (c. 450–325 BC) is marked by the re-introduction of long swords and the emergence of a new art style. A number of regions including East Yorkshire exhibit close continental links at this time. Contact between Brittany and south-west England is shown by pottery with stamped and rouletted ornamentation, and later with elaborate designs derived from Early La Tène metalwork (Cunliffe 1995). In south-east England, ceramic assemblages included angular tripartite bowls, some with low pedestal bases, which closely recall contemporary north French developments.

Continental influence diminished noticeably, but did not cease, during Middle La Tène (*c.* 325–150 BC). Innovations in sword technology and art styles indicate continuing contact. Increased regionalism is a feature of much of Europe at this period: most communities became less open to emulating outside fashions; Britain is no exception. Here, highly decorated regional pottery styles have no obvious external counterparts. British brooch types, including involuted and decorated forms, also diverged markedly from continental forms. Many of the masterpieces of insular La Tène art, like the Witham and Wandsworth shields, date to this time.

A major feature of the Late La Tène period (*c.* 150–20 BC) was the arrival of the first Roman imports, principally Dressel 1 wine amphorae and metal drinking services. At this stage there was still virtually no direct contact with the Roman world, and these goods were evidently introduced through indigenous exchange networks as cross-Channel contacts once again intensified. From 20 BC, however, south-east England was increasingly influenced by the Romanized culture emerging in northern France. Imported brooch, coin and pottery types were widely copied and the range of imports diversified. Differing attitudes to the body and changes in personal appearance are suggested by the use of toilet instruments, while the new vessel forms indicate differences in the way in which food and drink were prepared and served. A degree of literacy is implied by the use of Roman style inscriptions on coins, and by graffiti on pottery, although the latter could be the work of foreign traders.

## CURRENT PROBLEMS AND PERCEPTIONS

Little is known for certain about how Iron Age societies were organized. Until recently, this theme was usually approached by extrapolating from texts relating to the Celtic-speaking peoples of Gaul and (much later in time) Ireland. However, the archaeological record implies that the social and political organization of individual Celtic peoples differed significantly, while Classical authors consistently treat the Britons as distinct from the Gauls. Modern excavation has shown that the surviving Iron Age material is much less straightforward to interpret than was previously realized, for the ritual deposits placed in many settlement contexts produce a distorted and selective picture of everyday life (Champion and Collis 1996; Gwilt and Haselgrove 1997). We can no longer speak confidently of rich or poor inhabitants, or even of diet, without careful analysis of the formation processes of the archaeological record.

For the Early and Middle Iron Age, the existence of socio-political hierarchies has come under scrutiny, since even extensively excavated settlements yield remarkably little evidence of elites (Hill 1995a; 1995b). Unless visible signs of ranking were deliberately suppressed, relatively low levels of social differentiation are probably indicated. The reduction in the number of occupied hillforts after 300 BC nonetheless suggests some concentration of power at this time. Archaeologists are also actively questioning whether the substantial houses found on Iron Age settlements in northern Britain represent high status dwellings within a hierarchical social system, or served to express the identity of individual households in more egalitarian structures (Hingley 1992). In practice, no single model can possibly account for the strong regional differences apparent, and answers will have to be sought at increasingly local levels.

The view of the period as dominated by endemic warfare is being overturned. Although particular groups of hillforts were possibly constructed in response to military crises, and several sites show signs of conflict, warfare need not have been any more frequent than in other pre-historic societies. Indeed, evidence of wounding and violent death is not especially common in the known Iron Age burials. The construction of fortified enclosures appears to have been connected as much with status as with defence. Many settlements become increasingly ostentatious with time, but the embellishments were often confined to their most conspicuous sectors, suggesting that military considerations were not uppermost.

Debate continues over the relative importance of internal and external factors in the changes of the Late Iron Age. To what extent should this economic and social differentiation be regarded as a culmination of indigenous processes that were already underway by the Middle Iron Age? While Roman imperialism was increasingly influential in southern Britain from 20 BC, did the pre-existing cultural contacts with northern France have an equally significant role? Whether innovations such as coinage and literacy are symptomatic of profound structural changes, such as the emergence of a market economy, or centralized kingship, remains debatable. Much of the evidence is at best ambiguous. Coinage, for example, appears to have served largely for political, social and religious purposes, and few finds can be convincingly interpreted as losses from commercial transactions. Arguably, the combination of Roman expansion and indigenous developments has exaggerated the real degree of change by artificially highlighting the period and by rendering the Late Iron Age elites archaeologically visible in a way unknown since the Bronze Age. These are some of the key themes awaiting investigation.

## Key texts

Champion, T.C. and Collis, J.R. (eds) 1996. *The Iron Age in Britain and Ireland: recent trends.* Sheffield: J. R. Collis Publications.
Cunliffe, B.W., 1991. *Iron Age communities in Britain.* London: Routledge. 3 edn.
Cunliffe, B.W., 1995. *Iron Age Britain.* London: Batsford.
Gwilt, A. and Haselgrove, C.C. (eds.) 1997. *Reconstructing Iron Age societies: new approaches to the British Iron Age.* Oxford: Oxbow Monograph 71.
James, S.T. and Rigby, V., 1997. *Britain and the Celtic Iron Age.* London: British Museum Press.

## Bibliography

Bersu, G., 1940. 'Excavations at Little Woodbury, Wiltshire', *Proceedings of the Prehistoric Society* 6, 30-111.
Coles, J.M. and Minnitt, S., 1995. *Industrious and fairly civilised: the Glastonbury Lake Village.* Taunton: Somerset Levels Project.
Cunliffe, B.W., 1993. *Danebury.* London: Batsford/English Heritage.
Dent, J.S., 1985. 'Three cart burials from Wetwang, Yorkshire', *Antiquity* 59, 85–92.
De Jersey, P., 1996. *Celtic coinage in Britain.* Princes Risborough: Shire.
Ehrenreich, R.M., 1985. *Trade, technology and the iron working community in the Iron Age of southern Britain.* Oxford: British Archaeological Reports British Series 144.
Fitzpatrick, A.P., 1997. *Archaeological excavations on the route of the A27 Westhampnett Bypass, West Sussex: Volume 2: the cemeteries.* Salisbury: Wessex Archaeological Report 12.
Fox, C.F., 1932. *The personality of Britain.* Cardiff: National Museum of Wales. 2 edn.
Fox, C.F., 1946. *A find of the early Iron Age from Llyn Cerrig Bach, Anglesey.* Cardiff: National Museum of Wales.
Haselgrove, C.C., 1989. 'The later Iron Age in southern Britain and beyond', in Todd, M. (ed.) *Research on Roman Britain 1960–89*, 1–18. London: Britannia Monograph 11.
Haselgrove, C.C., 1998. 'Iron Age Britain and its European setting', in Collis, J. R. (ed.) *Actes du XVIII Colloque de l'AFEAF, Winchester, 1994.* Sheffield: Sheffield Academic Press.
Hawkes, C.F.C., 1960. 'The British Iron Age', in Frere, S.S. (ed.) *Problems of the Iron Age in southern Britain*, 1–16. London: Institute of Archaeology, Occasional Paper 11.
Hill, J.D., 1995a. 'The Iron Age in Britain and Ireland (c. 800 BC–AD 100): an overview', *Journal of World Prehistory* 9, 47–98.
Hill, J. D., 1995b. *Ritual and rubbish in the Iron Age of Wessex.* Oxford: British Archaeological Reports British Series 242.
Hingley, R., 1992. 'Society in Scotland from 700 BC–AD 200', *Proceedings of the Society of Antiquaries of Scotland* 122, 7–53.
Hodson, F.R., 1964. 'Cultural groupings within the pre-Roman British Iron Age', *Proceedings of the Prehistoric Society* 30, 99–110.
Lambrick, G., 1992. 'The development of later prehistoric and Roman farming on the Thames gravels', in Fulford, M. and Nichols, E. (eds) *Developing landscapes of lowland Britain; the archaeology of the British gravels: a review*, 78–105. London: Society of Antiquaries of London Occasional Paper 14.
Morris, E.L., 1994. 'Production and distribution of pottery and salt in Iron Age Britain: a review', *Proceedings of the Prehistoric Society* 60, 371–394.
Parfitt, K., 1995. *Iron Age burials from Mill Hill, Deal.* London: British Museum Press.
Peacock, D.P.S., 1968. 'A contribution to the study of Glastonbury ware from south-west Britain', *Antiquaries Journal* 46, 41–61.
Pryor, F., 1984. *Excavations at Fengate, Peterborough, England: the 4th report.* Northampton: Northamptonshire Archaeological Monograph 2.
Ralston, I.B.M., 1979. 'The Iron Age: northern Britain', in Megaw, J.V.S. and Simpson, D.D.A. (eds) *Introduction to British Prehistory*, 446–501. Leicester: Leicester University Press.
Sharples, N.M., 1991. *Maiden Castle.* London: Batsford/English Heritage.

Stead, I.M., 1991. 'Snettisham', *Antiquity* 65, 447–464.

Stead, I.M., 1996. *Celtic Art.* London: British Museum. 2 edn.

Stead, I.M., Bourke, J.B. and Brothwell, D., 1986. *Lindow man. The body in the bog.* London: British Museum Press.

Van der Veen, M., 1992. *Crop husbandry regimes. An archaeobotanical study of farming in northern England 1000 BC–AD 500.* Sheffield: Sheffield Archaeological Monograph 3.

Wainwright, G.J., 1979. *Gussage All Saints: an Iron Age settlement in Dorset.* London: Department of the Environment, Archaeological Reports 10.

while tombstones can indicate the origin of those troops, their life expectancy and family relationships (e.g. Figure 8.1). All three types of inscription can assist in the study of the movement of particular units or the careers of individuals, which, in turn, can contribute both to refining the chronology and interpreting the significance of historical events.

The major contribution of archaeology is in the elucidation of military installations in terms of date and function. When on campaign in hostile territory, or simply operating away from home base, the Roman army constructed temporary defended enclosures, referred to as 'temporary camps', for overnight protection. More are known from Britain than from any other province of the Roman Empire. They range in size dramatically, from 0.4 ha to 67 ha in area. The smaller examples are more likely to relate to the building activities of work parties involved in the construction or repair of military installations, but the larger camps can indicate the lines of march of troops on campaign, and are sometimes termed 'marching camps' (e.g. Ardoch below) (Figure 8.2). Semi-permanent works, often referred to as 'vexillation fortresses' and covering an area of some 8 ha, are occasionally attested. They are usually associated with campaigning and were perhaps linked to the provision of adequate supplies, though the precise nature of such sites is much debated (e.g. Red House, Corbridge, below and Figure 8.4).

After its conquest had been achieved, control of an area was usually consolidated by a more permanent military presence, though the nature and extent of this varies according to the political geography of the area concerned. Close military control was usually manifested in the form of a network of forts and fortlets linked by a road system. This pattern is seen in Wales, northern England and Scotland in the first and second centuries AD, although such close supervision of conquered territory is not recorded in south-eastern England (Figure 8.3). Here more sophisticated means of political control seem to have been applied immediately after the conquest, involving the use of diplomacy and the establishment of client or 'friendly' kings in an area where native political organization may have been more complex (Chapter 7) and where the opposition was, perhaps, less intransigent.

When establishing military control of an area, the Romans utilized a hierarchy of permanent military establishments. At its hub were the legionary fortresses, bases for some 5,000 citizen infantry who formed the core of the Roman army (e.g. Inchtuthil below and Figure 8.4). Only four legions were used in the invasion of Britain and, by the mid-80s AD, only three remained in garrison. Legionary movements fluctuated considerably in the early years of campaigning and conquest,

***Figure 8.2*** Aerial photograph of the fort (F), annexe (A) and temporary camps (C) at Malling, Perthshire.
*Source*: Crown copyright: Royal Commission on the Ancient and Historical Monuments of Scotland.

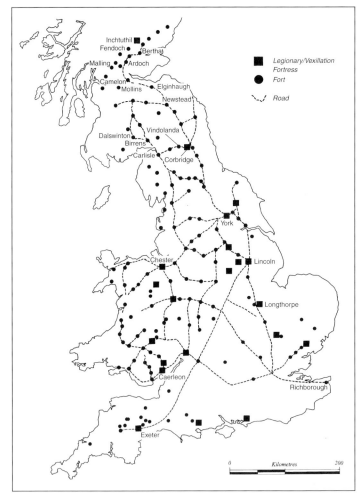

*Figure 8.3* Distribution of first-century AD Roman forts in Britain (NB not all sites were occupied contemporaneously).

eventually settling down in permanent fortresses at York, Caerleon and Chester. The bulk of the military garrison, however, was made up of auxiliary troops, including cavalry, sub-divided into units approximately 500 or 1,000 strong. These were non-citizen soldiers, recruited from the provinces of the Empire, who formed the main front-line and garrison troops. They were housed in forts that varied in size considerably from 0.8 to 4 ha in internal area (Figure 8.5). Three examples (Elginhaugh, Housesteads and *Vindolanda*) are described below. Indeed, there is still much debate about the relationship between auxiliary fort sizes and the different types of unit known, particularly in relation to the housing of cavalry horses inside or outside the fort. What is becoming increasingly clear, however, is that there is no simple correlation between auxiliary unit and fort, with units being split between different forts and/or different units occupying the same fort. The division of units is further attested by the frequency of use of much smaller installations, known as 'fortlets', usually less than 0.4 ha in internal area (e.g. Barburgh Mill below and Figure 8.6a). The distinction between a large fortlet and a very small fort can be difficult, but the former generally lacks any central administrative buildings.

The smallest permanent installations are watchtowers (Figure 8.6b). Though individual examples do occur, they are usually associated with frontiers and are best known along Hadrian's Wall (the so-called 'turrets') and the Gask frontier in Perthshire, as at Westerton, described below. They are not infrequently described as signal stations, though whether or not they were used to relay signals is much debated. Some capacity to pass on any information gained from look-outs would seem essential, without necessarily implying the existence of a system for relaying complex messages (Southern 1990).

Roman military architecture was remarkably consistent for long periods of time. However, some major changes become apparent from the late third century. New forts constructed at coastal locations around the south-east coast of England and in north and south Wales put greater emphasis on defence. They are provided with massive stone walls and projecting bastions (e.g.

Figure 8.5d), though their internal buildings, where known, were of timber. Late watchtowers, as attested along the coast of North Yorkshire, show similar developments as compared to their first- and second-century predecessors; that at Filey is described below (Figure 8.6c).

Fort sites can often be quite closely dated. Knowledge of the overall historical framework provided by the literary account and the epigraphic sources usually allows a general context to be established. Refinement of that chronology derives from the associated material remains, particularly the coins, pottery and, to a lesser extent, glass and metalwork. Study of Roman pottery, particularly the fine tablewares, and most notably the ubiquitous imported red glossware known as Samian, is so well developed as to allow quite close dating by that means alone in the first and second centuries AD. Occasionally, circumstances permit even closer dating when waterlogged conditions preserve structural timbers that can be dated by dendro-chronology.

## CHANGING PERCEPTIONS

The most substantive change in our perception of the military occupation of Britain since the Second World War has been brought about by aerial reconnaissance, which is the single most important method of discovering new archaeological sites from the Neolithic period onwards. The combination of the morphological distinction of Roman military sites and the primary Roman period interest of some major aerial photographic practitioners has resulted in a massive increase in our knowledge of the numbers, types and distributions of both temporary and permanent military installations. This, in turn, has greatly enhanced our understanding of the process of conquest and consolidation. Some 45% of all forts and fortlets in Scotland, for example, and the vast majority of all temporary camps in Britain have been discovered from the air since the last war (e.g. Figure 8.2).

Excavation techniques have developed significantly also, though their impact has been less dramatic and far-reaching. Military establishments were for long thought to be sufficiently regular in both form and lay-out to require only minimal examination. Thus, up to the 1970s, a process of small-scale sampling was deemed adequate to elucidate their history and development, as exemplified in the excavations at Fendoch (Perthshire), Birrens (Dumfriesshire) and Longthorpe, near Peterborough. It has since been realized that forts were less regular and standardized, and that their periods of occupation may be more complex. This requires more extensive investigation, as has been undertaken at, for example, Elginhaugh (Midlothian) and South Shields and Wallsend in north-east England.

Both of these developments have in turn contributed to an increasing emphasis being placed on archaeological evidence in its own right, more than simply as an adjunct to the literary sources that previously always took primacy. Such an approach is illustrated, for example, in the lengthy reassessment of the role of Agricola in the conquest of the north of Britain (Hanson 1991).

While the development of radiocarbon dating, so important for prehistory, has had little or no impact on Roman archaeology because of its imprecision, dendrochronology has had some significant impact where excavation has recovered quantities of waterlogged timber. Dating by matching tree-ring patterns on oak timbers to a master sequence can give a chronological precision equal to the best historical or epigraphic dating. It has been responsible, for example, for the pushing back of the long-accepted date for the establishment of the fort at Carlisle, contributing to the reassessment of the chronology of the conquest of the north. Other aspects of archaeological science are also proving significant. Most important has been the analysis of environmental evidence from excavations, both pollen and macro-fossil remains. These have

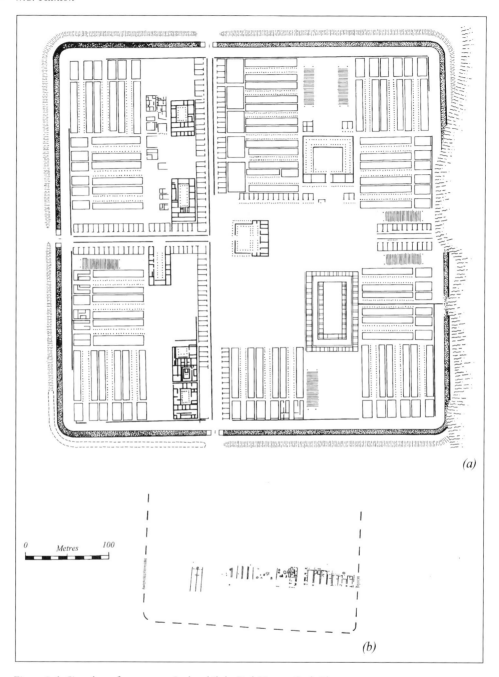

*Figure 8.4* Site plans: fortresses: a. Inchtuthil; b. Red House, Corbridge.

made considerable contributions to our understanding of the impact of the Roman army on the local environment, particularly the extent to which it was responsible for deforestation, as well as to considerations of the diet of the troops, and the logistics of their food supply (e.g. Breeze 1984; Hanson 1997).

## KEY DATA

### Inchtuthil, Perthshire

It is ironic that the most extensively known legionary fortress in Britain is that at Inchtuthil, which is both the most northerly and briefest occupied of all of the fortresses. A combination of aerial photography and limited excavation has recovered virtually the complete plan of the timber-built fortress (Figure 8.4a) (Pitts and St Joseph 1985). It covered an area of some 20 ha and was clearly intended to house a full legion. All of the barrack blocks had been built, along with the headquarters building, hospital, workshop, some of the granaries, and the houses for most of the junior officers. However, construction of the commanding officer's house had not commenced when the fortress was abandoned and dismantled as part of the Roman withdrawal from northern Scotland, probably in AD 87. The location of the fortress on the extreme northern frontier represents the consolidation of the conquests achieved by Agricola, but placing a legion in this exposed position also indicates the Roman intention to continue to advance.

### Red House, Corbridge, Northumberland

The full size of the fort at Red House is unknown, but its east–west dimension suggests that it should be interpreted as a vexillation fortress of some 10 ha. Excavation ahead of road building recovered traces of timber buildings, including a workshop, a large barrack block and several open-ended storage buildings (Hanson *et al.* 1979), while earlier work had identified the remains of a large bath building close by (Figure 8.4b). Occupation of the site was short-lived and seems to have been linked to the campaigns of Agricola, after which it was replaced by an auxiliary fort nearby.

### Elginhaugh, Midlothian

This timber-built auxiliary fort is the only example for which we have the complete plan recovered by excavation. Eleven barrack blocks, two of them probably for cavalry, are crammed into a space of only 1.2 ha, providing accommodation for some 780 men (Figure 8.5a). More limited examination of the annexe to the west indicated a complex development of ovens and storage buildings alongside the road, with perhaps open spaces for the tethering of horses elsewhere in its interior. Situated at the northern end of Dere Street, the main route into Scotland up the eastern side of the country, the fort was occupied as part of the consolidation of Lowland Scotland from probably *c.* AD 80 and, like Inchtuthil, it was demolished and abandoned in AD 87. Immediately thereafter, however, the fort enclosure seems to have been reused by the Romans as a collection point for livestock, perhaps linked to the continuing extraction of tribute from the local tribe, the Votadini (Hanson forthcoming).

### Housesteads, Northumberland

The auxiliary fort at Housesteads is perhaps one of the most famous in Roman Britain. It was attached to the rear of Hadrian's Wall when garrisons were moved up to the line of the Wall as part of the reassessment of its operation during the course of its construction. The fort covered an area of 2 ha and probably contained some 800–1,000 men. The original plan is not known in its entirety, and the apparently 'full' plan as often published is a composite of different periods derived from excavations at the end of last century. The fort was occupied almost continuously from the reign of Hadrian in the second century AD through to the end of the fourth century, or the beginning of the fifth. Its garrison in the third and fourth centuries, the first cohort of Tungrians, an infantry unit originally from modern-day Belgium, is attested epigraphically. By the third century, an extensive civilian settlement had grown up around the fort, with some of the buildings encroaching

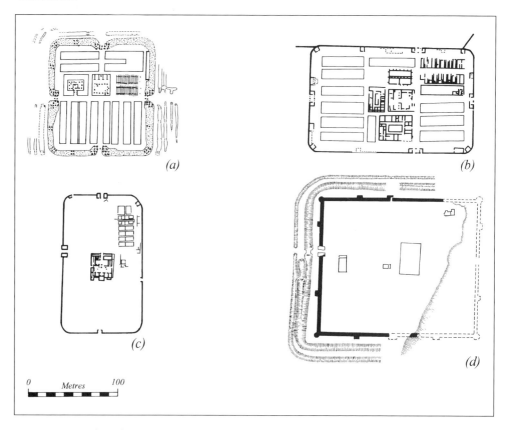

*Figure 8.5* Site plans: forts: a. Elginhaugh; b. Housesteads; c. *Vindolanda*; d. Richborough.

right up to its walls (Crow 1995). The stone walls of the fort, with associated gates and towers, as well as the headquarters building, commanding officer's house, granaries, hospital, latrine and some barrack blocks within it, have been consolidated and put on public display (see Figure 8.5b), along with some of the buildings of the civil settlement ('*vicus*') outside the south gate.

## Vindolanda (Chesterholm), Northumberland

The Roman fort at *Vindolanda*, situated only some 3 km south of Housesteads, has a complex history. It was founded in the Late Flavian period (later first century AD), presumably as part of the military consolidation in northern England, but some years after its initial conquest. In the second century AD, the fort continued in use as one of the garrison posts along the Trajanic Stanegate frontier, and, like Corbridge, occupation appears to have continued even with the construction of Hadrian's Wall and the moving of garrisons up to its line. The original timber-built fort was replaced in stone on a slightly different alignment probably in the later second century, and continued to be occupied through until the late fourth or early fifth (Figure 8.5c). The rampart walls and headquarters building of this stone fort have also been consolidated for public display, along with the external bath house and buildings of a civil settlement. The major importance of this site, however, derives from the excavation of the deeply buried earlier timber fort: its waterlogged state has preserved an exciting range of environmental evidence and organic artefacts, including writing tablets. These include elements of the fort's administrative archive and copies of private letters (Bowman 1994).

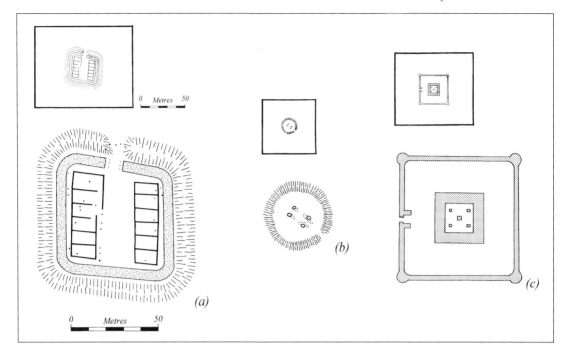

*Figure 8.6* Site plans: fortlet and towers: a. Barburgh Mill; b. Westerton; c. Filey. The plans in the boxed inserts are at the same scale as Figures 8.4 and 8.5.

## Barburgh Mill, Dumfriesshire

Dating to the period of the Antonine occupation of south-west Scotland, the fortlet at Barburgh Mill is the most completely excavated example of its type (Breeze 1974). The fortlet, which enclosed an area of less than 0.1 ha, contained two small timber barrack blocks, sufficient to house a single century (about 80) of infantry troops (Figure 8.6a). Its occupation relates to the close control of south-west Scotland in the early Antonine period, and did not continue beyond the late 150s or early 160s AD.

## Richborough, Kent

Possibly one of the landing sites on the east coast of Kent for the Claudian invasion of AD 43. Richborough became a military supply base immediately thereafter. An irregular enclosure was filled with timber-built granaries, though this function seems to have been short-lived. The association of the site with the original conquest seems to have been reaffirmed in the Flavian period with the construction of a monumental triumphal arch later in the first century AD. After a period of urban development, the site was reoccupied by the military in the mid-third century, with the apparent conversion of the monumental arch into a watchtower surrounded by triple ditches. Later in that century this was levelled and a new fort built, enclosed by massive stone walls over 3 m thick and at least 7 m high with projecting bastions, constituting one of a series of coastal defences that made up the Saxon Shore frontier (Maxfield 1989) (Figure 8.5d). Unfortunately, little is known of its internal buildings, which seem to have been mainly of timber. The well-preserved remains of the Late Roman defences, the base of the triumphal arch and elements of the ditch system of the earlier supply base are on public display.

## Westerton, Perthshire

The small single-ditched enclosure at Westerton contained a timber tower constructed on four massive posts (Figure 8.6b). The site is one of a number at regular intervals along the most northerly stretch of Roman road in Scotland (e.g. Figure 8.7), which collectively formed one of the earliest artificially demarcated frontiers in the Roman Empire, the Gask Frontier. This seems to demarcate a temporary halt during the conquest of Scotland in the Flavian period (Hanson and Friell 1995).

## Filey, North Yorkshire

This heavily fortified watchtower, most of which has now fallen into the sea, was constructed on a coastal promontory on the north side of Filey Bay. A massive stone-built tower was surrounded by a smaller stone wall with projecting corner bastions, beyond which lay a ditch cutting off the headland (Figure 8.6c) (Ottaway 1996). Associated finds date its occupation to the last years of the fourth century AD. The tower is one of several along the North Yorkshire coast that acted as an early warning system against seaborne raiders.

## Ardoch, Perthshire

The earthwork defences of this fort (Figure 8.7) are among the best preserved anywhere in the Roman Empire. The fort (1) was occupied originally in the Flavian period, as part of the consolidation of the conquest of Scotland, and it was reoccupied in the second century AD as an outpost fort beyond the line of the Antonine Wall. Excavations at the turn of the century revealed timber buildings in its interior, but the plan is poorly understood as the different phases of occupation were not distinguished (Breeze 1983). To the east of the fort is an enclosure (2) of uncertain function and to the north, adjacent to the Roman road (11), a timber watch tower (10 – for a more detailed plan of another example see Figure

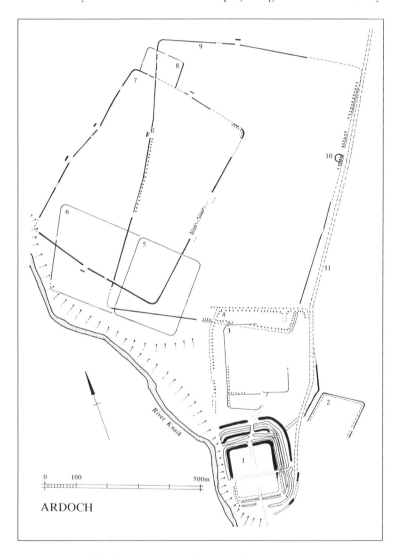

*Figure 8.7* Ardoch: fort, annexe, watchtower and temporary camps.

8.6b). Much of the outline of a large annexe is preserved, attached to the north of the fort, though little is known of what took place in its interior. Within, beyond and partly overlapping the annexe, is a series of temporary camps (3, 5–7, 9), some elements of which are still visible on the ground. The largest camp, covering 52 ha (9), is the latest and replaces a 25.5 ha camp and its attached annexe (8) that it partly overlies, though both probably relate to campaigning in the early third century by the Emperor Septimius Severus.

## INTERRELATIONSHIPS

The process of Romanization, or more correctly of acculturation between the Roman invader and the indigenous native population, is central to the study of Roman Britain and will be highlighted in Chapter 9. In the military context, the topic has three principal aspects:

- What was the impact of the Roman army on those areas that it occupied?
- What was the nature, extent and effect of contacts with peoples beyond the frontier once it had been established?
- What role did the army play in the process of Romanization?

The hypothesis that the Roman authorities played any part in the deliberate fostering of Romanization has come under considerable challenge in recent years. There is, however, sufficient evidence to suggest that the view that would explain the changes as entirely driven by the indigenous population is extreme (Hanson 1994 *contra* Millett 1990). If the Roman authorities did indeed promote and assist the process of Romanization, then the military, as the primary arm of that administration, are likely to have been involved. It has long been argued, for example, that fort sites may have influenced the subsequent location of Roman towns, though this is likely to have been a passive rather than proactive process. It is also possible that direct military assistance was given to urban building projects, even though the evidence for this is disputed (cf. Blagg 1984). More certain, however, is the indirect military role in the general acculturation process. Once the army of garrison became relatively static, the practice of inter-marriage and local recruitment will gradually have resulted in the army itself becoming increasingly Romano-British. Occasionally a tombstone can reveal something of this process, as for example that of Tadius Exuperatus from Caerleon in Gwent (Collingwood and Wright 1965, no. 369) (Figure 8. 1), who died while serving with the second legion on an expedition in Germany. He was commemorated beside the tomb of his father by his sister and mother, Tadia Vallaunius, whose *cognomen* (surname) is of Celtic origin. The fact that he took his mother's *nomen* (first name) probably indicates that he was the offspring of an illegal local liaison, since serving soldiers were not allowed to marry until the time of Severus. It is unfortunate, therefore, that relatively little is known about the nature, growth and development of civil settlements (*vici* and *cannabae*) outside Roman forts and fortresses, though on the northern frontier they appear to flourish during the lengthy period of peace through the third century that followed the Severan campaigns. Few have been extensively examined by excavation in recent years, though aerial reconnaissance has given some indication of the overall plan of several examples (e.g. Figure 8.8).

The military impact on Britain varies according to the area concerned. Because of the relatively short period of occupation involved, this impact is likely to have been very limited in the south-east and the extreme north. Whether the longer term presence of the army stimulated the local economy by encouraging the production of a surplus to supply the military market, or depressed it by placing demands on the local system that it could not sustain, depends upon both the natural environment and the social and technological development of the area concerned. In north-western England, for example, the effect of the military presence seems to have been largely

*Figure 8.8* Aerial photograph of the fort and *vicus* at Old Carlisle, Cumbria.

detrimental to the economic development of the indigenous population, whereas in south Wales and perhaps in south-eastern Scotland, the opposite was the case (Higham 1989; Hanson and Macinnes 1991). It is becoming increasingly clear, however, that the military impact on the local environment in the north, once thought to have been quite dramatic, is likely to have been relatively limited (Hanson 1997). Much of the forest seems to have been cleared as part of the long-term expansion of settlement and agriculture by the indigenous population, not to fulfil Roman building requirements; substantive disruption of the settlement pattern is not readily attested; and no major changes in agricultural production to cater for the Roman dietary preferences for beef and wheat are currently detectable.

The nature, extent and effects of contacts with peoples beyond the frontier are also much in debate. The first problem is that of defining the limit of Roman territory, which is not as straightforward as might at first appear (an issue discussed further below); the difficulty is further exacerbated by the fluctuations in the area involved. The second problem is the lack of data. Apart from a few scant references in the Classical literature, the evidence is restricted to the distribution of Roman artefacts on native sites (e.g. Macinnes 1989). Whether this material represents booty from raiding, gifts received to cement diplomatic relations, or is the result of trading contacts is difficult to determine. Two factors, however, are apparent. Firstly, apart from a number of coin hoards, the bulk of the material found north of Hadrian's Wall dates to those periods when direct Roman occupation was extended into Scotland. Secondly, the material is not evenly distributed within contemporary native society. In the main, greater access to Roman material amongst the upper social stratum of native society is indicated (e.g. Macinnes 1984).

## CURRENT PERCEPTIONS AND OUTSTANDING PROBLEMS

### The search for a frontier

Whether it was the original intention to conquer the whole of the island of Britain is uncertain. The Romans were most familiar with the south-east because of Caesar's two expeditions in 55 and 54 BC and continued diplomatic and trading contacts thereafter, the latter manifested archaeologically in the distribution of Roman artefacts, particularly Italian Dressel 1B wine amphorae (Peacock 1984; and see Chapter 7). Such contacts also ensured that the conquest of AD 43 was achieved and maintained with relative ease in the south and east, since it was supported by certain factions within native society. The creation of three client or friendly kingdoms, those of the Iceni, the Regnenses and the Brigantes, is an important feature of this early period. It underpinned Roman control of the Province and freed troops to concentrate on areas of greater resistance.

It has been argued that the initial plan was to occupy only the south and east of England; the identification of an early frontier along the Fosse Way, the Roman road from Exeter to Lincoln, is misconceived, however, and not supported by the chronology of the sites involved (Jones and Mattingly 1991). Moreover, troop deployments, particularly the presence of legionary and vexillation fortresses along the periphery of the area under direct Roman control, indicate the intention to continue to advance, rather than simply to police the area already overrun. In the context of the early consolidation of the Roman conquest, the idea of a frontier would have been psychologically unacceptable since it would, in effect, have implied that there was a definable limit to Roman expansion.

Continued conquest was slowed by less favourable terrain and increasing hostility from the indigenous tribes who had had no previous contact with Rome. It was further delayed by the Boudican rebellion of AD 60 and its aftermath, and a local uprising amongst the Brigantes in AD 69. Several of the limited number of forts known in south-eastern England seem to have been established as a direct consequence of the Boudican rebellion, indicating the need to re-establish Roman control.

When conquest and concomitant expansion was resumed in AD 71 under a new imperial house, the Flavians, it progressed rapidly over the next 15 years under successive governors. Roman military occupation was extended north and west across northern England, Wales and Scotland (Figure 8.3), and the conquest of the whole British mainland became a feasible proposition for Roman forces. However, the possibility that they might fail to achieve such a goal may already have begun to be considered. Tacitus indicates (*Agricola* 23) that a halt was made in the campaigns of conquest of his father-in-law, Agricola, and the line drawn across the most obvious geographical point, the Forth–Clyde isthmus. Supporting archaeological evidence remains problematic. It was once thought, for example, that Agricolan forts lay beneath many of the later fortifications along the Antonine Wall, but this belief can no longer be substantiated in most cases. Though several first-century forts are known across the isthmus, such as Mollins (Lanarkshire) and Camelon (Stirlingshire), both lying away from the later Wall line, not enough have been identified legitimately to confirm a first-century frontier line.

However, following the road north of the isthmus as far as the River Tay at Bertha (Perthshire), a series of forts, fortlets and timber watchtowers has been discovered that have all the hallmarks of such a frontier. When the Romans were imposing close military control over an area, forts and fortlets tend to occur at regular intervals of 25–32 km, usually referred to as a day's march apart. When frontier lines begin to emerge, this spacing is reduced to half or less, often with fortlets interspersed between the forts, and closer supervision provided by the construction of watchtowers. The unusual survival of a number of these towers along the Gask Ridge in Perthshire was noted around 1900, and subsequently their extent has been augmented by aerial survey and tested by excavation, indicating that they stretch for some 40 km at intervals of between 800 m and 1,500 m (Figure 8.9). There is still disagreement about the precise date and context of this system, but a link with Agricola's halt on the Fort–Clyde isthmus seems at present the best explanation and would make this the earliest artificially defined frontier in the Roman Empire.

Campaigning was resumed, probably as the result of a change of emperor, and the complete conquest of the island was clearly the intention. However, a serious military setback in Dacia in eastern Europe resulted in the withdrawal of troops from Britain to the Danube frontier and the concomitant failure to consolidate the conquest of the north, reminding us that Britain was just one small, remote province in a huge empire, and that decisions that affected it were not necessarily always taken entirely with local considerations in mind.

For the next 130 years, the history of the northern frontier involves the search for a convenient limit to Roman occupation. On the Continent, the great rivers of the Rhine and Danube provided ready demarcators of Roman territory. In Britain, the geographical choice lay between the isthmuses of the Tyne–Solway and Forth–Clyde, though with variations on this theme. These variations give some clue to the Roman attitude towards frontiers and their function, though these subjects are still much debated.

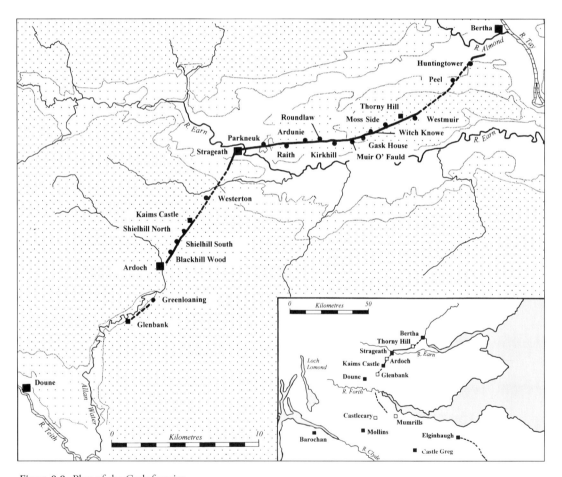

*Figure 8.9* Plan of the Gask frontier.

The exact location of the frontier at the end of the first century is not absolutely clear. It does not appear at present that the Tyne–Solway isthmus became the frontier immediately after the withdrawal from Scotland in the late 80s AD. At least part of Lowland Scotland continued to be controlled by a network of forts, the most northerly of which were Newstead (Roxburghshire) in the east and Dalswinton (Dumfriesshire) in the west. Moreover, Roman control and influence seems to have extended beyond them, for the abandoned site of the auxiliary fort at Elginhaugh was used by the Romans as a collection point for animals, presumably as part of the exaction of tribute from the surrounding area. Within 20 years, however, these northern forts were abandoned, the withdrawal probably brought about by the demands of an extensive military commitment beyond the Danube in Dacia, as the Emperor Trajan sought the conquest of that area. In Britain, the emergence of a frontier line across the Tyne–Solway isthmus is perceptible; this is usually referred to as the Trajanic or Stanegate frontier (Figure 8.10a). The latter term derives from the medieval name for the Roman road that runs from west to east between Carlisle and Corbridge. This frontier is manifested archaeologically in a decrease in spacing between posts along that road. New forts were constructed, including two, Haltwhistle Burn and Throp (both in Northumberland), which, in terms of their size, lie halfway between fort and fortlet. As on the Gask frontier, the closer spacing of larger installations seems to have been supplemented by the

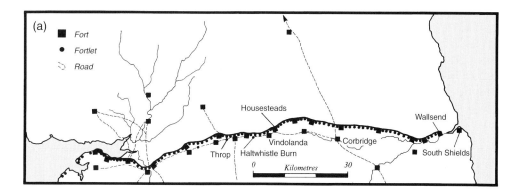

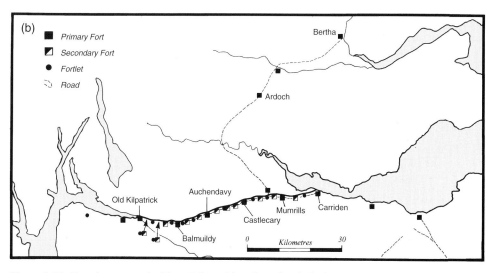

*Figure 8.10* Frontiers across the Tyne–Solway (a) and Forth–Clyde (b).

provision of watchtowers, though the system is still known only in embryo, being best attested in the central sector and at the western end (e.g. Jones 1979).

These dispositions represent the first stages in the creation of a frontier across the Tyne–Solway isthmus that eventually culminated in the elaborate and extensively studied provisions of Hadrian's Wall (Breeze and Dobson 1987) (Figure 8.10). Nonetheless, there is still a good deal to discover of its earliest development. It is clear that the original Hadrianic plan was merely an augmentation of the pre-existing frontier along the Stanegate by the construction of a running barrier of stone or turf. This connected a series of watchtowers (usually now called 'turrets') at intervals of 500 m, with garrisoned gateways every 1.6 km (1 mile) in fortlets, generally now referred to as 'milecastles'. Thereafter, the plan underwent continuous modification until its abandonment when the Romans expanded northwards to reoccupy Scotland in AD 139. The major change was the construction of forts on the line of the Wall itself, though only some of the forts to the rear were given up in the process. This was clearly a recognition that the linear barrier not only served to exclude unwanted incursion from the north, but made it more difficult for the Romans to deploy troops rapidly beyond it.

Given that the army had just left one linear barrier that was still undergoing modification, it ought not to be surprising that they should choose to construct another when the readvance into Scotland at the behest of Emperor Antoninus Pius had been completed. This was set across the Forth–Clyde isthmus. As originally conceived, the Antonine Wall seems to have been modelled on Hadrian's Wall in its developed form, with forts attached to the barrier at intervals of approximately 13 km and fortlets 1.6 km apart between them (Hanson and Maxwell 1986), although the absence of a system of watchtowers, the equivalent of the turrets on Hadrian's Wall, remains a problem. The Antonine Wall also underwent dramatic modification during its construction, with the addition of a series of smaller forts reducing the average spacing to some 3.5 km, and resulting in a denser concentration of forces than on any other linear frontier in the Empire (Figure 8.10b). Such a dramatic change can only have been in response to some perceived threat, though there is no direct evidence of it. However, occupation of the more northerly wall was relatively short-lived. By the 160s AD, the Romans had withdrawn to Hadrian's Wall, though details of the fluctuations involved and their precise dates remain in dispute (e.g. Hodgson 1995). Apart from the brief period of the Severan campaigns, when completion of the conquest of Scotland was again a possibility (Breeze 1982), Hadrian's Wall remained the northern frontier of the Province of Britain, though the distance over which control extended beyond it varies, as is indicated by the fluctuation in the occupation of outpost forts.

## The function of frontiers

Hadrian's Wall is perhaps the best known frontier in the whole of the Roman Empire, but it is far from typical of Roman frontiers. Most were not defined by linear barriers, and, among those that were, the provision of a massive stone wall was not the norm. Even where obvious demarcation lines were provided, whether manmade or natural, such as rivers, they do not necessarily define the limit of Roman occupied territory and rarely do they define the full extent of the territory over which Roman control was exercised. The provision of outpost forts as a regular feature of both frontier walls in Britain indicates that military occupation normally extended between approximately 8–40 km to the north of them. Moreover, it is quite clear that, for most of the third and fourth centuries, patrols exercised Roman military control considerably further afield. Where no obvious line was demarcated, the definition of the limit of Roman territory can be even more difficult. Indeed, it remains a matter of debate whether there was ever a precisely defined legal limit to the Empire, even though this might seem a necessary prerequisite for administrative purposes.

Roman frontiers were built and operated by the army, and military defence was clearly one of their prime functions, but, at least until the early fourth century AD in Britain, the process was both proactive as well as reactive. The Romans usually responded to threats to territory they occupied by undertaking a campaign against the aggressors, the principle best exemplified by the action of Agricola against the Ordovices in north Wales immediately upon his arrival in the Province as the new governor (Tacitus, *Agricola*, 18). Static defence from maintained positions was not normal Roman practice. When thoughts of completing the conquest of the island of Britain were given up and it was necessary to create a frontier, the Romans looked to natural features, such as the Forth–Clyde isthmus, for convenience of definition (Tacitus, *Agricola*, 23). Such features were at first augmented by a closer spacing of military garrisons than was the case when hostile territory was being controlled by a fort network, often utilizing smaller garrison posts, either small forts or fortlets. Other characteristic features were the provision of a system of watchtowers and of a lateral road connecting these various installations. This development can be seen on the Gask and Stanegate frontiers of late first- and early second-century date, as noted above. Only later, after Hadrian's reign, do we see the addition of a linear barrier as part of the system.

This sequence of development gives some indication of Rome's attitude to the function of frontiers. The provision of garrisons at closer intervals and of a regular system of watchtowers suggests a concern for the control of movement across the frontier, but there is no suggestion that a system of preclusive defence was intended. Even when linear barriers were added to the system, provision was made for regular gateways at fortlets located every 1.6 km on both Hadrian's Wall and the Antonine Wall. If the primary function of frontiers were to exclude, such an arrangement would have been both unnecessary and potentially disadvantageous, since gateways are a weak spot in any defensive circuit. On the other hand, the provision of a linear barrier would be a logical step if concern was to increase the level of control and the intensity of security. Such action would serve to funnel all legitimate movement through the gateways under the watchful eyes of the Roman garrison, making the levying of customs dues more readily achieved, and would also effectively exclude small-scale illicit movement, such as border raiding. Linear barriers are of little use against major incursions, since external forces could be massed at a selected location, easily outnumbering any local troops, and could readily breach the wall before sufficient defensive reinforcements could be summoned to the spot.

Whether or not the wall line was ever intended to be defended as a barrier in the way that the perimeter of a fort would have been is much disputed. Clearly, the original thickness of Hadrian's Wall (the so-called 'broad wall') could have accommodated a walkway, though there is no direct evidence that it was provided with the necessary parapet or crenellations. The reduction in the width of later sections of this wall to as little as 1.3 m, however, decreases the probability that it could have been used as a fighting platform. Evidence from the Antonine Wall is more difficult to assess since the details of the superstructure of the turf rampart are less certain. Analogy with the German frontier, however, where the barrier consisted of only a timber palisade, makes clear that the use of such barriers as elevated fighting platforms requires proof rather than being automatically assumed.

It has been further suggested that the provision of a linear barrier would provide greater protection to the local population within the Province, thus encouraging and facilitating the process of Romanization (Hanson and Maxwell 1986, 163). However, whether this was the intended function rather than an incidental side-effect remains unproven.

Debate about the function of the Saxon Shore is more fundamental, since its very identification as a frontier has been challenged. Recent reassessment of the evidence suggests that the forts there do not readily fit into any practical defensive strategy, but should better be seen as trans-shipment centres for the collection and distribution of state supplies (Cotterill 1993). However, various

*Figure 8.11* Distribution of Saxon Shore forts and late Roman forts and coastal watchtowers.

factors make it difficult to dismiss the current orthodoxy: the general distribution of the forts along the coast that faced the brunt of Saxon raiding (Figure 8.11); the way in which the forts seem to dominate access to important harbours or river mouths, a feature that is even more apparent against the background of the contemporary coastline where this is known (e.g. Maxfield 1989, 13–15); and the specific literary reference to defence against such attacks being the reason for the appointment of Carausius, under whose auspices most of the forts seem to have been built, to a command that spanned both sides of the Channel. Nonetheless, the absence of direct evidence for naval detachments at most of the forts remains a problem if their primary function was as defended strongholds for the fleet.

## ROMAN BRITAIN IN ITS WIDER SETTING

Two distinctive approaches to the study of Roman Britain are apparent. The first emphasizes the distinctive nature of the island and the importance of local conditions in determining the extent, nature and course of that occupation. The second stresses Britain's position in the wider Empire, of which it was only a small part, and the impact of broader policy decisions and actions elsewhere on events in the Province. This latter approach has become the orthodoxy in recent years, but has recently been subject to question (e.g. Freeman 1996). In fact, there is validity in both approaches, for although, on the one hand, the physical and political geography will have varied from frontier to frontier, on the other hand, all the provinces were constituent parts of a wider imperial system, administered by personnel who frequently moved between provinces (Hanson 1994). Thus, though local circumstances must have influenced decisions taken about the strategy and tactics involved in the occupation, the personnel making those decisions will inevitably have been informed by their experiences in other parts of the Empire. Moreover, comparative frontier studies do reveal various consistent approaches to the exercising of control in frontier zones, such as the use of client or friendly monarchs or the levying of customs duties, as well as highlighting local differences, such as the absence of gateways along the German frontier palisade or the more restricted depth of military dispositions behind the frontiers along the Rhine and Danube.

The influence of the wider stage of imperial politics on events in Britain has already been hinted at above, when the resumption of advance in the Flavian period after the halt on the Forth–Clyde isthmus seems to coincide with the accession of a new emperor. There are, however, several more specific examples of this process. It is now widely accepted that the major stimulus for the invasion in AD 43 was the need of the new emperor, Claudius, for the prestige of a successful military conquest, while the same principle seems to underlie the reconquest of Scotland under Antoninus Pius. Similarly, attention has been drawn to the effect of circumstances in other parts of the Empire on determining the limits of Roman control in the north of Britain. In the late first century AD, the transfer of troops to the Danube resulted in the withdrawal from northern Scotland; and in the early second century, Trajan's concentration on wars of expansion in Dacia may have resulted in further retrenchment on the northern frontier.

## Key texts
Breeze, D.J., 1982. *The northern frontiers of Roman Britain.* London: Batsford.
Breeze, D.J. and Dobson, B., 1987. *Hadrian's Wall.* London: Penguin.
Hanson, W.S., 1991. *Agricola and the conquest of the north.* London: Batsford. 2 edn.
Hanson, W.S. and Maxwell, G.S., 1986. *Rome's north-west frontier: the Antonine Wall.* Edinburgh: Edinburgh University Press. 2 edn.
Jones, G.D.B. and Mattingly, D.J., 1991. *An atlas of Roman Britain.* Oxford: Blackwell.

# Bibliography

Blagg, T.F.C., 1984. 'An examination of the connexions between military and civilian architecture', in Blagg, T.F.C. and King, A.C. (eds) *Military and civilian in Roman Britain: cultural relationships in a frontier province*, Oxford: British Archaeologial Reports British Series 136, 249–263.

Bowman, A.K., 1994. *Life and letters on the Roman frontier.* London: British Museum Press.

Breeze, D.J., 1974. 'The Roman fortlet at Barburgh Mill, Dumfriesshire', *Britannia* 5, 130–162.

Breeze, D.J., 1983. 'The Roman forts at Ardoch', in O'Connor, A. and Clarke, D.V. (eds) *From the Stone Age to the 'Forty-five.* Edinburgh: John Donald, 224–236.

Breeze, D.J., 1984. 'Demand and supply on the northern frontier', in Miket, R. and Burgess, C. (eds) *Between and beyond the Walls: essays on the prehistory and history of north Britain in honour of George Jobey.* Edinburgh: John Donald, 264–286.

Collingwood, R.G. and Wright, R.P., 1965. *Roman inscriptions of Britain.* Oxford: Clarendon Press.

Cotterill, J., 1993. 'Saxon raiding and the role of the late Roman coastal forts of Britain', *Britannia* 24, 227–239.

Crow, J., 1995. *The English Heritage Book of Housesteads.* London: Batsford/English Heritage.

Freeman, P., 1996. 'Roman frontier studies: what's new?', *Britannia* 27, 465–470.

Frere, S.S. 1987. *Britannia: a history of Roman Britain.* London: Routledge. 3 edn.

Hanson, W.S., 1994. 'Dealing with barbarians: the Romanization of Britain', in Vyner, B. (ed.) *Building on the past.* London: Royal Archaeological Institute, 149–163.

Hanson, W.S., 1997. 'The Roman presence: brief interludes', in Edwards, K.J. and Ralston, I.B.M. (eds) *Scotland: environment and archaeology, 8000 BC–AD 1000.* Chichester: Wiley, 195–216.

Hanson, W.S., forthcoming. *Elginhaugh: a Flavian auxiliary fort and its annexe.* London: Society for the Promotion of Roman Studies.

Hanson, W.S., Daniels, C.M., Dore, J.N. and Gillam, J.P., 1979. 'The Agricolan supply-base at Red House, Corbridge', *Archaeologia Aeliana* 5 ser 7, 1–97.

Hanson, W S. and Friell, J.G.P., 1995. 'Westerton: a Roman watchtower on the Gask frontier', *Proceedings of the Society of Antiquaries of Scotland* 125, 499–519.

Hanson, W.S. and Macinnes, L., 1991. 'Soldiers and settlement in Wales and Scotland', in Jones, R.J.F. (ed.) *Roman Britain: recent trends.* Sheffield: J.R. Collis Publications, 85–92.

Higham, N.J., 1989. 'Roman and native in England north of the Tees: acculturation and its limitations', in Barrett, J.C., Fitzpatrick, A.P. and Macinnes, L. (eds) *Barbarians and Romans in north-west Europe from the later Republic to late Antiquity.* Oxford: British Archaeological Reports International Series S471, 165–174.

Hodgson, N., 1995. 'Were there two Antonine occupations of Scotland?', *Britannia* 26, 29–49.

Jones, G.D.B., 1979. 'The western Stanegate and the development of the coastal frontier', in Dobson, B. (ed.) *The tenth Pilgrimage of Hadrian's Wall.* Kendal: Wilson, 28–29.

Keppie, L.J.F., 1991. *Understanding Roman inscriptions.* London: Batsford.

Macinnes, L., 1984. 'Brochs and the Roman occupation of lowland Scotland', *Proceedings of the Society of Antiquaries of Scotland* 114, 234–249.

Macinnes, L., 1989. 'Baubles, bangles and beads: trade and exchange in Roman Scotland', in Barrett, J.C., Fitzpatrick, A.P. and Macinnes, L. (eds) *Barbarians and Romans in north-west Europe from the later Republic to late Antiquity.* Oxford: British Archaeological Reports International Series S471, 108–116.

Maxfield, V.A. (ed.) 1989. *The Saxon Shore: a handbook.* Exeter: University of Exeter.

Millett, M., 1990. *The Romanization of Britain.* Cambridge: Cambridge University Press.

Ottaway, P., 1996. *Romans on the Yorkshire coast.* York: York Archaeological Trust.

Peacock, D.P.S., 1984. 'Amphorae in Iron Age Britain: a re-assessment', in Macready, S. and Thompson, F.H. (eds) *Cross-Channel trade between Gaul and Britain in the pre-Roman Iron Age.* London: Society of Antiquaries Occasional Paper New Ser. IV, 37–42.

Pitts, L. and St Joseph, J.K.S., 1985. *Inchtuthil: the Roman legionary fortress: excavations 1952–1965.* London: Society for the Promotion of Roman Studies.

Salway, P., 1981. *Roman Britain.* Oxford: Clarendon Press.

Southern, P., 1990. 'Signals versus illumination on Roman frontiers', *Britannia* 21, 233–242.

Todd, M., 1981. *Roman Britain (55 BC–AD 400).* Brighton: Harvester Press.

*Chapter Nine*

# Roman Britain

## Civil and rural society

## Simon Esmonde Cleary

### INTRODUCTION

One of the briefest of the epochs of Britain's past, the Roman period is also one of the most recognizable. To the archaeologist, this is because it saw the introduction of important and distinctive new classes of site, monument and artefact. More generally, it is also the period that bequeathed legacies such as roads and towns that still shape the map of Britain. It also marks the intrusion into Britain of Classical culture, the intellectual, literary and architectural vocabulary of which are embedded in modern European idioms. It can therefore seem comfortingly familiar, perhaps dangerously so for those whose business it is to investigate the 'otherness' of the past.

The distinctive dataset, links with the wider Classical world and some long-standing intellectual traditions mean that the study of Roman Britain has often been rather self-contained. At both the beginning and the end of the Roman period, however, an incoming group imposed itself on a numerically far superior indigenous population. The archaeological distinctiveness of Roman and of Anglo-Saxon material culture (Chapter 10) has meant that perhaps disproportionate effort has been expended on the minority at the expense of the less archaeologically obvious majority. One of the longest standing approaches to the analysis and explanation of the archaeology of the Roman period has been the concept of 'Romanization', analysing the nature and process of the interaction of Roman and indigenous culture to produce the synthesis known as 'Romano-British' (Millett 1990; see also Chapter 8 here). This was not a process whereby the imperial power imposed its culture, but one where the British population made choices about its relationship to that power and about how to display those choices through the adoption (or not) of Roman-style behaviour and its physical expressions. This approach can be undertaken only with an understanding of the Later Iron Age (Chapter 7 here) in order to identify and assess the changes resulting from the Roman conquest. The links between the two periods and the transition from one to the other are visible in the archaeological record, and currently the increasing emphasis on the role of the indigenous population can lead to the earlier part of the Roman period at least being seen almost as a continuation of the Iron Age by other means.

At the end of the Roman period, the interface between Roman Britain and Early Anglo-Saxon England is much less well studied and understood, for the two material cultures seem to have nothing in common, reinforcing the impression of ethnic, cultural and religious separateness gained from the written sources. More recent research and excavation are suggesting, however,

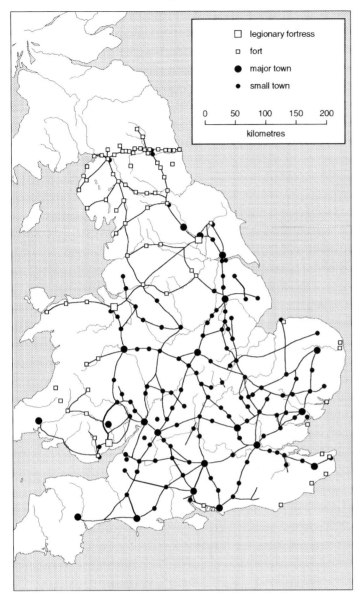

*Figure 9.1* Map of Roman Britain showing distribution of long-term military sites compared with civilian towns. Villas, temples and burials show the same overall distribution as the towns.
*Source*: Jones and Mattingly 1990

that again the relationship between the incomers and the indigenous population may not have been as adversarial as literary convention likes to portray. Even so, the study of the beginning of the Roman period is dominated by models of continuity, and that of its end by models of discontinuity.

## FRAMEWORKS

### Sub-divisions of the period

Though Roman Britain lasted for only some 400 years, its study has tended to fall into two parts: an *earlier* period running from the Claudian invasion of AD 43 down to the end of the second century, and a *later* comprising the third and fourth centuries through to the disappearance of Roman rule and material culture in the first half of the fifth century. Initially, this division and the concentration on the earlier period reflected a wider perspective of the Early Roman Empire (the Principate) as a period of military expansion and cultural vigour, with the later Empire as a period of military decline and cultural decadence. Nowadays, both the wider perspective and the more particular British expression of it are viewed somewhat differently. The earlier period sees the impact of Rome on the native populations and systems through military conquest and cultural adaptation. The later period traces the trajectory of Romano-British culture under the influence of internal factors and in response to wider changes in the Roman world during the period now known as Late Antiquity (*c.* AD 300–700).

### Geographical scope

Until recently, the archaeological study of the civil population of Roman Britain was largely concerned with the area south and east of a line from the Humber to the Devon Exe (cf. Jones and

Mattingly 1990). This stemmed from two largely unstated preoccupations. The first was that it was in the south and east that the Britons were visibly Romanized. Thus in the south and east it was possible to study the assimilation of the native population to a 'higher', Mediterranean-derived civilization. The second was that in the north and west, the same focus on the study of Roman-style monuments and material meant an almost exclusive concentration on military archaeology (Chapter 8), which also fitted into the separate sub-discipline of the study of the Roman army on an Empire-wide basis (Figure 9. 1). This led to a neglect of the archaeology of the civil population, which exhibited little or no sign of Romanization, and whose often insubstantial remains made for difficult, sometimes dull, digging.

## APPROACHES TO THE ARCHAEOLOGICAL RECORD

### Overview

As a result of those factors outlined above, the study of the civil population long concentrated on those site-, monument- and artefact-types that were archaeologically highly visible and attested to the influence of Rome on her most north-westerly province. Foremost amongst these were the towns, acknowledged hallmark of Graeco-Roman civilization. The effect of Rome on the countryside was seen in the spread of *villas*, the quasi-Roman residences of those with the means and the wish to define themselves as part of the new imperial order. Whereas town-dwellers and villa-owners can have formed only a tiny, if influential, fraction of the total population, the evidence of temples and shrines might stand for the more intangible but hugely important sphere of the impact of Rome on the realms of thought and belief of a wider spectrum of the populace. So also might the sculpture, mosaics and wall-paintings found in towns, villas and temples, where 'Roman' and 'native' elements might be disentangled, incidentally throwing light back onto the intractable problems of Iron Age religion (Henig 1984; 1995). Burial, though, so vital a source of information on demography, social structure and religious practice in so many periods of British archaeology, has until very recently been almost totally neglected by students of Roman Britain, though thousands of burials are known (almost all from the south and east) (Philpott 1991).

   The Roman period in Britain is also (in)famous for the huge numbers of artefacts that entered the archaeological record; their technological competence means that the inorganic ones persist in quantity (de la Bédoyère 1988). By far the commonest is pottery, traditionally much used as evidence for dating, but also available for analysis of, for instance, trade or exchange, site function, and the changing consumption of food and drink. Coins have also obviously been much exploited for their dating potential, but more recent studies have shown their usefulness for inter-site comparisons (Reece 1987). Other classes of artefact such as glass, metalwork and organic materials all have their own protocols of study.

### Developments since 1945

The study of Roman Britain since the Second World War has been affected by many of the wider developments in archaeological method and thought, though often less radically than for other periods. The application of techniques derived from the physical and chemical sciences has contributed relatively little to our understanding of the period. For instance, radiocarbon dating has been little used, since on the whole the dating derived from historically datable artefacts provides a cheaper and more secure framework. As has also been noted in regard to military installations (Chapter 8), dendrochronology can be even more precise and certain than artefacts, and is beginning to have an appreciable impact on the dating of sites with suitable conditions of preservation, such as within London. Another technique that has proved valuable is ceramic petrology, in its ability to source fabrics of the ubiquitous Romano-British pottery and thus help to establish patterns of distribution (Peacock 1982). The biological sciences, on the other hand, have made possible major advances in our understanding of the ecology of Roman Britain. This has enabled us to dispense with the traditional reliance on the Roman agrarian writers Cato, Varro and Columella, who were concerned with the Mediterranean slave agriculture of Italy, and replace it with an understanding based on the evidence from Britain itself. This has particularly been developed from osteology for wild and domesticated animals, and by palynology and palaeobotany for staple and relish crops and the overall management of the countryside and its resources such as woodland.

Most important and striking have been the changes in the intellectual framework within which the study of Roman Britain takes place. For the quarter-century or so after the Second World War, such study was strongly empirical, its analyses dominated by questions and approaches derived ultimately from the surviving literary sources along with epigraphic (inscription) evidence (e.g. Salway 1993). This was particularly true of the military archaeology of Roman Britain, but the tiny number of references to affairs in the civil side of the Province had a quite disproportionate effect. Excavation concentrated on 'Roman' sites such as towns and villas, and explanatory models were often drawn either from Classical authors (appropriate or not) or consciously or implicitly from the experiences of the modern British land-owning and educated classes. They projected back onto the Roman Empire the experiences and preconceptions of the elite of a modern imperial/colonial power.

The successive intellectual movements and fashions that have swept archaeology over the last 30 years or so have taken their time to dislodge this well-established tradition; some have failed to make headway against indifference or antipathy. In other cases, the close relationship between data and the generation and application of theoretical approaches has meant that approaches devised for other areas or periods have not been seen as appropriate for the Roman period, particularly when confronted with the great quantity and range of data from that period. Nonetheless, with the rise of a generation that has grown up in and after Britain's own retreat from Empire and that has been trained as archaeologists rather than historians, a change is coming about. Gradually, a Romano-British intellectual synthesis is being formed through the interaction of new ideas and approaches from external sources with the indigenous database and epistemology. Its characteristics include a marked concern for making explicit the theoretical approaches of both past and present work, be it excavation or analysis. Allied with this is a concern for the quantification of data, its statistical manipulation and graphic display, which are particularly welcome in such a data-rich period. This has been underpinning the development of an explanatory framework centring on social structures and development, reflecting the importance of the 'processualist' school of thought (Chapter 1) in recent British archaeology. It also seems particularly appropriate for investigating the processes that make up the phenomenon of Romanization. Romanization was also a matter of more than the social, however, and the concerns of post-processual thought with the symbolism and the *mentalités* of societies are beginning to impinge on Romano-British studies, as are other strands such as the archaeology of gender. The post-imperial consciousness of many workers is to be seen in the increasing commitment to the less visibly Romanized part of the Romano-British population, for instance in the north and west, and to the reasons and choices that lay behind the rejection (or non-acceptance) of a Romanized culture (cf. TRAC 1993). These theoretical developments co-exist, however, with a still strong, continuing empirical tradition, represented by the excavation and the publication of sites and of works on classes of material or other aspects of the archaeology of Roman Britain.

# TOWNS

Much excavation and publication has centred on towns, for they were central to the Roman way of life, and even today commendatory words such as 'civilized' and 'urbane' derive from Latin words for town. Their cultural importance, to say nothing of their administrative usefulness, caused the Roman authorities to encourage the development of towns. Thus the appearance, development and disappearance of towns reflects as nothing else the impact of Rome on Britain (Wacher 1995). Traditionally, Roman towns in Britain have been placed in a classificatory hierarchy based on their rank in the Roman administrative system, but to the archaeologist there is a simple, two-fold grouping on size and morphological grounds.

## 'Large' towns

The group of 'large' towns comprehends the major centres, those that the Romans ranked as *coloniae*, and the *civitas*-capitals. The *coloniae* were originally purposive foundations by the Roman authorities at Colchester, Gloucester and Lincoln, where veteran legionaries were settled; later York and probably London were given the title as an honour. A *civitas* was a unit of local government based on the territories of the late Iron Age tribes and administered by the Romanized tribal elite; each *civitas* was run from a principal town.

Despite differences in rank, these 'large' towns shared many characteristics. They were formally laid out on an orthogonal street-grid. They contained a range of public buildings in Roman-derived form for administration and leisure. Chief amongst these was the forum/basilica complex, which was the administrative seat of the governance of the *civitas*. Each 'large' town also had a set of public baths, not just places for getting clean but also principal centres for leisure and social activity. These would entail a water supply and a sewerage system for the town. Other buildings for leisure and entertainment might include an amphitheatre (for games and spectacles) or, more rarely, a theatre (for plays and mimes), along with temples. No certain example of a circus or hippodrome for horse and chariot racing has yet been found in Britain, and the theatres and amphitheatres tend to be small and unimpressive compared with continental examples.

All of these activities were derived from Roman culture and took place in Roman-style buildings, yet they represent a British phenomenon, for it would have been the local elites of the *civitates* who would have paid for them (not the Roman authorities). By choosing so to do, these elites demonstrated both to the Romans and to their social sub-ordinates their acceptance of Roman ways and of the Mediterranean ideal of euergetism (civic benefaction).

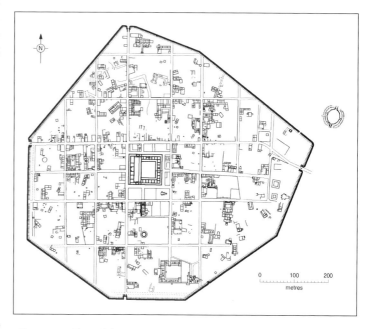

*Figure 9.2* Plan of the *civitas*-capital at Silchester, Hampshire, showing the grid plan, defences, public and private buildings.
*Source*: Boon, G.C., 1974. *Silchester: the Roman town of Calleva*. Newton Abbott: David and Charles

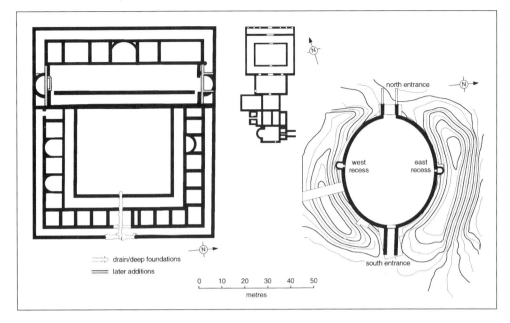

**Figure 9.3** Silchester: the forum (Hadrianic version), the baths (first period, late first century) and amphitheatre (stone phase, third–fourth century).
*Source*: Fulford, M., 1993 in Greep, S. (ed.) *Roman Towns: the Wheeler inheritance*. London: Council for British Archaeology Research Report 93; St John Hope, W.H.S. and Fox, G.E., 1905. 'Excavations on the site of the Roman city at Silchester, Hants in 1903 and 1904', *Archaeologia* 59: 2; Fulford, M. 1989, *The Silchester Amphitheatre*. London: Britannia Monograph Series 10

Initially, however, this acceptance did not extend to actually living in the towns for whose embellishment they were paying. Until the late second century, the domestic structures within these towns overwhelmingly consisted of the shops/workshops of the artisans and traders who made these towns centres of commerce. From the late second century, however, these towns were increasingly colonized by the large 'town houses' of the elite, so that by the fourth century they were dominated by these mansions for the private display of wealth, whilst the old public buildings fell into decay and disuse and the commercial life of the 'large' towns became less important to them.

Most of the 'large' towns of Roman Britain are now covered by medieval and modern towns, but Silchester (Hampshire) was not reoccupied and is a type-site for Roman provincial towns (Figure 9.2). The 40 ha within the defences were cleared at the end of the nineteenth century, revealing the overall plan, the various public buildings (Figure 9.3) and many private buildings, principally 'town houses' and some commercial premises along the main thoroughfare. The cemeteries lay outside the defences, thus separating the world of the dead from that of the living; they remain unexcavated. It is now appreciated that the plan bequeathed to us by the Victorian excavations is essentially that of fourth-century Silchester. For a better impression of development through time, one must turn to *Verulamium* (near St Albans, Hertfordshire), another abandoned Roman town, where the excavations before the Second World War by Mortimer Wheeler and subsequently by Sheppard Frere and others have revealed a complete sequence from the Late Iron Age oppidum (Chapter 7) to the town destroyed by the Boudiccan rebellion of AD 60/61, thereafter rebuilt, enlarged, embellished and ultimately declining to extinction through the late fourth and fifth centuries.

## 'Small' towns

By contrast, the 'small' towns of Roman Britain were local market centres, lacking the formal planning, public buildings and amenities, and the large houses of the wealthy. They ranged in size from clusters of buildings little differentiated in form, or probably function, from those on rural sites, up to major settlements comparable in extent with the 'large' towns (Burnham and Wacher 1990). Though more numerous than the 'large' towns, they have been the targets of less structured excavation and research. Characteristically, they grew up along roads or at road junctions, emphasizing the importance of communications for their commercial functions. Several also contained installations of the *cursus publicus* (imperial communications) and many had temples, some of which may have been the stimulus for the development of the settlement and suggest that some 'small' towns may have acted as religious foci for sub-divisions (*pagi*) of the *civitas*. In place of the public and the high-status buildings of the 'large' towns, the building-stock of the 'small' towns overwhelmingly consists of the shop/workshop type (Figure 9.4) already noted as the commercial and artisan premises at the 'large' towns. The evidence for the manufacture and distribution of imported and locally produced pottery and other artefact types out into the surrounding rural sites confirms the 'small' towns' role as market and trading centres.

The only commonly occurring public structures were defences, initially an earthwork and later replaced in stone like those at the 'large' towns. Unlike at the 'large' towns, these defences made no attempt to enclose the entire inhabited zone, leaving large extra-mural areas. Many 'small' towns had ordered cemeteries, but burials are also encountered close to and amongst the houses of the

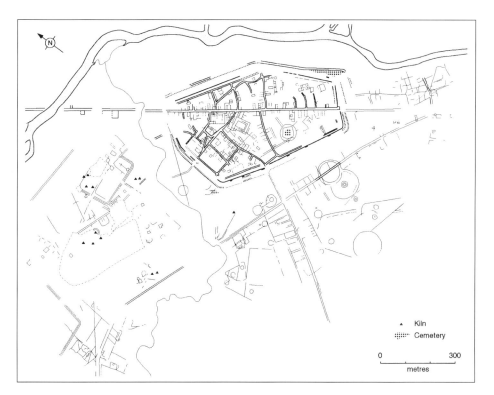

*Figure 9.4* Plan of a 'small' town at Water Newton, Cambridgeshire, showing the defended nucleus, intra-mural building types, extra-mural occupation, and pottery kilns.
*Source*: Burnham and Wacher 1990

living. It would seem that the 'small' towns were at their peak in the fourth century, correspond-ing with the decline in commercial dominance of the 'large' towns, as the latter came increasingly to be occupied by the houses of the elite.

## Villas and the countryside

One of the important features of towns at any period is that they act as channels for the diffusion of new ideas. This is evident in Roman Britain through the development in the south and east of villas, though even in these parts of the country there are variations in distribution with, for instance, clusters in the Cotswolds, central-southern England and the East Midlands and absences in the West Midlands, the Fenland and the Weald. *Villa* is a Latin word meaning 'farm', but in modern archaeological usage 'villa' has come to mean a rural site exhibiting Roman-style building plans and architecture, thus evoking integration into the imperial culture and probably also a closer involvement in the imperial economy than other, un-Romanized sites (Rivet 1969; Todd 1978; Hingley 1989). A problem is that the single term 'villa' is used to describe hundreds of sites ranging in date from the late first to the early fifth centuries and in size from cottage to palatial, suggesting in fact that form, function and social significance may have varied greatly through time. Furthermore, many villa excavations have concentrated on the principal residence and ignored the agricultural aspects of the site, though this is now changing for the better, and survey projects such as that at Maddle Farm (Berkshire) show how study of the Roman period may be integrated into and benefit from a multiperiod, landscape approach.

## The development of villas

The earliest Romano-British villas, of the second half of the first century, show their continental origins. The most famous but atypical is the great Flavian 'palace' at Fishbourne (West Sussex), with its Mediterranean plan, architecture, mosaics, other decor and formal gardens with water-supply. This is often claimed as the residence of the 'client king' (semi-independent native ruler) Cogidubnus. Contemporary villas are otherwise modest, sometimes little more than a single rectangular room – in effect a rectilinear version of the roundhouses of the preceding Iron Age – or two or three rooms (e.g. Lockleys and Park Street, both Hertfordshire), often ranged behind a 'winged-corridor' façade consisting of a passage or portico with projecting rooms at either end. This type of façade occurs commonly in Britain, Gaul and Germany, masking a whole variety of suites of rooms, indicating a desire to conform to the accepted formal frontage, whatever lay behind (e.g. Ditchley, Oxfordshire; Gadebridge, Hertfordshire; and Great Staughton, Huntingdonshire). Several of these early villas show continuity from Late Iron Age sites (e.g. Gorhambury, Hertfordshire) (Figure 9.5). Another characteristic villa building was the aisled building or aisled barn, a rectangular structure with two internal rows of posts; some idea of the appearance of these can be gained from the collapsed gable wall of one excavated at Meonstoke (Hampshire). Excavated examples suggest use for storage, for craft activity and for accom-modation (sometimes all at once). Aisled buildings are known either as the principal building of a small villa (e.g. Combley, Isle of Wight) or as subsidiary buildings in a larger establishment (e.g. Winterton, Lincolnshire), but are not a purely rural building type as they occur also in towns.

During the second century, the plans of villas became more complex, with the principal dwelling being extended and made more elaborate, and dependencies and agricultural buildings often arranged more or less formally around a courtyard as at Llantwit Major (Glamorgan) or Rockbourne (Hampshire). After an apparent lull in villa (re)construction during much of the third century, the late third and first half of the fourth centuries saw the hey-day of the villa in Britain. This was when the maximum number were in commission. It is also the period from which some of the best-known, largest and most luxuriously appointed examples date, such as Bignor (West Sussex) or Woodchester (Gloucestershire), which stand comparison with the great continental villas, though there were also some much more modest establishments of this date, such as Barnack (Cambridgeshire).

In the first spate of the provision of mosaics at the end of the second century, they were almost all laid in the new mansions in the 'large' towns. The main phase of mosaic laying in Britain, however, was not until the first half of the fourth century, and now the majority of these were laid at villas, with some also at residences in the 'large' towns, reflecting the shift in display to the private sphere and the growing importance of rural seats *vis-à-vis* the main towns. Many of these mosaics showed divine figures or mythical scenes, all of which were taken from Graeco-Roman, not Celtic, culture and religion (including Christianity). Until recently, it was assumed that a villa was the residence of a land-owning male aristocrat, his family and dependants. This accorded with the picture derived from the Roman agrarian writers and also unconsciously reflected the pattern of the modern British land-owning aristocracy: the villa seen as proto-country-house. More recently, it has been argued that some villa plans are more amenable to dissection as a series of units of differing size and status, and thus rather than reflecting the picture outlined above, might in fact show multiple occupancy of a single villa, perhaps by different branches of a descent group in a 'Celtic' fashion (Smith 1978). Though this suggestion is not universally accepted, it does illustrate how unstated preconceptions can influence interpretation, and how new approaches can be applied to old evidence.

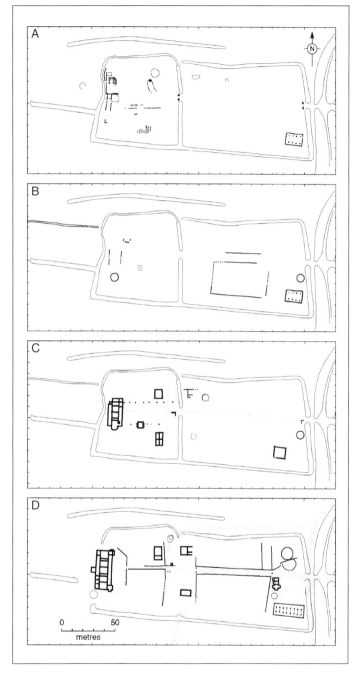

*Figure 9.5* Gorhambury, Hertfordshire. (A) The Late Iron Age settlement; (B) the Early Roman period settlement; (C) the second-century villa; (D) the villa in the third century.
*Source*: Neal, D.S. *et al.*, 1990. *Excavation of the Iron Age, Roman and Medieval Settlement at Gorhambury, St Albans.* London: English Heritage Archaeological Report 14.

*Figure 9.6* Settlement and landscape of the Roman period in the vicinity of Chalton, Hampshire.
*Source*: Cunliffe, B.W., 1976, 'A Romano-British village at Chalton, Hants', *Proceedings of the Hampshire Field Club* 33.

## Other rural settlements

One of the many benefits of aerial and other survey techniques has been to end dependence on villas for our view of the Romano-British countryside and its society. Instead of a number of isolated sites, archaeologists can now discern a landscape articulated into field-systems, and crossed by tracks and boundaries (Fulford 1990). It is now clear that the great majority of settlements were of the 'native farm-stead' type, that is enclosed groups of structures, usually of the prehistoric roundhouse tradition and yielding relatively little Romanized artefactual material (Hingley 1989). Alongside these dispersed, small settlements, perhaps the homes of extended family groups, there are also nucleated linear settlements, somewhat reminiscent of medieval village plans. These are best known in Somerset (Catsgore), Wiltshire (Chisenbury Warren, Nook) and Hampshire (Chalton) (Figure 9.6). Many non-villa settlements continue on the same site from the Late Iron Age, but there is increasing evidence that through the 400 years of Roman Britain, there was much settlement shift, boundary redrawing and the creation of new field-systems, so that the agrarian landscape of the fourth century would often have been markedly different from that of the first. Large-scale modern excavations in advance of gravel-extraction in the river valleys of lowland Britain at sites in the upper Thames Valley such as Claydon Pike, Lechlade (Gloucestershire), the Warwickshire Avon at Beckford (Hereford and Worcestershire) and Wasperton (Warwickshire) have enabled detailed studies of the shifting pattern of settlements within their contemporary landscapes.

It can seem at first sight that the majority of the rural population was little touched by the Roman way of doing things, though archaeologists should not slide too easily into thinking that there was no contact. Towns 'large' and 'small' would make available new products and new ideas. Links up the social hierarchy to Romanized landowners would also introduce new ways. Moreover, the ubiquitous demands of taxation, military supply and possibly military service would make these people aware of the imperial system. Though in their day-to-day lives there might be little direct evidence of Rome, the social, economic and mental frameworks within which those lives were conducted would have changed.

# RELIGION

Many rural sites yield evidence for religious observance, and the study of the archaeological and epigraphic evidence for religion and ritual have long been an important area for the assessment of the degree of continuity of native cult on the one hand, and the changes wrought by Roman introductions on the other (Henig 1984). Conventionally, religions in Roman Britain have been classified according to whether they related to the state pantheon of Rome, or were indigenous, or were imported eastern 'mystery' cults. The aspects of religion fossilized in the archaeological record reveal little about the actual belief- and value-systems of the religion or about the views and practices of the individual worshipper. For these, written evidence is required, hence the paradox that the imperial and mystery cults are relatively well understood, whereas the far more widespread indigenous cults are only obliquely illuminated.

The worship of the state deities, of *Roma*, of living and dead emperors and the imperial house was one of the ways in which Rome tried to impose some common loyalty and ideology on a vast and disparate Empire. In Britain, the bulk of the evidence for these observances comes from the military areas of the north and west. In part, this is a reflection of the political imperative of ensuring the loyalty of the army, but it also reflects the fact that the overwhelming majority of surviving inscriptions come from these areas. In the civil south and east, the 'epigraphic habit' does not seem to have caught on, the relative shortage of inscriptions being accentuated by the disappearance of Roman stone into later buildings. Nonetheless, the imposing Temple of the Deified Claudius at Colchester, which was the centre of the provincial cult, and fragmentary epigraphic evidence elsewhere, show that the state cults were observed. Serving as a priest of one of these cults would have been one of the prestigious posts open to members of the local elites.

For the bulk of the population, however, it was the cults with their origins in prehistory and often very localized that shaped their day-to-day lives and attitudes. The evidence for these is most easily identified at temples. Sharing a very similar distribution with towns and villas, temples were almost all built not to the Classical plan, like the Parthenon, but to the so-called Romano-Celtic plan of a square within a square, or sometimes to a double-circle or double-polygon plan. These temples were small and designed for the ministrations of priests or individual worshippers, not to contain congregations. Many temples stood within a precinct or *temenos*, sometimes containing ancillary structures as at Lydney or Uley (both in Gloucestershire) (Figure 9.7). These *temene* could have accommodated large numbers of

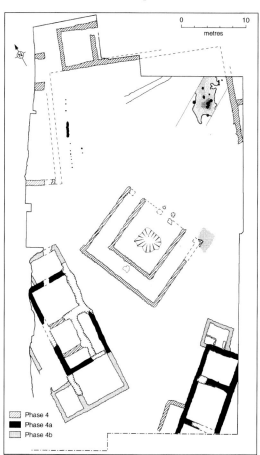

Phase 4
Phase 4a
Phase 4b

***Figure 9.7*** West Hill, Uley, Gloucestershire. The Romano-Celtic temple (centre) and ancillary buildings in the third/fourth centuries.
*Source*: Woodward, A. and Leach, P., 1993. *The Uley Shrines: excavation of a ritual complex on West Hill, Uley, Gloucestershire: 1977–9*. London: English Heritage Archaeological Report 17

worshippers at festivals. Also associated with temple sites are altars, sculptures and various forms of votive deposit, of which the single most interesting is the assemblage of over 12,000 coins, other offerings and inscribed curse-tablets (*defixiones*) from Bath (Cunliffe and Davenport 1988).

## Religion in relation to earlier practices

The study of pagan religion in the civil areas of Roman Britain has been much conditioned by the problem of the extent to which it represents a continuum from the ill-understood religious world of the Later Iron Age. This, as so often, has stemmed from epigraphic and literary sources. Inscriptions reveal the practice of *interpretatio romana*, the conflation of native with Roman deities, such as the goddess Sulis Minerva at Bath or the god Mars Rigonemetos (King of the Grove) from Nettleham (Lincolnshire). The better-known classical deity can be used as a guide to aspects of the native. Also called in aid are the early Welsh and Irish myth and hero stories, which give some insight into Celtic religious beliefs and practices. Sometimes these sources can provide a context for elements observable in the archaeological record, such as the importance of the number three, of the head, or of springs and other places involving water. They can also suggest some ways of approaching some of the otherwise inscrutable sculptures and symbols from Romano-British religious sites. It is clearly dangerous, however, to make simple links between sources of evidence so widely different in type, time and context (Wait 1985). More secure evidence for the continuance of Late Iron Age observances into the Roman period comes from those Romano-Celtic temples that overlie Iron Age predecessors, as at Hayling Island (Hampshire). Nevertheless, it should be remembered that worship at temples and the use of features such as altars and sculpture derive from Mediterranean practice. Even the deposit at Bath, though placed in a spring as in later prehistory, consisted of a range of objects very different from those in comparable Iron Age contexts, and the curse-tablets were inscribed throughout in Latin.

## Oriental cults; Christianity

A feature of the Later Roman period was the appearance of evidence for the oriental 'mystery' cults in the civil areas of the Province. These offered some form of salvation or life after death to those initiated into the cult, in return for right belief and action in this life. Though again more common at military sites, the civil areas have evidence for the worship of Isis and of Mithras from London, and from there and elsewhere for the cults of Cybele and of Serapis. Ultimately, the most successful of these religions was Christianity (Thomas 1981). There is increasing evidence for Christianity amongst the urban and land-owning rural classes in the fourth century.

Churches (albeit small ones) are suggested at Lincoln (Figure 9.10) and Silchester, and fonts are known from the Saxon Shore fort at Richborough (Chapter 8) and the 'small' town of Icklingham. From the 'small' town of Chesterton/Water Newton (Cambridgeshire) comes a hoard of Christian silver plate. The villas at Frampton and Hinton St Mary (Dorset) (Figure 9.8) and Lullingstone (Kent) had Christian mosaics and wall-paintings respectively. That Christianity should have made head-way amongst the upper classes in the fourth century is unsurprising, given the amount of imperial patronage and privileges the religion was granted. More difficult to assess is the spread of 'lower class' Christianity, due to problems in how to identify it if it did not leave substantial remains. Some large fourth-century cemeteries, such as Poundbury, Dorchester (Dorset), have been claimed as Christian on the basis of east–west inhumation with no grave goods, but in truth this just seems to have been the general rite in Late Roman Britain and is not necessarily related to religious affiliation, which had little effect on Roman burial practice. It was, of course, this Romano-British tradition of Christianity, reinforced from Gaul, that was to persist in the British Isles as 'Celtic' Christianity. Early in the fifth century, it also produced the Romano-Britons Pelagius the heretic and Patricius, better known as Patrick, apostle of the Irish.

## THE NORTH AND WEST

Towns, villas, temples and archaeologically visible burials are features
of the civil archaeology of Britain
largely confined to the south and
east. Their co-incidence in time and
space strongly suggests that they are
all inter-related aspects of the initial
adoption and adaptation of Roman
culture and its subsequent development into the Late Roman period
by the populace of these regions.
North-west of the Humber–Exe
line, however, these Romanized
elements were few and far between.
Some of the trading functions elsewhere performed by the towns may
have occurred at *vici*, the civilian
settlements attached to the garrison
forts (Sommer 1984), though to
judge by the paucity of Roman
material on native sites, exchange
with the indigenous people was not
one of the prime activities at the
*vici*.

## Settlements

In the north and west, the principal
settlement pattern continued to be
dispersed and the main settlement
type the enclosed farmstead, as in
prehistory. Aerial and other survey
has revealed large numbers of settlements of this type in north-eastern
and north-western England, the
Lowlands of Scotland and in Wales
and the south-west of England (e.g.
the Cornish 'rounds', with their
courtyard houses).

*Figure 9.8* Line drawing of the mid-fourth-century probable Christian mosaic from the villa at Hinton St Mary, Dorset.
*Source*: Tonybee, J., 1964. 'A new mosaic pavement found in Dorset', *Journal of Roman Studies* 54

A combination of aerial and ground survey in north-western England and south-western Scotland has shown very many of these sites to date to the Roman period, both to south and north of Hadrian's Wall (cf. Higham and Jones 1985). Whether this represents a higher density of settlement than in late prehistory and the early medieval centuries is more problematic, since in this area both these periods were aceramic and thus essentially undatable by field survey, so the apparent peak in the Roman period may be more a reflection of the availability of dating material than of actual population levels. Settlements still visible as upstanding monuments or on aerial photographs or which have been excavated show that the number of structures at a site could

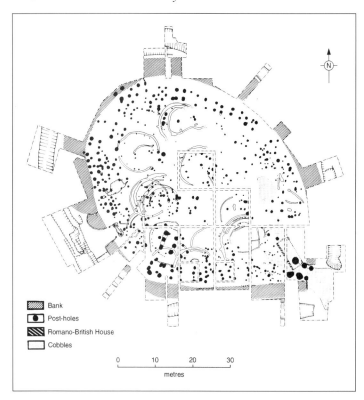

range from one roundhouse, as at Belling Law (Northumberland), to multistructure complexes such as Milking Gap (Northumberland) or Walesland Rath (Pembrokeshire) (Figure 9.9), usually interpreted as the residence of either a single nucleated family or, for the larger sites, an extended family or kin group.

## Economy and environment

In overall plan, building-types and artefacts, these settlements show little Roman influence. Explaining this phenomenon poses important questions about the interaction of Romans and Britons. In the past, the explanation was often seen as environmental determinism: the north and west are agriculturally poorer than the south and east, with an emphasis on pastoralism; but the north and west could sustain elaborate and expensive displays of status through building, as the abbeys and castles of the Middle Ages show. Environmental factors might thus help explain a relative

*Figure 9.9* Walesland Rath, Pembrokeshire, a settlement with Iron Age-style layout and structures, but of the Roman period.
*Source*: Wainwright, G.J., 1971. 'The excavation of a fortified settlement at Walesland Rath, Pembrokeshire', *Britannia* 2

difference but not the more absolute difference that is apparent between the north and west *versus* the south and east in the Roman period; social and economic factors must be adduced. An obvious difference between the two areas is the long-term presence in the north and west of the Roman army (Chapter 8). Though the army has often been seen as a principal instrument of Romanization, this is in fact unlikely. The auxiliary units that formed the majority of the garrison in the north and west were themselves of provincial extraction from all over the Empire, with a veneer of military Roman-ness added, such as in the use of the Latin language and the observance of the deities and religious festivals of the Roman state. They would give as reliable a guide to Roman civilization as a soldier of the French Foreign Legion to contemporary France. So lack of suitable role models may have been part of the explanation for the lack of Romanization.

## Romanization and its impacts

Another important answer lies in the process of Romanization. This normally took place by the conversion of the elite to Roman ways, with a consequent 'trickle-down' effect, as we have seen in the south and east. But the archaeological evidence for the north and west does not show clear evidence of a steep social hierarchy and the presence of an élite in later prehistory or in the Roman period: no elite, no Romanization? Did the very presence of the army and the consequent siphoning-off of ambitious young men inhibit the formation of an elite? There may also have been ideological factors at work, promoting the continuance of traditional means of social distinction at the expense of new, Roman-derived ones. Thus command over people or livestock may have been what mattered, and traditional means of display such as gift giving or ritualized feasting may have been preferred to building a villa with Roman-style dining room and using pottery. This may also hold good for some of the villa-less areas of the south and east such as the West Midlands.

There were, however, inescapable links between the military garrisons and the civilian population of the north and west through the needs of the former for supplies from the latter. The Roman army was, in part, fed, clothed and supplied through taxation, and there is evidence that in frontier provinces such as Britain this was often rendered in kind rather than coin. Over and above this, military units could purchase supplies, as could individual men. For convenience's sake, much of this would have been obtained from the regions in which the army was based, thus the army would have been an attractive market for local agriculturalists. The apparent peak in rural settlement in this period might in part result from this stimulus, for instance the Roman army ate meat and used huge quantities of leather, which would suit regions of pastoralism. In the previous chapter, a rather different perspective on these potential impacts is offered. Also vital was a supply of recruits. Once the army settled on permanent frontier systems, local recruitment would increasingly have been the case; but balancing this drain of young men would have been the soldiers' input into the local demography through their families, mainly resident in the *vici*. Thus economic and social links would undoubtedly have existed between military and civilian, even if they were not of a type that leaves much trace in the archaeological record.

## AGRICULTURE, INDUSTRY AND TECHNOLOGICAL DEVELOPMENTS

### Farming and foodstuffs

For a long time it was believed that the impact of a major civilization on Britain must have included substantial changes and improvements to the productive capacity and technology of the island. By far the most important single 'industry' in Roman Britain was agriculture, and modern work on archaeological evidence for the arable and pastoral regimes suggests that in fact there was considerable continuity from the Iron Age (Jones 1989). The principal grain crops remained spelt wheat (with some emmer in the north and west) and barley and oats. The Roman period did see a wider use of bread wheat, perhaps initially under military influence, though its rise to dominance was to be a post-Roman trend. If the staple crops changed little, there is evidence that the 'relish' plants – vegetables, herbs and spices – did see introductions in the Roman period, from cucumber to coriander, presumably reflecting Romanization of the cuisine. There is now good evidence for Roman-period viticulture in Britain. There is also some evidence for developments in the technology of crop production and processing, with the introduction of the coulter to speed the plough, the mould-board to turn the soil and the water-mill.

Likewise, the main domestic animal species remained the same: cattle, sheep and pigs (Grant 1989). There is, though, evidence for changes in their raising and consumption. Over time, there was a trend towards cattle at the expense of sheep, showing first at forts and 'large' towns, then spreading to villas and 'small' towns, again probably suggesting a change in dietary preference and cuisine. This is supported by evidence for changes in butchery practice between the Iron Age and the Roman period. The kill pattern of cattle and sheep tends, broadly, to be bi-modal, with a number killed young, presumably for meat, but many kept into maturity. In the case of cattle, this was probably for energy, reproduction, as a wealth-store and for the many products of the eventual carcass, and, in the case of sheep, for their wool.

Even if the basic crops and animals of British agriculture remained pretty stable through the Roman period, there are grounds for believing that the ways in which they were used changed significantly. For a start, the presence of the agriculturally idle mouths of the army, many town-dwellers and of the leisured élite would have affected crop production and animal husbandry and emphasized a system of producing and consuming sites. Moreover, there were changes in dietary preference, cuisine and the surroundings in which the Romanized section of the population consumed its food. Food and its consumption can be as much social statements as dress or speech, and what went on in the *triclinium* or *stibadium*, the formal dining-rooms of the villas and town houses of the early and late empires, may have transformed the use of apparently standard crops and animals almost out of recognition.

## Mineral extraction

Mineral resources were heavily exploited in the Roman period. The gold mines at Dolaucothi (Carmarthenshire) were opened up by the army. The lead deposits of the Mendips, the Peak District, Flintshire and Shropshire were all worked, initially by the army but later by civilian contractors. The principal interest here was in the small amount of silver in the lead, though the lead was a useful by-product. The copper deposits of north Wales and the copper and tin of Cornwall continued to be exploited. Iron was mined in the Forest of Dean and in the Weald, the latter by the *Classis Britannica*, the fleet.

## Other industries

Of other industries, by far the best known is pottery (Tyers 1996). The potter's fast wheel had been adopted in south-eastern Britain in the century before the Roman invasion, and ceramics comparable with those of the Roman world were being produced (Chapter 7). Outside this area, hand- or slow-wheel-made pottery was the norm, with much of the north and the west being aceramic. The Roman army introduced new forms such as the flagon and the *mortarium*, a grinding bowl. It was also responsible for a vastly increased supply of continental fine wares, especially 'Samian' (*terra sigillata*), a fine red table ware from Gaul, often with moulded decoration, and of amphorae, large vessels for the transport of Mediterranean commodities such as wine, olive oil and *garum* (fish sauce). This all betrays the impact of Roman eating and drinking habits.

Indigenous potters soon learnt to produce competent coarse and table wares in huge quantities. These were manufactured either in small production sites, perhaps as a cash-crop in slack periods of the agricultural year, or in major 'industrial' complexes such as those at Colchester and the lower Nene Valley in the second century, or East Yorkshire, the New Forest and Oxfordshire in the third and fourth centuries. The distributions show the importance of marketing through the towns. The fine ware was simple but competent earthenware, with colour-coat and slip decoration, occasionally with painted or impressed decoration. The coarse ware was generally undecorated, often grey. It should be remembered that though pottery is very common and much studied, it was a cheap commodity, and the well-to-do would have eaten and drunk from metalware such as bronze, pewter or silver. The pottery industry shows that incorporation within the Roman Empire did not lead to major technological innovation, but rather involved the systematic application of technically simple but tried and tested means of manufacture not very different to some already in use in the island; an example is the appearance of more developed kilns alongside the continuing use of simpler methods of firing.

## THE 'END' OF ROMAN BRITAIN

Given the durability of Romano-British buildings and the ubiquity of the artefacts, it seems surprising that such an influential culture seems to have disappeared in short order early in the fifth century. The decline and fall of Roman Britain are still poorly understood (Esmonde Cleary 1989), although several 'ends' can be recognized. The historical sources give a political and administrative 'end' in about AD 411, when the imperial government was no longer able to assert its authority in Britain. This also entailed an economic 'end', as the imperial taxation and expenditure system broke down, presumably bringing about a military 'end' soon after, as the army was no longer paid or supplied. The archaeological sources suggest an 'end' to general use of Roman-style material culture by the middle of the fifth century. Dating this process is very difficult, since the economic 'end' of Roman Britain meant that no new coins were supplied to the island, and part of the archaeological 'end' was the disappearance of the pottery industries. Thus the main dating indicators fail at a crucial juncture. Nevertheless, it is clear that by *c.* AD 450, the towns were no longer functioning as urban places, villas were abandoned, and Roman-style artefacts, such as pottery, were no longer being produced.

To approach an answer, it has to be remembered that Roman material culture in Britain was very much tied in with the Romanized elite and the urban populace. It was they who lived in villas, walked on mosaics, used coin and dropped pottery. It can be argued that in the Late Roman period, towns and the elite were heavily dependent on the imperial system for economic vitality and social position. If this was so, then the collapse of that imperial system would have taken precisely those groups so visible in the archaeological record as 'Roman' down with it. That the archaeological 'end' of Roman Britain should coincide so closely with the administrative and economic 'ends' of Roman governance in Britain would therefore be entirely understandable. The apparent enormity of the collapse of Romano-British culture thus becomes more comprehensible when it is appreciated that it primarily concerned a relatively small, influential and, above all, archaeologically highly visible segment of the population.

## CURRENT ISSUES IN THE STUDY OF ROMAN BRITAIN

It should be clear that the ways in which the archaeology of Roman Britain are undertaken and thought about are in considerable flux. Much of this is in response to wider trends in archaeology. For instance, the database for the Roman period was long thought to be of such quantity and quality that it almost spoke for itself. Increasing concern with site formation processes and their purposive rather than random nature, with taphonomy, with recovery, with absence as well as presence, and with statistical and sampling techniques, however, has made students of this period sharply aware of the patchiness and biased nature of the database. This awareness feeds into the current debates over Romanization, particularly the extent and nature of the impact of Roman ways on the non-elite and archaeologically less visible majority of the population. It is also increasingly recognized that the concept of Romanization risks imposing a false polarity between 'Roman' and 'indigenous' on the archaeological material. This is exacerbated by appreciation that much that archaeologists designate as 'Roman' in Britain would not look particularly so to an inhabitant of the City of Rome. There was no 'ideal type' of Roman: it was a series of provincial compromises. Equally, was there a stereotypical 'British'? The diversity of both Iron Age and Roman-period material culture strongly suggests not.

Other chronological problems need to be confronted. The concept of Romanization loses much of its explanatory power around the end of the second century. By then, the principal phase of the adoption of Roman-style culture is over, and subsequent developments cannot satisfactorily be explained only in such terms. For the Roman Empire in general, the third century is seen as a period of crisis, or at least major change. The archaeology of towns, villas, burials, artefacts and their significance in AD 300 is markedly different to that in AD 200. How can these changes be calibrated and explained? What of the ending of Roman Britain? If it is accepted that this

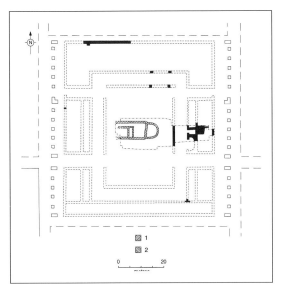

*Figure 9.10* The Late Roman timber churches in the forum plaza at Lincoln.
*Source*: Jones, M., 1995. (ed.) *Pre-Viking Lindsey*. Lincoln: Lincoln Archaeological Studies 1

was not inflicted by invading Anglo-Saxons, then responsibility shifts back to the Romano-Britons, within the context of the fall of the western Roman Empire. What of the archaeological evidence that Romano-British culture was already in marked decline in the late fourth century? If study of the archaeological record indicates the disappearance of a Romanized elite culture in the early fifth century, what follows is archaeologically near to invisible (Figure 9.10). What happened to the elite, and who or what succeeded it?

As well as chronology-based problems there are many more thematic ones, often relating to particular classes of site or material. The neglect of mortuary archaeology for the Roman period has been remarked on, though this is now changing for the better. Also remarked on has been the relatively limited range of approaches to the archaeology of religious sites and material. The increasing interest in the role of symbolism must mean that new perspectives on sculptural and other representations and on the whole field of 'art' need to be opened up, since this evidence represents very directly concerns and choices of the people who commissioned or made it. Many commonly occurring classes of artefact such as pottery or glass are now producing important and fascinating information, but others such as brooches await elucidation. These are just a small sample of classes of evidence that can still yield very valuable insights; it would be possible to repeat this exercise across the spectrum of Romano-British archaeology. The important message, though, is that a period that often seemed to have its evidence and its answers carved in stone was in fact as shifting as any other.

## THE WIDER SETTING

Roman Britain can be looked at in two ways. One is as a short period in the continuum of British archaeology. This may be the right approach for projects at the micro-scale, such as field surveys and many excavations, for instance at rural sites. Here the main problems lie in longer-term developments and perspectives, and the Roman-period evidence really makes sense only in that context. Alongside this tradition of insular archaeology is another approach which recognizes the fact that for some 400 years Britain was a part of a continental-scale Empire. At a very simple level, it is necessary to look at evidence from elsewhere in the Empire, in particular the western provinces, for such things as comparanda and parallels. Understanding the wider processes of change, development and decline can be possible only within the framework of the wider Empire of which Britain was a part. In that way alone can archaeologists hope to appreciate and understand the impact of Roman on British and British on Roman that makes this period so distinctive.

## Key texts
Esmonde Cleary, A.S., 1989. *The ending of Roman Britain*. London: Batsford.
Jones, G.D.B. and Mattingly, D.J., 1990. *An atlas of Roman Britain*. Oxford: Blackwell.

Millett, M.J., 1990. *The Romanization of Britain*. Cambridge: Cambridge University Press.
Salway, P., 1993. *The Oxford illustrated history of Roman Britain*. Oxford: Oxford University Press.

## Bibliography

de la Bédoyère, G., 1988. *The finds of Roman Britain*. London: Batsford.
Burnham, B.C. and Wacher, J.S., 1990. *The 'small towns' of Roman Britain*. London: Batsford.
Cunliffe, B.W. and Davenport, P., 1988. *The temple of Sulis Minerva at Bath, Volume 2: The finds from the sacred spring*. Oxford: Oxford University Committee for Archaeology Monograph 16.
Fulford, M., 1990. 'The landscape of Roman Britain: a review', *Landscape History* 12, 25–31.
Grant, A., 1989. 'Animals in Roman Britain', in Todd, M. (ed.) *Research on Roman Britain 1960–89*. London: Society for the Promotion of Roman Studies, 135–146. = Britannia Monograph Series 11.
Henig, M., 1984. *Religion in Roman Britain*. London: Batsford.
Henig, M., 1995. *Art in Roman Britain*. London: Batsford.
Higham, N. and Jones, G.D.B., 1985. *The Carvetii*. London: Duckworth.
Hingley, R., 1989. *Rural settlement in Roman Britain*. London: Seaby.
Jones, M., 1989. 'Agriculture in Roman Britain: the dynamics of change', in Todd, M. (ed.) *Research on Roman Britain 1960–89*. London: Society for the Promotion of Roman Studies, 127–134. = Britannia Monograph Series 11.
Peacock, D.P.S., 1982. *Pottery in the Roman world*. London: Longman.
Philpott, R., 1991. *Roman burial practices in Britain: a survey of grave treatment and furnishing*. Oxford: British Archaeological Reports British Series 219.
Reece, R.M., 1987. *Coinage in Roman Britain*. London: Seaby.
Rivet, A.L.F. (ed.) 1969. *The Roman villa in Britain*. London: Routledge and Kegan Paul.
Smith, J.T., 1978. 'Villas as a key to social structure', in Todd, M. (ed.) *Studies in the Romano-British villa*. Leicester: Leicester University Press, 149–185.
Sommer, C.S., 1984. *The military vici of Roman Britain*. Oxford: British Archaeological Reports British Series 129.
Thomas, C., 1981. *Christianity in Roman Britain to A.D. 500*. London: Batsford.
Todd, M. (ed.) 1978. *Studies in the Romano-British villa*. Leicester: Leicester University Press.
TRAC, 1993. *Proceedings of the Theoretical Roman Archaeology Conference*. Oxford: Oxbow Books.
Tyers, P., 1996. *Pottery in Roman Britain*. London: Batsford.
Wacher, J.S., 1995. *The towns of Roman Britain*. London: Batsford. 2 edn.
Wait, J.S., 1985. *Ritual and religion in Iron Age Britain*. Oxford: British Archaeological Reports British Series 149.

*Chapter Ten*

# Early Historic Britain

## Catherine Hills

### BACKGROUND

The second half of the first millennium AD saw the emergence of England, Scotland and Wales from what had been the Roman provinces of Britannia and the parts of modern Scotland that had remained outside the Empire (see Hill 1981). After the withdrawal of Roman authority in the early fifth century, Britain fell apart into numerous small warring groups led by chiefs of a variety of ancestries, both indigenous and invaders. However, by the seventh century, a number of larger kingdoms had emerged which formed the basis for the medieval kingdoms of England and Scotland; in England, the major kingdoms were Northumbria, Mercia, East Anglia, Kent and Wessex (Figure 10.1). By the eighth century, it seemed that the Midlands kingdom of Mercia, under King Offa, would form the core of a consolidated England, but Mercia fell victim to the ninth-century Viking invasions, and it was instead the kings of Wessex, Alfred and his descendants, who first created a strong West Saxon kingdom south of the Thames and then, during the tenth century, conquered the rest of England. In Scotland, the dominant people were originally the Picts, but the Scoti, rulers of the kingdom of Dalriada, centred on Argyll, who were of Irish descent, eventually imposed their rule on all of Scotland except for the regions in the north, including the Orkneys and Hebrides; these fell under Scandinavian rule from the end of the eighth century. In Wales, larger kingdoms did emerge, including Gwynedd and Powys in the north, Dyfed, Gwent and Brycheiniog in the south, but it was never united under one ruler except, ultimately, after conquest by the Norman and Plantagenet kings of England.

### TERMINOLOGY

The history of this period has always been complicated by its role in national creation myths, and it is difficult even to find a name for it that does not betray a specific perspective. The popular name 'The Dark Ages' is a term that derives from the way in which people of the Renaissance saw the time between the Classical world and their own world, in which the glories of Greece and Rome were seen to have been 'reborn'. In between was a black hole of medieval superstition and ignorance. This contrast between antiquity and the Middle Ages is now not so sharply drawn, and our ignorance of the early medieval world has lessened to the extent that the term 'Dark Ages' has almost disappeared from academic works.

Some terms are relevant only to parts of Britain. In England, 'The Anglo-Saxon period' is commonly used, taking its name from the dominant peoples amongst the fifth-century settlers.

*Figure 10.1* Map of kingdoms and tribal areas mentioned in text.

It is chronologically divided into 'Early' – roughly AD 450–650, 'Middle' – AD 650–800 and 'Late' – AD 800–1066. The division between 'Middle' and 'Late' is complicated by the arrival of Viking raiders and settlers (see Chapter 11). Alternative names given to the 'Early' period reflect the importance attributed by some scholars either to the movements of barbarian peoples into the former Roman Empire, hence 'the Migration period', or to Christianity, which can be seen as retrospectively defining the centuries before the arrival of the Augustinian mission in AD 597 as 'the Pagan period'.

Outside southern and eastern England, 'Anglo-Saxon' seems inappropriate. 'Pictish' is used instead in parts of Scotland, but oversimplifies complex and rather vague tribal organization. In the south-west, 'sub-Roman' is current because it has been argued that elements of the social and political structure of the Roman province survived there. 'Arthurian' is another term more current in popular than academic literature; it implies the existence of King Arthur or an 'Arthur-type figure' in the post-Roman period, usually in the decades around AD 500. 'The Later Iron Age' stresses continuity between later prehistory and the first millennium AD, while 'Early Christian' accentuates the role of the Church.

Attempts at neutrality include 'Early medieval' and 'Early historic'. However, 'medieval' can still be understood as meaning 'after AD 1066', and 'Early historic' suggests a very limited range of documentary sources, which is not true for the second half of the period covered in this chapter. Archaeological dating for this period is either imprecise, as with radiocarbon, or indirectly dependent on historical sources, as with coins. Dendrochronology, used to great effect in this period in Scandinavia, depends on the survival of wood, which has not yet been found in sufficient quantity in Britain.

Historically derived dates are still the main basis for chronology, yet the significance of these dates is open to considerable doubt. We might begin in AD 410, the date when traditionally a beleaguered emperor Honorius told Britain to look to its own defences; but had the withdrawal of troops begun much sooner? Did vestiges of Roman authority last much longer? Is this a reliably transmitted imperial letter? Why should that date have had any meaning in Scotland (see Chapter 8)? Alternatively, we could start with the arrival of the Anglo-Saxons in AD 449, a date that Bede, writing centuries after the events, gives us as the best sense he could make of the records at his disposal. He was a careful scholar, but he could have been wrong, and much ink has been spilt in inconclusive discussion of both these dates. At the other end, 1066 is agreed by all as the date when William, Duke of Normandy defeated and replaced the Anglo-Saxon kings as ruler of England, although that did not have an immediate impact on Scotland and Wales. Nor is it a date traceable in much of the evidence used by archaeologists. It can be seen in those places where the impact of an aggressive, intrusive, military aristocracy might be expected, most notably in the construction of castles, as well as in the scale of church building, and in the destruction of ordinary houses, but in other respects there was no change: house types, burial practice, pottery and even coinage continued uninterrupted. The year AD 1000, or perhaps 1050, might be better because neither carries the overwhelming historical message embodied in '1066'.

## SOURCES

Even from the earlier centuries, two major narrative sources survive, the *De Excidio Britanniae* by Gildas (Winterbottom 1978) and the *Historia Ecclesiastica* by Bede (Colgrave and Mynors 1969), although they could both be seen as casting as much darkness as light on the period, partly, paradoxically, because they are so persuasive in the picture they present. Both authors had messages to convey; neither was attempting to write 'objective' history and neither is easily verifiable outside their own writings, which themselves constitute the main sources for the periods about which (or during which) they wrote. For the fifth century, only one of them is really independent, since Bede drew heavily on Gildas for this period.

Gildas is usually described as a monk who wrote in the sixth century in south-western Britain, although this is not fully demonstrable. He was an educated British Christian cleric, but not necessarily a monk at the time of writing. His precise dates are not clear, although his life must have fallen within the second half of the fifth and the sixth centuries, and he probably lived in south-western Britain. What is clear is that the chapters of his work that are most often used today form only one part of a carefully constructed literary work, the main theme of which was a comparison of the Britons of his own day with the Israelites of the Bible. Gildas' account of the invasion of Britain by the Anglo-Saxons is presented within a framework of history in which assaults by barbarians were seen as punishments by God for the sins of the British. This had happened, he claimed, after the Romans had left (at a much disputed date in the fifth century), and the wickedness of Gildas' contemporaries made it likely that it would happen again unless they mended their ways. From Gildas we learn that barbarians invaded Britain in the fifth century, that they caused great destruction and that they took control of parts of the country. However, much of the detailed history that has been constructed from *De Excidio* has gone far beyond what can legitimately be learnt from it.

Bede is better documented. He was a learned Christian monk who lived and wrote at the monastery of Jarrow in Northumbria. He died in AD 635, having completed the *Historia* in 631. In this work, he told the story of the Anglo-Saxons' conversion to Christianity. His main aim was not to write a narrative history of the creation of the Anglo-Saxon kingdoms, although the information he provides is our main source for that history. He wrote from an Anglo-Saxon perspective and had a negative view of the British which he was able to support by reference to their own historian, Gildas.

Bede was not alone in his scholarship. From the later seventh century onwards, an increasing body of written documents of all kinds survives, both secular and religious in purpose, including poetry, chronicles, law codes, letters, charters and wills, gospel books, sermons, lives of saints, and even collections of riddles (Godden and Lapidge 1991). Late Anglo-Saxon England had a complex administration which used written records and which was taken over by the Normans. The Vikings may have torn holes in our knowledge of the ninth century, but the eighth century, and the centuries immediately before the Norman conquest, look as fully historical as those after it.

The archaeological evidence for the period is unevenly preserved in time and space, so that discussion of, for example, fifth-century Scotland will be based on different kinds of evidence from that of tenth-century Wessex, and will need to be conducted on different terms. Outside Anglo-Saxon England, there is relatively little archaeological evidence for the whole period, and what there is is not always precisely datable. Fortified strongholds, and the metalwork made for their rulers, predominate in the record. There are few lower status settlements, no towns and not many burial sites. By contrast, in England, cemeteries and the artefacts buried with the dead still provide the basis for research into the fifth to seventh centuries, although in recent decades settlement sites have been excavated more extensively. From the seventh century, burials ceased to be elaborately furnished and decline in importance as a source of information, while churches, sculpture and manuscripts emerge as an important class of evidence throughout Britain. At the same time, towns reappear for the first time since the Roman era, at first as coastal trading places but later as a network of administrative centres with, amongst other functions, that of mints for a re-established coinage.

## CHANGING PERCEPTIONS

Because the history of the period has always been bound up with national identity, more significance has been attached to the differences between peoples than to their similarities. The Anglo-Saxons have been seen as arriving in force from northern Germany, displacing the Romano-Britons of eastern and southern Britain, so that the English were and are a distinct

*Figure 10.2*  Perception of King Alfred.
*Source*: A.S. Esmonde Cleary

people from the Welsh and the Scots. This view suited not only the Anglo-Saxons but also the English of later centuries. In the sixteenth century, the Church of Bede was seen as the ancestor of the reformed Anglican Church, predating and avoiding the errors of medieval Catholicism. We owe much of our knowledge of Anglo-Saxon England to this idea, because it was what led Queen Elizabeth's archbishop, Matthew Parker, to seek out, preserve and study Anglo-Saxon manuscripts (some of his collection remains to this day in the library of Corpus Christi, Cambridge, Parker's college). Seventeenth-century Parliamentarians saw the Anglo-Saxon *witan*, the council consulted by the king, as the model for constitutional monarchy from which the Stuarts had wrongly departed. They and others after them also believed in an ancestral, free, democratic Germanic society, which by the nineteenth century had become the basis for the thesis that the English were a peculiarly blessed nation, suited to rule others around the world and distinctly superior to their Celtic neighbours. The Victorians saw King Alfred as the model of a virtuous, wise and patriotic king (Figure 10.2). The twentieth century, however, brought two wars with Germany and the end of empire. It began to seem better to play down the role of the Anglo-Saxons and to stress both continuity from Roman to medieval and the kinship of all the inhabitants of Britain with each other, rather than with ancestors of the German enemy.

This approach is supported by an alternative version of the history of the fifth century in Britain which can be derived, albeit in sketchy outline, from some (but not all) readings of Gildas. This allows for the survival of an extensive part of Roman Britain under British rule, preferably the rule of King Arthur or someone like him. The existence of Arthur as a real person at all, let alone as a great king, has been much, and inconclusively, debated. The story became popular after the Norman Conquest, because it seemed to provide an alternative to the defeated Anglo-Saxons' view of the history of Britain. It was popularized most vigorously by Geoffrey of Monmouth, who wrote his *History of the Kings of Britain* in the early twelfth century. At the end of the Middle Ages, Arthur was the name given by the Welsh Henry Tudor to his eldest son, and Arthur has persisted as a figure in myth and literature through the centuries. He had a brief vogue as an archaeological inspiration in the 1960s and early 1970s, with the excavation at South Cadbury ('Camelot'), and at other western British sites such as Glastonbury, Cadbury Congresbury, and the Roman city of Wroxeter, near Shrewsbury. Occupation of these sites in the fifth or sixth centuries was seen as evidence for the existence of sub-Roman leader(s) and for survival of a partly Roman way of life, thus providing a factual basis for the later Arthurian stories. In part, this was the inspiration for a more widespread search for 'continuity' from Roman to Saxon on both urban and rural settlement sites. In towns, this search has been largely unsuccessful, and has tended to confirm the traditional account of urban decline and destruction, although it has provided a more ambiguous and complex picture for the countryside (see below).

Under the influence of ideas associated both with processual and post-processual archaeology, social analysis has become important (e.g. Arnold 1988), partly because it offers an alternative to the agenda set by historians which is still focused largely on political history. Much research is still devoted to tracing migrations through distributions of metalwork or placenames, or to the development of kingdoms from pottery and coins. New ideas about the mechanisms behind change in material culture have, however, encouraged criticism and reassessment of the traditional equation of different types of pottery and brooches with different ethnic groups. Interest has shifted to the detection of social complexity, whether in terms of hierarchical ranking and status, or to the roles of different people in society according to such factors as age, gender, occupation, family or religious affiliation (e.g. Hines 1997).

Although some archaeologists would prefer to treat at least the earlier centuries as prehistoric, and although some historians would still prefer to disregard archaeology altogether, it is the existence of both kinds of evidence that is the greatest strength of the period. If the temptation to subordinate one kind of information to the other can be resisted, the combination of both allows each to provide different kinds of insight. Historical archaeology should be a key testing ground for both historians and archaeologists; the fact that instead it is often a poor relation is a result of the territoriality of academic disciplines, which should be continually challenged.

## KEY DATA

### Landscapes

Environmental evidence (e.g. Rackham 1994) has made it possible to approach the history of the landscape over the long term, and to put recorded events into a longer and broader perspective. It is no longer possible to imagine the complete disappearance of the population of Roman Britain: aerial and field survey have shown a density of occupation of lowland Britain during the Roman period that reached, or exceeded, that known for medieval England. A population of such size could not have completely disappeared, even in the face of prolonged war, famine and plague. It is true that the same surveys show a far less densely occupied land in the early medieval period, but not an empty one. The difference must partly derive from a genuine decline in population, but it is exaggerated by the difference between Roman and later people in terms of identifiable material culture. Romano-Britons seem to have created more rubbish than their successors, so that it is easier to find Roman sites than later ones. In Scotland and Wales, it is extremely difficult to identify early medieval sites at all because pottery was not made or used in large quantities, and when it was, it was of poor quality, not durable and not easily identifiable. That is not, however, taken as evidence for complete depopulation of those regions. Even in Anglo-Saxon England, where many sites have been identified, the majority are burials, so that when the practice of burying grave-goods ends around AD 700, archaeological evidence for the Anglo-Saxons declines, at a time when we have no other reason to suppose that the population was itself in decline.

We know that there was no regeneration of the primeval forest in which it used to be imagined that Anglo-Saxon settlers hewed clearings for their newly founded settlements in an otherwise empty land. There may have been abandonment of some fields, and a shift from arable to pasture, but no dramatic overall change in land use seems at present to be be attributable to the middle of the first millennium AD. Animal and plant species did not change at this point either, nor, as far as can be seen, did farming techniques. Even land divisions remained in use. Early maps show field boundaries, some still in existence, that underlie, and were therefore earlier than, Roman roads, but which must have continued in use through Anglo-Saxon, medieval and early modern centuries (Williamson 1993, Fig 2.1). If fields, plants and animals survived, so must some of the people.

The question now is not whether any Britons remained to form part of the population of 'Anglo-Saxon' England, but whether immigrants arrived in significant numbers or just as small groups of invading warriors who took over at the top, but did not replace the basic population (Higham 1992). In the west, it was never thought that the Britons disappeared, but there were Irish settlers in the south-west, and also the Scoti in Dalriada, more often interpreted as invading war leaders than as a folk migration.

## Cemeteries

Early medieval cemeteries have not been discovered in large numbers in western and northern Britain (Edwards and Lane 1992). Known burials in those regions are mostly unfurnished inhumations dated, often very approximately, by stratigraphy or radiocarbon. There is a variety of associated structures: round or square ditched enclosures, stone cists or cairns, and some evidence for reuse of prehistoric burial monuments. In as much as the limited evidence allows for argument, it suggests long-term continuity of practice from prehistoric and Roman-period burial ritual, consistent with continuity of population, and the gradual introduction of features connected with Christianity, such as enclosed graveyards and churches.

Anglo-Saxon cemeteries (e.g. Scull 1992) are numerous, highly visible and apparently intrusive, because they do not appear to be a development from past indigenous practice, but instead resemble burials found on the other side of the North Sea where they form part of a long local tradition of burial ritual. This has always seemed to be evidence for the immigration of large numbers of Germanic peoples across the North Sea to Britain. However, it is not clear what the native British burial practice was, since relatively few Iron Age or Roman burials have been excavated in Britain, except for a few urban Roman cemeteries. The change may not have been so complete. Many Anglo-Saxon cemeteries, especially in Yorkshire, are associated with prehistoric monuments such as Bronze Age barrows, and may represent newcomers laying claim to the ancestors of the lands they had taken over. The phenomenon might also represent a continuing veneration of monuments by people on lands that had always been occupied. All the same, there are such similarities between English and continental burials that there must have been a close connection between the respective peoples involved, and migration cannot be discounted as a partial explanation. This need not mean that all the occupants of 'Anglo-Saxon' burials were of Germanic ancestry. Britons might have adopted foreign customs through social or political expediency, or religious conversion.

In the east, the majority of the earliest burials were cremations. One of the largest cremation cemeteries excavated in England is Spong Hill, North Elmham, Norfolk (e.g. Hills 1976; McKinley 1994), where more than 2,000 cremations and 56 inhumations were excavated from a cemetery used in the fifth and sixth centuries AD (Figure 10.3). The bones were contained in hand-made pots, often elaborately decorated with incised, stamped or plastic decoration. It was possible to identify groups of pots decorated with the same tool, and therefore made at the same time, probably by the same person. Adults of both sexes and children had been buried there. Many of the graves also contained cremated animal bones, some of which might have been food offerings, but in many cases it seems that a whole animal, usually a horse, had been burnt on the pyre. These were young adult animals which must have been valuable, so that their sacrifice was a significant offering of wealth. The women buried had been laid out wearing their jewellery, glass beads and bronze brooches, the melted remains of which were then put in the pot with the bones. Men were not

*Figure 10.3* Cremation burials at Spong Hill.
*Source*: David Wicks, Field Archaeology Division, Norfolk Museums Service

equipped with anything distinctive, and were not accompanied by weapons. Also burnt were glass and bronze vessels, again representing the destruction of significant wealth, since they must all have been imported. There were also sets of miniature tweezers, razors and shears, often with full size or miniature combs, usually unburnt and found in graves of all ages and both sexes.

Similar cemeteries have been found elsewhere in eastern England, for example at Sancton in Yorkshire, Loveden Hill and Elsham in Lincolnshire, and Newark, Nottinghamshire. Comparison with the Continent shows a considerable overlap with finds from north Germany, in particular from Schleswig Holstein and Lower Saxony. The grave goods are very similar, and much of the pottery has the same decoration. The main point of difference is that stamped pottery is very popular in England, but not common in north Germany. Some of the stamps used on the Spong Hill pots include motifs such as animals, swastikas and runes, often carefully drawn, suggesting that, initially at least, stamped decoration had some meaning, although later it may have become purely ornamental. The similarities between Spong Hill and sites such as Issendorf, near Hamburg, relate not just to an initial settlement phase, but to much of the time that Spong Hill was in use. People did not get into their boats and sail to England, never to return. The communities on both sides of the North Sea remained in contact. The connections between them could have owed as much to the exchange of ideas and goods through trade, religion and political relationships as to migration.

In southern England, inhumation was always more popular, and it had superseded cremation everywhere by about AD 600. Late Roman burials had been mostly unfurnished inhumations, but the later fourth century saw the appearance in Britain and northern Gaul of inhumations accompanied by weapons and belt fittings. Although these have often been interpreted as the burials of Germanic mercenary soldiers, there is not really any reason to see them purely in ethnic terms, although it does seem to have been a fashion prevalent amongst a military elite, which included men of Germanic origin. These burials may have contributed to the development of the rite seen throughout western Europe and southern Britain between the fifth and seventh centuries. This was inhumation burial, often in large cemeteries arranged in rows, some bodies in coffins or stone sarcophagi. Men were buried with weapons, women with brooches and necklaces. In England these are attributed to Anglo-Saxons, in Gaul to the Franks, further south the Alemanni; but not all of those buried in this manner need have belonged to these ethnic groups.

## Regional variation in England

According to Bede, the settlers came from three of the strongest tribes of Germany: the Angles, Saxons and Jutes. To some extent, regional patterning, in the distribution especially of dress fasteners, seems to reflect this tripartite division, which is also detectable in regional names (Hills 1979). In East Anglia, the East Midlands and Yorkshire, women wore cruciform and annular brooches, and fastened their sleeves with metal clasps. In southern England, in Sussex, Wessex and Essex, they preferred round brooches and did not use clasps. Most of the ornaments in these regions are made of copper alloy. Some of them are decorated with a distinctive form of animal ornament (Style I), where animals and humans are represented by disjointed limbs and heads. In Kent, allegedly settled by Jutes from Denmark, there was a greater use of gold and silver and some very elaborate ornaments, such as the Kingston brooch, decorated with *cloisonné* garnets, glass and gold filigree (Figure 10.4). In Kent, the animal ornament used was often Style II, where the beasts had sinuous bodies like snakes or ribbons, tied in knots around each other. This style is also found in East Anglia, on some of the objects from Sutton Hoo (below). Some of the jewellery buried in Kentish graves had been imported from the continent.

There is a tripartite regional division, but its explanation may not be straightforward. The north-east/south, 'Angle/Saxon' divide appears already in the fifth century in the distinction between those areas practising cremation and those favouring inhumation. This difference seems to reflect the situation at the end of the Roman period, when eastern England seems to have been overrun sooner and more completely than the south, which preserved more of its Romano-British culture. It may have been accentuated by Scandinavian contacts in the sixth century, and again by the division between Danelaw and Saxon England of the ninth and tenth centuries (see Chapter 11). The distinctive Kentish culture belongs to the sixth and seventh centuries, not to the initial migration period, and owes far more to contacts with Frankish culture than Danish. Bede was rationalizing distinctions that existed in his own time but which may have had complex origins.

## Social analysis

Social analysis of Anglo-Saxon cemeteries has often focused on a few very elaborate, high-status burials. Most remarkable amongst these are those found at Sutton Hoo near Woodbridge on the coast of Suffolk (Carver 1992), where the burial mounds have attracted successive generations of investigators (Figure 10.5). Many were dug into and looted without record in the nineteenth century, three were opened in 1938 and 1939, and a systematic exploration of the site as a whole was carried out in the 1980s. The most spectacular deposit was that from mound I, excavated in 1939. This contained the remains of a ship and a lavish deposit of grave goods including a helmet, sword, shield, gold buckle, gold and garnet fittings, bronze and silver bowls, and a purse containing Merovingian coins. Because most of these coins do not carry the names of kings, it has not been easy to date them. The most recent analysis suggests a date for the assemblage of the

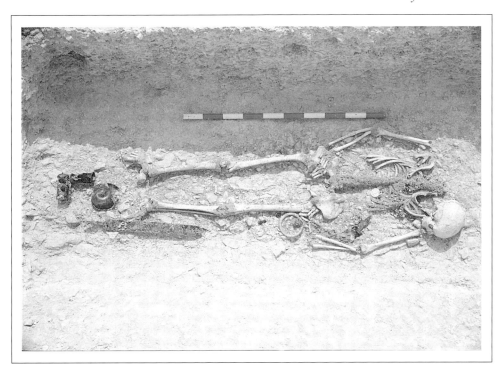

*Figure 10.4* Anglo-Saxon grave from Kent.
*Source*: Canterbury Archaeological Trust

coins, and probably for the burial, early in the seventh century. This would be too early for the most popular contender for occupancy of mound I, King Redwald of East Anglia, known to us from Bede as a lapsed Christian king who died in the 620s. Perhaps one of the other mounds did contain Redwald, but mound I is more likely to have been the grave of a predecessor. Another grave, excavated in 1991, contained a young man buried in a coffin with weapons, bronze and wooden vessels, and horse harness. In a grave beside him lay his horse. The status of others buried at Sutton Hoo was less exalted. A series of graves was found in the recent excavation campaign that contained

*Figure 10.5* Sutton Hoo from the air.
*Source*: C. Hoppit

the remains of individuals who seemed to have been executed. Some of these were contemporary with the rich burials, others probably belong to a later Saxon use of the site as a place of execution.

Attention has also been devoted to more subtle variations in status. Some graves contained sword, shield and spear, others spears only. Some had five brooches, others one or none. It is possible to use this variation to reconstruct pyramidal gradations of rank that compare well with those recorded in later law codes. However, some of the variation is regional or chronological, and some may be due to varying religious beliefs or the ancestral burial traditions of different families. Age and gender seem to structure some differences: the attribution of weapons to men and jewellery to women has been broadly confirmed by osteological sexing of the bones, and relatively few grave goods were buried with children. But not all men had weapons nor all women brooches, and each cemetery has practices different from its neighbour, displaying a wide variety of local preferences within a standard range, and making it very difficult to produce any but the most general patterns.

## Settlements

In western Britain and Scotland, a number of fortified sites have been identified on historical or archaeological grounds as being of early medieval date (Figure 10.6), including Dinas Powys in Wales, Tintagel in Cornwall, and Dunadd and Dundurn in Scotland (e.g. Campbell and Lane 1993). These sites are most often on hill tops or steep promontories, or on crannogs. They have produced imported Mediterranean pottery and glass, decorated metalwork, and evidence for the manufacture of similar metalwork. The nature of the sites as fortified strongholds and the presence of high-status objects makes it clear that these are elite residences, although they have not produced elaborate structural remains. They cannot yet be put in the wider context of the network of contemporary lower status farms and villages that must have existed, because these are still proving difficult to distinguish from similar settlements of much earlier or later date.

*Figure 10.6* Aerial view of fort at Dundurn, Perthshire.
*Source*: Ian Ralston

In Anglo-Saxon England, the situation is different. Many settlements are known, although often only from air photographs, as scatters of pottery from field survey, or from limited rescue excavations. Several sites have been extensively excavated, including West Stow in Suffolk, Mucking in Essex and West Heslerton in Yorkshire (Welch 1992, chs 2 and 3). The visibility of Anglo-Saxon settlements is partly caused by a commonly found type known as the *Grubenhaus*, or sunken featured building. The pit that characterizes this type of building usually produces a rich deposit of occupation debris: pottery, artefacts and animal bones. Earlier interpretations of these pits suggested that the Anglo-Saxons lived in squalor in holes in the ground full of rubbish, but more recently, partly as a result of experimental reconstructions at West Stow, they have been explained as underfloor spaces, essentially cellars, for storage and insulation, underneath perfectly habitable thatched wooden houses. Much of the material found in the pits therefore does not relate directly to the use of the building but represents later rubbish put there after it had gone out of use and been demolished. *Grubenhaeuser* were subsidiary buildings with a variety of domestic and industrial uses, while the most important buildings were larger rectangular 'halls' that did not have cellars.

At Mucking and West Stow, it has been argued that the settlements consisted of groups of farms that shifted their locations over time, because there is some chronological variation in the distribution of the finds. Even Mucking, therefore, which looks quite large on the site plan, was no more than a village, because the whole excavated area was not in use at any single point in time. At West Heslerton, however, it appears that the settlement was functionally and not chronologically zoned, with spatial separation of different activities and people. In some areas, industrial activities were carried out in or near *Grubenhaeuser*, whereas in others there were only 'halls', and elsewhere animal pens. On this model, the whole site was in use during at least parts of its existence, with a planned layout that the excavator describes as closer to a town than a village. The Anglo-Saxon occupation of West Heslerton is being investigated as part of research into the long-term use of the region. It succeeded settlements on the other side of the valley that were occupied through the Roman period and into the fifth century. The new location is explained partly in terms of alterations in land ownership and political control, which could have been connected with take-over by incoming Anglo-Saxons, but need not have represented wholesale replacement of the population. The underlying Roman structures may also have given the site some local significance, and influenced its siting.

*Grubenhaeuser* appear on the Continent before they arrive in Britain. Like cremation burials, they are usually taken as an indication of Germanic immigrants, but it is not clear why this type of building was developed on the Continent, where it is found as early as the second century in The Netherlands. It may have had as much to do with changing climate and agricultural regimes as with population movements. The main house type in use in northern Europe was the longhouse, a narrow, aisled timber building that had accommodation for humans at one end and animal stalls at the other. The absence of this kind of building from early Anglo-Saxon settlements in England is one of the strongest arguments against a simple replacement of Briton by immigrant Saxon. The rectangular buildings that do occur on Anglo-Saxon sites have a distinctive plan: they are near to double-squares, with opposed doors in the middle of the long sides and a narrow partition at one end. Both Romano-British and continental ancestry has been plausibly claimed for this building type.

There is some regional variation amongst settlement sites, not unlike that apparent in the burial record, in that *Grubenhaeuser* are more numerous in eastern England, whereas south of the Thames, at sites such as Chalton in Hampshire, 'halls' predominate. This may be partly due to a difference in date, in that earlier settlements seem to be found in the east, but this is difficult to demonstrate since sites that do not include *Grubenhaeuser* produce fewer finds and are harder to date. The use of the building technique in which walls are constructed by setting upright posts in a narrow trench seems to be relatively later than the use of separate posts. However, both occur on the same site at Chalton and at Cowdery's Down, near Basingstoke, which could each be partly seventh century in date. This is also observable at the site of Yeavering in Northumbria.

Yeavering was discovered from aerial photographs that showed a complex of rectangular structures on a river terrace hill below the Iron Age hillfort of Yeavering Bell, near Wooler in Northumbria. Excavations of this site in the 1950s produced a series of large, rectangular 'halls', some of massive construction, that had been burnt down at least twice. There was also a structure like a segment of an amphitheatre, burials, and possibly both a temple and a church. Clearly this site had distinctive functions: the buildings required much wood, labour and skill, and the 'grandstand' suggests meetings and ceremonies. It has been identified as *Ad Gefrin*, which Bede tells us was a 'villa regalis', a residence of King Edwin of Northumbria which was visited by bishop Paulinus in 626 when he came to preach Christianity to the Northumbrians. The buildings are consistent with such an interpretation, but there are very few finds, perhaps because the site was occupied only occasionally, or perhaps because the Anglo-Saxons, far from living in squalor, actually took pains to keep their houses, or indeed their royal residences, clean.

Yeavering has been interpreted as a 'palace' on historical grounds, and because of the range and size of the buildings found there. Other 'royal' sites have been identified from aerial photographs, including several not far from Yeavering including Sprouston, in the Tweed Valley, and also in southern England (Rahtz 1981). At Cowdery's Down, the size of at least one of the buildings (22 × 9 m) has allowed it to be added to the list of high status sites. One Late Saxon royal site, at Cheddar in Somerset, has been excavated. Although it is now possible to distinguish excavated sites in terms of status and function, discussion of settlement hierarchy still rests on a limited sample of excavated sites.

## Christianity

In the fourth century, Britain, like the rest of the Roman Empire, was officially Christian. It is difficult to know how deeply rooted belief had become amongst the population at large, or the extent to which it survived the end of Roman rule, but Gildas' account of the period was Christian, as were the rulers of south-western England and Wales to whom it was addressed. Ireland was converted from Britain, traditionally by St Patrick in the fifth century, and it was from Ireland that St Columba came to found a monastery on Iona in AD 563. This became one of the great centres of early Christian learning in Britain, and from Iona missionaries set out to convert the Picts and the Northumbrians. In 597, a mission led by Augustine, sent from Rome by Pope Gregory, reached England. Augustine had initial success in converting Ethelbert of Kent, but it was not until the middle decades of the seventh century that the other Anglo-Saxon kingdoms were converted, usually for reasons as much political as religious.

Archaeological evidence for Christianity takes various forms (see Webster and Backhouse 1991). At first, furnished burial continued, and the impact of closer contact with the Mediterranean world appears in new styles of dress and ornament such as necklaces with pendants, a few in the shape of the cross, and decorated pins, some linked by chains, used to fasten cloaks and head-dresses. Some prominent Christians were buried with objects; for example, St Cuthbert was interred with his pectoral cross, a portable altar and a comb. Kings and other landowners who endowed churches were buried in them, probably with elaborate clothing like that known from royal continental Christian burials, although comparable graves have not been found in Britain. Eventually, a standard pattern of Christian burial emerged throughout Britain, replacing the older variety of different burial and cemetery types with uniform, unfurnished, east–west orientated inhumations in enclosed cemeteries beside churches in the middle of villages. These were used over many centuries, some to the present day.

There was probably a tradition of wooden sculpture amongst the Anglo-Saxons, and perhaps among the other peoples of Britain, but only stone has survived. In the west, memorial stones of post-Roman date show influence from Gaul, and in Scotland, carved stones are the most distinctive monuments of the Picts, the earlier ones carrying symbols that clearly had a complex meaning and predate later Christian examples (Ritchie 1989). Anglo-Saxon England produced architectural sculpture, gravestones and free-standing stone crosses. The Mediterranean features of these crosses are clear: figures of Christ and the saints, vinescrolls, interlace and inscriptions in Roman letters; but the vines are inhabited by northern animals, and there are also inscriptions cut in runic letters (Wilson 1984). Stone crosses became a feature of early medieval Ireland, and in England they continued into the Viking period.

## Churches

The building of churches may sometimes have meant no more than the dedication of an existing timber hall to Christian worship. Benedict Biscop, however, founder of Jarrow and Monkwear-mouth, imported builders from France, because the crafts of building in stone, plastering, glazing windows and tiling roofs had disappeared from Britain. Timber, wattle and daub or drystone walls are the natural choice for northern builders, and the appearance of ashlar masonry and glazed windows would suggest strong continental influence, even if we had no documentation of the Conversion. Few, if any, early church buildings have been identified in Scotland (but see Whithorn, below), Wales or south-west England, but many churches from eastern and southern England can be shown to have been founded before the Norman Conquest, and to preserve part of their original fabric (Cherry 1981). These churches have characteristic tall, narrow proportions, round arches, small windows and towers, sometimes decorated with applied strips like those at Earls Barton and Barnack. Most are not very large, but they were richly decorated with sculpture, painting and embroidered hangings. Early churches survive as excavated foundations or as parts of standing churches mostly in Kent and Northumbria, including St Augustine's, St Martin's and St Pancras at Canterbury, and Jarrow, Monkwearmouth and the crypts at Ripon and Hexham in Northumbria. The church at Brixworth, in Northamptonshire, shows the way in which Anglo-Saxon builders reused Roman materials, in this case tiles for the arches. Foundations of Anglo-Saxon cathedrals have been discovered at Winchester and at Canterbury, the latter nearly as large as its Norman successor, but not underneath York minster. However, the great majority of identified Anglo-Saxon churches belong to the tenth and eleventh centuries; these are discussed further in Chapter 13.

## Monasteries

Early monasteries do not present the classic plan of the medieval Benedictine house, with its church, cloister and regular rectangular layout. Monastic houses seem to have been adaptations of contemporary secular building and settlement types, and are therefore not always easily distinguishable from them. Identification as a monastery depends either on historical sources, or on peculiarities of plan or finds that are argued to be more monastic than secular in character.

In the west, and particularly in Ireland, the monasteries may be slightly better evidenced, with clusters of round huts and small rectangular chapels, sometimes in remote and inconvenient places (Figure 10.7). Tintagel in Cornwall used to be interpreted on this basis as the site of an early monastery, but is now seen instead as a secular elite site (Thomas 1993). Whithorn in Galloway has traditionally been associated with an early British bishop, St Ninian, and recent excavations have shown occupation and burial for many centuries, beginning at least in the fifth century. One

*Figure 10.7* Model of the Anglo-Saxon monastery of St Paul, Jarrow, in the early eighth century. The appearance of the monastery is based on the results of excavation.

*Source*: South Tyneside Metropolitan Borough Council

grave appears to have become the focus of a shrine, later incorporated into a small building and subsequently, when the Northumbrians took over this region in the early eighth century, into a church. Other small, rectangular buildings were arranged in parallel rows. Similar buildings were found at Hartlepool and thought to be associated with Abbess Hild. The best known of early Anglo-Saxon monasteries is Bede's Jarrow (Cramp 1981), where excavations showed long, narrow, rectangular buildings arranged in something that approximates to a cloister. Similar features were seen at the sister monastery at nearby Monkwearmouth.

Other sites are less securely identified. Features that might be thought to rule out monasticism need not necessarily have done so. Cemeteries with men, women and children could be explained as belonging to double houses, with both monks and nuns, and very young oblates or schoolchildren, and the graves of the sick, cared for in the monastery. Animal bones, evidence of meat eating, might reflect a less than complete observance of dietary rules. At Brandon in Suffolk, a settlement of Middle Saxon date consisted of rectangular buildings, one associated with burials and interpreted as a church. Finds included imported pottery, ornamented pins, precious metal, and glass, both from vessels and windows. Flixborough in Lincolnshire also produced rectangular buildings, possibly including a church, burials, and a range of similar artefacts as well as a great quantity of animal bones. This is all consistent with secular high status. Both these sites have also produced evidence for literacy, which is normally associated with the church, in the form of writing implements, styli, and also an inscribed lead plaque and ring at Flixborough and a gold plaque, probably from a book cover, with the symbol of St John at Brandon.

It is in manuscript art that we can see most clearly the great achievement of the early Church in Britain in the fusion of three traditions: Mediterranean, Germanic and Celtic. The illuminated pages of the Lindisfarne Gospels or the Book of Durrow show a dynamic combination of Classical figures, Germanic interlaced animals and Celtic patterns. The skills that had previously been devoted to the creation of jewellery were now deployed in the service of the Church (Wilson 1984). This art cannot be attributed to any one of the peoples of Britain: it is neither Anglo-Saxon nor Celtic, and is often called 'Hiberno-Saxon', although that name does not allow for a Pictish contribution. The mobility of missionaries and craftsmen allowed the transmission of ideas from one secular or religious centre to another, so that it is often difficult to decide exactly where any one manuscript or artefact was created. The Lindisfarne Gospels are located by a written statement, but the Book of Kells has been attributed variously to Northumbria, Ireland and Iona. Manuscripts should not be studied in isolation from other art: book covers, reliquaries, chalices and other items of Church plate all demanded fine craftsmanship. Metalworking, painting, sculpture – either of stone or on the smaller scale of ivory – and embroidery all used similar designs, and shared some techniques.

## Towns and trade

Although urban centres do not fully emerge until towards the later part of the millennium (see Chapter 11), trade did not cease entirely in Britain between the early fifth and the late seventh century (Hodges and Hobley 1988). Mediterranean pottery arrived in the west during the fifth and sixth centuries, presumably accompanying perishable goods such as wine or oil. Anglo-Saxon graves in East Anglia contained imported ivory, glass and bronze vessels, and Kent was in close contact with Frankish Gaul. Trade may not have been on a scale sufficient to demand permanent markets, and none has yet been identified in Britain for this period, but their existence should not be ruled out. In Denmark, for example, such a site has been found at Lundborg on Fyn which functioned from the second century to the seventh. From the seventh century, local trade can be identified from the distribution of pottery, for example 'Ipswich' ware, which is found throughout East Anglia, around the east coast up the Thames to London (Wade 1988). In the Late Saxon period, it was succeeded by several wheel-thrown pottery types, including Thetford ware and Stamford ware, which was glazed.

Around AD 700, coastal trading places emerged all around the North Sea (Hodges and Hobley 1988). Hedeby and Ribe in Denmark, Dorestad in the Netherlands and Quentovic in France are paralleled in England by Hamwic, near Southampton, and Ipswich (Ottaway 1992). These were open, undefended sites, producing evidence for local manufacture and import of a wide range of goods. Similar sites have been identified outside the walls of Roman York and London (Figure 10.8). Because the place-name element *-wic* is common to many of them, they have sometimes been called by that name. They flourished in the eighth century and suffered from Viking raids in the ninth, after which decline set in and they either disappeared (like Quentovic), were relocated (like Hamwic and Hedeby), or retreated behind the old Roman walls (as at London and York). These places may have begun as seasonal fairs, but permanent structures and regular street plans appeared early in their history. The suggestion that they were deliberate foundations by rulers to control trade into their territories finds some support in the archaeological evidence, including the deliberate laying-out of streets and properties at one time, the restricted distribution of imported pottery and the limited diet suggested by the animal bones. Imported pottery may be a by-product of the wine trade. Rhenish pottery is found in eastern England, while pottery from northern France reached southern England (Hodges 1989, ch 4). Early medieval trading places have also been identified in the Irish Sea region.

In Britain, coins had gone out of use at the end of the Roman period. A few Byzantine and rather more Merovingian coins were used as ornaments, and during the seventh century a limited gold coinage was struck in Kent. The history of Anglo-Saxon coins really begins with the silver currency, often called *sceattas*, small dumpy coins that were in use from the later seventh century until a new, larger, thin silver penny was created in the later eighth century. Sceattas are found in some quantity in the coastal trading places. They also occur on other inland sites, including some that have produced many artefacts, often through metal detecting. These 'productive sites' have not so far shown much evidence for permanent occupation and may perhaps have been seasonal fairs. Late Saxon coins were a carefully controlled part of West Saxon government, minted only in specified places and regularly recalled for issue of new types (e.g. Vince 1990, ch 9).

***Figure 10.8*** Saxon London. A Middle Saxon road in the foreground with an alley leading away from the road, with the remnants of timber buildings on either side of the alley, found during excavations at the Royal Opera House.
*Source*: Museum of London Archaeology Service

## THE WIDER SETTING

After the end of Roman rule, Britain is sometimes seen as having been set adrift, cut off from Europe. This is a mistake. It would be better to see it instead as belonging to interrelated maritime zones, centred on the North and Irish Seas, each with many lines of contact to the rest of Europe and beyond. In the east, around the North Sea, contact with north Germany and Scandinavia was continuous and intense. Germanic settlement in the fifth and sixth centuries and Viking raids and settlement in the ninth and tenth were followed by a brief period when England was part of a Danish empire. Contact with western Europe and the Mediterranean world never entirely ceased, and was dramatically renewed in the seventh century with the Christian mission. At the end of the period, England became, as it was to remain throughout the Middle Ages, closely connected to the politics of western Europe, especially to the area that was to become France.

The western parts of Britain always retained some level of communication with western France and the Mediterranean, manifested partly by the distribution of imported pottery and maintained through the Church. The far north was, like England, subject to Viking raids and settlement that left parts of Scotland under Norse control for several centuries.

The medieval kingdoms of Britain, England, Scotland and Wales were already clearly defined by the time of the Norman Conquest. England by then was a centralized state with a complex system of government and administration. This was taken over and strengthened by the Normans. Just as the imposition of castles destroyed houses and changed parts of the plans of Anglo-Saxon towns, without ultimately replacing them, so Domesday Book records an Anglo-Saxon state under new lordship, changed but not replaced.

## Key texts

Foster, S.M., 1996. *Picts, Gaels and Scots*. London: Batsford/Historic Scotland.

Thomas, C., 1993. *Tintagel: Arthur and archaeology*. London: Batsford/English Heritage.

Vince, A., 1990. *Saxon London: an archaeological investigation*. London: Seaby.

Webster, L. and Backhouse, J., 1991. *The making of England. Anglo-Saxon art and culture AD 600–900*. London: British Museum Publications.

Welch, M.., 1992. *Anglo-Saxon England*. London: Batsford/English Heritage.

Wilson, D.M. (ed.) 1981. *The archaeology of Anglo-Saxon England*. Cambridge: Cambridge University Press. 2nd edn.

## Bibliography

Arnold, C.J., 1988. *An archaeology of the early Anglo-Saxon kingdoms*. London: Routledge.

Campbell, E. and Lane, A., 1993. 'Celtic and Germanic interaction in Dalriada: the seventh century metalworking site at Dunadd', in Spearman, R.M. and Higgitt, J. (eds) *The age of migrating ideas*. Stroud: Alan Sutton Publishing, 52–63.

Carver, M.O.H., 1992. 'The Anglo-Saxon cemetery at Sutton Hoo: an interim report', in Carver, M.O.H. (ed.) *The age of Sutton Hoo*. Woodbridge: Boydell, 343–371.

Cherry, B., 1981. 'Ecclesiastical architecture', in Wilson, D.M. (ed.), 1981, 151–200.

Colgrave, B. and Mynors, R.A.B., 1969. *Bede's Ecclesiastical History of the English People*. Oxford: Oxford University Press.

Cramp, R.J., 1981. 'Monastic sites', in Wilson, D.M. (ed.), 1981, 201–252.

Edwards, N. and Lane, A. (eds) 1992. *The early Church in Wales and the West*. Oxford: Oxbow Monograph 16.

Godden, M. and Lapidge, M. (eds) 1991. *The Cambridge companion to Old English literature*. Cambridge: Cambridge University Press.

Higham, N., 1992. *Rome, Britain and the Anglo-Saxons*. London: Seaby.

Hill, D., 1981. *An atlas of Anglo-Saxon England*. Oxford: Blackwell.

Hills, C., 1976. *The Anglo-Saxon cemetery at Spong Hill, North Elmham, Norfolk, Part I*. Gressenhall: East Anglian Archaeology Report 6. See also reports 11, 21, 34, 67, 69 and 73.

Hills, C., 1979. 'The archaeology of Anglo-Saxon England in the pagan period: a review', *Anglo-Saxon England* 8, 297–329.

Hines, J. (ed.) 1997. *The Anglo-Saxons from the Migration Period to the eighth century: an ethnographic perspective*. London: Boydell.

Hodges, R., 1989. *The Anglo-Saxon achievement*. London: Duckworth.

Hodges, R. and Hobley, B. (eds) 1988. *The rebirth of towns in the West*. London: Council for British Archaeology Research Report 68.

McKinley, J., 1994. *The Anglo-Saxon cemetery at Spong Hill, Part VIII: The Cremated Bones*. Gressenhall: East Anglia Archaeology 69. See also reports 6, 11, 21, 34, 67 and 73.

Ottaway, P., 1992. *Archaeology in British towns from Claudius to the Black Death*. London: Routledge.

Rackham, J. (ed.) 1994. *Environment and economy in Anglo-Saxon England*. London: Council for British Archaeology Research Report 89.

Rahtz, P.A., 1981. 'Buildings and rural settlements', in Wilson, D.M. (ed.), 1981, 49–98.

Ritchie, A., 1989. *The Picts*. Edinburgh: HMSO.

Scull, C., 1992. 'Before Sutton Hoo', in Carver, M.O.H. (ed.) *The Age of Sutton Hoo*. Woodbridge: Boydell, 3–22.

Wade, K., 1988. 'Ipswich', in Hodges, R. and Hobley, B. (eds) *The rebirth of towns in the West*. London: Council for British Archaeology Research Report 68, 93–100.

Williamson, T., 1993. *The origins of Norfolk*. Manchester: Manchester University Press.

Wilson, D.M., 1984. *Anglo-Saxon art*. London: Thames and Hudson.

Winterbottom, M. (ed.) 1978. *Gildas. The ruin of Britain*. New York: Phillimore.

*Chapter Eleven*

# The Scandinavian presence

## Julian D. Richards

### Background

For three centuries, beginning shortly before AD 800, the British Isles were subject to raids from Scandinavia. Initially these were hit-and-run affairs, targeted against vulnerable coastal sites, principally monasteries, such as Lindisfarne, Monkwearmouth and Iona. As the raiding parties gained in size and confidence, and as the need for reward increased, they seized land as well, although the rate at which raiding turned to settlement varied from area to area. Norse colonies were founded in the Northern and Western Isles of Scotland, and on the Isle of Man, although Wales appears to have avoided permanent occupation on a significant scale. For Late Saxon England, however, the Anglo-Saxon Chronicle provides a near contemporary, if one-sided, account of raids, annexations and Scandinavian invasions. It records the presence of a highly mobile Danish 'great army' in England from AD 865. Having captured York in AD 866, this army seized territory in Northumbria, Mercia and East Anglia. Within these areas, which became known as the Danelaw, many Scandinavians settled, although the raids resumed in the 980s, culminating in the invasion of England by a new army under the Danish king Svein Forkbeard in AD 1013.

Despite living in a war zone, or perhaps because of it, this was also a period of major social and economic change for the Anglo-Saxons. A network of fortified towns, or *burhs*, was founded in Mercia by King Offa, and in Wessex by Alfred and his successors. As places of royal control and protection, these towns were centres of minting and taxation, and trade and industry were encouraged to develop under their ramparts. Rural craft production of precious items gave way to semi-industrialized mass-production of standardized forms, often imitating Scandinavian artistic tastes. After some initial disruption and a shift to more easily defendable areas, the Middle Saxon *wics*, such as Hamwic (Southampton), London, Norwich, Ipswich and York also prospered. Most burhs and wics continued beyond the Norman Conquest to expand into fully fledged medieval towns (see Chapter 12). In the countryside, rural settlement was also reorganized. In many parts of England, Scandinavian settlement hastened the process of disintegration of those large estates that had been under direct royal or ecclesiastical control. Although some historians are reluctant to identify feudalism before the Norman conquest, many agree that the laying out of villages in the tenth century represents the beginnings of a manorial system (see Chapter 14). The contemporaneous boom in church building probably reflects the associated construction of private chapels attached to early manor sites (see Chapter 13).

## TERMINOLOGY AND CHARACTER

The period commencing AD 800 is often described as the Viking Age, although some explanation of the term is needed. Viking is an evocative word, but it was rarely used by contemporary chroniclers who preferred to use Norse, Dane, or even heathen, often interchangeably. The term Viking became widely used only in the nineteenth century, when translations of medieval Icelandic sagas captured the Victorian romantic imagination with tales of a heroic and mythical past. Some modern scholars go so far as to see the Vikings as inventions of the sagas, popularized by the Victorians, and maintained by contemporary nationalism. Whilst there can be little doubt that Scandinavian warriors did go on sea-borne raids from at least AD 800, it is worth acknowledging that this was, to some extent, part of a continuing process of migration that had also seen Scandinavian peoples colonize England within the shelter of earlier Germanic migration.

The Viking Age is normally thought of as ending in the mid-eleventh century. In England, it is conveniently marked by the death of the last great Viking leader, Harald Hardraada, and the subsequent victory of William the Conqueror, and is coincidental with the Late Saxon period. The Western Isles of Scotland and the Isle of Man, however, remained under Scandinavian rule until 1266, and Orkney and Shetland belonged to Norway until 1469.

For archaeologists, the Scandinavian presence in the British Isles is recognizable by its distinctive material culture. Burials accompanied by weaponry and jewellery in Scandinavian forms probably represent a first generation of pagan settlers, although their uneven distribution is also testimony to the extent of conversion amongst the settlers. In England, for example, where Christianized Danes formed the majority of the settlers, there are no more than 30 known burial sites, and most of these are solitary graves. Those from churchyards, such as those at Repton, Derbyshire, may represent a transitional conversion phase, and whilst their number might be increased by further churchyard excavation, the total would still remain relatively small. On the northern and western fringes, by comparison, there are many more pagan burials per head of population. On the Isle of Man alone, for instance, there are at least 15 burial sites. This may partly reflect the Norse preponderance in these areas, although the overtly pagan nature of some of the burials suggests that they may have also emphasized their 'Vikingness' to stress their ethnic differences in this colonial context (Myhre 1993; Richards 1991).

In some areas, such as Yorkshire and the Isle of Man, there is a flowering of stone cross construction, frequently combining pagan and Christian iconography, but Scandinavian stone sculpture is rare in southern England and in Scotland. The Viking Kingdom of York is also the centre of the distribution of the unique hogback stones, which appear to represent another distinctive colonial monument (Lang 1978).

Hoards of Viking silver are widely distributed throughout the British Isles, although their interpretation is far from straightforward. The largest, comprising over 40 kg of silver coins, bullion and arm rings, is that discovered in 1840 at Cuerdale, Lancashire, on the banks of the River Ribble (Figure 11.1); it has been interpreted as the pay chest of a Viking army, possibly recently arrived from Dublin in *c.* AD 905. Other smaller hoards from Scotland and the Isle of Man may also represent the personal fortunes of Viking leaders who were unable to pass on their wealth as gifts to their followers in order to buy their allegiance through reciprocity. It has also been suggested that some hoards as well as river offerings of weapons continued the pagan Scandinavian tradition of making gifts to gods that were never intended to be recovered. Other hoards may simply represent personal wealth buried, but never recovered, under the threat of advance of a Viking raiding party (Graham-Campbell 1992).

***Figure 11.1*** Cuerdale, Lancashire: part of the early tenth-century silver hoard.
*Source*: Trustees of the British Museum

There is little settlement evidence that can clearly be categorized as Scandinavian. Indeed, there is no reason why the buildings of Viking York should be any different from those of Saxon London, although the appearance in tenth-century York and Chester of town buildings with semi-sunken cellars, providing space for storage of traded and manufactured items, mirrors their occurrence in Danish towns. Similarly, the appearance of bow-sided halls, on high status rural sites such as Sulgrave, Northamptonshire, and Goltho, Lincolnshire, matches the Trelleborg-style halls of Denmark. It is likely, however, that so-called Norse farmsteads, with stone-footed buildings such as those discovered in Scotland and the Isle of Man, or that excavated at Ribblehead, North Yorkshire, simply represent a typical upland farmstead type that would have been familiar to both Norse settlers and natives (Richards 1991).

The identification of Scandinavian settlements raises the question of whether the majority of Viking Age inhabitants of the British Isles originated from Scandinavia or had merely acquired a politically correct Viking veneer. It is probably impossible to attempt to use material culture to identify race rather than ethnicity. Certainly in York it seems that Anglo-Saxon style disc brooches were decorated with Danish Jellinge style ornament, rather than Anglo-Saxon women adopting Scandinavian costume with the bow brooches needed to hold it in place. The established view has relied heavily upon linguistic evidence to support the idea that there was a substantial number of immigrants. In the former East Riding of Yorkshire, for example, it has been calculated that 48 per cent of placenames are of Scandinavian influence; the English language also adopted a number of Old Norse words into everyday usage. In the Isle of Man, it has been argued that Gaelic was completely supplanted by Norse and was restored only at the end of Scandinavian rule. However, such arguments beg the question of how many people are required to change a language, and linguistic studies have shown that a small but influential group can have an effect out of all proportion to their numbers. Similarly, arguments based on placenames often ignore the fact that placenames tell one only about who named the settlements, and sometimes about who collected the taxes, but not necessarily about who lived there. Certainly, the distribution of Scandinavian type placenames corresponds fairly well with the areas of recorded Danish settlements in Yorkshire, Mercia and East Anglia and the Wirral, although there are also further concentrations, such as that in the Lake District, for which there is no historical documentation.

It is perhaps intuitively unlikely that the newcomers arrived anywhere in the British Isles in such numbers, or replaced the local population to such an extent, so as to form a majority of the population. Irrespective of its size, however, the fact remains that the Scandinavian presence had considerable influence throughout the British Isles.

## CHANGING PERCEPTIONS

Since the Second World War, the saga-inspired view of horned-helmeted Norse raiders carrying off Anglo-Saxon treasure and women to their dragon-headed longships has gradually given way to a more positive image of the Scandinavian presence.

In particular, rescue archaeology within English towns has demonstrated the importance of the ninth and tenth centuries as a period of urban growth and industrialization. As a direct result of the Coppergate excavations in York and the presentation of an interpretative tableau of Viking Age York in the Jorvik Viking Centre, the modern scholarly and popular view sees Scandinavian settlers as homely entrepreneurs, trading from the fronts of their rather cosy, but smelly, workshops.

In common with other periods, there has also been a tendency to downplay the extent and impact of invasion and migration. From the 1960s, revisionist historians, notably Peter Sawyer, have questioned the reliability of figures for the size of the Danish armies given in the Anglo-Saxon Chronicle, and have suggested that these were generally small raiding forces (Sawyer 1971). They have also argued against simplistic interpretations of linguistic evidence to suggest that there was never a mass folk migration of Scandinavian settlers. Current archaeological and historical thinking emphasizes change at an elite level, but sees the vast majority of the population as unaffected by changes at the top. Most recently, post-processualist trends have encouraged archaeologists to question also whether artefact styles and cultural assemblages can be interpreted at face value. There is a growing tendency to treat the adoption of Scandinavian style ornaments as a symbolic fashion statement and to see Viking burial and sculpture as cultural signalling by a population anxious to be identified with a Scandinavian elite group (e.g. Myhre 1993).

Nevertheless, study of the period has been largely unaffected by developments in archaeological science or theory. Scientific dating methods have had little impact, and chronology still depends upon the detailed working out of typological trends from an art-historical standpoint. Most scholarly work is still at the stage of being focused upon data collection and cataloguing rather than interpretation. Environmental archaeology has enlarged our economic understanding through analysis of urban bone assemblages, but we still lack those rural sites in the urban hinterlands that might allow a picture of the full economy to be established. The agenda is still largely that set by the documentary sources. There is a tendency to use archaeological evidence as illustrations for a historical narrative and as resistance to more anthropologically based approaches, such as from those who might use Viking hoards to seek to examine gift exchange, for instance (see, for example, papers in Samson 1991). The documentary sources have also determined the popular view of the Vikings as the outsiders; few British today would identify themselves with Viking ancestors. The Anglo-Saxons, under Alfred, are the ancestral English; the Vikings are still the invaders.

## KEY DATA

## Burials

It is rare to find archaeological evidence that appears to relate to a specific historical event, and dangerous to look for it, but investigations at Repton, Derbyshire, appear to support an entry in the Anglo-Saxon Chronicle that claims that the Viking army over-wintered there in 873–874. Excavations by Martin Biddle located a D-shaped enclosure constructed so that the River Trent formed the long side, whilst the rest of the site was surrounded by a bank and ditch into which the monastery church was incorporated as a gatehouse. Some 50 m west of the enclosure, an earthen mound had been built over a massive, two-roomed stone structure, which may originally have been intended as a mausoleum for the Mercian royal family. The mausoleum had been reused as a charnel house, in which the remains of some 250 individuals had been interred. The bones were disarticulated when they were buried, with longbones stacked together and skulls placed on top. This suggests that they had been exposed or buried elsewhere, allowing the flesh to come off, before being collected together for reburial. Analysis of the skeletal remains shows that 80 per cent were robust males who died aged 15–45. The mass burial is dated by a group of five pennies deposited some time after 871. The form of the burial, its demographic characteristics, and its date all suggest that these were members of the Viking 'great army' with their womenfolk, although the absence of fatal injury marks suggests that they died from disease or starvation, rather than in battle.

Further Scandinavian burials were found near the east end of the church at Repton, including that of a man aged 35–40, who had been killed by a massive cut to the top of his left leg. He wore a necklace of two glass beads and a Thor's hammer silver amulet. By his side was a sword in a fleece-lined scabbard, a folding knife and a key, whilst a boar's tusk and jackdaw bone had been placed between his legs. A substantial posthole at the east end of the grave suggests that it had been marked by a wooden post (Biddle and Kjølbye-Biddle 1992).

At Ingleby, some 4 km south-east of Repton, fragmentary remains have been found of the only known Scandinavian cremation cemetery in England. The cemetery originally comprised 59 barrows, although of the 15 excavated, eight were found to be cenotaphs; others contained cremated animal as well as human remains, and in some cases the bodies may have been cremated on biers constructed of sections of ship's planking. It has been suggested that the Ingleby cremations may be amongst the earliest Viking burials in the British Isles. They are contemporaneous, however, with several of the cenotaphs. The cenotaphs may reflect a 'hedging of bets' by warriors whose bodies were perhaps buried by the church at Repton but to whom a mound was still erected in the pagan cemetery (Richards *et al.* 1996).

Pagan symbolism is also evidenced amongst many of the burials of first-generation Viking settlers on the Isle of Man. The graves of these first landtakers were frequently marked by coastal mounds that would have been visible from the sea. In the parish of Jurby, six out of eight of the quarterland farms (a quarterland was a unit of land division) on the coastal strip are distinguished by a prominently sited burial mound. At Balladoole (Figure 11.2), a stone cairn was erected forming the outline of a ship. The distribution of some 300 clench nails marks the location of an actual vessel, some 11 m in length. It appears that two corpses were buried in the boat, including a male accompanied by various personal items, a shield and riding equipment. The burial cairn was covered by a layer of cremated animal bones, including horse, ox, pig, sheep or goat, dog and cat. It had been cut into a Christian cist grave cemetery, some of whose occupants had been so recently buried that their limbs were still articulated. It is difficult to avoid the conclusion that such desecration was deliberate. At Ballateare, a circular mound covered a burial pit in which a young male had been placed. The body had been wrapped in a cloak held in place by a ring-headed pin. Various weapons had been placed outside the coffin, most of which showed evidence of deliberate mutilation. The sword had been broken in three pieces and replaced in its scabbard. A shield with two deep indentations to the boss had been placed on one side, and two spears had been broken and thrown in the backfill. A thin layer of cremated animal bone had again been thrown over the mound, but this time it also included the skeleton of a young female killed by a slashing blow to the top of her head. Most interpretations accept that this was a warrior accompanied to the afterworld by symbolic representations of various aspects of his property, including a slave girl (Bersu and Wilson 1966).

Ship burials are also known from other areas of Norse settlement, including the Northern and Western Isles. At Scar on the island of Sanday in Orkney, a small rowing boat, about 6.3 m long, was discovered eroding out of a cliff in 1991. Despite the sea damage, it is one of the best-recorded Norse graves from Scotland. Buried in the boat were a man in his thirties, a woman in her seventies and a child. The age difference makes it unlikely that they were a typical family group, but both adults had rich personal grave-goods, also making it unlikely that they were a master or mistress and slave. The man was armed with a sword and arrows, and had a fine comb and a set of 22 gaming pieces. The woman was wearing a gilded brooch and beside her was a whalebone plaque, a sickle, cooking spit, a small pair of shears and a steatite spindlewhorl (Ritchie 1993).

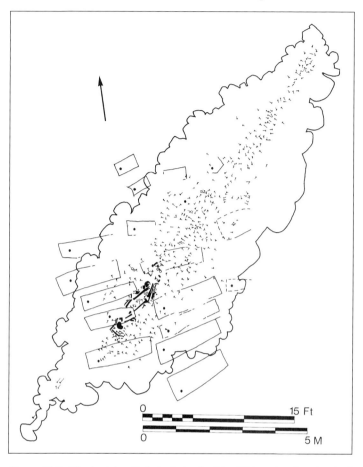

*Figure 11.2* The burial at Balladoole in the Isle of Man, showing clenched nails from boat and outlines of earlier Christian graves.
*Source*: Richards 1991

The reappearance of pagan burial in the British Isles appears to have been a relatively short-lived phenomenon, representing the first generation of Scandinavian settlers. Their successors rapidly adopted local burial customs and become archaeologically indistinguishable from those given Christian burial. At Raunds, Northamptonshire, 368 Christian burials have been excavated in a tenth- and eleventh-century graveyard clustered around a church within a rectangular ditched enclosure. All the graves were aligned east–west with the head to the west; none was buried with grave-goods. Most of the bodies were simply placed in holes in the ground, although slabs of limestone were used as pillow stones in about 60 per cent of the graves. There are indications of wooden coffins in some cases, and six elite burials were distinguished by being placed in lidded stone coffins. On the Isle of Man, over 300 Christian burials have been excavated in a cemetery to the north of St German's Cathedral, St Patrick's Isle, Peel. Most of them were in stone-lined cist graves, although the later ones simply have stone pillow slabs to protect the head, or are buried in wooden coffins. There are also at least seven Scandinavian burials of the tenth century, although only that of a high status female was accompanied by grave-goods, apart from items of dress. The woman had been laid with a cushion to support her head and was accompanied by various items

*Figure 11.3* The Middleton Cross, St Andrew's Church, Middleton, North Yorkshire.
*Source*: Dept of Archaeology, University of Durham

including a cooking spit, a work box or bag with two needles, a pair of small shears and a curious amulet. All of the Peel burials share the same alignment and style of grave construction, suggesting no break in continuity at this site, unlike Balladoole (Richards 1991).

In both the Danelaw and the Isle of Man, the Scandinavians also adopted the local custom of erecting stone crosses. This had previously been largely confined to monasteries and prestigious churches, but stone monuments now proliferated throughout northern and eastern England, and on the Isle of Man. Some fragments depict Viking warriors with their weapons. One of the best examples is at Middleton, North Yorkshire (Figure 11.3); other examples include Levisham and Weston in North Yorkshire, and Sockburn, Co. Durham. These figures may well represent the new landlords, and the distribution of crosses may indicate the presence, if not the centres, of new landholdings (Bailey 1980).

The subjects chosen by the sculptors or their patrons are particularly striking; many emphasize the parallels between Christian and pagan stories. At Gosforth, Cumbria, a Crucifixion scene is paired with *Ragnarok*, the last great battle of Norse mythology; Thorwald's cross at Kirk Andreas on the Isle of Man counterbalances Odin and *Ragnarok* with the triumph of Christ over Satan. The legend of Sigurd and his struggle with the dragon is another popular theme; the scene in which he roasts the heart of the dragon Fafnir and burns his thumb is found at Kirk Andreas and at Halton, Lancashire, and Ripon, North Yorkshire. At Nunburnholme, Humberside, there is a cross in which Sigurd has been recarved over a Eucharistic theme, drawing attention to the Sigurd feast as a pagan version of the Eucharist (Bailey 1980; Lang 1991).

Many of the graves of York's Viking Age elite discovered under York minster are marked by recumbent grave slabs decorated with Scandinavian style ornament; some have separate head and foot stones. These may be the predecessors of the distinctive so-called hogback stones, which were erected for a period of about 50 years from 920. Hogbacks are shaped like bow-sided buildings with ridged roofs and curved side walls, but their ends may be decorated with bearlike creatures, or sometimes wolves or dogs. They may also have been influenced by house-shaped shrines. Their distribution is concentrated in northern England but with outliers in Scotland, Wales and Cornwall. The best collection is in the church at Brompton, North Yorkshire, but the largest group is at Lythe, North Yorkshire (Lang 1978).

## Settlement

The stone monuments provide the best evidence for an influential Scandinavian presence in the British Isles. In the Danelaw, it is difficult to determine from excavated rural sites if they were occupied by Scandinavians. The upland farmstead at Ribblehead is frequently advanced as a Viking site (Figure 11.4). It comprises the stone footings of a longhouse, bakery and smithy set in an enclosed farmyard with an associated field system. The few artefacts recovered suggest a mixture of agricultural and simple craft activities. They included an iron cow bell, a horse bit, a spearhead, two iron knives and a stone spindlewhorl. Local materials were

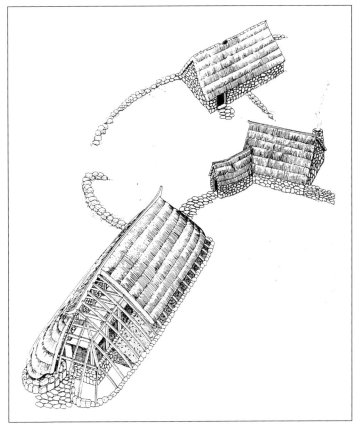

*Figure 11.4* Ribblehead, North Yorkshire: an artist's reconstruction of the Viking Age farmstead.
*Source*: Yorkshire Museum

used for most needs and the site was largely self-sufficient, although four Northumbrian copper coins, or *stycas*, attest to links with the urban markets to the east (King 1978).

At Doarlish Cashen, on the Isle of Man, a longhouse with wall benches was also discovered on marginal land at about 210 m above sea-level. Such settlements would undoubtedly have been familiar to Norse settlers but they are also standard upland building forms. In lowland England, it is becoming apparent that a number of villages were first established in the tenth century. At Furnells Manor, Raunds, Northamptonshire, a Middle Saxon settlement in a ditched enclosure was replaced by a large timber hall and an adjacent church in the early tenth century. At about the same time, the first regular tenements of peasant farmers were being laid out at Furnells and West Cotton in Northamptonshire and marked by ditched enclosures. At Goltho, an early ninth-century village was superseded by a fortified earthwork enclosing a bow-sided hall, a kitchen and weaving sheds. The manorial complex may have been founded by a member of the Saxon aristocracy, although the discovery of a Scandinavian style bridle bit could be used to suggest that it was a late ninth-century Viking foundation. Bow-sided halls are associated particularly with Viking Age Denmark, and are also found in most of the areas settled by Scandinavians. At Goltho, there was evidence that the hall, 24 m long by 6 m wide at the centre, was divided into three rooms, with a raised dais at one end and a cobbled hearth in the centre. During the late tenth and early

*Figure 11.5* Norse buildings at Jarlshof, Shetland.
*Source*: Historic Scotland

eleventh centuries, the site underwent considerable expansion. The hall was replaced by an aisled version without internal partitions, and the bower was enlarged with a latrine attached at one end. After the Norman Conquest, it developed into a motte-and-bailey castle (Beresford 1987).

In Orkney, Shetland and the Hebrides, it is easier to identify Norse settlements. Rectangular longhouses replace native houses based on oval or circular forms. Around the Bay of Birsay, Orkney, a likely seat of the Norse earls (Hunter 1986), are a number of Norse farmsteads. At the Point of Buckquoy at Birsay, a Norse farm had been built on top of the ruins of an earlier Pictish farm, and at first sight would appear to support a picture of conquest and replacement of the local population. However, the artefacts from the Norse occupation levels are not Scandinavian types but Pictish bone pins and decorated combs. These imply that the Viking newcomers were at least able to obtain equipment from a native population that had not been exterminated, and most probably inter-married with it. By contrast, the evidence from the Udal, North Uist, has been used to demolish the idea of social integration. Here the eighth-century native settlement was apparently replaced by an entirely Scandinavian culture. A short-lived defended enclosure was the first Viking Age structure; characteristic longhouses were then built amongst the ruins of five Pictish houses (Ritchie 1993).

At Jarlshof on Shetland, romantically named by Sir Walter Scott, a small Pictish community was replaced by a sequence of Norse longhouses in the ninth century. Houses over 20 m long by 5 m wide are known. The walls are built of stone rubble with a turf and earth core. Typically there are pairs of opposed doors placed in the long walls, stone-lined hearths and wall benches. At Jarlshof, the group of two or three houses and their outbuildings, perhaps representing an extended family unit, is unusual (Figure 11.5). In Scotland, the overall settlement pattern is dispersed, comprising individual farms. At Westness, Rousay, Orkney, excavations have revealed a fragment of a Viking Age landscape. A coastal cemetery contained more than 30 graves, some pre-Norse, but with two small boat burials. Nearby was a farm consisting of a substantial longhouse and two byres, one interpreted as a cattle byre with space for about 18 animals, and the other for sheep. Beyond the cemetery was a boat-house, or *naust*, comprising a three-sided building, open to the sea (Ritchie 1993).

# Towns

In northern and western Britain, there are no towns during this period, but in England the Scandinavian presence coincided with a period of urban growth. In the East Midlands there are five towns, Derby, Leicester, Lincoln, Nottingham and Stamford, which are described in the Anglo-Saxon Chronicle as Five Boroughs; they were once thought to have been specially fortified towns, established by the Danes after the partition of the Danelaw, and used by Alfred as a model for the burhs (below). However, they may not have become Danish strongholds until later, in which case they may have been modelled upon Alfred's foundations, rather than the other way round (Hall 1989).

There had been urban trading and manufacturing centres in England since the early eighth century. Sites such as Hamwic (Saxon Southampton), Eoforwic (York) and Lundenwic (London) developed under royal patronage around a waterfront where traders could beach their vessels and perhaps establish their booths in regulated plots. At most *wic* sites, however, the threat of attack in the Viking Age led the traders to seek protection within walled towns, and may also have disrupted trade.

The site of Hamwic was depopulated by the late ninth century and the focus of tenth-century occupation shifted to higher ground within the area that was to become the medieval walled town. In London, the exposed waterfront site along the Strand was abandoned and the area of the old Roman fortress was reoccupied in the tenth century, becoming known as Lundenburh (Vince 1990). In York, a single coin of the 860s is the latest find from the Fishergate site, outside the confluence of the rivers Ouse and Foss, whilst activity commences in Coppergate at about this time. It is impossible to say, however, whether this starts before the Viking capture of York in 866 as a result of people seeking the protection of the walled town, or whether it is a consequence of the Viking settlement. It does appear that York's Viking rulers renovated its Roman defences and remodelled its street system. They constructed a new bridge across the Ouse and built houses along Micklegate, 'the great street', leading to the new crossing point. In Coppergate, excavations between 1976 and 1981 of an area of deep, oxygen-free organic soils have provided some of the best preserved evidence of Viking Age urban life in the Danelaw. The Viking Age street was established by 930, and possibly as early as 900, with the delineation of four tenements, each 5.5 m wide. Initially, a single line of buildings was constructed along the street frontage, narrow end facing the street (Figure 11.6). These first buildings comprised timber wall posts and roof supports with wattlework wall panels. Each was about 4.4 m wide and 8.2 m or more in length. They had central clay hearths that would have provided both heat and light. There were probably doors at the front and rear of the properties, but windows are unlikely. In some cases, traces of wall benches were preserved. The finds suggest that these buildings served both as houses and workshops. In the late tenth century they were pulled down and replaced by substantial semi-basement structures with planked walls. Given that this occurred simultaneously along the street suggests that the tenements were under the control of a single landlord. The new buildings were probably two-storey structures with living accommodation above and extra storage and workshop space below (Hall 1994). The York examples are the best preserved in the British Isles, but cellared buildings also occur in other major towns such as London, Chester, Oxford and Thetford. They seem to be a response to the increased pressure upon urban space and the need to store goods in transit and stock-in-trade.

Although some of the largest towns developed as trading sites, a much larger group of towns was established as defended forts or burhs, probably as a direct response to the Viking threat. The earliest examples were founded in Mercia *c.* 780–90 by King Offa, possibly copying Carolingian practice. At Tamworth and Hereford, ramparts were erected to enclose a rectilinear area with one side protected by the river. At Chester, the surviving walls of the Roman fort were refurbished and probably extended down to the River Dee by Ethelflaed in 907. A substantial Hiberno-Norse

***Figure 11.6*** Excavated buildings at Coppergate, York.
*Source*: York Archaeological Trust

trading community developed near the waterfront. At Lower Bridge Street, at least five cellared timber buildings were erected in the tenth century (Mason 1985).

In Wessex, Alfred is credited with the establishment of a burghal system so that no part of his kingdom was more than 32 km from a fortified burh. When Edward the Elder reconquered England in 911–19, he extended the network and fortified a number of new sites. The Burghal Hidage, a tax assessment of *c.* 914–18, lists the Wessex burhs in the later years of Edward's reign, and indicates the extent of their perimeters. In Bath, Chichester, Exeter, Portchester (Hampshire), Southampton and Winchester, the burhs made use of Roman stone walls and gates. At Cricklade (Gloucestershire), Oxford, Wallingford (Oxfordshire) and Wareham (Dorset), new rectangular defences were erected on Roman models. The ramparts were initially of clay and turfs with timber revetment, and were probably crowned with timber palisades. In the late tenth or early eleventh centuries, the timber palisade was often replaced by a stone wall. At other sites, such as Lydford (Devon) or Malmesbury (Wiltshire), natural defences such as promontories or peninsular sites were utilized; at South Cadbury, the Iron Age hillfort was reoccupied. Within some of the larger burhs, a regular street system was laid out, and whilst the temporary forts were abandoned after the decline of the Viking threat, many of the larger burhs became permanent towns. They provided not only a haven for industry but also an urban market for its products, and for materials and produce imported from the hinterland. Winchester, unlike the earlier Hamwic, was part of a ranked hierarchy of markets. By the end of the tenth century, a number of specialized activities had developed in different sectors, reflected in street names such as Tanner Street, Fleshmonger Street and Wheelwright Street. The south-east quarter appears to have been a royal and ecclesiastical centre; a stone-built tower set in an enclosure on Brook Street may have been a residential compound of an elite group, its architecture reflecting their classical aspirations (Biddle 1981; Richards 1991).

## Industry

In the towns, the Scandinavians provided one of the main catalysts for urban growth and helped create the conditions by which England experienced what Richard Hodges describes as the First Industrial Revolution (Hodges 1989). Pottery is a case in point. During the Middle Saxon period, most pottery was manufactured locally by hand. By the early ninth century, only Ipswich ware was produced on an industrial scale and traded widely. From the mid-ninth century, changes began to occur at a number of centres. In York, there were the first steps towards a specialized pottery industry with increased standardization of forms and fabrics (Mainman 1990). In East Anglia, the Ipswich potters began to use a wheel to make cooking pots in what is known as the Thetford tradition. By 900, wheel-thrown pottery was manufactured over much of eastern England. This new pottery production was predominantly town-based: Northampton, Stamford, Stafford, Thetford and Winchester are all examples of new wares that take their names from towns in which kilns have been discovered. Stamford is notable for the introduction, in the late ninth century, of yellow or green glazing on spouted pitchers made in a fine, off-white fabric. The sudden appearance of glazing is coincidental with the Scandinavian presence in Stamford, but the technology appears to have been introduced from northern France or the Low Countries by potters who arrived in the wake of the Scandinavian takeover. Stamford ware was traded widely via coastal or riverine routes throughout the Danelaw; by the eleventh century it accounts for 25 per cent of all pottery in Lincoln and York. Its spread appears to have started with specialist industrial pottery; glazed crucibles are the first pottery to appear on tenth-century metalworking sites in Lincoln, Thetford and York.

Industrial-scale metalworking is also a feature of the new towns. The working of copper alloys and precious metals was hitherto restricted to high status sites such as the royal palace at Cheddar, Somerset, and generally appears to have been carried out only under lordly or ecclesiastical patronage. By the tenth century, it had become an urban enterprise; at Coppergate, for example, two adjacent tenements were occupied by metalworkers, and some 1,000 crucible fragments were found (Bayley 1992). The urban markets fuelled a large demand for mass-produced lead-alloy disc brooches decorated in a Scandinavian style. Iron working also spread to the towns, and whilst rural farmsteads still had their own smithies, it was in the towns that smiths experimented with new artefacts and new techniques. In York, for example, new types of knife were introduced and decoration proliferated (Ottaway 1992).

The urban communities are also characterized by manufacture in bone and antler, leather and textiles. In each case, raw materials would have been available in the immediate rural hinterlands and the urban craftsmen produced goods on a large scale for local demand. To date, the relationship between towns and their hinterlands is best studied from the urban evidence, particularly that provided by environmental archaeology. In York, the Middle Saxon traders occupying the Fishergate site appear to have been dependent upon the ruling elite for the majority of their food supply, and had little opportunity for trading with rural food-producers. The settlement at Fishergate seems to have had a narrow subsistence base. Cattle and sheep probably arrived in York on the hoof, although some pigs may have arrived as dressed carcasses. Minor animal components of the diet are very under-represented, and there are few wild mammals, birds and fish. In Viking Age York, by contrast, there was a great increase in the variety of foodstuffs available. Although there is little change in the staple meat species, there is a marked increase in those species identified as suitable for raising in backyards, such as pigs, geese and fowl. The fish bones show intensive exploitation of the river; plant remains, including moss, elder, blackberry, raspberry and sloe, reflect exploitation of local woodland resources. By the late tenth century, the exploitation pattern now has more in common with that seen in medieval York. Whereas the food supply of the Anglo-Saxon *wic* had been dependent upon a food rent system run by the elite, the Viking Age traders and craftsmen had greater freedom of operation than their controlled predecessors. Here we may see the emergence, therefore, of an independent mercantile urban class whose livelihood was based upon trade and exchange rather than redistribution (O'Connor 1994).

Commercial trade would have been dependent upon the development of a monetary economy. By the late tenth century, there were some 50–60 mints operating from burhs and major towns throughout England. The Isle of Man too began producing its own distinctive Hiberno-Manx coinage, although this may not have functioned as a full currency. The process was much slower in Scotland, and Scottish hoards indicate that a monetary economy was not operating in the fringes of the British Isles until much later. Scottish hoards, such as that from Skaill, Orkney, contain not only imported silver coins but also hack-silver (i.e. fragments of silver objects that have been chopped up to use simply as bullion) and ring-money (i.e. plain silver arm rings, which were a convenient way of carrying measurable wealth). In England, imported silver was converted into the official coinage. At each mint, a number of private individuals, or moneyers, took responsibility for the coinage on behalf of royal authority. Whilst coins carried the name of the ruler on their obverse, on the reverse the name of the moneyer appeared. Chester, being the entry point from Dublin, became an important centre for coin production, and 24 moneyers worked there from 924–39. Although not all those with Scandinavian names may have been settlers, it is still significant that by the reign of Ethelred, 75 per cent of York's moneyers, and 50 per cent of Lincoln's, bore Scandinavian names (see papers in Blackburn 1986).

## The church

In the countryside, it seems that Scandinavian settlers presided over the fragmentation of great estates, establishing manorial centres and accelerating the market in the buying and selling of land. Alongside this we see a boom in the creation of rural parishes and parish churches, notably in the tenth and early eleventh centuries. By the time of the Domesday Book, there were demonstrably over 2,600 local churches (Morris 1989). This explosion in church construction was a by-product of the quest for status of new landowners. The possession of a church was an important status symbol, as well as a source of income. Most of the manorial churches were new buildings, although some were adapted from existing minster or monastic sites. Many probably began as wooden buildings, but most were soon transformed into impressive stone buildings. The new churches generally started as simple, small, rectangular boxes to provide a nave, although chancels were often added later. At Wharram Percy, North Yorkshire, a small timber church was established in the tenth century, perhaps as a private chapel of an Anglo-Scandinavian lord. This was enlarged in the eleventh century by a small, two-celled church consisting of a nave and chancel. The church became a focus for burials of the early lords of the Percy manor, and later of the parish (Beresford and Hurst 1990). At Raunds, a small, rectangular, late ninth- or tenth-century church was erected on a stone foundation adjacent to the manorial enclosure. In the eleventh century, this building was replaced by a larger church, 15 m long, which by this time must have been serving the residents of the surrounding settlements who were buried in the graveyard.

Many of the new churches were founded by Scandinavian lords. The sequestration of monastic estates in the Danelaw may even have facilitated the creation of local churches, as some minsters lost control of their territories. At several Yorkshire sites, the lords chose to record their benefactions in a prominent position on the church sundial, for all to read. At Kirkdale, North Yorkshire, the inscription of 1055–65 commemorates a lord with a Norse name, Orm, who bought the redundant minster and erected a new church on its site. At Aldborough, Suffolk, a similar sundial records that 'Ulf ordered the church to be put up for himself and for Gunwaru's soul.'

## THE WIDER SETTING

The Scandinavian presence in the British Isles needs to be set in the wider context of the Viking World. The geographical extent of Scandinavian cultural domination is one of the most striking aspects of the Viking Age. The Norse travelled westwards across the North Atlantic to the fringes of the known world, founding colonies in the Faroes, Iceland, Greenland and even reaching the coast of Newfoundland; in the east, Swedish Vikings had established trading ports down the major river routes into the heart of eastern Europe (Graham-Campbell *et al.* 1994). These provide valuable comparisons for the Scandinavian presence in Britain, allowing archaeologists to study the nature of contact and its effects upon the native peoples. In some cases, the Scandinavians were occupying virgin territory; in others, they were moving into already intensively settled and exploited lands. On the whole, it appears that the secret of their success lay in their ability to change and to adapt to local circumstances, enabling the incomers to blend, chameleon-like, into the background in some cases, such as in the Danelaw, or to emphasize and develop a distinctive Viking cultural identity in others.

Developments in Scandinavia are of particular relevance to Britain, as Scandinavian expansion overseas can be understood only in the context of state formation at home. Denmark, the first of the Scandinavian kingdoms to appear on the historical stage, must serve as an example. The date of the emergence of a kingdom that encompassed all of present-day Denmark is a vexed question, but it is at least accepted that by the reign of Harold Bluetooth in the late tenth century, most of Jutland plus the islands of Fyn, Sjælland and that southern portion of Sweden known as Skåne were under the control of the Danish king. At the royal burial site at Jelling, Harold erected a runestone monument on which he claimed responsibility for the unification, as well as the conversion to Christianity, of Denmark. Harold established a system of ring forts, known after one of them as Trelleborg forts, in each part of his kingdom. At about the same time, we see the emergence of a class of warrior farmers whom we presume made up the king's armies. This group might also have been the landholders at sites such as Vorbasse, with its bow-sided, Trelleborg style halls. These sites have been termed magnate farms and, in parallel with Late Saxon England, are often interpreted as being farmed by tenant farmers on behalf of a lord to whom tribute and allegiance would be owed. This was the social and economic glue that bound the Viking raiding parties together.

The causes of Viking expansion have been much debated and have ranged from population pressure and a worsening climate at home to Viking skills at ship building and navigation. Whilst these factors may have contributed, the most satisfactory explanation rests upon internal pressures caused by shortage of resources. Our understanding of pre-Viking Danish society suggests that the giving of prestige gifts both to others and to the gods was one of the key means by which chieftains maintained their status. If the internal supply of gifts were to dry up, or fail to maintain pace with demand, the easiest solution would be to turn to external sources. During the initial stages of the Viking raids, Anglo-Saxon monastic treasures provided a ready means to reward one's war band.

Later, as Denmark developed into a state society, the desire for portable wealth was supplemented by a desire for territorial control. Similarly, the giving of silver arm rings was augmented by the giving of rights to land. The division of the great estates of England was accelerated by the presence of Scandinavians, sharing land tenure between their followers in return for continued allegiance and support.

## Key texts

Crawford, B., 1987. *Scandinavian Scotland*. Leicester: Leicester University Press.
Graham-Campbell, J., Batey, C., Clarke, H., Page, R.I. and Price, N.S., 1994. *Cultural atlas of the Viking world*. Abingdon: Andromeda Oxford Limited.
Hall, R.A., 1990. *Viking Age archaeology in Britain and Ireland*. Princes Risborough: Shire Publications.
Hall, R.A., 1994. *Viking Age York*. London: Batsford/English Heritage.
Richards, J.D., 1991. *Viking Age England*. London: Batsford/English Heritage.
Ritchie, A., 1993. *Viking Scotland*. London: Batsford/Historic Scotland.

## Bibliography

Bailey, R.N., 1980. *Viking Age sculpture in northern England*. London: Collins.
Bayley, J., 1992. *Non-ferrous metalworking from 16–22 Coppergate*. London: Archaeology of York 17/7.
Beresford, G., 1987. *Goltho: the development of an early medieval manor c. 850–1150*. London: English Heritage Archaeological Report 4.
Beresford, M. and Hurst, J.G., 1990. *Wharram Percy: deserted medieval village*. London: Batsford/English Heritage.
Bersu, G. and Wilson, D.M., 1966. *Three Viking graves in the Isle of Man*. London: Society for Medieval Archaeology Monograph Series 1.
Biddle, M., 1981. 'Towns', in Wilson, D.M. (ed.) *The archaeology of Anglo-Saxon England*. Cambridge: Cambridge University Press, 99–150. 2nd edn.
Biddle, M. and Kjølbye-Biddle, B., 1992. 'Repton and the Vikings', *Antiquity* 66, 36–51.
Blackburn, M.A.S. (ed.) 1986. *Anglo-Saxon monetary history: essays in honour of Michael Dolley*. Leicester: Leicester University Press.
Graham-Campbell, J. (ed.) 1992. *Viking treasure from the North-West: the Cuerdale hoard in its context*. Liverpool: National Museums and Galleries of Merseyside Occasional Papers 5.
Hall, R.A., 1989. 'The Five Boroughs of the Danelaw: a review of present knowledge', *Anglo-Saxon England* 18, 149–206.
Hodges, R., 1989. *The Anglo-Saxon achievement*. London: Duckworth.
Hunter, J.R., 1986. *Rescue excavations on the Brough of Birsay 1974–1982*. Edinburgh: Society of Antiquaries of Scotland Monograph 4.
King, A., 1978. 'Gauber high pasture, Ribblehead: an interim report', in Hall, R.A. (ed.) *Viking Age York and the North*. London: Council for British Archaeology Research Report 27, 21–25.
Lang, J.T., 1978. 'The hogback: a Viking colonial monument', *Anglo-Saxon studies in archaeology and history* 3, 85–176.
Lang, J.T., 1991. *Corpus of Anglo-Saxon stone sculpture: Volume 3. York and Eastern Yorkshire*. London: British Academy.
Mainman, A., 1990. *Anglo-Scandinavian pottery from 16–22 Coppergate*. London: Archaeology of York 16/5.
Mason, D.J.P., 1985. *Excavations at Chester: 26–42 Lower Bridge Street 1974–6: the Dark Age and Saxon Period*. Chester: Grosvenor Museum Archaeology, Excavation and Survey Reports 3.
Morris, R.K., 1989. *Churches in the landscape*. London: Dent.
Myhre, B., 1993. 'The beginning of the Viking Age – some current archaeological problems', in Faulkes, A. and Perkins, R. (eds) *Viking revaluations: Viking Society Centenary Symposium 14–15 May 1992*. London: Viking Society for Northern Research, 182–204.
O'Connor, T.P., 1994. '8th–11th century economy and environment in York', in Rackham, J. (ed.) *Environment and economy in Anglo-Saxon England*. London: CBA Research Report 89, 136–47.
Ottaway, P.J., 1992. *Anglo-Scandinavian ironwork from 16–22 Coppergate*. London: Archaeology of York 17/6.

Richards, J.D. *et al.*, 1996. 'The Viking barrow cemetery at Heath Wood, Ingleby, Derbyshire', *Medieval Archaeology* 39, 51–70.

Samson, R. (ed.) 1991. *Social approaches to Viking studies.* Glasgow: Cruithne Press.

Sawyer, P.H., 1971. *The age of the Vikings.* London: Edward Arnold.

Vince, A.G., 1990. *Saxon London: an archaeological investigation.* London: Seaby.

*Chapter Twelve*

# Landscapes of the Middle Ages

## Towns 1050–1500

## John Schofield

### PRINCIPAL CHRONOLOGICAL SUB-DIVISIONS

The period AD 1050–1500 in the British Isles is conventionally divided into three successive phases:

1  the development of towns and the countryside in a period of growth, 1050–1300;
2  the crises of the early and mid fourteenth-century, including the Black Death;
3  a long period of mixed fortunes from about 1350 to 1500, which comprised both decline for some towns and the rise of others, including in England the increasing dominance of London over a widening hinterland and a similar dominance in Scotland of Edinburgh.

In the eleventh century, there were already many towns in Britain, though the majority were in England, where Domesday Book records 112 places called boroughs in 1086. They were based on royal residences, or trading settlements, or the defended places of Saxons or Danes in the ninth and tenth centuries (Hinton 1990, 82–105). Some major centres such as London, Lincoln and York had longer histories, being Roman foundations of the first century AD.

In the towns, a period of comparative wealth and growth in the eleventh and twelfth centuries is illustrated by the range of civic and religious buildings that were constructed (Hinton 1990, 106–132; Platt 1978, 1–29). The great majority of urban defences in England and Wales, for instance, were built, or at least begun, before 1300. The Normans moved the seats of bishops to towns, which meant several new cathedrals, and established centres of secular authority. This usually meant the destruction of large areas of the Saxon towns to accommodate both cathedrals and castles (see Chapter 13). In the thirteenth century, the friars arrived in Britain seeking populous locations, and hospitals were founded in and around many urban places.

Weekly markets in the smaller towns are mentioned in the twelfth but especially in the thirteenth centuries; sometimes the grant of the market itself is recorded. The fair, on the other hand, was a wider kind of market, usually held once a year and lasting for at least three days and sometimes for as long as six weeks. As the market was the centre for exchange within the neighbourhood, so the fair was the centre for foreign wares, brought from outside the locality.

Between 1200 and 1500 about 2,800 grants of market were made by the English Crown, over half of them in the period 1200–75. Village markets and seasonal local fairs were augmented by weekly or bi-weekly markets held in centres of production, both existing towns and new towns. This was happening all over Europe, for instance in south-west France (the interface between the English and French kingdoms) and along the Baltic coast. Towns were valuable pieces of property, for the lord gained revenue from the court, tolls on merchandise, and from the demands of the market which benefited his own rural manors in the surrounding countryside (Platt 1978, 30–90). The main stimulus for economic growth in small towns may have been the needs of a local lord. Country landowners and religious houses acquired properties in the ports, where they could trade with the surplus of their own manors and farms, and have access to the market in imported luxuries.

In this early phase, the merchants of many small British towns participated in overseas trade, and London's dominance was largely a thing of the future. Ships still came to the river-ports of York, Lincoln, Norwich, Gloucester and Chester. Wine from the English lands in Gascony (south-west France) came to Boston in Lincolnshire; wool exports through the town rivalled those of the capital. Along the eastern and southern coasts, small and medium-sized towns fed their regions with imports, and shipped out the local produce. By the twelfth century, however, London was the primary distribution centre for inland trade, and its size and wealth began to dominate south-east England.

In Wales, by 1135, a boundary zone of castles and nascent towns had been established along the Marches from Cardiff to Chester. Towns flourished particularly in south Wales during the eleventh and twelfth centuries: places like Monmouth, Cardiff, Abergavenny, Brecon (where the first civil town was laid out in the castle bailey, a pattern found elsewhere in the Welsh zone), Carmarthen and Pembroke. This southern group was complemented by a second wave of fortress towns added in the north and west by Edward I's campaigns in the 1270s; the many medieval cellars of Chester probably date from this period, as the town became a supply base for the royal army.

In Scotland, by the eleventh century, there were also political and economic systems that could organize and support substantial centres of population, but urban history is obscure before the widespread introduction of the 'burgh' and its privileges by King David I (1124–53) and his successors. Some towns, like Edinburgh and Stirling, grew next to citadels, while others, such as Lanark, Selkirk and Dunfermline, are on unprotected sites.

In England, towards the end of the thirteenth century, there are signs of economic strain and social tensions, at least in the larger towns. The most important single industry was the making of cloth, but in the thirteenth century, in the face of the highly urbanized Flemish industry, England became an exporter of wool. Times were good, and many towns were established and prospered; the population rose in towns and in the countryside. Around 1300, however, fortunes changed. Crop failures and cattle disease caused widespread famines in 1315–25; a 50 per cent drop in production brought a 400 per cent increase in grain prices. England was at war with Scotland and from 1337 with France, which resulted in heavy taxes to pay for the king's campaigns. The Black Death of 1348, a Europe-wide epidemic of bubonic plague, was the *coup de grâce* to a country already weakened by political problems and natural disasters.

During the late fourteenth and fifteenth centuries, cloth went back to replacing wool as England's main export. By 1500, the bulk of the country's overseas trade was in English hands; so was the transformation of raw materials into finished products. Many towns, however, some sooner than others, went into decline. At Nottingham in 1376, houses were falling into decay; Bedford and Warwick similarly stagnated. At York around 1400, the textile industry was flourishing and the town's merchants engaged in overseas trade through the nearby port of Hull, but within 30 years, the textile industry had migrated to the countryside and wool exports had slumped. Hull could not compensate by more exports of cloth, for it faced Hanseatic opposition in the Baltic and London's interests in Flanders. Lincoln was declining more rapidly, initially from the effect of the plague and then from problems with its vital waterways, the Fosdyke to the Trent and the Witham to Boston.

Other towns, however, succeeded. Gloucester and Coventry switched attention from wool to cloth production. Salisbury and Norwich did likewise, and whole regions came to specialize in cloth: notably the south-west (Totnes; Castle Combe), East Anglia (Lavenham; Hadleigh) and the former West Riding of Yorkshire (Halifax and Wakefield). Ports also fared better, as demonstrated by the fortunes of Bristol and London.

## MAJOR AND TYPICAL DATA TYPES

Urban finds are of several kinds: ceramics (largely pottery); animal bones; human bones; buildings and loose building material; non-ceramic artefacts (in leather, wood and metals); and biological and botanical evidence. Buildings and streets are types of artefact, to be analysed in the same general ways as pottery or small finds. The town's archaeology is the result of a bundle of influences – climatic regimes, physical factors in the environment such as the influence of geology or gradual pollution, or biological factors (e.g. dietary differences between people).

The archaeologist studying medieval British towns must use maps and documents as well as the trowel (Aston and Bond 1974; Platt 1976; Schofield 1993; Schofield and Vince 1994). Medieval towns have, to varying degrees, the additional benefit of more records per square kilometre than

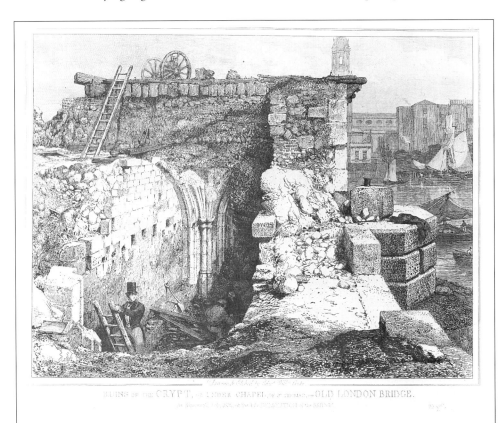

*Figure 12.1* The undercroft beneath the chapel on medieval London Bridge, revealed during demolition in 1832. Above the crypt are the road layers of the thirteenth-century bridge itself. Engravings like this are the earliest archaeological records of medieval towns.
*Source*: Guildhall Library, London

rural places, or than towns in previous centuries. Archaeology gives more depth on individual sites, while documentary study is wider and is effective at the level of larger units such as street or town. Engravings (for example, Figure 12.1) and other drawings by antiquaries of the eighteenth and nineteenth centuries are often useful for reconstructing lost or destroyed medieval buildings in many towns.

## CHANGING PERCEPTIONS SINCE THE SECOND WORLD WAR

In the first half of the twentieth century in Britain, urban history studies were dominated by a concern exclusively with constitutions and institutions; there was no attempt to think of towns as actual places. Urban archaeology in Britain began immediately after the last war in the bomb-damaged cellars of London, Canterbury and a small number of other towns, where medieval buildings and monuments had suffered destruction along with those of more recent centuries (Grimes 1968).

By the end of the 1960s, many archaeologists were concerned about the destruction of physical evidence for Britain's history in towns. This resulted in the survey *The Erosion of History* (Heighway 1972), which drew attention to the 'crisis in urban archaeology'. It argued that the most important English towns of all historical periods would be lost to archaeology in 20 years, if not before; half of the 906 historic towns remaining in mainland Britain were threatened with some sort of development, 159 of them seriously.

During the 1970s and early 1980s, archaeologists widened the debate and scope of their activities from being purely reactive to formulating strategic plans for individual towns (e.g. Carver 1980 on Worcester). In the 1970s, the practice of asking every developer to pay for dealing with the archaeology of his site in an appropriate way spread from London and the larger cities to a more general use everywhere (Schofield and Vince 1994). Since 1990, government policy has been to insist on preservation of historic strata wherever possible, and rescue archaeology has diminished. At the same time, the urban archaeologists have been digesting the vast haul of information from the last 30 years of rescue work, and new perceptions of the medieval town and what went on in it are being formed.

## KEY DATA: SITES AND ASSEMBLAGES

This chapter will briefly outline some of the recent thinking and discoveries concerning planned towns and planned parts of towns; urban defences; streets, markets and public buildings; suburbs and the waterfront areas of towns; houses and buildings on the domestic scale; evidence of manufacture and crafts; and the medieval urban environment. Castles, monasteries, and churches in towns are dealt with in the following chapter.

## Planned towns and planned parts of towns

From the modern street-plan of towns, or from maps showing their former state, we can identify certain layouts that were shared by new towns and by planned extensions to existing (pre-medieval) settlements. Three main variants have been identified. Firstly, in a small number of towns there is clear evidence of planning. A chequerboard pattern formed by at least four streets and nine squares is found rarely (Salisbury or Winchelsea) and must always have been exceptional. Ludlow, which now comprises a grid of streets, probably grew in a series of stages (Platt 1976, 38–44). A second grid-plan produced a ladder-like effect with two main streets in parallel (e.g. New Shoreham, Melcombe Regis). Thirdly, particularly in the years up to 1200, an urban castle might dominate the town plan to the extent of making it circular or D-shaped, following the castle's outer defences (Barnstaple, Pleshey).

A second group of apparently planned elements were more irregular, and concern the emphasis placed upon the market, especially as defensive considerations declined during the thirteenth century. Markets might be in the main street, causing its edges to bulge into a cigar-shape, or the meeting of two or three ways might produce a triangular space. These two market-forms are very common in towns, and one might ask what, if any, deliberate policy of planning they represent, apart from the initial decision to start the market.

Ideas of what may be termed medieval town planning are most evident in the new towns associated with Edward I. In the north at Berwick, and in Wales at Flint, Conwy and Caernarvon, he hoped both to keep the peace by establishing garrison towns but also to encourage it by promoting ports and markets, incidentally ensuring effective markets to feed the garrisons. These towns were therefore military units in which castle and borough were designed as a single concept. The castles have survived well in these Welsh towns, but unfortunately there is little evidence at present for ordinary houses in these specialized places; we have to look to contemporary foundations in Gascony in France, where there are many English and French towns called *bastides*, in which the medieval fabric survives to be studied.

Many town plans were composed of a series of topographical units of different periods. The clearest examples are those towns of great age, such as Abergavenny, Doncaster, Godmanchester and Hereford, but the apparent homogeneity of planned towns should also be regarded with caution. New towns might have been laid out systematically at first, but soon spilled over and developed their own idiosyncracies. In addition, as demonstrated in many 'planned' cases, the units of new settlement were based on field boundaries and ridges, as in the twelfth century at Stratford and Lichfield. In Scotland, cumulative phases of settlement from the twelfth to the fifteenth centuries and later are suggested at Perth by analysis of street-blocks and plot widths. The emphasis of wider European studies (Clarke and Simms 1985) has also been to emphasize the cumulative character of town plans, often with many stages from a Dark Age or Carolingian fortified centre, through markets, extensions and suburbs, to the fully expanded city of Renaissance times.

## Urban defences

The best way to understand a town's topography is to start with the outer boundary. Defences signified the town limits and the size or the intended size of the settlement. Extensions to circuits might therefore be caused by growth of population or expansion of building beyond original boundaries, as at Abergavenny, Bridgnorth and Southampton in the thirteenth century, or Cardiff and Pembroke in the fourteenth century. Only Bristol, Lincoln, Norwich and York developed extensions in several directions, which resemble the concentric rings of defences seen in continental cities, though there may be more examples to be identified. Rebuilding the defences to define a smaller area than before, which presumably reflects urban decay or retrenchment, is rare, but there are examples at New Winchelsea, where the defences in 1414–15 reduced the area of the town, and at Berwick-on-Tweed, where the Elizabethan circuit covered only two-thirds of the area of the fourteenth-century town. Alternatively, city walls might be built, or lines of defence strengthened, by joining together existing lines of the walls of stone houses and blocking up openings such as doors and windows, as is documented at Southampton and Edinburgh.

Roman defensive circuits were reused by medieval towns on the same sites, for instance at Canterbury, Lincoln, London and York. The walls were of masonry, and the surviving Roman gates formidable structures, so that it was usual for medieval gates to occupy the same sites as their Roman predecessors. At other towns, a defensive circuit originally of Anglo-Saxon date was partly or wholly reused by the medieval town, as at Barnstaple, Bridgnorth, Oxford or Totnes.

New medieval circuits or extensions were substantially of masonry in the larger towns such as Berwick, Bristol, Edinburgh, London (Blackfriars), Newcastle, Norwich, Oxford, Shrewsbury, Southampton, Stirling and Worcester. Gates of masonry were an essential part of these defences, and a good number survive, though some of the circuit walls have been lost. In a further group of towns, the gates were of masonry but the defences of earth and timber, giving both strength and prestige to the entry points into the town. This was the case, for instance, at Aberdeen, Coventry, Pontefract and Tewkesbury. At Banbury, there were four gates, but no walls; Glasgow also had gates across its streets, but no defences. Towards the end of the medieval period, town gates became increasingly ornamental and had little military significance. Similarly, few town walls in England or Wales were ever seriously tested in warfare; very few were ever rebuilt to take account of developments in the technology of warfare, such as the use of cannon from the late fourteenth century.

Defences performed many secondary functions besides protection of the town and exclusion of the outsider. Gates were used as accommodation for civic officers, as chapels, lock-ups and meeting-rooms. The defensive system included fishponds at Stafford and York, and a lake at Edinburgh; at Hereford and other towns, water from the town ditch drove mills.

## Streets, markets and public buildings

In some towns, the meeting of main roads, and the market, was to be found at the gate of the monastery or cathedral church, which took over the castle's role as epicentre of the place; this would have an effect on the neighbourhood round the new centre. Market life was also inextricably mixed with daily religious observance. Markets were held in or near churchyards, as at Llanelli or Haverfordwest; in many other places, churches lay in the middle of broad market streets.

The local ruler controlled the revenue of trade by establishing a market within a town, on only one site in the smaller and more typical towns. A central space, often near the main church, would be made available for stalls, which over time became permanent structures and buildings that in some cases survive today (as at Salisbury). By the late thirteenth century, covered specialized markets and civic warehouses for food, grain or cloth were to be found in larger towns. Recent work has reconstructed the mid-fifteenth-century Leadenhall market in London (Samuel 1989). The complex comprised a large market space surrounded by arcades, with ware-houses above; a chapel; and a grammar school, endowed by the rich mercer Simon Eyre. The larger places such as Bristol, Coventry and London had several specialized market places for different commodities.

The chief civic building would be the town hall or guildhall. This begins to appear in records in the twelfth and thirteenth centuries, when towns were straining towards self-government. During the fourteenth to sixteenth centuries, many were rebuilt in grander fashion, often in stone. Around the hall, used as a court and for assemblies, would be service buildings (especially kitchens for feasts) and rooms used for storing arms and keeping prisoners. Timber-framed public halls such as at Canterbury, Coventry, Leicester and Lavenham were adaptations of house designs, but the larger towns in eastern England, during the fifteenth century, could afford guildhalls in stone that are comparable with those in continental towns (London, King's Lynn, Norwich, York). Along with the structures (real and symbolic) of civic organization, there was the infrastructure of justice, punishment and control. The larger prisons, such as the royal Fleet Prison in London and the jail at Lydford (Devon), looked like castles; the Fleet had been built in the late eleventh century on an island in the broad stream that ran down the side of the City of London to meet the Thames.

## Suburbs and the waterfront

The actions of civic leaders in medieval towns can also be seen in the way in which the borders of towns, outside the line of the defences, were organized – the suburbs on land, and the waterfront zone along the town's river or its seafront.

Growth or decline in the suburbs of the town may be a reflection of its economic fortunes. The form of suburbs was usually dictated by existing approach roads and by the location of markets immediately outside the town gates, as illustrated most vividly by the space called St Giles outside the north gate of Oxford. During the eleventh and twelfth centuries, many of the older towns such as Canterbury, Winchester and York expanded their suburbs to reach their largest extent for several centuries. Prominent churches or bridges would be rebuilt as signs of prosperity. At Exeter, for instance, a suburb on Exe Island would have been promoted by the building of St Edmund's church and the contiguous Exe Bridge around 1200. Suburban expansion can be identified by areas of town called Newland, as at Banbury and Gloucester. After 1300, few if any towns expanded further, and many contracted in size. By the time of the earliest maps around 1600, great parts of their suburbs had reverted to fields.

Dangerous or obnoxious trades were often banned to the extramural areas. Blacksmiths, potters, tanners and fullers were found here, either excluded because of their smoke or noise, or taking advantage of the relatively open space (the bell-founders could dig for brickearth, the dyers stretch their cloths on frames called tenters). When the hospitals and friaries came in the twelfth and thirteenth centuries, they tended to form topographical obstacles rather than give encouragment to further growth (though there are exceptions: sometimes a friary would give a new tone to a suburb or neighbourhood, and richer houses would thereafter congregate around it).

Most suburbs were relatively poor, but some early developments were conspicuously wealthy, for instance in the western suburb of Winchester or outside the north gate at Gloucester. In a few cases, the town centre moved to what had previously been a suburb; at Hereford and Northampton, for example, the extramural market became the commercial centre of the town, and the later expansion of Leicester was around the East Gate.

The boundaries of suburbs, being the boundaries of the whole settlement, indicate general prosperity or decline of the town, and suburbs often offer 'clean-slate' sites, where the occupation is easier to understand because it is on virgin soil. This occupation is often of an industrial character. A relative concentration of housing along certain streets identifies the major axis routes to the town, and if the date of this settlement can be established by archaeological and other means, the date of development of that route (a trading route out to the hinterland in a particular direction) can be explored. Two excavations of medieval suburban sites in recent years demonstrate these qualities: that of the Hamel, Oxford, and Alms Lane, Norwich (Atkin 1985). Alms Lane in particular shows a good suburban sequence. In the tenth century, it lay north of and outside the Saxon town, and until about 1275 was used as a refuse dump for the crafts of the town, as shown by the artefacts. Wetland plants and bones of frogs and toads indicate the environment. From the late thirteenth century, as demonstrated by archaeological and documentary evidence, the site was owned and used by workers in leather, skinning, bone-working and especially iron-working. In about 1375, however, the land was levelled and became the site of housing from the expanding city, and suburban industries were pushed out.

Besides spreading out along approach roads, the town often spread in a rather different manner into the adjacent river or sea. A waterfront zone often developed as a narrow strip of reclaimed land along the river bank or shore, modifying it to suit the needs both of landing and exporting goods, and in time for housing, warehouses and other buildings, even churches. Thus many towns actually increased their area – in the City of London, perhaps by as much as 15 per cent – over the medieval period by pushing out into the water.

Such reclaimed areas, though usually without churches, can be identified at British ports such as King's Lynn, London, Newcastle, Norwich and Hull, and in many continental ports (Good *et al.* 1991). The remarkable survival of archaeological strata and especially finds in a waterfront zone gives the area a general importance for greater understanding of a town's history in a number of significant ways.

Firstly, the wealth of finds, especially of organic materials such as wood, leather and bone, is often accurately dated by a combination of dendrochronology (Figure 12.2) and coins. The finds often include trade waste (unfinished products) or industrial scrap. We know from documents that in many towns, rubbish heaps were not allowed to stand for more than a few days, and domestic and trade refuse was carted away. In the twelfth to fourteenth centuries, especially, it was used to infill behind the reclamation units (e.g. Milne and Milne 1982). The waterfront revetments (Figure 12.3) contain datable groups of medieval finds representative of life in the wider city, since backfilling the revetments acted as private and civic rubbish-tips. The series of catalogues of medieval finds from excavations in London, nearly all from waterfront sites, illustrates this most clearly (for example Crowfoot *et al.* 1992; Egan and Pritchard 1991). The waterfront sites also provide the basis for the construction of pottery chronologies on which so much other archaeological dating and inference depends.

Secondly, in many ports, the strip of land along the river has often been raised several times against the rising river, and this action buried many medieval buildings, the fairly complete plans of which may be recovered by excavation. At other ports, previous buildings are buried by attempts to reach the water as the port silted up. In towns such as London and Hull, the buildings and the finds in and around them may be further illuminated by documentary study of their owners and occupiers, including people of different social standing and of different trades.

Thirdly, overall, it is reasonable to suggest that the rate of reclamation in cubic metres is indicative

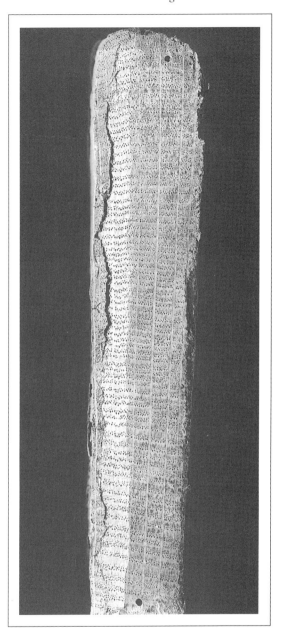

*Figure 12.2* An oak board from a twelfth-century waterfront excavated at Seal House, Thames Street, London, in 1974. The tree from which it came was cut down around 1160.
*Source*: Museum of London Archaeology Service

of activity and growth in the city at large; so that as our information increases from a programme of excavations, we may be able to relate the volume of reclamation (measured by archaeological contexts) with periods of growth in the city itself. This is one of the reasons for suggesting, from archaeological evidence, that the twelfth century was a time of urban growth. In London, the greatest amount of reclamation took place between about 1120 and 1220.

## Houses and buildings on the domestic scale

The shape and size of individual buildings clearly contributed to the outline and definition of properties, particularly along street frontages; by 1150, in London, the frontages of streets such as Bow Lane and Milk Street were continuous rows of buildings. Equally, properties can be defined by the way in which rubbish pits were dug in groups or lines (Schofield *et al.* 1990). In some cases, the street frontage was already indented or even slightly curved, taking account of encroachments or obstacles formed by prominent buildings. Some of these encroachments were buildings of stone, commonly with their gables against the street. The erection of a stone building by the street, often in the twelfth or thirteenth centuries (as for example also at Lincoln and Bury St Edmunds), would thereafter tend to anchor that part of the frontage for generations.

In Canterbury, London and Winchester, stone buildings near the street could occasionally be found by 1100; there are a number of twelfth-century examples, for instance in London at Well Court, also in Bow Lane, or on narrow waterfront properties immediately downstream of the medieval bridge site at New Fresh Wharf. In smaller but still important towns, the stone buildings tended to be in certain areas such as on or near the main street, or along the riverfront; some towns had areas where the small but economically significant Jewish community congregated, and they have been traditionally associated with stone houses. On the other hand, in towns such as Bury St Edmunds, there was a scattering of stone houses throughout, not in any one part.

Many houses in both large and medium-sized towns belonged to a distant lord, whether lay or religious (a monastery or bishopric). There were two purposes for such a house: the provision of accommodation for those engaged in the everyday affairs of the house or the see, such as the selling of produce or the buying of goods, especially luxuries; and as the residence of the institution's head when in town. These urban depots of religious institutions from out of the town, whether based in another town or in the countryside, are found in many of the larger centres, such as York, or

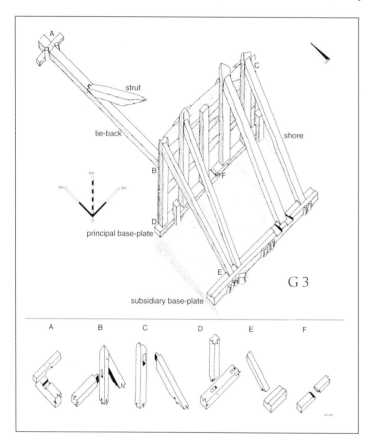

*Figure 12.3* A revetment of 1270–90 excavated at Trig Lane, London, showing its repertoire of carpentry joints. Sometimes timbers from medieval buildings formerly on land are found reused in the waterfront constructions, enabling details of the lost townscape to be reconstructed.
*Source*: Museum of London Archaeology Service

Edinburgh, where fifteenth-century ecclesiastical town houses have produced evidence of luxurious living, such as an unusual amount of imported German pottery; and in nascent county towns such as Shrewsbury.

In the majority of cases where their plans can be ascertained, the houses of religious and noble leaders were of courtyard plan. The hall of the property lay normally at the rear of a yard, though occasionally to the side on restricted sites, with a range of buildings (often separately let) fronting the street. Leaders of the merchant community in the larger towns, such as those who dealt in wine or some other aspect of royal service, also aspired to the style of house with a courtyard and an open hall of lofty proportions. Fourteenth- to sixteenth-century examples are known at Exeter, King's Lynn, London, Norwich and Oxford (Pantin 1962–3).

A smaller form of house, of three to six rooms in ground-floor plan, did not have a true courtyard with a formal gate to the street, though it might have a yard with buildings along one side, or an alley running the length of a long, narrow property. The latter arrangement is illustrated most clearly by properties on waterfront sites, such as in King's Lynn or south of Thames Street in London. Many had an alley down one side, and in consequence buildings were usually arranged down the side of the plot behind the street-range which commonly comprised shops, sometimes let separately. Along, usually at the side of, most waterfront properties ran the access alley from the street to the river and the main water supply. This originated for the most part as a private thoroughfare, in some cases becoming

*Figure 12.4* Medieval buildings survive in many British towns. Here, at the Cornmarket in Oxford, are three out of an original block of five houses that formed the street frontage of the New Inn. They were built, according to dendrochronology of the timbers, probably in 1386–7, and have been recently restored. Medieval buildings have much to contribute to the appearance of the town today.
*Source*: Julian Munby

public through time and custom. There were many variations on this long, narrow plan (e.g. in Hartlepool, Daniels 1990), and these houses do not conform easily to any type or standard design.

Smaller, and more uniform in its characteristics, was a house with two rooms on three or more floors. This type is known from documentary and archaeological evidence in London from the early fourteenth century; in several cases such houses form a strip, two rooms deep, fronting but separate from a larger property behind. Fourteenth-century examples are known from both excavation and from documents in London, and a block of three (originally five) still stand in Cornmarket, Oxford; they are dated by dendrochronology to 1386–7 (Figure 12.4).

The houses of the medieval poor have largely been destroyed without trace in almost every town. By the time the depictions of towns in engravings became commonplace, these humble dwellings had largely disappeared; and as they commonly lay along street-frontages, archaeological excavation has not uncovered them because of later street-widening and the digging of cellars, especially in the nineteenth century. Sometimes the existence of buildings, probably forming continuous

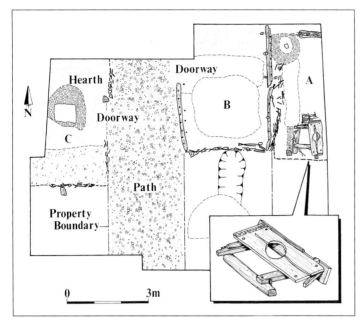

*Figure 12.5* Three houses and a latrine in thirteenth-century Perth at Kirk Close.
*Source*: Scottish Urban Archaeological Trust, from Yeoman 1995

facades and one room deep, may be inferred from the absence of rubbish pits near the line of the street. One-room timber-framed houses of thirteenth- or early fourteenth-century date have been excavated at Lower Brook Street, Winchester, and more substantial examples in stone of the fifteenth century at St Peter's Street, Northampton (Williams 1979). Work in Perth has uncovered graphic evidence of poor lifestyles, in single-room buildings with walls of posts and wattle which were probably both living and working space for cobblers and other artisans (Figure 12.5).

Medieval towns, to varying degrees, had building regulations that sought to prevent fires and improve sanitation and drainage. Sometimes the observance or flouting of these regulations can be seen in the archaeological record: for instance, walls only 1 m wide dividing properties in London. Buildings of stone lasted longer, and often formed links with former topographic arrangements among the comparatively restless mass of timber-framed buildings, which were easily taken down and reassembled, sometimes on a different site.

## Evidence of manufacture and crafts

Today, in many towns, we can see a Butcher's Row or Ironmonger Lane. It is usual to think of the craft areas of medieval towns as being clearly demarcated one from another; but this is only part of a more complex picture.

Certainly, a common feature of twelfth-century and later urban industries is their nucleation. Not only do some industries occur in towns but not in the surrounding countryside, but there are distinct zones within towns. The existence of these quarters in the twelfth century can be demonstrated both by street names, and also by the concentration of certain types of industrial waste, such as large, brass-melting crucibles and bronze-casting mould fragments from certain areas of the City of London. In Britain, as in France and Germany, such quarters seem to have been more prevalent in the twelfth and thirteenth centuries and significantly not later, when, after the plague, these local boundaries appear to have broken down.

Sometimes any zoning will be explicable in terms of the requirements of the industry. The fringes of a town will always be attractive to those industries that require large areas for storage or preparation, for example timber yards, pottery or tile kilns and tanneries. Most urban crafts, however, did not require distinctive workshops and many are therefore archaeologically almost invisible. We can study those industries that required the provision of heat, or abnormally high quantities of water or other unusual conditions. Medieval crafts that have left traces include the making of pottery and tiles, various stages in the manufacture of cloth, making salt, bells, tanning

*Figure 12.6* A piece of animal bone (a pig's jaw-bone) used for trying out artistic designs that were to be cut into leather or possibly metal objects. From an eleventh-century pit on the Milk Street site, London.
*Source*: Museum of London Archaeology Service

hides, burning lime for construction work, and blacksmiths' workshops. The majority of the evidence is from finished or half-finished pieces, or from manufacturing waste (Figure 12.6). Objects of fine workmanship fill our museums, and now we are beginning to understand how they were made (Biddle 1990; Blair and Ramsay 1991).

Were these industries efficient or innovative? We must be careful here, for these are modern terms. There is little evidence for technological innovations in British towns, though like all towns they probably acted as 'electrical transformers' (the phrase used by the French historian Fernand Braudel, for example in Braudel 1979) in transmitting and experimenting with new ideas from elsewhere in Europe and the Muslim world. Around 1200, increased sophistication in the production of pottery is apparent, and more complex joints in carpentry allowed the heightening of timber-framed buildings to two, three or more storeys to accommodate more people in towns (Milne 1992). Several luxury industries, such as the provision of marble tombs and brasses, were concentrated in the big cities. Literacy and schooling were always features of towns, and at the end of the period, printed books became more available. We would there-fore expect new fashions in architecture, or dress, to be apparent in the archaeological record of towns before appearing in the countryside. It is also likely that technological or fashionable changes moved along lines of communication from town to town, bypassing areas of relatively backward countryside.

## The medieval urban environment

Towns were small parts of larger rural landscapes, and very little food was grown within the walls. In medieval towns, we can study the way in which food was provided, the economic and therefore environmental relations between the town and its hinterland, and the lifestyle of the townsfolk as shown by their skeletons, and we can attempt to determine whether the quality of life in towns was different – either better or worse – than that in the contemporary countryside.

A number of studies of animal bones from urban sites show that cattle, sheep and pigs were the main sources of meat. Cattle would often be slaughtered when their usefulness as dairy animals was over; similarly sheep were usually kept for their wool, and a large proportion of sheep bones in towns indicates an emphasis on sheep farming in the surrounding area. Pigs roamed the yards and streets of many towns, and were tolerated as scavengers. Seeds of many plants also survive in dump deposits or in cesspits.

How good was the standard of living in medieval towns? Townspeople generally probably had a better diet than their neighbours in the countryside. If they had money, they could buy several kinds of bread, ale, wine, meat and fish. Fruit and vegetables came from town and suburban gardens. Over the period, there is some evidence that town dwellers ate more meat and less cereals or fish than their rural counterparts (Dyer 1989, 201–202).

Human skeletons from churchyards tell us about health and disease, but at present there are more questions than answers. Of vitamin deficiency diseases, only scurvy and rickets are detectable in skeletons. Scurvy (lack of vitamin C) is indicative of a restricted diet, and was epidemic in medieval Europe in winter months when fresh fruit and vegetables were unavailable. Rickets (lack of vitamin D) is a disease of children, enlarging the epiphyses (the ends) of growing bones; common among medieval skeletons, it was endemic in places that had little sunlight, and perhaps therefore it might be more prevalent in crowded parts of towns. The most common complaints suffered by excavated skeletons from medieval towns were osteoarthritis and problems with their teeth.

Infectious diseases that might have been particularly rife in towns include leprosy, tuberculosis and syphilis. The first two in particular were common in the medieval period, though it has also been suggested that the spread of pulmonary tuberculosis led to the decline of leprosy in the post-medieval period, since the tubercle bacillus seems to have given some immunity from the bacterium that causes leprosy. So far few sites in Britain have produced examples of leprous bones, though the disease was common enough for there to be about 200 leper hospitals in thirteenth-century England (Steane 1985, 96–7). Five cases of tuberculosis and some possible cases of syphilis were noted at St Helen's in York. Other diseases known to have been virulent in medieval Europe included amoebic dysentery and smallpox.

## CURRENT PERCEPTIONS AND OUTSTANDING PROBLEMS

Urban archaeology is good at establishing long sequences of layers that are often accurately dated by coins or dendrochronology, when timbers survive either in buried waterfront constructions or in standing buildings. We can quickly establish what was there, how it was built, what was left in each room or building, what date it was, and what each object was made of. Beyond this, the wealth of information gathered from the last 30 years of work in towns points to exciting new possibilities that are only now being explored.

The medieval town is a place where we can study social organization, understand the role of women and children, and find out more about political centres and the boundaries of their influence. Buildings represent both these functions: the castle is a centre for warfare, feasting and political control; but it also reflects social divisions – it symbolizes the political and social elite in its height, manner of construction and location of the walls that both defended and constrained the town. From the sheer numbers of artefacts we can begin to study consumer demand for products, popular culture and fashion, for instance in dress (Egan and Pritchard 1991). Here archaeological work, particularly on the spectacular array of objects found in dated contexts on waterfront sites, is showing the popularity of shoddy, mass-produced items in base metals, especially after 1300, and allows researchers to identify the varied quality of products of the various traditions of manufacture mentioned in documents.

A second area to develop is that of the town as an economic unit: in distinction to the surrounding countryside, the economy of an urban place will be non-agricultural, will use coins or tokens (Figure 12.7) instead of barter or exchange, and, at least up to 1500, will not yet have the features of industrialization that were to follow. How much did kings and nobles use towns to control the redistribution of significant goods – not only luxuries, but necessities such as food? Although there were probably no factories in medieval British towns, we should study the history of technology and see if towns had any role in spreading innovation or new techniques of production. This will mean more emphasis on the medieval consumer than on production or manufacturing sites.

Thirdly, archaeological investigation of medieval towns may bring to light medieval beliefs, superstitions and evidence of ritual (both religious and secular, for instance processions that brought together all the townsfolk) and may suggest how medieval people constructed their public and private worlds (Schofield and Vince 1994, 89–98). Sacred and profane spaces can be recognized; the medieval concepts of 'clean' and 'dirty', 'male' and 'female' might be deduced from the internal arrangement of buildings or the distribution of artefacts.

Between 1100 and 1340, a new urban society came into being in British towns. Much of this development was in the twelfth century, as shown by the expansion of suburbs and water-front areas, new stone houses, and the birth of a consumer culture. At the same time, towns were largely driven by the institutions or noble power centres within them, which were large constructions – castles, monasteries and lords' houses. They used towns to get luxuries,

*Figure 12.7* Late thirteenth-century tokens found on the London waterfront near Billingsgate. They were probably used as fractions of pence, prior to the official issue of halfpence and farthings. They bridged the gap between official coins and the ancient practice of bartering and exchange of goods, and by their presence show the increasing commercialization of medieval towns and the demand for small coins or something like them.
*Source*: Museum of London Archaeology Service

particularly from faraway places within Britain and abroad. There were links with many European cities and states, but one strong link was with south-west France (Gascony), which was part of the English kingdom.

No more new towns were established after Queenborough in Kent (a special case, being a naval base) by Edward III in 1368. At the start of this chapter, the period of economic downturn in the early fourteenth century and the Black Death in 1348–9 was given separate status, and since urban archaeology can most easily chart change, the traumatic changes of this period should be apparent in the archaeological record. However, more fieldwork is required to test this picture or up-and-down graph of fortunes that we have been offered by documentary historians.

The third part of the Middle Ages, from 1350 to about 1500, is poorly understood by comparison with the earlier period, in towns as in the countryside. In contrast with the period before 1340, this is the time of growing power of the craft guilds and the lessening of power of the lords and religious magnates. In both large and small centres, the archaeological strata of this later period are thin; the waterfront zones are increasingly unhelpful, as stone walls take over from timber revetments and the dated groups of artefacts become far less frequent. It seems the case that after the Black Death, because there were considerably fewer people in towns, several processes took place. Shops disappeared from central streets; some houses became larger, while the unwanted margins of settlement crumbled, decayed and were covered with their own version of

*Figure 12.8* Torksey, Lincolnshire: an aerial view of the shrunken medieval river port, in an angle of the River Trent (left) and the Foss Dyke (foreground). The town stretched from the Dyke to the later railway line 0.8 km away. In its heighday, it had three parish churches and two monasteries; now it is almost all fields.
*Source*: Cambridge University Committee for Aerial Photography; Crown copyright reserved

dark earth, the deposit normally associated with the Saxon centuries. Some towns, like Torksey in Lincolnshire, declined to almost nothing; now they are largely fields (Figure 12.8).

Archaeological and historical work is beginning to suggest that the period from 1350 to 1500 can be divided further. At first, up to about 1420, urban populations reproduced themselves and made up for the plague losses. Towns went through a period of self-selection, where one might decline, but a local rival rose (Wallingford overtaken by Reading, Torksey overtaken by Boston). The larger centres such as York, Norwich and King's Lynn went through a good period.

After 1420, more general decay set in, and even the larger towns declined. By the early sixteenth century, to take an extreme case, it was reported that a quarter of all the houses in Coventry were empty. At the same time, there was a fundamental change in the trading patterns around the south of Britain. The fifteenth century opened in a phase of prosperity for foreign commerce, which had slumped to less than half of its former value by the middle of the century, and then rose to new heights. The area of trading swung away from Gascony and Normandy, and withdrew from the Baltic, to a more concentrated North Sea axis centred on the Netherlands. These changes are evident in the character of imported objects on British sites. It was the port towns, some of them growing new functions for the first time, that survived in good shape into the sixteenth century – not only London and Bristol, but Newcastle, Colchester, Ipswich, Exeter and Chester. We are at present only dimly aware of all the factors at play here, and regional archaeological studies will show which areas retained vitality or exploited new markets. Even greater changes, to the topography of towns and to the lifestyles of townspeople, were about to follow in the 1530s with the dissolution of the monasteries and the religious changes collectively known as the Reformation.

## THE BRITISH EVIDENCE IN ITS WIDER SETTING

Although the rescue archaeology movement, in Britain and other European countries, has brought about the excavation and interpretation of sites of all periods from Palaeolithic to the modern, it has a special relevance for towns in Britain and for medieval archaeology. Urban archaeology as a discipline has grown up almost totally since 1945. Medieval archaeology as a subject has only a slightly longer history: in Britain, the first discussions of the concept date from about 1940. Rescue archaeology has also been active in medieval towns all over Europe (for examples of national reviews, see those for Germany and Sweden, in Fehring 1991 and Esgard *et al.* 1992). Though archaeologists in European countries, like their British counterparts, are now digesting the evidence of the last five decades, some common questions and answers are appearing. A critical question concerns whether archaeologists in medieval towns should try to apply theoretical models to their results, and whether these models should be derived from historical sources and deal with historical problems, or should be constructed totally by archaeologists themselves.

Did medieval towns advance the economic development of Britain or Europe? Some scholars think that towns were irritants in the basically rural feudal system of life-control, and that towns were instrumental in the campaigns for individual rights (first for men, and later for women). Braudel (1979) distinguished between three sorts of town: the *open* town, which is still attached to its parent agricultural world; the *subject* town, which is shaped by an external political authority (a bishop, prince or king); and the *closed* town, where those within the town take over power for themselves. Western European economic growth is seen to be pushed forward by the attempts of some closed towns to increase and maintain their fortunes. This three-part grouping, which could be applied to British towns, underlines clearly that British towns are part of a larger European phenomenon. Though small towns in England, Wales or Scotland were largely the built expressions of local interests, they were part of a larger European picture with many regional variations.

This historical model (and there are several others) is, however, ultimately unsatisfactory. Towns refuse to be pinned down and categorized simply, and other scholars have argued that there is nothing special about towns, no independent city variable: towns are sites where more general structures of power and struggles for power are dramatically expressed. It is true that the town can be profitably discussed as a social form in which larger systems of social relations are concentrated and intensified. What is fascinating is to see how this intensification brings out specialized forms of housing, ways of coping with density of settlement and its problems, and the consequences of variety in occupations or ethnic groups.

Some archaeologists (Carver 1987; Schofield and Vince 1994) have begun to construct a model that starts with the mountain of data now dug up from British towns. Let the data speak; see what it has to say. The extraordinary value of waterfront archaeology, the most important product of post-war excavations in European towns, has revolutionized the study of material medieval culture. It has shown how archaeology, aided by spectacular preservation of artefacts and the development of dendrochronology, has constructed a whole new area of study and debate with historians, and on its own terms.

## Acknowledgements
I am grateful to my students Vicky Snelling, Tom Dodd and Graham Cushmay for criticism of this chapter in draft.

## KEY TEXTS

Aston, M. and Bond, J., 1974. *The landscape of towns.* London: Dent.
Clarke, H., 1984. *The archaeology of medieval England.* London: British Museum.
Dyer, C., 1989. *Standards of living in the later Middle Ages: social change in England c 1200–1520.* Cambridge: Cambridge University Press.
Platt, C., 1976. *The English medieval town.* London: Secker and Warburg.
Schofield, J. and Vince, A., 1994. *Medieval towns.* London: Pinter Press.
Steane, J.M., 1985. *The archaeology of medieval England and Wales.* Beckenham: Croom Helm.

## Bibliography

Atkin, M., 1985. 'Excavations on Alms Lane', in Atkin, M., Carter, A. and Evans, D.H., *Excavations in Norwich 1971–78, Part II.* Gressenhall: East Anglian Archaeology 26, 144–260.
Biddle, M. (ed.) 1990. *Object and economy in medieval Winchester.* Oxford: Winchester Studies 7.ii.
Blair, J. and Ramsay, N. (eds) 1991. *English medieval industries.* London: Hambledon Press.
Braudel, F., 1979. *Capitalism and material life 1400–1800.* London: Fontana.
Carver, M.O.H., 1980. 'Medieval Worcester: an archaeological framework', *Transactions of the Worcestershire Archaeological Society* 7.
Carver, M.O.H., 1987. 'The nature of urban deposits', in Schofield, J. and Leech, R. (eds) *Urban archaeology in Britain.* London: Council for British Archaeology Research Report 61, 9–26.
Clarke, H.B. and Simms, A. (eds) 1985. *The comparative history of urban origins in non-Roman Europe,* Oxford: British Archaeological Reports 255.
Crowfoot, E., Pritchard, F. and Staniland, K., 1992. *Textiles and clothing c 1150–c 1450,* = Medieval finds from excavations in London 4. London: HMSO.
Daniels, R., 1990. 'The development of medieval Hartlepool: excavations at Church Close, 1984–5', *Archaeological Journal* 147, 337–410.
Egan, G. and Pritchard, F., 1991. *Dress accessories* = Medieval finds from excavations in London 3. London: HMSO.
Esgard, L., Holstrom, M. and Lamm, K. (eds) 1992 *Rescue and research: reflections of society in Sweden 700–1700 AD.* Stockholm: Riksantikvarieambetet.

Fehring, G.P., 1991. *The archaeology of medieval Germany*. London: Routledge.

Good, G.L., Jones, R.H., and Ponsford, M.W. (eds) 1991. *Waterfront archaeology: proceedings of the third international conference, Bristol, 1988*. London: Council for British Archaeology Research Report 74.

Grimes, W.F., 1968. *The excavation of Roman and medieval London*. London: Routledge.

Heighway, C., 1972. *The erosion of history*. London: Council for British Archaeology.

Hinton, D.A., 1990. *Archaeology, economy and society: England from the fifth to the fifteenth century*. London: Seaby.

Milne, G., 1992. *Timber building techniques in London c 900–c 1400*. London: London and Middlesex Archaeological Society Special Paper 15.

Milne, G. and Milne, C., 1982. *Medieval waterfront development at Trig Lane, London*. London: London and Middlesex Archaeological Society Special Paper 5.

Pantin, W.A., 1962–3. 'Medieval English town-house plans', *Medieval Archaeology* 6–7, 202–239.

Platt, C., 1978. *Medieval England: a social history and archaeology from the Conquest to 1600*. London: Routledge.

Samuel, M., 1989. 'The fifteenth century garner at Leadenhall, London', *Antiquaries Journal* 59, 119–153.

Schofield, J., 1993. *The building of London from the Conquest to the Great Fire*. London: British Museum. 2 edn.

Schofield, J., Allen, P. and Taylor, C., 1990. 'Medieval buildings and property development in the area of Cheapside', *Transactions of London and Middlesex Archaeological Society* 41, 39–238.

Williams, J.H., 1979. *St Peter's Street Northampton, Excavations 1973–76*. Northampton: Northampton Development Corporation.

Yeoman, P., 1995. *Medieval Scotland*. London: Batsford.

## Chapter Thirteen

# Landscapes of the Middle Ages

## Churches, castles and monasteries

### Roberta Gilchrist

#### BACKGROUND

Within a generation or so of the conversion to Christianity, each Anglo-Saxon kingdom had become divided into large parishes (*parochiae*) administered by a minster church. These minsters (from the Latin *monasterium*) were instigated by episcopal or royal initiative, and their siting was frequently coincident with royal vills; Welsh churches, by contrast, were established in association with secular *llys* (courts). These early minsters of the seventh to eighth centuries housed communities of priests or monks, living a collegiate or monastic lifestyle, who had pastoral responsibility for the inhabitants of the *parochia*. Between the tenth to twelfth centuries, large minster churches were supplemented by the proliferation of private, or proprietary, churches, with a resident priest who served a local community. It is now believed that there had been an immense shift in settlement patterns from the ninth century to the mid-eleventh century. It is supposed that complex, multiple estates based on Anglo-Saxon royal and ecclesiastical centres of the seventh to tenth centuries fragmented into smaller, self-contained local manors. The emergence of these manors, and the social class of local lords (*thegns*), created the small field churches of the late Saxon period; the evolution of the nucleated village sometime during the ninth to twelfth centuries provided the social impetus for the local community church. These local churches, the ancestors of parish churches, did not immediately have full rights, such as baptism or burial, but were subject to the authority of the old minsters, which presided as superior, or mother, churches. From the eleventh to thirteenth centuries, the *parochiae* of the minsters were broken down into smaller territories of individual parishes, giving rise to the parochial system of the Middle Ages (Blair 1988, 1–14).

Churches subsequently became the focal point for ritual and social life in a medieval community. They were used as a place of worship and regular meeting, for religious and seasonal festivals, baptism of infants, marriages, and burial of the dead. Chapels, known as chapels-of-ease, were built to serve parishioners who lived some distance from the parish church, and palaces, castles and manor houses often had private chapels that served the resident family and retainers. Some 12,000 English churches and chapels of medieval date survive today as standing buildings, in addition to several hundred ruined churches and the countless sites of former churches that exist only as buried archaeological deposits. The expansion of towns in the tenth to eleventh centuries also resulted in the proliferation of parishes, some of which were carved from the territories of earlier minsters. Towns that expanded in the late Saxon period can be ranked according to the number of churches that they once possessed: London 100+, Norwich and

Winchester 50+, York and Lincoln 40+ and Exeter *c.* 20 (Morris 1989, 178). These early parishes seem to have been based around clusters of households, rather than on more ancient land-holding patterns, the churches being established by ecclesiastical or secular authorities, often privately owned and patronized by lords, as they were in the countryside.

The administration and character of the Church in England was reorganized to a considerable degree as a result of the Norman Conquest. Anglo-Saxon dioceses (the ecclesiastical territories under the jurisdiction of a bishop) were largely retained and new bishops' sees were added in the twelfth century, contemporaneous with the reorganization of the Church in Wales and Scotland. The head of each diocese focused on an urban cathedral; these were a combination of two types of institution. Some were monastic cathedrals based around a community of monks headed by a prior, a form that had developed in Anglo-Saxon England, while others were secular cathedrals, in which a chapter of canons was led by a dean, an arrangement more common in Normandy and Brittany. Cathedral priories followed the rule of St Benedict, and their communities resembled the usual Benedictine arrangement (below), albeit on a much grander and larger scale. The secular cathedrals, in contrast, were staffed by prebends, priests who received a portion of the living. It became common to have a group of additional resident priests who were accommodated within the cathedral precinct, such as the Bedern at York, or the Vicars' Choral at Wells. The latter was built in 1348 and survives today as a planned street or terrace of individual houses, each with a hall below and chamber above, with a common chapel and refectory at the ends of the street, and a covered bridge providing direct access to the chapter house and cathedral church.

The medieval castle was the fortified residence of a lord. It served dual military and domestic functions, the latter including the accommodation of the lord's household and the administration of the estate. It also acted as a strategic point for gaining and maintaining control over a hostile territory. The castle was intimately linked with feudalism: a system of vassalage and land-holding that bound different strata of society together through bonds of loyalty. The king was the greatest overlord and landlord, and he rewarded his followers with lands, so that they owed him loyalty and became his vassals. They, in turn, secured the loyalty of a group of followers through a process of gift-giving. This system of reciprocity united medieval society, and ensured that armies could be raised, while at the same time allowing the king to retain ultimate control over his people.

The first Norman castles to be built were strongholds along the progress of William the Conqueror, starting on 28th September 1066. By the 1070/80s, the feudal system of military service was laid down and lands were transferred from Saxon thegns to Norman barons. By the time of Domesday Book in 1086, 20 per cent of land in England was held by the king, 50 per cent by the lay baronage and 30 per cent by the Church. The barons had been rewarded for their loyalty through gifts of land, and their status as lords entitled them to construct castles. The castle became symbolic of the office of lordship and the favour of the king, but conversely, a lord's castle could be destroyed or confiscated at the king's displeasure. Some 1,500 castles were built following the Conquest, although approximately half of these were small timber and earthwork constructions that had been abandoned by the early fourteenth century (Pounds 1990). Scottish kings were strategic in their support of castle-building: they established new lordships and associated castles where royal power was weakest, in the Highlands, Western Isles, Galloway, Lanarkshire, along the upper Clyde and over the north-east lowlands. Conversely, the royal stronghold of the south-east of Scotland saw few castles built.

The Normans also revitalized monastic life, introducing new continental orders and founding abbeys and priories in association with castles, towns and rural manors. A monastery was an exceptional medieval community, one that comprised celibate men or women who took religious vows to follow a set of strict rules that governed their lifestyle. The form and organization of the earlier Anglo-Saxon monasteries had been more fluid and diverse (seventh to ninth centuries), until a reform movement of the tenth century laid down rules to be observed in monasteries and nunneries (the *Regularis Concordia*), and more standard plans evolved that were based around the monastic cloister (Aston 1993; Coppack 1990; Greene 1992). The origins of this social movement can be traced back to the desert monasticism of fourth- and fifth-century Egypt, Palestine and Syria. Two basic forms of monastic life prevailed throughout the medieval world: the eremitic and the coenobitic. Eremitic monasticism (from *eremos*, the desert) followed the tradition of the hermit, in which an individual lived in isolation and sought a more challenging, aescetic spirituality, denying comfort and companionship. The more common, coenobitic, monasticism stems from the rule of St Benedict, written by Benedict of Nursia *c.* 525, at Monte Cassino in Italy. The Benedictine Rule emphasized communal living, and laid down precise requirements for the structure and routine of the monastery. It was to be self-sufficient in all things, so that ties and obligations to the outside world could be minimized, and the monks were to worship together, sleep in a communal dormitory and eat in a common refectory.

By a conservative estimate, at least 2,000 monasteries and religious houses were founded in medieval England, Scotland and Wales, with particular orders coincident with certain chrono-logical periods, associated variously with the town or countryside, and committed to a broad range of religious and charitable purposes (Knowles and Hadcock 1971). Benedictine and Cluniac monasteries were founded by the Normans in England (*c.* 1067–1130), and were often used as a means of consolidating their royal or baronial authority over Anglo-Saxon areas. Monasteries following the rule of St Augustine were established for more pastoral and charitable functions. Houses of Augustinian canons were set up on a smaller scale and by lower-ranking patrons, in areas that required pastoral care (*c.* 1100–1260). The Cistercians sought isolated and remote places, particularly in Yorkshire, Cheshire and Wales, in order to follow their reformed version of the monastic life (*c.* 1125–1220). Initially the Cistercians were devoted to a life of simplicity; until the fourteenth century they included lay-brothers in most of their monasteries who were responsible for manual work and management of the estates and granges (farms). Orders of friars arrived in Britain *c.* 1225, including the Franciscans and Dominicans, with new foundations into the early fourteenth century, aimed at preaching and educating the urban poor. In addition to the main orders for monks, canons and friars, there were corresponding houses for religious women, colleges, hospitals following monastic ordinances, preceptories of the Crusading Orders (the Templars and Hospitallers), Carthusian charterhouses (based on eremitic principles) and small hermitages (Gilchrist 1995). Most monasteries were established in the twelfth or thirteenth centuries, and continued in use for several hundred years, until the dissolution of the monasteries in England and Wales under Henry VIII (1535–40), and in Scotland by Parliament in 1560 when monasteries were confiscated and their buildings and lands sold or redistributed.

## KEY DATA

### Churches

Early written sources are generally limited to references to church sites in wills, charters, saints' lives, monastic chronicles and law codes. Domesday Book, compiled in 1086, enumerated churches in England according to their financial value: approximately 2,700 were recorded, but many seem to have been omitted from the list, with accuracy varying according to the methods used by the compilers of the survey in each county. From the twelfth, and especially the thirteenth, century a wider range of documentary sources was compiled, including bishops' registers, the records of church courts and, from the fourteenth century, churchwardens' accounts. By the fifteenth and sixteenth centuries, personal wills were regularly compiled that yield evidence of private bequests for building projects, the foundation of chantries and details of internal furnishings and fittings. Very occasionally, the foundation dates of churches can be recognized through the evidence of placenames or inscriptions (Morris 1983).

The archaeological recording of churches has yielded new evidence on the nature of their design and construction. Material for the building of masonry churches of Anglo-Saxon date had been obtained by canabilizing Roman sites for brick, tile and stone, until the eleventh- and twelfth-century expansion in church construction brought about a more systematic industry of stone quarrying. The skills of the carpenter are evident in rubble-built parish churches well into the twelfth century. Stone was used to imitate wood by producing the appearance of lathe-turning, through pilaster stripwork that mimicked timber joints, for instance in the tower at Earls Barton, Northants, and in the wooden or basketwork windows and templates that were used, such as those at Hales and Framlingham Earl, Norfolk (Rodwell 1989). Regional building traditions resulted from the availability of stone types and building material, in addition to the conscious promotion of cultural preferences, such as the round-towers of East Anglian churches.

Dating of extant medieval buildings has been carried out predominantly through stylistic or typological methods. Architectural style was regularly evolving from the late eleventh century to the fifteenth, so that it is possible to date certain diagnostic features to within 20–30 years, notably mouldings, capitals, window tracery and roofs. The dating of smaller parish churches can be more problematic in the earlier period (pre-1120) and from 1350–1500, when the date ranges achieved by means of stylistic methods can stretch from 50 to 100 years. An archaeological approach to the study of buildings, developed for particular application to Anglo-Saxon churches, is known as 'structural analysis': this consists of the close scrutiny of church fabric in order to discern the sequence in which constituent parts were added, modified or removed. This is a non-destructive approach that is based on the observation of vertical joints in walls, quoin types, fabric changes and blocked or inserted features (Taylor 1972).

Scientific methods of absolute dating are used less frequently on medieval excavated evidence, since after *c.* 1050, radiocarbon dates yield broader chronological ranges than those achieved through typological, stylistic or numismatic approaches. However, radiocarbon dates on human bone from the primary burials in parish churches have been important in establishing dates for the earliest structural phases, and dendrochronology, which has been used to date roofs, bell-frames and remains of timber scaffolding, has potential to establish firmer chronologies for transitional periods of architecture.

Where church sites have been extensively excavated, a primary phase has often been revealed to consist of a simple one- or two-cell church, sometimes constructed in timber. For example, single-celled timber churches have been recorded at Norwich Castle, Lincoln St Mark and Wharram Percy, North Yorkshire; two-celled timber churches are known from Thetford St Michael and Rivenhall, Essex, and a cruciform timber church was excavated at Potterne, Wiltshire. As churches evolved, these timber precursors were later either encased in a stone structure, or a stone successor was built adjacent to it (Rodwell 1989, 118). Excavations at Raunds, Northamptonshire, showed the changes and variations that might occur: a single-cell church was established *c.* 875–925, which was later enlarged to two cells, rebuilt again and reorientated in the eleventh century, and finally fell out of use *c.* 1200, when a church about 230 m away continued to function (Figure 13.1) (Boddington 1996).

The parish church and churchyard were closely integrated physically and socially with the community (Morris 1989). The seigneurial associations (i.e. feudal relationship with a lord) of early churches were sometimes retained into the later Middle Ages, with churches situated adjacent to later medieval manor houses, moated sites or castles. Churches were often associated with villages, in cases of planned villages placed close to a green or at the head of a street, forming the nucleus

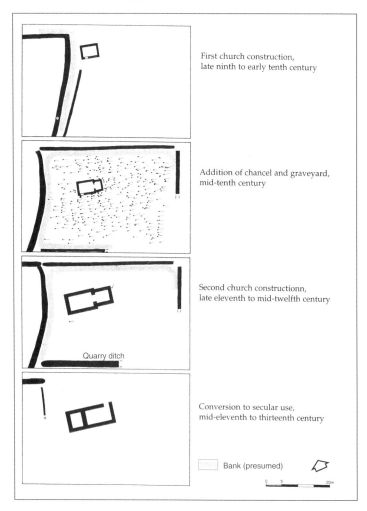

First church construction,
late ninth to early tenth century

Addition of chancel and graveyard,
mid-tenth century

Second church constructionn,
late eleventh to mid-twelfth century

Quarry ditch

Conversion to secular use,
mid-eleventh to thirteenth century

Bank (presumed)

0      5                    20m

*Figure 13.1* Sequence of church constructions at Raunds,
Northamptonshire, late ninth to thirteenth centuries.
*Source*: Boddington 1996, Fig. 5

of the settlement. Where villages evolved from the coalescence of a number of settlements, multiple churches might result, such as at Beechamwell, Norfolk, where the convergence of three settlements resulted in the co-existence of three parish churches in a single village. In eastern England, cases of multiple lordship occasionally resulted in the sharing of a single churchyard by two to three parish churches, such as at Rcepham, Norfolk. In regions of dispersed settlement, churches may have been founded in relative isolation, although this appearance may sometimes be deceptive. Agricultural shifts, such as a transition from arable to pastoral farming, could cause the movement of settlement to areas of free grazing, such as greens and parish boundaries. In such cases, early village sites were deserted and churches that now appear to be isolated in the landscape were once in close proximity to their communities. Churches in towns were placed in order to encourage easy access: on street corners, on main thoroughfares, at markets, bridges and at gates in town walls, so that travellers and pilgrims could visit them easily when beginning or completing a journey.

Between 1050–1150, there was a massive rebuilding of churches, translating timber-built, local churches to the more substantial parish churches constructed in stone. Excavations have shown that these early stone churches were of fairly simple form, consisting of one or two cells, often incorporating an apsed eastern end: examples include All Saints, Barton Bendish, Norfolk; Barrow, Lincolnshire; St Paul-in-the-Bail, Lincoln; and St Benedict, Norwich. A small number of three-cell early churches are known, incorporating an axial, or central, tower, while others had towers attached to the western end of the church. It has been suggested that such towers may have been reserved for the use of the lord who had built and owned the church, with the nave left open for public use (Morris 1989, 252–255). Moreover, the manorial residence of the lord seems to have been closely associated with the church. Excavations at Barton-on-Humber, Humberside, which retains a highly embellished Anglo-Saxon tower, revealed that the church of *c.* 970–1030 was erected just west of a large bank and ditch, which defined a sub-circular enclosure that may have been the manor or residence of the lord (Figure 13.2) (Rodwell and Rodwell 1982).

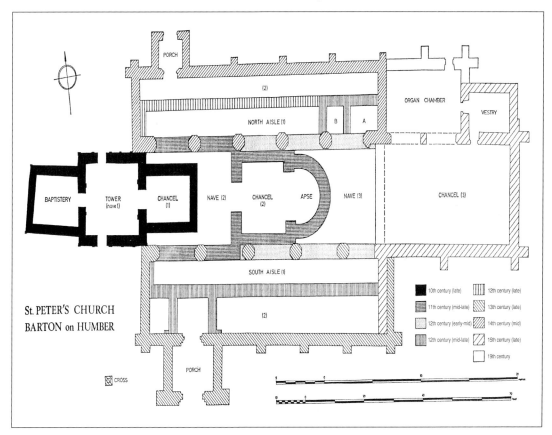

*Figure 13.2* Composite ground-plan of St Peter's church, Barton-upon-Humber, Humberside. The original church was of three cells (AD 990±70). In the mid-eleventh century, the old chancel was demolished and replaced with a rectangular nave and apsidal chancel, with the former nave serving as the tower. This church was replaced by *c.* 1200 by a large, aisled building that involved the extension of the nave, the addition of a south aisle and two chambers to the north side of the nave that were incorporated subsequently into a north aisle. In the thirteenth and fourteenth centuries the aisles were widened, and in the fifteenth century the chancel was rebuilt.
*Source*: Rodwell and Rodwell 1982, Fig. 3

Before the twelfth century, burial was prohibited inside parish churches, with the exceptions of the graves of founders and priests. After this, important patrons and wealthy individuals were able to attain burial in the church interior; this space was, however, commonly used for post-medieval graves and vaults, which sometimes riddle the interior of medieval churches (e.g. St Augustine the Less, Bristol). The first phases of the cemetery generally correspond with the foundation of the church, at least in eastern and southern England, while in places such as Winchester and Hereford the cathedral church retained the monopoly over burial of the dead until later in the Middle Ages. Excavation of cemeteries has yielded important information on inhumation practices, zoning of burial according to age or sex, and information from skeletons regarding demography, health and life-expectancy (e.g. St Helen-on-the-Walls, York; St Nicholas, Shambles, London) (see Rodwell 1989, 157–179). Some progress has been made in investigating the churchyard itself, for instance at Raunds and Wharram Percy, including evidence for the evolution of boundaries, and the development of paths and structures such as bell-houses, charnel houses (for the storage of bones), almshouses (hospitals, or residential homes for the poor) or anchorages (the dwellings of hermits).

At Barton-on-Humber, a ninth-century cemetery predated the church, and burials were systematically cleared in order to begin its construction. The later Anglo-Saxon cemetery had interments concentrated along the south side and at the east end of the church, with possible clusters of family groups. By the fifteenth century, burial inside the church at Barton was becoming more common, especially in front of the chancel and aisle screens (Rodwell and Rodwell 1982).

## Castles

Archaeological excavation has enabled a more rigorous study of the origins of the castle, and has expanded our knowledge of early timber castles considerably, as for example at Hen Domen, Montgomeryshire (Figure 13.3). Documentary sources for the construction of the first Norman castles include the Anglo-Saxon Chronicle and Domesday Book, which record the destruction of Saxon settlement in the wake of castle construction (e.g. Wallingford and Shrewsbury). The major source of information for work at royal castles is the building accounts maintained by the Exchequer: the Pipe Rolls detailed annual expenditure from 1155–1216, later continued by the Misae Rolls and Liberate Rolls (Colvin 1963). Further details can be gleaned from chronicles, charters, feudal documents, Inquisitions and sources such as the Assize Rolls, Liberate and Memoranda Rolls, Patent Rolls and Curia Regis Rolls.

It is generally agreed that the true castle had not existed in Anglo-Saxon England, and resulted instead from the process of conquest by the Normans. To some extent this conclusion rests on the definition of the castle, since the Saxon system of burhs included both fortified towns and the residences of thegns, where a bank and palisade protected the burgheat (e.g. Goltho, Lincolnshire). The Norman castle acted as a strategic point for gaining and maintaining control over a hostile territory; some measure of its success was due to the Norman use of cavalry, since the Saxons did not use horses for warfare. The earliest forms of the English castle had their origins in tenth-century France, where two essential components have been traced: the first-floor hall and the motte. However, in France and Germany, upper halls developed in the mid-tenth century for the purpose of defence. The classic site for discerning this evolution is Doué la Fontaine (Maine et Loire), where a ground-floor hall was destroyed by fire *c.* 925–50, and reconstructed as a first-floor hall. This was later turned into a keep by heaping material around the ground-floor, in the manner of a motte (Thompson 1995, 45–48).

Castles have been classified into standard types developing from the eleventh to the sixteenth centuries, although there is a wide degree of fluidity between types and variation between individual sites. Timber and masonry castles can be distinguished, the former consisting of ringwork and motte and bailey types, with the latter including a wide variety that developed chronologically from the tower-keep to the enclosure castle, concentric castle, quadrangular castle, courtyard house and tower house. In the later Middle Ages, forms of defensive structure were developed that no longer combined the dual features of residence and fortification that define the true castle. From the later fourteenth century, block houses were built to house guns and protect gunners on inland waterways (such as the Cow Tower, Norwich, 1398). From the late fifteenth and particularly the sixteenth centuries, artillery castles were built mainly at coastal sites to house heavy guns, usually arranged as multiple tiers of concentric defences (e.g. Dartmouth Castle, Devon, 1481).

At the heart of the castle was the hall: used as a public eating and meeting place, for administration and for sleeping. Aisles were added to halls from *c.* 1100 to provide additional space for larger households. A bi-polar arrangement had emerged by the second half of the thirteenth century, in which the upper end of the hall was screened to provide a private chamber for the lord's household, while a lower end fulfilled the need for storage and services. From the thirteenth century, a castle might contain several different halls, each the focus of an individual household, in addition to the great hall, which was the centre of ceremonial and administrative life. Freestanding halls were generally located at the ground-floor level, open to the roof, sometimes with an associated two-storey chamber block to provide private chambers (e.g. Boothby Pagnell, Lincolnshire). Upper halls, located at first-floor level, were common in twelfth-century tower-keeps and proto-keeps (such as Chepstow, Gwent), and again in the fourteenth to fifteenth centuries, as at Nunney, Somerset (Thompson 1995).

Excavation has improved our understanding of the technology of castle construction. Traces of temporary workshops were uncovered at Sandal, West Yorkshire, and Portchester, Hampshire, the latter consisting of two lead-melting hearths set into the floor of a hall, with a temporary smithy erected in a courtyard. At Sandal, the conversion of the castle from timber to masonry required lead- and iron-working hearths and horse- and oxen-drawn carts to move supplies; tracks from these vehicles were traced during the excavations (Mayes and Butler 1983). Lime kilns are commonly found at castles, ranging from basic pits to stone-built kilns, such as a thirteenth-century example at Bedford. A kiln for the production of ridge-tiles, *c.* 1240, was excavated at Sandal, and additional evidence for roof furniture included tiles, slates and finials. Lead and stone tiles were also commonly used for roofing materials. Worked stone and fragments of decorated wall plaster have been recovered from excavated castles, together with window glass, although this was not common in non-royal castles until the later thirteenth century (Kenyon 1990, 164–167).

Along the coasts of Britain, naturally defensible sites were used for castle building, such as Corfe, Dorset. The earliest castles sometimes reused Roman forts and Saxon burhs, in order to take advantage of ready-made defences and good networks of roads. Royal castles were predominantly urban, associated with towns in order to dominate the largest concentrations of population, and to ease the administration of a newly conquered land. The Norman barons held scattered parcels of land, rather than consolidated estates, and would build their castles at the centre of a concentration of lands, sited to take into account the availability of water, good communications and arable resources (Pounds 1990). Barnard Castle, Co. Durham, was sited on the boundary between woodland and grazing land, and its estate held a balanced range of land types and resources (Austin 1984). It was common to enhance the symbolism of lordship by twinning castles with parish churches or monasteries, especially Benedictine and Cluniac houses. Economic development was maximized by the Normans through foundations of new towns: up to one third of these grew up at the gates of castles. Grid-iron street plans developed at planned castle towns such as Castle Acre and New Buckenham, Norfolk.

Two major types of earthwork castles were constructed in Norman Britain: the motte and bailey, and the ringwork. The motte and bailey outnumbered the ringwork by as much as four to one; it was built during the first century after the Conquest and during the civil war between King Stephen and Queen Matilda (1138–53). The motte was an artificial mound of earth, surrounded by a ditch, and frequently associated with one or more baileys, which were enclosures surrounded by earthen banks. A timber tower was placed within or on top of the motte. Recent excavations have shown that the tower was sometimes the primary feature, with the motte formed around it by heaping up earth from the encircling ditch. This method of construction is shown on the Bayeux Tapestry and has been confirmed by excavations at South Mimms, Hertfordshire, where a wooden tower 35 m square was set on a flint footing and surrounded by a motte with a low flint wall around its base. Entrance to the tower was gained via a tunnel through the motte, and the motte was revetted with timber shuttering. The ringwork castle, in contrast, was a simple enclosure comprising a bank and ditch. In some cases, ringworks were filled in with later mottes, as at Aldingham, Cumbria, while at Goltho a motte was levelled in the twelfth century to serve as a raised platform for an aisled hall and domestic buildings (Beresford 1987). Timber buildings were

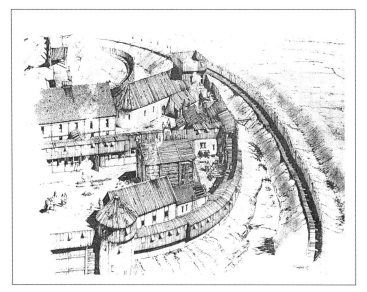

***Figure 13.3*** Reconstruction of defences and timber buildings at the castle of Hen Domen, Montgomeryshire, based on excavated structures dated to *c.* 1150.
*Source*: Higham and Barker 1992, Fig. 9.6

***Figure 13.4*** Castle Acre, Norfolk, a castle with inner and outer bailey connected by a bridge. The keep of the 1140/50s was converted from a weakly defended house dating from the eleventh century; refortification included heightening the perimeter bank and adding a curtain wall.
*Source*: Derek A. Edwards, Norfolk Air Photographic Library, Norfolk Museums Service

placed within the bailey or ring-work. At Hen Domen, a motte and bailey castle first established *c.* 1070, there were 50 timber buildings of simple construction excavated in the bailey, which was encircled by a double bank and ditch (Figure 13.3) (Higham and Barker 1992).

The first castles to be built in stone were the keeps, or *donjons*: free-standing towers of at least two storeys with a highly fortified core. The earliest English tower-keep was the White Tower of London, built in 1075, and clearly symbolic of the authority of the new Norman king. The hall was located at first-storey level, with an off-centre cross-wall placed to allow the division of space into further suites of private rooms. Additional facilities included a kitchen, garderobes (latrines) and a chapel. In some cases houses may have evolved into keeps, as shown by the development of Castle Acre, Norfolk (Coad and Streeten 1982). Excavation on the site evidenced a late eleventh-century stone structure surrounded by a weak ringwork. This was converted to a keep in the 1140/50s, which involved doubling the thickness of the internal walls, raising the interior and blocking the main entrance and the door through the spinal wall. Only the northern half of the building was completed as a keep; the southern half became a courtyard. A masonry curtain wall was added to the bank of the ring-work (Figure 13.4). Shell keeps were built on mottes that could not support the full weight of a tower-keep. These shells were simply masonry walls built around the perimeter of the summit of a motte, replacing the timber palisade (e.g. Totnes, Devon).

By *c.* 1200, the emphasis of defence was shifting away from the highly fortified core of the castle to its outer, curtain walls, and at the same time the increasing degree of social stratification within castle communities demanded a change in the nature of accommodation. Innovation resulted in part from changes in warfare, including the use of the crossbow, mangonel and trébuchet (early siege machines that used rope tension and counterpoise systems, respectively). Enclosure castles such as Framlingham, Suffolk, rebuilt from 1190–1210, exhibit a range of new features. This change included the development of mural towers placed at intervals along the walls, the increasing importance of gatehouses for the defence of entrances, and the introduction of new features such as barbicans (outworks protecting an entrance) and posterns (small, concealed gates in the curtain wall). The fortification of the curtain walls (*enceinte*) allowed the defence of a larger space, promoting an expansion in the size and facilities of castles. Enclosure castles provided accommodation for separate households, placed in buildings centred on free-standing, ground-floor halls, or within stacking chambers in towers. By this date, a castle might have possessed several chapels, halls and kitchens, providing a number of foci for different social groups or households, defined by different social levels, gender or generations of the lord's family.

During the thirteenth century, building work at royal castles concentrated predominantly on the improvement of royal apartments and domestic residences. This frequently took the form of households sited in the bailey, as excavations have shown at Castle Rising, Norfolk, separate from the accommodation of the original keep. Between 1277–1304, a series of castles was built on the

*Figure 13.5* Bodiam Castle, Sussex, a quadrangular castle dating to the last quarter of the fourteenth century. The castle comprises a symmetrical courtyard placed within water defences; it is set within an early designed landscape, including viewing terraces.
*Source*: R. Gilchrist

Welsh border by Edward I, during the period of the Welsh Wars. These concentric castles showed a renewed emphasis on the military considerations of castle design, while retaining the elements of comfort and privacy for the royal apartments. At Rhuddlan, Flintshire, for example, £10,000 was spent on the castle and town defences, beginning in 1277. The castle comprised an inner ward, which was a diamond-shaped courtyard containing the royal apartments, corner towers and two great gatehouses, and an outer ward that was wrapped around three sides of the inner one, and surrounded by a broad, dry moat.

The relative prosperity of the fourteenth and fifteenth centuries promoted the construction of new castles by a greater social range of people, including lesser aristocracy, gentry and wealthy merchants. This period witnessed an increase in licences granted by the crown to crenellate, perhaps indicating the pretensions of the lesser nobility who wished to achieve the appearance of a castle by fortifying their manor houses. During the last quarter of the fourteenth century, courtyard castles were built that elevated architectural display over the importance of defence. Their essential characteristics included ranges of stacking accommodation around a central courtyard, the use of decorative façades and an emphasis on symmetry that was absent in earlier buildings (Figure 13.5). It has been argued that these late medieval constructions were 'show castles', designed with a martial face to command prestige through pseudo-military features such as towers, gatehouses and crenellations (Thompson 1987). On the Scottish borders, the need for defence continued to be balanced with the desire for improved accommodation. Tower houses were built by aristocratic and gentry landowners between 1350 and 1600. These consisted of a hall and cross-wing, with the wing raised in the form of a tower. The tower was often rectangular in plan and of three storeys, with vaulted basements, an entrance at ground-level and a roof-walk with battlements. The hall and tower were surrounded by a courtyard that contained domestic offices.

## Monasteries

Foundation dates for monasteries are usually provided by documentary sources (in particular charters and chronicles); other useful sources include monastic registers and letter-books, account rolls, inventories, deeds and conveyances. The main monastic church and cloister often appear to be the best-preserved part of the monastery, frequently consisting of ruined buildings that were cleared for public display during the nineteenth century. However, in the case of rural monasteries, this central core may have made up only 20 per cent of the actual area of the precinct. The remaining 80 per cent was given over to non-religious purposes, including an inner and outer court that contained service buildings, industrial areas, fishponds and mills (Aston 1993; Coppack 1990). The ideal rural monastery was situated in an isolated river valley, providing shelter, fresh water, timber and land for cultivation. In order to achieve this, it was not uncommon for monasteries to relocate existing villages, and to canalize rivers in order to shift their course to suit the requirements of the monastery for water.

Norman foundations brought the fully developed monastic plan to Britain, which had evolved in Merovingian and Carolingian monasteries, and was depicted in the ninth-century plan of St Gall (Horn and Born 1979). This prototype for a monastery was probably drawn up for Haito, Bishop of Basle, in his *scriptorium* at Reichenau (Switzerland), around 820. The plan depicts the full range of facilities expected for a large, Benedictine monastery, including the domestic and industrial buildings, guest houses, an infirmary and school. The church and cloister continued to form the nucleus of most types of monastery throughout the Middle Ages, so that a familiar, repetitive plan can be recognized throughout Britain and western Europe (Figure 13.6). The cloister was normally to the south of the church, and consisted of a courtyard surrounded by covered walkways (the cloister alleys) that provided access to the three ranges of buildings that flanked the cloister. In the south range, opposite the church, was normally the refectory; to the west was the guest house or general offices and storage; to the east was the chapter house (where the community met daily), with the dormitory of the monks or nuns placed above it on the upper storey. Monastic churches were arranged on a cruciform ground-plan or a simple rectangle, the latter typical of many churches of canons and nuns. The church was divided into the presbytery in the east end, which contained the high altar; the choir, where the stalls of the monks or nuns were located, was in the vicinity of the crossing between the transepts; and the nave was situated to the west.

Excavation has shown that before permanent accommodation was built in stone, monasteries were in many cases provided with temporary timber buildings, for example at Fountains, North Yorkshire, and Sandwell, West Midlands. At Norton Priory, Cheshire, several phases of large timber buildings were excavated to the south-west of the cloisters (Figure 13.6). The actual cloister ranges themselves may have first been built in timber (Greene 1989). Construction of the stone buildings generally progressed starting with the church, built from east to west. Excavation at monasteries regularly reveals constructional evidence, including tile kilns, lime kilns and mixers, lead came and painted glass from windows, and bell-casting pits. Evidence can also be found for the destruction that followed the Dissolution, in particular the lead-melting pits for condensing lead stripped from roofs.

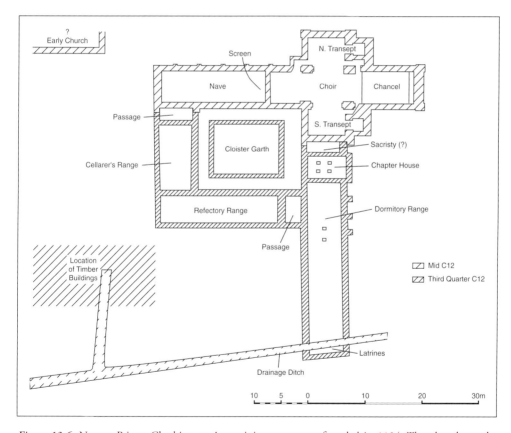

*Figure 13.6* Norton Priory, Cheshire, an Augustinian monastery founded in 1134. The plan shows the location of the temporary timber buildings in relation to the monastic plan of the twelfth century, prior to substantial reordering in the thirteenth century.
*Source*: Greene 1989, Fig. 36

The architecture of the church and some claustral buildings varied according to the filiation of the monastery, in other words, the monastic order to which it belonged. These variations included the ground-plan of the buildings and the nature of their architectural embellishment. For instance, the buildings of the Cluniacs were typically more highly ornamented than those of other orders (such as Much Wenlock, Shropshire), while those of the friars and the early phases of the Cistercians were simple, unadorned structures. The social composition of a monastery also affected its form. The inclusion of the lay-brothers in Cistercian monasteries required the provision of a second set of domestic accommodation. The west range of the monastery was therefore extended in scale to include the dormitory and refectory of the lay-brothers, with easy access to their space in the nave, as shown at Fountains (Figure 13.7). In order to serve the refectories of both the monks and the lay-brothers, a kitchen was placed in the angle between the west and south ranges. This required the monks' refectory to be turned at right angles in order to project from the cloister. A second complex was also required in the case of double houses, which were essentially nunneries that had a group of resident monks or canons attached. The orders of St Gilbert and Fontevrault were both based on this structure, and required separate cloisters for the nuns and canons, with that of the nuns joined to the main conventual church (for example at Watton, North Yorkshire). The ordering of space in the monastery was carefully arranged to divide social groups, separating monks from lay-brothers, canons from nuns, and all religious from secular (non-monastic) visitors. Even within the monastic choir and refectory, seating was carefully ordered according to seniority within the community.

*Figure 13.7* Fountains Abbey, North Yorkshire, from the north-east. The Cistercian monastery was founded in 1132, and rebuilt on a massive scale by the 1150s. The square cloister projects from the south of the monastic church; the accommodation of the lay-brothers was contained in the extended west range (shown here with lead roof); adjacent is the monks' refectory, which projects at right angles from the cloister.
*Source*: R. Gilchrist

Beyond the cloister, an inner court housed stables, store houses, laundries, gardens and ancillary structures. An outer court contained larger scale industrial and storage buildings and work areas that were subject to frequent remodelling, including dovecotes, kilns, malthouses, breweries and granaries, as shown by excavations at Thornholme, Lincolnshire. At Fountains, a masonry-built woolhouse has been excavated that underwent six phases of development, including conversion to a watermill for fulling and finishing cloth (Figure 13.8) (Coppack 1986). At Bordesley Abbey, Worcestershire, a series of timber-built mills had hearths located near the wheel. Associated with this complex were metal offcuts, but very little slag, indicative of water-powered metalworking (Astill 1989). Fishponds were common on the outer edges of the precinct, and some sites included elaborate pond complexes for management of fish, such as Marton, North Yorkshire. Some orders, in particular the Cistercian, also held specialized farms (granges) located some distance from the monastery. The plagues of the mid-fourteenth century caused a shortage of labour and recruits to serve as lay-brothers. As a result, such farms were increasingly leased out to tenant farmers.

The vocation of the friars to preach and educate the urban poor affected the form and location of their houses. Because they were relative latecomers to towns, they sometimes occupied the outer fringes, such as the Austin Friars at Leicester. Wherever possible, however, they would acquire a more central site, even if this meant moving when a new site could be purchased. The vocation to preach initiated the lofty preaching nave, a hall-like structure in which visibility and audibility were the priorities (e.g. the extant Dominican church at Norwich). The preaching nave was open to the public, and separated from the friars' choir in the eastern arm of the church by a screened space known as the 'walking place', which was often surmounted by a tower. Friaries followed the model of the cloister plan, but placed less emphasis on the regular ordering of space, requiring flexibility to fit their accommodation into more cramped

*Figure 13.8* Fountains Abbey, North Yorkshire, reconstruction of the thirteenth-century woolhouse excavated in the outer court. Drawing by Simon Hayfield from research by Glyn Coppack.
*Source*: Coppack 1986, Fig. 19

urban environments. A second, or 'little', cloister provided additional functions, including infirmaries, guest houses, industry or school rooms and almonries.

Monasteries of the military orders, the Templars and Hospitallers, are known as preceptories or commanderies. These acted principally as large agricultural holdings, amassing wealth to fund the Crusades to regain Jerusalem for the Christian West. The larger preceptories had churches with round naves, an unusual form of iconographic architecture that made a direct symbolic reference

*Figure 13.9* Little Maplestead, Essex, although now a parish church, this was the monastic church of a Hospitaller commandery, built *c.* 1245. The round nave was symbolic of the church of the Holy Sepulchre in Jerusalem. *Source*: R. Gilchrist

to the church of the Holy Sepulchre in Jerusalem (Figure 13.9). In Britain, preceptories seem to have been ordered more on the model of secular manors than on monasteries. Excavation at South Witham, Lincolnshire, showed that religious and agricultural buildings were contained in the same ditched enclosure, but were spatially separated. Domestic buildings in the south-eastern part of the site included halls and a chapel, while agricultural buildings were placed to the north and west, and fishponds were dug in the south-western corner.

Certain areas of the monastery were favoured for burial of the dead, including the chapter house, cloister garth (centre of the cloister courtyard), cloister alleys, the south transept and aisles of the nave. Place of burial was determined by social identity and status: the chapter house and eastern arm of the church were commonly reserved for abbots, priors or a monastery's founders or most significant patrons. Burial within the monastic precinct was not confined to religious personnel. Family groups were sometimes buried in chapels, such as that of the Uffords at the nunnery of Campsey Ash (Suffolk), and occasionally special areas were given over to the burial of children, for example the western end of the chapter house at the Dominican Friary in Oxford.

## THE SOCIAL LIFE OF BUILDINGS

Changes in belief, liturgy (formalized religious practices) and social *mores* can be read in the developing plan and fittings of the local parish church. The ground-plans of the earliest excavated churches indicate that a simple plan was common by the eleventh century, consisting of a nave and chancel: the chancel contained the altar and officiating clergy, while the nave held the local people who stood in observation and worship. A division of responsibility emerged that reflected this usage, with the maintenance of the nave being in the remit of the parishioners, and that of the chancel falling under the auspices of the priest or patron. The altar seems to have been placed at the western end of the chancel at St Mark, Lincoln, and Raunds, allowing easy visibility for those in the nave. The small scale of these churches implies an intimate setting and high degree of visibility and interaction between the priest and people. In contrast, during the thirteenth century, chancels were rebuilt in a more elongated form, increasing the distance between the altar and the nave, and reflecting the formalization of the liturgy at that time. The chancel received more elaborate features, such as *sedilia* (seats for the priests), Easter Sepulchres (for the Easter liturgy) and *piscinae* and *aumbries* (fixed ritual basins and book cupboards, respectively). The junction between the nave and chancel was marked by a decorated timber, or more rarely stone, screen that supported the rood, an image of the Crucifixion. Churches acquired fonts by the twelfth century, located in the western end of the nave to denote both entry to the church and initation to the life-cycle. By the fifteenth or sixteenth century, sermons had become an important element of the service, and pulpits were sometimes placed at the eastern end of the nave. Benches and fixed seating also began to appear at this time, with their arrangement reflecting the social hierarchy of the community itself. Factors such as social status, gender and age influenced the parishioner's visibility of the altar and masses.

Higher status churches were built with, or acquired, transepts, the two arms that project from the crossing of a cruciform (cross-shaped) plan. The transepts were used to house additional chapels or important burials. From the twelfth century, but more regularly from the thirteenth century, aisles were added to the south and/or north side of the nave. This new construction sometimes involved the piercing of existing side walls with an arcade, a series of arches supported by piers and columns, that would be screened to divide the envelope of the nave from the aisles. Aisles may have provided space for a growing population, but more likely reflect changes in the use of churches. Aisles were used to house separate chapels, or to provide special places for guilds and fraternities, groups linked by occupation, or devotion to particular saints or feasts. During the fourteenth and fifteenth centuries, private family chapels and mausolea became common in the spaces of the aisles, particularly as chantry masses – prayers for the dead that were believed to hasten the passage of the soul through Purgatory – became more popular.

Traditionally, castles have been studied from a purely military perspective, although there has been some recent discussion of the symbolic and iconographic content of castle architecture (Heslop 1991). Archaeologists are increasingly concerned with issues of daily life in castles and monasteries, including standards of living, social life, production and consumption of goods. Evidence for food preparation at castles includes a twelfth-century bread-oven excavated in the bailey at Hen Domen, corn-drying kilns at Stamford that were placed adjacent to the kitchen, a malthouse and kiln at Sandal, and a thirteenth- to fourteenth-century kitchen complex at Montgomery that included an oven and brewhouse. Investigation of animal remains can amplify our knowledge of the higher status medieval diet. In common with the monastic diet, this included a substantial amount of marine and freshwater fish, the latter having been a fairly precious commodity in medieval Britain. Remains of oysters from Okehampton, Devon, suggest that the shellfish was deliberately cultivated and harvested at three to four years (Kenyon 1990, 179–180). At Barnard Castle, Co. Durham, large quantities of the bones of deer suggest the production of venison on a commercial scale (Austin 1984). Daily life is revealed through the recovery of household artefacts, including sources of lighting, such as cresset lamps, candlesticks and lanterns; the usual range of wooden, pottery and glass vessels; and rarer forms of distillative glass and urinals, possibly indicating medicinal use. Personal artefacts recovered include jewellery, militaria, such as spurs and arrowheads, and artefacts revealing entertainment and leisure, such as the gaming pieces and musical instruments excavated at Castle Acre (Kenyon 1990).

Monastic sites have yielded a wide range of material: artefacts excavated at Kirkstall Abbey, West Yorkshire, included those linked with domestic activity, such as bronze, glass and pewter vessels, building fittings, including door furniture, roof tiles, water pipes, glass and lead cames, and personal items such as belts and strap fittings, jewellery, toilet implements and coins and jettons. Among the most commonly recovered artefacts are sherds of pottery, traditionally used to help assign dates to archaeological contexts. Pottery from Kirkstall Abbey was plotted by individual sherd, in order to help in understanding the degree of contamination and residuality of features, and to assist in interpreting the functions of different areas of the monastery (Moorhouse and Wrathmell 1987). The production and range of medieval pottery is relatively well understood, so that the presence of diagnostic fabrics can be used to reconstruct patterns of monastic production, consumption and trade. The form of the vessel, for example whether bowl, jug or cooking pot, will provide understanding of its use, and additional information can be gleaned from its surface condition (e.g. whether there is evidence of soot from cooking) and through residue analysis to determine its former contents. Glass vessels are less robust than pottery or wood, which survives in waterlogged deposits, but fragments of glass vessels can sometimes indicate the presence of activities such as medical treatment (urinals used for diagnosis), literacy (ink wells) and perhaps even alchemy, a chemical procedure that was believed to turn base metals into gold (Moorhouse 1993). Larger monasteries for men housed *scriptoria* for copying manuscripts, and considerable archaeological evidence can be found for monastic literacy. For instance, parchment prickers, lead dry points, book plates and book clasps were all recovered from St Andrew's, York, and a number of sites have yielded evidence for pigments used in manuscript illumination, including the Carmelite friary at Linlithgow, West Lothian, mixed in oyster shells that served as convenient palettes.

Monastic libraries were repositories for knowledge from the Classical and Arabic worlds. This informed the monks' knowledge of technology and attitudes towards medicine, in particular. Next to the cloister was the monastic infirmary, which consisted of a large aisled hall with a chapel at the eastern end. The partially extant example at Christchurch, Canterbury, stretches to *c.* 75 m in length. Diet and hygiene were carefully regulated in the monastery, and a meat-enriched diet was provided for sick and elderly monks in the infirmary. Every monk was expected to visit the infirmary up to seven times each year for blood-letting, which was believed to maintain good health. Concern with sanitation, in addition to ideas about spiritual purity, led to a strong emphasis in monasteries on provision of fresh water (Coppack 1990; Greene 1992). The main requirements were threefold: supply, distribution to buildings in the cloister and courts, and removal of waste. Especially in towns, it was necessary to transport water over long distances through lead or ceramic pipes, and to filter water from pollutants and contaminants by means of settling tanks.

The long-term nature of occupation at monastic sites, together with their emphasis on the formalized use of space, can give the impression of a static continuity and uniformity. Archaeology has in fact demonstrated a substantial diversity between different monastic orders, male and female houses and larger and smaller monasteries. A considerable degree of change can be observed particularly for the fifteenth and sixteenth centuries. At some houses, space became less strictly regulated, with buildings around the cloister being used for a variety of domestic activities, such as baking and brewing, and for storage of grain. The coenobitic ideal of the communal life broke down as the concept of privacy evolved, and religious belief shifted towards the importance of the individual. In some monasteries, this is reflected in the partitioning of formerly communal dormitories and infirmary halls, and in extreme cases, such as Elstow, Bedfordshire, the withdrawal of small groups from the rest of the community to eat and live together in separate households. Evidence of animal bones suggests that prohibitions on diet were broken in all but the strictest of monasteries, while the recovery of personal artefacts and costly imported items suggests that earlier vows to eschew wealth and private property had been breached.

## THE WIDER VIEW

There are considerable parallels between British and continental evidence, particularly in the case of monastic orders that had their origins or mother house in France. Monasteries developed from models established in Carolingian Europe, with close resemblance of the British examples from the tenth century onwards. However, castles and parish churches evolved along slightly different lines from their continental counterparts. Fortified hill-top settlements, mottes and *donjons* appeared in France and Germany from the mid-tenth to the eleventh centuries, and towers on conical mounds were built at the same time in southern Germany and Italy. The motte and bailey form declined in all of north-western Europe by the twelfth to thirteenth centuries, when it began to flourish in southern and eastern Europe (Fehring 1991, 118). Continental parishes formed much earlier due to Carolingian reforms, with a two-tier system of mother churches and parish churches from *c.* 800. This structure developed in England (and in Italy) much later, with full parochial rights for village churches accruing from the eleventh to the thirteenth centuries.

However, the pace and precise character of parochial development is likely to have varied between localities. Regional variations can be detected, such as the more tenacious survival of the minster system in north-western and south-western England, and the absence of evidence for minster frameworks in the areas of Viking settlement such as Yorkshire and East Anglia. The consensus of current opinion favours a seigneurial origin for most local churches, in other words, their foundation by a local lord. It has been argued that they began as privately owned churches, possibly motivated by the financial gains to be made by the lord retaining a portion of tithes and soulscot (paid for the burial of corpses) (Blair 1988, 12). While economic gain may have played some part in motivating local lords to construct churches, social expectations must also have played a role. The proprietary church became symbolic of thegnly rank, and represented a pious act that it was believed would improve one's chances of salvation. The current picture of church origins also neglects the possibility that local communities either demanded that churches should be provided for them, or instigated such building projects themselves.

Considerable debate still surrounds the issue of the origins and development of the parish church and the castle (e.g. Blair and Pyrah 1996). In some quarters, there has been a recent concern to investigate the domestic and ideological dimensions of castle life over that of military functions, while the priorities of monastic archaeology have shifted away from religious and social elements to focus on landscape and technology. Furthermore, the development of environmental archaeology has made a substantial contribution to our understanding of medieval life. Particularly in the case of monastic excavations, the evidence of pollen and plant and insect remains has been used to reconstruct former environmental conditions. Animal bones and plant macrofossils have yielded new information on the high status medieval diet, and skeletons excavated from ecclesiastical sites have provided insights on health and demography. It is especially when investigating the standards of daily life that archaeology makes its own unique contribution to medieval studies.

Monastic studies have successfully incorporated a more integrated, landscape approach that is still lacking in investigations of parish churches and castles. Research and recording of all three types of settlement have assisted in refining a distinctive archaeological method for the study of standing buildings. In contrast to these advances, there has been comparatively little interaction between archaeological theory and the practice of medieval archaeology, an omission that is gradually being redressed.

## Key texts
Greene, J. P., 1992. *Medieval monasteries.* London: Leicester University Press.
Kenyon, J.R., 1990. *Medieval fortifications.* London: Leicester University Press.
Morris, R., 1989. *Churches in the landscape.* London: Dent.
Pounds, N.J.G., 1990. *The medieval castle in England and Wales. A social and political history.* Cambridge: Cambridge University Press.
Rodwell, W., 1989. *Church archaeology.* London: Batsford/English Heritage.

## Bibliography
Astill, G., 1989. 'Monastic research designs: Bordesley Abbey', in Gilchrist, R. and Mytum, H. (eds) *The archaeology of rural monasteries.* Oxford: British Archaeological Report 203, 277–292.

Aston, M., 1993. *Monasteries*. London: Batsford.

Austin, D., 1984. 'The castle and the landscape', *Landscape History* 6, 69–81.

Beresford, G., 1987. *Goltho: the development of an early medieval manor, c. 850–1150*. London: HBMCE.

Blair, J. (ed.) 1988. *Minsters and parish churches: the local church in transition, 950–1200*. Oxford: Oxford University Committee for Archaeology Monograph 17.

Blair, J. and Pyrah, C. (eds) 1996. *Research designs for church archaeology*. York: Council for British Archaeology Research Report 104.

Boddington, A., 1996. *Raunds Furnell. The Anglo-Saxon church and churchyard*. London: English Heritage.

Coad, J.G., and Streeten, A.D.F., 1982. 'Excavations at Castle Acre Castle, Norfolk, 1972–77: country house and castle of the Norman earls of Surrey', *Archaeological Journal* 139, 138–301.

Colvin, H.M. (ed.) 1963. *The history of the king's works: 1–2. The Middle Ages*. London: HMSO.

Coppack, G., 1986. 'The excavation of an outer court building, perhaps the woolhouse, at Fountains Abbey, North Yorkshire', *Medieval Archaeology* 30, 46–87.

Coppack, G., 1990. *Abbeys and priories*. London: Batsford/English Heritage.

Fehring, G.P., 1991. *The archaeology of medieval Germany: an introduction*. London: Routledge.

Gilchrist, R., 1995. *Contemplation and action. The other monasticism*. London: Leicester University Press.

Greene, J.P., 1989. *Norton Priory: the archaeology of a medieval religious house*. Cambridge: Cambridge University Press.

Heslop, T.A., 1991. 'Orford Castle, nostalgia and sophisticated living', *Architectural History* 34, 36–58.

Higham, R. and Barker, P., 1992. *Timber castles*. London: Leicester University Press.

Horn, W. and Born, E., 1979. *The plan of St Gall*. Berkeley: University of California Press.

Knowles, D. and Hadcock, R.N., 1971. *Medieval religious houses: England and Wales*. London: Longman.

Mayes, P. and Butler, L., 1983. *Sandal Castle excavations 1964–1973: a detailed archaeological report*. Wakefield: West Yorkshire Archaeology.

Morris, R., 1983. *The church in British archaeology*. London: Council for British Archaeology Research Report 47.

Moorhouse, S., 1993. 'Pottery and glass in the medieval monastery', in Gilchrist, R. and Mytum, H. (eds) *Advances in monastic archaeology*. Oxford: British Archaeological Report 227, 127–148.

Moorhouse, S. and Wrathmell, S., 1987. *Kirkstall Abbey Volume 1. The 1950–64 excavations: a reassessment*. Wakefield: West Yorkshire Archaeology.

Rodwell, W. and Rodwell, K., 1982. 'St Peter's Church, Barton-upon-Humber: excavation and structural study, 1978–81', *Antiquaries Journal* 62, 283–315.

Thompson, M.W., 1987. *The decline of the castle*. Cambridge: Cambridge University Press.

Thompson, M.W., 1995. *The medieval hall: the basis of secular domestic life 600–1600*. London: Scolar Press.

Taylor, H.M., 1972. 'Structural criticism: a plea for more systematic study of Anglo-Saxon buildings', *Anglo-Saxon England* 1, 259–72.

*Chapter Fourteen*

# Landscapes of the Middle Ages

## Rural settlement and manors

## Paul Stamper

### FRAMEWORKS

To most British archaeologists and historians, the Middle Ages (Middle, that is, between the Classical world and that of the Renaissance when the term was first used) begins in 1066 with the Norman Conquest of England. While many would admit that this over-emphasizes the significance of what was essentially a political coup, the later eleventh century fell anyway in a period of significant changes sufficient by themselves to define a new age. At various times over the previous century or so, parish churches had proliferated, fully integrated manorial estates had evolved, nucleated settlements and open field systems had been established in all parts of lowland England, and Romanesque (Norman) architecture had arrived. There is less agreement about when the Middle Ages ended, although historians generally take as their marker the Battle of Bosworth in 1485 which brought to a close the Wars of the Roses. Archaeologists, more attuned to the material world, tend to see the medieval world continuing until the 1540s, when the Dissolution of the monasteries not only brought down those key medieval institutions but also saw a redistribution of something like a third of the land of England, as monastic estates were sold off into lay (non-religious) ownership.

Those five centuries pivot about the mid-fourteenth century, and especially the first and most awful visitation in 1348–9 of bubonic plague, the Black Death, which killed a third of the country's population. This accelerated and accentuated changes that were already afoot (Platt 1996). Labour, until then plentiful and cheap, was no longer so. More importantly, as the land of the dead was redistributed, far fewer families had to live at bare subsistence level and prey to starvation if their meagre acreage of crops failed. The greater availability of land similarly enabled the more enterprising peasants to start to put together larger holdings, and to begin to take on the characteristics of the modern farmer.

There is one other pivotal development that significantly affects the study of the Middle Ages, and this is the explosion in written record keeping that occurred in the thirteenth century. Within the space of a few decades around the middle of that century, title to land, estate accounts, and legal proceedings all began routinely to be made in writing – a technology previously very restricted in its application. Before then, little was recorded in writing other than the doings of kings and their battles, but thereafter for many half-acres we know their full tenurial history and for many estates their productivity down to the last bushel of grain and piglet. Michael Clanchy has calculated that in the thirteenth century alone 8 million charters (deeds) may have been produced for England's peasants. The figure is barely credible, yet plausible, and some measure of the scale of the transformation that he has characterized as the move from memory to written record.

This vast new dataset inevitably alters the role of archaeology in the study of the later Middle Ages, although opinion is divided in what way. Does archaeology become a tool to be used more selectively, given that documents tell us so much? Or does the availability, as it were, of written cross-checks open up the opportunity to have a far deeper and more critical understanding of, or dialogue with, the archaeological evidence? That such a fundamental question remains unresolved is a mark of the relative youth of the discipline of medieval archaeology, which, as will be seen, developed only after the Second World War. Prehistorians had banded together to found a national Prehistoric Society in 1935, but not until 1957, when the Society for Medieval Archaeology was established, was there an archaeological 'period' society and journal for the Middle Ages. That annual publication, *Medieval Archaeology*, remains the key periodical for the study of the archaeology of the Middle Ages in north-west Europe.

The archaeological data available to the medievalist, both in range and quantity, is very similar to that which faces the Romanist. Although in some parts of the country little pottery was in use at the time of the Norman Conquest, by the twelfth century pottery was generally plentiful and, it would seem, cheap – certainly the coarser unglazed wares used for cooking and storage. In the thirteenth century, glazed vessels, especially jugs, became increasingly common and more spectacular in decoration, and scatters of sherds in the ploughsoil remain the best indicator in the countryside of the location of habitation sites. Excavation of such invariably recovers a wide range of manufactured goods – tools, fixtures and fittings, and dress items – manufactured from stone, bone, and all kinds of metal, although predominantly iron and bronze. Where soil conditions permit, as with the sites of any period, it will also yield a wide range of environmental remains, which can range from the bones of oxen and horses to charred, waterlogged or mineralized seeds. Little of this data can be securely dated on stylistic grounds, and even the most distinctive forms of glazed pottery can only be allocated, with any confidence, to a 50-year date band. The medievalist is therefore fortunate that the economy was quite heavily reliant on money, and that even peasants close to the bottom of the social spectrum routinely handled, and lost into what in time became archaeological deposits, datable small denomination coinage.

The most precise dating available to the medieval archaeologist is dendrochronology (i.e. dating using tree rings), although obviously that technique is applicable only where a standing structure with substantial original timbers is being studied (Figure 14.1), or where conditions have resulted in the survival of

*Figure 14.1* Pillar-and-stall coal mining exposed at Coleorton, Leicestershire, during modern opencast operations, dated by tree-ring analysis of pit props and shaft timbers to between 1450 and 1463. The workings are in a coal seam 3 m thick, which in the area shown is at a depth of 30 m. The long, thin 'pillars' of solid coal were left by the miners to support the roof. Access was gained to the seam not from the outcrop (although this was only 250 m to the left of the photo) but from carefully constructed timber-lined shafts sunk vertically from the surface.

*Source*: R.F. Hartley, Leicestershire Museums, Arts and Records Service

waterlogged or charred timbers. In general, scientific methods have had only a limited impact on medieval archaeology in the field, although undeniably, and as with sites of all periods, they assume a much greater importance in the laboratory when finds are subject to microscopic study and analysis. Techniques that are routinely used outdoors include archaeomagnetic dating, where burnt clay features such as kilns, ovens and hearths are encountered, but rarely radiocarbon dating because the very broad date brackets do not offer a 'tighter' date than that given by, say, pottery.

A medieval villager lived in a landscape of whose administrative complexity he was probably more aware than his modern-day equivalent. Each Sunday he would go to the church of his parish, the place where ultimately he would be buried. To that church he owed a tenth – a tithe – of all he produced on his holding, whether it be grain, hay or lambs. Once in a while, especially if doing duty as churchwarden, he might see the archdeacon, representative of the bishop and the greater Church beyond. During his life he would undoubtedly occasionally become aware of other systems of administration: of royal officials such as the county sheriff, tax collectors and travelling justices; of the county Quarter Sessions where, from the later fourteenth century, Justices of the Peace dealt with matters including murder, assault and riot; of the county coroner to whom matters including suspicious deaths and discoveries of treasure had to be reported; of the Church's courts for those accused of moral and ecclesiastical offences; and of Forest courts, to which those who lived in the extensive areas deemed forest came if charged with poaching deer, damaging trees, or bringing land into cultivation without permission.

The administrative unit most familiar to the villager, however, was the manor. Essentially this was the estate on which he lived and held his land. To its owner, the lord of the manor, in return for his holding he owed a money rent or labour services, that is a set number of days' work on the lord's own land. Although there were considerable variations both regionally and over time in the classes of peasantry and their obligations, by and large a distinction can be made between those who were 'free' – that is those, usually the minority, who owed only a money rent for their holding and in whose lives the lord had relatively little opportunity to interfere – and those servile tenants who were obliged to do labour services and who, at least in theory, often held their farm only during their own lifetime, after which it passed back to the lord to be reallotted. In many parts of the country, such men were called 'copyholders', that is they held their house and land according to an agreement made in the manor court of which they received a written copy. Such courts, termed 'courts baron', were held at regular intervals, perhaps monthly, and were at the heart of rural life. For here not only was the surrender and transfer of holdings dealt with but also the regulation of agricultural land and the appointment of officials. Those might include a hayward to look after fences and the manor's grazing land and, most importantly, a reeve, responsible for collecting any dues owed to the lord and acting as the main channel of communications between the lord and his tenants.

Parish and manor were therefore entirely separate: the first was the territory that supported a church through the payment of tithes, while the second was a lay estate comprising the land of the lord and that of his tenants. Both varied greatly in size and complexity, and many parishes, especially those established earlier rather than later in the era of parish formation in the later Saxon period, contained several manors. That having been said, it was perhaps commonest for parish and manor to be co-extensive – that is to have the same boundaries – reflecting the origin of so many parish churches as the private or estate chapel of a local lord.

Those frameworks, an appreciation of which is essential for the student of medieval society, have long been well understood; they survived little changed until the earlier nineteenth century and have been, and remain, the subject of intensive enquiry by historians. What then has archaeology to contribute to the study of rural settlement?

The first point that can be made is that, traditionally, few historians exhibited any interest whatsoever in material culture, whether it be the layout of a village's fields, the design of its houses or the range of their contents. That was especially so with regard to peasant society, which was assumed to be (in every sense) rude, crude and unworthy of scholarly investigation. In fairness to historians (and this is the second point), medieval documentary sources tend anyway to touch only indirectly on these matters. Even after the making of written records proliferated in the thirteenth century, narrative and descriptive passages of ordinary life are few and far between, and most documents are terse, factual memoranda: of the transfer of property, of misdemeanours and punishments, and of grants of permissions. If these do mention, say, a house, a mill, or a pig, it is rare for there to be any descriptive gloss given.

Furthermore, although the mention or otherwise of items in documents can indicate the date of change – when windmills first appeared or when large-scale goat keeping declined – they rarely offer direct explanation. Archaeology's ultimate access to a much larger dataset, and to one with a degree of detail denied the historian, makes the investigation of explanation far more feasible.

That such an approach is now possible owes much to a small number of scholars who, between the early 1950s and the 1980s, not only established the techniques for studying the medieval countryside but also gathered much of the evidence and formed many of the interpretations that underpin our understanding of it (Hurst 1986). Although as early as the 1840s John Wilson had excavated a medieval village, Woodperry, Oxfordshire, recording foundations, pottery and small finds, his lead was not followed up; only in the 1930s, when Martyn Jope excavated a peasant house at Great Beere, Devon, and Rupert Bruce-Mitford began to dig at the deserted village of Seacourt, Oxfordshire, was there a renewed interest in the possibilities such excavations offered. With survey, a similar pattern can be seen, of early landmarks not pursued. From the 1850s, Ordnance Survey surveyors were occasionally mapping in some detail medieval settlement remains, although these aroused little comment, while in 1924, O.G.S. Crawford published the first air photograph of a deserted medieval village, Gainsthorpe, Lincolnshire. In terms of more holistic landscape work, there was very little, although John Hurst has drawn attention to the work of amateurs such as Ethel Rudkin in Lincolnshire, Helen O'Neil in Gloucestershire and Tony Brewster in Yorkshire, who brought to bear techniques including fieldwalking, air photography, experimental archaeology, and excavation in pioneering individual studies.

Although it is to simplify matters, the publication of three books in the mid-1950s provided a vital catalyst for medieval landscape studies. In the 1940s, two economic historians, Maurice Beresford and William Hoskins, had independently begun to seek out on the ground and on air photos (the available number of which expanded hugely as systematic post-war surveys were released) medieval and later landscapes which they had encountered in documents and, in particular, on hand-drawn estate maps. Beresford's *Lost Villages of England* appeared in 1954 and his *History on the Ground* in 1957, and Hoskins' *Making of the English Landscape* in 1955.

## VILLAGES, HAMLETS AND HOUSES

Among the most important points those books established, despite the scepticism of some senior colleagues, was that not only were large numbers of villages deserted in the Middle Ages but that their remains, readily identifiable as earthwork house platforms, hollow ways and banks and ditches, were to be seen in many parts of the country, sometimes in profusion. However, when the historians attempted to excavate individual houses, the results were disappointing, not least because of the primitive methods used. In one celebrated instance, Beresford searched for walls with a gargantuan coke shovel borrowed from the local railway stationmaster.

The defining moment in medieval rural archaeology came in 1952 when a Cambridge post-graduate, John Hurst, precociously engaged in the study of medieval pottery, visited one of Beresford's excavations, at Wharram Percy, deep in the high chalk landscape of the east Yorkshire Wolds (Beresford and Hurst 1990). Appalled by the historians' trenching, Hurst agreed to take over responsibility for the excavations, thus unwittingly launching not only one of the most celebrated partnerships of post-war archaeology but also what, over the whole course of its 40-year existence, was undoubtedly one of the most influential all-round projects in European archaeology. During that time, the project was the archaeological flagship of the Deserted Medieval Settlement Research Group, founded in the latter part of 1952, which was later to change its name as perceptions altered and interests broadened to the Medieval Village Research Group in 1971 and to the Medieval Settlement Research Group in 1986.

As excavations proper commenced at Wharram in 1953, Hurst abandoned the then 'industry standard' method made famous by Sir Mortimer Wheeler of digging a regular chequerboard of trenches separated by broad baulks whose sections recorded the vertical stratigraphy. Instead, and for the first time on a British medieval site, the technique of open-area excavation was adopted and the whole area of House 10 was opened up at once. Its excavation occupied summer seasons throughout the 1950s, as did a similar campaign on House 6 in the 1960s. The archaeology of both sites was complex, and its interpretation has changed radically over the years. That in itself is testimony to another innovation at Wharram, of meticulous recording: stone-by-stone planning, and the noting of the position of every find, even pottery, in three dimensions. When the turf and the shattered chalk destruction rubble was removed and picked apart, what was exposed was apparently not the single-phase 30-m long buildings that the earthworks had suggested but short, misaligned lengths of walling interpreted as evidence of the frequent rebuilding of what must therefore have been structurally flimsy buildings. Only in the 1980s, and following detailed work on the area's vernacular architecture, was Stuart Wrathmell able to reinterpret the same evidence, and to demonstrate that these had been cruck-framed houses, sturdy and long lived, standing for perhaps two centuries (Figure 14.2). What the excavators had found were the short lengths of walling between each timber cruck, walls that had no structural function (the roof being supported by the cruck frames), and which were replaced piecemeal as needs be.

The study of vernacular architecture – that is of ordinary houses and cottages constructed from locally available materials using traditional building techniques – has made a massive impact in general on the study of medieval housing, especially now that dendrochronology has supplied large numbers of precise dates. In Kent, for instance, admittedly a county where the tradition of timber-framed building was strong, it is now reckoned that there remain some 2,500 open-hall houses of late thirteenth- to late sixteenth-century date, most post-dating 1370, when rebuilding began with a vengeance after a 30-year gap following the Black Death. The sheer number strongly indicates that these represent not atypical structures, the survival of which can be explained by the use of exceptional materials or techniques, but the perfectly ordinary farmhouses of an emerging late medieval sub-gentry class (Pearson 1994). Documentary research has also played a part in advancing our understanding of peasant building, for although references to structural details are relatively infrequent, when collected together on a regional basis, significant patterns can emerge. In the West Midlands, for instance, the historical evidence has enabled Dyer (1986) to characterize late medieval houses as well-carpented, of two or three bays, erected around cruck principals and founded on low stone plinth walls. It is now clear that in many parts of the country the late medieval peasantry was living in well-built houses, many of which have survived to this day.

Returning to archaeology, from the mid-1960s, open-area excavation began on villages other than Wharram, both of single plots ('tofts') and more extensively (for a review and references see

*Figure 14.2* Daily life in a late medieval cruck-built longhouse of the type excavated at Wharram Percy. One or more rooms provided living accommodation, the main room an open hall heated by an open fire on a central hearth. Lofts may have provided storage space, and perhaps a sleeping space for children. At the other end of the house, and divided from it by a cross-passage that ran between the house's main doors, was a byre where animals were stalled in the winter, and a central drain carrying slurry through a hole in the end wall. A screen along the cross-passage would normally have divided off the byre end.
*Source*: Beresford and Hurst 1990, 40. Drawing by Peter Dunn

Astill 1988). Partly by design, and partly through the accidental pressures of rescue work, these were in many different parts of the country, and most usefully in areas with very different geophysical characteristics. Longhouses – structures with one or more living rooms, separated from a byre for animals by a cross-passage – were long thought to be the ubiquitous peasant house type, and certainly they were more widespread in the Middle Ages than later, when they came to be almost wholly associated with the upland farms of western and northern Britain. In lowland Britain, for instance, medieval examples have been found by excavation in Northamptonshire at Lyveden, in Gloucestershire at Upton, in Wiltshire at Gomeldon and in Sussex at Hangleton. Documentary evidence provides further occasional examples, for instance from Worcestershire, where in 1440 at Northfield a tenant agreed to build 'a hall . . . and a chamber at the front end of the hall with a byre at the rear end' (Dyer 1986, 25). In upland Britain sites include highland 'fermtouns', or hamlets (Figure 14.3), such as at Rosal in Sutherland and Lix in Perthshire, where survey combined with excavation identified a number of cruck-roofed longhouses (Yeoman 1991). Hound Tor, Devon, a granite-built hamlet sited high (335 m) on Dartmoor, was abandoned in the fourteenth century. Here the settlement latterly comprised an irregular group of farms, each with a longhouse at its centre and with substantial grain-drying kilns among the associated structures. An equally inhospitable site was West Whelpington, Northumberland, sited on a dolerite outcrop 40 km north-west of Newcastle. This, however, was a large settlement, probably established as a planned village around a green *c.* 1100, and in the later thirteenth century with as many as 35 bondage (servile) tenancies, each with an average of 20 acres of land and 2 acres of meadow. At that time, the houses were of a type described by the excavators as 'proto-longhouses', but after the village was burnt, probably by the Scots in the wake of Bannockburn in 1314, it was rebuilt with houses of a new type. These were probably laid out through the initiative of the lord, and comprised four main terraces of longhouses, in all *c.* 28 dwellings, facing onto the

***Figure 14.3*** Home Farm, Wardhouse, Aberdeenshire. A Scottish fermtoun, or farming hamlet, surrounded by ridge and furrow, sometimes in Scotland called *runrig.*
*Source:* Aberdeen Archaeological Surveys

green (Figure 14.4). Encroaching on the green were simpler, cottage dwellings and, added in the sixteenth century, a defensive pele tower. In Scotland, a terraced row of three cruck-built longhouses of the mid-thirteenth century, again argued by the excavator to represent seigneurial investment, was found at Springwood Park, about 35 miles south-east of Edinburgh (Yeoman 1995, 115) (Figure 14.5). Longhouses arranged end-to-end make the point that medieval building types do not fall conveniently into hard and fast types, and that the known range is likely to extend still further with excavations in the future. Terraced rows, although not of true longhouses, have also been found in village excavations at Thrislington, Durham, and Burton Dassett, Warwickshire.

A move away from longhouses in the later Middle Ages has sometimes been demonstrated by excavation. At Gomeldon, the twelfth-century longhouse was later replaced by a courtyard farm with separate buildings for people, animals and other farming activities. The same transition may also have been glimpsed at Hangleton, where, in the thirteenth century, both longhouses and farms were in use at the same time. Elsewhere, animals seem never to have been accommodated in the main house, and during the later Middle Ages this tradition, of functionally discrete buildings set around a courtyard, seems to have become established even in areas where earlier longhouses may have been common. Within this general courtyard, layout differences reflected variations in local building materials and farming systems. In Hampshire, on the clay-with-flints soil at Popham, the fourteenth-century structures were built on flint sleeper walls, with the houses ranging in size from 7.2 x 4.4 m to a three roomed structure of 15 x 5 m, with a hearth in the central room. Most were aligned on the village street, with post-built barns and byres behind. At Greynston (or Grenstein), Norfolk clay lump (sun dried clay and straw blocks) was used as the main building material in a farm complex of a house with two yards, both set about with barns, a cattle shed and outbuildings. Houses were also clay walled in the villages of Goltho, Lincolnshire,

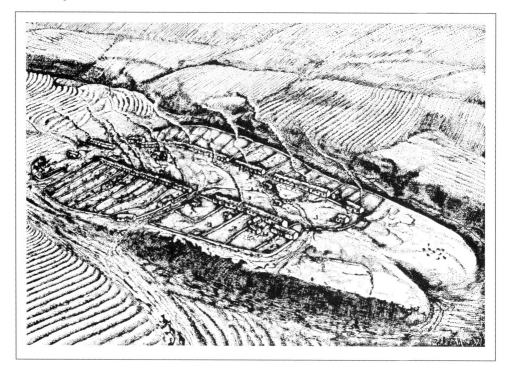

***Figure 14.4*** The village of West Whelpington, with terraced rows facing on to the green, as it may have been in the early fifteenth century.
*Source*: Drawing by Howard Mason

and Barton Blount, Derbyshire, here the material being raised around a timber framework to create houses of two or three rooms. Outside, cattle were over-wintered in crewyards enclosed by the house, barn, and any other agricultural buildings. Late medieval courtyard farms around crewyards have also been found in excavations at Wawne, Humberside, and can be recognized elsewhere as earthworks (at Towthorpe, for instance, another village in Wharram Percy parish), with the crewyards, lowered by successive annual scourings out of the winter's accumulated manure, appearing as distinct hollows.

Archaeology has also identified other aspects of farming regimes. On the Cotswolds, Dyer has recently recognized the distinctive earthwork remains of sheepcotes, long sheds in which sheep were housed during bad weather and during lambing (Dyer 1995). All manner of animal sheds and pens, although difficult to identify with certainty, have been claimed by excavators (Astill 1988, 58), such as the 1.5 · 1 m animal cot found abutting a wall at Cosmeston, Glamorgan. Drains and sumps show the need to keep yards dry, to maintain water holes (some originating as quarry pits) and wells, and to collect and retain water, especially when stock was kept in. Grain-drying ovens, such as those found at Hound Tor, are common discoveries, if varying widely in form and capacity. Stack stands and rick ditches attest to the need to keep stored crops dry, as do structures interpreted as granaries (e.g. Burton Dassett). Astill has suggested that the average size of corn barns on peasant holdings may have risen in the fourteenth and fifteenth centuries, evidence of increasing prosperity and perhaps even of the retention of corn until the market price rose. Excavation has also begun to produce good samples, usually charred, of corn, peas and beans, which in some cases have allowed the agricultural regimes on individual sites to be characterized. At Cefn

Graeanog, Gwynned, for instance, charred macrofossils indicate that the arable effort in the twelfth and thirteenth centuries was directed towards the cultivation of oats (*Avena* sp.). Such a fact is often (as there) already known from the documentary evidence, and what is more exciting is the unique opportunity such finds present of assessing the quality of medieval crops (Bell 1989).

Manor houses themselves have been studied by archaeologists through excavation, by architectural historians who have looked at standing examples, and by

*Figure 14.5* Thirteenth-century terraced longhouses at Springwood Park, Roxburghshire, each *c.* 4 · 10 m.
*Source*: Drawing by Alan Braby

historians using documents, usually financial accounts of construction and repair. What these studies show is that, despite the huge variations in the details of manorial complexes – regionally, over time, and in scale – the same elements tend to be ever present. At the heart of the complex would be a hall, scene of communal eating, with the lord and his retinue seated on a raised dais above socially inferior servants, tenants and guests, as well as other functions such as weekly or monthly manorial courts. From the 'high' dais end of the hall, there was usually direct access into the lord's private accommodation, formed of various chambers and usually including a solar or great chamber, a first-floor room over a cellar that acted as the family's main living room as well as serving in many cases as the lord's bed chamber. Grouped in a rough courtyard arrangement would be other buildings: perhaps a chapel; the kitchen, generally a detached building in order to reduce the risk of fire; stables; barns; and other farm buildings. On bigger manors, the farm buildings were usually grouped in a separate court or courts, with gardens and orchards forming still further elements of the complex. Especially in the thirteenth and fourteenth centuries, a moat was often dug around the manorial complex; excavation has shown that most were only shallow, but with a thorn hedge on the inner bank this would have been enough to deter most would-be thieves. Crime was a serious problem in medieval society, especially when times were hard: Norfolk had a murder rate that exceeded that of modern New York.

Only a few common themes emerge from excavations of medieval rural houses. Most obvious is the change in the twelfth and thirteenth centuries from dwellings built wholly of wood to ones where at least the lowest parts of the walls, even if only a course or two, were built of stone. This can be seen, for instance, at Foxcotte, Hampshire, where a change from post-built structures to ones raised off unmortared flint sleeper walls took place in the late thirteenth or fourteenth century. At Goltho and Barton Blount, the change was almost resisted, although even here padstones began to be put under the posts in the later Middle Ages. The adoption of stone footings was definitely a fundamental technical advance that greatly lengthened the life of the structure by preventing the lower parts of the structure, and especially the bases of the main trusses or the sill beam, rotting through being in direct contact with the ground. Initially this was seen as either a 'natural' progression (the Whig interpretation of archaeology) or a response to the declining availablity of structural timber as fields were enlarged at the expense of woods (Stamper 1988). Dyer, a historian, has argued rather that this change marks the emergence, documented in the written record in about the thirteenth century, of professional carpenters. Each explanation relies on (and demands) a different explanation of the medieval economy and society; in the last case, for instance, that a specialized, market economy had filtered down to the base of rural society, and that there was sufficient money in circulation to support a range of professional specialists. Another common theme, picked up by Wrathmell (1989), appears to be the movement of the main hearth in the late Middle Ages from the centre of the living room to against the cross passage wall. This was presumably to allow a firehood to be installed, although for what ultimate pupose is as yet unknown; whether it was to improve the living environment within the house by creating a fire with better (and safer) 'draw', or whether it was to allow the space above the living room to be converted into a loft. At Caldecotte, Hertfordshire, the next and final stage in the process was observed, with the insertion of wall chimneys before the settlement was deserted in the sixteenth century. It may also be the case that in the later Middle Ages the standard of fittings and fixtures improved, and at both Wharram and West Whelpington, lead-camed glass windows began to appear in the fifteenth century (Wrathmell 1989, 257).

One other development noted on a wide range of sites is the appearance of better defined boundaries in the early Middle Ages. Hatch, near Basingstoke, Hampshire, was an 'open' settlement in the late Saxon period, largely without internal boundaries between properties, and remained so until the twelfth century when ditches were dug to define the individual tenements. In a review of the evidence that demonstrated how widespread this trend towards ever more clearly defined boundaries was, especially in the late thirteenth and fourteenth centuries, Astill remarked that 'in chalk areas the tofts must have resembled stockades' and in general that 'The impression is that walking down the village street it would have been difficult to see in to the individual tofts, for most of the banks, walls or hedges would have been at head height' (1988, 52–53). This clearer definition of individual ownership in villages mirrored developments in the wider countryside, as the rising population increased pressure on resources of all kinds. Woods, moors and heaths that had previously been intercommoned, available for use by all the surrounding communities, came to be physically apportioned between them. Ditches and walls, or in woods linear clearings called trenches, were created to mark these new boundaries in what in many parts of Britain marked the last chapter in the allocation of the countryside into precisely defined territories.

Thus while it is possible to identify common themes in the vernacular buildings of medieval Britain, what emerges instead is an impression of great variety. Local, vernacular building styles, such as that identified by Austin in south-west England (Austin 1985), may have been just as marked in the early and high Middle Ages (the eleventh to later fourteenth centuries) as later. Those variations presumably reflect the availability (or otherwise) of local building materials and skilled carpenters, changing farming systems and differing levels of wealth and social status as well as innate local traditions.

As well as investigating variety in the plan and form of individual houses, archaeologists and geographers have also studied the settlements of which they formed a part. Here the work of Brian Roberts has been especially influential, and has now expanded from early work in the north-east to encompass all of England, for instance in an ambitious attempt to define for the whole of England discrete areas of rural settlement types defined in a hierachy of *Settlement Provinces, Sub-Provinces* and *Local Regions* (Roberts 1987). Almost equally ambitious has been an attempt to map village types in the East Midlands and to investigate their relationship both to natural factors, such as soil type, and to historic ones, such as the influence of the Scandinavian settlements (Lewis *et al.* 1997). The principal classificatory division that is usually applied is between nucleated and dispersed settlements, that is between, on the one hand, landscapes of villages and large hamlets and, on the other, those of scattered hamlets and farmsteads. Within each broad group there are many variants in plan form, which range over the whole scale from large villages with uniform properties clearly laid to a predetermined plan to settlements that sprawl in disorder and where there has apparently never been a seigneurial or communal attempt to control the use of space.

The main research exercise of the 1990s that centred on a single village and its territory was the Shapwick Project, set up in 1988 to examine a 1,284 ha parish in the centre of Somerset that runs up from the wetlands of the Somerset Levels to the Polden Hills 3 or 4 km away. The principal hypothesis that the Project set out to test was that the present village and its medieval open field system originated in the late Saxon period, and replaced an earlier pattern of dispersed farmsteads each with its own individual fields. As with the Wharram Project, with the last two years of which it overlapped, Shapwick has been a largely voluntary exercise conducted by academics including Mick Aston and Chris Gerrard assisted by large numbers of specialists, students and voluntary helpers. A wide range of techniques has been employed, some, like excavation, field walking (on a heroic scale), earthwork survey, documentary research, air photography and hedgerow dating, well established, others quite innovative, certainly in a British medieval context (see e.g. Selkirk 1997). Shovel pit testing – the sieving of samples of topsoil where the landscape is predominantly pasture for pottery, flints and other finds – has proved remarkably effective in locating sites. Also being tested in the mid-1990s was the possibility of locating aceramic settlements through geophysical and geochemical survey methods, including the identification of heavy metals in the soil.

The continuing population growth seen in the twelfth and thirteenth centuries inevitably led to changes in the pattern of rural settlement. Individual properties were sub-divided, most frequently to accommodate sons unable to find or afford their own holdings or to accommodate retired parents from whom the holding had been taken over. The 'newlands' found in some village plans indicate that, presumably with the initiative or at least acquiescence of the lord, it was sometimes possible for a settlement to expand, although unless new arable land could be added to the village's fields, the result would be a reduction in average farm size. Especially in areas of dispersed settlement, secondary or 'daughter' settlements were sometimes established in areas until then considered as of only marginal use. In the Fenlands of East Anglia, for instance, linear villages were established along drove roads, and comparable developments can be seen in the Somerset Levels wetlands. The most developed studies of dispersed and secondary settlements, however, have been those undertaken in 'wood-pasture' areas, such as those of the Weald of Kent and the West Midlands. At Hanbury, Worcestershire, much of the parish was farmed in the early Middle Ages from houses clustered around hamlets called 'Ends', such as Morweysend and Brookend, tenanted by customary tenants required to do labour services for the lord. However, in the two centuries after the Norman Conquest, a large acreage of woodland was felled in the parish – some 1,000 acres, an eighth of its total area, in the thirteenth century alone – and brought into cultivation. Many of the new cultivators, it has been argued, stood apart from the older inhabitants of Hanbury both in being freemen and in that they lived in 'Green' hamlets such as Gallows Green and Mere Green.

For all this better understanding and more accurate description of settlement types, the most fundamental questions remain how, when and why villages emerged as perhaps the most quintessential (although not ubiquitous) element of the countryside. Archaeology has played a major part here, field walking being used to establish, for instance, the very dispersed nature of settlement in the mid-Saxon period, even within areas later dominated by nucleated villages, and thereby establishing a *terminus post quem* for village formation. Much of the most important work has been undertaken as a part of the Raunds Project, focused on a series of excavations in and around a small Northamptonshire town and the field survey of 40 km² of the surrounding area. The excavations have shown how in the early and middle Saxon periods, the settlement was 'open' – without boundaries and apparently lacking planning (see also Chapter 10). A major change took place in the early tenth century, affecting all aspects of settlement, as rectilinear enclosures were laid out, probably (as at West Cotton nearby) to a standard width of 20 m, and a new building technique was adopted using foundation trenches. One of the new buildings was much longer (37 m) than the rest and has been identified as a manor house, another major addition to the settlement at this time being a church.

In fact it now seems likely that the replanning extended beyond the villages to encompass the whole landscape, and that the bringing together of estates' tenants from their previously dispersed farms and small hamlets into much larger settlements went hand-in-hand with the creation of new, integrated, arable land-holding patterns, the great open field systems of medieval England.

## OPEN FIELDS

Across most of lowland medieval England, settlement land was divided up in such a way that while individuals grew and harvested their own crops, it was within a communal system. Each holding enjoyed, at least in theory, a fixed allocation of resources and rights: so much arable land, so much meadow, so many loads of wood, and so on. The most important feature of the system was that the whole of the settlement's arable land was organized in a single rotation, with one-third or one-half left uncropped (fallow) each year. That fallow was used as communal grazing land, as was the remainder of the arable land once the crops were cut. This system is known variously as the three- or (if half the land was left untilled) two-course rotation, or the open-field system – the latter name because each of the 'open' fields would have been entirely without visible internal boundaries: a prairie to rival anything in modern Norfolk. Another feature of arable farming in the Middle Ages, certainly in areas of heavier soils, was the ploughing of lands into ridges of between 5 m and 15 m in width. In a period without underdrainage, this was a deliberate technique to raise as much soil as possible into a relatively dry raised bed (ridge), separated from the next by a furrow that helped drain it. The technique produced whole landscapes of 'ridge and furrow' that in many parts of the countryside remained intact until relatively recently, when EEC policies encouraged farmers to plough up land that had been down to grass since the end of the Middle Ages and, incidentally, to erase these most tangible remnants of the medieval countryside.

The mapping of ridge and furrow, and comparison of those results with detailed surveys and field books compiled while the systems were in use, has done much to elucidate the origins and operation of the open fields. The most important work has been that of David Hall in Northamptonshire (Figure 14.6). This has shown how in the early Middle Ages, individuals' allotments of strips fell in a regular cycle (in other words, in a village of 32 households, every thirty-second strip belonged to the same tenant), and that those cycles can be related to eleventh-century fiscal returns. Another recent observation, made first in Yorkshire and later in the Midlands, is of evidence for what have been termed 'long lands'. These are individual strips that run for up to 2,000 m, sometimes right across townships, through and underneath what can be deduced to be later sub-divisions of the arable land into furlongs. These 'long lands' appear to represent the first stage of the great replanning of the countryside *c.* 900, and their discovery is very exciting.

To what extent this replanning of the countryside, embracing the creation of new villages and the reordering and reapportioning of large parts of the farming landscape (further reflected in the proliferation of charters with boundary clauses), required lordly coercion, rather than peasant co-operation or initiative, is unknown, although in a more hierachical and frequently taxed society there may have been many advantages in a tenantry where each had an equal share of the resources and each the same obligations. Glenn Foard has gone so far as to suggest a precise context for the

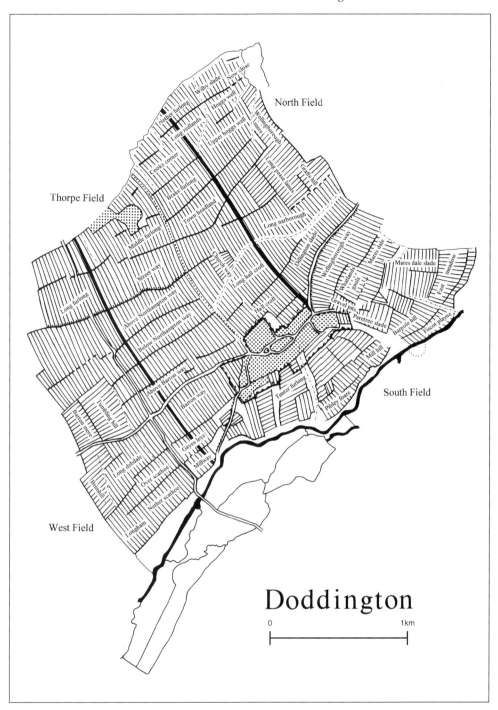

*Figure 14.6* The open fields of Doddington, Northamptonshire, reconstructed by David Hall from earthwork survey combined with documentary evidence. The arable lands seem originally to have been almost 1.6 km long; later they were divided into the much shorter, named, furlongs.
*Source*: David Hall

replanning: the imposition in the first half of the tenth century of a new local administrative organization following the reconquest of the Danelaw by Wessex. This established the hundred as the standard local unit of administration and the hide, nominally 48 ha, as the basic unit on which fiscal and military obligations were based. Newly divided up, the landscape then became 'a record in itself of dues; a regional imposition for national administrative purposes'. This revelation of a great replanning of the countryside in the late Saxon period, at least equal to that which followed the enclosures of a millennium later, is one of the great discoveries of British archaeology of the later twentieth century.

Just as methodological advances have led to a better understanding of the lowland agricultural landscapes of the Middle Ages, so they are likewise beginning to unravel the stone walled countryside of upland areas. At Roystone Grange, in the White Peak of Derbyshire, a multiperiod landscape criss-crossed with dry stone walls of various prehistoric to post-medieval dates, careful examination of wall types, and of their relationship to each other and to dated features and sites, has allowed the reconstruction of the local countryside at different times. One phase of walling, for instance, seems to relate to the establishment of a Cistercian grange – a monastic farm – at Roystone in the later twelfth century, while a later one apparently dates from the enclosure of the moorland *c*. 1600 (Hodges 1991, ch. 2). Similarly, work in the Lakeland valleys for the National Trust has been equally successful in identifying several phases of walling, which has in turn led to the ascription of functions to the different zones of field. The most significant type of wall, the head dykes or ring garths that run continuously along the valleys, separating the cultivated land from the rough pastures above, is now seen as having been established here in the eleventh or twelfth century.

## INDUSTRY

Over the last generation, a much better understanding of medieval industry has been arrived at, largely through the application of what may broadly be termed archaeological techniques, including, alongside excavation, the study of industrial landscapes and the scientific and technical studies of objects, by-products and residues (Blair and Ramsay 1991). With the iron industry, for instance (Geddes 1991), it can now be seen that by the twelfth century ore was having to be got via tunnels, trenches and bell pits, presumably because the easily available surface deposits had been worked out. While there were few changes in smelting techniques between the Romano-British period and the late Middle Ages, blast furnaces were introduced from abroad in the late fifteenth century. Newbridge, Sussex, is the earliest known; Henry VIII commissioned cast-iron ordnance from here in 1496, and within a short time the product range included domestic items such as firedogs, fire backs and tomb slabs. Water-powered forges, where a water wheel was used to drive bellows and hammers, appeared earlier, the first example being set up at Chingley, Kent, in the early fourteenth century. Archaeology has also shown, in excavations at Bordesley Abbey, Worcestershire, how water power was harnessed from the late twelfth century to provide power in a smithy housed in a mill equipped with wooden cogs and stone bearings (Astill 1993). While relatively few smithies have yet been excavated, the microscopic analysis of slags and hammer scales seems likely to enable a far fuller understanding both of the spatial organization within individual complexes and of the techniques employed there. The gradual advances in iron-working technologies were reflected in the ever-broader range of iron and steel goods manufactured, some advances at least being demand-led. The clergy, for instance, needed accurate time-keeping devices, and between 1280 and 1300 iron horologia begin to be mentioned; the earliest surviving example is that of 1386 in Salisbury Cathedral (Geddes 1991, 178–179).

One of the most interesting studies published to date that demonstrates something of the complex interrelationships between different industries, natural resources and human controls, has been that by Foard (1991) of the medieval pottery industries of Rockingham and Whittlewood forests, Northamptonshire. Here, in the twelfth and thirteenth centuries, what were two of the East Midlands' main pottery industries became concentrated in woodland villages, close to coppice woods that could supply fuel for the kilns. Not surprisingly, the distribution of the pottery industry in those forests broadly matches those of the similarly wood-dependent medieval iron- and charcoal-producing industries, in Rockingham concentrated around Stanion village and the Lyveden hamlets and in Whittlewood around the villages of Potterspury and Yardley Gobion (Figure 14.7). At a local level, however, distinct variations in the distribution can be seen. In Rockingham, it appears that the potters avoided (or were excluded from) those settlements where iron-working and charcoal burning were large-scale and well established – places such as Weldon, Fineshade and Corby – presumably because no coppice wood was available for a major new consumer. Foard has also observed that whereas the iron-working villages generally lay within the legally defined royal forest, the potters' villages lay outside, and that whereas iron production was centred primarily on royal manors, pottery manufacture generally took place on the lesser manors of other lords.

## TRANSPORT

One of the popular images of medieval Britain is of a land with quagmire roads and where communication was difficult. In fact, as documentary evidence of the movement of royal and other aristocratic households from one manor to another shows, that was not the case; Edward I's household, for instance, averaged 32 km a day when on the move (Hindle 1982, 10). While for bulky and weighty goods such as stone and timber, transportation by water was clearly preferred, with rivers and minor waterways utilized far more than later, study of the Lincolnshire limestone industry has demonstrated that carriage by road was perfectly feasible and the extra costs not prohibitive for major projects (Alexander 1995). Most essential to

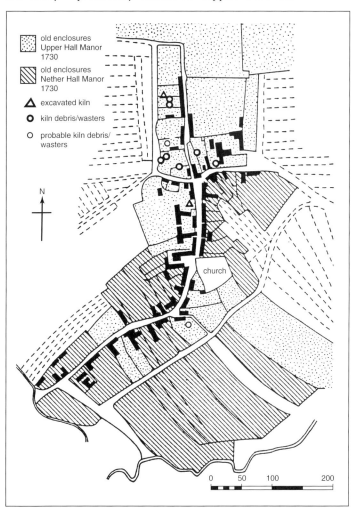

*Figure 14.7* Stanion, Northamptonshire, based on a map of 1730, showing how medieval industrial activity concentrated on Upper Hall Manor. *Source*: Foard 1991

*Figure 14.8* The timber piers of the great bridge built in the 1090s across the Trent at Hemington, Leicestershire. *Source*: Leicestershire Museums

the national transport network was the construction and maintenance of bridges at major river crossings. Numerous stone examples still survive, of course, while in the early 1990s dramatic evidence of bridge building was found at Hemington, Leicestershire, where gravel digging revealed three bridges that had succesively spanned the Trent between the eleventh and thirteenth centuries (Cooper *et al.* 1994) (Figure 14.8). Each was over 50 m long, the earlier two entirely of timber and the last supported on massive stone plinths 9.6 m in length.

At a local level, the study of patterns of communication in the post-Roman period is being used in a methodologically innovative study of the landscape around Yatesbury and Avebury, Wiltshire. Topographical, cartographic, documentary and archaeological evidence is here being used to dissect and date the pattern of Roman, Saxon and later roads, for once using the study of communications to provide the chronological and spatial frameworks for a broader study of the landscape, rather than as a dissociated or secondary venture.

## OVERVIEW

Over the last generation, excavation, fieldwork and documentary research – much, incidentally, undertaken by amateurs or by professionals in their holidays – has transformed our understanding of the medieval countryside. What has emerged is a picture not of a single countryside, fixed and unchanging, but of a landscape that was varied and dynamic, and at times highly sensitive to changing external circumstances. Population growth or contraction, expanding or declining market opportunities, climatic change, soil exhaustion, war, pestilence and famine, all at one time or another had an effect on housing and farming in Britain. Sometimes one of those things touched much, even if not all, of the country at the same time. At other times, the effect was more piecemeal, reflecting the wide variety of local farming and settlement regions that together made up medieval Britain. As work progresses, those regions will become more clearly defined and better understood; that is the challenge for the next generation of researchers.

## KEY TEXTS

Astill, G. and Grant, A., 1988. *The countryside of medieval England.* Oxford: Basil Blackwell.
Dyer, C., 1989. *Standards of living in the Middle Ages: social change in England c. 1200–1520.* Cambridge: Cambridge University Press.
Miller, E. and Hatcher, J., 1978. *Medieval England: rural society and economic change 1086–1348.* London: Longman.
Platt, C., 1978. *Medieval England: a social history and archaeology from the Conquest to A.D. 1600.* London: Routledge and Kegan Paul.
Taylor, C., 1983. *Village and farmstead: a history of rural settlement in England.* London: George Philip.

# BIBLIOGRAPHY

Alexander, J.S., 1995. 'Building Stone from the East Midland Quarries: Sources, Transportation and Usage', *Medieval Archaeology* 39, 107–135.

Astill, G., 1988. 'Rural Settlement: The Toft and the Croft', in Astill, G. and Grant, A. *The countryside of medieval England*. Oxford: Basil Blackwell, 36–61.

Astill, G., 1993. *A medieval industrial complex and its landscape: the metalworking, watermills and workshops of Bordesley Abbey*. London: Council for British Archaeology Research Report 92.

Aston, M., Austin, D. and Dyer, C., 1989. *The rural settlements of medieval England*. Oxford: Basil Blackwell.

Austin, D., 1985. 'Dartmoor and the upland village of the south-west of England' in Hooke, D. (ed.), *Medieval villages: a review of current work*. Oxford: Oxford Monograph 5, 71–77.

Bell, M., 1989. 'Environmental archaeology as an index of continuity and change in the medieval landscape', in Aston, M., Austin, D. and Dyer, C. (eds) *The rural settlements of medieval England*. Oxford: Basil Blackwell, 269–86.

Beresford, M. and Hurst, J.G., 1990. *Wharram Percy deserted medieval village*. London: Batsford.

Blair, J. and Ramsay, N. (eds) 1991. *English medieval industries*. London: Hambledon Press.

Cooper, L., Ripper, S. and Clay, P., 1994. 'The Hemington bridges', *Current Archaeology* 140, 316–321.

Dyer, C., 1986. 'English peasant buildings in the later Middle Ages', *Medieval Archaeology* 30, 19–45.

Dyer, C., 1995. 'Sheepcotes: evidence for medieval sheepfarming', *Medieval Archaeology* 39, 136–164.

Foard, G., 1991. 'The Medieval pottery industry of Rockingham Forest, Northamptonshire', *Medieval Ceramics* 15, 13–20.

Geddes, J., 1991. 'Iron', in Blair, J. and Ramsay, N. (eds) *English medieval industries*. London: Hambledon Press, 167–188.

Hindle, B. P., 1982. *Medieval roads*. Princes Risborough: Shire Books.

Hodges, R., 1991. *Wall-to-wall history. The story of Roystone Grange*. London: Duckworth.

Hurst, J. G., 1986. 'The medieval countryside', in Longworth, I. and Cherry, J. (eds) *Archaeology in Britain since 1945*. London: British Museum, 197–236.

Lewis, C., Mitchell-Fox, P. and Dyer, C., 1997. *Village, hamlet and field. Changing medieval settlements in central England*. Manchester: Manchester University Press.

Pearson, S., 1994. *The medieval houses of Kent: an historical analysis*. London: Royal Commission on the Historical monuments of England.

Platt, C., 1996. *King death: the Black Death and its aftermath in late medieval England*. London: UCL Press.

Roberts, B.K., 1987. *The making of the English village*. London: Longman.

Selkirk, A., 1997. 'Shapwick', *Current Archaeology* 151, 244–254.

Stamper, P.A., 1988. 'Woods and parks', in Astill, G. and Grant, A. *The countryside of medieval England*. Oxford: Basil Blackwell, 128–148.

Wrathmell, S., 1989. 'Peasant houses, farmsteads and villages in north-east England' in Aston, M., Austin, D. and Dyer, C. (eds) *The rural settlements of medieval England*. Oxford: Basil Blackwell, 247–267.

Yeoman, P., 1991. 'Medieval rural settlement: the invisible centuries', in Hanson, W.S. and Slater, E.A. (eds) *Scottish archaeology: new perceptions*. Aberdeen: Aberdeen University Press, 112–128.

Yeoman, P., 1995. *Medieval Scotland*. London: Batsford/Historic Scotland.

## Chapter Fifteen

# The historical geography of Britain from AD 1500

## Landscape and townscape

## Ian Whyte

### BACKGROUND

This chapter covers the period from *c.* 1500 until the start of the most rapid phase of industrialization around 1830. During this period, the British landscape was transformed dramatically. The most important background influences were the sustained growth of population following the post medieval decline, along with growing prosperity for at least some social groups. Between the sixteenth and nineteenth centuries, the population of England and Wales trebled, and in Scotland more than doubled. In the countryside, this encouraged the commercialization of agriculture, with wide-ranging implications for the rural landscape. In the towns, it generated growth and structural changes. Major developments occurred in the technology and scale of many industries, leading to the creation of new industrial landscapes and regions. All these changes influenced, and were in turn affected by, developments in transport. In 1500, society in England was predominantly rural with only *c.* 5 per cent of the population living in large towns. Wales and Scotland were even more lightly urbanized. By *c.* 1830, Britain was well on the way to becoming a society dominated by urban population and industry. The British landscape may be, as has often been claimed, a palimpsest, but it is a palimpsest dominated by post medieval features. It is impossible to present a full landscape history of such a complex period in a single chapter; attention will therefore focus on the main themes in landscape evolution, together with the various approaches that have been adopted in studying them.

### APPROACHES AND TECHNIQUES

The 40 years since the publication of W.G. Hoskins' classic work, *The Making of the English Landscape* (1955), have seen considerable advances in our understanding of how the British countryside changed from the sixteenth to the nineteenth century. There has been an upsurge of interest in industrial archaeology, and in post medieval archaeology in general (Crossley 1990; Rackham 1986; also Chapter 16). The Society for Post Medieval Archaeology was established in 1967, and the reviews of research in its journal demonstrate the range of current activity. Less work has been undertaken on the north of England compared with the south, less work on Wales and Scotland than for England (Whyte and Whyte 1991).

There has been a widespread belief that archaeological techniques, especially excavation, were inappropriate to a period for which historical sources were seemingly abundant and for which there were so many extant buildings and structures (Atkin and Howes 1993). Multiperiod landscape surveys still sometimes limit the study of the post medieval period, assuming that this can be studied from documentary sources. More recently, however, it has been appreciated that historical documents are silent on many aspects of society and economy after AD 1500. For instance, many industrial processes and the sites associated with them are not described in contemporary records and are only recoverable by means of field survey and excavation. Even as late as the eighteenth century, the volume and quality of surviving documentation diminishes as one moves from southern England northwards and becomes even more sparse for Scotland and Wales. Nevertheless, the late sixteenth century sees the period of detailed cartographic sources begin. Large-scale surveys become increasingly common, although full map coverage of the landscape was not achieved until the Ordnance Survey's 6-inch maps in the nineteenth century. In Scotland, however, estate plans are not common until the later eighteenth century.

Post medieval archaeology has tended to emphasize field survey and the examination of surviving structures rather than excavation. Partly this reflects lack of resources, but it also emphasizes the fact that landscape remains from this period are often abundant and readily identifiable. However, a post medieval dimension has been recognized in urban archaeology only relatively recently (Robertson 1990). Post medieval layers have often suffered considerable damage from nineteenth-century cellars and more recent construction. The preponderance of rescue excavations on urban sites with limited time and resources as well as deep stratigraphy has often led to the use of the JCB rather than the trowel as a means of removing inconvenient post medieval strata in order to reach medieval and Roman layers more quickly.

Until recently, the archaeology of the Industrial Revolution focused primarily on technology. Since the 1980s, there has been increasing interest on the broader social, economic and landscape effects of industrialization, such as the archaeology of navvy settlements associated with major construction projects (Morris 1994). Since the term 'industrial archaeology' was first coined in 1955, the subject has remained largely a part-time amateur interest, away from mainstream archaeology (Palmer 1990). Definitions of the chronological scope of archaeology often stop short at the start of the era of industrialization, and it has been argued that industrial archaeology will be assured of a significant role if, instead of being seen as a thematic topic, it is considered as a period discipline involving the archaeology of the industrial era and not just of industrial monuments.

## RURAL SETTLEMENT

Approaches to the study of post medieval settlement include the investigation of specific sites, the study of settlement landscapes and the analysis of broader aspects of settlement patterns. Settlement plans are sometimes treated as if they had evolved with only limited changes from their original form. The excavation of the deserted village at West Whelpington in Northumberland has demonstrated the change that could occur in settlement morphology (Evans and Jarrett 1987; 1988). Replanned from its original layout in the later fourteenth or early fifteenth century after destruction by the Scots, the village was subject to another reorganization with a reduced number of holdings *c.* 1675 before being abandoned in the 1720s. Change rather than stability may indeed be a characteristic feature of settlement layouts.

Settlement desertion has a range of underlying causes. Deserted villages have been recorded in every century from the twelfth to the twentieth. Cowlam is only one of a number of deserted settlements in the Yorkshire Wolds that was abandoned *c.* 1680 due to the amalgamation of its holdings (Brewster 1988). In Northumberland, the peak of desertions fell in the century between 1660 and 1760, as older gentry families were bought out by wealthy merchants and lawyers keen to make a profit on their investment. The eighteenth century saw the addition of industrial villages – textile settlements like Styal in Cheshire, mining and quarrying settlements. Settlement change in post medieval times was related to environmental changes as well as human activity. Parry's (1977) work in charting the progressive lowering of cultivation limits in south-east Scotland from the fourteenth to the eighteenth century, and the associated abandonment of field systems and settlements, linked to climatic deterioration, has yet to be followed up in other parts of Britain.

In Scotland, medieval or later rural settlements with their field systems form landscapes that cover extensive areas in the upland fringes and, in parts of the Highlands, at low level. The Royal Commission has undertaken important field surveys backed up by a limited amount of excavation (Hingley and Foster 1994). This has allowed some regional and chronological variations in building types to be established. The extensive nature and complexity of these landscapes make them highly distinctive within a north-west European context. In the West Highlands, Dodgshon (1993) has shown that the clachans (hamlet clusters) associated with runrig (open fields in fragmented occupation), which preceded the nineteenth-century crofting townships, were not the ancient settlement pattern that was once believed. They were preceded by an earlier dispersed settlement pattern associated with enclosed fields. The transition to runrig associated with clachans did not begin until late medieval times and was still incomplete in the eighteenth century.

Roberts and Wrathmell (1994) have mapped rural settlement characteristics for England based on the first edition of the 1-inch Ordnance Survey Map from the early and mid-nineteenth century. They have identified three broad settlement provinces: a central one with large numbers of nucleations; and two others to the south and east, and to the north and west with more dispersed settlement. These divisions fit broadly the champion/wood-pasture and ancient/planned countryside distinction that other landscape historians have identified. At a more local scale, Roberts has sub-divided each region on the basis of settlement, terrain and other variables.

In upland areas of the north and west, the practice of sending livestock to summer hill grazings, accompanied by part of the community who lived in temporary huts, survived into the seventeenth century or later. Shieling systems are recorded in Northumberland into the early seventeenth century, and the foundations of clusters of shieling huts can still be seen. In Wales, shielings in the Brecon Beacons may date from the same period. In the Scottish Highlands, shielings continued in widespread use until the later eighteenth century. Documentary sources and landscape evidence show that some temporary shielings were converted to permanent settlements in the seventeenth and eighteenth centuries under pressure of population (Bil 1990). The use of shielings over much of the Highlands ended with the introduction of commercial sheep farming, but in areas like Lewis, which were unsuited to sheep farming, shielings continued in use into the early twentieth century and still survive as upstanding structures rather than as grassed-over foundations (Figure 15.1).

## BUILDINGS AND STRUCTURES

Excavation of deserted settlements from late medieval and post medieval times is beginning to show that, even in northern England, peasant dwellings were often substantially built and long-lived. Impressions gained from Wharram Percy that late medieval and early modern peasant houses were flimsy affairs, built to last only a generation, may be misleading. The 'revolution' in housing that occurred from the Tudor period was, in some cases at least, more one of layout rather than construction standards. At West Whelpington, a change from timber-walled houses to ones with stone walls to eaves level occurred in the fifteenth and sixteenth centuries, possibly due to a lack of timber (Evans and Jarrett 1988). Such dwellings were built to last for centuries. On other sites, 'rebuilding' may have involved only repairs to non-load-bearing walls with the cruck frames still in place. Houses of this type may have required more regular maintenance than their successors with mortared stone walls and slate roofs but were not necessarily less durable. They were demolished in the eighteenth and nineteenth centuries not because they were no longer usable but because they could not be readily converted to accommodate current fashions in housing and rises in living standards.

Post medieval housing styles first appear in southern England before 1500, generated by profits from production for the London market and rents that lagged behind rising prices. Medieval halls were floored over and chimneys and staircases installed to provide greater privacy, comfort and warmth. Brick began to replace wattle and daub with timber

*Figure 15.1* Shieling huts, Lewis, Scotland, probably dating from the late nineteenth or early twentieth centuries. *Source*: I. Whyte

framing, while glass was used more extensively. Even within southern England there was a mosaic of rural economies, some of them less well integrated into the market than others, so that there can be distinct local variations in the timing of housing improvements. Regional variations in the evolution of peasant houses from medieval times onwards are still far from clear. In the North York Moors, for example, a sizeable group of modified longhouses survives, but in the Yorkshire Pennines, if such houses were common in medieval times, few now exist. Longhouse layouts continued, with upgraded standards of comfort in parts of England, such as Devon, into the eighteenth century, while laithe houses, with farmhouse and outbuildings constructed as a continuous range but without a common entrance, continued to be built in the Yorkshire Pennines and the Lancashire lowlands well into the nineteenth century.

The 'Great Rebuilding' of rural England, first identified by Hoskins, took a century or more to penetrate to many parts of northern England. In less prosperous areas, like Wales and especially Scotland, traditional housing styles and construction techniques remained in use through the eighteenth century and later. Many people continued to live with their animals in longhouses. Only gradually were such dwellings upgraded, with the byre being turned into storage accommodation. Upland Wales preserves many farmhouses that at their core have a converted longhouse. In Scotland, the change to better quality housing came only in the second half of the eighteenth century in the Lowlands, and the nineteenth century in the Highlands. In the Outer Hebrides, traditional 'black houses', typified by the surviving one at Arnol in Lewis, were occupied as late as the 1960s. Excavation is especially important in areas like northern England and Scotland, where housing standards were poorer and ordinary domestic buildings from the sixteenth, seventeenth and early eighteenth centuries have virtually disappeared from the landscape.

With the end of private warfare under the growing power of the Tudor state, country mansions began to replace medieval baronial castles. Excavation has played little part in the study of the evolution of English country houses, apart from vanished royal palaces like Nonsuch, Surrey, but, as with churches, there is much scope for the detailed survey of surviving structures. The shake-up in landholding with the Dissolution of the monasteries provided many gentry families with additional land and income. In some cases, the domestic buildings of monasteries were converted to secular uses; elsewhere they provided useful quarries for building stone. The country house and its surrounding parklands, emphasizing the control of great landowners over the

*Figure 15.2* Montacute House, Somerset; a fine example of a Tudor country house.
*Source*: I. Whyte

*Figure 15.3* Excavation of a sixteenth-seventeenth-century deserted bastle house and *fermtoun* site, Glenochar, upper Clydesdale.
*Source*: I. Whyte

countryside and its inhabitants, have come to epitomize the traditional English rural landscape (Figure 15.2). The distinctive, sometimes whimsical styles of the Tudor period with their exuberant decoration gave way to more sedate Jacobean and then to full classicism as the influence of Palladio spread. Inigo Jones, Surveyor of the King's Works from 1615, was the first architect to introduce the fully-fledged classical style to England. In the later seventeenth century, the taste for classical styles began to gather momentum, producing some monumental Baroque houses like Blenheim, Oxfordshire. In the first half of the eighteenth century, a more restrained Palladianism spread throughout Britain. By the later eighteenth century, the Gothic style was beginning to become popular. The houses of the gentry changed more slowly than those of the aristocracy. Many medieval moated sites continued in use, while hall houses with screens passages were still being built in southern England in the sixteenth century.

In the far north of England and in Lowland Scotland, fortified houses, ranging from baronial castles through tower houses to modest bastles, continued to be occupied and even constructed into the early seventeenth century. The study of late medieval Scottish castles has been dominated by architectural historians, and only recently have archaeologists started to make a contribution. Excavations at sites like Smailholm, Borders and Threave, Dumfries and Galloway have established that the modern appearance of such structures is misleading. They were not isolated structures but were accompanied by halls and ranges of service buildings (Tabraham 1988). Fortified bastle houses went out of use in Cumberland and Northumberland following the pacification of the Border after 1603. Recent surveys and excavations in upper Clydesdale have shown that such houses were more common in southern Scotland than has been supposed (Figure 15.3). In Scotland, they continued in use for another half century or more. The last Scottish tower house was completed as late as 1661. Some of the later Scottish fortified houses did, however, place as much emphasis on style and architectural embellishment as on defence, adapting French chateau features to Scottish layouts in a distinctive style that reaches its apogee in castles like Crathes (Figure 15.4) and Craigievar, Aberdeenshire. Following the Restoration, Scottish landowners began to convert their castles, remodelling irregular facades and adding more spacious accommodation blocks, as at Traquair House, Peeblesshire. By the end of the seventeenth century, the first classical mansions were being built in Scotland by Sir William Bruce. By the later eighteenth century, Scottish architects like Robert Adam were influencing the style of country houses south of the Border. During the eighteenth century, the new trends spread to the Highlands where the use of fortified houses continued until the Jacobite rebellion of 1745. From the 1740s, new-style mansions, such as Inveraray Castle, Argyll, began to appear in the Highlands.

Churches have been studied more for evidence of their origins and medieval development than for their post medieval history. Relatively little attention has been given to studying how they adapted to population change after 1500. In parts of northern England, where medieval parishes were huge, rapid population growth in the sixteenth and seventeenth centuries led to the splitting of parishes and the

*Figure 15.4* Crathes Castle, Aberdeenshire. A late sixteenth-early seventeenth-century Scottish fortified house.
*Source*: I. Whyte

establishment of new churches. In areas of rural depopulation, as at Wharram Percy, this period saw a contraction of the church, with aisles and side chapels being abandoned as parish population dropped. From the late seventeenth century, there was a rapid increase in the number of non-conformist chapels and meeting houses, a class of building that has only recently been the subject of serious research and which is particularly vulnerable to destruction and conversion.

Military architecture changed rapidly in the sixteenth and seventeenth centuries under the impact of artillery. Henry VIII's system of defences along the east and south coasts, begun in the late 1530s, was obsolete before it was finished, its round gun platforms, well seen at Camber Castle, Sussex, having been superseded by angled bastions. These were introduced in the earthwork forts constructed in Scotland during the campaigns of the late 1540s; the fort at Eyemouth, Berwickshire is the best preserved example. The new military technology was preserved more massively in the rebuilt defences of Berwick. Earthworks from the Civil War period, generally linked to sieges, have mostly been obliterated by urban expansion. Forts in the Scottish Highlands, designed to counter the Jacobite threat, have mostly disappeared. Only smaller outposts such as Ruthven Barracks and Glenelg, Highlands, have survived in anything like their original form. The ease with which Fort Augustus and Fort George, Inverness-shire, were captured during the 1745 Rebellion prompted the construction of a much larger and powerful Fort George east of Inverness. It survives intact as the best British example of an eighteenth-century artillery fortification.

## LANDSCAPE

Approaches to the study of landscape have been largely empirical and qualitative, with explanations usually grounded in economic change. From the sixteenth century, with the advent of more detailed written surveys and estate plans, it becomes possible to quantify rates of landscape change, measuring changes in elements like boundaries, field and holding sizes, and different categories of land use, but such approaches are still at a pioneer stage (Hunn 1994).

The pace of landscape change over much of England was continuous, though accelerating, from the sixteenth to the early nineteenth century. However, there were often sharp contrasts between adjacent parishes, some of which were enclosed in Tudor or Stuart times while others remained in open field until the early nineteenth century. In Lowland Scotland, the medieval landscape of scattered fermtouns and infield-outfield survived with only limited changes into the eighteenth century. Landscape change, beginning on the home farms of some estates in the later seventeenth century, continued through the first half of the eighteenth century but accelerated dramatically from the 1760s. The countryside in most parts of the Lowlands was transformed within two generations, leading to the observation that the Scottish rural landscape is one of revolution rather than evolution.

The greatest visual change in the British countryside between the sixteenth and the nineteenth centuries involved enclosure, with a shift from communal farming in open fields to individual decision making (Butlin 1982). By the end of our period, only a few open field systems were left, including the famous example at Laxton in Nottinghamshire. In the past, the emphasis of landscape change has been on Parliamentary Enclosure in the later eighteenth and early nineteenth centuries as part of a package of developments conventionally labelled the 'Agricultural Revolution'. More recently, it has been realized that enclosure in the sixteenth and seventeenth centuries, often piecemeal and poorly documented, was more important in changing the landscape in many areas. Unfortunately, while it is possible to estimate how much enclosure was accomplished before Parliamentary Enclosure, it is much harder to determine how much of this post dated 1500.

Although Tudor enclosure brought population displacement and social problems to parts of Lowland England, in other districts, such as Lancashire, Cumbria, and the Welsh borders, many open field systems, less extensive and less complex in their organization, were enclosed unobtrusively by private agreement, often over several generations (Porter 1980). Extensive areas in the Home Counties were enclosed early under the influence of the London market. In the later seventeenth and early eighteenth century, a similar process affected the country around the rapidly growing industrial area of Tyneside. The build-up of population during the sixteenth century encouraged the enclosure of land from waste by unauthorized squatting in some upland and wood pasture areas, producing patterns of small, irregular enclosures similar to medieval assarts (intakes from the waste), often easy to identify in the landscape but frequently difficult to date.

By the early seventeenth century, the government had dropped its opposition to enclosure. In succeeding decades, schemes proceeded more commonly by agreement than by the dictates of individual landowners. The seventeenth century also witnessed substantial reclamation of land, particularly in the Fens where some 142,000 ha of land were drained between the 1630s and 1670s. The Dutch engineers' work in digging a new channel for the Bedford River 21 m wide and 34 km long was a major engineering achievement. Shrinkage of the drying peat surface created drainage problems that were tackled by the construction of hundreds of windmills. There was also considerable reclamation of heathland and low-lying clay soils at this period. Another innovation, the floating of water meadows, has left many traces in the present landscape of counties like Dorset, Hampshire and Wiltshire.

The final phase of enclosure in England and Wales occurred from the mid-eighteenth century to the early nineteenth, with four-fifths of the activity concentrated into short bursts in the 1760s and 1770s, and during the French wars from 1793 to 1815. Estimates of the amount of land involved run to as much as 2.73 million ha of common field arable. This amounts to some 21 per cent of England, a huge area that nevertheless emphasizes how much enclosure had already taken place, much of it in the sixteenth and seventeenth centuries. Parliamentary Enclosure of upland waste changed the landscapes of many parts of northern and western England, with regular fields on the fellsides bounded by stone walls contrasting with the smaller, irregular pattern of earlier enclosures in the valleys. Some 0.9 million ha were involved. Although Parliamentary Enclosure acts operated at the level of the individual parish, the use of standardized procedures for surveying the ground and marking out the new allotments produced a distinctive uniformity of landscape, with square and rectangular fields bounded by hawthorn hedges and wide, straight access roads. As new compact farms replaced fragmented, open field holdings, farmsteads located in villages were moved out to the new compact holdings. The landscape of thousands of parishes was transformed within five years or so. Sometimes, however, Parliamentary Enclosure followed the boundaries of the former open field strips, preserving their gentle reverse-S shaped curves in the modern field pattern (Turner 1980).

Between 1660 and 1695, the Scottish Parliament passed a series of acts encouraging estate improvement, particularly enclosure and the division of commonties, pastures in shared ownership between two or more landowners. The face of the countryside was transformed by the new, rational planned landscapes. New farmsteads of superior design were built. Planned estate villages, acting as local market centres and foci for rural industry, were established in large numbers. The old farming system, even in the most fertile parts of Lowland Scotland, had included much uncultivated land. With improvement, much additional land was brought under cultivation, especially on the divided commonties, while reclamation of lowland peat bogs, as in the Carse of Stirling, also had a great impact on the landscape.

In the southern and eastern Highlands, agricultural improvement and landscape change began earlier in the eighteenth century and proceeded more gradually than further north, creating a balanced farming system with larger farms and smaller crofts. Surplus population readily found work in nearby Lowland towns. In the far north and west, however, change came later and more catastrophically. The traditional farming system began to intensify under the impact of population pressure from the sixteenth century onwards, leading in some areas to the abandonment of plough cultivation in favour of hand tillage. The clearance of people from interior glens to make way for the new sheep farms led to the creation of planned crofting townships on the coast, frequently using land that had not previously been cultivated. The geometric layout of crofting townships, sometimes involving the realignment of existing runrig touns on the same ground but in other instances laid out fresh, are still a prominent feature of the landscape of the Hebrides and the West Highlands (Whyte and Whyte 1991).

In the early nineteenth century, high grain prices encouraged an expansion of cultivation throughout Britain. Straight ridge and furrow in moorland and upland fringe areas often marks this phase of temporary, opportunist cropping. Much land remained in cultivation through to the mid-nineteenth century. During this period of 'high farming', there was tremendous investment in land improvement, including undersoil drainage, along with the construction of new architect-designed steadings and improved farm workers' cottages on many estates, a legacy that is still evident in the landscape today.

From the sixteenth century to the nineteenth, there was an evolution in the appearance of the parks surrounding country houses (Currie and Locock 1993). Before the mid sixteenth-century,

*Figure 15.5* Garden and landscaped park, Mellerstain, Scottish Borders.
*Source*: I. Whyte

gardens had been small, often walled, incorporated into courtyard layouts or within defensive perimeters. From the reign of Henry VIII, these gave way to formal gardens on a far grander scale (Figure 15.5), while parks began to be developed in more diverse ways than merely as deer sanctuaries. While many medieval parks disappeared and were converted to agricultural uses, new ones were laid out on some estates, often with profound consequences for the local population as well as the landscape. The creation of landscaped parks sometimes involved the removal and rebuilding of entire villages. In the later seventeenth century, British gardens were influenced by those at Versailles; by the early eighteenth century, French influences were considered unpatriotic and went out of favour. Less formal garden designs became fashionable, under the influence of ideas regarding the picturesque, with a wealth of temples, grottoes and statues. The work of Capability Brown represented a reaction against this fussiness with his use of grass, trees and water on a sweeping scale. Although his ideas dominated the second half of the eighteenth century, they gave way to a greater emphasis on the formal once more under Humphry Repton and the creation of more varied scenes with the introduction of exotic trees and plants. Aerial and ground survey as well as excavation have identified a range of earthwork features associated with gardens (Daniels and Seymour 1990).

## INDUSTRY

Although industry is traditionally considered separately from agriculture, it is important to appreciate that for much of the period under consideration agriculture and industry were closely related, complementary rather than competing elements of a dual economy in a predominantly rural landscape. In 1500, most industry was small in scale, operating at the level of the individual workshop or craftsman, and widely dispersed, although textile manufacture, mining and ironworking had more marked concentrations. Population growth led to unrestricted squatting on waste land in many parts of northern England, with smallholders spinning and weaving cloth as an adjunct to subsistence agriculture. This produced the densely settled landscape of small farms and thickly scattered weavers' cottages that is a feature of many parts of the southern Pennines, such as the area around Haworth, West Yorkshire.

The iron industry, centred on the Weald in south-east England, still used primitive bloomery forges in the early sixteenth century. The introduction of the blast furnace, used first in the Weald at the very end of the fifteenth century and only spreading to areas like south Wales and Shropshire by the 1560s, involved an increase in the scale of operations and required a more careful choice of site. As the available charcoal resources, produced from carefully managed coppice woodlands, became inadequate to support further growth in the Weald, the industry moved to more remote areas like the West Midlands, the Forest of Dean, south Wales and Furness.

Mining for non-ferrous metals affected the landscape of many upland areas. In the sixteenth and early seventeenth centuries, mining technology was relatively simple, with veins being worked by levels or open stopes. Ore was crushed by hand. Much of this early working has been obliterated by later developments. In addition, it can be difficult to distinguish genuinely old workings from later small-scale trials. Improved drainage equipment using horse- and water-power allowed deeper working during the seventeenth and eighteenth centuries, while these power sources were also applied to crushing machinery. A feature of remote mining areas was the continued reliance on water power because of the expense of importing coal. Surviving waterwheels like the one at Killhope in Weardale, the water-bucket pumping engine at Wanlockhead, Dumfries and Galloway, and the remains of complicated systems of sluices at Coniston, Cumbria, are a testimony to the ingenuity of engineers in husbanding the limited water power resources of these high-lying areas. Cornish tin mining began to be steam powered early in the eighteenth century because of the ease with which coal could be brought from South Wales. The chimneys and engine houses associated with Cornish tin mines remain a powerful image in the landscape today (Figure 15.6). Prospecting using the technique of hushing – constructing artificial reservoirs high up

*Figure 15.6* Engine house of tin mine, Helston, Cornwall.
*Source*: I. Whyte

on hillsides and then releasing the water in a flood to strip off the topsoil and expose potential veins – scarred many hillsides in upland mining areas, while the fumes from lead and copper smelters blighted the soil and killed the vegetation. Later smelters were constructed with long flues leading to distant hilltop chimneys, to take the poisonous fumes as far from settlements as possible. The peak of production in many upland mining areas was reached in the mid nineteenth-century before a catastrophic fall in prices due to the opening up of large overseas ore deposits caused rapid contraction.

Coal mining also remained small scale and widely scattered until well into the nineteenth century, though deeper mining, requiring more sophisticated drainage, ventilation and winding technology, was being undertaken on some sites from the seventeenth century. Early mining by levels and shallow bell pits has mostly been obliterated in the main coalfields but is sometimes exposed in section with modern opencast extraction. Remains of early coal mining survive where the landscape has been protected, as in estate parks or in remote locations where the seams were too thin to be worth working in later times.

The lime industry also grew with increasing demand not only for the building trade but for agricultural use. Simple clamp kilns covered in turf leaving rings of stones or low mounds gave way to more sophisticated draw kilns where coal and lime could be fed in continuously. Many small kilns in field corners in areas like the Yorkshire Dales are associated with the enclosure of waste and the expansion of cultivation in the eighteenth and nineteenth centuries.

The need of industries for water power continued to attract them to remote, sometimes upland, locations where suitable water resources were available. The eighteenth century saw important developments in the efficiency of water-powered machinery; late eighteenth-century county maps and early Ordnance Survey maps show the tremendous density of water power sites in areas like the Pennine valleys and the southern Lake District, and the remains of many small mills with their weirs and lades may still be found on the ground. The first true factories, like Arkwright's mill at Cromford in Derbyshire, built in 1771, were sited primarily for access to water power. Such remote communities had to be self-sufficient with shops and other facilities, while industrialists had to provide good quality housing at reasonable rents to attract and retain workers, a tradition creating 'model' communities like New Lanark, Lanarkshire, and Styal, Cheshire. Only gradually did the development of steam power start to draw industry on to the coalfields and into the larger towns.

In the sixteenth and seventeenth centuries quarrying had been a widespread, small-scale activity, poorly documented and, as yet, little studied. As the demand for building stone became more specialized, the industry became more localized. Rapid urban growth created a huge demand for building materials. Roofing slate from the West Highlands, the Lake District and, above all, north Wales came to dominate, with flagstones from the Pennines and Caithness. Portland stone was a prestige material for London builders. Granite, especially valued for heavy-duty structures like piers and lighthouses as well as for its ornamental value, was quarried on a large scale only from the nineteenth century, when steam-powered cutting equipment was developed. In Cornwall, the mining of china clay gave rise to one of the most distinctive landscapes associated with mineral extraction.

## TRANSPORT

Transport developments were also a powerful force for landscape change. Road transport remained essentially medieval in character until the later seventeenth century and beyond, with roads mostly worn by use rather than deliberately constructed. The statute labour system, instituted in 1555, was largely ineffective. In upland areas, transport was mainly by pack horse. Narrow pack horse tracks with laid cobbles were constructed in the Pennines, Lake District and Wales. Narrow pack horse bridges with low parapets were built while many medieval bridges remained in service.

The great era of turnpike (toll road) construction occurred in the later eighteenth and early nineteenth centuries. The roads that were improved or realigned at this time still form the basis of the modern A and B road network in most parts of Britain. Not every turnpike was well aligned, well constructed or well maintained, but overall they were a tremendous improvement, allowing faster, easier and cheaper movement of people and goods, including bulky items like coal, and generating a great increase in traffic. While the roads themselves have been upgraded, the milestones and toll houses, often with a characteristic 'house style' peculiar to individual turnpike trusts, are still prominent landscape features. Even more pronounced is the legacy of bridges from the eighteenth and nineteenth centuries, many still carrying today's traffic without alteration. The droving of cattle from Wales, northern England and as far away as the Western Highlands to London and the industrial towns of England reached its peak in the late eighteenth and early nineteenth centuries. The drove roads that they used kept to high ground as far as possible and remain a prominent feature of Britain's upland areas today. The stances where drovers rested their herds each night were often provided with alehouses, some of which survive today as remote Pennine inns. The droving trade declined rapidly in the 1840s with the establishment of a national railway network.

In the later eighteenth century, canals transformed the landscape even more profoundly than turnpikes (Ransom 1984). The earliest canals developed out of schemes to improve navigible rivers by dredging and installing locks to regulate and raise water levels. Canals like the Sankey Navigation, designed to supply coal to Liverpool, for which an act was passed in 1755, had a specific purpose but soon became used by more general traffic. The scale of new engineering works associated with canal construction was first evident in the Bridgwater canal, completed in 1761, designed to bring coal from the third Duke of Bridgwater's mines at Worsley into Manchester.

**Figure 15.7** Mullion Cove, Cornwall, typical of many small British harbours from pre-industrial times.
*Source*: I. Whyte

By the end of the century, trans-Pennine canals like the Huddersfield, Leeds–Liverpool and Rochdale canals were tackling gradients using flights of locks and long tunnels, while elsewhere steam-powered inclined planes and vertical lifts were used.

Railways had antecedents stretching back at least as far as canals. By the late seventeenth century, colliery tramways were becoming common on Tyneside. In the early nineteenth century, the extension of some of these tramway systems and a broadening of their role to include carrying general freight and passengers demonstrated that they could be competitive with other forms of transport even without steam locomotion (Ransom 1984). Extensive tramway systems were developed in the early nineteenth century in some areas like Brecon Forest, linking coal and iron deposits and encouraging agricultural improvement. However, the introduction of more effective steam locomotives in the later 1820s and 1830s encouraged the first true railways. The opening of the Liverpool–Manchester line in 1830, primarily to carry passengers, was a major landmark. By the end of the 1840s, a national railway network was beginning to take shape with almost every major town in England connected to the railway and two lines linking England and Scotland. The impact on the landscape, with cuttings, tunnels and bridges, was even more dramatic than that of the canals because of the much greater mileage involved. They created a number of new urban centres at important junctions such as Crewe and Swindon. They also caused profound changes in existing towns, as the construction of lines, sidings and stations with associated railway hotels required the demolition of huge areas of property including many historic buildings as well as large areas of slums.

Over the same period, marine transport was also transformed. Excavation has made only a limited contribution to the study of harbour developments. The development of Britain's major ports has been relatively well chronicled but there is still much research to do into the history – and the physical remains – of a great many small ports (Jackson 1983; Figure 15.7). Sequences of harbour developments can be best seen on difficult estuaries like the Lune or the Tay where growth of trade and increases in the size of vessels forced the construction of successive harbours further and further downstream (Bowler and Catchart 1994).

## TOWNSCAPES

Urban archaeology has made great advances in the last 30 years, but much of the effort has gone into the search for the Roman origins and medieval development of towns rather than their post medieval features (Crossley 1990). Few excavations have been directed specifically at post medieval sites and problems. The predominance of rescue excavations in urban archaeology has made it difficult to devise proper research strategies. Excavation has often been piecemeal, involving part of a building plot or even merely part of a building. Nineteenth-century cellars have sometimes destroyed all levels above the medieval ones. Excavation has tended to focus on the tails of burgage plots rather than on street frontages, and many finds have come from pits rather than from structures, their origins not easily attributed. In towns like Norwich, a change in the way in which rubbish was disposed from the mid-seventeenth century, with disposal in the suburbs, has led to a paucity of artefacts in later levels (Ayres 1991).

As with the countryside, new sources become available from the sixteenth century for studying the evolution of townscapes. Bird's eye views start to provide valuable information on townscapes from the later sixteenth century, while increasingly accurate and detailed town maps and plans were produced from the seventeenth century.

In 1500, towns throughout Britain were still suffering from the long period of decline and decay that had affected them throughout late medieval times. They remained small, within their medieval boundaries, often with ruined buildings and reduced populations testifying to their lack of trade and industry. In England, the sixteenth century saw the start of a massive phase of urbanization that was to transform towns and, on a wider scale, the entire countryside. In 1550, only 3.5 per cent of the population of England and Wales lived in towns of over 10,000 inhabitants. By 1600, this figure had risen to 5.8 per cent, by 1700 to 13.3 per cent and by 1800 to over 20 per cent. In Scotland, urban growth started from a lower baseline but had reached almost the same level as England by the early nineteenth century, although the growth of large towns represents only the tip of the iceberg. Population growth in the later sixteenth century also affected many medium-sized towns and smaller market centres. However, there was considerable variation when particular towns began to expand and change. Infilling of the existing built up area was often gradual. York still retained a considerable amount of open space within its medieval walls into the nineteenth century.

The growth of urban population in the sixteenth and seventeenth centuries did not necessarily involve physical expansion. The bird's eye views of English county towns drawn by John Speed *c.* 1610 show that there was plenty of space within the existing medieval limits to be infilled. Most of London's huge population increase in the sixteenth and early seventeenth centuries was accommodated by intensified construction within the existing built up area (Thompson *et al.* 1984). Urban growth occurred by the expansion of suburbs, by the colonization of streets and market areas and by the intensification of development on existing building plots. The increasingly tight packing of working-class housing into the tails of burgage plots behind street frontages led to severe overcrowding with problems of water supply and waste disposal, eventually producing some of the worst slum housing – court dwellings and back to backs – of the Industrial Revolution, bad enough in small towns, awful in larger ones like Manchester.

The Reformation often produced major townscape changes. In Gloucester, *c.* 16 per cent of the medieval town was occupied by friaries and the abbey. Following the Dissolution, their buildings were converted to residential and industrial uses, although Anglican cathedral closes developed as distinct enclaves in many towns. Almshouses, hospitals and other charitable foundations replaced the charity formerly provided by the Church, while increasing civic pride led to the construction or rebuilding of guild halls, town halls and market halls. The discovery and excavation of the Rose

Theatre and part of Shakespeare's Globe has added a major new dimension to our understanding of Elizabethan theatre. The debate over the preservation of the remains of the Rose Theatre generated a lot of media attention and helped to give urban archaeology, especially post medieval archaeology, a higher public profile (Orrell and Gurr 1989). At a later date, coaching inns, with their high arches and courtyards, were another addition to the urban scene.

The 'Great Rebuilding' in the English countryside had its urban counterpart. The evolution of urban housing styles closely paralleled those in the countryside, with modifications to allow for more cramped sites. In many English county and market towns, the later sixteenth and seventeenth centuries saw a move from timber frame with wattle and daub towards the use of brick and stone. This reflected growing prosperity but also in some cases rebuilding in more fireproof materials after major conflagrations. In Scotland, population pressure and shortage of space on a physically cramped site led to the replacement of timber-frame houses by stone tenements in Edinburgh during the early seventeenth century. Tenement housing was found in Glasgow and Dundee too at this period, while flatted housing was also a feature of St Andrews and other small Fife burghs where pressure on space was much less. It may reflect a different housing tradition with an acceptance, in a generally poorer country, of lower housing standards.

As with the post medieval countryside, far more is known about the housing conditions of wealthier urban dwellers than those in the poorest social groups. In the sixteenth and seventeenth centuries, towns had distinctive social areas, with wealthier residents living in central locations and much of the poorer population living in peripheral areas. At a smaller scale, occupational groups were often located in distinct clusters. Urban housing continued in an essentially vernacular style well into the seventeenth century, with buildings designed individually rather than as part of larger schemes (Crossley 1990). Influences in urban planning began to reach England in the early seventeenth century. Inigo Jones' Covent Garden, a square with houses on three sides designed with uniform facades, the first true urban residential square in Britain, was built from 1630, the first of many such developments in London. New residential developments in the capital began to spread westwards in the later seventeenth century: the Earl of Southampton laid out Bloomsbury Square in 1661 and many others followed. Most of the late seventeenth- and early eighteenth-century squares in London were built piecemeal, although general building guidelines were imposed. Progress continued through the eighteenth century, with Bedford Square, *c.* 1775, being the best preserved of London's Georgian squares. Under the patronage of George IV, as regent and king, John Nash designed or refashioned parks, palaces, squares and streets into a brilliant sequence from Regent's Park to Buckingham Palace. Regent's Park itself was laid out as a garden suburb, dotted with isolated villas.

Similar developments spread to provincial towns as landowners began to appreciate the profitability of releasing land for speculative building. If work transformed much of the British landscape in the eighteenth and nineteenth centuries, leisure also made its contribution. Spa centres such as Bath and Tunbridge Wells began to develop from the later seventeenth century when continental ideas concerning the efficacy of taking spring water as a cure became popular, creating new centres and adding a new function to existing ones. In the early eighteenth century, Bath in particular became fashionable. The work of John Wood, father and son, from 1727 turned it into one of the finest towns in Europe. In Queen Square, started in 1729, the houses were treated on a monumental scale, with whole sides designed with palace facades. Royal Circus, begun in 1754, was the first circular space in British town planning. Royal Crescent, from *c.* 1770, made striking use of a hillside site (Figure 15.8). In the later eighteenth and early nineteenth centuries, dozens of squares and crescents were built in other British towns, though rarely on the scale of Bath. The New Town of Edinburgh, begun in the 1750s, was an exception. The fragmented pattern of freeholds around many towns sometimes defeated grandiose schemes.

*Figure 15.8* Royal Crescent, Bath: classical urban symmetry.
*Source*: I. Whyte

The crescent at Buxton, Derbyshire, demonstrates the effect of new urban design on a smaller centre. Sea bathing also had its attractions: Scarborough developed from the early eighteenth century, and royal patronage encouraged the development of Brighton and Weymouth in the late eighteenth century, by which time Blackpool was just beginning to achieve local prominence as a summer resort.

The development of industrial towns in the late eighteenth and early nineteenth centuries was often, by contrast, unplanned and piecemeal. In areas like south Wales and Lancashire, new towns mushroomed from nothing within a few years. Factory owners still often lived close to their workers but only a few laid out planned housing developments for them, like Sir John Morris, the copper magnate, at Morriston near Swansea from *c.* 1793.

## CONCLUSION

Despite limitations of space, it is hoped that this chapter has been able to convey the sheer range and vitality of the changes that occurred in landscapes and townscapes during a period that has often been written off as a mere appendage to the concerns of 'proper' archaeology. In future, the application of archaeological approaches and techniques to the remains of the early modern period and even the industrial era seems more assured. Increasing interest in Britain's industrial past, witnessed by heritage attractions and industrial museums, should help to place archaeology within this period on a firmer footing, a trend already evident in the work of many archaeological research and rescue units.

### Key texts

Crossley, D., 1990. *Post medieval archaeology in Britain*. Leicester: Leicester University Press.
Dodgshon, R.A. and Butlin, R.A. (eds) 1990. *An historical geography of England and Wales*. London: Academic Press. 2 edn.
Hoskins, W.G., 1955. *The making of the English landscape*. London: Hodder.
Rackham, O., 1986. *The History of the countryside*. London: Dent.
Whyte, I.D. and Whyte, K.A., 1991. *Scotland's changing landscape 1500–1800*. London: Routledge.

### Bibliography

Atkin, M. and Howes, R., 1993. 'The use of archaeology and documentary sources in identifying the Civil War defences of Gloucester', *Post Medieval Archaeology* 27, 15–42.
Ayres, B., 1991. 'Post medieval archaeology in Norwich: a review', *Post Medieval Archaeology* 25, 1–24.
Bil, A., 1990. *The shieling 1600–1840. The case of the central Scottish Highlands*. Edinburgh: John Donald.
Bowler, D. and Catchart, R., 1994. 'Tay Street, Perth: the excavation of an early harbour site', *Proceedings of the Society of Antiquaries of Scotland* 124, 467–489.

Brewster, T.C.M., 1988. 'Cowlam deserted village: a case study of post medieval desertion', *Post Medieval Archaeology* 27, 21–109.

Butlin, R.A., 1982. *The transformation of rural England c. 1580–1800.* Oxford: Oxford University Press.

Currie, C.K. and Locock, M., 1993. 'Excavations at Castle Bromwich Hall gardens', *Post Medieval Archaeology* 27, 111–199.

Daniels, S. and Seymour, S., 1990. 'Landscape design and the idea of improvement 1730–1900', in Dodgshon, R.A. and Butlin, R.A. (eds) *An historical geography of England and Wales.* London: Academic Press. 487–520.

Dodgshon, R.A., 1993. 'West Highland and Hebridean settlement prior to crofting and the Clearances', *Proceedings of the Society of Antiquaries of Scotland* 123, 419–439.

Evans, D.H. and Jarrett, M.G., 1987. 'The deserted village of West Whelpington, Northumberland, part 1', *Archaeologia Aeliana* 15, 199–308.

Evans, D.H. and Jarrett, M.G., 1988. 'The deserted village of West Whelpington, Northumberland, part 2', *Archaeologia Aeliana* 16, 139–192.

Hingley, R. and Foster, S. (eds) 1994. *Medieval or later rural settlement in Scotland.* = Medieval Settlement Research Group Report 9. Edinburgh: Historic Scotland.

Hunn, J.R., 1994. *Reconstruction and measurement of landscape change. A case study of six parishes in the St. Albans area.* Oxford: British Archaeological Reports 236.

Jackson, G., 1983. *The history and archaeology of ports.* London: World's Work.

Morris, S.M., 1994. 'Towards an archaeology of navvy huts and settlements', *Antiquity* 68, 573–584.

Orrell, J. and Gurr, A., 1989. 'What the Rose can tell us', *Antiquity* 63, 421–429.

Palmer, M., 1990. 'Industrial archaeology: a thematic or a period discipline?', *Antiquity* 64, 275–285.

Parry, M.L., 1977. *Climatic change, agriculture and settlement.* Folkestone: Dawson.

Porter, J., 1980. *The making of the central Pennines,* Ashbourne: Moorland.

Ransom, P.J.C., 1984. *The archaeology of the transport revolution 1750–1850,* London: World's Work.

Roberts, B.K. and Wrathmell, S., 1994. 'The monuments protection programme: medieval settlements programme', in Hingley, R. and Foster, S. (eds) *Medieval of later rural settlement in Scotland.* = Medieval Settlement Research Group Report 9, 12–16.

Robertson, J.C., 1990. 'Moving on from holes and corners: recent currents in urban archaeology', *Urban History* 20, 1–13.

Tabraham, C.J., 1988. 'The Scottish medieval towerhouse as lordly residence in the light of recent excavations', *Proceedings of the Society of Antiquaries of Scotland* 118, 267–276.

Thompson, A., Grew, F. and Schofield, J., 1984. 'Excavations at Aldgate 1974', *Post Medieval Archaeology* 18, 1–148.

Turner, M., 1980. *English parliamentary enclosure.* Folkestone: Dawson.

*Chapter Sixteen*

# The workshop of the world

## The industrial revolution

## Kate Clark

### THE INDUSTRIAL REVOLUTION AND INDUSTRIAL ARCHAEOLOGY

The industrial revolution, and its causes, is a topic engraved on the heart of every schoolchild. The great takeoff into sustained growth, during which Britain was transformed from a sleepy agricultural economy into the first industrial nation, has been a topic of endless fascination, not least to those economists interested in finding out how other nations might undergo a similar transformation, or how Britain might reverse its current decline. Studies of the industrial revolution have in general been dominated by economic historians whose primary interest is large-scale, macro-economic transformations based on statistical measures of economic indices. Only recently have social historians and historical geographers begun to look more closely at the idea, asking not only whether or not a revolution took place, but also whether small-scale social, domestic or local sources of evidence might not be as useful a source as macro-economic indicators.

Archaeology, unfortunately, has played a relatively minor role in this debate, perhaps because the subject is by its nature empirical and local and therefore unfashionable, or perhaps because in its early stages the archaeology of the industrial period, whose serious study is a very recent phenomenon, has been more concerned with identifying sites than considering the wider historical implications of the data (Clark 1987). It is probable that as mainstream archaeology focuses on these later periods, it will contribute to the wider study of the industrial revolution.

### The nature of the industrial revolution

Few historians agree on the dating, origin, causes and nature of the industrial revolution, but most would accept that during the period between the middle of the eighteenth century and perhaps the second quarter of the nineteenth century, Britain underwent an economic and social transformation.

Agricultural output per hectare increased, as did the amount of land in cultivation; the first was as a result of changes in methods of husbandry and crop rotation, the latter following enclosure of the former open-field system. Coal replaced wood as a fuel, and steam replaced water as the predominant source of power for industry, making possible manufacturing on a much greater scale than had hitherto been viable. A 'wave of gadgets', as the historian T.S. Ashton has called it, swept Britain, with innovations in the manufacture of textiles, in the construction of canals, in iron smelting and puddling, in the use of iron in construction, the manufacture of porcelain and the introduction of the rotative engine. Many of these increased the gap between what could be achieved mechanically and what could be achieved by an individual alone. The factory system replaced more traditional forms of working, as people were brought together into single workplaces. Towns grew as population moved from the countryside to work in the new factories, but also as the population itself increased. Real income *per capita* grew, as self-sufficiency diminished, and people relied more upon obtaining food and consumer goods from others.

Britain sought and exploited new overseas markets throughout Europe, Africa, America and the Far East, becoming a major world trading power. Profits from this, and the notorious triangular trade between Britain, Africa and the Caribbean, provided capital for investment as well as new industrial opportunities for processing raw materials for re-export. London became the financial centre of the world, and capital was diverted into industrial enterprises.

In Britain, the landscape was transformed by the pattern of enclosure and by massive increases in the exploitation of raw materials, leaving great scars across the countryside, whilst in towns, houses were built for the newly industrialized workforce, and factories, warehouses and other industrial buildings added whole new quarters to what had been small market towns. The focus of settlement moved from the south and east, to the north and Midlands, and the population grew, perhaps as a result of changing marriage patterns or more likely falling death rates due to improved health. Transport of goods and people became easier as the roads were turnpiked and straightened, the navigable reaches of rivers were linked by a network of canals, and the beginnings of the railway system were laid down (see Chapter 15).

Accompanying all this physical change were alterations in the financial and political institutions of Britain, in the role of the State, the nature of capital and banking, and in the system of privileges and monopolies that had dominated trade.

There is no single agreed date for either the beginning or the end of this process – the start of the process is variously placed in the mid-sixteenth century, in 1750 or in the early 1780s as the point at which statistical indicators move significantly upwards; at the other end there is even less agreement on whether one cuts off in 1802, marking the end of a major watershed, or extends the process through the nineteenth century when sectors such as brick-making were finally mechanized.

## Interpretative models of the industrial revolution

The following is a sweeping and fairly conventional version of a complex process. Historians have many different views on why this transformation took place, and indeed whether it was quite such a transformation as the history books might suggest (Hudson 1992).

Early nineteenth-century observers were aware of the way in which society was changing; whilst some were impressed by the ingenious machinery and the personalities of the great inventors, others were worried by working-class organization and the atmosphere of distrust between workers and capitalists that had grown out of the appalling conditions accompanying industrialization. The idea of a 'revolution' came from French writers at the end of the eighteenth century, who themselves had seen extraordinary changes in their own society, and was perhaps best formalized in English history by Arnold Toynbee in his *Lectures on the Industrial Revolution* in 1884, outlining the basic model of economic transformation set out above.

This interpretation was questioned during the 1930s, when writers such as J.U. Nef, looking at the coal industry, saw a more evolutionary process at work, recognizing that it was necessary to look back into the sixteenth and seventeenth centuries in order to understand the changes of the eighteenth. Coal was already replacing wood as fuel in a range of manufactures in the sixteenth century, and the transport systems, mining techniques and capital formation that accompanied the growth in coal production were essential preconditions for later industrialization. Others writing during the Depression saw the industrial revolution as one wave in a pattern of economic cycles, whereas in the more optimistic 1950s, writers such as Rostow identified the preconditions for growth that he hoped might be applied to the economies of other developing nations. Against this view, others saw industrialization as something that was a product of exploitation, with Britain succeeding only at the expense of the economies of dependent states. Subsequently, dynamic entrepreneurs, technological innovation and capital formation have all been identified as prime movers in precipitating change. Underlying all of this was a search for the causes of the industrial revolution.

In contrast with this approach, social historians have looked at small-scale, local changes, and feminists such as Maxine Berg have paid more attention to the role of domestic organization and women's working patterns. In a period of industrial decline, more pessimistic historians have seen the industrial revolution as a 'limited, restricted piecemeal phenomenon in which various things did not happen or where they did, they had far less effect than was previously supposed', although the information revolution has brought a new fascination with the impact of technological change (Hudson 1992, 37). Historical geographers have borrowed heavily from social theory when looking at industrialization, moving from positivist, environmentally determinist approaches to structural and symbolic ones as they debate the role of humans versus environments in shaping industry (Grant 1987).

What unites almost all of the traditional historical views of the period is the lack of reference to industrial archaeology or indeed, with the exception of some historical geographers, any adequate use of physical evidence for the period in general.

## INDUSTRIAL ARCHAEOLOGY

### Origins and development

The origins of industrial archaeology lie in the nineteenth-century fascination with technology. The enthusiasm for travelling to industrial areas was shared between foreign spies seeking technical information, fellow industrialists, artists, writers and those seeking the curious and unusual. Many eighteenth-century writers left descriptions of the way in which the landscapes and towns of Britain were changing, the origins of the physical remains that they saw and the impact of the new industries on society. The Great Exhibition of 1851 celebrated the industrial achievements of some of Britain's best known firms, and became a showcase for their products. Items were collected that represented outstanding contributions to the development of engineering and technology, such as early locomotives, and became the nucleus of museum collections which remain important, but neglected, sources for industrial archaeology. The founding of the Newcomen Society in 1919 provided a forum for the study of all aspects of technology, as well as creating a new awareness of the importance of industrial monuments and their conservation.

Industrial archaeology as a branch of archaeology rather than a tradition of technical history dates only to the 1950s, however, when evening classes and local societies sprang up, devoted to the study of industrial remains. Those who took part in the classes often did fieldwork of their own, and one of the key themes in the work of this period is identification and cataloguing of sites. There are a good number of excellent regional and national accounts of industrial remains in Britain (e.g. Falconer 1980; Trinder 1994; the David and Charles regional industrial archaeology series, and the county guides published by the Association for Industrial Archaeology). National bodies such as Royal Commissions in England, Scotland and Wales have taken particular interest in recording industrial remains either regionally or thematically (e.g. Hay and Stell 1986; McCutcheon 1980), and a formal Industrial Monuments Survey is now housed with the RCHME in Swindon. The Council for British Archaeology also took an early initiative by establishing an Industrial Archaeology Research Committee to look at listing and protecting industrial sites, and today the Association for Industrial Archaeology promotes the subject and publishes a journal devoted to the subject. Interest in industrial archaeology cannot be separated from the broader conservation agenda, and Historic Scotland, CADW and English Heritage as well as the National Trust are all active in the field (Palmer and Neaverson 1995).

The scope of industrial archaeology has never been clearly defined: it may refer on the one hand to the archaeology of industry of all periods, whether prehistoric or modern, and on the other, to all of the archaeology of the period of the industrial revolution, whether it be country houses, industrial sites, railway locomotives or the growth of cities (Figure 16.1). The term 'historical archaeology' is widely accepted abroad but not commonly used in Britain, as it is often argued that archaeology of all of the past 2,000 years is to some extent dependent upon written sources. In this chapter, the term industrial archaeology is used to refer to the archaeology of the late second millennium AD – of the period during and after Britain's industrial trans-

*Figure 16.1* Study of industrial archaeology is often associated with museums. The entrance to Beamish Museum.
*Source*: Kate Clark

formation. No end date has been chosen, and even the archaeology of the twentieth century is a new area, where relatively little archaeological research has yet been undertaken (Trinder 1993).

## Current perceptions and outstanding problems

If archaeology is seen in terms of explicitly archaeological field methods, i.e. the use of stratigraphy and the rigorous analysis of physical evidence in time and space, then one attempt to meet this ideal might be cited. A survey of the Ironbridge Gorge, Shropshire (Alfrey and Clark 1993), set out to explore the use of archaeology in understanding a complex landscape over several hundred years. The survey brought evidence for buildings of all types – vernacular, polite, industrial and commercial – together with the archaeology of the landscape in which they were set, and used methods of landscape analysis to show the way in which the area changed from the medieval period to the present day, and to provide a context for some of the best known developments in the industrial period. The strength of the methodology was that it was possible to go beyond the traditional concept of the site to look at landscape as an entity; the weakness of the work has been cited as the resource implications of such intensive study. One of the themes that emerged from the work was that even in an area said to be the 'cradle of the industrial revolution', adaptation and reuse of sites, the approach of make do and mend, predominated throughout its history. Innovations such as the first iron bridge (Figure 16.2) have to be seen in the context of a pre-existing landscape and not as isolated events.

*Figure 16.2* The Iron Bridge, Shropshire: the first iron bridge in the world.
*Source*: Ben Osborne

Industrial archaeology also shows that there are some types of historical question that physical evidence can address, and some that are best left to documentary historians. Industrial archaeologists can rarely see the work of individuals or the large-scale changes in economic output cited by economic historians. However, field evidence does demonstrate processes such as the take up of innovations, or the decisions made by industrialists in siting industries. It shows how industrial complexes changed through time, and stresses the importance of links not only between different industries, but between different aspects of the economy, such as settlement and industry, or transport and urbanization.

This agenda remains largely empirical, and there have been relatively few attempts to set out a theoretical agenda for industrial archaeology. One possibility is to look towards other disciplines for theoretical modelling such as mainstream history, where there has been an emphasis on the role of social history, and in particular domestic patterns of work in understanding industry. However this area is rarely well documented, and small-scale archaeological investigations of individual houses or communities and their use of space and material goods might provide an alternative view of such patterns. Architectural history has in the past been dominated by traditions of documentary research, connoisseurship and attribution; the analysis of the fabric of structures of the industrial period, whether factories, country houses or furnaces, may provide a complementary source of evidence.

Prehistoric and later archaeology might provide a source of theoretical approaches for industrial archaeology, although when writing about a period with such good documentary evidence it is difficult to make assertions about hierarchies, power, symbols or conflict based on archaeology alone look anything other than mundane.

## THE ARCHAEOLOGY OF THE INDUSTRIAL REVOLUTION

### Pre-industrial landscape of Britain

Archaeology suggests that the changes in British industry in the latter half of the eighteenth century were neither sudden nor particularly revolutionary. However, they did take place on a large scale, and in order to understand precisely what happened, it is necessary to look first at the archaeology of Britain in the years before 1750. As Trinder notes, Britain presented a 'busy, thriving, trading and manufacturing nation' (Trinder 1987, 51), with a variety of industries scattered about the countryside. Pottery and glass-making, woollen textiles production, ironworking and non-ferrous metals were all well established, some in expanding market towns and ports serving overseas trade, whilst other industries, such as fulling in the countryside, made use of water power (Crossley 1990). The overall pattern was not, however, one that was very different to other European countries, and it was only after 1750 that the face of Britain began to change visibly.

## Raw materials

The development of the British coal industry in the years prior to 1750 was to have a significant impact on the wider process of industrialization. The expansion of the coal industry not only enabled industries to move from dependency on timber or charcoal, but also created much of the transport, capital and settlement infrastructure on which later industrialization was based. This infrastructure is very apparent in the archaeological record.

In order to understand the development of coal-production, it is important to realize that there are different types of coal in Britain – domestic coals, coking coal that can be used in furnaces, steam coal and anthracite. The earliest coals to be exploited were the low sulphur domestic coals, which could be burnt comfortably in a grate without emitting noxious fumes. This coal was also used for industrial purposes on a large scale from the sixteenth century onwards for burning lime, malting, glass-making and baking. The demand for coking coals grew considerably during the late eighteenth century, following the discovery of ways in which to use such coal in iron-making.

Early coal mines consisted of adits, or short tunnels into the seam where it outcropped near the surface, but little evidence for these survives on the surface. In areas such as the Clee Hills in Shropshire, or Rudland Rigg in North Yorkshire, regular patterns of circular spoil mounds are surface evidence for the short shafts or bell pits dug from the surface down into the coal below. One of the biggest problems with any evidence for mining is the difficulty of dating surface evidence such as this without some access to below ground works; the large open-cast coal mines dug in recent years have often exposed, and destroyed, archaeological evidence for the techniques used in early coal mines. In 1991, a timber pit prop from Lounge colliery in Leicestershire dating to between 1450 and 1463 provided one of the earliest accurately dated coal mining finds in Britain, and showed that pillar and stall workings dated to the late fifteenth century.

Mines provide only a tiny fraction of the evidence for coal mining. Coal was bulky and road transport difficult, and hence one of the earliest solutions was the use of wooden wagons or railways pioneered in Newcastle early in the seventeenth century. At Bersham, Clwyd, archaeologists have excavated a 40 m length of wooden waggonway *in situ* that was associated with the nearby ironworks and probably used for transporting coal and ironstone (Grenter 1993). Elsewhere, historic tramways survive in the landscape as old routes or footpaths, and occasionally as large pieces of engineering, as at the Causey Arch near Durham – a huge masonry tramway bridge that demonstrates the sophistication of, and level of investment in, many of these early tramway routes.

Coal mining also created a new demand for labour that could not always be satisfied from by-employment amongst traditional agricultural villages near the coalfields. From the seventeenth century onwards, new communities are found in coal-mining areas and can be evidenced from scattered plots of land. Many, such as those in the Forest of Dean, the Potteries and the Black Country, became the nuclei of later industrial areas.

## Iron

One of the great breakthroughs in industrialization was the increasing use of iron as a material in construction, in engineering and even in ship-building. Wrought iron had been produced in small quantities since prehistoric times in bloomeries, but it was only with the introduction of the charcoal blast furnace in *c.* 1500 that iron was produced in large quantities, both as cast iron straight from the furnace, or converted into the more flexible wrought iron at the finery forge.

Archaeological survey and excavation of charcoal furnaces in the ore-bearing areas of Sussex, Kent and Surrey, such as that at a sixteenth-century furnace at Chingley in Kent (Cleere and Crossley 1985), have shown how such furnaces developed and operated in the area where they were first introduced from Europe. It has been demonstrated that the use of blast furnaces spread from there to the Midlands, Wales in the seventeenth century, and only much later into the Forest of Dean, where bloomeries persisted until *c.* 1700. This is a pattern that illustrates a very common phenomenon in the industrial period – namely that the adoption of new technology within an industry is rarely automatic, nor is the spread of technology to new places a steady or straightforward process.

The transition from charcoal smelting to coke smelting, often held to be one of the major factors behind increased iron production during the eighteenth century, is an equally complex process. In 1709, Abraham Darby began to smelt iron using coke rather than charcoal at an old charcoal furnace at Coalbrookdale in Shropshire that he adapted for the purpose (Clark 1993). However, it is important to note that the iron Darby produced was suitable for castings, but could not be converted into the more flexible wrought iron. It was not until much later that a means of using coke to produce iron that could be converted to wrought iron was discovered, and coke production began to expand rapidly. The transition is illustrated in archaeological excavations at Rockley in Yorkshire (Crossley 1990, 166), where the site of a seventeenth-century water-powered bloomery was reopened and used with coke in the late eighteenth century. In some areas, such as Furness in Cumbria, coppicewood for charcoal production was plentiful, and charcoal iron smelting persisted until 1867.

A number of charcoal or coke iron furnaces survive across Britain, but the furnace was only one element in a working industrial complex that would have included casting houses, blacking mills, grinding mills for cleaning off castings, pattern-making shops and offices, almost all of which have now disappeared. One of the best preserved charcoal iron complexes is that at Bonawe, Argyll, where buildings for storing charcoal and ore survive, as well as the furnace and associated water power system (Figure 16.3). Archaeological excavations over a large area at Newdale in Shropshire illustrated the extent of a works devoted to remelting iron for castings – the site included back-to-back workers' cottages, air furnaces, a casting building and forge, all without any form of water power.

Steel was essential for producing sharp blades. Most steel was imported until the introduction in the seventeenth century of a German method of cementation that has since been identified from excavations at Derwentcote in Co. Durham. Crucible steel production (where metal is heated in pots) can be seen at Abbeydale Forge in Sheffield, but steel was produced only on a very large scale, and thus cheaply after the introduction of the Bessemer converter in 1856.

*Figure 16.3* Ironworks at Bonawe, Argyll.
*Source*: Kate Clark

## Non-ferrous metals

As with iron, the exploitation of non-ferrous metals expanded greatly

during the eighteenth and nineteenth centuries. Copper, tin and
lead had been worked on a small
scale for centuries, but new demands
were created by, for example, ship
building, tin plating or the metal
trades of Birmingham or the need
for engines.

In the Derbyshire Pennines, for
example, lead occurs as veins in the
limestone, and early mining can
be traced where it follows the ore
in long rakes that criss-cross the
landscape; at Charterhouse in
Somerset, continuity in mining is
suggested from the Roman period
until the nineteenth century. In
order to process lead ore, it has first
to be crushed and then washed, and
associated with such rakes are often

*Figure 16.4* Landscape at Parys Mountain, Anglesey, showing the legacy of copper working.
*Source*: Kate Clark

found remains of stamp mills and buddles, used to wash the ore, such as the complex excavated at
Killhope, Co. Durham (Cranstone 1989).

Copper mining on a large scale began in 1568, and continued until largely superseded by
imported ores at the end of the nineteenth century. Copper occurred in workable quantities in
Cornwall, Devon, Anglesey and the Lake District, and perhaps one of the best surviving
landscapes is at Red Dell Beck in the Lake District, where crushing and stamping works, adits,
shafts and waste heaps survive. The spectacular landscape of Parys Mountain, Anglesey, is all that
remains of what was once the largest copper working in Europe, where working continued until
1815, with a few subsequent revivals (Figure 16.4). The nearby harbour at Amlwch developed in
the eighteenth century as a port for shipping the copper ore out to smelters sited closer to sources
of coal.

Such sites also demonstrate the general principle that the final smelting of minerals such as
iron, lead or copper rarely took place in areas where they were mined. Field evidence suggests that
fuel, or easy access to fuel via a good transport network, was a more important determinant of
location. Relatively little copper smelting took place in Cornwall; most of it occurred in areas such
as Swansea in south Wales, where there were plentiful supplies of cheap coal.

At Gawton in West Devon, archaeological survey of a quay, copper mine, lime kilns and arsenic
works show how copper mining operated together with a variety of other activities at a site that
had the advantages of both raw materials and transport. Another complex associated with copper
mining is Aberdulais Falls in West Glamorgan, where ironworking and tinplate manufacturing
were also found. Such sites are very common and illustrate how difficult it is archaeologically to
isolate the evidence for single industries from their contexts.

## Power systems

The processing of minerals in any quantity depended upon a ready supply of power, as indeed did
the functioning of many other industries. The move from water power to steam power is one of
the factors commonly cited as being responsible for the large increases in output in British
manufacturing in the latter part of the eighteenth century. Archaeological evidence, nevertheless,

suggests that water power remained important for industrial purposes until well into the nineteenth century, and well after the steam engine had become firmly established (Cossons 1987).

Waterwheels were cheap, easy to install, and could drive rotative machinery well before steam engines could; only after the 1840s were steam engines built that were more powerful. The technology of the waterwheel was well established by the sixteenth century, and by the early eighteenth century simple undershot wheels were common. Key technical developments in waterwheel technology through the eighteenth and early nineteenth century include improvements to the buckets, and more elaborate means of driving wheels to take advantage of different conditions. The water turbine was developed after 1820 by Benoit Fourneyron in France to take advantage of low heads of water, and the technology spread, perhaps illicitly, to Northern Ireland where they were manufactured by the MacAdam brothers of Belfast in the 1840s. Water turbines remain in use today for the generation of hydro-electricity.

Many waterwheels survive in Britain, and at many sites field survey of the associated leats, sluices and tailraces, and analysis of the relevant falls is often the only source of evidence for the precise way in which the system worked. At Quarry Bank Mill, Styal in Cheshire, more explicitly archaeological techniques have been used to untangle the sequence of use of water, steam and gas as sources of power at a large textile mill complex. Although a steam engine was installed at the site in 1810, waterwheels remained in use there until 1889 when water turbines were installed, demonstrating that various sources of power often coexisted (Milln 1995). Archaeological analysis has also been used at Bordesley, Worcestershire, where remains of a water-powered needle mill were identified. Through time, many industrialized valleys developed extremely complex water power systems, often with steam engines being used not to drive the machinery directly (although such technology was available) but to pump water back up, so it could be recycled back around the earlier dams and waterwheels. Indeed, Cossons (1987) argues that the decline in water power may have had more to do with the diversion of water by land drainage schemes, or for urban domestic consumption, than the inefficiency of water power itself.

Whilst water power remained common in rural areas until the nineteenth century, and indeed survived in some places until the twentieth century, in urban areas the take-up of steam was more widespread. This illustrates the ultimate advantage that steam had over water power – it was a flexible, movable source of power that could be set up where required. Despite the importance of water power (and its greater legibility in the archaeological record), the application of steam engines to industrial uses from mining, and mineral production, through to textiles, manufacturing and transport, undoubtedly made possible much higher levels of productivity, and ultimately freed many areas of manufacturing from dependency upon human and horse power.

Newcomen engines remained in use for pumping coal mines where fuel was relatively cheap and where vertical motion was the main requirement. However, the improvements in steam engines created by Watt's patents of the late eighteenth century resulted in engines that used less fuel and thus were cheaper, and could turn as well as lift. Textile mills, forges, metal works, glass making, breweries and water works all found ready uses for such engines, and by 1800 nearly 500 had been built. Steam engine development did not stop with Boulton and Watt, and throughout the nineteenth century a series of patents resulted in smaller, more powerful and yet more portable engines. Reciprocating steam engines were used for electricity production in the 1880s, but only began to become redundant with the patenting of the steam turbine in 1884, which was immediately useful for electricity generation.

The portability of steam engines is illustrated by the earliest surviving engine, a Newcomen engine that today stands in Dartmouth. It was moved there, having been used successively at Griff Colliery in Warwickshire, at Measham in Leicestershire and at Hawkesbury Junction on the

Coventry Canal. Such portability makes it very difficult to interpret the archaeological evidence for steam engines on the basis of site remains alone. The vast majority of engines do not survive *in situ*, and those engine bases that do survive may have been modified either as their engines were adapted, or replaced, and as engines became smaller and less dependent upon built features such as engine houses.

By contrast, engine houses do tend to survive. The Cornish pumping engine was a higher pressure, single acting engine developed specifically for mining. An archaeological survey of such engine houses in Cornwall has produced a methodology for classifying them as a single building type within the wider context of crushers, waste heaps and mines that survive in the Cornish landscape (Johnson *et al.* 1995) (Figure 16.5). Cornish mining technology was very distinctive, and was exported to other parts of the world in the nineteenth century, including South Australia, where Cornish-style engine houses may still be seen today.

In contrast to steam, remains of the gas and electricity industries survive somewhat better, although they are increasingly under threat, and should also be seen as relevant to the study of the industrial revolution. The way in which the Iron-bridge power stations, opened respectively in 1932 and 1969, were designed, built, and altered through

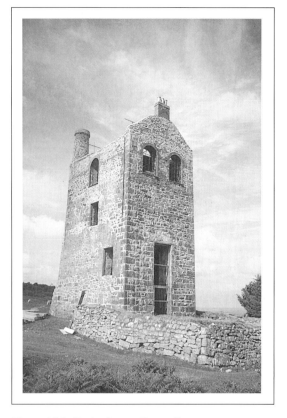

*Figure 16.5* Engine house, Cornwall.
*Source*: Kate Clark

time, and the associated impact on the local landscape, which already had a long history of industrialization, are explored by Stratton (1994).

The application of power to industrial processes provides a context for the development of the factory system whereby production became highly organized, and labour specialized.

## Textiles

The most potent symbol of the factory system is the multistorey textile mill, with its steam engine or waterwheel powering several floors of spinning machinery. The spinning and weaving of woollen cloth and the production of lace and hosiery were common amongst the textile industries in Britain in the early part of the eighteenth century. However, major innovations in textile machinery for spinning yarn, culminating in spinning mules of over 1,000 spindles, revolutionized the scale of yarn production. Weaving remained hand operated, often in association with spinning mills, until the development of an effective power loom in the early nineteenth century. It was the displacement of once highly skilled hand loom workers that generated the Luddite machine smashing, exacerbated by the depression following the Napoleonic wars. Many of these developments applied to cotton, but were extended to woollen production, hosiery and lace.

The textile mill buildings provide a graphic illustration of the changing nature of textile production, and stand as one of the most visible reminders of the industrial revolution. Early production took place in the home, assisted by factors who purchased materials in bulk, and 'put out' work. Large windows on the top storeys of buildings in many small towns, such as Newtown, Powys, indicate that lofts were used for weaving. The earliest purpose-built mills, such as Lombe's factory in Derby, were well lit, five storeys high, long and narrow, with line shafting to carry power from an engine, and lots of repetitive spaces supported by brick or cast iron columns. Because they were vulnerable to fire, most of the earliest mills have now been burnt down or altered almost beyond recognition. Most were simple, brick structures, and although largely functional, the use of classical detailing such as pediments and clock towers became common. Such buildings were generally located on streams, and thus concentrated in areas where water power was available. In the 1780s a form of fireproof construction, involving cast-iron beams and shallow brick jack arches, was developed. This was used at Stanley Mill in Gloucestershire, a 'fire proof' woollen mill, where the use of Palladian windows and decorative cast iron also illustrates the architectural pretension of the mill complex.

Steam was applied to spinning in 1785, making possible factory buildings in towns, close to sources of labour and materials. The mill buildings of the Ancoats area in Manchester exemplify the way in which urban areas became transformed by concentrations of multistorey textile complexes, although there is plentiful evidence to show that 'out-working' persisted as a mode of operation (by the mid-nineteenth century only half the textile workers operated in factories). A survey of Yorkshire textile mills places rural water-powered mills in their landscape context, and demonstrates the importance of looking at where and how mills were built as well as studying the buildings themselves (Giles and Goodall 1992).

It is easy to forget that mills were usually only one element in a large industrial complex that might include single-storey weaving sheds, dye houses, engine houses, carding buildings, offices and a multitude of other small structures needed for the factory's operation. In Manchester, the huge textile warehouses represent the role of marketing and distribution in the industry. At Saltaire in Bradford, West Yorkshire, the mill became part of a social experiment where the mill owner, Titus Salt, built rows of houses for employees, adding a church, hospital, baths and schools. Such structures are usually very vulnerable, and archaeology can play a role in ensuring that the more obvious structures are placed in their context.

## Building technology

Textile mills are only one of a wide range of new building types that began to appear in the late eighteenth century as a result of industrialization. Some categories were very specific and a direct reflection of the process they housed, such as iron furnaces or gas holders, whilst other buildings depended upon a vocabulary of features that were designed to provide light, shelter, access, fire-proofing and perhaps power for industrial processes. Building technology evolved rapidly as early building types were found to be unsuitable for industrial processes, and often burnt down or were shaken to bits. The introduction of iron to support buildings, fire-proofing, and new construction techniques involving the use of concrete and rolled steel, zig-zag north light roofs to bring in more light, and the use of steel framing all created extraordinarily innovative buildings. It should not be assumed that all such buildings were purely functional and without pretension. The earliest eighteenth-century factories made use of the Palladian idiom in their deployment of pediments and ornate roofs, and the industrial buildings of the Victorian period – such as the Egyptian style Temple Mill – illustrate all of the major themes in the architecture of the period.

## Workers' housing

Industries depended upon people, and many historians have commented upon the population changes in Britain during the period of industrialization. The population grew, and the centres of population moved, and although archaeology may not be able to resolve the reasons behind these changes, the study of changing settlements can provide some of the details. Prior to the development of mass transport, few people lived far from their place of work, and most industrial areas are characterized by workers' housing. Early dwellings seem to have been small, single-storey cottages, perhaps with lofts, built of local materials. Some were self-built by workers who squatted on former common or waste land; others were thrown up by speculators or investors, including the companies themselves. A study of workers' housing in West Yorkshire uses surviving buildings to show these different building processes at work, illustrating how the unbridled and chaotic development of industrial housing influenced the utopian designs of reformers such as Salt, and the later council-built housing of the twentieth century (Caffyn 1986).

Uncontrolled development and overcrowding, particularly in towns, soon led to health problems such as the great cholera epidemics of the mid-nineteenth century. Reform was slow, but did come eventually in the form of legislation to ensure sanitation in towns, and also the provision of services such as gas, water, drains and transport.

## Transport

The changing pattern of settlement is intimately bound up with the development of new transport networks in the latter part of the eighteenth century. Canals, roads, railways, ports and harbours were all upgraded in order to cope with increased movement in goods and people. With the communication came new termini and often new towns, such as Swindon, Wiltshire, on the Great Western Railway.

At the end of the seventeenth century, the only really efficient form of transport for bulky industrial goods such as coal was by coastal route and along navigable parts of the river network.

*Figure 16.6* Anderton boat lift, Cheshire.
*Source*: Kate Clark

Some rivers were made more navigable by the introduction of locks, and a canal was built near Exeter in 1566, but the big boom in canal building occurred during the late eighteenth century when, for example, Brindley's canal over the river Irwell in Manchester linked mines with the Mersey. Canal mania developed between 1789–93, resulting in the estuaries of the Thames, Severn, Humber and Mersey being linked, the Pennines traversed and London linked with the Midlands and the north. Nigel Crowe's surveys of the buildings of Britain's canal network demonstrate the variety of structures that were needed to support this enterprise (Crowe 1994).

Ingenious devices were constructed to cope with the differences in height on canals. In many cases, flights of locks were used, but in some cases, inclined planes powered by water or by steam engines lifted boats bodily up and down sloping railway tracks (Figure 16.6). The Anderton boat lift near Norwich built in 1865 was a similar device that lifted boats physically, using hydraulic rams and later electricity.

Roads were heavily rutted and impassable at many times of the year. Private trusts had been set up to build turnpike roads in the early nineteenth century, but their great period of geographical expansion was between 1750 and 1780. Real improvements came only after the introduction of new techniques for road construction – the use of tar and crushed stones and Telford's road improvements. Today mileposts, toll-houses and the occasional buried surface encountered during road improvement are reminders of the turnpiking process.

*Figure 16.7* Reconstruction of a coal waggon on a wooden waggon way, Causey, Durham.
*Source*: Kate Clark

Wooden railways had been in use since the early seventeenth century for transporting coal. In 1767, iron rails were adopted laid on top of wooden frameworks, and were themselves superseded by 'L' shaped tracks from the 1780s. Horse-drawn tramways were built extensively well into the 1830s, in association with canals and collieries, and occasionally for public use (Figure 16.7). The earliest experiments in using steam locomotion were undertaken by Richard Trevithick in 1802, but it was only in 1829 with George Stephenson's use of steam that the fortunes of the locomotive began to turn.

Canals, roads and indeed railways all faced the problem of crossing rivers or valleys while remaining level. Bridge and aqueduct technology was another area of innovation during the late eighteenth century, when engineers devised new methods, including the use of cast iron on the first iron bridge at Ironbridge in Shropshire. The history of these and many of the other great iron structures tends to be dominated by the great engineers who built them: John Rennie (1761–1821), Thomas Telford (1757–1834) and John Smeaton (1724–92). However, it is important to remember the role of the firms they worked with: William Hazeldine, the Coalbrookdale Company and, in the nineteenth century, the Butterley Company and others whose day-to-day experience in using cast iron was likely to have been equally important in creating practical designs.

## Agriculture

Two major changes transformed the agricultural landscape between the middle of the eighteenth century and the end of the nineteenth century. The first was the process of enclosure of the former open fields as a result of privately sponsored parliamentary Acts (placed in the wider context of rural changes in the previous chapter); the second was the industrialization of agriculture itself. Both are clearly visible in the archaeological record. The increased productivity of the land was needed to feed the growing industrial populations.

In the late eighteenth century, consolidated holdings and capital investment, as well as an interest in improving farming, seem to have resulted in fine model farms. This was particularly the case in Scotland, where sweeping changes after the Jacobite rising of 1745 and the systematic enclosure by large estates, led to a programme of farm improvement. George Meikle, from East Lothian, experimented with applying horse power to threshing; steam was introduced early in areas such as East Lothian and Yorkshire where coal was cheap.

One way of increasing productivity was through the application of fertilizer, and much of the industrial archaeology of agriculture can be seen to relate to fertilizer production and distribution. During the 1850s, a boom in agricultural prices and new research into the science of farming created an optimism that is translated in some extraordinary groups of buildings. Cattle were brought in and fed for much of the year on new feed compounds, their manure collected and taken to the fields. At Leighton, Powys, during the 1850s, John Naylor erected cattle sheds, circular piggeries, a root house, engine houses, and other buildings. Manure was collected from the stockhouses, mixed with bone meal ground on the site, and pumped up to an enormous slurry tank where it was then fed onto the fields. There was a funicular railway, a decorative poultry house, a saw mill, gas works and brickworks and a broad gauge railway taking ricks directly into the huge barn (Figure 16.8). Archaeological investigation shows the way in which the systems were designed to work together on the steep hillside, and also suggests that the scheme was very short-lived (Wade Martins 1991).

The elaborate tramways of the Brecon Beacons also relate to this period of high agricultural optimism. Archaeological survey has shown how a network was originally constructed to bring lime to the uplands as part of a large scheme of agricultural development, but the enterprise failed, and the tramways were adapted in order to serve the industrial areas of the Swansea valley (Hughes 1990). Lime was very important as a source of fertilizer, and the kilns at Calke Abbey, Derbyshire, illustrate the importance of lime as part of the workings of a large estate (Marshall 1992).

## Consumer goods

Probate inventories, compiled when people died, were lists of possessions that are often used by historians to explore changes in material culture. Archaeology, however, can also provide a source of information

*Figure 16.8*  The great barn at Leighton, Wales, constructed in the 1850s and designed so that hay ricks could be brought in on a broad gauge railway.
*Source*: Kate Clark

*Figure 16.9* Kilns at Gladstone Pottery Museum, Stoke-on-Trent.
*Source*: Kate Clark

for how people lived. Eighteenth-and nineteenth-century ceramics are often the subject of research by collectors and art historians, anxious to establish firm attributions for individual pieces. The archaeological study of ceramics for the industrial period, however, has concentrated much more on methods of production (Baker 1991) (Figure 16.9) – there have, for example, been many excavations of kilns in major ceramic-producing areas such as Stoke-on-Trent in the Midlands. Only recently have traditional excavation reports begun to deal seriously with post eighteenth-century ceramics (Figure 16.10).

The production of tin-glazed wares, stonewares and domestic earthenwares was established in Britain by the end of the seventeenth century (Draper 1984). Pottery production was transformed, however, in the latter half of the eighteenth century when the new fashions for drinking tea, coffee and chocolate were being initially satisfied by the importation of blue and white porcelains from China. Local manufacturers were desperate to recreate these, and started making white stonewares with incised blue decoration. Firms in Worcester, and later at Caughley and Coalport in Shropshire, in Liverpool and in Nantgarw, Gwent, experimented with, and finally succeeded in making, hard and soft paste porcelains in Britain, applying hand-painted and later transfer-printed blue designs in imitation of the Chinese wares. These were, however, specialist wares. The first successful mass production of ceramics was undertaken by Josiah Wedgwood, who developed and patented a cream coloured earthenware that was cheap to produce, and could be coloured. 'Queensware', as it was called, was successfully marketed throughout Britain, and the predominance of creamwares in archaeological assemblages throughout the parts of the world with which Britain had trading contacts is particularly notable.

## INDUSTRIAL AND HISTORICAL ARCHAEOLOGY

In compiling this brief survey, it has not always been easy to see how distinctively archaeology is contributing to our understanding of the period. The problem is not lack of application – much hard work has been done in the field and in the library, and many good inventories compiled – but one of defining how archaeology might best be utilized and which approaches should be taken.

The theoretical basis for the archaeology of the past two centuries is much better developed in countries outside Britain such as the United States of America, Canada and Australia, where it has long been recognized that the archaeology of the historical period is a proving ground for methodological developments (Connah 1988). In such countries, industrial archaeology is a sub-set of the wider field of historical archaeology.

In Australia and New Zealand, historical archaeology deals with the buildings, landscapes and artefacts of the whole period from pre-colonial

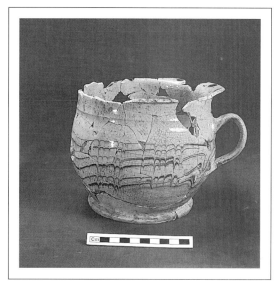

*Figure 16.10* Slip-glazed chamber pot: an example of the ordinary domestic ceramics that became important in the second half of the eighteenth century.
*Source*: Kate Clark

contact until the present day. Key themes in Australia include the tension between imported and locally developed technology, the role of the penal system, the process of clearance and the development of distinctive building types. The process of colonization, whether successful or failed, is an area that has been explored in a number of countries, including Canada, Sweden and the Caribbean (Dyson 1985). It is to America or Australia that the archaeologist interested in the material culture of the eighteenth and nineteenth century, and in particular ceramics, should turn, because here sequences of artefacts tend to be better published, and better dated. More recent American studies are dominated by themes such as women's roles, consumer behaviour, ethnicity and urbanization, and it is argued, for example, that struggles between different groups in society, be they women and men, slaves and planters, capitalists and workers, may all be seen in the use of pottery and material culture, in town planning or in the design of buildings. In an age that has seen a new fascination with the impact of information technology, the relationship between people and technology, or the way in which innovations are adopted, has also gained a new relevance.

The other factor that has shaped industrial archaeology has been the need to consider, rank, research, defend and care for industrial monuments as part of the wider spectrum of heritage conservation. On the Continent, major conservation initiatives in France and in the Ruhr in Germany have generated a renewed interest in the remains of the period, and in Britain, the systematic surveys of English Heritage's Monuments Protection Programme have greatly enhanced our understanding of the range of sites that remain. Perhaps the emphasis on the 'industrial' aspects of historical archaeology are particularly strong in Britain because, as Cossons argues, it was an epoch when Britain 'for a brief period of perhaps five generations, held the centre of the world stage as the first industrial nation, birthplace of the Industrial Revolution' (1987, 10).

The subject matter for industrial archaeology is vast, and the contribution of archaeology is limited only by the number of archaeologists who are prepared to tackle it. The impact of the new technologies of the nineteenth and twentieth centuries have barely been touched upon, nor have the major social issues of the time. The relationship between Britain and the rest of the world as expressed in material culture, is poorly understood from this end. Yet if archaeologists are to make an impact on the history of the past two centuries, two things are vital: firstly that we go beyond catalogues and begin to interpret our evidence; and secondly that we are more rigorous about our archaeological methods, and have the courage to be more openly critical of our own data.

## Key texts

Cossons, N., 1987. *BP Book of industrial archaeology.* Newton Abbott: David and Charles (3 edn 1996).
Crossley, D., 1990. *Post medieval archaeology in Britain.* Leicester: Leicester University Press.
Hay, G.D. and Stell, G.P., 1986. *Monuments of industry: an illustrated historical record.* Edinburgh: HMSO.
McCutcheon, W.A., 1980. *The industrial archaeology of Northern Ireland.* London: HMSO.
Trinder, B., 1994. *The Blackwell encyclopedia of industrial archaeology.* Oxford: Blackwell.

## Bibliography

Alfrey, J. and Clark, C., 1993. *The landscape of industry. Patterns of change in the Ironbridge Gorge.* London: Routledge.
Baker, D., 1991. *Potworks: the industrial architecture of the Staffordshire potteries.* London: RCHME.
Caffyn, L., 1986. *Workers' housing in West Yorkshire 1750–1920.* Wakefield: RCHME and West Yorkshire Metropolitan Council.
Clark, C., 1993. *English Heritage book of the Ironbridge Gorge.* London: Batsford.
Clark, C.M., 1987. 'Trouble at t'mill: industrial archaeology in the 1980's', *Antiquity* 61, 169–179.
Cleere, H.F. and Crossley, D.W., 1985. *The iron industry in the Weald.* Leicester: Leicester University Press.
Connah, G., 1988. *Of the hut I builded. The archaeology of Australia's history.* Cambridge: Cambridge University Press.
Cranstone, D., 1989. 'The archaeology of washing floors: problems, potentials and priorities', *Industrial Archaeology Review* 12:1, 40–49.
Crowe, N., 1994. *The English Heritage book of canals.* London: Batsford.
Draper, J., 1984. *Post-medieval pottery 1650–1800.* Aylesbury: Shire Publications.
Dyson, S.L., 1985. *Comparative studies in the archaeology of colonialism.* Oxford: British Archaeological Reports International Series 233.
Falconer, K., 1980. *Guide to England's industrial heritage.* London: Batsford.
Giles, C. and Goodall, I.H., 1992. *Yorkshire textile mills 1770–1930.* London: RCHME.
Grant, E.G., 1987. 'Industry: landscape and location', in Wagstaff, J.M. (ed.) *Landscape and Culture.* Oxford: Blackwell, 96–117.
Grenter, S., 1993. 'A wooden waggonway complex at Bersham Ironworks, Wrexham', *Industrial Archaeology Review* 15:2, 195–207.
Hudson, P., 1992. *The industrial revolution.* London: Edward Arnold.
Hughes, S., 1990. *The Brecon Forest tramroads: the archaeology of an early railway system.* Aberystwyth: RCAHMW.
Johnson, N., Thomas, N., Herring, P. and Sharpe, A., 1995. 'The survey and consolidation of industrial remains in Cornwall – a progress report', *Industrial Archaeology Review* 18:1, 29–38.
Marshall, G., 1992. 'The history and archaeology of the Calke Abbey Lime-yards', *Industrial Archaeology Review* 15:2, 145–176.
Milln, J., 1995. 'Power development at the northern end of Quarry Bank Mill, Styal, Cheshire', *Industrial Archaeology Review* 18:1, 8–28.
Palmer, M. and Neaverson, P., 1995. *Managing the industrial heritage.* Leicester: Leicester Archaeology Monograph 2.
Stratton, M., 1994. *Ironbridge and the electric revolution.* London: John Murray.
Trinder, B., 1987. *The making of the industrial landscape.* Stroud: Alan Sutton.
Trinder, B., 1993. 'The archaeology of the British food industry 1660–1966: a preliminary survey'. *Industrial Archaeology Review* 15:2, 119–139.
Wade Martins, S., 1991. *Historic farm buildings.* London: Batsford.

*Chapter Seventeen*

# Reeling in the years

## The past in the present

## Timothy Darvill

## INTRODUCTION

Fragments of antiquity are all around us, components of the modern world that, by chance or design, have survived to become part of the fabric of everyday life. As earlier chapters in this book illustrate, archaeological remains, whether single objects, structures, or the complicated stratified layers revealed through excavations, provide the raw materials from which each successive generation of archaeologists constructs an understanding of the past; but archaeological remains are much more than this. Britain is an old country that has been continuously occupied for over 10,000 years. Thousands of archaeological sites in Britain are still in use, in many cases perpetuating the purposes for which they were originally built. Ancient churches are probably the most obvious and widespread examples, but they head a long list that also includes houses, mills, bridges, roads, tracks, and many different kinds of boundary. Tens of thousands of sites have fallen out of use yet remain to be seen in the countryside, in villages, and in towns (Darvill 1987), and every day archaeological remains are brought back into the light of day after hundreds or thousands of years of lying hidden or forgotten in the ground.

Archaeological remains are real things that can be seen, encountered, experienced, explored, touched and engaged with in all sorts of ways by individuals and groups, whether in the town or the countryside (Figure 17.1). Because of this, archaeological remains have a contemporary social context that gives them political, economic and ideological meanings, while making them susceptible to control, manipulation and negotiation.

This chapter considers the ways in which archaeological remains are treated by archaeologists in Britain today, especially in relation to the social context and competing demands placed upon the material itself (Harrison 1994; Hunter 1996). The philosophies, theoretical perspectives, practices and professional skills discussed here are collectively known as archaeological resource management.

## BACKGROUND

Archaeological resource management as currently practised in Britain is a relatively new branch of archaeology (Hunter and Ralston 1993), although its roots penetrate deep into the history of the discipline as a whole. As long ago as AD 1533, Henry VIII appointed John Leland as the first, and as it turned out only, 'King's Antiquary'. He was commissioned to search England and Wales for surviving antiquities and monuments, which he did between 1534 and 1543, although he never

*Figure 17.1* Ancient monuments in the countryside: a Bronze Age round barrow cemetery on King Barrow Ridge, Amesbury, Wiltshire.
*Source*: Timothy Darvill

published the results. Leland died insane in 1552, but the idea of cataloguing, recording and trying to preserve archaeological remains endured. In the seventeenth, eighteenth and nineteenth centuries, interest in the preservation and care of monuments can be glimpsed in the writings of antiquaries such as William Camden (1561–1623), John Aubrey (1626–1697), William Stukeley (1687–1765) and James Douglas (1753–1819). All, however, were operating in the intellectual traditions of the Age of Enlightenment and the political climate of conservatism. It was not until the scientific revolution, positivist thinking and Liberal political reforms of the mid-nineteenth century that things started to change.

Concerns about the destruction of archaeological remains, and the need to protect them, appear in numerous antiquarian accounts printed in the later nineteenth century. At a meeting of the International Congress on Prehistoric Archaeology held in Norwich in August 1868, a committee was set up to try to prevent the destruction of monuments in Brittany, and soon after a Committee of the Ethnological Society was formed for the purpose of describing and preserving the prehistoric monuments of Britain and Ireland.

In 1870, John Lubbock, later Lord Avebury, introduced into Parliament a Bill that later became the first piece of ancient monuments legislation, *The Ancient Monuments Protection Act 1882*. Although limited in its coverage and powers, it established precedents for state control over the destiny of important archaeological sites. On January 1st 1883, General Pitt Rivers, a well-known and established archaeologist, took up the post of the first Inspector of Ancient Monuments, a role he continued until his death in 1900.

The impact, expansion and periodic re-enactment of Ancient Monuments legislation from 1882 down to modern times has been well documented and discussed (Saunders 1983). The early date of the first Act is, however, important as it came much earlier than, for example, specific legislation for the preservation of National Parks in England and Wales (1949), historic buildings (1953), the countryside (1968) and wildlife (1981). Its limitations in relating only to important monuments listed in a 'schedule' and its focus on the 'preservation' of remains through the control of works are factors that have certainly conditioned, and in many ways constrained, the development of approaches to the care of archaeological remains in Britain.

Massive wartime devastation of historic cities such as London, Bristol, Winchester, Exeter and Southampton prompted the need for substantial archaeological provision during redevelopment. Indeed, the need had been recognized even before the end of the war when, in March 1944, the Council for British Archaeology was founded to promote British archaeology in all its aspects. The principle that became established in Britain was what later became known as 'rescue archaeology' – the rapid recording of archaeological sites immediately in advance of their destruction. This is all that could be done in a political climate and legal framework that promoted a presumption in favour of development.

During the 1950s and early 1960s, a substantial group of itinerant rescue archaeologists moved from site to site, excavating and recording remains, often in difficult and frustrating conditions

(Rahtz 1974). In a few areas, permanent excavation 'units' were established, Winchester being among the first in 1961, soon followed by Southampton, Oxford, Lincoln, Colchester and others; but this was not enough. In 1960, the Royal Commission on Historical Monuments sounded a warning bell about the destruction of archaeological sites in the English countryside through the publication of a book entitled *A Matter of Time*, but its message was never really acted upon. The pace of construction and reconstruction continued unabated into the 1970s, and new threats came into play, for example the development of the motorway system, expanded mineral extraction, and the extensification of forestry.

In January 1971, an organization calling itself RESCUE was formed with the aims of increasing public awareness of the destruction of archaeological remains, improving legislation for the protection of remains, and pressing for more state funding for excavation and recording programmes (Rahtz 1974). In all these things they were successful, especially in starting to raise public expenditure for rescue excavation: in England, expenditure rose from £450,000 in 1972, passing £1m by 1975, £5.2m by 1985, and reaching a peak of £7.5m in 1994–5.

In America, similar problems were being encountered, sometimes on an alarming scale. In the ten year period to 1972, for example, it was estimated that 25 per cent of all known archaeological sites in Arkansas had been destroyed (McGimsey 1972, 3). 'Salvage archaeology', as it is called in the US, was commonplace and widespread, but even by the early 1970s there was disenchantment with the approach. As McGimsey put it: 'The archaeologist cannot afford to continue to let the engineer, the farmer, and the urban developer determine where he is to utilize the limited resources at his command.' (ibid., 18). What emerged instead was 'cultural resource management', an approach that advocated preservation and protection as the primary objective, followed by the controlled and carefully reasoned exploitation of archaeological remains (Fowler 1986). In this view, archaeological remains were seen as existing not primarily for archaeological research as and when archaeologists felt like it, but rather as something rather more valuable that was a community resource for which there was shared responsibility (Cleere and Fowler 1976; Fowler 1977; Thomas 1971). It was the translation of these principles across the Atlantic into Britain during the 1980s, mixed with Britain's own traditions of rescue archaeology, that provides the basis of modern archaeological resource management in what can now be seen as the post-rescue era (Fowler 1978; Thomas 1977). At the core of this sector of the discipline in Britain, three key principles have emerged:

- Sustainability of the archaeological resource so that there is a representative sample of material for future generations to utilize.
- Plurality of endeavour so that there is a balance between preservation of material for the future through conservation and protection, and exploitation for the present through excavation and research.
- Informed decision making about the relative importance of specific archaeological sites and finds and what should happen to them. This usually involves some kind of assessment or evaluation process.

The majority of archaeologists working in Britain are employed in the field of archaeological resource management. A survey of the profession by RESCUE in 1991 revealed that 46 per cent of archaeologists worked in local authorities, 38 per cent in contracting units, 7 per cent in national heritage agencies and 8 per cent in universities. Archaeology has become a highly professionalized discipline, and within archaeological resource management there are clearly defined role sets – the three 'c's: *curators* who are responsible for the overall well-being of the resource, *contractors* who carry out archaeological investigations and surveys, and *consultants* who advise and guide individuals and organizations on archaeological matters.

What unites everyone, however, is a concern for the raw material of archaeology, the stuff of the discipline that is in, on or under the ground which has come to be understood as the archaeological resource.

## WHAT IS THE ARCHAEOLOGICAL RESOURCE?

Defining what constitutes the archaeological resource is far from easy, and has both intellectual and practical dimensions. At a theoretical level, what is of interest to archaeologists largely depends on the interpretative frameworks within which they work. In Britain, as in other western societies, archaeology is distanced from the societies that created the things that are studied; as David Lowenthal suggests, 'the past is a foreign country' (1985). Archaeological remains are examined with detachment and from numerous viewpoints. Thus within the processual perspectives of the 'New Archaeology' of the 1960s and 1970s, the archaeological resource was the material against which theories were tested. In the post-processual archaeologies of the 1980s and 1990s, it is not so much the individual elements that are important as the totality, the materials and their context from which broadly based narratives can be constructed.

In practical terms, there are problems and issues too. The core is easy, as things like Palaeolithic hand-axes, Neolithic long barrows, Roman villas and deserted medieval villages are widely recognized as being within the archaeologist's domain. But where does it stop? What about hedgerows and boundaries that are still in use but which were first built in prehistoric or Saxon times? Is a historic building or ancient church archaeological? And what about a peat-bog? The problem is that, in operational terms, much of what is of interest to archaeologists is also of interest to others. The boundaries of the subject are blurred, and archaeological interests overlap with history, sociology, landscape geography, anthropology, ethnology, architectural history and others beside. Peter Fowler once argued that the whole of Britain should be seen as one enormous archaeological site, and in a sense he was right. Since earliest times, people have lived, worked and been buried within a space that, in social terms, is infinite because it stretches outwards in all directions from the focus of an individual's existence: their home or home territory. While space is socially infinite it is, however, physically constrained. There is only so much of it and the distribution of activities within space is uneven and discrete. What the archaeologist normally finds are hot-spots or nodes where evidence of the activities that took place are rich enough, or substantial enough, or well-preserved enough to be visible and recognizable. This is the archaeological resource, but there is no neat embracing definition of it; it is effectively whatever archaeologists recognize as relevant to their work at any given point in time. In this sense, the intellectual or theoretical constitution of archaeological work drives and defines its practical application.

While the exact definition of what the archaeological resource comprises evolves and develops, a number of common characteristics can be recognized:

* Finite: there is only so much of it, even though we do not know exactly how much.
* Immovable: context and relationships are critical to understanding and appreciating archaeological material. While individual objects and sometimes whole sites have been moved, doing so destroys their authenticity, setting and context.
* Non-renewable: archaeological material does not regenerate itself. Once destroyed it has gone for ever. It could be argued that because the social process continues, more archaeology is being formed all the time, but this is an extension to the record, not a replacement or replenishment of it.

- Fragile and vulnerable: archaeological remains are easily toppled and broken, buried remains can be segmented or the environments that surround them inadvertently changed.
- Integrity is consequent upon completeness of survival: the value of the resource lies partly in our ability to interpret it and read it. Legibility is therefore important and the more complete the surviving pieces the more that can be done with them.
- Each element has spatial, temporal and socially determined relationships with other elements. The material that comprises the resource was created as part of a set of social processes that were not confined to single sites or places.
- Attributed meaning: archaeological objects do not have inherent meaning; people and society give them meaning.
- As a whole what is represented is a unique record of human achievement over the whole duration of human existence.

Within these common characteristics, it is recognized that three main kinds of archaeological deposits and situations can be identified, partly as a result of conditions of survival and partly because of the intrinsic nature of the material itself. These provide useful pragmatic categories for dealing with remains:

- Single monuments: the most familiar items that archaeologists are concerned with, including relatively discrete structures such as round barrows, long barrows, Roman villas, deserted villages, mines or glasshouses.
- Urban deposits: composite deposits created in heavily occupied areas from Roman times through to the present day. Especially important is the way in which they build up within a restricted area and become reworked over and over again.
- Relict landscapes: potentially the most important kind of data for archaeology, especially for earlier periods, relict landscapes comprise groups of related monuments and structures bound together as though in some form of articulation (natural or man-made), even though the archaeological deposits may not themselves be continuous.

One major problem with all three forms is the extent to which we know what we have. No one is ever able to see the complete picture, and there is no way of really knowing how much archaeology there is to find. For this reason, the resource has to be conceptualized and quantified in a carefully structured way. Figure 17.2 shows a diagram representing the main elements. The outer box represents what, within any particular definition of archaeology, there is to know about the 'original resource'. Part of that material is recorded in various ways. Britain is very fortunate to have numerous and long-standing lists and inventories of ancient monuments held at national and local level by government agencies and local

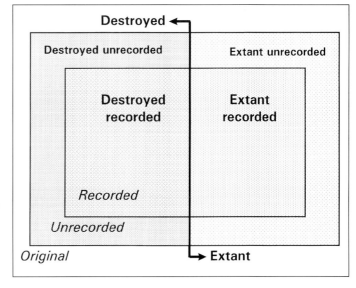

*Figure 17.2* Diagram showing the main components of the archaeological resource.

authorities (Larsen 1992). This can be referred to as the 'recorded resource'. In England, for example, the recorded resource is currently estimated at about 900,000 items, including stray finds, place-name records, and many other relatively ephemeral pieces of information. About 600,000 items refer to what could be called archaeological monuments of one sort or another: sites and structures (including ancient buildings) that contain archaeological deposits (Darvill and Fulton 1998).

Part of the original resource and the recorded resource remains extant and is therefore able to be investigated or looked at. That part of the original resource that is extant but not yet recorded is the target for surveys and studies whose objectives involve the discovery of new sites. That part of the original resource that has been destroyed but was recorded before being lost is now known only through the records themselves, which range in quality from the very comprehensive to the almost incomprehensible. The resource destroyed without record will never be known about and is now completely lost. In large measure, how we see the archaeological resource and how it will expand in future, comes down to its importance and how it is valued by society today.

## WHY DO WE VALUE THE ARCHAEOLOGICAL REMAINS?

Importance and value are two rather different things. The former applies differentially to particular elements of the archaeological resource, in the sense that some things are regarded as more important than others. In determining whether remains are of sufficient importance to merit designation under the prevailing national legislation (see below), remains are judged against the following criteria: survival/condition, period, rarity, fragility/vulnerability, diversity, documentation, group value and potential, which can be systematically applied (Darvill *et al.* 1987). More general measures of importance have also been suggested, for example the idea of 'legibility' in the case of urban deposits (Carver 1996).

Value, however, is rather different as it relates to broad, socially defined perceptions of what is good, right and acceptable (Darvill 1995). It applies not so much to individual sites or monuments, but rather to the resource as a whole. In Britain, a series of value-sets relating to archaeological remains can be seen developing from medieval times onwards, but in present-day society there are three main value systems, or value gradients as they are sometimes known: use value, option value and existence value. The following sub-sections look briefly at each in turn.

### Use value

This system is based upon the fact that demands are placed upon the archaeological resource by contemporary society. The values are based on consumption, even though the act of consumption is also creative. Society's ability to use the archaeological resource depends on two things, both contributed by experts

*Figure 17.3* Visitors at Stonehenge, Wiltshire.
*Source*: Timothy Darvill

with expert knowledge. First is the existence of some evidence, record or memory of things to be drawn upon. Second is our ability to attribute meaning to what we have. Such meanings are not necessarily right or wrong, they are attributed as part of the process of recognition, derivation and renegotiation into a future state.

The focus of this value set is the evidential nature of the resource as something that can be exploited to develop a tangible return. Ancient things (here including structures and relationships as well as objects) are taken out of their original social context and given a new context and a new set of meanings within another society: history is used to make history. Kristian Kristiansen (1993) has presented a very useful critical analysis of the way in which the past is used in the present, emphasizing in particular the interdependence of archaeology and politics in the widest sense. The following contemporary uses of archaeological remains are especially common:

- Archaeological research: one of the most obvious uses we make of the archaeological resource is for archaeological research, the discovery of information or knowledge about the past.
- Scientific research: all sorts of scientific research uses data from archaeological sites.
- Creative arts: artists, writers, poets and photographers draw inspiration from archaeological monuments and translate and renegotiate the material world into visual, literary or oral images.
- Education: archaeological resources play a substantial role in the general education of children and adults.
- Recreation and tourism: ancient monuments are used for recreation, tourism and indeed entertainment. Some monuments are very heavily visited by domestic and overseas tourists (Figure 17.3).
- Symbolic representation: archaeological sites are widely used as symbols of various sorts. Stonehenge is probably the most widely recognized; it has featured in advertisements for things as diverse as lawnmowers, cigarettes, computer consultancy services and photographic materials.
- Legitimation of action: the ascription of meaning to archaeological evidence is not always left to archaeological scientists. Archaeological evidence is frequently used to support or legitimize particular propositions, especially politically motivated propositions.
- Social solidarity and integration: archaeological remains bolster social solidarity and promote integration.
- Monetary and economic gain: the use of remains for monetary gain, both legitimate and otherwise, is among the oldest known calls on the monuments and objects we have.

## Option value

Turning now to the second value system, something rather different is encountered. Here emphasis is on production rather than consumption, but the process of production is deferred because the temporal context of this value system is not the present but rather some unspecified time in the future. It shows a particular respect for those individuals and communities who will come after us (our children's children) and who might expect to use the resource in the future or at least may wish to do so. Axiomatic to this value system is the physical preservation of things in order to achieve the notional preservation of options. It is a focus that lies at the very heart of the 'green debate' (Macinnes and Wickham-Jones 1992).

Option values hinge on a projected understanding that future generations will both want to and be able to make some use of the resource or resources in question; in other words, that we have a duty to those who follow. But identifying the interest base of these values is rather difficult, not least because specific uses cannot be predicted; there will always be new questions about the past to be addressed, new data needed to renegotiate the future with, and new techniques and methodologies with which to investigate the past. Certainly that has been the experience of the last few decades. The more fundamental interests related to this value set are perceptual rather than functional:

- Stability: adherence to option values as the justification of action inhibits change and enhances the perception of stability, timelessness and tradition. Recreation and restoration of times past is an important dimension. Elements of the past become celebrated for what they might be rather than what they are.
- Mystery and enigma: not knowing about the past may be as important as knowing about it. The attraction of places such as Stonehenge is probably the fact that relatively little is known about their use and social context.

## Existence value

The third value system relates simply to the existence of the resource. The temporal context is the present, although in this case the spatial context is not necessarily very clearly defined. Central to the realization of these values is the recognition of feelings of well-being, contentment and satisfaction: the so-called 'feelgood' factor. These feelings are triggered in people who may never expect to use or see the resource itself, simply by knowing it exists. Thus at one end of the value gradient is the elation of knowing that all is well because everything is safe, that viability and diversity are being maintained, and that existence is assured. At the other end is despondency because the resource is under great threat, viability and integrity are marginal, diversity is low, and continued existence endangered. Two interests stand out for special attention:

- Cultural identity: there is an active reflection of feelings of belonging in the use of references to ancient monuments in place-names and the periodic festivals and celebrations on anniversaries and 'special' occasions.
- Resistance to change: every generation believes that the world is changing uncontrollably and at a more rapid pace than ever before. Maybe this is true. But a predominant theme of protests against change is the galvanizing of interest in some previously almost unnoticed structure or institution. Such things are not recognized until they are threatened, but the force of the arguments for their retention is a reminder of the latent strength of existence value.

Running through so many of these ideas is that values are supported by a constructive tension between different systems in the minds of individuals. This carries through into the demands placed upon archaeological materials. John Barrett has argued that the proper role for archaeologists is the construction of histories (1995), and in many ways this is the most widely recognized and obvious element of archaeological work, the things that archaeologists find are the props and scenery for such stories. But is archaeology just a form of history? What archaeologists make may be a kind of history, but what they actually see through their excavations, surveys and technical studies is something else. In his Inaugural Lecture as Professor of European Archaeology in the Institute of Archaeology, London University in 1946, Gordon Childe argued that archaeology was a social science, in effect the recording of the longest-lived non-repeatable survey of social change ever. Certainly what archaeologists record is a series of glimpses into the behaviours and actions of individuals and groups at different times in the past. Such differences in what archaeologists do impact on how they do it.

## THE CONCEPT OF 'MANAGEMENT' IN ARCHAEOLOGY

The fact that archaeological remains are recognized and given value by society means that choices have to be made about what to do with ancient sites, structures and finds. The contemporary world is full of competing demands; change is the natural state of things and provides the engine that drives society forward. Change is the process by which archaeological deposits are both created and destroyed, and the context in which choices, sometimes very difficult choices, have to be made: do we keep this Roman villa or construct a new wing for the local hospital?

It would be nice to think that everything can be preserved, but that is Utopian. The concept of management in archaeology is all about managing change – the contrived regulation of situations for the fulfilment of defined objectives. These objectives flow from the general guiding principles of archaeological resource management already noted, and can be summarized as follows:

- To retain the rich diversity of archaeological remains that is known to exist in the landscape.
- To make the archaeological heritage satisfy the demands made upon it by society as a whole.
- To reconcile conflict and competition for the use of land containing ancient monuments.

In addition to its intellectual context, archaeological resource management must also fit within the legislative frameworks that relate both to its practice and to the materials with which it is concerned. As already noted, the scope and range of legislative controls is itself a reflection of society's interest and concern for the past (Figure 17.4). Today, legislative controls for archaeology fall into two main spheres: firstly, planning and environmental legislation; and, secondly, ancient monuments legislation (Ross 1991). All find expression at three main levels – international, national and local.

## Planning and environmental legislation

The key concept here is that of 'development', which in Britain is taken to mean: 'the carrying out of building, engineering, mining or other operations in, on, over or under land, or the making of any material change in the use of any buildings or other land' (*Town and Country Planning Act 1990* S55(1)). All development is regulated in two main ways, through strategic planning and development control.

Strategic planning takes place at a regional and local level through the construction, debate and agreement of development plans for a specific area (e.g. a town, district or county). The confirmed plans set out the framework within which development will take place, and include projections of future needs and a means of achieving those needs through the allocation of land for such things as house building, mineral extraction, waste disposal, road construction, energy supply, recreational provision and so on. Included in the scheme should be a detailed consideration of the expected impact on archaeological remains and how such impacts can be minimized through the careful selection of allocated land.

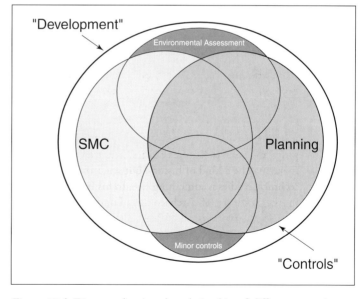

*Figure 17.4* Diagram showing the relationship of different controls over developments impacting on archaeological deposits. SMC = scheduled movement consent procedure (see p. 307).
*Source*: Timothy Darvill

Development control relates to the decision-making process as it applies to individual schemes. Here international legislation provides the top layer of guidance. In 1985, the European Commission introduced a *Directive on Environmental Assessment* (Directive 85/337/EC), which was implemented in the United Kingdom as *The Town and Country Planning (Assessment of Environmental Effects) Regulations 1988*. This provides for the full review of the impact of large and potentially damaging schemes, including reviews of archaeological remains that might be affected. The Directive was revised in 1997 (*Directive N 97/11/EC*), and this in turn will carry through into new legislation in the United Kingdom in due course.

At regional and local level, development control is carried out through the granting of planning permission by local authorities. In determining applications for planning permission, the authorities must give consideration to a wide range of factors. National Planning Policy Guidance notes set out the parameters within which decisions can be taken, and in England PPG16, entitled *Archaeology and Planning*, explains the main considerations (similar guidance is provided for Scotland and Wales in separate documents). In particular, the desirability of preserving nationally important sites *in situ* is made a material consideration, and rescue archaeology is identified as a second-best option where preservation *in situ* is not possible. In granting planning permission, the local planning authority has the power to impose a planning condition that makes provision for an agreed programme of archaeological works (a so-called mitigation strategy) to be carried out prior to the development taking place. Such works would normally be undertaken at the developer's expense.

In England, approximately 480,000 planning applications were submitted to local planning authorities in 1994/5, of which 88 per cent were approved outright or subject to conditions. Processing all these amounts to a very considerable amount of work, especially when it is recognized that nearly 2 per cent of applications had archaeological implications, with perhaps a little under 1 per cent having direct archaeological impacts on recorded remains. Of course, the definition of development is not all-embracing, and many things that are archaeologically damaging fall outside the definition, or are excluded from it by other pieces of special-purpose legislation (e.g. works carried out by public utility companies). Equally, there is provision for the preservation of archaeological remains within other legislation, for example as part of the designation of environmentally sensitive areas (ESAs), and, most recently, for England and Wales, through the reporting of stray finds set out in the *Treasure Act 1997*.

## Ancient monuments legislation

At an international level, the main pieces of guiding legislation are the World Heritage Convention and the Valletta Convention. *The Convention Concerning the Protection of the World Cultural and Natural Heritage*, the World Heritage Convention, is a UNESCO convention, adopted by the General Conference in Paris on the 16th November 1972. It was ratified by the UK Government in 1984, and to 1997 some twelve cultural World Heritage Sites within the UK have been inscribed, including: Studley Royal Park and Fountains Abbey, Stonehenge and Avebury, Canterbury Cathedral and St Augustine's Abbey, The City of Bath, Durham Castle and Cathedral, The City of Edinburgh, The Tower of London, Blenheim Palace, The Palace of Westminster and Westminster Abbey, the castles and town walls of King Edward I in Gwynedd, Ironbridge Gorge and Hadrian's Wall. The primary aim of the Convention is to draw up a list of sites and monuments considered to be of such exceptional interest and such universal value that their protection is the responsibility of all mankind. This is achieved by encouraging international collaboration and making the conservation, management and presentation of World Heritage Sites the direct responsibility of the government of the state in which the designated site lies.

The *European Convention on the Protection of the Archaeological Heritage (revised)* was opened for signature in January 1992 in Valletta, Malta, by the Council of Europe (O'Keefe 1993). The UK Government has yet to ratify the Valletta Convention, but once this is done, its clauses will inform the future development of archaeological legislation in the United Kingdom. The definition of archaeological sites in the convention is broad, including structures, constructions, groups of buildings, developed sites, movable objects, and monuments of other kinds whether situated on land or under water (Article 1). Emphasis is placed on the need to maintain proper inventories of recorded sites; the information is subsequently used in the planning process to ensure well-balanced strategies for the protection, conservation and enhancement of sites of archaeological interest.

At a national level, the main legislation is the *Ancient Monuments and Archaeological Areas Act 1979*, amended for England by the *National Heritage Act 1984*. This legislation relates to sites or monuments that are explicitly recognized as being of archaeological importance. Three such classes of monument are defined: scheduled monuments, of which there are currently about 16,000 in England, 5,300 in Scotland and 2,700 in Wales; guardianship monuments, of which there about 440 in England, 330 in Scotland and 125 in Wales; and Areas of Archaeological Importance, which are confined to five historic towns in England (Canterbury, Chester, Exeter, Hereford and York). Apart from guardianship, where the objective of direct management is total preservation of the site, the other designations are methods of controlling change as a means of achieving preservation. In the case of scheduled monuments, control is achieved through a scheduled monument consent procedure, whereby permission is needed to undertake any kind of works likely to damage the monument. Such permissions may be subject to conditions, including the full archaeological investigation and recording of remains prior to works commencing.

Dealing with all these legal and advisory frameworks, together with numerous policy statements issued by public bodies and interested parties, the process of decision making has become highly complicated. Moreover, one of the fundamental principles of archaeological resource management is that decision making should be properly informed. Accordingly, what has become known as the 'management cycle' has developed as a consolidated, repeatable, and widely applicable system to guide the acquisition of information and the decision making process (Darvill and Gerrard 1994, 157). Figure 17.5 shows the management cycle in schematic form with eight main stages:

- Appraisal: define the problem or issue. In the case of a development programme, this would first involve the definition of the development site boundaries and the nature and scale of what was to be done.

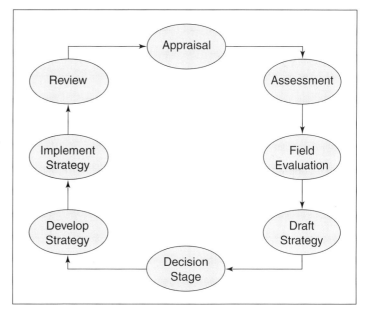

*Figure 17.5* Schematic representation of the management cycle applied to archaeological situations.
*Source*: Timothy Darvill

- Assessment. This represents the first substantial piece of work in the management cycle, usually desk-based, and will most likely be undertaken according to a project design or specification established at the appraisal stage.
- Field evaluation. This stage involves the close examination of the archaeological resource, sometimes through excavation, to determine, as far as practicable, the principal physical characteristics of the quality, extent, survival, condition and fragility of the deposits, as well as details of form, interpretation, date and archaeological potential.
- Strategy formulation. This stage involves the construction of an archaeological management or mitigation strategy or detailed project design of some kind, based on the information and conclusions documented by the field evaluation.
- Decision. Here a competent authority will decide whether the strategy as formulated should proceed or not. In the context of a development proposal, this stage will primarily be through the planning system, although where scheduled ancient monuments are involved, the decision will also be through the scheduled monument consent system. In the case of research programmes, the project design will probably be the basis of funding approvals.
- Strategy development. Using comments and information from the decision phase, the strategy itself can be developed and expanded, with more detail added if necessary.
- Strategy implementation. In archaeological terms, this is the most visible element of the work, as it involves what most people would regard as the real business of archaeology: excavations, surveys, technical studies, and so on. In the case of a development scheme, this often happens in three phases:

  *Pre-construction works*: preparatory works for the preservation or conservation of deposits, and the total or selective excavation of areas before groundworks get under way.

  *Intra-construction works*: small-scale excavations, watching briefs, and recorded observations undertaken in parallel with groundworks and the activities of construction contractors on the site.

  *Post-construction works*: archaeological operations carried out after the development is complete, including on-site operations such as the establishment and maintenance of long-term conservation or preservation measures, and off-site operations such as the analysis of finds and records from earlier phases of archaeological work, the conservation of fragile finds, the preparation of general and academic reports and accounts of the work, and the deposition of the archive and finds in an appropriate museum.

  For research programmes, the implementation stage will comprise the execution in series or in parallel of the various pieces of data-collection, followed by an analysis and reporting stage.

- Review. The final stage in the cycle is a review of what has been done and whether it has achieved what was intended. In some cases, this stage may last several years, with regular monitoring to see that aspects of the scheme are working.

In all these stages, professionalism is increasingly important. Since its creation in 1982, the Institute of Field Archaeologists has been concerned with the promotion and raising of professional standards. Its membership, which represents over one-third of all professional archaeologists in the UK, work to an agreed set of 'standards' for archaeological projects. However, what no legislation, policy, guidance or standards can deal with is the political and emotional aspects of the process. Both are surprisingly important. In the case of planning decisions, it is not the professional advisers who make the decisions but elected representatives as council members who sit on planning committees. It is these groups who ultimately decide whether archaeological considerations must give way to social, economic or ideological pressures, or *vice versa*; and the general public have an increasingly strong voice in these discussions too, as the case of the Rose Theatre in London illustrates very clearly.

The Rose Theatre is one of four Tudor/Jacobean playhouses known to have existed on London's South Bank, its exact site being well known. In 1988, the local planning authority granted planning permission for the development of the site as offices, with a voluntary agreement between the developers and the Museum of London to allow and fund two months' excavation before development commenced. However, once the remains of the theatre were uncovered and found to be in reasonably good condition, public pressure to preserve the site became intense, with groups of well-known actors and others staging protests, lobbying Parliament to schedule the remains, and forming the Rose Theatre Trust to pursue legal actions through the courts to prevent development. English Heritage stepped in with temporary measures to preserve the remains while a solution was found, and helped develop a long-term preservation scheme which involved the redesign of the building on new foundations and the creation of a sub-basement in which the remains of the theatre could be protected and conserved (Biddle 1989; Wainwright 1989).

What the Rose Theatre case highlights is, firstly, the intensity of public interest and concern for the archaeological heritage, and, secondly, the fact that even when the proper procedures have been followed there are no easy answers to satisfy everyone. An important element of archaeological resource management has become the skill of finding ways of satisfying more than one demand at a time, balancing competing interests. The tools available to do this comprise what are called 'management options'. These can be deployed either in series or in parallel for maximum effect, the full range of such options being very considerable, and expanding. Broadly, however, they fall into three groups: protection, conservation and exploitation.

- Protection. This involves minimizing or guarding against the adverse affects of some kind of identifiable threat to the archaeological resource. The main source of such threats comes from disturbance of the ground in which ancient structures and deposits lie.

   In urban areas, construction works such as the excavation of basements, foundations, soakaways, drains and lift-shafts are all common causes of such disturbance, as too is the laying of pipelines or groundworks connected with the creation of level surfaces for car-parks and playing fields. These can be anticipated and a balance achieved between the economical construction of buildings and the constraints (archaeological and otherwise) of the site. There are a number of ways in which the preservation of archaeological deposits can be achieved, many of which require an engineered solution to the problem of supporting large structures on small but strong foundations.

   In the countryside, the main threats are from agriculture and extensive land-use such as forestry. Here protection can be provided either by creating local micro-environments for recognized monuments, for example by taking them out of cultivation, or by fencing and marking them (Figure 17.6). Intensive threats in the countryside, from quarrying, mineral extraction and road construction, for example, require similar protective measures to those used in urban areas, and here again engineers are becoming increasingly imaginative in what can be achieved.

   Protection, however, is a static response. The threat needs to be anticipated, and in developing ways of averting damage, other inadvertent consequences sometimes emerge.

- Conservation. This, by contrast, is a dynamic response and involves establishing a positive relationship between processes of change and the maintenance of the archaeological resource. Typically this involves the adoption of land management regimes that promote the stability of buried or upstanding archaeological deposits, and keeping in check any events that might cause the accelerated decay of such remains (Figure 17.7). Conservation requires constant vigilance and the availability of skills not only to recognize signs reflecting the onset of accelerated decay but also to do something about it. In the case of small-scale effects, the process is straightforward. Visitor erosion where footpaths cross archaeological sites is one of the most widespread examples, where the opportunity to move the main path slightly or divert users to allow the regeneration of vegetation cover may be all that is needed. Bigger problems are more difficult, among the worst being tree-throw in strong winds, and coastal erosion. The National Trust in particular is at the forefront of developing new approaches to these kinds of problems in the countryside, and much innovative research is carried out on their properties.

•  Exploitation. Many demands are placed upon the archaeological resource by today's society. These range from access to ancient monuments for educational and recreational use, promotion of the archaeological heritage as a tourist attraction and visitor facility, and the exploration of the past through research and study. All represent perfectly legitimate claims, and need to be taken into account when considering the long-term future of the resource. Intensive exploitation of the archaeological resource through excavation or restoration for public display can be as destructive as developing the land for a completely non-archaeological objective.

Making accessible some of the more tangible remains of the past often finds public support. Within the development process, and in countryside management, there are numerous opportunities to make aspects of the local archaeological resource accessible. Nor need presentational work always be archaeologically destructive. There is often enough visible already to allow the creation of a 'heritage trail', whether as a self-guided facility or as part of a more structured experience. In almost any development there is scope to mark the positions of earlier buildings in coloured brick, or perpetuate historic alignments, or reconstruct important features. Sociologically, such things serve to strengthen the 'existence' value of the historic elements of cultural heritage.

The number of publicly accessible archaeological sites, museums, heritage centres and historical attractions has risen dramatically in recent decades, and with increases in available leisure time within the population as a whole, historic sites and displays are an important destination for trips and visits. A survey by the British Tourist Authority revealed that in 1995 historic houses and monuments were collectively the second most popular kind of attraction after museums and galleries. The top ten historic houses and monuments comprised: the Tower of London, Windsor Castle, Edinburgh Castle, the Roman baths in Bath, Warwick Castle, Stonehenge, Shakespeare's birthplace, Hampton Court, Leeds Castle and Blenheim Palace.

Whether in public or private hands, there is a range of attractions that run from the almost untouched site opened-up for visitors with

*Figure 17.6* Protecting monuments: wooden barriers in place around a section of Iron Age rampart at Badbury Rings, Dorset.
*Source*: Timothy Darvill

very little razzmatazz, through to the intensively marketed 'heritage attraction' where 'the past comes alive' in a way that is more theatre than exhibition (Figure 17.8). Across this spectrum there is also a visible shift from the authentic at one end to the fabricated at the other. Motivation and purpose is an important consideration when judging these kinds of facility. Some wholly fabricated reconstructions, like Butser Hill Iron Age farm in Hampshire or Bede's World in Jarrow, Tyne and Wear, are serious scientific experiments, carefully researched, and packaged in a way that maintains their integrity as well as providing a good visitor experience. The highly popular Jorvik Centre in York comes close to this too, being a reconstruction based on, and situated exactly over, the excavated remains of one small part of the Viking city.

*Figure 17.7* Conservation in action: restoration and consolidation in progress at Lulworth Castle, Dorset.
*Source*: Timothy Darvill

Simple structures and monuments in the countryside are hard to present to the public to everyone's satisfaction, and raise many interesting issues of interpretation. To what extent should the things presented be authentic? Do the visiting public discern between what is real and what is not? Again the picture is far from simple, with progression from the wholly authentic, through the restored, to the reconstructed (Figure 17.9), and on again to the totally fabricated. At Guardianship properties managed by English Heritage, the policy is to consolidate as found, in other words not to add anything or take anything away but simply to make safe whatever is there when they take the site over. Even this can be misleading, however, because the Victorians in particular were great restorers and some of what is visible at well-known monuments today is little more than 100 years old. Moreover, painstaking research is often needed to spot the additions. The Rollright Stones in Oxfordshire provide a good example (Lambrick 1988). This well-known and much visited stone circle today comprises about 73 upright stones in what appears to be an almost perfect ring. Studies by the Oxford

*Figure 17.8* Heritage at work: the Morwellham Quay Heritage centre, Devon.
*Source*: Timothy Darvill

*Figure 17.9* Reconstructing archaeological remains: Roman gatehouse at South Shields, Tyne and Wear.
*Source*: Timothy Darvill

Archaeological Unit, however, revealed that at least a third of the stones had been repositioned in AD 1882, and that another third of them were leaning or displaced at this time. Two stones were probably added. Of the stones visible today, only about one-third are in the same positions they occupied in the seventeenth century AD.

Social, political and ethical issues are also important, as Stonehenge, Wiltshire, demonstrates time and again. While for decades the main stone circle was accessible to the public, it was closed off in 1983 when visitor numbers rose to over 800,000 per year. The site had become a victim of its own success in the sense that the experience everyone came to see was clouded because so many other people were there too. Interest in the site at the summer solstice followed a similar course. Until the early 1980s, various groups including latter-day druids, hippies, travellers, and many others gathered to witness the sunrise and make festival. Since 1985, the Stonehenge area has been inaccessible to the public over the solstice, much to the dismay of almost everyone (Chippindale 1986; Chippindale *et al.* 1990). Now there are new plans for the conservation and management of Stonehenge and its surroundings, including the closure of the road that runs past the site, the removal of existing visitor facilities at the stones, the creation of an archaeological park containing not only Stonehenge but also many associated monuments, and the re-siting of visitor facilities to a new site beside a main road anything up to 3 km away (Wainwright 1996).

Despite widespread acceptance that something needs to be done about the present arrangements at Stonehenge, and a broad consensus that facilities close to the stones are inappropriate, new conflicts have broken out. On one side are those who argue that the site is Britain's best and most important prehistoric monument, part of a World Heritage Site, and so should be easily accessible to the public with appropriate explanations of what is known about it. On the other side are those who argue that it is all so important and precious that nobody should be allowed near the good bits in case they damage them in some way, and that if people really want to see it then the infrastructure to transport them around must be so well hidden that it does not spoil any views or get too close to the stones. The final solution will eventually err to one side of this argument or the other: both at once is impossible and so compromise seems inevitable.

As an essentially academic subject, archaeology is driven forward by the results of research and new discoveries (Figure 17.10). There has been much debate about what constitutes research in this sense, who should do it, and who should be setting the agenda; but much of the discussion misses the point that all archaeological work that involves the investigation or examination of original data is research in one sense or another. To try to sub-divide and partition archaeological research rigidly into discrete elements is futile, but two very broad and by no means mutually exclusive groupings can be recognized: problem-orientated research and development-prompted research.

Problem-orientated research arises from the definition of a potentially interesting problem and a methodology that allows it to be explored. The work may involve the application of particular methodologies, including perhaps excavation, at a local or regional level, depending on the nature of the problem under investigation. Funding for this kind of work usually comes from public sources through government agencies, local authorities, charitable trusts or universities. Naturally there is considerable competition for the relatively limited sums available.

Development-prompted research arises from the need to investigate deposits that in the normal course of events will be destroyed. This is

*Figure 17.10* Archaeological excavations at Silchester, Hampshire. *Source*: Timothy Darvill

usually because the preservation of a monument, or part of it, is not feasible or is deemed to be of secondary importance to the benefits of the works that will replace it. Superficially, this is 'rescue excavation', at one time rather euphemistically called 'preservation by record'; but to compare modern rescue excavation with that undertaken in the 1960s and early 1970s is rather unfair. Much earlier work was literally rescuing what could be salvaged; nowadays the skill of the archaeological curator specifying the work and the archaeological contractor carrying out the work lies in getting the best information possible from the opportunity available, being selective within defined research parameters.

A popularly perceived down-side to development-prompted research is that investigations are tied to particular development sites which, if the archaeologist has a totally free hand, may not be the first they would choose to excavate. This view is naive and ill-informed. It tries to force development-prompted research into the same frameworks as problem-orientated research, without admitting that both approaches have distinct but different benefits. Much the same arguments were presented in the 1960s and 1970s when a massive motorway construction programme prompted numerous archaeological surveys and excavations. In retrospect, the considered results of that phase of archaeological research completely changed understandings of settlement patterns and estimates of population density for almost every period of Britain's past. Numerous problem-orientated research programmes have arisen as a result of motorway archaeology projects, perhaps more than anything else underlining the need to invigorate archaeological research from as many different sources as possible.

## CONCLUSION

The past gets out of date very quickly, not so much because of new discoveries (although these are always important) but because of new ideas, new models and new explanations. How long the explanations and accounts presented in this book will stand up remains to be seen, but alongside a continuing concern for explanation there is, as this chapter seeks to show, considerable interest in the raw data on which explanations are built. Society continually steals bits of its past to shape its future, sometimes to construct knowledge and create history, at other times out of an interest in physical remains to provide the focus for a day out.

## KEY TEXTS

Darvill, T., 1987. *Ancient monuments in the countryside.* Historic Buildings and Monuments Commission for England Archaeological Report 5. London: English Heritage.
Harrison, R. (ed.) 1994. *Manual of heritage management.* Oxford: Butterworth Heinemann.
Hunter, J.R. and Ralston, I.B.M. (eds) 1993. *Archaeological resource management in the UK: an introduction.* Stroud: Alan Sutton and Institute of Field Archaeologists.
Hunter, M. (ed.) 1996. *Preserving the past: the rise of heritage in modern Britain.* Stroud: Alan Sutton.
Ross, M., 1991. *Planning and the heritage.* London: Spon.

## Bibliography

Barrett, J.C., 1995. *Some challenges in contemporary archaeology.* Oxford: Oxbow Books.
Biddle, M., 1989. 'The Rose reviewed: a comedy (?) of errors', *Antiquity* 63, 753–760.
Carver, M., 1996. 'On archaeological value', *Antiquity* 70, 4556.
Chippindale, C., 1986. 'Stoned Henge: events and issues at the summer solstice 1985', *World Archaeology* 18, 38–58.
Chippindale, C., Devereux, P., Fowler, P., Jones, R. and Sebastian, T., 1990. *Who owns Stonehenge?* London: Batsford.
Cleere, H. and Fowler, P., 1976. 'US Archaeology through British eyes', *Antiquity* 50, 230–232.
Darvill, T., 1995. 'Value systems in archaeology', in Cooper, M.A., Firth, A., Carman, J. and Wheatley, D. (eds) *Managing archaeology.* London: Routledge, 40–50.
Darvill, T. and Fulton, A., 1998. *MARS: The monuments at risk survey of England, 1995. Main Report.* Bournemouth and London: Bournemouth University and English Heritage.
Darvill, T. and Gerrard, C., 1994. *Cirencester: town and landscape.* Cirencester: Cotswold Archaeological Trust.
Darvill, T., Saunders, A. and Startin, B., 1987. 'A question of national importance: approaches to the evaluation of ancient monuments for the Monuments Protection Programme in England', *Antiquity* 61, 393–408.
Fowler, D., 1986. 'Conserving American Archaeological Resources', in Meltzer, D.J., Fowler, D.D. and Sabloff, J.A. (eds) *American Archaeology Past and Future.* Washington: Smithsonian Institution, 135–162.
Fowler, P.J., 1977. 'Land management and the cultural resource', in Rowley, R.T. and Breakell, M. (eds) *Planning and the historic environment II.* Oxford: Oxford University Department of External Studies 131–142.
Fowler, P.J., 1978. 'The business of archaeology', in Darvill, T.C., Parker Pearson, M., Smith, R.W. and Thomas, R.M. (eds) *New approaches to our past: an archaeological forum.* Southampton: Southampton University Archaeological Society, 1–10.
Kristiansen, K., 1993. 'The strength of the past and its great might: an essay on the use of the past', *Journal of European Archaeology* 1, 3–32.
Lambrick, G., 1988. *The Rollright stones: megaliths, monuments, and settlement in the prehistoric landscape.* Historic Buildings and Monuments Commission for England, Archaeological Report 6. London: English Heritage.
Larsen, C.U. (ed.) 1992. *Sites and monuments. National archaeological records.* Copenhagen: The National Museum of Denmark.
Lowenthal, D., 1985. *The past is a foreign country.* Cambridge: Cambridge University Press.
McGimsey, C.R., 1972. *Public Archaeology.* New York and London: Seminar Press.
Macinnes, L. and Wickham-Jones, C.R. (eds) 1992. *All natural things. Archaeology and the green debate.* Oxford: Oxbow Monograph 21.
O'Keefe, P.J., 1993. 'The European convention on the protection of the archaeological heritage', *Antiquity* 67, 406–413.
Rahtz, P.A. (ed.) 1974. *Rescue archaeology.* Harmondsworth: Penguin.
Saunders, A.D., 1983. 'A century of ancient monuments legislation 1882–1982', *Antiquaries Journal* 63, 11–33.

Thomas, C., 1971. 'Ethics in archaeology', *Antiquity* 45, 268–274.

Thomas, C., 1977. *After RESCUE, what next?*. London: Council for British Archaeology (First de Cardi Lecture).

Wainwright, G.J., 1989. 'Saving the Rose', *Antiquity* 63, 430–435.

Wainwright, G.J., 1996. 'Stonehenge saved?', *Antiquity* 70, 9–12.

# Index

Illustrations are indicated by page numbers in *italics* or by *illus* where figures are scattered throughout the text.

Abbeydale Forge (Sheffield) 286
Aberdeen 215
Aberdulais Falls (W Glam) 287
Abergavenny (Gwent) 211, 214
Abingdon Ashville (Oxon) 120
accessibility, monuments 310–12
*Ad Gefrin* 188
Adam, Robert 269
aerial photography 3, *4*
Agricola 138, 141, 143, 149, 153
agriculture: Neolithic 58–9, 60–1, 62, 74–5; Early Bronze Age 85, 91; Later Bronze Age 103, 105, 109, 110; Iron Age 115–16, 125, 129; Roman 171–2; early historic period 181–2; medieval 247, 254–5; post-medieval 266, 271, 280, 293; *see also* diet, field systems, subsistence
*Ahrensburgian* industry 31–2
Aldborough (Suffolk) 207
Aldermaston Wharf (Berks) 99
Aldingham (Cumbria) 235
Aldwincle (Northants), enclosure *118*
Alfred 176, *180*, 194, 204
almshouses 276
Alt Chrysal (W Isles) 84
altars, Roman 138, 168
amber 19, 80, 89, 106
Amlwch (Anglesey) 287
Ammianus Marcellinus 138
amphitheatres 161, *162*
An Corran (Skye) 43
*Ancient Monuments Protection Act 1882* 298
Anderton boat lift *291*, 292
Angles 184
animal bone deposits, ritual: Neolithic 58, *70*, 71, 74; Early Bronze Age 87, 89; Later Bronze Age 101, 109
animal husbandry *see* agriculture
antler-working: Upper Palaeolithic 16–17, 21;

Mesolithic *41–2*, 43, 45, 50; *see also* bone-working
Antonine Wall 136, 149, *151*, 152, 153
Antoninus Pius 152, 155
Arbury Camp (Cambs) 121
archaeological resource: defined 300–2; management of 297–300, 304–13; value of 302–4
archaeological theory 5–7
ard agriculture 61, 91
Ardoch (Perths) *146*, 147
Areas of Archaeological Importance 307
army, Roman *see* Roman army
Arnol (Lewis) 267
art: Upper Palaeolithic 23, 24, 28, *32*; Mesolithic *42*, 43, 44; Iron Age 128, 131; Roman 174; early historic period 184, 190–1, 196; *see also* sculpture
Arthur 178, 180–1
artillery emplacements 1, *2*, 234, 269
Ashgrove (Fife) 81
astronomical theories 92
Atkinson, R.J.C. 61
Aubrey, John 298
Augustine, St 188
Aulus Plautius 136
Avebury (Wilts): Neolithic period 60, 72–3, 74; Bronze Age period 90; communications study 262; World Heritage Site designation 306
Aveline's Hole (Som) 43–4
Avington VI (Berks) 30
axes: Mesolithic 38; Neolithic 59, 64, 65–6, 71; Early Bronze Age 78, *80*, 83, 92; Later Bronze Age 107
Aylesford (Kent) 124

Badbury Rings (Dorset) *310*
Bagendon (Glos) *122*
Baldock (Herts) 120, 123, 124
Balfarg (Fife) 62, 73
Balladoole (Isle of Man) 198, *199*, 200
Ballateare (Isle of Man) 198

Banbury (Oxon) 215, 216
Bancroft *116, 119*
banjo enclosures 117
barbed points *see* harpoons
Barburgh Mill (Dum & Gall), fortlet 140, *145*
Barnack (Cambs) 89, 165, 189
Barnard Castle (Co Durham) 235, 243
Barnhouse (Orkney) 65
barns: Roman 164; medieval 254; post-medieval *293*
Barnstaple (Devon) 213, 214
Barrow (Lincs) 232
barrows: Iron Age 123; Scandinavian 198; *see also* long barrows, round barrows/cairns
Barton Bendish (Norfolk) 232
Barton Blount (Derbys) 254, 255
Barton-on-Humber (Humb), church 232, *233*, 234
Barvas (W Isles) 84, *85*
bastle houses *268*
Bath (B&NES): Roman period 168; early historic period 204; post-medieval period 277, *278*; World Heritage Site designation 306
bath houses 143, 161, *162*
Bathampton Down (B&NES) 120
batons, Upper Palaeolithic 17, *20*, 21
battle axes, Bronze Age 80, 89
beads: Upper Palaeolithic 17, 32; Mesolithic *42*, 43, 44, 54–5; Bronze Age 80, 89; Iron Age 125, 126; early historic period 182
Beamish Museum (Co Durham) *283*
Beckford (Worcs) 166
Bede 178, 179, 184, 185, 188
Bedford (Beds) 211, 235
Beechamwell (Norfolk) 232
Beer (Devon) 19
beetle studies 13, 15, 24, 29
Belgae 114, 115, 130
Belle Tout (Sussex) 85
Belling Law (Northumb) 170
Benedict Biscop, St 189
Benie Hoose (Shetland) 84–5
Beresford, Maurice 250–1
Bersham (Clwyd) 285
Bersu, Gerhard 6, 115
Bertha (Perths) 149
Berwick-on-Tweed (Northumb) 214, 215, 269
Bigbury (Kent) 121
Bignor (W Sussex) 165
Birrens (Dum & Gall) 141
Birsay (Orkney) 202
Bishopstone (Sussex) 117
Black Death 211, 224, 247
Black Patch (E Sussex) 100, *101*
Blackpool (Lancs) 278
Blashenwell (Dorset) 49
Blenheim (Oxon) 268, 306

block houses 234
bloodstone 47, 51
boats: Mesolithic 44; Bronze Age 84, *104*, 105, 106; Iron Age 131; early historic period 184; Anglo-Scandinavian 198, *199*, 202; *see also* ports, underwater archaeology
Bodiam Castle (Sussex) 237
Bodmin Moor (Corn) 91, 101
bog bodies 124
Bolsay Farm (Islay) 48, 50–1
Bonawe (Argyll), ironworks *286*
bone-working: Upper Palaeolithic 16–17, 20–1; Mesolithic 50; *see also* antler-working
Book of Durrow 190
Book of Kells 191
Boothby Pagnell (Lincs) 235
Bordesley (Worcs) 241, 260, 288
Boston (Lincs) 211, 225
Boudiccan rebellion 136, 149, 162
Bradford (W Yorks) 290
Brandon (Suffolk) 190
Braughing-Puckeridge (Herts) 121
Brecon (Powys) 211
Brecon Beacons (Powys), tramways 293
Breiddin (Powys) 102, 120
Brewster, Tony 250
bridges: medieval *262*, 274; post-medieval 274, 283, *284*, 285, 292
Bridgnorth (Shrops) 214
Bridgwater canal 275
Brigantes 136, 149
Brighton (Sussex) 278
Brindley, James 292
briquetage 126
Bristol 212, 214, 215, 225, 233
Brixworth (Northants) 189
brochs 113, 117, 130
Brockhill (Surrey) 25
Broken Cavern (Devon) 25, 26
Brompton (N Yorks) 201
brooches: Iron Age *114*, 131, 132; Roman 174; early historic period 182, 184, 186, 196
Brooklands (Surrey) 125
Broom Hill (Hants) 43, 54
Broomend of Crichie (Aberdeen) 90
Brouster (Shetland) 84
Brown, Capability 272
Bruce, Sir William 269
Bruce-Mitford, Rupert 250
Brycheiniog, kingdom of 176
Bryn y Castell (Gwynedd) 125
Bu, house plan *116*
building technology 221, 290
buildings, domestic: Mesolithic 43, *49*; Neolithic 63, *64*, 65, 75; Early Bronze Age 84, *85*, 86, 91, 93; Later Bronze Age 99, 100, *101*, 102, 105; Iron Age 115, *116*, 117, 120–1, 132;

Roman, 162, 164, 166, *170*; *see also* villas; early historic period 187–8; Anglo-Scandinavian 196, *201–2*, 203, *204*; medieval (rural 250–1, *252*, 253–4, *255*, 256; urban 217, *218–20*, 221, 224); post-medieval (rural 266–7, *268–9*; urban 276, 277, *278*, 290–1)

*burhs* 194, 203–4, 206, 234, 235

burials: Upper Palaeolithic 21–3, 28; Mesolithic 43–4; Neolithic, 60, *66*, 67, *68–9*, 70, 71; Early Bronze Age *86–8*, 89–90, 91, 93; Later Bronze Age 95, 99, 100, 108; Iron Age 113, 123, *124*, 130; Roman 159, 162, 163–4, 168, 174; early historic period 179, 182–4, *185*, 186, 188–9, 190; Anglo-Scandinavian 195, 197–8, *199*, 200–1, 202; medieval 233–4, 242; post-medieval 233

burnt stone mounds 102–3

Burton Dassett (Warks) 253, 254

Burton Fleming-Rudston (E Yorks) 123

Bury St Edmunds (Suffolk) 31, 218

Bush Barrow (Wilts) 89

butchery: Upper Palaeolithic 20, 28; Mesolithic 45, 46

Butterley Company 292

Buxton (Derbys) 278

Cadbury Castle (Som) 120, 180

Caerleon (Gwent) 140, 147

Caernarvon (Gwynedd) 214

Caldecotte (Herts) 256

Calke Abbey (Derbys) 293

Callanish (Lewis) 60, 73

Camber Castle (Sussex) 269

Camden, William 298

Camelon (Stirling) 149

Campsey Ash (Suffolk) 242

canals, 275, *291*, 292

*cannabae* 147

cannibalism 23

Canterbury (Kent) 306, 307: Iron Age oppidum 121; Anglo-Saxon churches 189; medieval period 213, 214, 215, 216, 218, 244

Carausius 137, 155

Cardiff (Glam) 211, 214

Carlisle (Cumbria) 141

Carmarthen (Carmarth) 211

Carn Brea (Corn) 70

Carn Euny (Corn) 130

Cass Ny Hawin (Isle of Man) 38, 43

Cassington (Oxon) 86

Castle Acre (Norfolk) 235, *236*, 243

Castle Combe (Wilts) 212

Castle Rising (Norfolk) 237

castles (*illus*) 11, 234–8, 243, 244–5: function 229; replacement of 267–9; Welsh 211, 214, 237–8, 306

Castletown Roche (Ireland) 78

Catsgore (Som) 166

Caughley (Shrops) 294

causewayed enclosures 59, 60, 75: ditch deposits 67, *70*, 74; interpretation 61–2, *70*, 71–2

Causey (Co Durham) 285, 292

Cefn Graeanog (Gwynedd) 254–5

cemeteries: Mesolithic 43–4; Early Bronze Age 90, 91, 93; Later Bronze Age 99, 100; Iron Age 123–4, 130; Roman 162, 163, 168; early historic period (*illus*) 179, 182–6, 188–9, 190; Anglo-Scandinavian 195, 198, 199, 202; medieval 233–4, 242; *see also* burials

cereal cultivation *see* agriculture

cereal exploitation, ?Mesolithic 54

Chalton (Hants), settlement *166*, 187–8

chambered tombs 59–60, 66, 67, *68*, 90

chapels, nonconformist 269

charcoal 261, 272, 285–6

Charterhouse (Som) 287

Cheddar (Som) 20, 188, 205

Chepstow (Gwent) 235

chert 19, 25, 51

Chester (Ches): Area of Archaeological Importance designation 307; Roman fortress 140; Anglo-Scandinavian period 196, 203–4, 206; medieval period 211, 225

Chichester (W Sussex) 204

chiefdom societies 89

Childe, V. Gordon 5, 77, 304

china clay mining 274

Chingley (Kent) 260, 286

Chisenbury Warren (Wilts) 166

Christianity: Roman 168, 169; early historic period 179, 182, 188–9; *see also* churches, monasteries

chronology 2–3

Church Hole (Derbys) 17, 21, 23

churches: Roman 168, *174*; early historic period 188–9, 228; Anglo-Scandinavian 206–7; medieval (*illus*) 228–9, 230–4, 242–3, 244–5, 249; post-medieval period 269; *see also* Christianity, monasteries

Chysauster (Corn) *119*

Cill Donnain (W Isles) 84, *85*

cists: Bronze Age 87, 91; Iron Age 124; early historic period 182; Anglo-Scandinavian 199

*civitas*-capitals *161*, 162

clachans 266

Clandon barrow (Dorset) 89

Clark, Grahame 6, 45, 61

Clarke, David, L. 6

Claudius 155, 167

Clava cairns (Highland) 72

Claydon Pike (Glos) 166

Cleaven Dyke (Perths) 72

Clee Hills (Shrops) 285

clothing, Bronze Age 80

Cnoc Coig *see* Oronsay
coaching inns 277
coal mining: medieval *248*, 285; post-medieval 273, 281, 285, 288
Coalbrookdale (Shrops) 286
Coalport (Shrops) 294
coffins: Bronze Age *87*; early historic period 184, 185; Anglo-Scandinavian 198, 199
Cogidubnus 164
coins/coinage: Iron Age (Celtic 122, 123, *129*, 130; Gallo-Belgic 128, 130; function 132–3); Roman 159, 168; early historic period 179, 184–5, 191, 206; Viking 195; medieval *223*, 248; *see also* currency bars
Colchester (*Camulodunum*, Essex); Iron Age oppidum *122*, 123, 130; Roman period 136, 161, 167, 172; medieval town 225
Coleorton (Leics), coal mining *248*
Collfryn (Powys) 117, *118*
*coloniae* 161, 162
Columba, St 188
Combley (Isle of Wight) 164
Coney Island (Co Armagh) 85
Coneybury (Wilts) 58, 64, 73
Coniston (Cumbria) 273
conservation, industrial sites 295; *see also* archaeological resource, management of
Conwy (Gwynedd) 214
copper mining: Bronze Age 78, 104, 105, 106; Iron Age 128; Roman 172; post-medieval *287*
copper/copper alloy-working: Early Bronze Age 78; Later Bronze Age 100, 102–3, 105, 106–8; Iron Age 125, 128; Anglo-Scandinavian 205; medieval 220; post-medieval 287
Corbridge (Northumb), fortress 139, *142*, 143
cord rig 113
Corfe (Dorset) 235
Corlea (Ireland) 78
Cosmeston (Glam) 254
Cothill Fen (Oxon) 54
Coulererach (Islay) 38, 50–1
court cairns 67
courtyard houses 117, 130, 169
Coventry (W Mids) 212, 215, 225
Cowdery's Down (Hants) 188
Cowlam (Yorks) 265
Craigievar (Aberdeen) 269
crannogs 3, 113, 186
Crathes Castle (Aberdeen) *269*
Crawford, O.G.S. 250
cremations: Neolithic 60, 67, 71, 72; Early Bronze Age 82, 86–7, 88, 90, 91, 93; Later Bronze Age 95, 100, 102, 108; Iron Age 123, *124*, 130; early historic period 182, *183*, 184; Anglo-Scandinavian 198
Creswellian industry *16*, 17–24
Cricklade (Glos) 204

Crickley Hill (Glos) 62, 71, 120
Croft Ambrey (Heref) 120
crofting 271
Cromford (Derbys) 274
Crosskirk (Caithness), broch *116*, 130
Cuerdale (Lancs), hoard 195, *196*
Culduthel (Highland) 89
culture history 5–7
Culverwell (Dorset) 48–9, 53, 55
Cunliffe, Barry 115
cup and ring marked stones 91
currency bars 125
curses 168
cursus monuments 59, 60, *71*, 72, 91
*cursus publicus* 163
Cuthbert, St 188
Cwmystwyth (Dyfed) 78

daggers, Bronze Age 92
Dallican Water (Shetland) 44
Dalmore (W Isles) 84, *85*
Dalriada 176, 182
Dalswinton (Dum & Gall) 151
Dalton Parlours (W Yorks) 117, *119*
Danebury (Hants) 120, *121*, 123
Danelaw 194, 203
Daniel, Glyn 92
Darby, Abraham 286
Dartmoor (Devon), land division 91, 101, *102*
Dartmouth (Devon) 234, 288
dating methods 2–3
David I 211
Deepcar (Yorks) 43, 51
defences, medieval 214–15
demography: Mesolithic 55; Neolithic 62, 74; Bronze Age 99; Iron Age 129; early historic period 181; medieval 247, 257, 262; post-medieval 264, 269, 270, 276, 281
dendrochronology 3, 5, 141
Denmark, kingdom of 207
Derby (Derbys) 203, 290
Dere Street 143
Derwentcote (Co Durham) 286
deserted medieval villages 250–3, *253–4*, 265
development control 305–6
diet: Roman, 148, 171–2; early historic period 205; Anglo-Scandinavian 205–6; medieval 221–2, 243, 244, 245; *see also* agriculture, feasting
Dinas Powys (Glam) 186
Dinorben (Clwyd) 102
Dio Cassius 138
dioceses 229
disease 222, 291; *see also* Black Death
Ditchley (Oxon) 164
DNA 22, 44

Doarlish Cashen (Isle of Man) 201
documentary sources *see* historical sources
Doddington (Northants) *259*
Dolaucothi (Carmarth) 172
domestication 31–2, 59, 62
Don Valley (Aberdeen), aerial view *4*
Doncaster (Yorks) 214
Doniford Cliff (Som) 31
*donjons* 236, 244
Dorchester-on-Thames (Oxon) 72
Dorset Cursus *71*, 72
Douglas, James 298
Douglasmuir (Angus) 117, *119*
Dover (Kent): boat 84, *104*, 105, 106; metalwork 106
Down Farm (Dorset) 86, 90
Downton (Hants) 50
Dragonby (Lincs) 117
Droitwich (Worcs) 126
drove roads 274
Dryburn Bridge (E Loth), Iron Age settlement 117, *119*
Duddingston Loch (Edinburgh) 107
Duggleby Howe (Yorks) 67
Dunadd (Argyll) 186
Dundee (Angus) 277
Dundurn (Perths) *186*
Dunfermline (Fife) 211
duns 113
Dunstan Park (Northumb), Iron Age house plan *116*
Durham (Co Durham) 306
Durrington Walls (Wilts) 58, 61, 72, 73
Dyfed, kingdom of 176

Earls Barton (Northants) 29, 189, 231
East Anglia, kingdom of 176, 185, 194
East Chisenbury (Wilts) 101
economy *see* agriculture; industry; markets; subsistence; technology; trade/exchange systems
Edinburgh: defences 214, 215; growth of 211; houses 219, 277; World Heritage Site designation 306
Edlington Wood (Yorks) 21
Edward I 211, 214, 238, 306
Edward the Elder 204
Edwin 188
Eildon Hill North (Roxburghs) 120
Elderbush Cave (Staffs) 29
Eldon's Seat (Dorset) 120
Elginhaugh (Midlothian) 140, 141, 143, *144*, 151
Elsham (Lincs) 183
Elstow (Beds) 244
employment, archaeological 1, 299
enclosure, fields 270–1
enclosures: Neolithic 58, 60, 70–4; Bronze Age

86, 90–1, *100*, 101; Iron Age 115, 117, *118*, 120–2, 130, 132
environmental archaeology 5
environmental evidence: Upper Palaeolithic 14–15, 24, 29; Mesolithic 35–7, 44, 46, 52–3, 54; Neolithic 60, 62; Bronze Age 91–2, 103; Iron Age 115; Roman 141–2, 160; medieval 245; *see also* molluscan studies, pollen studies, woodland clearance
Eoforwic *see* York
Ertebølle culture 63
Essendon (Herts) 123
Ethelbert 188
Ethelflaed 203
Ethelred 206
Etton (Cambs) 67, 71
Ewart Park (Northumb), metalwork 96, *98*
excavation units 299
exchange systems *see* trade/exchange systems
Exeter (Devon): Area of Archaeological Importance designation 307; *burh* 204; churches 229; houses 219; suburbs 216; trade 225
Eyemouth (Borders) 269
Eynsham (Oxon) 86

factories 274, 281, 289–90
fairs, medieval 210; *see also* markets
feasting: Neolithic 58, 71; Bronze Age 101, 103, 109, 111; Iron Age 122, 124, 128
*Federmesser* industries 26, 27
Fendoch (Perths) 141
Fengate (Cambs) 61, 99, 117, *119*, 120
feudalism 194, 229
field systems: Neolithic 61; Bronze Age 99, 100, 101, *102*, 103, 110; Iron Age 113, 129; Roman *166*; early historic period 181–2; Anglo-Scandinavian 201; medieval 258, *259*, 260, 266; post-medieval 266, 270–1, 280, 293
fieldwork 7–8
Filey (N Yorks), watchtower 141, *145*, 146
fire, Mesolithic use of 52, 54
Fishbourne (W Sussex) 164
Fisherwick (Staffs) 117
fishponds 215, 241
Fison Way (Norfolk) 123
Flag Fen (Cambs) 99, 105, 106, 107
Flagstones (Dorset) 59, 72
Flint (Clwyd) 214
flint assemblages: Upper Palaeolithic *16*, 18–19, 21; Final Upper Palaeolithic (*illus*) 24–7, 28, 29–32; Mesolithic (*illus*) 37–40, 43, 45–52, 54; Neolithic 59, 65; Early Bronze Age 78, 80, 81, *82*; Later Bronze Age 104; *see also* microwear analysis
flint mining 65–6, 104
Flixborough (Lincs) 190
fonts 168

food *see* agriculture, diet
footprints, Mesolithic 38
fora/basilicae 161, *162*
Fort Augustus (Highland) 269
Fort George (Highland) 269
fortlets, Roman: described 140, *145*; distribution 139, 141, 149, *150*, 152–3, *154*
fortresses, Roman 139–40, *142*, 143, 147
forts: Roman (*illus*) 139–55; post-medieval 234, 269
Fosse Way 149
Fountains Abbey (N Yorks) 239, *240–1*, 306
Fox, C.F. 114
Fox Hole (Derbys) 17, 21
Foxcotte (Hants) 255
Framlingham (Suffolk) 237
Framlingham Earl (Norfolk) 231
Frampton (Dorset) 168
Frere, Sheppard 162
friaries 216, 230, 240, 241
Froggatt (Derbys) 21
frontiers, Roman 149, *150–1*, 152–5
funerary monuments/rites *see* burials, cemeteries, chambered tombs, cists, cremations, long barrows, passage graves, portal dolmens, round barrows/cairns
Furnells (Northants) 201
Furness (Cumbria) 286

Gadebridge (Herts) 164
Gainsthorpe (Lincs) 250
gardens, post-medieval *272*
Garrod, Dorothy 16
Gask frontier 140, 146, 149, *150*, 153
Gatehampton Farm (Oxon) 30–1
Gawton (Devon) 287
Geoffrey of Monmouth 180
geographical information systems 4
geophysical survey 4
Gildas 178–9, 180, 188
Glasgow 215, 277
glass making: Iron Age 125, 126, 129; post-medieval 284
Glastonbury (Som): Arthur 180; lake village *119*, 120
Gleann Mor (Islay) *48*, 50
Glenbatrick (Jura) 47
Glenelg (Highland) 269
Glenochar (S Lanarks) *268*
Gloucester (Glos) 161, 211, 212, 216, 276
Godmanchester (Cambs) 214
gold mining 104, 172
gold-working 78, 80, 89
Goldcliff (Gwent) 117
Goldington (Beds) 87
Goltho (Lincs): castle 234, 235; houses 196, 201–2, 253, 255

Gomeldon (Wilts) 252, 253
Gorhambury (Herts) villa 164, *165*
Gosforth (Cumbria) 200
Gough's Cave (Som) 14–15, 16–17, 19, 20; art 23–4; burials 22–3, 28, 44
Gouy Cave (France) 23
Gransmoor (E Yorks) 14, 15
Gravelly Guy (Oxon) 120
Great Beere (Devon) 250
Great Orme (Gwynedd) 104
Great Staughton (Hunts) 164
Green Low round barrow (Derbys), grave goods *82*
Greynston (Grenstein, Norfolk) 253
Grime's Graves (Norfolk) 65–6
Grimsby (Humb) 128
*Grubenhaeuser* 187–8
guardianship monuments 307, 311
guildhalls 215, 276
Gurness (Orkney) 130
Gussage All Saints (Dorset) 128
Gwent, kingdom of 176
Gwithian (Corn) 86, 91
Gwynedd, kingdom of 176

Haddenham (Cambs) 70
Hadleigh (Suffolk) 212
Hadrian's Wall 136, 140, *151*, 152, 153, 306; *see also* Housesteads, *Vindolanda*
Hales (Norfolk) 231
Halifax (Yorks) 212
Halton (Lancs) 200
Haltwhistle Burn (Northumb) 151
Hambledon Hill (Dorset) 62, 67, 71, 72
Hamwic (Hants) 191, 194, 203, 204
Hanbury (Worcs) 257
Hangleton (Sussex) 252, 253
harbours *275*, 291; *see also* ports
Hardwick (Oxon) *116*, *118*, 120
Harlow (Essex) *123*
Harold Bluetooth 207
Harold (Harald) Hardraada 195
harpoons: Upper Palaeolithic 17; Mesolithic *41*, 43, 48
Hartlepool (Cleveland) 190, 219
Hasholme (E Yorks) 131
Hatch (Hants) 256
Haverfordwest (Pemb) 215
Hawkes, C.F.C. 114
Haworth (W Yorks) *272*
Hayhope Knowe (Roxburgh) *118*
Hayling Island (Hants) *123*, 168
Hazeldine, William 292
hazelnuts 43, 54
Hazleton long barrow (Glos) 62, 63, 67
Heathery Burn (Co Durham) 102
Heathrow (G London) 7, *123*

Helston (Corn), tin mine *273*
Hemington (Leics), bridge *262*
Hemp Knoll barrow (Wilts) *87*
Hen Domen (Mont) 234, *236*, 243
henges 58, 59, 60, 75; burials 67; interpretation 61–2, 72–4; later monuments in relation to 90, 91
Hengistbury Head (Dorset): Upper Palaeolithic site 25–6, 28; Mesolithic site 50, 51; Iron Age port 131
Henry VIII 297
Hereford (Heref): Area of Archaeological Importance designation 307; cemeteries 233; defences 203, 215; suburbs 216; town plan 214
Herodian 138
Hexham (Northumb) 189
hide-working: Upper Palaeolithic 21, 28; Mesolithic 45, 46, 49, 50; Bronze Age 104; Iron Age 126
Hild, St 190
hillforts/hill top settlements: Bronze Age 102, 115, 120; Iron Age (*illus*) 113, 114, 120–3, 128–30, 132; early historic period *186*; *see also* oppida
Hinton St Mary (Dorset) 168, 169
historical sources: Roman period 136–7, 138–9, 160; early historic period 178–81; medieval period (castles 234; churches 230–1; landscape 247–8, 250; monasteries 238; towns *212*, 213); post-medieval period 264–5 (industry 284; landscape 270; towns 276); *see also* inscriptions
hoards: Early Bronze Age 89–90; Later Bronze Age (*illus*) 95–8, 103, 107–8, 111; Iron Age 113–14, 123, 128; Roman 168; Anglo-Scandinavian 195, *196*, 197, 206; *see also* votive deposits
Hodson, F.R. 114–15
Honorius 137, 178
horse burial 185
Horsehope (Peebles) 109
Hoskins, William 250
hospitals: medieval 210, 216, 230; post-medieval 276
Hound Tor (Devon) 252, 254
houses *see* buildings, domestic
Housesteads (Northumb) 140, 143, *144*
Howe (Orkney) 130
Hull (Humb) 211, 217
human bones, Upper Palaeolithic *22*, 23, 28; *see also* burials
hunting *see* subsistence
Hurst, John 251
Hurst Fen (Suffolk) 61, 64
huts *see* buildings, domestic

Iceni 136, 149
Icklingham (Suffolk) 168
Inchtuthil (Perths), fortress 139, *142*, 143

industrial archaeology 265, 280, 282–4, 295–6
industry: Roman 172; early historic period 194, 204–6; medieval 211, 216, 220–1, 223, 260–1; post-medieval 264, 265–6, 272–4, 280–96; *see also* technology
Ingleby (Derbys) 198
ingots, iron 125
inscriptions: Iron Age 132; Roman *138*, 139, 167, 168; *see also* historical sources
invasion theory 6; Bronze Age 81–2, 91; Iron Age 114–15, 130
Inveraray Castle (Argyll) 269
Iona (Argyll) 188, 194
Iping II (Hants) 49, 50
Ipswich (Suffolk) 191, 194, 225
Ireland, archaeological research 9
iron ore mining/extraction 125, 129, 172, 260, 261
iron-working: Iron Age 125; Anglo-Scandinavian 205; medieval 260–1; post-medieval 272, 284, 285–6, 287
Ironbridge (Shrops) 283, *284*, 289, 292, 306
Irthlingborough barrow (Northants) 87, *88*, 89, 90

Jarlshof (Shetland) 6, 102, *202*
Jarrow (Tyne & Wear) 179, 189, *190*
Jewish communities 218
Jones, Inigo 268, 277
Jope, Martyn 250
Julius Caesar 114, 149
Jurby (Isle of Man) 198
Jutes, 184

Kelvedon (Essex) 123
Kendrick's Cave (Gwynedd) 28, 32
Kent, kingdom of 176, 188
Kent's Cavern (Devon) 13, 16, 17, 19, 21
Killhope (Co Durham) 273, 287
kilns: grain-drying 243, 252, 254; pottery 128, 172, 205, *294*; tile 235, 239; *see also* lime kilns
Kilphedir (Suth) 117
King Barrows (Wilts) 87
kingdoms, early historic period 176, *177*
King's Lynn (Norfolk) 215, 217, 219, 225
Kinloch (Rum) 38, *40*, *47*
Kirk Andreas (Isle of Man) 200
Kirkdale (N Yorks) 207
Kirkstall Abbey (W Yorks) 243
Knap of Howar (Orkney) 60
Knighton Heath (Devon) 95

Lakenheath Warren (Suffolk) 21
Lanark (Larnarks) 211
land boundaries/division: Early Bronze Age 91, 92–3; Later Bronze Age 95, 101, *102*, 103;

Iron Age 113, 121, *122*; medieval 256, 260; *see also* field systems
land reclamation 270
landscape archaeology 3, 283
Langdale (Cumbria) 65–6
Langford (Notts) 87
lathe 125
Lavenham (Suffolk) 212, 215
Laxton (Notts) 270
lead mining 104, 105, 128, 172, 273, 287
lead-working 205, 239, 273, 287
leather-working *see* hide-working
Lechlade (Glos) 166
legislation, archaeological 298, 305–8
Leicester (Leics) 203, 215, 216, 241
Leighton (Powys), barn, *293*
Leland, John 297–8
Levisham (N Yorks) 200
Lichfield (Staffs) 214
Liddle (Orkney) 102
lime kilns 235, 239, 273, 287, 293
Lincoln (Lincs): Roman period 161, 168, *174*; Anglo-Scandinavian period 203, 205, 206; medieval period (churches 229, 231, 232, 242; defences, 214; houses 218; trade 211)
Lindisfarne (Northumb) 194
Lindisfarne Gospels 190–1
Lindow Man 124
*Linearbandkeramik* culture 63, 74–5
Links of Noltland (Orkney) 65
Linlithgow (W Loth) 244
literacy 132, 190, 221, 244
Little Maplestead (Essex), church *242*
Little Waltham (Essex), Iron Age settlement 117, *119*
Little Woodbury (Wilts) 6, 115
Liverpool (Lancs) 294
Lix (Perths) 252
Llanelli (Dyfed) 215
Llanilid (Glam) 15
Llantwit Major (Glam) 164
Llyn Cerrig Bach (Anglesey) 123
Llyn Fawr hoard (Glam) 96, 125
Loch Lang (S Uist) 44
Loch Olabhat (N Uist) 63, *64*
Lockington barrow (Leics) 87, 89
Lockleys (Herts) 164
Lodsworth (W Sussex) 127
Lofts Farm (Essex) *100*
London: Roman period 136, 161, 168; early historic period 191, *192*, 194, 203; medieval period (bridge *212*; castle 236; churches 228, 233; defences 214–15; Guildhall 215; houses 218, 219, 220; trade and industry 211, 215, 220, 225; waterfront 216–17); post-medieval period 276–7; World Heritage Site designation 306

long barrows (*illus*) 58, 59–60, 61–2, 66–9; later monuments incorporate 72, 91
Longthorpe (Cambs) 141
Lounge colliery (Leics) 285
Loveden Hill (Lincs) 183
Lubbock, John 298
Ludlow (Shrops) 213
Lullingstone (Kent) 168
Lulworth Castle (Dorset) *311*
Lydford (Devon) 204, 215
Lydney (Glos) 167
Lythe (N Yorks) 201
Lyveden (Northants) 252, 261

maceheads 59, 80
Machrie Moor (Arran) 54, 92
Maddle Farm (Berks) 164
Maes Howe (Orkney) 59, 65, 68, 73
Magdalenian industry 18, 19
Maglemosian industry 38, 46
Maiden Castle (Dorset) 6, 71, 120–1
Malling (Perths), fort *139*
Malmesbury (Wilts) 204
Manchester 290
manor houses 255
manorial system 194, 228, 231–2, 249
Marden (Wilts) 72
markets: Roman 162, 163; early historic period 191, 204; medieval 210–11, 214, 215, 216; *see also* trade/exchange systems
Marton (N Yorks) 241
masks, antler *42*, 43
mattocks, antler *41*, 43, 54
Meare (Som) 120, 126
Meikle, George 293
Melcombe Regis (Dorset) 213
Meldon Bridge (Scottish Borders) 73
Mellerstain (Scottish Borders), garden *272*
Melsonby (N Yorks), house plan *116*
Meonstoke (Hants) 164
Mercia 176, 194, 203
metal detectors 97
metalwork: Early Bronze Age 78–9, *80*; Later Bronze Age 95–6, *97–8*, 106–8, 110; Iron Age 113, *114*, 125, *126*, 128, 131; early historic period 182–3, 184–6; *see also* hoards
metalworking *see* copper/copper alloy-working, gold-working, iron-working, lead-working, silver-working, tin-working
microwear analysis 46, 50
middens; Mesolithic 37–8, 43, 44, 47–8, 53; Bronze Age 101
Middleton (N Yorks), cross *200*
Midhowe (Orkney) 67
military defences, C20 1, *2*, 9; *see also* camps, castles, fortlets, fortresses, forts, watchtowers
Milking Gap (Northumb) 170

Mill Hill (Kent) 124

mining *see* china clay mining; coal mining, copper mining, flint mining, gold mining, iron ore mining/extraction, lead mining, *see also* quarrying

moated sites 231, 255, 268; *see also* castles

Moel-y-Gaer (Powys) 102, *116*, 120

Mold (Clwyd) 80

Mollins (Lanarks) 149

molluscan studies 60, 91

monasteries: early historic period 188, 189, *190*, 191, 228; Anglo-Scandinavian period 206, 207; medieval 229–30, 238–42 (material from 243–4; properties of 211, 218–19; study of 11, 245); post-dissolution 267, 276

Monkwearmouth (Sunderland) 189, 190, 194

Monmouth (Gwent) 211

Montacute House (Som) *268*

Montgomery (Mont) 243

Morris, Sir John 278

Morriston (Glam) 278

Morton (Fife) 43

Morwellham Quay (Devon) *311*

mosaics, Roman 164, 165, 168, *169*

Mother Grundy's Parlour (Derbys) 23, 25

mottes 234, 235–6, 244–5

Mount Batten (Devon) 131

Mount Gabriel (Ireland) 78

Mount Pleasant (Dorset) 60, 62, 72, *73*, 78, 90

Mount Sandel (Co Antrim) 43, *49*, 54

Much Wenlock (Shrops) 240

Mucking (Essex) *100*, 187

Mullion Cove (Corn) *275*

Nab Head (Dyfed), finds from *42*, 43, 54–5

Nantgarw (Gwent) 294

Nash, John, 277

Naylor, John 293

Ness of Gruting (Shetland) 84

Nettleham (Lincs) 168

New Buckenham (Norfolk) 235

New Lanark (Lanarks) 274

New Shoreham (Sussex) 213

Newark (Notts) 21, 183

Newbridge (Sussex) 260

Newcastle (Tyne & Wear) 215, 217, 225

Newdale (Shrops) 286

Newstead (Roxburghs) 151

Newtown (Powys) 290

Ninian, St 189–90

Nonsuch Palace (Surrey) 267

Nook (Wilts) 166

Normanton Down (Wilts) *86*, 89

North Ferriby (Yorks) 106

North Gill (N Yorks) 52

Northampton (Northants) 205, 216, 220

Northfield (Worcs) 252

Northton (W Isles) 84, *85*

Northumbria 176, 188, 194

Norton Fitzwarren (Som) 83

Norton Priory (Ches) *239*

Norwich (Norfolk): *wic* 194; medieval period (defences 214, 215, 234; guildhall 215; houses 219; religious buildings 228, 231, 232, 241; suburbs 216, 217; trade 211, 212, 225); post-medieval period 276

Nottingham (Notts) 203, 211

Nunburnholme (Humb) 200

Nunney (Som) 235

Oakhanger (Hants) 47, 49, 51

Offa 176, 194, 203

Okehampton (Devon) 243

Old Carlisle (Cumbria), fort *148*

O'Neil, Helen 250

oppida 113, 121, *122*, 162

Oram's Arbour (Hants) 121

Ordovices 153

Orkney 195

Oronsay midden sites *41–2*, 43, 44, 47–8, 53

Orsett (Essex) 70

Oxford (Oxon): defences 204, 214–15; friary 224; houses 203, *219*; suburbs 216

parishes 206, 228–9, 245, 249

Park Street (Herts) 164

Parker, Matthew 180

parks, post-medieval 271, *272*

Parys Mountain (Anglesey) *287*

passage graves 59–60, 68, 75

Patrick, St 168, 188

Paulinus, St 188

Paviland Cave (W Glam) 13

Peacock's Farm (Cambs) 61, 64

Peel (Isle of Man) 199–200

Pelagius 168

pelt processing 20

Pembroke (Pemb) 211, 214

Penard (Glam), hoard 96

Perth (Perths) 214, *220*

Peterborough (Cambs), excavation *7*

Petters Sportsfield (Surrey) 107

phallus, Mesolithic *42*, 43

Picts 137, 176, 178, 188, 189, 202

Piggott, Stuart 61, 92

Pin Hole (Derbys) 23

Pitt Rivers, General 298

Pixie's Hole (Devon) 25, 26, 28

placenames 196

planning: medieval 211, 213–14, 231, 235; post-medieval 274, 278, 291; *see also burhs*

Pleshey (Essex) 213

ploughs, Iron Age 125; *see also* ards

pollen studies: Upper Palaeolithic 15, 24, 29;

Mesolithic *36*, 44, 46, 47, 52, 54; Neolithic 60, 62; Bronze Age 91; Iron Age 115; Roman 141, 160; medieval 245
Pontefract (Yorks) 215
Poole Harbour (Dorset) 128
Popham (Hants) 253
population *see* demography
portal dolmens 67
Portchester (Hants) 204, 235
ports: Iron Age 131; early historic period 179, 191, 203; medieval 211–12, 216–18, *224*, 225; post-medieval 275, 287, 291; *see also* trade/exchange systems, *wics*
Post Track (Som) 65
Potterne (Wilts) 101, 231
Potterspury (Northants) 261
pottery: Neolithic 58, 59, 60, 71, 75; Beaker 60, 77, 78, 80–1, *82*; Early Bronze Age 80–2, *83–4*, 93; Later Bronze Age 96–7, 98, *99–100*, 105, 106; Iron Age 114, *124*, *127*, 128, 131–2; Roman 141, 159, 160, 172, 174; early historic period 181, 182, *183*, 186, 191, 205; medieval 243–4, 248, 261; post-medieval 294, *295*
pottery making: Bronze Age 105; Iron Age 125, 126, 127–8, 129; Roman 172, 173; Anglo-Scandinavian period 205; medieval 221, 261; post-medieval 284, 294–5
Poundbury (Dorset) 168
power systems 274, 280, 287–9
Powys, kingdom of 176
preceptories 241, *242*
preservation *see* archaeological resource, management of
prisons 215
publications 8–9

Quanterness (Orkney) 67
quarrying 65–6, 80, 127, 274
Queenbrough (Kent) 224
querns 113, 125, 126–7

radiocarbon dating 3, 6, 10; Upper Palaeolithic 13–14, 17–18, 25, 26, 29; Mesolithic 46, 47, 48, 49; Neolithic 60; Bronze Age 82, 96, 97; Iron Age 115
Radley oval barrow (Oxon) *66*, 67
railways 275, 291, 292, 293
Ram's Hill (Berks) 83
raths 113
Raunds (Northants): Anglo-Scandinavian period 199, 201, 206, 231; medieval period 231, *232*, 233, 242; project 257–8
Reading (Berks) 225
Red Dell Beck (Cumbria) 287
red ochre 28, 44
Redditch (Worcs), military defences *2*
Redwald 185

Reepham (Norfolk) 232
Reformation 276
Regnenses 149
religion: Roman 138, 167–8; medieval 223; *see also* Christianity
religious sites *see* burials, churches, monasteries, temples/shrines, votive deposits
Rennie, John 292
Repton (Derbys) 195, 197–8
Repton, Humphry 272
rescue archaeology 7, 298–9, 306, 313; urban 213, 225, 265, 276
resource management *see* archaeological resource, management of
Rhuddlan (Clwyd): castle 238; pebble, Mesolithic *42*, 43
Ribblehead (N Yorks), farmstead 196, *201*
Richborough (Kent) *144*, 145, 168
ridge and furrow 258, 271
Ring of Brogar (Orkney) 65, 72, 73
ring-ditches 59, 60
ringworks 234, 235–6
Rinyo (Orkney) 65
Ripon (N Yorks) 189, 200
Risby Warren (Humb) 31
Rivenhall (Essex) 231
Riverdale (Kent) 30
roads: Roman *140*, 163; medieval 261–2; post-medieval 274, 291, 292; *see also* trackways
Robin Hood Cave (Derbys) 17, 19, 20, 23, 24
rock art 91
Rockbourne (Hants) 164
Rockingham (Northants) 261
Rockley (Yorks) 286
Rollright Stones (Oxon) 92, 311–12
Roman army: evidence 135–41; impact 147–8, 169–71; occupation, perception of 141–7; *see also* camps, fortlets, fortresses, forts, frontiers, watchtowers
Roman camps (temporary) *139*, 141, *146*, 147
Romanization 147–8, 170–1, 173–4
Romsey (Hants) 43
Rosal (Suth) 252
Rosinish (W Isles) 84, 91
round barrows/cairns: Neolithic 59, 60, 66–8; Bronze Age *86–8*, 89, 90, 91; reused 182
roundhouses *see* buildings, domestic
Roxby (N Yorks) 117, *119*
Roy…stone Grange (Derbys) 260
Rudkin, Ethel 250
Rudland Rigg (N Yorks) 285
Rudston (Yorks) 72, 90
Runnymede Bridge (Surrey) 99
Ruthven Barracks (Highland) 269

St Albans (*Verulamium*, Herts): oppida *122*, *123*, 124, 130; Roman period 136, 162

St Andrews (Fife) 277
Salcombe (Devon) 84, 106
Salisbury (Wilts) 212, 213, 215
Salmonsbury (Glos) 121
Salt, Titus, 290, 291
salt industry: Bronze Age 103, 104, 109, 110;
    Iron Age 113, 125, 126
Sancton (Yorks) 183
Sanctuary, The (Wilts) 74
Sandal (W Yorks) 235, 243
Sandwell (W Mids) 239
Sankey Navigation 275
Saxon Shore forts 145, 153, *154*, *155*
Saxons 137, 179–80, 184
Scar (Orkney) 199
Scarborough (N Yorks) 278
scheduled monuments 307
Scilly Isles (Corn) 27, 101
Scoti 137, 176, 182
sculpture: Roman 168, 174; early historic period
    179, 189; Anglo-Scandinavian 195, *200*, 201
sea-levels 35, 36, *37*, 44
Seacourt (Oxon) 250
Seamer Carr (N Yorks) 31–2, 44
seaside resorts 278
Selkirk (Scottish Borders) 211
settlement: Neolithic 63, *64*, 65; Early Bronze Age
    84, *85*, 86; Later Bronze Age 96–7, 98–9,
    *100*–1, 102, 110–11; Iron Age (*illus*) 113,
    115–24, 128–30; Roman (*illus*) 161–6,
    169–71; early historic period 179, *186*, 187–8,
    194; Anglo-Scandinavian (*illus*) 194, 196–7,
    201–5; medieval, rural (*illus*) 247–62;
    post-medieval, rural, 265–6; *see also* buildings,
    domestic, towns, villages
Severus, Septimus 136–7, 138, 147, 152
shale objects: Mesolithic *42*, 43, 54–5; Bronze Age
    80, 87, 89, 104, 106; Iron Age 113, 120, 125,
    129
Shapwick (Som) 257
Shaugh Moor (Devon) 87
sheepcotes, 254
shell middens *see* middens
shelters *see* buildings, domestic
Sherbourne (Dorset) 24
Shetland 195
shielings 266, *267*
Shrewsbury (Shrops) 215, 219, 234
shrines *see* temples/shrines
signal stations, Roman 140
Silbury Hill (Wilts) 60, 74
Silchester (Calleva, Hants) *122*, 161–2, 168, *313*
silver-working 172
Skaill (Orkney) 206
Skara Brae (Orkney) 60, 65
Smailholm (Borders) 268
Smeaton, John 292

Snettisham (Norfolk) 123, 128
social organization: Mesolithic 54–5; Neolithic
    61–2, 70; Early Bronze Age 89–90; Later
    Bronze Age 108–9, 111; Iron Age, 128–30
    132–3; early historic period 181, 184–6;
    medieval 222–3, 249
Sockburn (Co Durham) 200
Somerset Levels 61, 64–5
souterrains 117
South Cadbury (Som) 180, 204
South Lodge (Dorset) 86, 90, 100
South Mimms (Herts) 235
South Shields (Tyne & Wear) 141, *312*
South Street long barrow (Wilts) 61
South Witham (Lincs) 242
Southampton (Hants) 204, 214, 215
spas 277–8
Speed, John 276
Spong Hill (Norfolk) 182, *183*
Springfield Lyons (Essex) 100, 107
Springhead (Kent) 30
Springwood Park (Roxburghs) 253, *255*
Sproughton (Suffolk) 30
Sprouston (Scottish Borders) 188
Stackpole Warren (Dyfed) 85
Stafford (Staffs) 205, 215
stalled cairns 68
Stamford (Lincs) 203, 205, 243
standing stones 86, 91
Stanegate 144, 151, 152, 153
Stanion (Northants) *261*
Stanley Mill (Glos) 290
Stansted (Essex) *118*, 123
Stanwick (N Yorks) *122*
Stanydale (Shetland) 84
Staosnaig (Colonsay) 43, 48, 54
Star Carr (Yorks): case study 6, 45–6; economy
    43, 52, 54; environmental evidence 36–7; finds
    from 38, *39*, *41–2*, 43, 44, 50
steel 286
Stephenson, George 292
Stirling (Stirlingshire) 211, 215
Stoke-on-Trent (Staffs), kilns *294*
stone rows and avenues 60, 72, 74, 91
stone and timber circles: Neolithic 59, 60, 72–3,
    74; Bronze Age 86, 91–2
Stonea Camp (Cambs) 121
Stonehenge (Wilts): Neolithic period 58, 59, 67,
    72, 73–4; Bronze Age period 77, 78, 80, 89,
    90, 91–2; managing *302*, 306, *312*
Stones of Stenness (Orkney) 65, 72, 73
Strabo 130
strategic planning 305–9
Stratford (Warks) 214
Street House (Cleveland) 68, *69*
structures *see* buildings, domestic
Studley Royal Park (N Yorks) 306

Stukeley, William 298
Sturminster Marshall (Dorset) 84
Styal (Ches) 266, 274, 288
subsistence: Creswellian 19–21; Final Upper
    Palaeolithic 27–8; Younger Dryas 31–2;
    Mesolithic 45–6, 52–4, 55; *see also* agriculture
suburbs, medieval 216
Sulgrave (Northants) 196
Sun Hole (Som) 22
Sutton Hoo (Suffolk); Bronze Age house 85;
    Anglo-Saxon burials 184, *185*
Svein Forkbeard 194
Swaffham Prior (Suffolk) 30
Swansea (Glam) 287
Sweet Track (Som) 64–5
Swindon (Wilts) 291
Symonds Yat East Rockshelter (Glos) 25, 26, 28

Tacitus 138, 149
Tadia Vallaunius 147
Tadius Exuperatus 138, 147
tallies, bone 24, 28
Tamworth (Staffs) 203
Taunton (Som) 96
technology: Upper Palaeolithic 15–17, 24–6,
    29–31; Mesolithic (*illus*) 38–43; Neolithic 59,
    65; Bronze Age 78–84, 104–8; Iron Age 125–8;
    *see also* industry
Telford, Thomas 292
temples/shrines: Iron Age 117, 121, 122, *123*,
    130; Roman 159, 161, 163, *167*, 168; early
    historic period 188
territories, Iron Age 121–2, 129
Tewkesbury (Glos) 215
textile production: Bronze Age 99, 103, 104–5,
    110; Iron Age 126, 129; medieval 211–12;
    post-medieval 284, 288, 289–90
Thames, River 99, 107, 114
Thatcham (Berks) 36, 38, 43, 46–7, 50
theatres 161, 276–7, 309
Thetford (Norfolk) *123*, 203, 205, 231
Thom, Alexander 92
Thornholme (Lincs) 241
Thorpe Thewles (Cleveland) 117, *119*
Threave (Dum & Gall) 268
Three Holes Cave (Devon) *16*, 19, 25, 26, 28
Three Ways Wharf (G London), flints 29, *30*
Thrislington (Co Durham) 253
Throp (Northumb) 151
Thwing (Yorks) 100
timber circles *see* stone and timber circles
tin mining: Bronze Age 78, 104, 105, 106; Iron
    Age 128; Roman 172; post-medieval *273*, 289
tin-working 107, 287
Tintagel (Corn) 186, 189
tombstones, Roman *138*, 139, 147
torcs 123, 128

Torksey (Lincs) *224*, 225
Totnes (Devon) 212, 214, 236
tourism 310–11
tower houses 238, 268–9
town halls *see* guildhalls
towns: Roman (*illus*) 159, 161–4, 173; early
    historic period 179, 180–1, 191, 194;
    Anglo-Scandinavian period 194, 197, 203–5;
    medieval (*illus*) 210–26, 235; post-medieval
    264, 276–8, 281
Towthorpe (N Yorks) 254
trackways: Neolithic 61, 64–5; Bronze Age 78;
    Iron Age 113; Roman 166; medieval 274; *see
    also* roads
traction 103, 109
trade/exchange systems: Mesolithic 54–5;
    Neolithic 65; Early Bronze Age 83, 84; Later
    Bronze Age 97, 100, 104–6, 108; Iron Age 115,
    122, 125–8, 129, 131–2; Roman 148–9, 160,
    162, 163, 169, 172; early historic period 179,
    183, 191, 194; Anglo-Scandinavian period 194,
    197, 203–6; medieval 210–12, 215, 223, 225;
    post-medieval 281; *see also* coins/coinage,
    industry, markets, technology
tramways 275, 285, 292, 293
transport: medieval 261–2; post-medieval 264,
    274–5, 285, 291–2; *see also* boats, roads,
    trackways, wheeled vehicles
Traprain Law (E Loth) 120
Traquair House (Peebles) 269
Trethellan (Corn) 86
Trevisker (Corn) 86
Trevithick, Richard 292
Tunbridge Wells (Kent) 277
Twywell (Northants) *119*

Udal (N Uist) 202
Uley (Glos), West Hill *167*
Ulva Cave (Mull) 53
underwater archaeology 3
Upton (Glos) 252
urban archaeology *7*, 213, 225, 265, 276

Vale of Pewsey (Wilts) 19
Valletta Convention 307
*Verulamium see* St Albans
*vici* 147, *148*, 169, 171
Viking raids 194–5, 197
villages (*illus*) 228, 231–2, 250–8, 265–6
villas, Roman 159, 164, *165*, 173
*Vindolanda* (Chesterholm, Northumb) 138, 140,
    *144*
Votadini 143
votive deposits: Early Bronze Age 90; Later
    Bronze Age 99–100, 107–9, 110–11; Iron Age
    114, 123, 130; Roman 168; Anglo-
    Scandinavian 195

waggonways *see* tramways
Wakefield (Yorks) 212
Wakerley (Northants) *118*
Wales, field archaeology 8
Walesland Rath (Pemb) *118, 170*
Wallingford (Oxon) 204, 225, 234
Wallsend (Tyne & Wear) 141
Walton-on-the-Naze (Essex) 21
Wanborough (Surrey) 123
Wanlockhead (Dum & Gall), 273
Wareham (Dorset) 128, 204
warfare 109, 128, 132
Warwick (Warks) 211
Wasperton (Warks) 166
watchtowers, Roman (*illus*) 140–1, 145–6, 149, 152, 153
water meadows 270
Water Newton (Cambs) *163*, 168
waterfronts, medieval 216–18, 226
Watton (N Yorks) 240
Wawne (Humb) 254
Wayland's Smithy (Oxon) 61, 68
Wedgwood, Josiah 294
weights, Iron Age 125
Wells (Som) 229
Welwyn Garden City (Herts) 124
Wessex, kingdom of 176, 194, 204
Wessex burials 77, 78, 89
West Brandon (Co Durham) *116*, 117, *118*
West Cotton (Northants) 201, 258
West Heslerton (N Yorks) 6, 187
West Kennet (Wilts): avenue 60, 72, 74; long barrow 61, 67, *68*, 90; palisade enclosures 60
West Stow (Suffolk) 187
West Whelpington (Northumb) 252–3, *254*, 256, 265, 266
Westerton (Perths) 140, *145*, 146
Westhampnett (Sussex), cremation *124*
Westness (Orkney) 202
Weston (N Yorks) 200
Westward Ho! (Devon) 49
wetlands 5
Wetwang Slack (E Yorks) 123, *124*
Weymouth (Dorset) 278
Wharram Percy (N Yorks) 6; Anglo-Scandinavian period 206; medieval period 231, 233, 251, 256, 257; post-medieval period 266, 269
Wheathampstead (Herts) 121
wheeled vehicles: Bronze Age 102, 105, 109; Iron Age 123, *124*, 128
Wheeler, Mortimer 6, 162
Whithorn (Dum & Gall) 189–90
Whittlewood (Northants) 261
*wics* 191, 194, 203
Wilburton (Cambs), hoard 96, *97*
Wilson, John 250
Winchelsea (E Sussex) 213, 214
Winchester (Hants): churches 189, 229, 233; defences 204; houses 218, 220; industry 204–5; suburbs 216
Windmill Hill (Wilts) 66–7, *70*, 71
Winnall Down (Hants) 117
Winterslow (Wilts) 87
Winterton (Lincs) 164
Wood, John 277
wood-working 105
Woodchester (Glos) 165
Woodhenge (Wilts) 73
woodland clearance: Mesolithic 52–3, 54; Neolithic 59, 60, 63, 64; Bronze Age 91; Iron Age 129; Roman 142, 148
Woodperry (Oxon) 250
Worcester (Worcs) 215, 294
World Heritage Sites 306
Worsley (Manchester) 275
writing tablets, Roman 138, 144
Wroxeter (Shrops) 180

Yardley Gobion (Northants) 261
Yatesbury (Wilts) 262
Yeavering (Northumb) 6, 188
York: Area of Archaeological Importance designation 307; Roman period 137, 140, 161; early historic period 189, 191, 194, 203; Anglo-Scandinavian period (art/sculpture 195, 196, 200; defences, 203; houses 196, 203, *204*; trade 197, 203, 205–6); medieval period (churches 229, 233, 244; defences 214, 215; Guildhall 215; health 222, 233; houses 218–19; suburbs 216; trade 211, 225); post-medieval period 276
Yoxie (Shetland) 84